Four More Screenplays
by
Preston Sturges

Four More Screenplays

by

Preston Sturges

Introductions by
BRIAN HENDERSON

Foreword by
TOM STURGES

UNIVERSITY OF CALIFORNIA PRESS
Berkeley Los Angeles London

University of California Press
Berkeley and Los Angeles, California

University of California Press
London, England

Copyright © 1995 by
The Regents of the University of California

Library of Congress Cataloging-in-Publication Data

Sturges, Preston.
    Four more screenplays / by Preston Sturges; introduction by Brian
Henderson; foreword by Tom Sturges.
       p.   cm.
    Includes bibliographical references.
    Contents: The Palm Beach story—Triumph over pain/The great
moment—The miracle of Morgan's Creek—Unfaithfully yours.
     ISBN 0–520–20365–8 (pbk.: alk. paper).— ISBN 0–520–08126–9
(cloth: alk. paper)
    1. Motion picture plays. I. Title.
PN1997.A1S85   1995
791.43′75—dc20   95–14874
                                               CIP

Printed in the United States of America

1 2 3 4 5 6 7 8 9

The paper used in this publication meets the minimum requirements of American National Standard for Information Sciences—Permanence of Paper for Printed Library Materials, ANSI Z39.48–1984 ⊗

The publisher gratefully acknowledges the contribution provided by the General Endowment Fund of the Associates of the University of California Press.

Contents

Foreword

My initial inspiration for a series of books publishing the screenplays of my father, Preston Sturges, came just after a screening of one of his earliest films at a festival held at the Los Angeles County Museum of Art. *The Power and The Glory,* made in 1932, was one of Spencer Tracy's first starring roles and the film that Orson Welles sometimes credited as the precursor to *Citizen Kane.* I sat down hoping to see a great work, but rather than cinema for the ages, what appeared on the screen was simply a mess. One section was missing entirely, another was greenish, another was in French, and the beautiful dialogue was scratchy and dusty and hard to make out whenever the music was playing. The program notes explained that the principal factors contributing to the demise of the film were the original being on nitrate (decaying as we watched) and that a safety copy was destroyed in a studio fire in the fifties.

It was not an evening of celebration, needless to say. And I left the museum knowing that if I did not do something, my father's entire life's work would simply and silently disappear, frame by frame, line by line, and laugh by laugh. The beginning of the solution was to preserve the words, to find a way to get the screenplays published in book form, exactly as he had written them and exactly as cast and crew had read them. Nobody had ever tried that before.

Five Screenplays by Preston Sturges, the companion to the volume you hold in your hands, was published by the University of California Press in 1985, and it was the first step in the ultimate preservation of my father's cinematic work and life's legacy. The book received an extraordinary reception and focused a great deal of attention on my father and his writings. Over the course of the next year or so, he went from cult status to slightly grander cult status, but then a lot of things started to happen that have ensured he will have the chance to be remembered forever.

MCA/Universal, Paramount, and 20th Century-Fox struck new 35 mm prints of several films (and have since released them on both video and laser disc). Two different biographies were written and published, and my mother found a way to finish his autobiography, using his own words, and that was published, too. PBS made his life the subject of an American Masters Series documentary that won an Emmy for (how fitting) its writing. A lost play was found and mounted off-off-Broadway to much fanfare and hoopla, and a building was named in his honor on the Paramount lot as part of their 75th anniversary celebration. Film festivals have been staged all over the world, and New York's Film Forum put together one of the most complete and extraordinary retrospectives I have ever seen.

It has been an amazing run, and there are two more events yet to come: the third and final book of screenplays (written but not directed by . . .) and the movie of his life. I am working on both now.

Many individuals contributed to the events of my father's post-life career and each has made their own contribution for which my father would be very grateful if he were only here to say so. These people are, in no order whatsoever, Jim Curtiss, Brian Henderson, Bruce Goldstein, Lilace Hatayama, Ken Bowser, Todd McCarthy, Nancy Cushing-Jones, Louis Feola, Marlene Swartz, Deborah Rosen, Allan Mayer, Chick Callenbach, Ed Dimendberg, Karen Cooper, Michelle Nordon, Diane Jacobs, Priscilla Bonner Woolfan, and Sandy Sturges. On his behalf, may I say thank you once again.

Tom Sturges
Spring 1995
Hollywood, California

Introduction

Four More Screenplays by Preston Sturges: the "more" in the title refers to an earlier volume, *Five Screenplays by Preston Sturges,* which was published in 1985.[1] The Introduction to that volume included a survey of critical writing on Sturges that ranged from the classical essays of James Agee, André Bazin, Manny Farber, and Andrew Sarris to more recent work by Stanley Cavell, Richard Corliss, Sturges biographer James Curtis, and others. This survey might be updated to include a number of books on Sturges that have appeared since 1985. Among this number is James Harvey's 1987 study, *Romantic Comedy in Hollywood: From Lubitsch to Sturges.*[2] Harvey says of Sturges that he "wrote and directed one marvellous movie after another—eight extraordinary films in four years [at Paramount], and each one an 'original'—a burst of achievement without precedent or parallel in Hollywood memory."[3]

In August 1989, the 42nd Locarno International Film Festival was devoted to a Preston Sturges retrospective—the largest ever assembled. The event was accompanied by the publication of a book with essays by André Bazin, Siegfried Kracauer, Manny Farber, Penelope Houston, and others.[4] In 1990, there appeared *Preston Sturges by Preston Sturges,* adapted and edited by Sandy Sturges. This invaluable book is the first publication of Sturges's unfinished autobiography, "The Events Leading up to My Death,"[5] which is skillfully interwoven with Sturges's letters and other writings to bring to completion the story of his life. To read of Sturges's life and work in his own words—at once imaginative and ironic—is an unexpected treat.[6]

Two biographies of Sturges have appeared in recent years: *Madcap: The Life of Preston Sturges,* by Donald Spoto (1990), and *Christmas in July: The Life and Art of Preston Sturges,* by Diane Jacobs (1992).[7] These books may be said to complete the biographical project begun in 1982 with the publication of *Between Flops: A Biography of Preston Sturges,* by James Curtis.[8] For scholars, researchers, and other writers on Sturges, the existence of three biographies is a most valuable resource; consulting all three is essential.

Tributes to Sturges have also been paid in recent years by a number of

1

writers, directors, and producers. Their remarks have less to do with assessing Sturges's achievement than with acknowledging his ongoing influence and example. A high-profile instance is Joe Roth, who created and headed a production company called Morgan Creek Productions before becoming Chairman of 20th Century-Fox Films. Also a sometime director, Roth keeps on his office shelf "a photo of his directorial idol, Preston Sturges, playing pool."[9]

Another filmmaker—Paul Shrader, I think—mentions in an interview how sorry he feels for directors who claim to be making a film in the Preston Sturges manner. Writer-director Ron Shelton (*Bull Durham, Blaze, White Men Can't Jump, Cobb*) may never have spoken of a Sturges influence himself, but interviewer Garrett White makes that connection a number of times. For instance, White first found Shelton in the second-story bar of the Imperial Gardens, which, he notes, "was formerly the Player's Club, owned and operated during Hollywood's golden era by prototypical writer-director Preston Sturges, whose name has often been invoked in descriptions of Shelton's writings."[10] White says later in the piece that an early Shelton script "showed his great eye for kooky details in the American landscape—as with Sturges, always treated with a mixture of tenderness and humor."[11]

In her remarkable book, *Love Trouble Is My Business,* Veronica Geng alternates humor pieces she wrote—mainly for the *New Yorker*—with brief, serious essays on the circumstances, often quite personal, in which they were written. She says, in the essay that follows the first story,

What I most love to do is to be frivolous and then swerve into blatant sincerity. I have no idea why. My hero is Preston Sturges, whose great movie comedies of the 1940s take all kinds of daring plunges from farce to sentiment. He had inexhaustible strategies for making a situation yield its opposite and switch direction. So he could allow that the world runs on greed, delusion, and injustice while he revelled in the crazy exceptions that prove the rule. Certainly I didn't have racial prejudice in mind when I started writing the story ["The New Thing"], but when the chance came to shift gears this way, it was something I felt free to do because I'd seen Sturges do it.[12]

In the August 1990 issue of *Sight and Sound,* Penelope Houston, who was retiring after thirty-five years as editor of that journal, published a column called "Double Takes." It concluded with a brief section headed "Kockenlocker's Farewell." The grace of that farewell was due not a little to the resort she made to the scripts and films of Preston Sturges.

Some years ago, I did a stint on this column as Kockenlocker. I chose the pseudonym for the scene in *The Miracle of Morgan's Creek* where the Kockenlockers debate the probability of the soldier Betty Hutton has so inconveniently mislaid being called Ratziwatski. (Momentarily, Ratziwatski seemed an inviting alternative; but wiser counsels, as they say, prevailed.) There was also a certain feeling, possibly fellow-feeling, for officer Kockenlocker, the gallant if neanderthal smalltown policeman clinging to his sense of order and reason in the face of everything a Preston Sturges script could throw at him.

2

Once, watching on a movieola the scene in which Kockenlocker (William Demarest) tries to persuade Eddie Bracken to break out of his jail, I laughed so excessively that I fell off my stool, thereby I suppose achieving the condition known as rolling in the aisles. A kind of female Kockenlocker then employed by the National Film Archive appeared in the doorway, sighed theatrically, and made off with the rebuke, "No one *laughs* at the films we show here."

This is my final issue as editor of SIGHT AND SOUND, after what long-serving readers may well regard as an unconscionable time. I considered marking the occasion with an article on some such subject as film magazines, their present and future prospects, but it began to look more and more like "Brother, Where Art Thou?," the dismal movie Sullivan is longing to make at the start of *Sullivan's Travels*.

As far back as *Close Up*, no film magazine with any kind of serious intentions has probably been able to survive without some sort of patronage or subsidy. Certainly, SIGHT AND SOUND could not have lasted ten minutes without the support of the BFI. But for a variety of reasons, the future for this type of magazine now looks particularly insecure: too many in Europe and America have gone under, or have kept going only through compromise.

"There's nothing like a deep-dish movie for driving you out into the open," Veronica Lake warns Sullivan. It didn't seem quite the moment for achieving the same effect with a deep-dish article. Friends suggested a reminiscent piece, but that looked an invitation to self-indulgence. All in all, it seemed as well to leave the last word to Kockenlocker.

On a last, personal note, I would like to thank all our contributors. I'm particularly pleased and grateful to be publishing in this issue articles by Lindsay Anderson, my mentor when I took over as editor of SIGHT AND SOUND, and David Robinson, a colleague from early years. And I'm grateful to Susan Ray, Nicholas Ray's widow, for sending us "On Directing," making a kind of companion piece to an article by Nicholas Ray which we published in 1956, my first year as editor.

KOCKENLOCKER[13]

Sturges wrote and directed twelve films. The first eight were made for Paramount Pictures: *The Great McGinty* (1940), *Christmas in July* (1940), *The Lady Eve* (1941), *Sullivan's Travels* (1942), *The Palm Beach Story* (1942), *The Great Moment* (1944), *The Miracle of Morgan's Creek* (1944), and *Hail the Conquering Hero* (1944). In two years of "partnership" with Howard Hughes, Sturges wrote and directed only one film: *The Sin of Harold Diddlebock* (1946).[14] For 20th Century-Fox Films, Sturges wrote and directed *Unfaithfully Yours* (1948) and *The Beautiful Blonde from Bashful Bend* (1949). In Paris he wrote and directed French and English versions of *Les Carnets du Major Thompson* [*The French They Are a Funny Race*] (1955).

Most critics and other viewers regard Sturges's last two films as failures.[15] Thus his extremely high reputation as a writer-director rests on ten films. This volume collects the shooting scripts for four of these: *The Palm Beach Story, Triumph over Pain/The Great Moment, The Miracle of Morgan's Creek,* and *Unfaithfully Yours.* The shooting scripts for five others were collected in the 1985 volume mentioned above: *The Great McGinty, Christmas in July, The*

*On the set of HAIL THE CONQUERING HERO: a surprise
cake for Sturges's forty-fifth birthday (August 29, 1943).*

Lady Eve, Sullivan's Travels, and *Hail the Conquering Hero.* Absent from
both volumes—alas!—is the shooting script for *The Sin of Harold Diddlebock,* the rights to which are still tied up in the Howard Hughes estate.

The four scripts printed in this volume appear exactly as Sturges wrote
them, photocopied form the latest version of each. As studio production
scripts, they follow a prescribed format—they were designed to be used not
only by the director and the actors but also by budget personnel, set design-
ers, the costume department, the camera and sound crews, and others. The
three scripts for Paramount are divided into "sequences" that are marked "A,"
"B," "C," "D," "E," "F," "G," "H," "J," "K," and so on. (There are no sequences designated "I," perhaps to avoid confusion with the Roman numeral.) The use of the term "sequence" does not lend itself to rigorous definition. A new sequence heading usually marks a shift in time and/or setting, but
other temporal and/or spatial shifts may take place within a sequence. Considered overall, the sequence is simply a convenient division of the script—
and hence of the film-to-be—into large sections. Of the scripts in this volume,
The Palm Beach Story has eight sequences, *Triumph over Pain* nine, and *The
Miracle of Morgan's Creek* eleven. The script for *Unfaithfully Yours,* made
at 20th Century-Fox, has no breakdown into sequences. The number of sequences in a script does not correspond to its overall number of pages or to
the running time of the finished film, as the following table indicates:

	Number of pages	Number of sequences	Running time of film
Down Went McGinty[16]	134	9	81 min.
The New Yorkers	111	6	70 min.
The Lady Eve	155	10	97 min.
Sullivan's Travels	145	10	90 min.
The Palm Beach Story	157	8	88 min.
Triumph over Pain	160	9	83 min.
The Miracle of Morgan's Creek	156	11	99 min.
The Little Marine	137	5	101 min.
Unfaithfully Yours	154	—	105 min.

A studio production script contains a good deal of information besides scene-setting descriptions and dialogue. For instance, each page of a script bears the date on which it was completed or, more precisely, on which it was typed at the studio. This date is placed at the bottom left of the page in all the scripts printed below except *Unfaithfully Yours,* in which it is printed at the middle of the top of the page. *The Palm Beach Story* has the same date marking on each page; the pages of *Triumph over Pain, The Miracle of Morgan's Creek,* and *Unfaithfully Yours* do not all have the same date markings. Each page of the scripts printed below (except *Unfaithfully Yours*) is also designated by the letter of the sequence in which it is located. The pages of sequence A are designated "A-1," "A-2," et cetera. The pages of the sequences after sequence A are marked both by the sequence in which they occur and by their place in the overall script. Thus the first page of sequence B of *The Miracle of Morgan's Creek* is marked "B-1 (6)," indicating that it is the first page of sequence B and the sixth page of the script as a whole; the last page of the script is marked "L-17 (156)." (In addition, of course, each script page in this volume is paginated consecutively by numbers placed at the bottom of the page.) Page references in my introductions to each of the four scripts always refer to the overall numbering of the script in question; thus "(page A-1)" for the first page of *The Miracle of Morgan's Creek,* "(page 156)" for its last page, et cetera. It should also be noted that, for better or worse, the terms "screenplay" and "script" are used interchangeably throughout this introduction and the individual introductions to the four scripts.

Finally, like all studio production scripts, the screenplays printed here are organized according to the successive shots of the film-to-be. These shots are numbered according to the sequence in which they occur—"A-1," "A-2," et cetera. (Needless to say, there is a possibility for confusion between such shot designations and the sequence page numbers. In the introductions below, references are always to page numbers unless otherwise specified.) Following the shot number, the subject of the shot is described in capital letters. At the beginning of a sequence—or of a new scene within the sequence—this description always includes the setting of the shot which appears in underlined capital letters, presumably for the benefit of production staff members. If the setting is clear from the description of the first shot of a sequence or scene, it is not repeated in the subsequent shots of that passage. If the shot includes camera movement or character action, or if a particular demeanor of actors or quality of objects, et cetera, is desired, that is specified in lowercase below the shot designation. ("Dialogue continuities," which are transcripts of a film's dialogue taken down after a film has been shot, omit all such information, everything indeed except dialogue.)

Preserving the notation of studio production scripts makes for a rather crowded page, but it has its advantages. The general reader will find them highly readable and will have immediate access to Sturges's superb dialogue. In smoothed-over, continuous scripts—those published without the original page numbers or breakdowns into shots—it is often hard to find things. For scholars, teachers, and students, reproduction of an original script preserves its value as a research document, whereas an "adapted" script becomes an additional puzzle to be solved and thereby compounds the problems of interpretation. In any case, Sturges himself did not adapt or otherwise prepare his screenplays for publication in his lifetime; to attempt to do so for him would be presumptuous.

Sturges was the sole major Hollywood director who filmed only his own original screenplays. *The Great Moment* draws its facts from a published biography, but otherwise, Sturges—his last two films aside—never adapted his screenplays from someone else's story, novel, or play. The exception of *The Lady Eve,* based on a story by Monckton Hoffe, only proves the rule. The story is so completely transformed by Sturges that screen credit to its "original author" seems ludicrous. (Even as a nondirecting screenwriter in the thirties, Sturges preferred, as often as possible, to discard prior work by other writers and start all over again.) It is perhaps not surprising that Sturges as writer-director was not able to meet such exacting standards for much more than a decade—no one else was able to sustain them for even that long.

Separate introductions follow for each of the screenplays collected in this volume, detailing their genesis and development. For the most part, these introductions treat Sturges's direction as, in effect, the final stage of script revision. This perspective leaves out much of what is usually defined as direction, but the fact that Sturges directed his own scripts is enormously important in itself. Negatively speaking, it means that no other person altered the script in question by adding or subtracting things (however small), by imposing a questionable pace, by selecting the wrong cast members, or by guiding them incorrectly. The most common—and bitter—complaint of Hollywood writers of all eras is that their work has been distorted by other writers and/or the director. Sturges had the opportunity to alter his dialogue, even to omit scenes or to change the order of scenes if he chose to, during shooting or in the editing. His own brilliance and tireless revising aside, this opportunity resulted in

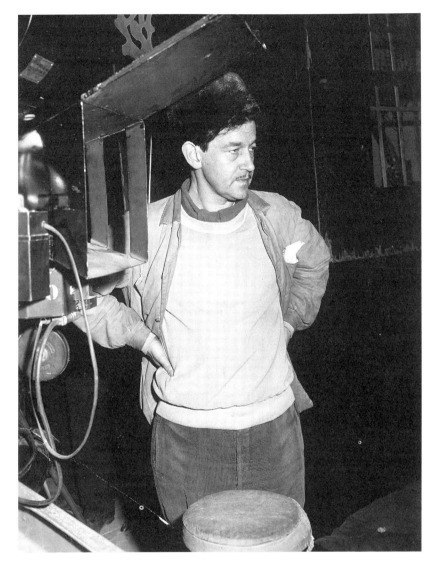

Getting it right: Sturges on the set of
THE MIRACLE OF MORGAN'S CREEK.

a final polish and perfection that few scripts have ever enjoyed. It is for these reasons that the introductions below frequently venture forward from the early versions of Sturges's screenplays, to the final versions printed here, to the actual film versions—for they constitute a single process of revision.

It should be pointed out, finally, that there are many differences in dialogue, most of them minor, between the final scripts and the films, and that the majority of these are not noted in the introductions. There simply was not space to do so. (Note, however, that, unless otherwise indicated, the passages of dialogue quoted in the introductions have been corrected to accord with the film version.) An excellent activity for prospective screenwriters, students, or anyone else interested in Sturges's work is to see one of his films with script in hand and to make notations of differences.

It is worth noting that my contributions to this book are based mainly on the 125 boxes of Preston Sturges papers that are housed in the Special Collections Department of the Graduate Research Library at UCLA. Thanks to a ninety-page index—prepared by the Special Collections staff—this material is very easy to access. Staff members are also very helpful in guiding researchers to what they need.

*   *   *

In Volume 1 of the Sturges screenplays, I included a biographical sketch of his life and career up to the point at which he began to rewrite *The Great McGinty* preparatory to filming it. As there are now three full-length biographies of Sturges, there is really no need for a continuation of that sketch here. Instead I will share, for what they are worth, a few items more or less on the periphery of Sturges's life that I have come across here and there and which I have not found in the biographies.

All three biographies rely extensively on interviews and correspondence with Priscilla Woolfan, whose maiden name was Bonner; she and her husband Bertie—who was also Sturges's personal physician—were Sturges's very intimate friends from 1933 up until his death in 1959.[17] Priscilla's sister was Marjorie Bonner, the woman who essentially rescued Malcolm Lowry when he met her in Los Angeles after his horrific Mexican experience. Eventually they married and collaborated on a number of works. From Dollarton, British Columbia, in January 1950, Lowry wrote:

My very dear Priscilla:

[T]hank you very much indeed for the French review [of *Under the Volcano*] and please thank Preston very sincerely for his courtesy and interest in translating it. But apart from liking it (as the reviewer says of the book) God what a gloomy ghoul it makes me sound! Especially when I think that my ambition was much as the famed Sullivan—to be a humorist. Won't even Preston think it a bit funny? Just a little bit, I hope, or I shall be hurt. (Though for that matter I see no reason why he should have to translate the book, as well as the review.) I am recently in receipt of some two dozen more French reviews . . . all of which are presently lost—just at the moment I had assembled them to send to you. I had also some months previously marked a very long very intelligent very enthusiastic resume of Preston's work particularly in relation to *Unfaithfully Yours* that was sent to me by my mother and which appeared in the *Illustrated London News*. Particularly though it was an appreciation of *Unfaithfully*

Sturges and Claudette Colbert on the set of
THE PALM BEACH STORY; *Sturges demonstrates*
what his script calls "the look."

Yours—a film I missed when abroad unfortunately. I thought Preston probably had so
many of such things that he didn't bother to look at them any longer: then I thought
damn it, no—he writes his films too, as well as directs them: perhaps having been
glutted with praise upon the directorial swings he could—sentence impossible—
escritorial roundabouts—what am I saying? But it is New Year after all. I meant well
but preserved the notice so faithfully that even as mine, I lost it—temporarily, I hope.
I put things away (or if I don't Margie does.)[18]

A different "look" for the male rival: Sturges and Rex Harrison during the filming of UNFAITHFULLY YOURS.

Lowry was not the first or the last writer to get Sturges tangled up in his prose (and projections)—perhaps just the best one. He concludes his letter to Priscilla: "*Mad Wednesday* hasn't reached here yet, but we'll be right in to see it when it arrives—hope it goes well; of special interest to me because I saw a bit of it being made, and very excellent too."[19] In Fall 1945, Marjorie and Lowry took a trip to Mexico; his November 1945 thank-you note to Priscilla from Cuernavaca indicates that they had stayed with the Woolfans in Hollywood on their way down from Canada.[20] This was surely the time Lowry saw a bit of *The Sin of Harold Diddlebock* being filmed. Sturges began shooting *Diddlebock* on September 12, 1945, and finished early in 1946. Howard Hughes had delayed the film's release for four years, and had also, besides altering it, renamed it *Mad Wednesday.* (See note 14.)

Sturges recalled his first meeting with Frank Lloyd Wright in a letter he wrote to the architect on July 6, 1945:

I remember precisely the day we met, the Palm Beach Story set where the meeting occurred, the trucking shot I was making at the time, and the spot where I placed my chair for you, so you could watch. I remember taking you to lunch and offering to send you a print of "The Good Fairy," which subsequently proved impractical, as the film had shrunk.

The Palm Beach Story was shot from late November 1941 to late January 1942, and Wright followed up his visit with a postal telegram dated February 12, 1942:

We have been sitting on the edge of our chair awaiting the film you so generously promised to give us could we perhaps have it for next Sunday when we want to show off for some friends I enjoyed meeting you as much as I did knowing you in your work with lots of love.

Over the next several years Sturges sent Wright prints of a number of his films at Taliesin West. The first, it seems, was *Sullivan's Travels,* which he sent later in February. Wright wrote back on February 23, 1942:

Sullivan's Travels reached us last evening and I can't refrain from sending a small bouquet. But, the superlatives have long since been exhausted by Hollywood itself— even "terrific." I don't quite yet know how to paint the lilly [*sic*] or gild fine gold, so understatement is inevitable.

It is enough to say that the creative touch that is yours and endears you to me is rampant in the whole thing. Forgive the foreboding, but I hope your "haymaking" in good weather won't result in any let-down of such quality. A box-office failure, or two, wouldn't matter at all if "the quality" was responsible for failure. It might well be—as things are.

But your devoted friends here as elsewhere, I am sure, could love you for such failure and feel damn'd sorry for any cheap success you might have.

A brief note from Wright on May 30, 1945, said "Thanks for *Hail the Conquering Hero!* A remarkable portrait of America by America herself. Give us more—oh, much more of the sort-."

The next exchange, written by Sturges to Wright at Taliesin in Spring Green, Wisconsin, had to do with some misunderstanding that arose between the two men. "I have before me your astonishing letter of June 30," Sturges begins.

I hope its deeply insulting tone made you feel better. It made me quite ill. Not that I mind having enemies. I have quite a lot of them. But I know why I dislike them and I know why they dislike me. I have known all about you for many years . . . the hotel that survived the earthquake . . . the fundamental rightness of your work . . . even the house you built for a cousin of mine out here.

This is followed by the passage, quoted above, in which Sturges recalls the meeting on the set of *The Palm Beach Story*; then:

I was delighted to receive word of encouragement about "Hail the Conquering Hero." I acknowledged it immediately, addressed you as "My dear friend," because you had called me "Dear Preston," and then, since I had had the pleasure of meeting your charming granddaughter, mentioned it to you in words which tried to recapture the momentary dismay I felt, as a man approaching fifty, who is told by a pretty girl that her grandfather is a great admirer of his. Since I have apparently wounded you deeply, I apologize for the result. I cannot apologize for my intent.

I enclose your letter to me, I don't want it in my files. I also enclose the other letters, so that you may read them again. I think you had better reconsider this matter and then sit down as quickly as possible and tell me that you are sorry. Being yourself, you will really have to.

Wright's offended letter, missing from the one hundred-plus large, overstuffed boxes of Sturges papers, must have been one of the relatively few items he managed to expunge. Which is more remarkable, Sturges's preferring the praise of a young woman to that of Frank Lloyd Wright, or his admitting that fact to the old man himself? Wright was duly disarmed and rewarded Sturges, on July 17, 1945, with by far his ripest letter.

Dear Preston: I am delighted. You are what I thought you were—after all—and how happily I apologize.

You see, Preston, "the tragedy of old age is that it is not old"—and I thought you were making game of an old man under pretext of your fear of old-age, yourself. But don't you worry!

You will be doing some of your best things at eighty and if you can believe me, out of my experience, life will be as much richer and better worth living as you grow older as you put yourself whole-heartedly and sincerely into your creative work. You do just that. And so I know what is true of me is going to be true of you—no matter what or how it may seem to you at times.

Yours is the creative mind and the magic touch of it exists in our goddamn country and in spite of its fool self it does. You and I prove it.

I was the more miffed, too, because I don't write fan letters. You had the only one I ever wrote to the movies so I send it back to you. It was a swell understatement of what I feel about you in your work. Everything you have done (I think I have seen it all) has freshness, humor, and true vitality. The only man I put in your category is Rene Clair when he is in France. In America you have the advantage over him—because, Preston, how American you are!

Cheer up, man!

This country needs a son like you—whether she knows so or not. She can learn—maybe? She is hard up now with the brood of hypocrites and liars-for-a-living she has to put up with. Her integrity is in real danger.

But men like you (yes, me too) will shame her back where she belongs.

To you—

"Frank"
Frank Lloyd Wright

A respectful if superficial exchange has turned, by virtue of Wright's seeming misreading, into something else. Wright has goaded Sturges into opening up and declaring himself, and Sturges then does the same to Wright—"being yourself, you will really have to [apologize]." Wright in turn says, "You are what I thought you were—after all . . ."

12

Sturges responded on July 21 with a cordial, patently relieved letter.

I am enormously pleased to have your charming letter. I was quite certain that you would write, not only because I had confidence in you, but also because I have a great confidence in truth. It rises to the top, becomes apparent and must be believed. From here in I am certain there will be no further misunderstandings. I always liked the story of the man who heard a noise downstairs at night, went down and found his close friend prying open his cash box. He said: "Wait a minute, I've got the key here," and opened the box without any further questions. He knew that since the man was his friend, he could not be robbing him, and whereas he didn't know exactly why he came in through the window instead of ringing the doorbell, he took it for granted that his friend had some private reason which would be explained later.

I am building a new room onto my restaurant, which will be called the Fourth Dimensional Room. The name is a joke, but the room will be quite practical in that one of its walls, containing a revolving bandstand, will be movable, making it a very small room when there are a few customers, and a very large room when there are many. When it is finished I will send you pictures of it, which may amuse you.

In the meantime, good luck and good wishes to you, and if someone tells you I said something terrible about you, don't believe it, because I won't have.

Sturges seems willfully blind to the import of Wright's advice on the renunciations and freedoms of old age. Does he, like a hero of Greek tragedy, refuse to heed the words of Tiresias, or to understand the clear voice of the oracle? Perhaps he was reluctant to tempt fate by discussing the issue, or felt that it was futile—either you lived to be eighty-something or you didn't. Sturges later predicted that he would live no longer than his mother's sixty years.[21] In any case, Sturges may well have suspected that practicing his art in old age was not a likely eventuality. The last item in the file is a letter Wright sent Sturges on March 29, 1948.

Dear Preston: The Diddlebock satirical circus went on in our little theater and the uproarious laughter of 60 apprentices from 20 different nations was something good to hear. They wanted it again next day—many said they hated to see it go back.

Nice of you (and an idea) to put Harold Lloyd back on the screen in this fashion. Satire like this refreshes me and it is a great Sturges gift.

A similar gift ruined Rene Clair in France? They couldn't take it. And may ruin Sturges with our "business sanctimony." It is evidently and refreshingly ruined by him in this "better than a circus."

Affectionately,

Frank

N.B. Is there anything funnier than your flash of the presidential physiognomies above the Diddlebock desk?
(Congratulations to H. Lloyd)

The sad coda to Wright's wishing Sturges a long creative life is already known to many readers. Both men died in 1959: Sturges at 60, Wright at 91.

Sturges biographer James Curtis argues that it was *Triumph over Pain,* renamed by the studio *The Great Moment,* that seems to have ended any prospect for good relations between Sturges and George Gard (B. G.) DeSylva—always called "Buddy"—who in early 1941 had replaced William Le Baron as Paramount's chief of production. DeSylva had opposed the project from the outset and, when the finished film confirmed his dislike, had it comprehensively reedited. (See the introduction to *Triumph over Pain/The Great Moment* below.) Indeed, the producer's animosity toward Sturges extended even to projects he did favor—*The Miracle of Morgan's Creek* and *Hail the Conquering Hero*—and seemed to dissolve only after Sturges had left the studio. All I can add to this topic, which is treated in detail in all three Sturges biographies, is to note a number of similarities between the two men.

As a member of the enormously successful songwriting team of Brown, DeSylva, and Henderson, DeSylva had written a large number of hits, many of them now standards. He also wrote a musical and several songs with George Gershwin, and a musical with Victor Herbert. Sturges had seriously tried songwriting at several points in his career and, in fact, wrote most of the songs used in *Miracle* and *Hail.* Although legend has it that the practice in Hollywood was common, both men had affairs with their secretaries: Sturges with Jean La Vell, DeSylva—according to his *New York Times* obituary—with Marie Ballentine. In 1947, DeSylva acknowledged paternity of their son Stephen. (In one instance at least, Sturges proceeded inversely—his affair with Bianca Gilchrist came first, her secretarial assistance later.) Both men also died young: DeSylva at fifty-four in 1950; Sturges, as mentioned, at sixty in 1959. In fact, ill-health—perhaps the heart ailment that led ultimately to his death—led DeSylva to give up his position as head of production on September 15, 1944, which was two months before the release of *The Great Moment.* DeSylva became head of an independent unit which released its films through Paramount, but in fact his last production was *The Stork Club* in 1945.

DeSylva had done successful producing in Hollywood and on Broadway, where, in 1939–1940, he had three hit shows running simultaneously. Nevertheless, as composer or collaborator on five hundred songs and writer of the books for several musical comedies and reviews, he was certifiably "a creative type." In theory, when such people become producers, they are more likely than others to be sympathetic to "creative personnel." However, in practice, there is no evidence supporting this proposition and some disturbing evidence to the contrary. Douglas Gomery says of the year (1935–1936) that director Ernst Lubitsch spent as head of production at Paramount:

While in charge, Lubitsch adopted a "retake and remake" procedure whereby a feature could be put back into production after principal photography had been completed if Lubitsch deemed there were ways to improve it. He centralized story purchases in his office and took a very tough line *vis-a-vis* his fellow directors.[22]

To judge from *Fun in a Chinese Laundry*,[23] his autobiography, director Josef von Sternberg would rather have suffered actual martyrdom than to blame another for the blight of his Paramount career after *The Devil Is a Woman* (1935). But in his distanced way, curious about but unsurprised by human behavior, he lets it be known that Lubitsch played a role in his departure from the studio.[24] As producer of *Vendetta* for California Pictures, Sturges hired Max Ophuls to direct the film. Later, though acting under direct orders from Hughes, Sturges fired Ophuls, but he did so, according to Diane Jacobs, "as if it were his own idea."[25] He himself was fired soon afterward when Hughes dissolved the partnership.

In a larger perspective, DeSylva and Sturges were both foot soldiers in corporate war games. Gomery says that the Paramount corporate leadership pursued a two-pronged strategy in the mid-forties: first, to move "from Lubitsch-like European products to far more profitable American material" and second, to minimize its risk in feature production by relying on spillover fame through the use of talent and properties from other entertainment sectors.[26] The Hope-Crosby "Road" pictures were the most profitable of the decade for Paramount. And from Hope-Crosby to Dean Martin and Jerry Lewis, big Paramount moneymakers of the fifties, is a far shorter step than it appeared at the time.

The wrangling over *Triumph over Pain*—and, even more, its ultimate fate— may have caused Sturges more pain than any of his other projects as writer or as writer-director. This is a paradox since the film itself reflects Sturges's lifelong concern with minimizing pain and maximizing pleasure—an interest that he no doubt shared with most of the people who have ever lived. High among his pleasures was receiving praise for his work. As he once put it,

It so happens that the good opinions of critics, either stage or film, have always meant as much to me as the air I breathe. I live for good reviews and am drunk with pleasure when I get them. They affect me like catnip does a cat and any rumors to the effect that I am a deep drinking man or jolly tosspot were probably started by someone who had seen me rolling around on the floor after I had read a good review.[27]

Besides work success and its pleasures, Sturges also spent a good deal of his time in the pursuit and enjoyment of romantic adventures. He also loved well-prepared food, especially if it was consumed in amusing and/or distinguished company. To secure this end he built a restaurant and spent a fortune to keep it open. Regarding drink, Sturges was as careful and discriminating, as attuned to the nuances of cause and effect, as he was regarding any of his other pastimes. On April 28, 1951, he wrote a brief letter to Mr. Roy Ald of New York City. Unfortunately, Mr. Ald's letter of inquiry has not survived.

My dear Mr. Ald:

Thank you for your letter. I drink Old-fashioneds made with Early Times Bourbon, plain rather than seltzer water and no bitters. It has of course a slice of orange and a maraschino cherry. A strong drink like this is absorbed immediately through the lining of the stomach and its cheerful effects leave with a reasonable promptness. Diluted highballs, beer and things like that pass through the stomach and are absorbed very slowly down in the basement. They stay with you forever . . . hence the horror of a beer or champagne drunk.

*   *   *

I am grateful to Tom Sturges for initiating the Sturges screenplay project and for his effective assistance in many other respects. Sandy Sturges very generously lent her time and spirit to the project; she aided my research in countless ways and also made valuable comments on the manuscript as a whole. I am grateful to the staff of the University of California Press, above all to Ernest Callenbach, who expertly guided the project in its early stages; to Ed Dimendberg, who very effectively saw it through to its conclusion; to Michelle Nordon, the book's superbly attentive project director; and to Nomi Kleinmuntz, its excellent copy editor. I also wish to thank the staff of the UCLA Special Collections Department for their gracious assistance with my work in the Sturges Collection. For generous support of my research on Sturges, I am grateful to the National Endowment for the Humanities for a Travel to Collections award; and to the New York State/United University Professions Professional Development and Quality of Working Life Committee for two awards. My greatest debt is to Sarah Ulen Henderson, who painstakingly assessed every sentence of the introductions and, in countless cases, suggested superior versions. Finally, I would like to thank Sam and Charlie for their support and good cheer.

NOTES

1. Brian Henderson, ed., *Five Screenplays by Preston Sturges* (Berkeley: University of California Press, 1985).

2. James Harvey, *Romantic Comedy in Hollywood: From Lubitsch to Sturges* (New York: Knopf, 1987).

3. Ibid., 509.

4. *Preston Sturges,* edited by Roland Cosandey (Editions du Festival international du film de Locarno, 1989).

5. The best account of the circumstances of the writing of this work is Donald Spoto, *Madcap: The Life of Preston Sturges* (Boston: Little, Brown, 1990), 251–256.

6. *Preston Sturges by Preston Sturges,* adapted and edited by Sandy Sturges (New York: Simon and Schuster, 1990).

7. Diane Jacobs, *Christmas in July: The Life and Art of Preston Sturges* (Berkeley: University of California Press, 1992).

8. James Curtis, *Between Flops: A Biography of Preston Sturges* (New York: Harcourt Brace Jovanovich, 1982).

9. Patrick Goldstein, "Joe Roth—A 20th Century Man," *Los Angeles Times* (March 16, 1990), F36 (article begins on F1).

10. Garrett White, "Between Hits," *L.A. Style* (December 1989), 214.

11. Ibid., 216.

12. Veronica Geng, *Love Trouble Is My Business* (New York: Harper & Row, 1988), 6–7.

13. Penelope Houston, "Double Takes," *Sight and Sound* 59, no. 4 (August 1990): 248–250.

14. The umbrella of the partnership—in which only Hughes was protected from the rain—was California Pictures. Hughes had a controlling interest in the company, and its charter also gave him the power to dissolve the partnership whenever he wished. (Hughes informed Sturges of the dissolution on October 30, 1946.) *Diddlebock* was released briefly by Hughes in 1947, then withdrawn and held by him until 1950, when he released it in an altered version as *Mad Wednesday.* Fortunately, Sturges's version survived intact and is now nearly always the one shown in retrospectives and on television.

15. I consider *The Beautiful Blonde from Bashful Bend* a most interesting—and possibly influential—experiment. See Brian Henderson, "Cartoon and Narrative in the Films of Frank Tashlin and Preston Sturges," in Andrew S. Horton, ed., *Comedy/Cinema/Theory* (Berkeley: University of California Press, 1991), 153–173. As for *Les Carnets du Major Thompson/The French They Are a Funny Race,* it is considerably overdue for reevaluation from a contemporary perspective.

16. The titles listed are those of the five final Sturges scripts collected in Volume 1 and the four collected in the present volume. At some point between the completion of the final scripts and the release of the films that Sturges directed, *Down Went McGinty* was retitled *The Great McGinty, The New Yorkers* became *Christmas in July, Triumph over Pain* became *The Great Moment,* and *The Little Marine* became *Hail the Conquering Hero.* As far as I have been able to determine, Sturges had no objection to any of these changes except that of *Triumph over Pain,* in which case his opposition was entrenched and persistent.

17. See, for instance, Diane Jacobs, *Christmas in July,* 141–447 passim.

18. Harvey Breit and Marjorie Bonner Lowry, eds., *Selected Letters of Malcolm Lowry* (London: Jonathon Cape, 1967), 187–188.

19. Ibid., 188.

20. Ibid., 53.

21. Jacobs, *Christmas in July,* 417.

22. Douglas Gomery, *The Hollywood Studio System* (New York: St. Martin's Press, 1986), 39.

23. Josef von Sternberg, *Fun in a Chinese Laundry: An Autobiography* (New York: Macmillan, 1965).

24. Ibid., 134–135; 265–267. On p. 38, von Sternberg is explicit: "Most of the films he [Lubitsch] made failed to appeal to me. He knew that, and one day when he was placed in charge of the studio where both of us worked, he was quick to liquidate

me as soon as he could." But on p. 135 he says, "We nevertheless became very good friends long before he died."

25. Jacobs, *Christmas in July,* 350.

26. Gomery, *The Hollywood Studio System,* 40.

27. Curtis, *Between Flops,* 149.

The Palm Beach Story

The earliest material on *The Palm Beach Story* in the Sturges papers are one hundred and fifty-five "yellow pages and notes" written between September 3 and November 1, 1941. They are all headed *Is That Bad?*—which was the project's title until the completion of the first screenplay version on November 3, whereupon it was renamed *The Palm Beach Story*. A second screenplay version dated November 8 was followed by the final script of November 21, 1941, which is reprinted below. Filming began on November 24 and was completed in late January 1942. The film had its world premiere in London in the summer of 1942 and was released in America in December of that year.

Sturges's first note on *Is That Bad?*—written September 3—was a summary of its opening scene. Gerry "muffs the breakfast" one morning in her suburban house: she burns the toast, breaks the cream bottle, and, falling asleep on the sofa, lets the coffee boil over. The smell of the coffee wakes her husband, Tom, "who departs minus breakfast and half dressed for the commuter train which he misses." Tom comes back to tell his wife off and in so doing misses the second train. He catches the third train, arrives late for work, and is fired. When he returns home that night, Gerry tells him she is no good for him and that, besides, they don't love each other anymore. To prove her point she kisses him passionately, which, under the circumstances, only irritates him. "You see," she says, "some men would give their life for that." What Gerry says next gives her morning's farce in the kitchen a shrewd twist:

You can't afford to have a wife like me . . . I'm like a very nice expensive car that gives you about six miles to the gallon . . . only you haven't got the gallon. . . . As a cook and a housewife I am certainly a phooey. . . . And as a good provider and the lord of the manor you are certainly a phooey.

Gerry wants a divorce, indeed has wanted one for years but something has said, "Wait until he has crashed through, wait until he has made a success." She continues:

19

The one strength I had, I mean being pretty and being able to make men do what I wanted . . . was the one strength I couldn't use any more because I was married. . . . What you should have been is a gigolo, and what I should have been . . . it's such an ugly word, isn't it?

Tom tells her to be serious, Gerry insists on divorce, and they are off on a long dialogue that moves toward her actual departure. Sturges does not reach that point in his first day's notes, and was not to do so for some time; in the meantime, he worked and reworked the opening scene and took notes on possible alternatives.

He wrote on September 5, for example, "Wife throws wedding ring out the window to prove she is on the level about divorce" and,

Picture starts with apartment house manager showing apartment to prospective tenants while our hero and heroine still occupy it. This should sell the fact that they are broke [no period in original]

On September 7, Sturges wrote a page and a half of Tom and Gerry dialogue of uncertain relation to that of his first day's notes:

TOM: I have the right to go out with the boys once in a while.
GERRY: (Wearily) With the boys or with the girls . . . it doesn't matter, darling. I could walk in and find you wrestling with a handful of what your little heart desires . . . or a half-a dozen of them, and it just . . . wouldn't matter.
TOM: Yes? Well you let me catch you . . .
GERRY: I'm not going to let you catch me . . . simply because I'm not going to do anything, because that doesn't interest me either. You don't seem to realize that the whole subject is entirely different from the woman's standpoint than from the man's . . . If some girl makes eyes at you or shows you her knees more than twice a day you nearly burst a blood vessel and strut in here at night like Brigham Young in a new necktie . . . but a pretty woman, darling, never sees any kind of look *but* that kind.

This passage does not appear in any script version but one of its points, at least, holds true for all of them. Infidelity, real or suspected, is not the cause of Tom and Gerry's breakup—as it is of Jerry and Lucy's in *The Awful Truth* (1937)—or even a source of tension—as it is for couples in many Lubitsch films. Tom and Gerry's root problem really does seem to be financial; their chief dispute is what to do about it.

On September 8 Sturges wrote three more pages of dialogue between Tom and Gerry, which concludes with Gerry telling Tom that he has not noticed her new dress and also that she bought it, and paid their rent, with money she was given by someone named the Wienie King. The very name of this character, mentioned here for the first time, apparently galvanized Sturges for he proceeded immediately to write a nine-page draft of Gerry's encounter with the Wienie King, much of which is reasonably close to the final script (pages A-3 to A-14). This draft, headed "Sequence 'A,'" is the first one of the project to appear in full script apparatus, which includes—besides the sequence heading itself—page numbers, shot numbers, and shot descriptions.

The Main Titles are superimposed over a panning SHOT FROM
A HIGH BUILDING DOWN on a residential section of New
York City. The CAMERA ZOOMS onto a CLOSER SHOT of
an apartment house.

DISSOLVE TO:

A-1   A SIGN: "APARTMENT TO LET"

DISSOLVE TO:

A-2   AN ELEVATOR DOOR OPENING

A dried up prune of an apartment house manager, male, steps
out of the elevator leading an old gentleman and his wife. The
CAMERA TRUCKS AHEAD OF THEM.

What follows is the first version of the dialogue among Wienie King, wife,
and manager as they walk down the hall (shot A-2). The next shot, A-3 (RE-
VERSE SHOT FROM INTERIOR OF A STUDIO APARTMENT), brings
the party inside Tom and Gerry's duplex apartment. The wife and the manager discuss how dirty the apartment is; the Wienie King wonders why the
ceiling is so high.

A-3   (Continued)

The CAMERA PANS UP to Geraldine leaning over the balcony.
She is a very pretty young woman in a negligee.

A-4   THE GROUP BELOW [Dialogue]

The manager and the Wife walk away OUT OF THE SHOT [to
the kitchenette]

A-5   GERALDINE – ON THE BALCONY

She turns and goes into her bedroom.

A-6   CLOSE SHOT – THE HUSBAND [not yet called the Wienie
King]

[After speaking to his retreating wife]
He crosses to the balcony stairs and climbs up them. He reaches
the top and pokes at the ceiling with his rubber-tipped cane.

A-7   CLOSE SHOT – THE HUSBAND

He lowers his cane to the floor and reacts suddenly to something
he sees. He comes a little CLOSER TO THE CAMERA and
looks again.

A-8   SHOT OF THE BEDROOM FROM THE HUSBAND'S
ANGLE

Inside the bedroom we see a dressing table, the foot of a footless
bed and a very pretty pair of ankles and feet encased in mules.

21

The Wienie King glimpses Gerry unawares: when she turns to enter her bedroom she does not know that he is about to climb the stairs. She does not close her door, so he is able to discover her lying on her bed in her negligee smoking a cigarette. This provocative view of Gerry is complemented by an emphasis on the Wienie King's voyeurism. Poking the upstairs ceiling with his cane, he "reacts suddenly to something he sees"; he "comes a little closer to the camera and looks again." "Closer to the camera" suggests not only his physical proximity to it but also the camera's identification with his peeping; the next shot, blatantly fetishistic, is what the Wienie King sees: a pair of ankles and feet cut off from the rest of Gerry's body by the door or frame line.

> A-9   THE HUSBAND – FROM INSIDE THE BEDROOM
>
> He approaches the door warily and stops in surprise.
>
> THE HUSBAND
> Hello.
>
> A-10   GERALDINE – ON THE BED
>
> She is smoking a cigarette.
>
> GERALDINE
> Hello.
>
> A-11   THE HUSBAND – IN THE DOORWAY
>
> THE HUSBAND
> What are you doing here?
>
> He advances to the edge of the bed and the CAMERA PANS
> GERALDINE INTO THE SHOT.
>
> GERRY
> I might ask you the same question but I suppose I haven't the right to.

The Wienie King approaches the bedroom door and sees Gerry on the bed; he "stops in surprise" and says hello. Not protesting or covering herself, Gerry returns his greeting. As he enters the room and advances toward her, the viewers again see what he sees. the camera "pans Geraldine into the shot," that is, moves horizontally along her body. The Wienie King moves to the edge of the bed and a bit later sits down, uninvited but unopposed. Gerry says she "hasn't the right" to question his presence there. This is a reference to her rent problem, but its odd other implication—that he has the right to enter her bedroom without warning—reinforces the seductive dimension of the scene.

After a page of further conversation, the Wienie King produces "a roll that would choke a horse" and, over Gerry's protests, presses five hundred dollars in her hand for the rent and throws "a couple more hundreds" on her bed for a new dress. He then "waves his stick at her and walks out leaving a stupefied

Gerry examining the money." The Wienie King returns to his wife and the manager and tells them, after some misunderstanding due to his deafness, that the lady now has money to pay the rent and won't be moving out after all. How does he know? "(Cackling) Because I just give it to her." After this scene Sturges cuts back to:

> A-13 GERRY SITTING ON THE EDGE OF HER BED
>
> She is looking Past the CAMERA completely mystified. The money lies beside her. She turns her head slowly almost to the point where she can see the money, then closes her eyes and reaches for it with her left hand. Her hand just misses the money. She tries again and says a little prayer. She misses it again. Now she opens her eyes, looks to heaven and makes another try. Her hand lands on the money. She looks at it quickly, then clutches her heart, picks up the money and examines it once more, then throws it in the air, slips out of her dressing gown and runs into the bathroom.
>
> FADE OUT:
>
> <u>END OF SEQUENCE "A"</u>

The Wienie King scene made a fine opening for the script as a whole but did not by itself provide sufficient motivation for Gerry to leave Tom. On September 10, two days after drafting the scene, Sturges returned to this problem:

The last thing goes wrong for the young man, his business collapses and his wife chooses this moment to tell him she is leaving him. He says: "That's fine, that makes everything complete. That's all I needed."

This brief note is the most pointed conjunction so far of Gerry's departure with Tom's business failure. The exact nature of Tom's economic failure and of Gerry's reaction to it, and the relation of both to Gerry's leaving, were issues that were to occupy Sturges through his second script draft, which he completed November 8. The note is interesting also in that it presents, for a moment at least, Tom's point of view. Gerry dominates nearly every scene with Tom in all versions of *The Palm Beach Story*; but in such cases it is useful, indeed crucial, to consider events from time to time from the other character's point of view. This allows the screenwriter, or dramatist, to build that character's perspective—and the audience's reaction to him or her—into the scene, which also controls the range of the dominant character's actions.

Two more pages of Tom-Gerry dialogue on September 10 are followed by the first mention of the film's later events, some idea of which Sturges had apparently had in mind for some time.

Gerry has succeeded in doing everything she wanted for Tom. The Vallee Character is going to put Tom's invention on the market, and now he wants to marry Gerry which seems to be the fruition of all of Gerry's plans. There remains only the somewhat difficult scene of telling Rockefeller that Tom is not her brother but her husband . . . or does Tom think they could get a divorce without Rockefeller finding out about it? (P.S. Note: "But Darling, I'm leaving you anyway . . . we don't love each other," is her rejoinder to all of his objections to the scene)

This is the first time any mention is made of Tom's having invented something. It is not inconsistent with his also having a job, which is referred to in many more notes and script drafts to come. He is by no means yet the unemployed inventor of the final script and film. Sturges has also apparently not yet come up with Tom's airport idea, which the phrase "put on the market" does not quite fit. The question about Tom that follows—"could they get a divorce without Rockefeller finding out about it?"—suggests his complicity at some point in Gerry's fortune-hunting, a possibility that Sturges played with for some time before rejecting it firmly. It is not as simple as that, however, because Gerry keeps maneuvering Tom into the role of a cuckold-pimp by seeking to make him the beneficiary of her attractiveness to other men. In the final script and film, certainly, Tom keeps repudiating this role and trying to get Gerry to call off her campaign. Still, despite his best efforts, he finds himself in something like a pimp's shoes. (This may be why, taken together with Gerry's defection itself, he is angry so much of the time.) Casting bears on the issue as well. Joel McCrea could probably not be perceived by audiences as other than moral and honorable in all circumstances—a point that cuts in two ways. *Because* McCrea will not be perceived as even a circumstantial pimp, Sturges can put him into one dubious situation after another, something one might not do with an actor whose screen image more closely fit the bill—the older Robert Taylor or Tyrone Power, for example. On the other hand, to see an actor-persona who can do no wrong in scenes both uncomfortable and compromising, makes for a fine tension.

The passage also contains Sturges's first mention of "Rockefeller," the character later called John D. Hackensacker IV—the final script changes it to III—and of the actor who eventually played him, Rudy Vallee. James Curtis reports that in August 1941 Sturges's New York friend Charles Abramson visited him in Los Angeles. They went to see a Ronald Colman film and, arriving early, saw an hour of the second feature, *Time Out for Rhythm,* a musical comedy featuring, among others, Vallee. Curtis continues:

The New York *Times* described Vallee's dry performance as "petulant." But Sturges noted that whenever Vallee, who had a relatively small part with little to do, opened his mouth, the audience roared with laughter. Sturges turned to Abramson. "This guy's funny and he doesn't realize it."[1]

At home, later that night, Sturges summoned his secretary Edwin Gillette, began dictating, "and suddenly there was a new character," Abramson later recalled. "What was that?" he asked. "That's the new part for Rudy," said Sturges. Word that Sturges was interested in him somehow reached Vallee, who promptly had his agent contact the director. Lest this be insufficient, however, Vallee wrote to Sturges on September 12:

Possibly Stanley Bergerman did not convey to you my personal feelings.
I would walk from here to Moscow and back if I could be a part of one of your productions. "The Lady Eve" is responsible for my great admiration of your craftsmanship
and even if nothing eventuates for me that was a picture I shall long remember.

Cordially yours,

Sturges had already used Vallee's name in his notes—even before the character he was to play had a name—but had not got far enough with the script
to commit himself, let alone the studio. He replied on the 15th.

Thank you very much for your amiable note of September 12th.
Stanley Bergerman *had* conveyed your message to me, and if the part works out I will
tell you about it later.
In seeing *Time Out for Rhythm* I thought I perceived how you should be used in pictures. It gave me the idea of showing a gentleman on the screen . . . with the qualities
and some of the faults that the word might imply.

On September 12 Sturges wrote a page and a half of dialogue for the latter part of the film: Tom is angry that Gerry has introduced him—presumably
to "Rockefeller" and his sister—as Captain McGlue. The next day, however,
Sturges was once again struggling with the initial dialogue between Tom and
Gerry. Five more pages of dialogue end with

> He kisses her again and during the kiss flips her off the ground
> and into his arms.
>
> GERRY
> (After the legal limit)
> Nothing but . . . habit.
>
> TOM
> (Starting upstairs with her)
> A bad habit, hunh?
>
> GERRY
> Very . . . very . . . bad . . . and wicked . . . and stupid . . . and
> young . . . and impractical and . . .
>
> He seals her lips with another kiss.
> FADEOUT:

Sturges retained this ending to the scene, with slight changes, in the final
script (pages 31–32) and in the film. "Starting upstairs" is the closest one could
come in Hays Office Hollywood to explicit sex. The long verbal battles between Tom and Gerry, in which issues fundamental to their marriage are discussed—now humorously, now painfully—end with their making love. This
tells us that, in spite of everything, Tom and Gerry are still attracted to each
other—a point that must be made early on if they are to get back together by
the end of the film. In the short run, however, a dilemma resulted: where does
the story go from here? What, notably, will now cause Gerry to leave?

The next day Sturges avoided this impasse, or sought a way around it, by considering the plot as a whole:

A young woman works her way to Palm Beach to see what life holds for her: a husband or adventure. She has left her husband because together they could not succeed. She chose Palm Beach because it contains more wealth in the shape of rich men per square mile than any other locale

The day after this, September 14, Sturges began a new episode, apparently designed to remotivate Gerry's departure following her intimate evening with Tom. In four pages of dialogue, a flirting Gerry tries to sell a Mr. Hodge—actually Tom's employer for three years—on a Diesel engine invented by "her brother," that is, Tom, who has tried without success to show it to Hodge hundreds of times. Gerry invites Hodge to lunch. He usually has crackers and milk at his desk but she suggests instead "steak and oysters and asparagus out of season . . . and champagne." The next day Sturges wrote seven pages of dialogue—set on train, then yacht—between Gerry and "John D., IV," as he is here called, and also introducing John's sister Edith, an early version of the Princess. On the 16th, he rewrote and expanded the scene between Gerry and Mr. Hodge—this time she admits the invention is her husband's. Rather than agree to help him, however, Hodge tells her Tom is fired, saying:

the man who hides behind his wife's skirts and has her do his dirty work for him is not the Hodge Brothers' type.

It was her own idea, Gerry tells Hodge; it doesn't matter, says he, "the whole matter reeks with unhealthiness." "I hope they choke you, you old milkshake!" she says, referring to his milk and crackers, whereupon he cancels the two weeks' severance pay he had ordered his secretary to include in Tom's final check. At this, "weeping and furious," Gerry

suddenly snatches a picture from the wall and brings it over Mr. Hodge's head and down around his shoulders. This knocks him to the floor and she sees that it has loosened his hair. Snatching the toupee from his head, she tears it in four, throws it in the wastepaper basket, then, as a last thought, picks up the wastepaper basket and jams it over his head.

This scene dissolves to one in which Tom is being thrown out of Hodge Brothers with a check in his hand. Somewhat dazed, he sees Gerry, who "snaps out of a woebegone expression and flashes her most cheerful smile"— she says she's come to have lunch with him. Tom asks "very suspiciously" if she knows anything about his having been fired. She says she does, in a way, and "laughs her prettiest laugh," which ends the scene.

Imminent, but not quite arrived at, is an angry Tom's outburst and Gerry's abrupt departure for Palm Beach. This, or something like it, is implied in a note of September 20, in which Sturges asks himself where the story as a whole is going:

To keep the story on the tracks and moving forward, the girl must want to do something, preferably for her husband. Thus, when she tries to further her husband's cause and succeeds only in getting him fired, the story is excellently interesting. Even the digression: the proving to her husband that a pretty woman can go anywhere for nothing, is good, but having arrived at where she was going, the lady must want something again immediately and have to surmount obstacles to get it. Only this wanting something keeps the story and the interest moving. This leaves us merely to find out what a handsome young woman in Palm Beach wants. Does she want her husband from New York to join her? Does she want to help him? If so, how? Does she want to find a rich husband for herself and possibly a rich wife for her husband? (This would be new, and Palm Beach would be just the place to find them both.) Does she want a divorce? Florida requires three months' residence.

NOTE: When Gerry arrives in Jacksonville with John D. IV we might demonstrate the value of having nothing as a leverage over one's friends. If Gerry had anything John D. could leave her to her own devices, but having nothing, she has a hold on him. He would like to give her five hundred dollars and wash his hands of her, but she will not be brushed off so inexpensively . . . and refuses the five hundred. Would she take a thousand? She would not. Well, what is he to do? Why doesn't he just leave her to her fate, she suggests. "You know perfectly well that I can't," says the exasperated John D. IV. He explains to her who he is and what his responsibilities are in the world. When she realizes whom she almost sent away her knees turn to water

That Sturges calls Gerry's train trip to Florida a digression is intriguing. Perhaps he wished to keep a steady focus on Tom and Gerry's relationship even on the train and in Palm Beach. He did not anticipate at this stage—or later?—that Rudy Vallee as John D. Hackensacker III and the Ale and Quail Club would not only distract attention from the couple's problems but quite overwhelm them in most viewers' experience, and memory, of the film.

If Gerry makes the trip to prove that a pretty woman can go anywhere for nothing, to whom is the proof offered? To her husband, who has little regard for her abilities; and to herself, to restore a self-confidence weakened by her husband's doubts and by the fiasco of her Hodge initiative. Upon her arrival in Palm Beach, however, another impasse looms for Sturges. If the only thing that will keep the story moving is Gerry's wanting something, then the critical issue becomes: What is it that she wants? Each answer to this question is a possible plot turn: that her husband arrive; that she help her husband in some way; that she find a rich husband for herself and perhaps a rich wife for her husband; a divorce.

Ultimately, of course, the problem will be resolved not by anything that happens in the Palm Beach scenes but by recasting the initial Tom-Gerry dialogues in order to provide an altered motivation for her departure. In the final script and film, Gerry heads for Palm Beach not primarily to show that she can get there on her own, but to leave the marriage itself. If Gerry assures Tom resentfully that she can make out very well by herself, she does so to stress his blindness to her charms—he does not notice her new dress—which is one of her principal justifications for leaving. If she does prove in the end that a pretty woman can go anywhere with nothing and for nothing, she has not set out to do so—she had wanted to bring more than the clothes on her back (see pages 38–40).

Sturges's work for the next six days bears no discernible relation to the fundamental script questions he had posed on September 20. Instead he seems to be reasking a question he had regarded as settled—why Gerry leaves Tom in the first place. On the twenty-third, for instance, he wrote a one-page addition to the initial Tom and Gerry scene in which she says, "I tell you we don't mean anything to each other any more . . . I don't love you . . . you don't love me . . . we're invisible to each other," but a note the next day has her say, "I'd like to have a little respite from financial worry while I'm still young enough to enjoy it." A page written on the twenty-fifth sketches a draft of Tom's interchange with the train porter in Palm Beach. A half-page exchange on the twenty-seventh has Gerry telling Tom that she is now engaged to John D.

TOM
(After a pause)
Well I've been engaged to you, you know, and if my memory . . .

GERRY
(Quickly)
That was entirely different.

Infidelity is not an issue in the breakup itself but emerges as one after Tom and Gerry part company. This note—and others later—make clear that neither party succumbs.

Also on September 27 Sturges made this note:

Gerry told Tom that together they defeated each other and the immediate happenings after their separation seemed to substantiate her contention. A few minutes after Gerry's departure on the Palm Beach Limited sans ticket, sans money, sans clothes thusly proving her other contention i.e.: that a pretty woman does not abide by the rules of ordinary mankind, Tom walked into a bar and ordered a drink.

Still later on the twenty-seventh, Sturges wrote a seven-page, eight-scene outline of the script as it had developed to date—from the Wienie King scene in the beginning to Tom's exchange with the porter in Palm Beach. Half of the outline was devoted to the New York scenes, dealing with the events leading to Gerry's departure; half to the events on the train and in Palm Beach.

At this point the Palm Beach events are, for the most part, sketchy and incomplete. For example:

6. Ale and Quail sequence, ending with Gerry losing all her clothes. The next morning she meets a young man with a little expense book. He lends her a dressing gown and buys her breakfast. He is somewhat embarrassed to go into the dining car with her in a dressing gown. She says: "Maybe you should wear one too, they'd think we were honeymooners."

28

Sturges then launches into a detailed, two-page treatment of the Jacksonville store scene, mentioned here for the first time, in which the young man buys Gerry clothes and a ruby bracelet, and she finds out who he is. This is followed in turn by a very brief summary of the yacht scene,

In which he tells her something about himself. She then tells him a few things about herself . . . not quite one hundred per cent truthful. She says she ran away from a convent and married while she was still too young to know what she was doing.

The young man asks about the brute she was married to. She says he wasn't really a brute but the young man concludes nevertheless, "the man was obviously a hound." The final event of the outline takes place at the train station in Palm Beach: The porter explains to Tom that the woman he is seeking got off the train at Jacksonville and continued her journey by yacht. How long does it take a yacht to get to Palm Beach, asks Tom. That depends upon what its occupants are doing, replies the porter. "With the right girl it could take quite some time."

The summary of the New York scenes crystallized—although Sturges makes no mention of it—several problems in the first part of the script. Before he "tosses a lot of money on the bed," the Wienie King tells Gerry that she's a sucker to be poor while she's young. "When Tom comes home Gerry tells him she is going to leave him . . . that she is tired of being poor," then she gives him some of the same arguments the Wienie King has given her. "The only thing that hurts me," says Gerry after she has made her point, "is to leave you worse off than I found you. If you would just let me help you a little before I left you . . . then I wouldn't mind going so much . . ." The only influence she has is over men—when she and Tom were in love she could not use this to help him, but now . . . "My mind recoils at what it thinks you are trying to say," says Tom. "It refuses to understand you." Gerry replies, "It wouldn't necessarily have to be anything bad . . . you have no idea what a long-legged gal can do . . . without doing anything." The scene "ends in a seduction, by which device Tom tries to prove to her that she still loves him."

At breakfast the next morning, however, Gerry reiterates her decision to leave. She resolves to do something for Tom first—perhaps to get him a raise—but Tom tells her to keep her nose out of his business. She resents the implication that nothing she can do could help him and says she will not be there when he gets home. Tom says that's a fine way to send a man to his office and departs, slamming the door. The outline continues:

Scene in which Gerry has Tom fired. It may be as written or it may start with her telling Mr. Hodge that she is leaving Tom and for him to please keep an eye out on him . . . she wouldn't want him to drink himself to death. . . . Consider also Tom coming in and catching Gerry and Mr. Hodge so that Mr. Hodge thinks he is being badgered and fires Tom instantly for this reason.

Scene in Pennsylvania Station: Gerry's sudden impulse to leave Tom immediately. She gets on [the] train by looking worried. When Tom wants to follow her they close the gates in his face. He goes into a bar to get drunk.

Sturges's work over the next several days tinkered with elements of the September 27 outline but did not alter its structure or basic premises. In the outline the Wienie King tells Gerry she should be rich while she's young; in a scene draft of the 28th he advises her in a somewhat different vein:

Trouble with people is they ain't courageous enough . . . always skeered to do what they want to do . . . always forgit they only goin' to live oncet . . .

The speech inspires the Wienie King to do something that he wants to do, which is to help a pretty lady in distress. Its main function, however, is to supply Gerry with a motive—or a push—to do what *she* wants to do, which is to leave Tom for richer pastures. "Just remember one thing," the Wienie King concludes. "OBEY THAT IMPULSE."

The terms of the advice are different, but Gerry, no less a parrot in this version than in the outline, passes the advice along to Tom later in the scene: "Did you know that you should always obey an impulse?"

> TOM
> You obeyed one when you married me.

> GERRY
> And I'm very glad of it . . . I've loved it . . . but now that we've had our fun . . . there's work to be done . . . say, am I talking in rhyme or something?

> TOM
> You're talking through your hat.

Gerry complains to Tom, as she does in the outline, that, although she tried, he wouldn't let her help him in his career; in this version, however, she cites examples. Tom would say, for instance, "What were you smiling that way for while you were dancing with that guy?" who often turned out to be the president of a company.

> GERRY
> So today, instead of being the vice-president of the Vitreous Bath Tub Company or sales manager for the Jersey City Hide Works, or high up in the Perth-Amboy Fish Meal Factory, all of which I could have got you easily, darling . . . and many more . . . you're a draftsman for Hodge Brothers.

> TOM
> And that isn't good enough for you, I suppose.

> GERRY
> That's right.

> TOM
> All you're interested in is how much a man makes.

GERRY

It isn't all I'm interested in . . . but it's a fairly good indication of
his intelligence . . . [handwritten:] and I love an intelligent man.

On September 29 and 30, Sturges wrote six pages on the Palm Beach part
of the script, including this description of Tom and Gerry's first scene alone
in the Hackensacker home ("It really *is* like a hotel," notes the script):

Here comes the placing of the idol on the mantlepiece [*sic*]. Another seduction scene
now takes place. When Tom wakes up in the morning Gerry is already gone. At this
point the Princess calls him to come over and have breakfast with her. She sends the
car and also tells him that Gerry is out fishing with Snoodles.

The young man of the outline, also referred to there as John D., here acquires
a pet name—Snoodles—before he has a proper one, and Edith in the outline
has become the Princess here. These two have serious designs on Gerry and
Tom, respectively, hence "the idol on the mantelpiece," which becomes in the
final script:

a little Staffordshire group that might be called "Innocence" . . . a boy and a girl and a
lamb . . . or a young girl with an armful of lillies . . . or a bride and groom looking
away from each other. (page 122)

Idol or group, the piece is used by Tom and Gerry to stand for their threatened fidelity, which, unlike the statue itself, remains unbroken.

Calling for a seduction just as the idol is placed on the mantelpiece is a
most interesting suggestion, but one which Sturges never pursued. If Tom
were to seduce Gerry at this point in the action, then the seduction could not
be used for the film's conclusion, which, it is true, Sturges had not drafted or
even outlined yet. When Gerry gives in to her feelings for Tom in the final
script and film—even as John D. Hackensacker serenades her below—she
knows she must give up Hackensacker. "I hope you realize this is costing us
millions," she says to Tom. Why must she give him up? Why couldn't Gerry
sleep with Tom at night and go fishing with Hackensacker in the morning?
Because in the gender politics of screwball comedy—and that of Hollywood
films more generally—the heart must always go with sex, and vice versa, particularly for women. Sturges was already pushing Hollywood censorship with
Gerry's quest itself; her simultaneous relationships with two men, even if one
is not sexual, would not get by. Also, in terms of the plot, if Tom's seduction
does not prompt Gerry to go back to him at this point, why will it do so later?
A Gerry who might decide on her own to return—simply because she wished
to do so—is far away at this point in the project and perhaps was not quite
fully achieved at any time.

On October 1, Sturges wrote a brief draft of a scene between Snoodles and
Tom, which he heads "CONCERNING THE BRACELET" and concludes
with this note:

When Gerry finds out she's still in love with Tom he says:

TOM
Yes, but can we do this to Snoodles?

This is Sturges's last explicit notation in a Tom-the-pimp vein. It is interesting that Tom's affection for John D., which is present nowhere in the film, here retards his taking back Gerry—the goal of all his striving—the moment she changes her mind in his favor.

On the same day, Sturges made this note:

1. Premise: That a pretty woman can do anything she wants and go anywhere she likes without money.

2. That a pretty woman can use her appeal for the advancement of her husband.

This brief note crystallizes a dilemma that had underlain Sturges's work on the script from the beginning. Which of the two *is* the film's premise? Can they be reconciled in a single plot and, if so, how? The note reveals, more subtly, Sturges's predisposition toward didacticism in the project: he is out to demonstrate, affirm, or substantiate some premise, even if he is not sure exactly which one.

Sturges did not articulate a more fundamental dilemma underlying his work up to this point. He was committed to Gerry as the film's protagonist but had not so far developed her into a character who could take decisive action—who had ideas of her own, rather than reflected or repeated ones—and whose goals and motivations were not confused or opaque or both. Consequently, after a month's steady work, the basic story was far from resolved. The emphasis of the notes from the very beginning was on Gerry's incompetence. She muffs the breakfast on Sturges's first day's work and goes on muffing things for nearly a month to come, including, notably, the Mr. Hodge incident and all other attempts to help her husband. Her actions seem to confirm Tom's low opinion of her and to justify his desire to keep her out of his work situation. For her part, Gerry berates her husband for earning too little, even suggesting his inferior intelligence because he does not make more money. Her leaving him just for a better lifestyle is, in Hollywood terms anyway, morally dubious. At the same time, Gerry does not actually act on her plan. She is highly indecisive—she insists several times she is going to leave, then does not. When she finally does go, it is "suddenly" and "on impulse." Her unpreparedness for the trip is not Tom's fault, as it is in the final script and film, but the result of her own poor planning. Also, she does not leave to pursue her own goals, but to prove something to her husband. She backs into change and departure, unlike the film's Gerry, who may not know where she is going but proceeds under her own steam and acts on what she believes to be best for herself—and for Tom.

From October 2 through 5, Sturges wrote nothing on the project. When he resumed on the fifth, his two-part problem—an unresolved story and an undefined Gerry—began, slowly, to move toward a solution. It would take him over a month, however—until the second script draft of November 8—to realize fully, and consolidate, the needed changes.

On October 6 Sturges wrote a three-page draft of the yacht scene, including a prefatory note:

On the yacht trip between Jacksonville and Palm Beach Gerry tells Hackensacker that her husband won't give her a divorce without a payment of (she looks around the yacht) a hundred thousand dollars.

Gerry's suggestion that her freedom can only be bought, introduced here, leads to some of John D.'s best lines, which are also sketched here for the first time:

> HACKENSACKER
> (Horrified)
> You mean he wants to sell you! . . .
>
> GERRY
> How much did this yacht cost you?
>
> HACKENSACKER
> That has nothing to do with it . . . a woman after all is not a uh . . . whatever she may be . . . a ~~boat~~ vessel . . . how does he want it?
>
> GERRY
> Uh . . . in cash.
>
> HACKENSACKER
> So I won't stop the check . . .
>
> GERRY
> I suppose he figures that I'm all he has . . . and that if he doesn't get anything out of me . . . why he'll never get anything out of anything.
>
> HACKENSACKER
> (Raising a finger)
> There is a name for such vermin . . . but I won't sully this beautiful morning air by mentioning it. . . . I mean to say: chivalry isn't dead . . . It's decomposed! . . . out of condition as I am . . . if I should ever meet that rat . . . I'd thrash him within an inch of his life.
>
> GERRY
> I hope you never meet him.
>
> H.
> I suppose he's very large.
>
> G.
> He is.

H.
That's one of the peculiarities of this life: that the men who are
most in need of a beating up are always enormous!

Later on October 6, Sturges launched a new scene, to be placed early in
the script, in which Tom seeks support from the mayor of the city for an invention he is trying to market: "an elevated airport in the middle of the city,"
which he describes as "a floating terminal . . . made of steel webbing like a
spider's web." The mayor's only concern during their conversation is the
appropriate mode of dress for a party he has to attend that evening. When he
finally grasps Tom's point, he says scowlingly, "I just built the biggest mu-
nicipal airport in the world . . . maybe you haven't heard about it?"

Sturges follows that scene with one between Tom and his apartment house
manager, in which Tom learns that Gerry has paid their overdue rent. In it
Tom walks straight up to the manager to talk to him "about that rent." (As
Sturges increases Tom's economic difficulties in later drafts, he has a hiding
Tom call to the doorman to make sure the manager is not there so he can
sneak into the building undetected.) The Tom-manager scene is followed by a
one-line scene in which Gerry tells him to put on his dinner jacket because
she is taking him "to dinner and then the theatre and then supper," at which
point the draft ends.

On October 7 and 8, Sturges wove what he had done so far into a revised
draft of sequence "A," which is comprised of the Wienie King's visit and its
immediate aftermath. This draft contains a number of small improvements in
dialogue and action and, more important, a revised version of the initial encounter between Gerry and the Wienie King. The changes begin with Gerry's
first view of the invading threesome below. This time she stays on the balcony long enough to see the old man start to climb the stairs.

A-9   CLOSE SHOT – GERALDINE

She reacts to the old man's coming up the stairs, hurries into her
room and closes the door.

A-10   THE OLD MAN REACHING <u>THE TOP LANDING</u>

He takes three pokes at the ceiling, then crosses to the bed room
door and goes in. He stops suddenly.

A-11   THE INDIGNANT GERALDINE RECLINING <u>ON HER BED</u>

She was in the act of lighting a cigarette.

GERRY
Well, you seem to have your nerve.

She lights the cigarette, blows out a cloud of smoke and puts the
match down.

A-12   THE HUSBAND – <u>IN THE DOORWAY</u>

THE HUSBAND
(Amiably)
Hello . . .

He advances and the CAMERA PANS HIM INTO THE SHOT
with Geraldine.

After asking what she is doing there and whether she goes with the apartment, the Wienie King tells her she has very pretty legs.

GERRY
(Pulling her wrapper tighter)
Thank you . . . I might ask what <u>you</u> were doing here . . . only I
happen to know.

More private as well as more modest than in the September 8 version of the scene, Gerry now closes her door and is indignant that the Wienie King comes in anyway. Now it is she who speaks first and challenges *his* presence. Gerry's wrapper, in keeping with the new tone, replaces the negligee she wore in the earlier version. The camera has also begun to shift from the Wienie King's point of view to Gerry's: the initial shot of Gerry is now a close-up rather than a pan up to her from the first floor. There is now no shot of Gerry or her feet from the Wienie King's point of view, and the camera pans the Wienie King into a shot of Gerry rather than the reverse.

The dialogue between Gerry and the Wienie King that results in his giving her the money remains unchanged, as does the ensuing scene in which he returns to his wife and the apartment house manager and tells them that "the lady don't want to rent," et cetera. The next scene, however—in which Gerry is shown alone, reacting to her sudden riches—has changed considerably.

A-16   GERRY – <u>IN HER ROOM</u>

   She crosses to the telephone and dials a number. As she waits
   for a reply--

A-17   <u>A GLASS DOOR IN A CHEAP OFFICE BUILDING</u>

   On it we read: THOMAS JEFFERS ENTERPRISES and below
   this: Engineers, Patents, Inventions

   We hear a phone ringing. The CAMERA PANS DOWN
   SLOWLY onto a notice to vacate attached to the door with a
   thumb tack. The phone continues to ring.

A-18   GERRY AT THE TELEPHONE

   She hangs up, gets to her feet, suddenly throws the money in the
   air, peels off her wrapper and hurries to her dressing table.

   FADE OUT:

   <u>END OF SEQUENCE "A"</u>

On October 9 Sturges wrote six pages of dialogue between Gerry and "Her Thoughts," to be placed just after the Wienie King has given her the seven hundred dollars and left. She got the money because of her pretty legs, she is getting older, Tom isn't going to amount to anything, he won't accept her help, says Her Thoughts. "We're in love" and "He'll get there some day," Gerry responds; but Her Thoughts' cynical practicality seems to carry the day. Sturges is struggling here both with the reasons for Gerry's departure and with finding the right dramatic mode in which to communicate them. He still seems uncertain about Gerry's attitudes and, ultimately, her character.

On October 12, Sturges wrote a page and a half, mainly description, showing Tom and Gerry in their seats at a theater after their dinner out on what is left of the Wienie King's money. The scene was not used in any script draft but is itself a wry comic set piece. It also shows Sturges still seeking to invent reasons for Gerry to leave Tom and at the same time to suggest the bond of intimacy that will ultimately reunite them.

> DISSOLVE TO:

B-22   TOM AND GERRY – <u>IN THEIR SEATS IN A THEATRE</u>

> We see about twenty other spectators. Tom looks glumly at the stage from which some English voices are playing a sad scene. Gerry looks sadly at the stage also. Now she looks compassionately at Tom and he returns her glance. He looks pleadingly at her, opens his mouth to say something and hiccups violently. He scowls back at the people who scowl at him, composes himself, glowers at the stage and hiccups again. Again he exchanges glances with his neighbors and Gerry tries to look as though she doesn't know him. He hiccups again, turns to scowl at the man at his left and hiccups in his face. He begins to look rather desperate.

> > GERRY
> > (Whispering)
> > Hold your breath.

> Tom takes a very deep breath and starts holding it. This attracts the attention of his neighbors who watch him to see how long he can hold it. Gerry watches him also. His eyes begin to bulge and the sweat comes out on his forehead. Suddenly he lets it go so hard it nearly blows the hair off a bald-headed gentleman in front of him. At this moment he releases the grandfather of all hiccups and one wing of his collar flies open. Gerry starts to get hysterical. Now panting, hiccuping and sweating he tries to fasten his collar. To do this he has to untie his tie. Eventually he gets the collar badly fastened together and the tie tied in a very lopsided manner. He gives Gerry one beautiful look and hiccups again and both sides of the collar fly open. Gerry becomes wildly hysterical. Tom starts doggedly to fasten himself together

but now his collar button is gone, having fallen down inside his shirt. He feels around for it then with a miserable look at Gerry unfastens his shirt and reaches inside for the collar button. It slips down further inside his clothing and he starts reaching into his trousers for it. Now he does a sort of shimmy interrupted by a look and a hiccup at the gentleman on his left, then stamps his feet alternately to shake the button down his trousers. Unsuccessful, he rises quickly, stamps a couple of times, snarls an apology at the people behind him and stamps once more.

Now he sits down again, rolls his trouser leg above the knee, pinches the collar button through the trousers with one hand and starts reaching up through the trousers with the other. This makes a very tight fit and his hand gets caught. While he is struggling to release his hand, the manager taps him on the shoulder and beckons him outside. As Tom opens his mouth to explain he hiccups. Now a policeman leans into the scene, taps him on the shoulder, then motions him out through a nice white glove.

This is Sturges's last free-form note on what became *The Palm Beach Story*. The next day—October 13—he left off writing notes and draft scenes and devoted his energies to the writing of the project's first complete screenplay version. Between October 13 and November 4, he wrote what became sequences "A" through "H" of the November 3 script.

The November 3 sequence "A" includes a revision, for what turned out to be the last time, of the initial encounter between Gerry and the Wienie King. Written on October 13, this version, like the October 7 version, begins with shot A-9, which it carries over unchanged:

CLOSE SHOT – GERALDINE

She reacts to the old man's coming up the stairs, hurries into her room and closes the door.

In the new A-10, however, the old man no longer walks right into Gerry's bedroom; he now "puts his hand on the knob." Sturges cuts from this to

A-11   GERRY – IN HER BEDROOM

PAST HER we see the door opening and she backs hurriedly into a closet and closes the door.

A-12   THE OLD MAN WANDERING AROUND THE BED ROOM

He picks up an atomizer and squirts some perfume on himself.

A-13   GERRY OPENING THE DOOR OF THE CLOSET

She reacts to the swiping of her perfume, etc.

What changes most significantly in the October 13 version is the addition of an elaborate silent play between Gerry and the Wienie King before they

The bird on her wrapper sings; she doesn't. Robert Dudley as the "Wienie King" corners Claudette Colbert as Gerry in THE PALM BEACH STORY.

speak to each other. This silent action swings the power struggle that has been at stake between them in all three versions decisively in Gerry's favor. The battle of looks that began with the old man spying on Gerry unawares now has Gerry spying on him unawares; with the power of the look in both cases goes the power of the scene.

The Wienie King now explores Gerry's environment thoroughly before he finds her. Moving from bedroom to closet to bathroom, her intimate spaces, he smells her perfume—even sprays it on himself—examines her lipstick and tastes it, and finally, although he does not intend to do so, "flushes" her in the shower stall where she is now hiding, forcing her to reveal herself when he starts to turn on the water. He tracks Gerry in her lair; the tracking and hunt are mutual, however, since Gerry sees the Wienie King coming up the stairs and observes every move he makes thereafter. She outmaneuvers him until he reaches for the faucet; even at this point, however, it is she who throws open the shower curtain, revealing herself and confronting the interloper.

As before, Sturges follows the Wienie King back to his wife and the manager after his conversation with Gerry, then cuts back or, as the script says, "dissolves to" Gerry in her room. Now her reaction to the gift she has received is somewhat different from before:

She looks at the money like a child looking at a cake. She thinks for a moment, then hurries to the telephone and dials a number.

GERRY
(Into the telephone)
Hello, this is Mrs. Jeffers . . . I want to have my hair done, please, and a manicure . . . yes . . .
(She looks at a clock)
all right, thank you.

She hangs up and rises, then sits down and dials another number.

GERRY
(Into the telephone)
Hello, this is Mrs. Jeffers . . .
have you still got that silver lamé dinner dress with the draped top? . . . oh will you hold it for me till I get there . . . thank you.

She rises and thinks another moment, then dials another number.

Sturges cuts here, as before, to the "cheap office building" in which Tom works, with the sound of a phone ringing and a notice to vacate on the door. In the cut back to Gerry, Sturges has her hang up, "look once more at the money," then rise happily, peel off her wrapper, and reach into her closet for a dress. With that the sequence ends.

Money in her hand again at last, Gerry thinks first of herself, then, as an afterthought, of Tom. Putting herself first is consistent with the new Gerry, but having her use the money for instant gratification is like the old Gerry, who seems unable to plan or, more fundamentally, to think. When the later Gerry uses her money to pay the bills—and even to buy a new dress—she is advancing toward her longer-range goal of leaving a marriage that is frustrating her.

The rest of the November 3 script's sequence "A" is, with one major exception, a slightly revised composite of scenes and passages written earlier and traced in detail above. The exception is the title sequence and brief introduction to the film that appear here for the first time, and are carried over unchanged in the November 8 script and with a half-page deletion in the November 21 script (pages A-1 to A-3). The title sequence and brief introduction comprise, with the last two pages of sequence "H" (pages 156–157)—the last two pages of the script—a kind of framing story, which will be discussed below. As was often the case with Sturges (*The Great McGinty, The Miracle of Morgan's Creek*), the framing story was written last—the revised sequence "A" on November 3, sequence "H" on November 4. It also coincided, in this case, with the project's title change. Pages written through November 2 are headed *Is That Bad?*; those written on the third and fourth are headed *The Palm Beach Story*. On October 13 Sturges wrote an unfinished version of sequence "B" that he later incorporated, with changes, into the November 3 script. This version begins, as did the earlier draft, with Tom's visit to the mayor of the city. It refines and expands the dialogue of the scene but leaves it otherwise unchanged. A partial exception is that here, for the first time, Tom has brought with him "a small model, very much simplified, of a miniature city with his steel net landing field over it." That scene is followed by a slightly revised version of Tom's scene with the doorman, and this is followed by a revised version of the initial dialogue between Tom and Gerry—which is full of cross-outs and written-in changes. This crucial part of the script is not yet close to being settled. After six pages of dialogue, for instance, Tom erupts in anger, which he does in no earlier or later version:

B-22   (Continued)

TOM
(Suddenly)
Look: if you don't like me as a husband, now would be as good a time as any to say so. I've taken about all the guff from you that I intend to, and if I'm not satisfactory . . .

GERRY
Why don't you put on your dinner jacket and take me out to dinner?

TOM
Because I don't feel like eating. I'm going out by myself . . . and get drunk.

GERRY
Well, you'd better take some money because the last time we were . . .

TOM
I don't need any of your ill-gotten gains, thank you.

GERRY
Ill-gotten gains . . . aren't you ashamed of yourself.

TOM
You ought to be ashamed of yourself.

He starts out.

GERRY
But I've already bought the theatre tickets.

TOM
Well, sit in them yourself.

He slams the door.

DISSOLVE TO:

B-23   GERRY – IN A THEATRE SEAT

There is an empty seat next to her. Next to this sits a large prosperous business man. Next to her sits

40

This is as far as Sturges got on October 13. In the November 3 sequence "B," the dialogue of Tom's scene with the mayor is revised somewhat but the doorman scene remains unchanged. The long dialogue scene between Tom and Gerry that follows—the heart of the sequence—has been consolidated and developed but has still not yet achieved anything like final form. Gerry tells Tom about the Wienie King and his gift and Tom is disturbed. He proposes to return the money to the Wienie King "and tell him what I think of . . ." Gerry replies that she does not know where he lives or even his name,

> and I don't think they'd give the money back: I mean the grocer
> and the drugstore and all, after they waited so long for it . . .

                              TOM
That's right, rub it in.

                              GERRY
> I'm not rubbing anything in. It isn't your fault if you haven't any
> talent for making money . . . some people are just born without it
> like some people are just born without a sense of smell—and go
> through life eating rotten eggs.

At this point Tom says, as in the October 13 version of the scene, "Look: if you don't like me as a husband, now would be as good a time as any to say so . . ." Also as before, Gerry suggests he put on his dinner jacket and take her out to dinner; her theater plans have been dropped. Again Tom refuses; he's going to get drunk and doesn't want her ill-gotten gains to help him do it. Rather than have Tom storm out, however, Sturges now has Gerry keep the conversation alive in an ingenious way.

                              GERRY
Tom.   -

                              TOM
What?

                              GERRY
> You said something a minute ago . . . now might be as good a
> time as any . . . while we're still young . . . and can make other
> connections.

                              TOM
When did you get this idea, this afternoon?

                              GERRY
> I've had it a long time but something always said: "Wait till he
> crashes through . . ."

"We looked so nice in the church," Gerry muses later in the conversation.

> They said, "My, what a handsome couple" . . . It should have
> ended there with "and they lived happily ever after" and some fi-
> nale music . . . instead of wondering where the rent was coming

from . . . wondering where our meals were coming from . . . unable to reciprocate for the generosity of our friends . . . with torn
stockings and run-down heels and sleezy dresses . . . in <u>spades</u> we
lived happily ever after!

                    TOM
Aren't you forgetting a little thing called love? . . .

                    GERRY
You mean that thing that happens in the spring . . . to increase the
population? . . . I haven't forgotten it . . . I'm <u>glad</u> I married you
for the stupidity of it and the youngness of it . . . with our champagne tastes and our near-beer income . . . taking everything for
granted . . . but we're not going to be young always and it isn't
quite so romantic to be <u>old</u> and poor . . . we're not going to get
anywhere.

                    TOM
How do you know?

                    GERRY
If a man hasn't succeeded at thirty-five, there is no reason to expect he is going to set the world on fire at fifty-five . . . Men don't
get smarter as they get older . . . they just lose their hair.

Tom, who seems reduced in the passage to feeding his wife straight lines,
remarks that Gerry hasn't been "such a big help" either. This prompts her to
recall the times she tried to help him by using her attractiveness to men but
"every time . . . you tried to punch the man in the nose."

                    TOM
Listen: you want a divorce?

                    GERRY
The only thing that hurts me about it is to leave you worse off
than I found you . . . if you could just be sensible about things . . .
I mean now that we don't love each other any more . . . we could
stay together for a little while . . . and by the time we parted I
would have made a success of you, darling . . . or at least you'd be
well on the road to it.

                    TOM
My mind refuses to understand what you are suggesting,
Geraldine . . . it recoils from what you're trying to imply.

                    GERRY
I'm not implying anything at all . . . You have no idea what a
long-legged gal can do . . . without doing anything.

                    TOM
You want a divorce.

GERRY
I'd much rather stay and help you. Like this afternoon . . .

Tom and Gerry go out to dinner, during which they continue their conversation, then return to their apartment, where they talk further and then not only "start upstairs," at which point the earlier draft stopped, but arrive there:

> He [Tom] seals her lips with another kiss and walks into the bedroom. He kicks the door to with his heel.

FADE OUT:

END OF SEQUENCE "B"

The November 3 sequence "B" established its definitive form: a three-stage conversation between Tom and Gerry, set in apartment, restaurant, and apartment, in which they end the evening by making love. The only thing that stops their conversation—in which nothing is resolved—is Tom's kicking the bedroom door closed or, in both earlier and later versions, his starting upstairs with Gerry.

There are no drafts of sequence "C" in the yellow pages and notes, but Sturges had taken notes on certain scenes that were later included in "C," and had drafted one of those scenes in detail—Gerry's efforts to help Tom by ingratiating herself with his boss, which results in Tom's losing his job. In the November 3 sequence "C," in which for the first time Tom is an unemployed inventor, the point of an episode like this seems dubious. Sturges was still committed to it, however, apparently as remotivation for Gerry's departure after the couple's evening of love. It appears, transformed and in a new context, in the November 3 script. It begins the morning after Tom and Gerry have their long three-part argument and spend the night together.

C-1   TOM – SHAVING WITH AN ELECTRIC RAZOR – <u>IN THE</u> <u>BATHROOM</u> – (DAY)

> He is partially dressed and whistling violently but somewhat off key. He seems very cheerful.

TOM
I'll get your breakfast in a minute, honey.

C-2   GERRY – <u>IN BED</u>

> She listens to the whistling for a moment, rather disagreeably, then sits up, puts on some mules and a wrapper and starts out of the room. As she passes the bathroom she tosses a line to him.

GERRY
Very proud of yourself, aren't you.

> She goes out.

C-3   GERRY – COMING DOWN <u>THE STAIRS IN THE STUDIO</u>

       She crosses the room and goes into the kitchen.

Sturges follows this with a single-spaced page-and-a-quarter description of the comic disaster that results when Gerry attempts to make breakfast. This is a reemergence of his initial note on the project of September 3, but more detailed and fully realized and, of course, situated in a very different context. Tom approaches the kitchen hungrily and finds Gerry sprawled on the floor with a bowl on her head and smoke everywhere. Somewhat later Gerry sits at her dressing table finishing her makeup when Tom comes in "with a nice breakfast on a tray." "You see, there's nothing to it, really," he says. Gerry suggests he get a job in a lunchroom and shut up, then says,

    I'm still going to leave you. Everything I said last night was true and just because you took me out and got me drunk doesn't alter the situation in the slightest.

                 TOM
    Will you stop?

               GERRY
    They arrest people for things like that, you know: "FIEND ATTACKS CO-ED."

    This is so stupid they both burst out laughing.

               GERRY
        (Accepting a cup of coffee)
    What are you selling this morning, the airport or the one-minute dry-cleaning machine?

                 TOM
    You don't have to get funny; we'll be rich.

               GERRY
    Yes, but will we enjoy it by then? [etc.]

    How did you come out with the Mayor? . . . You were too jealous to tell me.

                 TOM
    The same way I came in.

               GERRY
    Who are you seeing this morning?

                 TOM
    I'm going to try to see Groeble of the American Steel Cable Company . . . but he's very hard to see. I've been up there about ten times.

GERRY

Why don't you let me see him for you . . . I'll bet he's easy to see.

TOM

If it's all the same to you I'd appreciate it if you'd keep your nose
out of my business.

Gerry does go to see Groeble, of course. The long sequence in which she
does so begins in Groeble's outer office with his male secretary coolly telling
Tom he does not know whether Groeble will get to him. A Mr. Jessemer enters and is treated with great affection by the secretary. Tom seats himself
under a drawing of a suspension bridge that hangs in the waiting room. "Now
he looks sharply to the left and starts out of his chair." There is a cut to the
double doors of the office—"Gerry is just coming in. She looks around a little
guiltily, then smiles on seeing Tom." Tom argues with her "in a stage whisper"
and "through clenched teeth." Mr. Jessemer is told to go in but Gerry beats
him to the door and asks if she can go in first, which he beamingly allows.

> Mr. Jessemer turns, laughs triumphantly at Tom who laughs back
> with some nervousness. The two of them march to the Secretary's
> desk. The latter joins in the laughter.

MR. JESSEMER
(Philosophically)

Ah, well . . . pleasure before business.

> He roars at this and the Secretary nearly expires. Mr. Jessemer
> now slaps Tom on the back vigorously. Tom starts to laugh out of
> politeness, then bends a very displeased look on Mr. Groeble's
> door. Mr. Jessemer has a new paroxysm at this and pounds Tom
> on the back.

In the inner office, Groeble talks salaciously to his old friend while signing
a letter then looks up with a grin to find Gerry. His jaw drops open but then
he is all charm and welcome. Gerry invites him to lunch; he usually has milk
and crackers in his office but he agrees to go. She suggests steak and oysters
and asparagus, with champagne, and they slip out a side entrance. Tom, in the
outer office, demands to see Groeble, immediately. When the Secretary puts
him off, Tom says his wife is in there. The flustered Secretary buzzes, finds
no one, then tries unsuccessfully to stop Tom as he moves toward the inner
office, which he finds empty. Tom demands to know where his wife is and,
when he gets no answer, grabs the Secretary by the nose and puts his hand
over his mouth. The Secretary bites him, whereupon "Tom makes a threatening gesture as if to hit him and the Secretary bares his teeth like a horse and
stands his ground." Sturges dissolves from this stagelike tableau to the fashionable restaurant where Gerry and Groeble are having lunch.

Four water carafes have been arranged on the table and the four corners of a napkin are stretched to the carafes. Mr. Groeble holds two corners, Gerry holds one corner with her left hand and a perplexed head waiter holds the fourth corner.

"You see, this is steel mesh," says Gerry. "Like chicken wire . . . only stronger," suggests Groeble. "Much stronger," says Gerry. "It lets the light and air through to the buildings which are down here, see . . . and the smoke out." She goes on to explain that the planes come from any side to land, the passengers get out and go down an elevator. Suppose the plane should miss the field? "Maybe you don't realize how big this is," she says. It could cover whole cities? Gerry responds: "If necessary." They order two more B and B's, as Gerry discusses the ninety-nine thousand dollars necessary to build a demonstration of the airport. Since Groeble already has the steel cable, it would cost much less than that.

"And your husband thought of this all by himself, hunh?" says Groeble. "Bright boy. . . . We could use a boy like that. . . . Why, this opens an entirely new field for the steel cable business . . . you get a little tired waiting for them to build suspension bridges." Gerry: "Then you'll really consider giving him a job?" Groeble (indignantly): "Give it to him! He's got it!" "They raise their B and B's," notes Sturges. "Bravo" says the head waiter.

DISSOLVE TO:

C-24   THE SECRETARY – <u>AT HIS DESK IN GROEBLE'S OUTER OFFICE</u>

He is bathing his nose with a handkerchief and some ice from a glass. Now he glares across the room.

C-25   TOM – SITTING ANGRILY NEAR THE WALL

Tom looks to his right and the CAMERA PANS OVER onto an enormous man in his shirt sleeves and an eyeshade. His pockets are stuffed with pencils. Now the CAMERA PANS BACK to Tom. He looks to his left. The CAMERA PANS onto a very large janitor in striped overalls who returns his look. The CAMERA PANS BACK to Tom.

C-26   THE SECRETARY

He puts the handkerchief down, rotates his nose and mutters:

THE SECRETARY
You just try something.

Now his head turns toward the door and he leaps to his feet.

C-27   MR. GROEBLE AND GERRY – ENTERING ARM IN ARM

Their last B and B has made them very gay.

46

GERRY
(Waving limply at Tom)
Oh, hello, darling. I have the most wunnerfull news for you.

Tom leaps from his seat, saying, "Oh, you have! Well, I . . ." He trips over the janitor's extended leg and goes flat on his face. The janitor and the large draftsman leap on him instantly. Groeble tells Tom to stop it and asks what he thinks he is doing there. "Listen, you little squirt," Tom begins. Groeble points a finger at him and says,

You're fired . . . I wouldn't touch your rotten invention even if it
was good . . . that's gratitude for you . . . good day, madam.

Gerry tries to stop him but Groeble bids her good day again and leaves.

GERRY
(Calling after him)
Thanks for the lunch.
(She reaches out for Tom)
I'll take him.

The plaintive quality of Gerry's last words to Groeble is both odd and affecting. It may seem inconsistent with the confident Gerry of the final script and film, but that Gerry too is an interesting mixture of hard and soft qualities.

The November 3 script follows the Groeble debacle with a shot of Tom and Gerry walking down Thirty-third Street. Tom says, "You fixed it so I can *never* see him . . . my last hope . . . the one man in the country . . ." Gerry replies, "I know." "And you fixed it for me," continues Tom. "That's right," Gerry answers. "I fixed it so that you had a job . . . and he was going to build your demonstrator and . . ." "How was I to know?" "You weren't supposed to . . . that's why your parents made you dumb . . . so you wouldn't understand things and could botch up deals that more intelligent people had arranged for you . . . people who loved you . . ."

TOM
(Repentantly)
Listen, Gerry . . .

GERRY
(Violently)
Oh, go away from me, you big, stupid gook . . . I'm through with you!

She starts up the steps of the Pennsylvania Station.

TOM
(Seizing her arm)
Listen, Gerry . . .

GERRY
(Shaking her arm loose)
Let go of me!

TOM
Where are you going?

GERRY
I'm going to divorce you . . . this place is full of trains going
somewhere and I'll go somewhere and divorce you.

TOM
Will you stop talking like a child . . . You can't go anywhere; you
haven't got any money.

GERRY
I don't <u>need</u> any money . . . only stupid gooks like you need
money . . . I can go anywhere I like. Goodbye.

She kisses him quickly. She hurries up the steps and he follows.

There is a cut at this point to the interior of the station as Tom and Gerry
continue their conversation. "Listen, Gerry," says Tom. "Go fly a kite . . . I'm
really through with you . . . this is the end . . . go peddle your papers." "Listen, Gerry . . ." "No I won't. This is final: I want to help you . . . you won't
let me help you . . . I help you . . . you gum it up. All right . . . goodbye . . .
I'm going to divorce you." "Will you stop it." "I tell you I'm going to divorce
you . . . I'm perfectly cool, free, white and over twenty-one and I'm going
away to get a divorce. I'm tired of you."

Gerry stops at an information desk and asks for the quickest place to get a
divorce. Nevada takes six weeks, Palm Beach three months, she is told, but
the latter has a beautiful climate. Tom asks Gerry if she'll come back to the
apartment to talk it over.

GERRY
I will not; you'll just get me soused again and . . . talk me out of
it . . . I know your . . . persuasive ways.

Tom says "Listen, honey" once more and tries to take her arm. Gerry starts
to run and says good-bye. Tom hurries after her and Gerry tells a railroad policeman he is trying to molest her. From this point to the end of the sequence,
the November 3 script corresponds quite closely to the latter part of the sequence in the November 21 script (pages 40–49)—Tom is ejected from the
station by a policeman, Gerry appears forlorn and is finally given a free ticket
by the millionaire members of the Ale and Quail Club, who are boarding the
train to Palm Beach.

Different versions of Gerry and different story ideas lie side-by-side in the
November 3 script's "A," "B," and "C" sequences. It is true that Gerry controls as never before both the Wienie King scene and her long conversation
with Tom. A partial exception is that here it is Tom who first mentions di-

THE PALM BEACH STORY

vorce; Gerry has been thinking of it for some time but is not the one to introduce it into the conversation. At the end of sequence "B," Gerry is not—as she is in later versions—poised on the brink of leaving Tom. Here, she wishes to remain for a time in order to help his career. This is a plausible goal and we expect that it will be pursued in sequence "C" in a manner consistent with the new Gerry. In fact the character of Gerry now seems to lose most of the definition that Sturges had labored for six weeks to realize, regressing at times all the way back to the earliest versions.

First of all, Gerry is upset that she spent the night with Tom, sniping at him "rather disagreeably" and accusing him later of having gotten her drunk and then taking advantage of her condition. In the final script and film Gerry blames neither Tom nor herself for getting drunk or making love; she moves ahead in pursuit of her goals without—in the short run, anyway—a look back. Gerry has said in an earlier conversation with Tom that she is no cook, but, even so, in this version she attempts to make breakfast and makes a colossal mess. The later Gerry does not try things she knows she's not good at; she sticks to her strong suit (men). Tom has asked her not to interfere with his business but Gerry barges into Groeble's office anyway. He is a crucial prospect for supporting Tom's invention and she does a fine job of selling it to him. She has not alerted Tom to her campaign, however—even though she knows he is jealous—so her good work is undone. As a result Gerry's anger turns into a "sudden impulse to leave Tom immediately," as the September 27 outline described it, hence her departure sans clothes, sans money, and sans everything. In the final script and film, Gerry leaves Tom partly to free him of the responsibility of supporting her, but otherwise leaves his career in his own hands. She leaves hurriedly, hoping to avoid Tom's attempts to stop her, but she takes a bag of clothes and other necessities. (She takes no money because she does not have any.) This is not a sudden impulse but the rushed execution of a planned action.

The November 3 script is a document in transition. This is literally the case in that Sturges did not stop or even pause when he finished it but went to work, even as it was being typed, on what became the November 8 script. It is transitional also, as mentioned, in that different story directions and different versions of the Gerry character appear in it side-by-side. These differences lie almost entirely in sequences "A," "B," and "C," which correspond in all script versions to the events that lead up to Gerry's departure for Palm Beach. It was on these three sequences that nearly all of Sturges's efforts from the 3rd to the 8th were concentrated. Thus the November 3 script devotes 83 of its 207 pages to "A," "B," and "C"; the November 8 script, 48 of its 160 pages. Arithmetic suggests what is in fact the case, that sequences "D" through "H" changed relatively little in the revision—from 124 pages in the November 3 script to 112 pages in the November 8 script. This of course continued the trend of the early notes, discussed above, in which 117 of 155 pages were devoted to the events that became "A," "B," and "C." Admirers of the film may hardly believe that the passages they most like—those with the Ale and Quail Club and with John D. Hackensacker and his sister—were virtually dashed off by Sturges, while the parts almost no one discusses, or revels in, occupied the vast bulk of the revision process.

The November 8 script eliminates the Groeble passage entirely—twenty pages in one swoop. It also cuts Tom's whistling, Gerry's resentment over her night with him, and her fiasco in the kitchen. Cut from sequence "B" is Gerry's announcement of her plan to stay on a while to aid Tom's career. Gerry's arguments now press toward their logical conclusion of departure and divorce and, the morning after the night with Tom, leave she does. The note she pins to Tom provides the rationale not only of her own actions but of the new script itself.

> Darling—
> Just because you got me soused last night doesn't alter the logic of the situation. Goodbye, good luck, I love you—
>
> > Gerry

*　　　　*　　　　*

The November 21 script—the final script, reprinted below—makes many improvements in the November 8 script but does not alter its basic structure. For that reason, and since the November 21 script is reprinted in this volume, I will proceed directly to a comparison of the final script and the film.

The release print of the film eliminates shots A-14 through A-18 (pages A-2 to A-3) so that the film proceeds from "THEY LIVED HAPPILY EVER AFTER—OR DID THEY?" to a series of year titles—1937, 1938, 1939, 1940, 1941—and from there to A-19, the "Apartment for Rent" sign. Eliminated are the cuts from kitten to cat, from little rose bush to big rose bush, and from new 1937 car to old jalopy—further indications that years have passed between the wedding of the couple in the credits and the beginning of the main story. Since the years elapsed are counted out in titles, these shots are redundant; they are also not funny. Ernst Lubitsch was able to make this sort of visual contrast—and redundancy itself—amusing, as in the montage of black-to-white gowns, parasols, decor, lap dogs, et cetera, to indicate the passing of the main character's period of mourning in *The Merry Widow*. What delights and makes us laugh in Lubitsch is the obviousness of the contrast itself, its exaggeration to a precisely calibrated degree, and its superb cinematic realization. With anything less than Lubitsch's astonishing control of the medium and the audience, it does not work. A minor note: since dialogue continuities contain no information about visuals, it is impossible to know whether Sturges cut these shots before shooting the film, or shot, then cut them, in the final edit stage.

Gerry's scene with the Wienie King was shot very much as the script indicates. Eliminated in the final edit, however, was the King's dialogue with his wife and the apartment manager following his scene with Gerry (pages A-13 to A-14). Why cut this scene? Because to focus on the Wienie King's reactions to his encounter with Gerry requires a subsequent refocus on Gerry when she looks at the money and calls Tom. In any case, there is no need to follow the Wienie King after his scene with Gerry. He will appear just once more in the film—when he gives Tom the money to fly to Florida. His role as an eccentric fairy godfather to Gerry and an irascible one later to Tom is enhanced by cutting this scene: he seems to appear and disappear magically. Above all, the focus of the crucial early part of the film is kept firmly where it belongs—on the impact of the Wienie King's gift on Gerry and Tom.

The brief scene in Tom's office that ends sequence "A," treated differently in each script version and in the film, was settled only in the final edit. The November 3 script has Gerry call a beauty parlor and a dress shop and then "she rises and thinks another moment, then dials another number." The script cuts at this point to a glass door in "a cheap office building." A telephone rings as the camera pans down from Tom's name on the door to a notice to vacate. Gerry "rises happily and peels off her wrapper" and reaches into her closet for a dress as the scene fades out and the sequence ends. In the November 21 version (pages A-14 to A-16), Gerry looks at the money for a moment then hurries to the telephone and gives the operator Tom's number. This is an important change: here Gerry thinks first not of having her hair done or of buying a new dress, but of sharing her good news with her husband— "Darling, the most exciting thing has happened."

The scene is also important for what it tells us about Tom's character and his economic predicament, both of which bear on Gerry's reasons for leaving him and thereby on the film's plot. The scene is introduced in all versions by Gerry's phone call to tell Tom the news of her good fortune, although, also in all versions, that news is not conveyed. Sturges saves that for the Tom-Gerry confrontation of sequence "B." Gerry's call allows us to see Tom in his workplace before he hears the news, and gives Gerry time to pay their bills and to reflect on the longer-range implications of the Wienie King's gift. That she and Tom are momentarily "free and clear" allows her to act on her apparently long-standing resolve to leave the marriage. This does not seem to cross her mind in the euphoria following her receipt of the money but, by the time Tom comes home, she has decided to go.

A small but interesting point: in the November 8 and 21 scripts Sturges replaced the dial phone, specified in the November 3 script, with an operator-controlled one, for Gerry's call to Tom. This seems a matter of filmic pacing, that is, of the viewer's sense of how long things should take. In the November 3 script, Sturges cut from Gerry to a shot of Tom's empty office with a telephone ringing. In that version the call must seem to transmit instantly, hence the dial phone. In the November 8 and 21 scripts, Sturges cuts from Gerry to a shot of Tom trying to sell a prospective client on his airport: Tom speaks several lines before the phone rings and a few more before he picks it up. Having an operator place Gerry's call creates the sense of a brief delay, allowing the scene at Tom's office to begin. When Tom asks Gerry to tell him her news later, Sturges cuts to Gerry's reaching into her closet for a dress and then, for the first time in these scripts, cuts back to Tom's office for the final scene of sequence "A." Sturges might have had Gerry dial the number, Tom pick the phone up immediately, and the entire dialogue with the prospective client follow the brief cut back to Gerry. However, ending one scene before you launch the next creates a dead space between them, which also requires the second scene to begin from a complete stop; Sturges overlapped and interwove scenes wherever he could. His mastery of construction was equal to, but much less appreciated than, his flair for dialogue; but it is the construction of his films, arduously arrived at, that gives Sturges's dialogue its maximal power and savor. The direct dial versus operator point indicates that there are at least two levels of construction to which the best screenwriters devote attention: the level of the large movements of the film and that of the small.

The November 21 script has the landlord of Tom's office drop by to see about the rent (page A-16). He agrees to wait until Tom is through talking to his prospective backer and just stands there while he does so—"I ain't in a hurry," he says. This scene was shot by Sturges with a little added dialogue— Tom begins his "let's-start-again" spiel to the prospect and continues for a few sentences before the scene fades out. Having thus expanded the script to include the landlord and shot the scene accordingly, Sturges cut it in the final edit, which ends with the prospect's line, "I'm retired." (The landlord, included in the publicity still that appears below, does not appear in the film.) Tom's having a rent problem at his workplace as well as at his home goes back to the eviction notice pinned on his office door in the November 3 script. The November 8 script, however, included neither eviction notice nor landlord. Tom explains his airport idea to the prospect, who appears in that version for the first time, until he puts on his hat to go, whereupon Tom proposes to begin his explanation again. "Go ahead," the prospect says, "My time ain't worth anything . . . I'm retired." He removes his hat and the scene and sequence fade out. By cutting the landlord scene in his final edit, Sturges in effect restored the November 8 script's ending—in both versions, Tom has no office rent problem.

Why did Sturges vacillate on this matter? That Tom should be as seriously in arrears of his office rent as he is of his apartment rent is logical—how can he keep up an office when he cannot pay his rent at home? Having Tom proceed from his office rent problem to his home rent problem, in his scene with the doorman, emphasizes his plight effectively. He is not only a failure, he is a virtual bankrupt who will soon find himself and his wife on the street with no place to live and no visible means of support. (This emphasis also makes Gerry's departure more acceptable to the viewer.)

The answer may lie in fundamental contradictions in the November 3

*A publicity still from THE PALM BEACH STORY: Joel
McCrea as Tom shows his model airport to a
"prospect" as his rent-seeking landlord, who does
not appear in the film, looks on.*

script, which were discussed above. A subtle conflict in that script is the eviction notice on Tom's office door and the Wienie King's role as fairy godfather
to Gerry and Tom. A financial problem that is not resolved by the Wienie
King's money would spoil his magic and retrospectively diminish Gerry's
scene with him. On the other hand, wouldn't Gerry have saved some money
for Tom's office rent rather than take him out to dinner or buy clothes for herself? Most important of all, the Wienie King's gift makes Gerry and Tom,
momentarily at least, free and clear, as they presumably have not been for a
long time; a state of affairs that decides Gerry to act on her apparently long-
held decision to leave the marriage. These and other script elements, clarified
at last after months of work, become messy again if Tom's office rent problem is thrown in, too.

The logical problem remains—how has an impecunious man prevented his
eviction from his office? Indeed Gerry suggests at one point that Tom sleep in
his office once she's gone, to live more cheaply and make ends meet. Sturges
cut Tom's office problem because the logical inconsistency of doing so is preferable to its alternatives. So much else is happening so quickly that the viewer
simply accepts, or overlooks, it. Tom will soon fly to Florida anyway and the

office question will fade away. This is one of the most difficult, not to say maddening, aspects of screenwriting—to know just when illogic serves better than logic.

At the outset of sequence "B" (pages 17–18), Tom tries to sneak past the apartment house manager with the aid of the doorman. There is no need to sneak, the doorman tells him, Gerry has paid the rent with money an old man gave her. "What do you mean, an old man gave her the money?" says Tom, and there the scene ends; the five remaining lines of the scene were shot but cut in the final edit. A consequence of the cut is that the doorman scene in the film seems truncated: it ends abruptly and off-balance. Since the exchange is mainly expository, however, and transitional to the scene with Gerry that follows, playing the scene to its conclusion is not necessary. Doing so would also bring the film to a small halt, requiring that it start up again with Tom and Gerry. Far better to end the exchange as Sturges does, with Tom's interrogative. Unanswered by the doorman, that question now propels the film forward to his confrontation with Gerry, to whom, in any case, it is really addressed. The question is parried by Gerry, who stands before him in a new evening dress, even before he has a chance to ask it—"I said: I'm taking you to dinner . . . so hurry up and put on your dinner jacket" (page 18). This takes some of the wind out of Tom's sails, but he asks his question anyway, noting that the whole building is buzzing about the old man's gift. This information, conveyed by the doorman in the cut passage, would have been repetitious if we had heard the doorman say it. The doorman had made another remark, also deleted, to the effect that people in the building wish Gerry's visitor would drop in on them. This would have worked to let Gerry off the hook, in that it characterizes her behavior as only human. This is a reasonable perspective, to be sure—even, despite the Park Avenue setting, of a Brechtian sort—but it tends to undercut both the drama and the comedy of the dialogue between Tom and Gerry before it takes place.

Gerry's response to Tom's interrogation about the Wienie King moves quite quickly—and with admirable logic—to woman's place in male-dominated society. She notes that sex always enters into a woman's relations with men, "from the time you're about so big . . ." One of her amplifying remarks, "I even think I got it from a corpse once at a funeral" was changed during shooting to "from a statue in the park" and then cut altogether. "Got what?" says Tom. "The look," says Gerry, rolling her eyes. "How's about this evening, babe?" The line that follows this was shot but cut: "Sometimes they say it and sometimes they don't, but it gives you a fine opinion of men on the whole." Also cut are Gerry's remarks a bit further on,

> As if I had to pick out an old bunny like that . . . if I wanted to cut a caper. He did me a lot of good . . . I'd almost forgotten . . . You have no idea how it makes a girl feel to have a man say, "It's a privilege to be living in the same world with you . . . here is my fortune . . . help yourself."

This passage was not specifically targeted in the censorship documents I was able to locate, although it may have been elsewhere. Its sentiments are in any case implicit in Gerry's actions—the Wienie King's devotion does bolster her confidence enough to make the break with Tom. But the cut passage also seems to rub Tom's nose in his poverty and failure more callously than anything Gerry says in the film; it is thereby inconsistent with the latent love between them that the film insists on. They will be back together by the end of the film—indeed she will twice be shown missing him that very night—hence the initial rupture cannot be shown to be too acrimonious or bitter. (Like Jean in *The Lady Eve,* Gerry will scheme for a fortune in the first half of the film, then get it and give it up for true love in the second half.)

Gone too is Gerry's line "I don't want to have to pay people to dance with me . . . I'd rather they paid me . . ." (pages 24–25). Perhaps the most important cut in the sequence, however, occurs at the opening of the restaurant scene (page 27). Gerry is arguing that she and Tom have become invisible to each other, citing Tom's remark, "Oh, is that a new dress?" which ended the preceding scene. The line in question, however, is Gerry's "Don't you see how much more useful I'd be to you if our relationship was more like . . . brother and sister . . ." (page 27). This does little more than summarize the plot to come, but G. M. Shurlock of the Hays Office took exception to it in his three-page letter of December 6, 1941. He requests that the speech be "rewritten to the effect, 'Don't you see how much more useful I'd be to you if instead of being married we were more like . . . brother and sister . . .'" What is "offensive" here is the notion of a husband and wife having the relation of brother and sister, particularly where the "usefulness" of the relation is emphasized. Sturges sidestepped the question by cutting the line altogether, beginning the restaurant scene with Tom saying "You'll always be a sister to me, hunh?" This seems to answer a suggestion by Gerry that we haven't heard but it does not matter—the rest of the passage makes her idea clear enough. It also has the advantage of seeming to cut to a conversation already under way, which is also a continuation of issues we have heard them discuss earlier. It is well observed in a more general way as well: topics are less often introduced between marriage partners than merely returned to without preamble.

Shurlock's overriding concerns are stated in a paragraph that precedes the brother-sister point and other specific objections:

As you know, the industry at all times has tried to avoid giving offense to the American public and particularly to recognized civic and religious groups, where these groups have made it manifest that certain themes or treatments thereof give them offense. Of late, they have let it be known that stories centering around the theme of a light treatment of marriage and divorce, in connection with detailed discussions thereof, has been a source of serious complaint. In accordance with this, we earnestly request that you give full consideration to our suggestions below, where it might be asked that you help minimize what might be called "constant irritation" of a sensitive public.

The content of Shurlock's letter may not be surprising, but its timing is. By December 6 *The Palm Beach Story* had been shooting for twelve days and was scheduled for thirty more. It would have been quite difficult at this date to rewrite even the pages not yet filmed. Since Luigi Luraschi, Paramount's in-house censorship expert, was in constant contact with the Hays Office, more-over, the studio had good reason to suppose censorship matters had been set-tled by the Office's memos of November 25 and 26, which arrived before shooting started and hence could be easily honored. One wonders if Shurlock had taken his time in reading the script, or if he had awakened one night and realized what he had, in essence, approved by remaining silent.

In any case, Sturges happily ignored two other Shurlock directives. They appear in the film as written in the November 21 script.

Page 28: Please change Gerry's line, "Just because I'm a useless wife . . ." to "Just be-cause I'd stop being your wife . . ."

Page 30: On reconsideration, in order to avoid the sex flavor objected to in pictures of this sort, we must insist that Gerry's line, "I wasn't thinking about the roof . . ." be omitted.

The Hays Office's delay in responding to the script seems to have worked in Sturges's favor. (Perhaps the confusion following the bombing of Pearl Harbor did also.) By December 5 the passages in question had already been shot. The brother-sister line was part of a scene that could be abbreviated by cutting, but the other two would have required extensive, and expensive, re-takes. (War Production Board economy directives were not far away.)

The November 3 sequence "C" was 39 pages long, the November 8 se-quence, 16 pages, and the November 21 sequence, 17 pages. Gone from the later versions were Gerry's breakfast disaster, the long Groeble episode, and other passages. What was left after these purgings? A sequence of transitional passages: Gerry leaves Tom; Tom gives chase; each hurls obstacles in the other's way, until Gerry eludes Tom in Pennsylvania Station; Gerry wangles a ticket from the eccentric millionaires of the Ale and Quail Club, and their train pulls out for Palm Beach as the sequence ends. Passages of this sort serve to get characters from one place to another; they must do so plausibly, in a man-ner consistent with each character, and, wherever possible, amusingly. The suc-cess of such a sequence depends more than other kinds do on directorial real-ization—blocking, pace, camerawork, editing, et cetera. Sometimes, as in much of the lower-depths prowling in *Sullivan's Travels,* the script is thrown out altogether. Even where a script is fairly closely followed, as it was in *The Palm Beach Story,* action descriptions are little more than balloons to be filled in by the director during shooting.

In all script versions, the Ale and Quail Club is identified as such only at the end of sequence "C." As the train begins to move, Gerry waves wistfully to her husband, who is restrained by a policeman whom she herself summoned. The camera pans down from her tentative farewell to "A card in the first window. It reads: 'THE ALE AND QUAIL CLUB; PRIVATE'" (page 49). Followed by the fade-out that ends the sequence, the shot of the card signals trouble to come. In the film Sturges introduces the name of the club much earlier. Hunting horn music is played when we first see members of the club queuing up at a gate in Pennsylvania Station, and is repeated, ominously, over the shot of the card later. As they board the train to Palm Beach, each of the members of the club reacts to Gerry's ticketless plight in his own way, then identifies himself to the ticket taker as, for instance, "Kraft, Ale and Quail." Sturges also cuts earlier than was indicated in the November 21 script—directly after the first four members have gone by—to a brief scene in which the conductor (Al Bridge) is told by the Pullman Conductor that "the Club" is on board again. "You're telling me," the conductor replies sourly and vows trouble if they start something this time. These changes help to establish the identity of the club early on and thereby to prepare the viewer for sequence "D," which the club's members dominate. What point would have been served by keeping the viewer in the dark about the club until the very end of sequence "C"? Was the shot of the sign that ends the sequence supposed to be a surprise revelation or a harbinger of the mayhem to come? It works partly as both in the film, but would have worked as neither had the viewer been unprepared.

"D" is the longest sequence in the November 21 script, as it was in the November 8 script before it. It comprises, to be sure, the manifold activities of the Ale and Quail Club—drunkenly arguing with the conductor, serenading Gerry with campfire favorites, shooting up the train, organizing themselves as a posse to search the cars for Gerry with dogs and guns until the conductor forces them back into their car and then disconnects it from the rest of the train. However, the sequence also includes Gerry's first night away from home and her first meeting with John D. Hackensacker III, as well as shots of Tom alone at home and his own encounter with the Wienie King.

The members of the Ale and Quail Club are played by some of Sturges's most distinctive players—William Demarest, Robert Warwick, Torben Meyer, Vic Potel, Jimmy Conlin, Robert Grieg, Dewey Robinson, Jack Norton, Chester Conklin, Roscoe Ates, and Sheldon Jett. This ensemble creates a far more vivid and cohesive impression than the studio group that follows Sullivan around in *Sullivan's Travels*. Viewers have remembered the uproarious Ale and Quail scenes fondly and admired them as a distinctive Sturges creation— who else could have conceived, scripted, or properly directed such sublime antics? The highly disparate players operate plausibly as an eccentric group and it is the group that is remembered more than the individual players. However, the studio people in *Sullivan's Travels* are remembered neither as a group nor as individual players. Are the members of the club, and the people who play them, more individuated than the studio gang in the earlier film? It is not clear. It may be that beneath all the differences, including the great success of the Ale and Quail Club and the relative failure of the studio group, the method of treating the supporting players is rather similar.

The dialogue between Mr. Hinch (Robert Warwick) and Gerry (pages 59–62) was shot as written but cut almost entirely in the final edit, which retains only his last few lines about the size of his pajamas and Gerry's lack of luggage. Hinch, who travels with a valet, is a pompous fellow given to orotund speechifying, even if he tends to jump from topic to topic. In the deleted footage he seems to have vague ideas about seducing Gerry, whom he may see as an attractive stray of whom he can take advantage. He is stung—"laughing from one side of his face only"—at Gerry's unintended suggestion that he is old (page 61). It may be only to please his vanity that he imposes himself on her—she tries to push him out the door but he keeps his foot in. Sturges may have felt these points not worth making, or that they distracted attention from essential ones. He may also have feared that the Hinch episode would derail the viewer's good feelings about the Ale and Quailers. But, the role of Hinch was perfect for Robert Warwick, who had played one of the producers in *Sullivan's Travels*; to see the scene that was filmed, probably long since destroyed, would be a treat.

Sturges dissolves from Hinch's last lines to a shot of Gerry getting into bed in the pajamas he has lent her. In the film she does not sniffle, as the script indicates, but does look lonely and despondent, a mood enhanced by the club's mellow version of "Old Folks at Home" in the background. At this point in the script (page 62), Sturges dissolves to Tom in his seat in the airplane flying down to Florida to meet Gerry. In the final edit, however, Sturges placed Tom's scene with the Wienie King at this point and saved the dissolve to Tom in the airplane for a later point. The script places the Tom-Wienie King scene at the beginning of sequence "D" (pages 50–52) and, indeed, the initial editing of the film retained that placement.

> Tom comes in slowly and we see him silhouetted against the lighted hall. He turns on one lamp, closes the door and crosses to the studio window and looks over the city. Now he goes to a console for a cigarette. While lighting the cigarette he notices a pair of gloves next to the cigarette box. He picks them up gently and looks at them, then lifts them to his face and smells of them. He clenches his fists. The doorbell rings. Tom looks toward the door for a moment, then crosses and opens it, revealing The Wienie King. (page 50)

Located at the outset of sequence "D," Tom's return to his and Gerry's apartment and his dialogue there with the Wienie King immediately follow Gerry's tentative good-bye wave from the train. We presume in this context, in the absence of counterindications, that he has just returned from the train station. Viewers might see his sadness at this point related as much to his misadventures in Pennsylvania Station as to his missing his wife; when in this scene Tom gets angry again (at his wife's departure? at his making a fool of himself?), the ambiguity is perpetuated and the elegiac mood shattered. Also, Tom's jumping at the chance to fly down and meet his wife seems premature at this point or, perhaps, as much an extension of his anger as a desire to recover the woman he loves. Finally, the script's arrangement requires a cut from Tom's scene with the Wienie King to the boisterous encounter between the club members and the conductor over tickets.

Sturges's final-edit placements are superior in every respect. Holding the cut back to Tom until later in the sequence allows Gerry's feelings—and his own—to ripen. Neither can know immediately how much the loss of the other will mean. Some of Gerry's misadventures in the meantime may have helped her to realize this, but it is mainly her feelings for Tom at that moment that make her doubt her course of action. Tom also needs time to repent his anger and to rediscover his tender feelings for Gerry. Sturges cuts back to a sad, reflective Tom—his fist-clenching was removed during shooting—from a sad, reflective Gerry, and this allows him to cut back to her in the same state. Thus the scene works to affirm the bond between the two characters—we are reminded that they love each other and will probably end up back together. The scene is necessary to affirm this bond through the separation and trials to come, one of which, in the person of John D. Hackensacker III, Gerry is about to encounter.

Tom's return to the apartment has an elegiac mood that parallels Gerry's own as she tries to go to sleep on the train. Sturges did alter the beginning of the scene, however, to make it fit even better into its new context. In the film Tom comes in, walks to the phone, picks up the receiver and says, "Any calls?" then slowly puts it down. It has been only hours since Gerry left, but he is clearly hoping that she has phoned or telegraphed. The cut from Tom back to Gerry is followed in turn by the scene of the club's serenading of Gerry while one drunk (Jack Norton) and one disaffected member (William Demarest) begin to shoot up the train. Here Demarest calls his caroling clubmates a bunch of sissies and then a bunch of coeds. The censors were sure that "sissies" would not get by the British censors so Sturges specifies a "protection take" using the word "fatheads." The dialogue continuity indicates that this "alternate" take was shot and, presumably, that it was used in prints bound for Britain.

Gerry flees the great train shoot-out by running to the Pullman car and, after some fumbling, finds an empty upper berth. Trying to climb into it, she steps on the face of John D. Hackensacker (Rudy Vallee). The full Ale and Quail entourage pursues her—they call themselves a posse—but their dogs somehow miss her, finding her scent instead in Hackensacker's berth. The conductor catches up with them and soon after strands their car on a sidetrack. Gerry settles into her berth and, as a big close-up and romantic music make clear, thinks once again of Tom. It is here that Sturges cuts in the brief shot of an airplane and a second shot, linked by a dissolve, of Tom sitting inside, looking irritated. (The shots were moved from D-20 [page 62] to D-87 [page 79].) A second cut to Tom in the plane was called for at D-87 but either was not shot or was removed during editing. The opening scene takes the place of the first airplane shot and the first airplane shot takes the place of the second. (Or perhaps the first shot was cut and the second remains—in the first one we apparently would have seen Tom put up his collar.) There is a cut back from Tom to Gerry and this shot of her ends the sequence. Again their bond is affirmed, as is their inevitable meeting in Florida and the resumption of fireworks between them.

Why did Sturges originally want two cuts to Tom on the airplane? Perhaps to suggest that he and Gerry are moving in parallel directions and therefore that their remeeting is indeed inevitable. But it might also have appeared that he is pursuing her in anger or indeed that he is actually seeking revenge.

As for Gerry, she has met Hackensacker but she still dreams of Tom and misses him. Of course she does not yet know that Hackensacker is rich, let alone how rich, or who he is. When Tom does show up she will be quite irritated with him for meddling. But for now she misses him.

Sequence "E" changed very little from draft to draft. The first version of the sequence, which appears in the November 3 script, was written in five days—October 25–29, 1941. This was carried over with minor dialogue changes in the November 8 script and with additional dialogue changes in the November 21 script. The most important changes were made during shooting and editing but, once again, they were almost entirely in the dialogue. From the October draft to the finished film, no scenes were added or cut or transposed. The dialogues between Gerry and the porter and between Gerry and John D. Hackensacker were substantially in place in the first draft—indeed a number of their lines were already pointed and balanced in the best Sturges manner. Achieving this level of excellence for virtually all the film's dialogue was, of course, the cumulative result of the various revision stages.

In sequence "E," Gerry begins again from zero, for the second time in the film. The first time was when she left for the station without her suitcase, thanks to Tom, and once on the train she loses even the clothes on her back. Wearing the pajamas she borrowed from Mr. Hinch, Gerry sticks her head out of her upper berth to ask the porter (Charles Moore) about her clothes. She does not know that the Ale and Quail car has been disconnected, but we do, so Sturges cuts needless exposition by picking up their conversation in midstream. This is a favorite Sturges technique for accelerating the pace of his films, indeed for jumping the viewer into the heart of a scene instantly. Even the first draft of the scene in question had begun with the porter's response to a demand by Gerry that we do not hear:

THE PORTER

No, m'am.

GERRY

What do you mean, my clothes aren't there? They're in Stateroom
"B" in the private car right behind the diner . . . the club car and
my ticket and my handbag and my lipstick and everything.

THE PORTER

No, ma'am.

This exchange, which continues for three pages in the same vein, is of the
kind one thinks of as Faulknerian: one character, uneducated and socially inferior, doggedly clings to a single truth, reasserting it calmly whatever pressures are applied. This infuriates, and finally drives to apoplexy, the more sophisticated and articulate character, who is conducting the interrogation. Such
scenes are Faulkner's version of the irresistible force confronting the immovable, and implacable, object, except that in his fiction, the immovable object
is never budged and the irresistible force sputters itself to exhaustion.

Reshooting was next to impossible at the final edit stage unless a producer
suggested it, in which case it was mandatory. As an alternative, scenes were
sometimes cut from within, providing of course that the film-ends could be
joined plausibly and without a break in continuity. This occurred with the dialogue between Gerry and the porter; it was shot as written then partly cut in
the final edit—from Gerry's "Don't stand there saying 'no, m'am' . . ." (page
80) to the porter's second "No, m'am" (page 81). This excision from the middle of the scene was possible because the last line before the cut passage and
the first line following it dovetail. Helping to make them fit is the porter's re-
iteration of the phrase "No, m'am"—he says it five times overall—and Gerry's
impatient mockery of it, presumably added in the shooting process since it
does not appear in the script. In the film, therefore, the passage quoted above
is followed immediately by this:

GERRY

'No ma'am' . . . you just didn't look.

PORTER

(Doggedly)

Yes, m'am, I looked but I didn't see it 'cause it warn't there . . .
that's why I didn't see it.

GERRY

I suppose it just blew up, etc.

John D. comes along and says hello to Gerry—in the script, she says
hello first, which might have seemed a bit like hustling on her part to get out
of a jam. At any rate, manifestly pleased to be a knight in armor, John D. immediately involves himself in Gerry's predicament, proposing, besides a letter
of protest to the president of the company, that "as soon as we come to a town,

*John D. to the rescue: Rudy Vallee, Charles Moore, and
Claudette Colbert in* THE PALM BEACH STORY.

I could jump over to a store and jump back." "With a Mother Hubbard,"
replies Gerry, whom we know from the dress she bought earlier to be fashion-
conscious; the full, loose gown referred to is the best she feels she can expect
him to come back with if she is not there to be fitted. Besides, Gerry continues, she hasn't got any money. "Oh, I have money," says John D. "Oh, you
have?" Gerry replies. "Oh yes." The matter-of-fact way Vallee says this per-
suasively suggests the man he is supposed to be. For the moment, however,
John D. brightly suggests gathering articles of clothing from women on the
train, which he and the porter do, and the result is as awful as Gerry expects it
to be. Starting with "some button shoes with pearl gray tops" the camera tilts
up slowly and deliberately toward "a hat with roses on it": a parody portrait
of a floozie. Rather than appear thus in public, Gerry is next seen entering the
dining car wearing a Pullman blanket skirt, a blouse made of Hinch's pajama
top and something else, perhaps a pillow case, wrapped around her head.

The breakfast dialogue, like the yacht exchange later in the sequence, is
one of the highlights of the film. There was some pruning in the final edit—
two lines on page 88, six on 89—but otherwise the scene plays as Sturges
first wrote it. Both deleted passages have John D. say in reference to the fact

that Gerry has no ticket, "That presents quite a problem," a line he actually says three times (pages 88–89). Gerry responds in each case in the faux-naif manner she used to get a ticket from the Ale and Quailers: "I can't think of any solution," "It would take an Einstein," and "Don't tell me you found a way out." Striking all but one of these exchanges would have overcome the problem of repetition, but Sturges in fact cut all three, feeling perhaps that even one instance of the line might have hit the wrong note. In the film, John D. is penny-pinching in general but is genuinely smitten with Gerry; she, for her part, drops no hints and aims for no quick scores—such as a free train ticket. Her wheedling coyness in the cut passages violates the character of Gerry that the earlier scenes established.

Similarly, John D.'s three "quite a problem"'s show him as painfully reluctant to spend money, even if he is, or is about to be, in love. His buying Gerry clothes worth thousands and a ruby bracelet in the next scene, and a chip off the Hope Blue later, might seem in that case too quick a reversal—how stimulating can one breakfast with a new acquaintance be? The next scene, in the store, pivots on the French-accented saleswoman, whose mercenary prompting gets big laughs from most audiences. (Unfortunately the actress is unnamed in the film's cast list.) John D. gets carried away buying things for Gerry, but he cannot, given his character, be the one to initiate the spree. Gerry, conditioned by life with Tom, is embarrassed by the spending, which she also regards, or claims to do, as morally dubious. She even doubts, based again on life with Tom, that John D. can pay the bill. A catalyst is needed to propel both parties beyond their inhibitions; hence the saleswoman, who expertly manipulates each of them. The store proprietor (Julius Tannen), worried about payment as the couple heads toward the door, becomes weak-kneed when John D. hands him his card. The November 3 and 8 scripts have the proprietor make a speech of astonishment and apology to "Mr. Hackensacker." In the final script and film, however, he can barely utter the first syllable –"*Mis*ter Ha. . . ." The name of utmost wealth, our society's definition of the sacred, cannot be uttered.

The scene on the yacht that follows the buying spree is equally as good as the breakfast scene on the train. Colbert and Vallee play uncannily well together. It is not chemistry exactly because we cannot imagine them as a romantic couple. It is perhaps that the players are so comfortable in these particular roles—they do not just fit them, or vice versa, they inhabit the roles completely. Joel McCrea is quite appealing as Tom but his performance, while excellent, is of a different kind: off-balance, uncertain how to proceed, uncomfortable in his own skin. As for Mary Astor, the role of the Princess was, as she later wrote, "not my thing. I couldn't talk in a high, fluty voice and run my words together as he [Sturges] thought high-society women did, or at least *mad* high-society women . . ."[2]

Notable among further cuts in dialogue is this exchange between Gerry and John D. (page 101):

No, I mean that the person who marries me, the lady, for my money . . . would still have to be the right person. She'd have to be able to spend like a drunken Indian, of course, but at the same time . . .

GERRY

Write it in the book.

JOHN D.

Something like that. And when we travelled . . .

GERRY

You take the upper . . . I'll take the chair car.

John D. laughs at this and launches into his ideas about marriage. With the intervening passage cut, he seems to be laughing at Gerry's simile "like a horse in the bedroom" and/or at his own response, "I wasn't thinking exactly of that . . . but it will serve." Again, the two ends of a passage cut in the final edit dovetail quite well. Besides his "chivalry" and "beating up" lines, quoted above, John D. has other good lines here: "I rather enjoyed it," referring to Gerry's stepping on his face, and "There are a lot of inconveniences to yachting that most people don't know anything about."

Less noticeably, John D. makes many references to his family here and in the prior scene at the clothing store. He spoke there of his uncle, "the crazy one in the family," and his grandfather, who was called "a burglar or something." In answer to a question of Gerry's, he says the yacht is his—"Actually it was my grandfather's but he didn't like it . . . he only used it once." When he finally discloses his name to Gerry, he feels a need to add, "I'm not my grandfather, of course . . . he's dead anyway. I'm John D. the Third." He clarifies Gerry's confusion later by repeating that he is John D. the Third—"The Fourth will be my son . . . when I marry." Even writing his accounts in his little book is a family trait—"It used to please my grandfather . . . it's just a habit. It's nonsense really . . . I write things down but I never add them up."

Sturges had to cut a number of lines that equated John D. Hackensacker too openly with the Rockefeller family. These items gone, the link is still unmistakable, down to John D. Rockefeller's legendary tightness, including his tipping with bright shiny dimes. John D. to Gerry: "Do you happen to remember how much tip I gave the taxi driver?" ". . . from his face, I think it was ten cents," says Gerry. The porter complains to Tom later that Gerry's companion gave him a "dime (tip) from New York to Jacksonville," adding, "She's alone but she don't know it."

Besides the specifics, however, John D. is an instance of a recurring Sturges character type defined by Manny Farber:

His young millionaires are like heavily ornamented bugs, born out of an Oliver Twist world into a sad-faced, senile youth as moldy with leisure and tradition as an old cheese. Incapable of action, his obsolete multimillionaires gaze out into a world that has passed them by but to which they are firmly anchored by their wealth.

A pathetic creature in the last stages of futility, Vallee's sole occupation consists of recording, in a little black book, minute expenditures which are never totalled—as though he were the gently demented statistician of an era that has fallen to pieces for no special reason and has therefore escaped attention.[3]

John D.'s emphasis on his family reveals the uncertainty, even the pathos of his situation. His search for an identity seems to consist of family comparisons—he's not crazy like his uncle, a burglar like his grandfather, or a compulsive marrier and flirt like his sister. He keeps an account book like his grandfather and, like him, doesn't like yachting. He places himself in a chain that includes forebears and a son, but—knowing as we do that Gerry loves Tom—we wonder if he will pass along his family name or if it will end with him. He and his sister are two sides of their family's imminent extinction. They and their family line would be revitalized by marriages to Gerry and Tom, but that is possible only in an impossible ending. Sturges provides such an ending by inventing for the film's finale a twin of Gerry to marry John D. and a twin of Tom to marry the Princess. Fairy-tale farce aside, however, John D. and Maude would be left to languish at film's end.

Sequences "F," "G," and "H," the final three of the film's eight sequences, are set in Palm Beach. They comprise slightly less than a third of the final script (pages 106–157); like *Chinatown* (1974)—in this respect only—*The Palm Beach Story* takes most of its duration to arrive at the site of its title. If the Palm Beach section of the film seems more important than its sequence and page numbers indicate, it is perhaps because, in a sense, a new film begins there, centering on four potential lovers rather than just two actual ones.

Sequence "F," like "C" before it, is a sequence of transitions. "C" comprised Gerry's leaving Tom, his futile attempts to stop her, and her boarding the train to Palm Beach. "F" includes Tom's arrival in Palm Beach by air, Gerry and John D.'s arrival by yacht, and the Princess's picking them up in "a glistening motor boat coming along side" (page 108). Tom meets Gerry, John D., and the Princess on the pier and all parties then proceed to the Hackensacker estate, where the rest of the film takes place.

The November 21 script begins the sequence with a shot of "THE STREAMLINER – PULLING INTO WEST PALM BEACH." In the film we see instead a crowded shot of a Pullman car in a station with passengers alighting and welcomers greeting them, all of them crisscrossing the frame in various directions. We can see in the back, if we look closely, a tall man conversing with a shorter one. This long shot is followed by a medium shot of Tom interrogating the same porter who had earlier told Gerry about the missing railroad car. All script versions begin wth the porter's answer to what we assume was Tom's question about his wife: "Yassuh, I know who you talkin' about . . . you mean de young lady who lose all her clothes." In the film we hear not Tom's initial question but his explanatory addendum to it: "She's a tall, dark-haired girl with big eyes." This description, which more or less fits Colbert, could not have been included before her casting was certain. In this case, as in others, the shooting process revealed the need for a clarifying line not anticipated by the screenplay.

The script specifies that the porter "has his hat on and is going home," as he answers Tom's questions, an arrangement that Sturges changed during shooting. Holding a suitcase in his left hand and flowers in his right, Tom questions the porter while the latter is still assisting people off the train. This staging is better, more dynamic than the script's, in which the porter has finished work and just stands there conversing with Tom. Tom learns to his dismay not only about the lost clothes but also that the woman in question got off the train in Jacksonville and then headed, on her companion's yacht, for Palm Beach.

The script's specification of a shot in which the yacht is anchoring (F-6 on page 107) is cut in favor of a long shot of a quai with a man standing on it; a closer shot reveals him as Tom, still carrying flowers and looking out to sea. "Hey, let me use those a minute, will you?" he says to a man passing by with binoculars, a line that was added during shooting. We see through "the traditional binocular-shaped matte" a ship's captain giving orders to some men putting a boarding ladder in place. The binocular matte wavers briefly to the right side of the captain then to the left, then moves quickly far to the left to discover John D. and Gerry leaning happily on the rail. The shot, as though from a hidden camera, seems to be seeking scandal among the rich, as does the *Spy* magazine team in *The Philadelphia Story*. A cut back to Tom shows him reacting very angrily and then returning the binoculars.

The film adds to the script's three shots of the Princess's arrival by motor boat (pages 107–108) an additional four, the director perhaps having been stirred by sea air and the boating ambience. Sturges cuts several times back and forth between Gerry and John D. on the yacht and the Princess drawing near them in the motor boat, and breaks up their dialogue accordingly. Three script pages are largely taken up with the Princess's chattering as she comes up the boarding ladder and meets Gerry (pages 109–111). The script calls for a single shot of the Princess here but in shooting and editing, Sturges included a comic shot of Toto falling off the boarding ladder and two close-ups of the Princess, returning each time to the same group shot of all the characters in the scene. The Princess's first close-up occurs at her line to Gerry, "Don't tell me he doesn't even know your name," the second at her speech ending, "We'll look for new husbands together." The cut back to the group shot here allows Sturges to excise her next line, possibly for censorship reasons, "We can swap private info and have a wonderful time."

Sturges then cuts to Tom leaning on the railing of the quai and from this to a group shot of the other characters in a motor boat moving toward him. This arrangement allows him to omit several more lines of dialogue—everything before the Princess's "Did you have to get him drunk?"—that were both shot and included in the dialogue continuity. Deleted from the other end of the motor boat shot, after another cut to Tom, is another of the Princess's lines, "Well, introduce me to him will you . . . I'd like to cut a carpet with him."

Gerry runs up the gangplank to give Tom a piece of her mind out of the hearing of the others. Cut from this dialogue during shooting was Gerry's "you know I'm fond of you"—she is much too angry to say anything like that here—and "but I want to do everything for you that I can." This is also far too nice a thing for her to say at this point and invokes the possibility of a shady collusion between them too explicitly. Tom puts his arms around Gerry just as the Princess joins them so Gerry introduces him as her brother. The Princess invites him to stay "with us," saying, "We practically run a hotel anyway" but her addendum to this remark, "except the museum where Grandfather lives," was cut during shooting.

The Princess offers her arm to a reluctant Tom, who takes it, and the two walk on ahead of the others. Gerry and John D. discuss the Princess's evident attraction to Tom as they continue to walk away from the pier—he's more delighted at the prospect than she is, even though a moment earlier Gerry had announced to all within earshot that Tom was unmarried and "entirely free."

One of the Princess's speeches in this regard is an example of Sturges's efforts to improve his dialogue at every script and filmmaking stage. In this case, a slight change during shooting made a good line remarkable. In all three script versions, the Princess introduces Tom to Toto, her casual lover and/or admiring hanger-on. Tom, to whom the Princess is instantly attracted, has just been introduced by Gerry as Captain McGlue.

THE PRINCESS
This is Captain McGlue, Toto . . . I'm going to see more of him and less of you from now on. (page 115)

This becomes in the film:

Toto, this is Captain McGlue.
I'm going to see more of him and
less of you from now on.

The shifting of a single word turns prose into a brief and amusing poem. The first line now puts its final stress on "Captain McGlue," emphasizing the absurdity of the name by meter and word placement. The Princess's second line, unchanged, expresses as before the quickness of her decision to drop Toto and pursue Tom; but "you" now makes a rhyme with "McGlue" that is pleasing in its lopsidedness, and also accents, precisely by excluding it from the rhyme, the phrase "from now on." Hanging alone, outside the rhyme, the three words now realize formally what they also mean denotatively: the blissful extension into an indefinite future of a new romantic attachment. (That the romance is mere fantasy only increases the intensity of the speaker's wish.) "From now on" also avoids, on behalf of the entire speech, the triteness of rhyme itself, turning it into blank verse.

The film's sequence "G" begins, as do all of the script versions, with a shot of the Princess making up "at an extraordinary dressing table and watching her brother in the mirror" (page 118). The mirror itself is extraordinary, of such height and breadth that much of the scene is played between two Princesses and two John Ds. This mirror shot mirrors, or is mirrored by, the film's final shot, in which two Gerrys and two Toms appear—the second Gerry marrying John D. and the second Tom the Princess. Symbolically considered, the doubling of John D. and the Princess in the mirror is both unproductive—it frees neither from the self-defeating impasse in which each is held—and unprocreative—it will not avoid the extinction of the Hackensacker line that his virginity and her promiscuity threaten. The film's-end doubling of Tom and Gerry, on the contrary, is productive—it solves their own problems, and those of their twins and the Hackensackers as well—and procreative—it leads to the formation of two new sexual couples and enables a third (Tom and Gerry) to remain one, making it likely that the family lines of all six characters will be perpetuated.

"Why don't you marry her, she's lovely," says the mirror Princess to her mirror brother at the fade-in to sequence "G." Once again Sturges begins a scene with a response to lines, here presumably spoken by John D., that we do not hear. The Princess here encourages her brother's affection for Gerry; it is only when he reverts to caution, suggesting a test marriage with rented or borrowed children, that she reverts to teasing, which she began as she came aboard his yacht in sequence "F" and will continue, relentlessly, into the Tom and Gerry scene that follows.

Sturges cuts from the actual brother and sister to the fraudulent brother and sister, Tom and Gerry, who are in the midst of their first conversation alone since Gerry left their apartment several days earlier. Sturges begins with Tom in mid-rant: "But why 'Captain McGlue'? Of all the idiotic names . . ." (page 119). Tom's topic here is new—the name Gerry has just stuck him with—but his exasperation is not; neither is Gerry's alternating between defensiveness and confidence about what she is doing. The two take up their wrangling in Palm Beach virtually where they left off in Pennsylvania Station. This seems right on the one hand since neither has been shown to have changed in the interim, but wrong on the other because—well-dressed in luxurious surroundings and, for the moment at least, free of money worry—Tom and Gerry are situated at last in the setting that they, and screwball comedy, require. The film may now be read retrospectively as its central couple's search for the right costumes, setting, and situation for screwball comedy.

When Tom's expostulations on "McGlue," then on "Captain," conclude, Gerry says,

> I'm sorry, darling. I really meant it for the best.

> TOM
> I know you did . . . that's what's so irritating about it. (page 120)

This extraordinary exchange, rather lost in everything else that is going on, is the crystallization, if not the "Oh, say, can you see . . . ," of happily-married arguments, in which good intentions that miss the mark disappoint both parties. When Tom asks where she got the brother idea, Gerry says she introduced him as such because he had his arms around her at the time. This sets Tom off on a tirade about who else has had his arms around her—by which he means John D. Gerry replies, when she has a chance, "Naturally, he *will* put his arms around me . . . when and if we're engaged . . ." Eliminated during shooting, however, was Gerry's knife-turning completion of this thought "and you'll just have to get used to it" (page 121).

In the November 21 script, Gerry puts on the mantelpiece a "little Staffordshire group," to signal her continued fidelity to Tom and, she notes pointedly, his to her. In the film she hands the statue to Tom to place and his silent compliance in doing so seems to seal a pact between them—a renewed marriage vow perhaps.

According to the script, Gerry shifts topics "suddenly" at this point (page 122), to ask Tom where he got the money to fly down.

TOM

From the same place you got yours only I didn't have to kiss him good-bye.

GERRY

Oh, the Wienie King.

TOM

He wanted us to get back together, I guess . . . don't you think we owe it to him? Look: why don't you let me go out there and punch this guy in the nose just once.

GERRY

Because I've left you, darling . . . for both our good . . . just because I don't hate you doesn't mean I haven't left you. I have the right to do that, and if you'll only be sensible and sweet . . .

TOM

And brotherly.

GERRY

We're bound to come out on top.

TOM

All right, but don't you think as your brother I could poke him in the nose for that bracelet?

GERRY

(Laughing) You dope!

TOM

[To a knock at the door] Come in.

JOHN D.

Excuse me.

Sturges followed the script in shooting this passage but abbreviated it considerably in the final edit. He did this by moving up John D.'s entrance to where it follows Gerry's line "Because I've left you, darling. . . ." Sturges cuts at this point to a shot of the door, which John D. opens and briskly walks through without knocking. As he does so, we hear Gerry say, "for both our good." This cuts out, most important, Gerry's later line, with Tom's interjections, "If you'll only be sensible and sweet [Tom: And brotherly.], we're bound to come out on top. [Tom: All right . . .]."

The cut dialogue suggests a pact between Tom and Gerry of a rather different sort from the mutual fidelity they have just sworn. Her remarks not only show Gerry scheming behind John D.'s back while her romance with him is going on, they also make Tom complicit in her scheme—"all right," he says, to her implication that they might both benefit at John D.'s expense. His agreement makes Tom again something of a pimp, in which context his repeated wish to punch John D. in the nose "for that bracelet" hardly makes sense. Taking those lines out may have been to restore Tom's integrity or to deflect his complicity in Gerry's scheme; it was widely assumed, rightly or wrongly, that audiences would not tolerate a hero tarnished in this way.

Censor G. M. Shurlock objected to Gerry's plan to benefit Tom by attracting rich men to herself, although he did not raise the issue of Tom's complicity. As we have seen, Sturges gradually reduced this element throughout the revision process, eliminating it entirely only in the final edit. Addressing Gerry's behavior alone, Shurlock astutely suggested that her quest becomes more, not less, unsavory if she still loves Tom and hopes to benefit him by her schemes. He insisted, therefore, that Gerry be unsuccessful "in her morally questionable procedure of trying to get money to finance her husband's projects." Sturges did not agree—the ending Shurlock was urging implied virtually another film—and did not go along with it. As noted, he was most likely aided in this resolve by the fact that Shurlock's memo was sent on December 6, 1941, by which time shooting had been under way for two weeks and the objections of two earlier censorship memos, sent November 25 and 26, had already been, for the most part, accommodated.

Sturges had already made a number of small changes de-emphasizing and/ or distracting attention from Gerry's scheme, a process Shurlock's memo may have encouraged him to continue. Among the changes was the cutting of several references Gerry makes to her plan *while* it is going on. In the film itself she makes no remark that unequivocally suggests she is scheming behind John D.'s back. The elimination of Tom's complicity bears on this issue as well. If Gerry cannot speak of her scheme to Tom, then she cannot speak of it at all—in whom else might she confide? And if she cannot speak of her scheme, then the audience cannot be sure of what she is thinking. Viewers may be obliged to assume, therefore, that Gerry is genuinely considering marriage to John D. The fact that she mentions on several occasions the one hundred thousand dollars for Tom's airport project may be understood generally as a kind of divorce settlement and specifically as unfinished business in her relationship with Tom—harking back to her resolve to leave him as well off as she found him and, if possible, a success rather than a flop.

John D. bursts in on Tom and Gerry without knocking, something he may never have done before but he is now brimming with good feeling and high spirits and is not to be deterred. He asks "Mac," that is, Tom, if he brought a tuxedo, invites him to spend the season with his sister and himself, and is serene, even pleased, when Tom truculently raises the bracelet issue. "There's nothing the matter with my intentions," he is eager to assert, "as Mac will be the first to admit." Indeed the only thing that might embarrass Tom are "the lovely things I want to say to him about you . . . your face . . . your form, things a brother is naturally blind to." Sturges has Tom interrupt here and cuts to him for his line, "Is that so?" which was added during shooting. Designed to mollify a brother, John D.'s words infuriate a husband, particularly his fleeting inventory of Gerry's face and figure.* Tom's aggressive interruption serves to distract the viewer's attention from John D.'s remaining remarks, which are further undercut by Vallee's flat, run-on delivery, and by Sturges's cutting away from him—once again to the door, for the entrance of the Princess— before he finishes his sentence. Three times John D. has tried to propose his trial marriage idea—and to seek Tom's permission—and three times he has been interrupted by characters with other agendas. This time it is his sister, who wants to poke fun at him.

"What's buzzin', cousins . . . what's the dirt?" says the Princess as she breezes in. "Never mind, Maude. It's just a little something I want to discuss with Mac," John D. replies.

THE PRINCESS
(LAUGHS) My dear, when you hear what it is, you'll simply
expire. [John D.: Maude!] It is too, too excruciating! [John D.:
Maude! . . . please!] He wants a miniature marriage with you . . .
[Tom: A miniature what?] Go away, Toto, this is not for children.
You know, everything up to the dissolve, and then . . . Good night,
sweetheart, I'll see you in the morning . . . [John D.: Maude,
please!] [Tom: What's this?] The boy wants to bundle! [Tom:
Bun . . . ?] [John D.: Maude!] And then he's going to make you
cook and sew and wash the windows and then . . . and then he's
going to get some little brats to see if you know how to change
them! [Gerry: But how?] He's going to rent them! (pages
126–127)

*Mistaken identity is integral to comedies from the Greek classics to *Desperately Seeking Susan*; in the best hands, including Shakespeare's and—why not?—Sturges's, it is not merely a plot device but a tool of discovery, which shapes, among other things, scene construction and the formation of characters.

"My Dear, when you hear, you'll simply expire"; Mary Astor to Claudette Colbert as Joel McCrea and Rudy Vallee look on in THE PALM BEACH STORY.

John D.'s attempts to introduce his trial marriage idea are parried, terminally, by the entrance of his sister, who makes of the idea an uproarious joke. John D. is made to look ridiculous, but not as ridiculous as he would have looked had he actually proposed his idea himself. Being foiled in this endeavor preserves John D., if anything will, both as a believable rival to Tom and as a plausible participant in screwball comedy. However, the fact that John D. addresses his proposal to Tom, to seek his permission, reveals his adherence to antique rules of the game of love, which may disqualify him for the genre after all. The men and women of screwball comedy are in the arena on their own; they seek no one's permission to battle for love. In any case, his proposal defeated, John D. rises to the occasion immediately and magnificently; the Princess drags Tom away and John D. says to Gerry:

> I'm afraid I'm . . . there's no use trying to conceal it now . . . I might have guessed it on the train . . . I certainly should have known it in Jacksonville . . . and on the yacht . . . the trial was as much for you as for me . . . and however ridiculous I may seem there's nothing ridiculous about the way I feel (he kneels) in my heart . . . I'm madly in love with you. (page 128)

Moved by the speech, Gerry says "Oh . . ." softly and puts her hand on John D.'s chin. At this point, an angry Tom reappears at the door, the Princess, whom he's hardly aware of, still on his arm. He says nothing but stares at the kneeling John D. with the force of the Commendatore in *Don Giovanni*. As the Princess leads him away again, Tom does not turn in the direction they are walking but continues to stare at John D. The latter, who quickly gets off his knees when the unsmiling Tom appears, says to Gerry when he is gone, "You know, I'm not sure that Mac likes me." Gerry assures him that Tom is always like that, which is true enough, because he thinks no one is good enough for her. Agreeing heartily, John D. gets down on one knee again, whereupon the scene fades to the interior of a nightclub. John D. gets in proposal position twice but does not propose, as though, failing to have a practice marriage, he is practicing the activity that leads to it.

The nightclub scene (pages 129–139) is, almost literally, the centerpiece of sequence "G" (pages 118–147). It is also the heart of the screwball comedy comprised by sequences "F," "G," and "H"—that obligatory passage in which all the romantic principals go out on the town together and, in various combinations, dance and/or converse:

> Tom and the Princess (130)
> Gerry and John D. (130–132)
> Tom and the Princess (133–134)
> All four characters at their table (134–137)
> Tom and Gerry (137–138)
> All four conversing on the dance floor (138–139)

Sturges shot the nightclub scene with minor dialogue changes then, as in other instances noted, made more substantial changes in the editing. The first major divergence occurs at Gerry's line comparing Tom's airport to a tennis racket and John D.'s asking, "But would it be strong enough . . . I mean, after all, a tennis racket . . ." Gerry's subsequent explanation of the airport's steel cables and John D.'s responses (pages 131–132) are eliminated. Instead Sturges cuts to Tom and the Princess as she tells him about the $99,000 that Gerry's husband demanded for her freedom, and the fact that John D. plans to pay it (page 133)—several lines are cut from this conversation also. At this point Sturges cuts back to John D. telling Gerry, "I might be able to help him . . . in fact I will be able to . . . It's built" (page 132). Intercutting the two conversations is more lively than letting them play sequentially and, since they concern the same topic, links them thematically also. Sturges cut Gerry's explanation of the steel cables holding up the airport and her subsequent comparing of them to the Brooklyn Bridge as, no doubt, needless elaboration—we are not interested at this point in Tom's invention itself, which has long since become a given of the plot. They are perhaps a holdover from the sequence of Gerry and Mr. Groeble in the November 3 script. We stay with John D. and Gerry until his line, "It's built," whereupon Sturges cuts back to

Tom and the Princess at his line, "You mean her husband won't divorce her unless he gets ninety-nine thousand dollars?" (page 134). This eliminates three needless speeches between them at the bottom of page 133; four more are cut on 134. Only five of the script's twelve speeches for the scene made their way into the film, but these are sufficient. Tom presses the Princess to say that Gerry told her about her husband's wife-for-cash scheme; continuing to flirt relentlessly, the Princess in effect refuses.

Breaking each exchange in two and—with considerable trimming—intercutting them, makes for an admirably fluid passage that also builds tension. Gerry secures funding for her "brother's" invention from John D., while Tom learns from the Princess of Gerry's earlier scheme to get John D. to pay off her "rotten husband." The rising tension is not limited to the nightclub scene or even to sequence "G." It proceeds also from Gerry's frequent attempts to help Tom in the past and his refusals to let her do so, from Tom's failures as inventor and provider, and hence from the causes of Gerry's leaving him in the first place—in short, to the central themes of the film.

Following a brief shot of Toto at the table, "looking bored," the script has Gerry and John D. reach the table only a moment before Tom and the Princess do, so that Gerry burbles immediately to Tom: "Darling, I have the most wonderful news for you. Snoodles is going to build your airport." In shooting the film, Sturges had Gerry and John D. reach the table well before the other couple and gave them two short speeches:

GERRY
Oh, Snoodles, that's wonderful . . . Tom wi . . . eh, Mac will be
wild with excitement . . . You know, when you've waited so
long . . .

JOHN D.
Not at all, not at all, I'm delighted to have the opportunity . . .

This exchange repeats in somewhat different form what has already passed between John D. and Gerry. This sort of backing up, often to remotivate characters for an upcoming scene that builds on earlier events, is common enough in plays and films of all kinds; it is rare, almost nonexistent, in Sturges. It is rhythmically necessary here, however, both to provide an interval before the confrontation that is coming and to show Gerry and John D.'s excitement at the idea.

Gerry excitedly tells Tom her news but even then the tension is sustained. Tom remains silent—stunned perhaps, and attempting to sort things out. What begins to snap him out of it is John D.'s cheerful, happy remark:

Well, that gives us a lot to look forward to, doesn't it? I don't
know as I told you or not, Mac, but your sister and I have progressed considerably since this afternoon.

"Is that so?" says Tom, for what seems like the fifth time in the sequence. Who has not found oneself in a social situation in which fatigue, preoccupation, or the essential wrongness of the occasion locks one into repeating some nonsensical expression like "I see," "Is that so?" or "Yes, yes!" To become aware of what one is doing, contrary to the canons of self-knowledge, is to turn difficulty into calamity. Tom has been one step behind the action all evening, often repeating phrases just uttered in an attempt to understand them, particularly in the scene in which John D.'s intentions toward Gerry become clear (pages 126–128): "A miniature what?" "What's this?" "Bun[dle]?" "Just a minute . . . I—I . . ." "I . . . I . . . bake a . . . ?"

After saying "Is that so?" to John D., Tom asks Gerry about her husband's having demanded money in return for her freedom. She tries to play down the idea—"I'm not sure he actually meant it"—but John D. calls the "husband" a "human bacterium," adding, however, that he will probably pay it: "Ninety-nine thousand dollars isn't a small sum . . . on the other hand it isn't large." "I should say not," adds the Princess, rattling off three men's names, presumably her ex-husbands, who probably got larger payoffs than the sum Gerry's soon-to-be "ex" demanded. The name Baron Itsk, the third that the Princess mentions, corresponds to some word in Toto's language and involves them in a verbal byplay that, in this case, has a structural function. By further trivializing an already trivial conversation, it prepares the way for Tom's long speech, the most serious moment in the second part of the film.

> I'm awfully sorry to hear that about Tom. I knew he was a failure and a dreamer, I guess, but I didn't know he was a skunk. It's very kind of you to want to build the airport . . . I mean the model of it . . . I guess I was a little too . . . stunned to say thank you but you know how it is when you've been waiting for something for a long time . . . there's only one trouble with the whole set-up . . . something Gerry neglected to tell you . . . and that is that I'm not alone in this invention . . . that human bacterium we were talking about, her husband, has had exactly as much to do with it as I have, so you see if you help me you'd be helping him too, and I know that nothing could be further from your wish . . . [to Gerry] How about dancing with your brother? (pages 136–137)

Dancing with him, Gerry calls Tom a fathead—"Don't you ever get tired of being noble?" "I've got you the money twice already," she concludes—an unintended commentary on the double-identity plot that she herself set in motion. (In truth Tom is neither the money-grubbing husband nor the just-passing-through brother in whose names she got the money.) After another angry speech by Gerry, Tom says,

> The way you are is the way you have to be, honey. That's the way I am and if I'm supposed to be a flop . . .
>
> GERRY
> You're not going to be a flop. Nobody who's been married to me for five years is going to be a flop. You're going to get your airport if I have to build it for you myself . . . after I'm married.

75

TOM

"After you're married" . . . that's a funny thing to hear your wife
say . . .

Tom's last remark was added during shooting. It replaces the far less satisfactory script passage in which Tom refuses in advance to accept money from
Gerry after she's married and she responds at length that she'll invest in his
project anyway through a blind and he'll never know whose money he is accepting (page 138). She discusses possible devices for accomplishing this,
then fantasizes about their passing each other in cars some day whereupon
she'll tell him which investor had been working for her, his mouth will fall
open and she will laugh, and each will then drive off. Gerry's curious fantasy
incorporates elements of the ending of Chaplin's *A Woman of Paris* (1923), in
which the cars of a former couple pass each other on a country road but neither ex-lover sees the other. Chaplin's film is considered by many to be the
first sophisticated treatment of male-female relations in the American cinema.
Chaplin was a friend of Sturges, and Colbert herself was born in Paris. However, the passage is digressive at a crucial stage of the action and, even worse,
presents a discordant view of both characters. Tom's a priori refusal seems
spiteful, if not cruel, and Gerry's fantasy seems uncharacteristically masoch-
istic, particularly since it is her actions that have driven the plot at every point
and Tom has had to react.

John D. interrupts Tom and Gerry in their dance with his solution to the
problem of Tom's partnership with Gerry's husband on the airport project:
"I've got it. I'll build it and his share will be more than ninety-nine thousand
dollars so he'll have to release you." "Whose share?" asks Tom. "That scoundrel she's married to!" says John D., adding a bit later, "Now shall we change
partners?"

The film has the partners change, then cuts to a shot of Toto staring sul-
lenly in the direction of the dancing couples as he deals himself a hand of
solitaire. This is followed by a dissolve to Tom and the Princess arriving back
at the Hackensacker mansion. Eliminated during shooting, on censorship
grounds, was the following final exchange on the dance floor:

GERRY

(To Tom)
I told you you'd get someplace some day.

THE PRINCESS

He can get there tonight if he likes -- I understand there's a
preacher in Arcadia who stays open very late . . .

The Hays Office, not surprisingly, found the Princess's line "unacceptably
sex suggestive and [it] could not be approved in the finished picture." The
censor's reasoning here is of interest:

May we note that in the previous script [the November 8] this speech of the Princess
was buried in the middle of a long discussion and hence was thought to be proportion-

ately inoffensive. In the present script, it serves as a tag of a scene and, accordingly, assumes importance, which increases its offensiveness unduly.

Since the Princess has come on hard to Tom from the moment they met in sequence "F," her mention of marriage seems an odd thing for a censor to object to. However, since she takes little seriously this too may well have been perceived to be a joke. Rich men in the movies marry women they haven't slept with, in order to do so; and the Princess might too. However, she might also continue trying to seduce Tom and then make up her mind about marrying him. In any event, her next scene with Tom works better without the immediate marriage prospect in the air.

Saying good night to Tom, the Princess says, with characteristic double entendre, that he has renewed her faith in mankind.

TOM
There's nothing like saving your faith.

THE PRINCESS
[Laughs] You are too, too divine.

As though half-noticing her for the first time, Tom says,

You're a very embarrassing lady. If I weren't a little bit mixed up at the moment, I'd take you up on a few of your dares and make you say papa.

THE PRINCESS

Papa . . .

For the first and only time in the film, Tom speaks, if in the subjunctive, of having sex with the Princess. To do so is to make her say papa, which is at once (1) to subject her to male, literally patriarchal, authority, her freedom from which is "embarrassing"; (2) to subject her to Tom's individual authority; (3) to achieve her capitulation or defeat in a physical struggle, as in a wrestling match; and (4) to compel her acknowledgment and acceptance of all the above. The usual acknowledgment of defeat in a contest of strength— "saying uncle"—is revealingly adapted by Sturges to the more immediate male antecedent.

Considered in terms of character, Tom's choice of words is also revealing in regard to his situation. He has been unable to provide for his wife and unable to hold her. He is a flop as a patriarch, as he acknowledged to the Princess while they were dancing. Imagining sex with her has the effect of recouping these and earlier losses at least in fantasy.

The Princess's reply to Tom's remarks is devastating: she says "papa" immediately. Of course she is ironic here as she is in nearly everything else she says in the film, but in human mating, highly evolved, subjunctive and ironic statements are themselves crucial positionings. Saying "papa" in advance of the seduction serves to get the patriarchy, dominance, and struggle issues out of the way immediately. It thereby challenges Tom to have sex with her free of his cultural and individual agendas.

With this Tom and the Princess part company, and Tom overhears John D. saying good night to Gerry. John D. tells Gerry he has a surprise for her in a few minutes and asks her to leave her balcony window open in preparation for it. Just then a crash is heard inside—Tom has smashed the statue on the mantelpiece. Gerry comes in and angrily accuses him of infidelity:

> So you couldn't even wait a decent interval . . . you and your
> Princess . . . You big pull-over!

The usual expression may be push-over, but the Princess seems determined not to knock Tom down and away, but to pull him over onto herself. Tom explains that he has broken the statue only because it was handy, an elliptical answer that the viewer understands because Tom has heard John D.'s balcony remark; Gerry's understanding it without further explanation is less comprehensible. But her response to its destruction has revealed too much of her feelings for Tom, so she covers up by castigating him for following her to Palm Beach—"you should have given me a little time to get used to the idea." Tom replies that

> you can't blame a man for trying to hold onto something that he
> loves . . . that he always has loved . . . always will love.

"You're just going to make me cry," Gerry says. She soon reverses herself, however.

> No . . . when you make a decision you have to stand by it . . . and
> you can't let . . . memories get in the way of it. It's all over . . .
> and I know it's for the best . . .

The next line in the script does not appear in the film—"He'll [John D.] have to find out who you are someday . . . but by then he'll like you so much he won't care." Gerry here plans to marry John D., but it seems nonetheless one more instance of her scheming and of Tom's pimplike, if silent, complicity; if the other instances were cut, this had to go too.

Gerry goes into her room and, before closing the door, kisses "her brother" good night. Sturges notes:

> As if the touching of their lips were a cue, which it is, the strains
> of a glorious orchestra drift up from the lawn below. (page 145)

Tom and Gerry "separate slowly," walk to the window and look down. What they see is the orchestra from the Everglades Club arranged on the lawn. "Like many another amateur conductor," Sturges notes in the script, "John D. is leading it with his hand." In the film John D. does not lead the group at all, he merely holds the sheet music for his vocal. As a professional with his own orchestra, Vallee may have objected to conducting by hand. The script notes that John D. "sings the number with great distinction," but does not identify it. What Vallee sings, of course, is "Goodnight, Sweetheart," a 1931 song by English bandleader Ray Noble and two collaborators, the American version of which was written, and very successfully recorded, by Vallee. Earlier in the film, John D. sang in Gerry's ear while they were dancing. "By a fortunate happenstance," Sturges comments in the script, "the orchestra is playing a tune owned by Paramount" (page 130). That tune, "Isn't It Romantic?" was owned and used over and over again by Paramount in its films of the thirties and forties, often as a kind of aural wallpaper. Rogers and Hart wrote it for Paramount's *Love Me Tonight* (Mamoulian, 1932).

Intercut in their separate quarters, Tom and Gerry close their balcony windows but still hear John D.'s song. Neither seems ready for sleep. Gerry cannot undo her dress and, after many attempts and even more misgivings, goes into Tom's room and asks for his help. The hooks are undone and so is Gerry's resolve:

> she turns and throws her arms around his neck. Now she pulls his
> head down and crushes his lips against hers. (page 147)

After another kiss, she says, "I hope you realize this is costing us millions." A shot of John D. as he "hits the high note that finishes the song" is followed by a brief shot of Tom and Gerry embracing; as they do, sound and image fade out together.

Sequence "H" is brief, a mere nine pages, despite its formidable task of wrapping up a chaotic film. As the sequence opens, the "caged canary bird" in the Princess's room sings "Goodnight, Sweetheart" and Toto enters, dressed for polo and cheerful despite his drunken fall out of her car the night before. The Princess urges Toto to go to Havana—alone—but he refuses. John D. comes in with a spectacular diamond ring for Gerry, and the Princess shows him a watch, chain, and pen knife for Tom.

These links to the night before prepare us for the most important one— Tom and Gerry in their respective suites packing for their return to New York, the doors between them thrown open. Gerry "picks up the bracelet, looks at it lovingly, then hollers over her shoulder: 'I suppose I'll have to give the bracelet back, won't I?'" (page 151). This is marital conversational catch, played without looking, but her words are intercepted by John D., who has entered unheard carrying his ring box behind his back. (He did knock several rooms back but no one heard him.) "Why?" he asks Gerry, who looks startled for a moment; "Oh, Dear," she says—an Alice about to leave Wonderland—before answering his question.

> Oh Snoodles, I'm so very fond of you . . . You're such a lovely,
> generous, good-natured man . . . really a woman's ideal . . . only
> you shouldn't have sung last night. [John D.: What?] Here's your
> bracelet; I'm going back to my husband. (page 151)

She explains that it was not her husband who wanted the $99,000, but she who wanted it for him. John D. shows her the ring, which stuns her; she asks

THE PALM BEACH STORY

to have one more look and that Hackensacker "then put it away forever . . . there's a limit to what a woman can stand." Tom enters looking cheerful—for the first time in the film; he slaps John D. on the back saying, "Hello, there, Snoodles, how's every little thing?" "I'm very unhappy, as a matter of fact." "You'll get over it," says Tom, to which John D. replies,

> I'll never get over it as long as I live . . . I had such hopes . . . such plans . . . (page 153)

In sequence "E," John D. talks a great deal about his family—his grandfather, his great-grandfather, his uncle, his father. He even speaks of his own children-to-be, as though the existence of John D.'s I through III guarantees that there will be a IV. In sequence "G," John D. looks forward, speaks of the future again and again, for the first time.

> [on the airport project] Well that gives us a lot to look forward to, doesn't it? (page 135)

> [To Gerry] I think this is the happiest night of my life . . . You've freed me of a certain timidity from which I've always suffered . . . and now with you . . . and Mac . . . and the airport . . . I see great days ahead full of fun . . . and everything. (page 141)

The Princess reminds the disappointed John D. that he still has the airport "and you and the Captain and I will be as busy as bird dogs . . . won't we, Captain?" (page 154). When Tom says that isn't possible, John D. wants to know why not; he turns to Gerry and says,

> I still have . . . I always will have . . . the deepest affection for you . . . certainly nothing has happened to spoil my friendship with your brother . . . being with him . . . will remind me of you.

GERRY

Well, you see . . .

JOHN D.

What now?

GERRY

He isn't exactly my brother. [Tom: No.]

JOHN D.

He isn't exactly your brother?

GERRY

No . . . He's my husband.

JOHN D. and the PRINCESS

Your husband!

THE PRINCESS

Well, no wonder! I thought I was losing my grip.

80

The Princess's line is "susceptible of a very offensive double meaning"—
as the censors said of another of her lines, and as Mary Astor's seemingly
embarrassed laugh perhaps appreciates—but the censors did not catch it.

Putting it all together, John D. says to Tom, "Then, it's the Jeffers Airport . . . that's it, isn't it?" Tom says—incredulously, one supposes—"The
Jeffers Airport?" a line added in shooting but cut in editing. In the film it is
the Princess alone who responds to John D.'s inquiry:

> Are you still talking about the airport? You really take it on the
> chin, don't you?

> JOHN D.
> Why not? If an idea has merit, it has merit . . . sentiment and
> business don't belong in the same bed . . . After all grandfather
> loathed oil, you know . . . it made his eyes water but that didn't
> stop him from making billions out of it.

> TOM
> You mean you still want to go through with the airport?

> JOHN D.
> Why not . . . on a purely business basis, of course . . . Right now
> I don't like you . . . although I may get over it later . . . Right
> now I need something to occupy my mind . . . the airport is some-
> thing . . . if not exactly what I hoped for . . .

Sturges cuts here from a shot of all four principals to a closer shot of John
D. and the Princess, each looking across the other at the object of his/her desire. "I'll be lonely without you, Gerry," says John D.; "Oh, Captain . . . and
thou!" adds the Princess. Sturges cuts back to the group shot as brother and
sister each continue to look at their beloveds. "I don't suppose you have a sister," says John D.; "Only a twin sister," Gerry replies.

> JOHN D.
> A twin sister!

> GERRY
> Oh, didn't you know about that? That's how we were married in
> the beginning . . . both being twins.

> TOM
> Of course that's another plot entirely.

> PRINCESS & JOHN D.
> Both twins!

John D. and the Princess here change places so that each now stands next
to his/her beloved.

> PRINCESS & JOHN D.
> she
> Are you a twin? Well what's he doing?

81

TOM & GERRY
Well . . . nothing . . . you see . . .

The film dissolves here to a shot of Tom and Gerry standing at an altar; the camera pans to their right to reveal John D. standing next to another Claudette Colbert and another Joel McCrea standing next to the Princess, and last, least, and as always on the outside, Toto standing next to the Princess. All the men are in formal wear; the Princess and the second Colbert wear white wedding dresses. The minister stands in the middle of the two new couples, on the right half of the screen, which indicates that Tom and Gerry are not being remarried, as some critics have supposed. (If not divorced, why remarry?) Toto too stands in the marriage line and he is not being married. The arrangement may fail in logic, but it allows the final shot to serve not only as plot resolution but also as a kind of curtain call for the characters/players.

NOTES

1. James Curtis, *Between Flops: A Biography of Preston Sturges* (New York: Harcourt Brace Jovanovich, 1982), 160.
2. Ibid., 161.
3. Manny Farber, *Negative Space* (New York: Praeger, 1971), 101–102.

A   S C R E E N P L A Y

by

Preston Sturges

"THE PALM   BEACH STORY"

1   9   4   1

Paramount Pictures - Hollywood

Preston Sturges

<u>SEQUENCE "A"</u>

<u>During</u> the Main Titles we see:

A-1   AN ELDERLY MAID - TELEPHONING EXCITEDLY - (DAY)

         Now a shadow edges over her. Her eyes widen, she
         screams, throws the telephone wide and falls in a
         dead faint.

A-2   A BEST MAN - <u>OUTSIDE A CHURCH</u>

         He stands under a canvas marquee, looking at his
         watch. Now Joel McCrea, dressed as a groom, comes
         out and talks to him excitedly. They rush PAST THE
         CAMERA and jump into a taxicab which pulls away,
         just as a fatherly-looking character rushes out and
         looks at <u>his</u> watch.

A-3   CLAUDETTE COLBERT - <u>IN A CLOSET</u>

         She is in her chemise. Her hands are bound behind her
         and she is gagged up to the eyes with a towel. Now
         she starts to kick at the door.

A-4   INSERT: HER FOOT COMING THROUGH THE DOOR

A-5   THE MAID

         She sits up, sees the foot and falls in a dead faint
         again.

A-6   CLAUDETTE COLBERT - <u>IN A BEDROOM</u>

         She is getting into a bridal gown as fast as she can.
         The maid comes into the room, sees her and falls in a
         faint. Claudette runs out of the room.

A-7   JOEL McCREA - <u>IN A TAXICAB</u> - WITH A ROUGH LOOKING
         COMEDIAN

         He is dressed as a bridegroom except for some striped
         pants which he has difficulty in putting on.

A-8   CLAUDETTE - RUNNING OUT OF <u>A HOUSE</u> AND HAILING A TAXI-
         CAB

         She tries to hook herself up while getting into it.

-11-21-41

A-9   A BISHOP - IN FRONT OF AN ALTAR

        He looks at his watch, then smiles a sickly smile at
        the guests.

A-10   THE OLD MAID

        She gets up off the floor and comes out of the bed-
        room. Now her eyes widen as she sees the gagged
        Claudette coming through the hole she has kicked
        through the closet door. The maid falls in a faint.

A-11   THE BISHOP - IN FRONT OF THE ALTAR

        He looks at his watch once more, shrugs helplessly,
        then licks his lips and opens his mouth to speak.
        At this point we hear the shrieking of brakes, fol-
        lowed by the shrieking of some other brakes and a
        bang. The Bishop looks hopefully over the heads of
        the guests, then with a smile of relief, waves to
        somebody far away and high up. The organ thunders
        into the Wedding March. (Surely the Main Titles are
        over by now.)

        DISSOLVE TO:

A-12   TRUCKING SHOT - AHEAD OF JOEL AND CLAUDETTE

        as they come, panting down the aisle. As they smile
        at each other happily --

A-13   LONG SHOT OF THE WEDDING PARTY - THROUGH A GRILL ON
        WHICH WE READ IN PRETTY VALENTINE LETTERS:

                        AND THEY LIVED HAPPILY
                        EVER AFTER

        The CAMERA PULLS BACK through another grill and we
        read:

                        OR DID THEY?

        DISSOLVE TO:

A-14   A VERY SMALL GRAY AND WHITE KITTEN

        It SLOWLY DISSOLVES INTO a fully grown cat.

A-15   A TINY LITTLE ROSE BUSH

        It SLOWLY DISSOLVES INTO a large bush covered with
        roses.

-11-21-41

A-16   A CALENDAR WHICH SAYS: JUNE 1, 1937

The leaves start falling off and it SLOWLY DISSOLVES
INTO a calendar which says: February 2, 1942.

A-17   A SHINY NEW 1937 CAR

It SLOWLY DISSOLVES INTO an old jallopy.

A-18   A TITLE

It reads:

> In other words: five
> years have passed.

FADE OUT:

FADE IN:

A-19   A SIGN - "APARTMENT FOR RENT"

DISSOLVE TO:

A-20   AN ELEVATOR DOOR OPENING

From it emerge a sour looking apartment house manager
and the Wienie King and his wife. The CAMERA TRUCKS
AHEAD OF THEM as they move down the hall.

> THE WIFE
> We just want it as a little roost in
> case we miss the train or something...
> We have the big place in Yonkers.

> THE MANAGER
> Of course.

> THE WIENIE KING
> What did he say?

> THE WIFE
> (Hollering)
> He said, "Of course."
> (Then to the Manager)
> We're from Texas originally.

> THE MANAGER
> Of course.

> THE WIENIE KING
> What did he say?

A-20   (Cont'd)

> THE WIFE
> He said, "Of course."

> THE WIENIE KING
> Why does he keep saying the same
> thing all the time?

> THE WIFE
> (Apologetically)
> My husband is a little deaf.

> THE MANAGER
> Of course.

> THE WIENIE KING
> What did he say?

> THE WIFE
> He said: "It's as quiet as a tomb
> here"... Just what we're looking for.

> THE HUSBAND
> I don't mind a little life... We'll
> be dead soon enough.

He pounds on a wall with his cane.

> A DISTANT VOICE
> Come in.

> THE WIENIE KING
> Concrete.

> AN ANGRY HEAD
> (Popping out of a
> door behind them)
> I said, come in!

> THE WIENIE KING
> I'm fine, thanks, how are you?

> THE WIFE
> I hope all your tenants aren't as
> disagreeable.

> THE MANAGER
> I can assure you they're not. The
> building is friendly, efficient and
> quiet.

The voice of a lady opera singer does a piercing
arpeggio and a dog starts to yap.

11-21-41   (Continued)

A-20   (Cont'd)

                        THE MANAGER
            She got in by mistake. She's leav-
            ing first thing in the morning.

                        THE WIENIE KING
            What?

                        THE MANAGER
                    (Cupping his hands)
            She's leaving first thing in the
            morning.

                        THE WIENIE KING
            Who, my wife?... You going home to
            see your mother?

Before anybody can answer, the arpeggio is repeated
much higher.

                        THE WIENIE KING
                    (Pleased, holding up
                     a finger)
            What's that, a canary? I love birds.

                        THE MANAGER
                    (Cupping his hands)
            She's leaving the first thing in the
            morning.

                        THE WIENIE KING
            You don't have to shout and your best
            friend ought to tell you a little
            secret... just speak in a low clear
            voice.

                        THE MANAGER
                    (In a low, clear and
                     boiling voice)
            I said, she's leaving in the morning.
            She got in by mistake but tomorrow
            she flies away.

He accompanies the word "flies" with a flying motion
of his crossed hands, as one makes a shadow pigeon on
a sheet.

                        THE WIENIE KING
                    (Crossly)
            I understand it's a bird... What about
            it... I like birds.

11-21-41   (Continued)

A-20   (Cont'd)

                        THE MANAGER
                    (Forcing himself to
                      smile politely)
                It's just here.

He raps perfunctorily on the door and opens it and
leads the way.

A-21   REVERSE SHOT FROM - INT. A STUDIO DUPLEX

This is composed of a two-story studio, a dinette and
kitchenette on one level and a bedroom, dressing room
and bath on the balcony above. A winding stair leads
to this. The Manager, the Wienie King and the Wife
come TOWARD US.

                        THE WIENIE KING
                    (Pointing to the
                      ceiling with his
                      cane)
                What's the ceiling so high up for?

                        THE WIFE
                    (Running her finger
                      along a ledge)
                You don't seem to keep your apartments
                very clean.

                        THE WIENIE KING
                What's on the balcony?

                        THE MANAGER
                    (Almost as if it
                      gave him pleasure)
                The former tenants have not been get-
                ting the service... a little matter
                of delinquency... in the rent.

                        THE WIENIE KING
                What did he say?... I don't like him
                to talk to me.

                        THE WIFE
                    (Cupping her hands)
                He says the former tenants haven't
                been getting any service... that's
                why the place is dirty... they didn't
                pay their rent.

The CAMERA WHIPS UP TO Geraldine, leaning over the
balcony. She is a very pretty young woman in a
negligee.

11-21-41

A-22   THE MANAGER AND THE ELDERLY COUPLE - FROM GERALDINE'S
            VIEW POINT

                       THE WIENIE KING
             I don't mind a little dirt. That's the
             trouble with women: always fussing
             around, looking for something to pick on.

                       THE WIFE
             You can tell me later, Arthur.

                       THE WIENIE KING
                (Walking toward the
                stairs)
             Never satisfied with things the way the
             Lord made 'em.
                (He starts up the stairs)

His wife and the Manager start for the kitchenette.

                       THE WIENIE KING
             Dirt is as natural in this world as
             sin and disease and storms and twisters...

A-23   CLOSE SHOT - GERALDINE

            She reacts to the old man's coming up the stairs,
            hurries into her room and closes the door.

A-24   THE OLD MAN - REACHING THE TOP LANDING

            He takes three pokes at the ceiling and crosses to
            the bedroom door and puts his hand on the knob.

A-25   GERALDINE - IN HER BEDROOM

            PAST HER we see the door opening and she backs' hur-
            riedly into a closet and closes the door.

A-26   THE OLD MAN - WANDERING AROUND THE BEDROOM

            He picks up an atomizer and squirts some perfume on
            himself.

A-27   GERALDINE - OPENING THE DOOR OF THE CLOSET

            She reacts to the swiping of her perfume.

11-21-41

A-28   THE OLD MAN - AT THE DRESSING TABLE

          He puts down the atomizer and picks up another one.
          He smells of it and adds a little of this to the first
          perfume.

A-29   GERALDINE - PEEKING OUT OF THE CLOSET

          She glares at him.

A-30   THE OLD MAN - AT THE DRESSING TABLE

          He picks up a lipstick and examines it.

A-31   GERALDINE

          She narrows her eyes, wondering what he's going to do
          with it.

A-32   THE OLD MAN - AT THE DRESSING TABLE

          He puts the lipstick to his lips and tastes of it, by
          taking some off on his finger.

A-33   GERALDINE

          She is very indignant.

A-34   THE OLD MAN - AT THE DRESSING TABLE

          He puts down the lipstick and, still smacking his
          lips, wanders out into the balcony.

A-35   GERALDINE

          She comes out of the closet and goes cautiously to
          the dressing table. She peeks out onto the balcony.
          Suddenly she hears something behind her. The door
          from the bathroom is opening. Geraldine hurries out
          onto the balcony as the old man comes into the room
          from the bathroom. He looks around to make sure this
          is the same room and peeks onto the balcony.

A-36   GERALDINE - BACKING INTO THE BATHROOM

          Suddenly she turns and looks toward the bedroom door.

11-21-41

A-37   THE OLD MAN - IN THE BEDROOM

He goes into the bathroom.

A-38   THE BATHROOM

The old man comes into it, tries the faucets and
tastes of the tooth paste.

A-39   GERALDINE - IN THE BATH TUB BEHIND THE SHOWER CUR-
TAIN

She puts her hands on her hips.

A-40   THE OLD MAN - AT THE WASH BASIN

Still smacking his lips he crosses to the bath tub,
examines the shower curtain, then looks for the
faucet to turn on the shower. At this, Geraldine
sweeps the curtain back majestically and glares at
him.

> GERRY
> Is there anything else you'd like
> to try?

> THE WIENIE KING
> (Amiably)
> Hello. What are you doing in the
> bath tub with your wrapper on?

> GERRY
> I might ask you what you're doing
> in my bathroom...only I suppose
> you have the right, really.
> (She steps out of
> the tub)

> THE WIENIE KING
> (Helping her out)
> I don't suppose you go with the
> flat...I guess that would be too
> much to hope for...you have very
> pretty legs.

> GERRY
> (Pulling her wrapper
> tighter)
> That's very generous of you...I'm
> glad you like my perfume, too.

11-21-41

(Continued)

A-40 (Cont'd)

> She walks into her bedroom and the old man follows
> her.

A-41   <u>THE BEDROOM</u> - GERALDINE AND THE OLD MAN COMING IN

>   THE WIENIE KING
>   You have a lovely clear voice
>   ...like a bell. If I were
>   married to you I could hear
>   everything you said, almost...
>   but you wouldn't enjoy it...
>   besides, I'm already married.
>
>   GERRY
>   (Laughing a little)
>   So am I.
>
>   THE WIENIE KING
>   Me too. Anyway I'd be too old
>   for you...cold are the hands
>   of time that creep along relent-
>   lessly destroying slowly but
>   without pity that which yester-
>   day was young. Alone our memo-
>   ries resist this disintegration
>   and grow more lovely with the
>   passing years...that's hard to
>   say with false teeth.
>
>   GERRY
>   (Laughing)
>   You're a funny old man.
>
>   THE WIENIE KING
>   I didn't get it but you looked
>   very pretty while you said it.
>   (Now he gets a thought)
>   Say, if they're showin' us the
>   flat and you're still in it you
>   must be broke, hunh?
>
>   GERRY
>   (Shrugging)
>   It doesn't matter.
>
>   THE WIENIE KING
>   What did you say?
>
>   GERRY
>   (A little louder)
>   Yes.

11-21-41   (Continued)

93

A-41 (Cont'd)

>   THE WIENIE KING
> Is that varmint rentin' it out
> from under you?

>   GERRY
> Yes.

>   THE WIENIE KING
>   (Cackling)
> I know how you feel. I used
> to be broke too, when I was
> about your age...but I didn't
> have a figger like you got...I
> had to use my brains.
>   (He cackles)
> You'll get over it...you'll
> get over bein' young too...one
> day you'll wake up and find
> it's all behind you...gives you
> quite a turn...makes you sorry
> for a few of the things you
> didn't do...while you still
> could.

>   GERRY
> Are you sorry?

>   THE WIENIE KING
> How much rent do you owe?

>   GERRY
>   (Gently)
> That isn't really your business.

>   THE WIENIE KING
> I can't hear you; you're mumbling.

>   GERRY
>   (More distinctly)
> I said, it isn't really your
> business.

>   THE WIENIE KING
> I'm in the sausage business...
> don't worry about me.
>   (He reaches into his
>   pocket and produces
>   a roll that would
>   choke a crocodile)
> This will be a hot one on my
> wife. She's down there fussin'
> around...pokin' her snoot in

11-21-41   (Continued)

A-41 (Cont'd)

                        THE WIENIE KING (Cont'd)
                other people's business...with
                that varmint eggin' her on...
                        (He starts peeling
                        bills off the roll)

                        GERRY
                        (Looking fascinated
                        at the roll)
                Don't be silly.

                        THE WIENIE KING
                You say five hundred would cover
                it?

                        GERRY
                Don't talk nonsense, please.

                        THE WIENIE KING
                        (Pressing the five
                        hundred in her hand)
                I can't hear you...you're mumbling
                again...you shouldn't mumble with
                such a lovely voice...I wouldn't
                do this for everybody.

                        GERRY
                        (Trying to give
                        the money back)
                Look, this joke has gone far
                enough...

                        THE WIENIE KING
                You say that isn't enough...
                Well, how much do you need?

                        GERRY
                You're just embarrassing me.

                        THE WIENIE KING
                That's all right, don't mention
                it...it's a privilege to do a
                little favor for such a beauti-
                ful lady... It makes me feel
                young again.

                        GERRY
                Yes, but how do you suppose it
                makes me feel...I haven't seen
                anything like this in so long...
                        (Her lips tremble
                        a little)

11-21-41   (Continued)

A-41 (Cont'd)
                              THE WIENIE KING
                    If you're talking about the money,
                    forget it. I'm cheesey with
                    money...invented the Texas Wienie...
                    lay off 'em, you'll live longer...
                    here.
                         (He peels off a couple
                          more hundred and puts
                          them in her hand)
                    Buy yourself a new dress too...and
                    a new hat...you're a nice girl...
                    so long.

          He turns to go. Geraldine grabs him impulsively
          and kisses him on both cheeks.

                              THE WIENIE KING
                         (Crowing like a
                          rooster)
                    Yippee!...Hot dog!

          He pounds his stick on the floor and hurries out.

A-42   CLOSE SHOT - GERALDINE

          She looks at the money in stupefaction.

A-43   THE WIFE AND THE MANAGER - AT THE FOOT OF THE STAIRS

                              THE WIFE
                         (Starting up the
                          stairs)
                    Well, I suppose with a thorough
                    cleaning...
                         (Now she looks up)

A-44   THE WIENIE KING - COMING DOWN THE STAIRS

                              THE WIENIE KING
                    You don't have to climb up...
                    The lady don't want to rent.

          By now the CAMERA HAS PANNED HIM INTO THE GROUP with
          the others.

                              THE MANAGER
                         (Waspishly)
                    Oh, she don't, doesn't she!
                    Well, maybe I'll have something
                    to say about that.

11-21-41
                                             (Continued)

A-44 (Cont'd)

> THE WIENIE KING
> What did he say?

> THE WIFE
> He says she hasn't any choice
> in the matter.

> THE WIENIE KING
> (Belligerently)
> What do you mean, she hasn't
> any choice in the matter? I
> tell you she's going to pay
> her rent and stay.

> THE MANAGER
> And I've heard that one before.

> THE WIENIE KING
> What did he say?

> THE WIFE
> He says he don't believe she has
> the money.

> THE WIENIE KING
> Does he want to bet?

> THE WIFE
> How do you know she has the
> money?

> THE WIENIE KING
> (Delightedly)
> Because I just give it to her.

He busts out laughing, pounds his cane and leads
his indignant wife out.

A-45   GERALDINE - IN HER ROOM

She looks at the money for a moment, then hurries
to the telephone.

A-46   GERRY - AT THE TELEPHONE

> GERRY
> Will you get me Longacre 5-6599,
> please.

11-21-41   (Continued)

A-47   TOM AND THE PROSPECT - <u>IN TOM'S OFFICE</u>

      They are looking at a not too well made miniature of
      Tom's suspended air port. As we watch, a plane
      slides down a wire and lands on the netting.

                   TOM
          You see, it's simple and practical,
          it's strong, it's safe, it lets
          the light and air through, it's
          nearly invisible from below...

      The phone rings.

                   TOM
          (Looking at the phone)
          ...it's in the middle of the
          city instead of out in the sticks
          somewhere...just a minute.
          (Into telephone)
          Yeah?

A-48   GERRY - <u>AT THE TELEPHONE</u>

                   GERRY
          (Into the telephone)
          Darling, the most exciting thing
          has happened.

A-49   TOM - <u>AT THE TELEPHONE</u>

                   TOM
          (Into the telephone)
          Look, honey, I'm just in the middle
          of a talk with a gentleman here...
          could you tell me later?

A-50   GERRY - <u>AT THE TELEPHONE</u>

                   GERRY
          All right, dear.

      She hangs up the phone, looks at the money again,
      laughs happily and peels off her wrapper. As she
      reaches into her closet for a dress --

      DISSOLVE TO:

A-51   TOM AND THE PROSPECT - <u>IN TOM'S OFFICE</u>

                   TOM
          Of course this is the big one, but
          to build a working model in some

A-51 (Cont'd)

> TOM (Cont'd)
> field somewhere or a village...
> that small planes could actually
> land on...would only cost about
> ninety-nine thousand dollars...
> after that we'd be on velvet.
> Every municipality, every town,
> every city needs one...my patent
> is basic...

> THE PROSPECT
> Ninety-nine thousand dollars is
> a lot of money.

> TOM
> It isn't what it costs...it's
> what it brings you back...

> THE PROSPECT
> (Putting on his hat)
> You see I got ninety-nine thousand
> dollars now, but if I build this
> thing...

> TOM
> Look: let's start again at the
> beginning....

> THE PROSPECT
> Go ahead...my time ain't worth
> anything...I'm retired.

He removes his hat as another gent enters.

> TOM
> You want to see me about something?

> THE GENT
> About the rent.

> TOM
> Well... you'll have to wait...I'm
> busy.

> THE GENT
> Go ahead. I ain't in a hurry.

> TOM
> (Indicating)
> Gentlemen, here is the future - let
> us turn our clocks ahead and enjoy
> it now.
> (The gent looks at his
> watch)

FADE OUT:

END OF SEQUENCE "A"

FADE IN:

B-1   EXT. TOM'S AND GERALDINE'S APARTMENT HOUSE - (NIGHT)

A superbly uniformed doorman stands near the curb.
Tom comes INTO THE SHOT behind him, peeks into the
lobby, then calls to the doorman.

> TOM
> (Confidentially)
> Hey, Mike...come here a minute.

The doorman crosses to Tom and the CAMERA FOLLOWS him.

> TOM
> Take a gander inside and see if
> the manager's gone to dinner,
> will you. I don't want to meet
> him face to face.

> THE DOORMAN
> Sure, but if it's the rent you're
> thinkin' about you can go in and
> whistle up his nose...it's paid.

> TOM
> (Astonished)
> It's paid! What do you mean,
> it's paid?

> THE DOORMAN
> It's paid.

> TOM
> Who paid it?

> THE DOORMAN
> Your wife.

> TOM
> My wife!

> THE DOORMAN
> It sure wasn't mine...an old man
> give her the money.

> TOM
> An old man gave her the money!
> What do you mean, an old man
> gave her the money?

> THE DOORMAN
> Just what I'm telling you.

11-21-41   (Continued)

B-1 (Cont'd)
>   TOM
> How do you know about this?

>   THE DOORMAN
> The whole building knows about
> it... They wish he'd drop in
> on them.

>   TOM
> Who?

>   THE DOORMAN
> The old man.

Tom's expression becomes very ferocious and he
hurries into the building.

DISSOLVE TO:

B-2   GERRY IN A BEAUTIFUL DINNER DRESS - IN THE STUDIO
       OF THE APARTMENT - (NIGHT)

>   GERRY
>   (Repeating as to
>   a child)
> I said: I'm taking you to
> dinner and then the theatre
> and then supper, so hurry
> up and put on your dinner
> jacket.

B-3   TOM - PAST GERALDINE

>   TOM
> Just a minute... What's all
> this malarkey about some old
> man paying the rent for you...
> that the whole building is
> buzzing with?

>   GERRY
> It isn't malarkey, dear...
> here's the receipted bill...
> you see it says "Paid."...
> and I paid the grocer and the
> butcher and the drugstore and
> then I got this dress and had
> my hair done and six pairs of
> stockings and some new shoes
> and here's fourteen dollars
> in change... that's for you.
> Isn't that wonderful?

11-21-41   (Continued)

                              TOM
                     (Stiffly, being very
                      careful not to touch
                      the money)
                    Sensational, but you haven't
                    quite answered my question.

                             GERRY
                    What question, dear?

                              TOM
                    Why this alleged old man gave
                    you -- how much was it?

                             GERRY
                    Seven hundred dollars.

                              TOM
                    Seven hundred dollars...why?

                             GERRY
                     (Innocently)
                    No reason.

                              TOM
                     (Sarcastically)
                    Is that so... He just... Seven
                    hundred dollars...
                     (He waves his
                      arm)
                    just like that...

                             GERRY
                    Of course.

                              TOM
                     (With heavy
                      sarcasm)
                    I mean sex didn't even enter
                    into it.

                             GERRY
                     (Surprised)
                    But of course it did, darling...
                    I don't think he would have
                    given it to me if I had hair
                    like excelsior and little short
                    legs like an alligator... sex
                    always has something to do
                    with it... from the time
                    you're about so big...
                     (She indicates)

                              TOM
                    I see.

B-3 (Cont'd)

               GERRY

And wondering why your girl
friends' fathers are getting so
arch all of a sudden...nothing
wrong, just an overture to the
opera that's coming.

               TOM

I see.

               GERRY

You don't, really, but from then
on you get it from taxi drivers,
bell boys, cops, delicatessen
dealers, visiting noblemen, and
I even think I got it from a
corpse once...at a funeral.

               TOM
             (Exasperated)
Got what?

               GERRY

The look.
             (She rolls her eyes
             and mimics)
"How's about this evening, babe?"
Sometimes they say it and sometimes they don't, but it gives
you a fine opinion of men on
the whole.

               TOM

So this gent gave you the look.

               GERRY

The Wienie King? At his age, darling, it was really more of a blink.

               TOM
             (Frigidly)
Really. This is very illuminating.

               GERRY

You don't have to get rigid about
it. It was perfectly innocent,
I assure you.

               TOM

And where did you meet this Wienie
King?

               GERRY
             (Starting to laugh)
You'll die laughing when you hear
where.

-11-21-41   (Continued)

B-3 (Cont'd)

> TOM
> (Between clenched
> teeth)
> All right -- convulse me.

> GERRY
> (Holding onto him to
> control her mirth)
> In the bath tub!
> (She cascades in
> laughter)

> TOM
> (Snarling like an
> angry dog)
> The bath tub!

> GERRY
> Yes, isn't that charming?

> TOM
> Delicious! What were you
> doing in the bath tub?

> GERRY
> Hiding from him.

> TOM
> Hiding from him! What kind
> of games do you play around
> here while I'm out?

> GERRY
> I wish you'd seen the expres-
> sion on his face.

> TOM
> I'm glad I didn't. How much
> water was there in the tub?

> GERRY
> I was <u>standing</u> in the bath tub,
> foolish.

> TOM
> (With glazed
> eyeballs)
> You were <u>standing</u> in the bath tub!

> GERRY
> In a blue wrapper, you fool. He
> was just a funny little old man
> in a funny hat, darling. He just
> sat and talked for awhile on the
> edge of the bed...

B-3 (Cont'd)

> TOM
> Oh, he's on the bed now, is he!

> GERRY
> Well, there aren't any chairs
> in the bedroom, darling.

> TOM
> What was he doing in the bedroom?

> GERRY
> He wanted to rent the apartment,
> but when he found out we were
> broke he gave me seven hundred
> dollars and left.

> TOM
> Just like that.

> GERRY
> (Guiltily)
> Well... I did kiss him goodbye.

> TOM
> Now the truth is coming out.

> GERRY
> The truth! As if I had to pick
> out an old bunny like that...
> if I wanted to cut a caper. He
> did me a lot of good... I'd
> almost forgotten... You have no
> idea how it makes a girl feel to
> have a man say, "It's a privilege
> to be living in the same world
> with you... here is my fortune...
> help yourself."

> TOM
> He said that? -- You just tell me
> where this sausage king lives.
> I'll take him back his money and
> tell him what I think of...

> GERRY
> I don't know where he lives,
> darling... I don't even know
> his name, and I don't think
> they'd give the money back: I
> mean the grocer and the drug-
> store and all, after they
> waited so long for it... and
> you really couldn't blame them.

B-3 (Cont'd)

                TOM
That's right, rub it in.

                GERRY
Tom.

                TOM
Yes.

                GERRY
It's wonderful to have the rent
paid, isn't it, and the bills
settled up...you feel free and
clean and...I like that feeling.
I wish it were always like that.

                TOM
Don't you think I do?

                GERRY
I'd almost forgotten what it was
like....I don't look forward to
being in debt again...and slink-
ing past everybody...I dread it.

                TOM
It isn't going to be for always.
Everybody's a flop until he's a
success. Something is bound to
come through. I've got too many
good ideas...

                GERRY
Now that everything is paid up
you could move...

                TOM
Well, where would we go?

                GERRY
       (Avoiding his eye)
I wasn't thinking about me....
I just meant you.

                TOM
       (Slowly)
Oh...You mean...the bust up?

                GERRY
Unhunh.

                TOM
When did you get this idea...
this afternoon?

                GERRY
I've had it a long time, but something always said: "Wait till he

-11-21-41   (Continued)

                          GERRY (Cont'd)
          crashes through, wait till he's
          made one success," but you'll
          never make a success with me
          around...I'm just a milestone
          around your neck.

                          TOM
                     (Automatically)
          Millstone.

                          GERRY
          I'm no good for you, darling...
          oh, I don't mean I'm not good
          for somebody...but I can't cook
          or sew or whip up a little dress
          out of last year's window curtains...
          or a turban out of your old gold
          stockings...I'm like a car that
          only gives seven miles to the
          tankful...only you haven't got
          the tankful.

                          TOM
          You're sure you haven't got a
          tankful.

                          GERRY
                     (Ignoring him)
          You see by yourself you could
          live so simply...I mean just a
          little room anywhere or move in
          with your brother...or even use
          a couch in your office...and you
          wouldn't keep slipping back all
          the time...and you could balance
          what you earned and look the world
          in the eye...and maybe even get
          ahead a little.

                          TOM
          Thanks, and what will you be doing?

                          GERRY
          That's no problem...you can always
          find a good provider...if you really
          want one...he may not look like
          Charles Boyer....

                          TOM
                     (Coming closer)
          We'll get ahead some day.

                          GERRY
          I don't want it someday, I want it
          now while I can still enjoy it...I
          don't want to pay people to dance

-11-21-41   (Continued)

B-3 (Cont'd)

> GERRY (Cont'd)
> with me...I'd rather have them
> pay me...Anyway, men don't get
> smarter as they get older...they
> just lose their hair.

> TOM
> Gerry.

> GERRY
> Well I would. I'm very tired of be-
> ing broke, darling...and feeling so
> helpless about...having my hands
> tied...I could have helped you so
> many times, but every time I tried
> to you tried to punch the man in the
> nose. Like this afternoon...that
> poor little old man and his seven
> hundred dollars...suppose I'd got
> you the ninety-nine thousand.

> TOM
> Don't talk rot.

> GERRY
> How about that president of the
> smelting company.

> TOM
> That wolf!

> GERRY
> He's still the president of a
> smelting company...and we might
> have been in the smelting business
> now...and paying our rent.

> TOM
> Lovely.

> GERRY
> He liked you very much...he said.

> TOM
> The less you talk about that hyena
> the better I will like it.

> GERRY
> (Shrugging)
> Well...but that's what's so irrita-
> ting...to know that I could get you
> some place and without doing any
> harm, either...you have no idea
> what a long-legged gal can do with-
> out doing anything...and instead of

-11-21-41   (Continued)

                          GERRY (Cont'd)
          that I have to watch you...stamping
          around proudly...like Sitting Bull
          in a new blanket...breathing through
          your nose...while we both starve to
          death.

                          TOM
          Thanks.

                          GERRY
          You don't have to keep saying thanks
          all the time, I'm not being so nice.

                          TOM
                  (Angrily)
          Well...if you want a divorce .you're
          certainly entitled to it...I don't
          know where the money's coming from
          but...

                          GERRY
          Oh, the next husband always pays
          for that.

                          TOM
                  (Flaring up)
          Oh, you have him all picked out,
          have you!

                          GERRY
          You're such a child.

                          TOM
          He wouldn't happen to be in the
          sausage business by any chance,
          would he?

                          GERRY
                  (Shrugging)
          I may not even get married again...
          I might become an adventuress.

                          TOM
          I can just see you starting for
          China in a twenty-six foot sailboat.

                          GERRY
          You're thinking of an adventurer,
          dear...an adventuress never goes on
          anything under 300 feet...with a
          crew of eighty.

                          TOM
          Yes!...well you let me catch you
          on somebody's yacht...

-11-21-41   (Continued)

109

B-3 (Con't)

                GERRY
At least I wouldn't have to worry
about the rent...oh, I'm sorry...
let's go and have some dinner.

                TOM
How can you think of food at a
moment like this?

                GERRY
Because I'm a woman, maybe...and
a little more practical than you
are. Will you put on your dinner
jacket or shall I take off my new
dress?

                TOM
Oh, is that a new dress?

Gerry merely looks at him.

DISSOLVE TO:

B-4   TOM AND GERRY - IN A BOOTH IN A LITTLE RESTAURANT -
      (NIGHT)

There is music playing in the background. They have
finished their dinner. There are coffee cups, brandy
glasses and after-dinner mints on the table. Gerry
wears her new dress and Tom his dinner jacket. They
are both slightly, Oh, very slightly, swacked.

                GERRY
I tell you we don't mean anything
to each other any more...I don't
love you...you don't love me...
we don't even see each other any
more...we're invisible to each
other...I put on a brand new dress...

                TOM
I'm very sorry I didn't notice the
dress!
        (He starts to pour him-
         self another drink)

                GERRY
Don't you see how much more useful
I'd be to you if our relationship
was more like....brother and sister...

                TOM
You'll always be a sister to me, hunh?

                GERRY
I know it sounds stupid...but I'm a
rotten wife...I can't sew, I can't
cook...

-11-21-41   (Continued)

B-4 (Cont'd)

> TOM
> You certainly can't.

Gerry gives him a slight look before continuing.

> GERRY
> Just because I'm a useless wife
> doesn't mean I wouldn't be very
> valuable as a sister...<u>very</u>
> valuable.

> TOM
> I remember that pot roast you tried...

> GERRY
> (After a slight look)
> The boys who wanted to take me out
> would naturally have to be in your
> good graces...

> TOM
> (Gravely)
> Naturally.

> GERRY
> Or I wouldn't go out with them.

> TOM
> (Savagely)
> I'll say you wouldn't!

> GERRY
> And then they'd probably offer you
> partnerships...

> TOM
> In the smelting business.

> GERRY
> You could have your choice...I
> don't begin and end with a smelter.

> TOM
> I refuse to understand what you're
> talking about, Geraldine.

> GERRY
> They'd work you in on deals and
> let you in on good things that
> were happening in the market and
> all that kind of business.

> TOM
> Monkey business!

-11-21-41   (Continued)

B-4 (Cont'd)

GERRY
Well, very few pretty girls'
brothers have ever failed, you
know...if they knew enough to
come in out of a hail storm.

TOM
In the first place I don't happen
to be your brother 'and in the
second place may. I ask where all
these men are coming from...who
are going to...faint at your feet.

GERRY
You think there aren't any.

TOM
I didn't say there weren't any...
I just said, where are they?

GERRY
They're around...they're always
there, and they make new ones
every year.

TOM
I don't want to be rude, honey, but...

GERRY
You're not being rude, dear...you're
just being yourself. You see: You're
married to me...that's like saying
you're blind to me. For a long time
I've been a part of you, something to
snuggle up to and keep you warm at
night...like a blanket...but you can't
see me any more than you see the back
of your neck. I put on new dresses...
I change my hair...

TOM
Would you mind not looking quite so
gorgeous while you say all this
stuff?

GERRY
You're just plastered.

TOM
Yes, well I'd better get you home
before you fall apart...
     (Now he becomes very
     formal)
or do you object to spending the
night under the same roof with me?

B-4 (Cont'd)

>   GERRY
>   I wasn't thinking about the roof.

>   TOM
>   Come on.

>   GERRY
>   Wait a minute...I'd better pay the
>   check.

She puts out her whole fourteen dollars. As Tom
reacts --

DISSOLVE TO:

B-5   <u>THE APARTMENT</u> - (DIMLY LIT)

Tom and Gerry come in a little unsteadily.

>   TOM
>   (Indicating)
>   I'll sleep on the thing, there.

>   GERRY
>   Well, you <u>know</u> we don't love each
>   other any <u>more</u>...
>   (She starts working
>   on the back zipper
>   of her dress)
>   ...We're just habits...bad habits...
>   They don't make these zippers as
>   well as they used to...and when
>   love is gone there's nothing left
>   but admiration...respect.
>   (After a look)
>   I think this thing is stuck...Will
>   you see if you can undo it?

>   TOM
>   You don't think that is a little
>   intimate, do you?

Gerry shrugs, walks over and turns her back to him.

>   TOM
>   (After trying
>   in the dark)
>   Come over to the light.

They cross and he sits on a chair. As he works
violently on the zipper she sits on his knees. He
closes one eye and eventually opens the zipper.

11-21-41   (Continued)

B-5 (Cont'd)

        GERRY
Did you get it?

        TOM
It doesn't mean anything to you
any more to sit on my lap, hunh?

        GERRY .'
No.
     (Her lips tremble)

        TOM
Or if I kiss you there?

He kisses one of her vertebrae.

        GERRY
No.

        TOM
Or here?

He moves a vertebra.

        GERRY
    (Squirming a little)
Nothing.

        TOM
    (Putting his arms
    around her and
    kissing her again)
Or here?

        GERRY
    (Squirming)
Well, you know I'm...ticklish.

        TOM
Then why is your breath coming
faster?

        GERRY
Because you're...squeezing me.

Now he takes her in his arms and kisses her on the
lips.

        TOM
    (After the legal
    limit)
That doesn't mean anything any
more, hunh?

B-5 (Cont'd)
                           GERRY
                    Almost...nothing.

                           TOM
                    (Standing up with
                    her in his arms)
                    Nothing, hunh?

He starts for the stairs.

                           GERRY
                    Almost nothing...nothing but
                    habit...a bad habit.

                           TOM
                    (Starting upstairs
                    with her)
                    It is, hunh?

                           GERRY
                    Very,..very...bad...and wicked
                    ...and stupid...and useless...
                    and young...and impractical...
                    and...

He seals her lips with another kiss.

FADE OUT:

                    END OF SEQUENCE "B"

11-21-41

FADE IN:

C-1   CLOSE SHOT - TOM ASLEEP - IN THE BEDROOM OF THE
       STUDIO APARTMENT - (DAY)

       He smiles happily and snores a peaceful snore. The
       CAMERA PANS OVER to the other side of the bed but it
       is empty. Now it PANS to Gerry at her dressing
       table. She is dressed for traveling, a suitcase is
       at her feet. She looks back at Tom then continues
       writing on a paper.

C-2   INSERT: THE LETTER AND GERRY'S HAND FINISHING IT

       The reading of this is punctuated by Tom's snores.

                    "Darling -
                         Just because you got me
                    soused last night doesn't alter
                    the logic of the situation.
                    Goodbye, good luck, I love you --

                                        Gerry

C-3   GERRY FINISHING HER NOTE

       As she looks at Tom sentimentally we hear a terrific
       snore. Now she rises, picks up a pin, crosses on
       tip-toe to a place beside Tom and pins the note into
       his hip.

                         TOM
                    (Sitting straight up
                    in bed)
            Wow!
                    (Then rubbing his hip)
            What's the big idea?

                         GERRY
                    (Dismayed)
            Goodbye, darling...read the note...
            God bless you and take care of you.

       She picks up her suitcase and runs out of the room.

                         TOM
            Hey!

       He closes one eye and tries to focus on the note,
       then starts to get out of bed.

11/21/41   (Continued)

116

C-3   (Cont'd)

> TOM
>
> Wait a minute!

He pulls the quilt around him and tears out of the
room.

C-4   TOM - HURRYING DOWN THE STAIRS

He trips on the pajamas and shoots OUT OF THE SHOT.
We hear a crash and a bang.

C-5   TOM - PICKING HIMSELF UP OFF THE FLOOR

He steps out of the pajamas, pulls the quilt tight
around him and his foot yanks on a lamp cord which
pulls the lamp off a console. Now he hurries out of
the room.

C-6   GERRY - ARRIVING AT THE ELEVATORS

She pushes the bell and waits nervously. Now she
turns in alarm.

C-7   TOM - RUNNING DOWN THE HALL TOWARD US

> TOM
> (Near us)
> Will you wait a minute?

C-8   GERRY - PAST TOM

> GERRY
> No I won't. I've made up my mind
> and it's best for us both, darling
> ...while we're still young enough
> ...to make other connections.

C-9   TOM - PAST GERRY

> TOM
> You've still got a hangover and
> you're forgetting a little thing
> called love, honey. I love you
> and you love me.

He holds his quilt with his left hand and puts his
right hand on her shoulder. A near-sighted old lady
now approaches down the hall.

11/21/41   (Continued)

C-9   (Cont'd)

>TOM
>
>That's all that really matters...,
>that's all you can take with you...
>everything else is...

The old lady now screams and Tom pulls his quilt
around him with both hands.

C-10   GERRY - PAST TOM

>TOM
>(Turning to the old lady)
>I'm so sorry.

As he turned the elevator door opened silently and
Gerry stepped into it.

>TOM
>Please accept all my apologies
>uh...

He turns back and sees the elevator door closing.

>TOM
>Gerry!

Now he pulls up his quilt and sprints PAST THE CAMERA.
The old lady puts her hands to her eyes and screams
again.

C-11   THE STUDIO APARTMENT

Tom enters and flies up the stairs. He reappears
from his room a moment later pulling on his pants.
We hear a whistle far below and Tom sticks his head
out the window and looks down.

C-12   VERTICAL DOWN SHOT - GERRY WALKING UP THE STREET
CARRYING HER SUITCASE

She is near a policeman.

C-13   LOW CAMERA - CLOSE - UP AT TOM

>TOM
>(Hollering)
>Hey, officer!

C-14   CLOSE HIGH CAMERA SHOT ON THE POLICEMAN

Gerry walks INTO THE SHOT. They both look up.

11/21/41   (Continued)

C-14   (Cont'd)

                    THE POLICEMAN
        Hunh?

Gerry looks irritated.

C-15   CLOSE LOW CAMERA SHOT ON TOM

                    TOM
        Hold that woman...she stole
        my suitcase!

C-16   HIGH CAMERA SHOT - GERRY AND THE POLICEMAN

                    GERRY
                (Indignantly up at Tom)
        Why you lying...
                (She shapes her lips to say
                "bandit" just as the policeman
                drops a hand on her shoulder)

                    THE POLICEMAN
        This one?

C-17   LOW CAMERA SHOT - UP AT TOM IN THE WINDOW

                    TOM
        That's right, I'll be right down.

He disappears inside the building.

DISSOLVE TO:

C-18   GERRY SITTING ON THE SUITCASE NEXT TO THE COP

                    GERRY
        Do I look like a suitcase stealer
        to you?

                    THE COP
        It isn't how you look it's how
        you behave that counts in this
        world...I mind the time...

He licks his lips to relate the anecdote. They both
turn as Tom COMES INTO THE PICTURE.

                    GERRY
        Wise guy.

                    TOM
        Thanks for holding her, officer.

C-18 (Cont'd)

> THE COP
> You want to prefer charges or
> something disagreeable like that?

> TOM
> (Amiably)
> No, no, I prefer not to...this is
> my wife, Mrs. Jeffers...Mr. Milligan.

> THE COP
> The name happens to be O'Donnell if
> it's all the same to you and I've
> got a good mind to charge you with
> false arrest only I don't know if
> I could make it stick.

> GERRY
> Why don't you try?

> THE COP
> It's too nice a morning...the
> heck with it...Why don't you
> learn to get along together...
> I had to.

He strolls OUT OF THE PICTURE.

> GERRY
> (Picking up her suitcase)
> Now what?

> TOM
> (Taking ahold of the
> suitcase)
> Now will you come back upstairs
> and stop talking nonsense?

> GERRY
> No, I will not. Give me back my
> suitcase...it was hard enough to
> make up my mind to do what I
> know is right...and if I don't
> do it now I'll probably never be
> strong enough again. Now give me
> my suitcase.

> TOM
> (Hanging onto it)
> Gerry, will you stop talking like
> a fool. Where are you going, to
> visit your sister in Long Island?

> GERRY
> (To a passing cab)
> Taxi!...no, I'm going to get a
> divorce.

11-21-41

(Continued)

C-18 (Cont'd)

>   TOM
> How can you get a divorce with-
> out any money? How can you go
> any place? Why don't you be
> sensible? You just got a hang-
> over. Why don't you...

>   GERRY
> I don't need any money. I've
> already told you that a girl...
> Taxi!

A cab pulls up to the curb.

>   THE DRIVER
> Yes, m'am.

>   GERRY
> Where's the best place to get a
> divorce?

>   TOM
> Gerry, for heaven sake...

>   THE DRIVER
> Well, lotta people go to Reno,
> Nevada, but it's Palm Beach for
> my money...at this time of year...
> you got the track...you got the
> ocean...you got the palms...
> three months...you leave from
> Penn Station.

>   GERRY
> I'm in awful trouble, I haven't
> got a dime...would you take me
> down there for nothing?

>   THE DRIVER
> Where, to Palm Beach?

>   GERRY
> No, just to the station.

>   THE DRIVER
> Why certainly. Hop in, babe.

>   TOM
>   (To the taxi driver)
> Listen, you...

>   THE DRIVER
> Listen what?

>   GERRY
> Give me my suitcase.

11-21-41   (Continued)

C-18 (Cont'd)

> THE DRIVER
> Give the lady her suitcase.

> TOM
> Listen, you.

Gerry yanks on the suitqase which flies open, depositing its contents on the sidewalk.

> GERRY
> Now look what you've done.

> TOM
> What I've done!

He stoops to pick up the things.

> THE DRIVER
> Yeah...what you done.

> GERRY
> (To the driver)
> Go ahead.

She jumps into the cab which nips away from the curb.

> TOM
> (Standing up with the
>   suitcase)
> Hey!

> THE COP
> (Walking INTO THE SHOT)
> What's the trouble now?

> TOM
> (Slaming the suitcase
>   to the sidewalk)
> Taxi!

We hear the shrieking of tires.

> TOM
> (Running OUT OF THE SHOT)
> Pick up that stuff, willya?

C-19   CLOSE SHOT - THE COP

> THE COP
> Well I'll be.

DISSOLVE TO:

C-20   INT. OF THE PENNSYLVANIA STATION - HIGH CAMERA SHOT
        DOWN ON THE ACTIVITY

C-21   CLOSE SHOT - GERRY COMING DOWN THE STEPS

        A moment later Tom runs in and overtakes her.

                        TOM
                Will you stop behaving like a
                chicken with its head off. You
                can't go anywhere,...you haven't
                got any money...

                        GERRY
                I got this far, didn't I?

                        TOM
                Well...Gerry...

                        GERRY
                Where's my suitcase?

                        TOM
                Listen, honey.

                        GERRY
                    (Starting to run)
                Goodbye.

        She runs OUT OF THE SHOT. Tom looks around in some
        embarrassment, then hurries after her.

C-22   GERRY - LOOKING BACK OVER HER SHOULDER

        She hurries to a railroad policeman.

                        GERRY
                    (To the Officer)
                Officer, this man is trying to
                molest me. Please make him stop.

                        THE OFFICER
                Oh, he is, is he?

                        GERRY
                    (As she leaves)
                Thank you so very much.

        She walks out of the SHOT sedately.

                        THE OFFICER
                    (Making a dive for
                    the passing Tom)
                Just a moment, laddy boy. What
                are you chasing in such a hurry?

11-21-41   (Continued)

C-22 (Cont'd)

As Tom opens his mouth to speak:

> THE OFFICER
> You leave the dames alone in the
> Pennsylvania Station and the Penn-
> sylvania Station will leave you
> alone...or vicy versy...you get me?

> TOM
> (Trying to release
> himself)
> That happens to be my wife, you
> dumb cluck.

> THE OFFICER
> (Narrowing his eyes)
> Oh, I'm a dumb cluck now, am I?

> TOM
> I tell you that's my wife.

> THE OFFICER
> I've heard that one before laddy.

Tom opens his mouth.

> THE OFFICER
> And whatever you say, I've had
> that pulled on me before too...
> including the "dumb cluck".

> TOM
> Listen, officer.

> THE OFFICER
> (Turning him around
> and starting to walk
> him out)
> So why don't you just go home and
> sober up and try to keep your mind
> off women...it's more wholesome...
> you'll get further...you'll save
> your money...consider the great
> men of history...

> TOM
> (Struggling)
> Listen, you triple-plated moron...

> THE OFFICER
> (Flashing fire from
> his eyes)
> Or I can show you another side of my
> personality entirely, laddy...I like
> peace but I ain't morbid about it...

C-22 (Cont'd)
>He opens a door and prepares to shove Tom through it.

> THE OFFICER
> Now you get out of the Pennsylvania
> Station and stop annoying the janes
> around here before I lock you up.
> Go on now!

>He shoves Tom out and closes the door. Tom starts
>to come in again and the Officer takes out his hand-
>cuffs.

C-23   INSERT: A SIGN THAT SAID "PALM BEACH LIMITED"

C-24   GERRY - LOOKING UP AT THE SIGN

>Now she comes forward and the CAMERA PANS HER INTO
>THE SHOT which includes the gate and the Gateman.
>She looks at the Gateman, then comes up beside him.
>She looks up at the departing time on the gate which
>is 4:58, then up at the big clock in the station.

C-25   INSERT: THE BIG CLOCK

>It says 11:53

C-26   GERRY AND THE GATEMAN

>Passengers with fishing rods and hunting equipment
>are going by. Gerry looks down from the clock and
>begins showing signs of great distress. She bites
>her lips, bites her nails, shifts her weight from
>one foot to the other and is in every way the portrait
>of a damsel in distress. The passengers going by be-
>gin to look at her with some worry.

> THE GATEMAN
> Anything the matter, lady?

> GERRY
> (Very worried)
> Oh, I'll be all right...I'm sure
> they'll come with my ticket.

> DR. KUCK
> (He is a middleaged
> gentleman with two
> gun cases on his
> shoulders)
> Did somebody forget your ticket?

C-26 (Cont'd)

> GERRY
> (Vaguely)
> I'm suro I'll be all right...it's
> just that I...have to get to Palm
> Beach.

> DR. KUCK
> That's too bad.

He goes through with his porter and the CAMERA FOL-
LOWS HIM DOWN a few steps. Here he hesitates, looks
around toward Gerry, then continues on down.

C-27   GERRY

She is getting more and more nervous. A tall business man with a droopy mustache with two guns on his
shoulders whose name is McKeewie goes by.

> GERRY
> I'm sure they'll come.

> MR. McKEEWIE
> (In surprise)
> I beg your pardon.

He curls his mustache.

> GERRY
> (Anxiously)
> I'm so sorry; I was talking to the
> Gateman. I said I'm sure my ticket
> will come...it must come.
> (She closes her eyes
> fervently while say-
> ing the latter)

> MR. McKEEWIE
> (Hypnotized)
> Oh, yes...it must...by all means.

He passes down the steps in a trance. Behind him appears a tiny little good natured man, also with guns.

> MR. ASWELD
> You say your ticket didn't come yet...
> you haven't got much time.

> GERRY
> (Closing her eyes)
> I'm sure it will be all right...it
> must be.

11-21-41

(Continued)

                    MR. ASWELD
       Well... if there's anything I can do...

He passes on, revealing a very large stout man who
raises his eyebrows at Gerry and clears his throat.
He also has guns on his shoulders.

                    MR. OSMOND
               (He clears his throat)
       Hum.

                    GERRY
       I'm sure it will be all right.

She looks anxiously up at the clock. Mr. Osmond
clears his throat and passes through. Next to appear
is Mr. Hinch.

                    MR. HINCH
               (Noticing Gerry's
                distress)
       Is there something the matter, madam?

                    GERRY
       Nothing that anyone can help me with...
       I'm afraid...it's just that...
               (She smiles bravely)
       ... it looks as if my ticket isn't
       going to get here in time.

                    MR. HINCH
       Well... my gracious... there ought to
       be some solution to that problem.

                    GERRY
       I ... can't think of any.

                    MR. HINCH
       My gracious!

Suddenly he gets a thought and darts down the stairs.
Gerry watches him go, then looks back up at the clock.

                    THE GATEMAN
               (To Gerry)
       You'd think one of them would offer
       a lady a ticket.

                    GERRY
               (Shocked)
       Oh... but I couldn't accept it.

                    THE GATEMAN
       Why not?... rich millionaires...
               (Now confidentially
                he adds)
       Look, if your ticket don't come....

11-21-41   (Continued)

                        127

C-27 (Cont'd)

                  GERRY
Yes?

                THE GATEMAN
I don't want this to go no further,
you understand... but there's a guy
by the name of Ed 'who's the conductor of this train...

                  GERRY
Yes.

                THE GATEMAN
I done him a favor once...

                  GERRY
Oh.

C-28   THE CONDUCTOR ED, THE PULLMAN CONDUCTOR AND THE
        BRAKEMAN OF THE TRAIN - <u>IN FRONT OF A CAR</u>

               THE PULLMAN CONDUCTOR
              (Faintly amused)
I see we got the Club again, Ed.

                THE CONDUCTOR
              (Sourly)
You're telling me.

He follows with a bitter glance, a gentleman in a
hunting hat with guns on his shoulder.

                THE CONDUCTOR
Just let 'em try and start somethin'.

A valet goes by with eight hunting dogs on leashes.

                THE BRAKEMAN
              (Laughing)
Hot dog!

C-29   GERRY AND THE GATEMAN

                THE GATEMAN
              (Out of the side of his
               mouth)
And seein' as how I done him this
favor, he could always let you ride
as far as... Manhattan transfer,
maybe... or something.

11-21-41   (Continued)

C-29 (Cont'd)
>   GERRY
> I wouldn't want to get you in trou-
> ble... and I have a feeling it will
> be all right.

She looks down through the grating at the platform below.

C-30   HIGH CAMERA SHOT - DOWN ON MESSRS. KUCK, McKEEWIE,
ASWELD, OSMOND AND HINCH: ALSO A FEW MORE

Their heads are together and they are conferring
busily. They look up toward us occasionally.

C-31   GERRY AND THE GATEMAN

>   GERRY
> I'm sure it will be all right.

She looks up at the clock, then back straight into
the eyes of a large gentleman who straightens his tie
and passes through.

C-32   A DOOR OF THE STATION

Tom comes through cautiously. His coat collar is up
and the brim of his hat is turned down. He looks
around, then starts forward rapidly.

C-33   THE OFFICER - BY THE DOOR WHERE TOM WENT OUT

He gazes around vaguely. Suddenly he stiffens,
sets his jaw and starts forward.

C-34   GERRY AND THE GATEMAN

She looks up at the clock once more. The Gateman
does likewise.

C-35   THE BIG CLOCK

It says 11:57$\frac{1}{2}$.

C-36   GERRY AND THE GATEMAN

>   THE GATEMAN
> Just go through and tell Ed...

11-21-41   (Continued)

Now he stops and they both look down the stairs. We
hear some pounding of footsteps.

C-37   MR. McKEEWIE, MR. ASWELD AND MR. HINCH POUNDING UP
        THE STAIRS

        The CAMERA BRINGS THEM INTO THE SHOT with Gerry and
        the Gateman.

                         MR. ASWELD
                Did it come yet?

                         GERRY
                    (Bravely)
                No... but it's all right.

                         MR. McKEEWIE
                    (Indignantly)
                What do you mean, it's all right?

                         MR. HINCH
                    (Raising a finger)
                It's far from all right.

                         MR. ASWELD
                We have a wonderful idea...

                         MR. McKEEWIE
                The other members and myself, having
                talked it over...

                         MR. HINCH
                You see, we have a private car.

                         MR. ASWELD
                We have tons of tickets.

                         GERRY
                Oh, I could never accept.

                         MR. ASWELD
                We're just going to Savannah to shoot
                quail.

                         MR. HINCH
                But if you wanted to go any further,
                why we'll gladly...

                         MR. McKEEWIE
                Gladly.

                         MR. ASWELD
                You can be our mascot,...you must
11-21-41   be our mascot...   (Continued)

C-37 (Cont'd)

> GERRY
> (To the Gateman)
> Do you suppose it's all right?

> THE GATEMAN
> All right?... It's perfect.

> GERRY
> (To the gentlemen)
> Then, thank you for your chivalry, gen-
> tlemen; I accept with pleasure.

> MR. McKEEWIE
> (Bowing)
> The pleasure is ours... this is Asweld
> of the American Aswaldocan...Mr. Hinch,
> you've heard of Hinch's Emulsion, I
> presume... and I am McKeewie of the
> Seventh National.

> GERRY
> And I am Mrs. Thomas Jeffers, alias
> Geraldine.

> THE THREE GENTLEMEN
> (Delightedly)
> Geraldine!

> GERRY
> (To the Gateman)
> And thanks for your chivalry.

> THE GATEMAN
> Any time... from eight to twelve.

> A VOICE
> All aboard!

> THE GATEMAN
> (Quietly)
> They're coming, Ed; keep your hair on.

He starts to close the gate after Gerry. Now he looks
off toward pounding steps.

C-38   TOM - APPROACHING FULL SPEED, FOLLOWED BY THE OFFICER

The CAMERA PANS him INTO THE SHOT with the Gateman.

> TOM
> (Breathlessly)
> Let me through there!

C-38 (Cont'd)

> THE GATEMAN
> You got a ticket?

> TOM
> No, but...

> THE GATEMAN
> (Closing and locking
> the gate)
> No ticket, no passag.

> THE OFFICER
> (Seizing Tom)
> Oh you will, will you!

> TOM
> (Grabbing the gate
> and looking down)
> Gerry!

C-39   HIGH CAMERA SHOT - CLOSE ON GERRY - ON THE PLATFORM
BELOW

She is being piloted toward a car door by Messrs.
McKeewie, Asweld and Hinch. She looks up and hollers,

> GERRY
> Goodbye, darling.
> (She blows him a kiss)
> Goodbye.

The three gentlemen look up vaguely and also wave.

C-40   CLOSE SHOT - TOM - GLARING DOWN BETWEEN THE BARS OF
THE GATE

> THE OFFICER
> All right, come on now.

C-41   GERRY - ON THE MOVING PLATFORM OF THE CAR

She waves a little sadly. Now the CAMERA PANS DOWN
ONTO a card in the first window. It reads:

> "THE ALE AND QUAIL CLUB
> PRIVATE"

FADE OUT:

END OF SEQUENCE "C"

11-21-41

THE PALM BEACH STORY

SEQUENCE "D"

FADE IN:

D-1   INT. OF THE STUDIO APARTMENT - (DARK)

Tom comes in slowly and we see him silhouetted
against the lighted hall. He turns on one lamp,
closes the door and crosses to the studio window and
looks out over the city. Now he goes to a console
for a cigarette. While lighting the cigarette he
notices a pair of gloves next to the cigarette box.
He picks them up gently and looks at them, then lifts
them to his face and smells of them. He clenches his
fists. The door bell rings. Tom looks toward the
door for a moment, then crosses and opens it, revealing The Wienie King.

                    THE WIENIE KING
                  (Walking right in)
          Hello, where's that pretty gal
          with the nice figger who lives
          here I seen yesterday?

                    TOM
          Who are you?

                    THE WIENIE KING
          I'm fine, thank you, how are you?
          You must be her husband, where is she?

                    TOM
          What is that your business?

                    THE WIENIE KING
          I'm in the sausage business. I
          wanted to tell her we moved in after
          all...we got the green apartment
          down the hall where the opry singer
          moved out. I hate opry, I love
          birds, though. We wanted to take
          you both to dinner, where is she?

                    TOM
          She's gone. She left for Florida.
          She's going to divorce me.

                    THE WIENIE KING
          You say she's gone?

                    TOM
          That's right.

                    THE WIENIE KING
          Good for her...pretty gal like that
          can get anybody...don't have to hang
          around a man who can't pay the rent.
                  (He cackles)

11-21-41   (Continued

133

D-1 (Cont'd)

>   TOM
>   (Shaking a finger under his nose)
>   Look, you old rattle-brains, you've
>   made enough trouble around here without
>   getting insulting about it, so why don't
>   you...
>   (He starts to push him out)

>   THE WEINIE KING
>   (Shaking his stick at him)
>   Don't you threaten me, you big
>   baboon, I'm twicet your age and
>   only half as big but I'm awful
>   mean with this shillelah...I'll
>   beat your brains out afore you
>   can say...

Tom starts to laugh.

>   TOM
>   I guess you didn't mean any harm.
>   It was probably very kind of you
>   as a matter of fact.

>   THE WIENIE KING
>   (Relenting)
>   So she went and left you, hunh?

>   TOM
>   That's right.

>   THE WIENIE KING
>   How did she go, by train?

>   TOM
>   That's right.

>   THE WIENIE KING
>   Then why don't you fly down in an
>   aerioplane and meet her with a
>   bowkay of roses in your hand when
>   she gets off and bring her home?

>   TOM
>   Because I'm not in the sausage
>   business.

>   THE WIENIE KING
>   So am I. It's a good business,
>   too, if you know where to buy the
>   meat cheap. That's my secret but
>   I ain't tellin' nobody...ain't you
>   got the price of an aerioplane
>   ticket.

>   TOM (Bellowing)
>   NO!

D-1 (Cont'd)
                         THE WIENIE KING
                 Then why didn't you say so instead
                 o' standin' there like a stinkweed...
                 that gal is too good to lose...
                        (He produces his enormous roll)
                 ...how much do you need?

          DISSOLVE TO:

D-2   A TRAIN - ROARING THROUGH THE NIGHT

          DISSOLVE TO:

D-3   THE VESTIBULE OF A CAR

          The conductor, the brakeman and the Pullman Conductor
          enter, move into the next vestibule and open the door
          of the club car. Their ears are smitten by music,
          shouts of laughter and the howling of dogs. They
          exchange a look, then go in.

D-4   THE CONDUCTOR, THE BRAKEMAN AND THE PULLMAN CONDUCTOR
          - COMING TOWARD US THROUGH A CORRIDOR

          They stop and look into a compartment.

D-5   THE DOG COMPARTMENT

          This has been arranged with canvas and wood for the
          occupancy of the dogs who are barking and howling
          excitedly at the music.

D-6   THE CONDUCTOR, THE BRAKEMAN AND THE PULLMAN CONDUCTOR
          - IN THE CORRIDOR

          They exchange another look; the Conductor twiddles
          his finger in his ear and they come forward until
          they can see into the car.

D-7   INT. OF THE CLUB CAR

          A wild party is in progress. In the foreground the
          colored bartender is shaking drinks frenziedly and
          keeping the phonograph going. In the background a
          dance is going on. Gerry is being cut in on by the
          twelve members of the Ale and Quail Club, each one
          of which dances worse than the other eleven put to-
          gether.

11-21-41

D-8   CLOSE SHOT - GERRY - DANCING

         She is beginning to look a little woozy.

D-9   THE CONDUCTOR, THE BRAKEMAN AND THE PULLMAN CONDUCTOR
         - LOOKING ON

                              THE FIRST MEMBER
                          (Approaching with two
                            drinks)
                   Harya... come on in... here.

                              THE CONDUCTOR
                              (Severely)
                   Not while we're on duty, thanks.
                   Who's the head man here?

                              THE FIRST MEMBER
                   You mean the prejdent of the
                   club?

                              THE CONDUCTOR
                   Whoever has the tickets... we
                   don't care.

                              THE SECOND MEMBER
                              (Turning)
                   Hey, Ozzie... front and center.

D-10   MR. OSMOND

         He comes forward and the CAMERA PANS him into the
         group.

                              THE FIRST MEMBER
                   Thiz Mr. Osmond.. Prejdent o'
                   th' Ale an' Quail Club.

                              THE CONDUCTOR
                   How are ya.

                              MR. OSMOND
                   Ulp!

                              THE CONDUCTOR
                   It's about the tickets.

                              MR. OSMOND
                   Aha.
         With some difficulty he puts a pince-nez on his nose
         and starts pulling an interminably long ticket out
         of his breast pocket.

11-21-41   (Continued)

D-10 (Cont'd)
                              MR. OSMOND
              Ulp.

        His pince-nez falls off his nose, at which he drops
        the ticket. Solemnly he puts the pince-nez back on
        his nose and starts pulling a handful of very long
        tickets out of his breast pocket.

                            THE CONDUCTOR
              How many are in the party?

                              MR. OSMOND
              Ulp.

                              MR. ASWELD
                  (Arriving)
              Have a drink, boys.

                            THE CONDUCTOR
              Not on duty, thanks.

                          THE PULLMAN CONDUCTOR
              Thanks just the same.

                            THE CONDUCTOR
              How many members to this club?

                            THE FIRST MEMBER
              Well, there's me and Ozzie and
              you...
                  (He points to the
                   other member)
              ...that makes three.
                  (Now he points to
                   the conductors)
              And you two...that makes five...

                            THE CONDUCTOR
              We're not members of the club.

                            THE FIRST MEMBER
                  (Belligerently)
              Why not?

                            THE SECOND MEMBER
              Isn't good enough for you, hunh?

                              MR. OSMOND
                  (Pulling out tickets)
              Ulp!

        His collar comes undone. He starts fastening it,
        at which his pince-nez falls off. He starts re-
        adjusting the pince-nez.
11-21-41   (Continued)

                              137

D-10 (Cont'd)

> THE CONDUCTOR
> All right, let's get this
> straight. How many members
> are there?

> THE FIRST MEMBER
> (Pointing rapidly)
> One, two, three, four, five..
> five.

> THE CONDUCTOR
> All right; that makes three.
> Now let's go on from there.

> THE FIRST MEMBER
> You tryin' to make a liar outa me?

> THE SECOND MEMBER
> (Indicating the two
> conductors)
> Mr. Prejdent... I move that these
> membersh be exshpelled.

> MR. OSMOND
> Ulp!

The other side of his collar flies open.

> THE FIRST MEMBER
> Shecond th' motion.

> THE SECOND MEMBER
> All those in favor say "Aye."

D-11   GERRY AND THE OTHERS - DANCING

They all holler "Aye!"

D-12   GERRY- DANCING WITH MR HINCH

> GERRY
> What's happening?

> MR. HINCH
> (Who carries his liquor
> well)
> The meeting has been called to
> order... We have just voted on
> something.

> GERRY
> On what?

D-12   (Cont'd)

> MR. HINCH
> I don't know... but you always
> vote "Aye" anyway... it saves
> arguments.

> DR. KUCK
> May I cut in?

D-13   MR. OSMOND, THE MEMBERS AND THE CONDUCTORS

> THE CONDUCTOR
> All right, we're expelled...

> MR. McKEEWIE
> (Arriving)
> Have a drink, boys.

> THE CONDUCTOR
> (Pointing to the
> new arrival)
> All right, that's four.

> THE PULLMAN CONDUCTOR
> Check.

> THE FIRST MEMBER
> That's six... one, two, three,
> four, five, six... Whassa matter
> with you, you cockeyed?

> THE CONDUCTOR
> It ain't me that's cockeyed.

> THE FIRST MEMBER
> (To the Other Member)
> Wise guy!

> THE SECOND MEMBER
> (Belligerently)
> Lookin' for trouble, hunh?

At this point Mr. Osmond takes command of the situation. He soothes each of the members with a gesture
and raises a finger under the Conductor's nose and
shakes it in the negative.

> MR. OSMOND
> Ulp!
> His pince-nez falls off.

D-14   GERRY AND DR. KUCK

> DR. KUCK
> (Solemnly)
> Possibly I can be of some help...

11-21-41   (Continued)

D-14 (Cont'd)

>   MR. HINCH
>   (To Gerry)
>   Mr. Osmond doesn't always carry
>   his liquor to perfection... oik!
>   Excuse me.

>   GERRY
>   That's quite all right... eek!

>   DR. KUCK
>   (Philosophically)
>   Ah, well... even in the best of
>   families... wrlump!

>   MR. HINCH
>   Let's see if we can get them
>   straightened woop!

They start forward.

D-15   MR. OSMOND, THE THREE MEMBERS AND THE TWO CONDUCTORS

>   THE CONDUCTOR
>   (Wearily)
>   All right, now let's start again...

Gerry and Mr. Hinch join the scene.

>   MR. HINCH
>   Just a moment, officer.

>   THE CONDUCTOR
>   I'm not an officer, I'm the con-
>   ductor of this train.

>   GERRY
>   Hello, Ed.

The Conductor reacts slightly to this, steals a look
at the Pullman Conductor, then looks back at Gerry.

>   THE CONDUCTOR
>   (Warily)
>   How are you?

>   GERRY
>   (Enjoying the joke)
>   How's every little thing?

>   THE CONDUCTOR
>   Fine... Now if we can just get
>   this ticket situation straightened
>   out.

11-21-41   (Continued)

MT   THE PALM BEACH STORY   D-9

D-15   (58)

DR. KUCK
That's very simple...We are twelve
...that is to say, we are thirteen.
          (This last with a bow
          to Gerry)
Mr. Hinch and eight dogs.

          THE FIRST MEMBER
Who's a dog?

          HINCH
Quiet, Ernest.

He reaches for Mr. Osmond's breast pocket.

          MR. HINCH
All the tickets are right here...
          (He starts pulling
          tickets out)
... this is our president: Mr.
Osmond.

          MR. OSMOND
          (Letting out a quick
          one)
Oop!

          MR. HINCH
          (Producing a chocolate
          bar)
Mr. Osmond is a man who doesn't
believe in taking chances.
          (He pulls out some
          more tickets and a
          bag of gum drops)

          DR. KUCK
Mr. Osmond is now in his fourth term...

          MR. HINCH
There we are.

He starts pressing the mass of paper streamers in the
Conductor's hands. Mr. Osmond reaches into the mass
and retrieves his gum drops.

          MR. HINCH
I think we had to buy thirty
tickets to get the car... which
should be more than sufficient.

          THE CONDUCTOR
          (To Gerry)
You going to Savannah?

          GERRY
Well, I was actually going to...
Palm Beach.

-11-21-41   (Continued)

D-15 (Cont'd)
                    MR. HINCH
          Piffling, piffling... the Club
          will be more than overjoyed...

At this moment all eyes turn to Mr. Osmond who seems
to be suffering the beginnings of an epileptic fit.
He grasps the bar, his chest heaves, he rolls his
eyes wildly, he opens and closes his mouth, then suddenly shouts in stentorian tones.

                    MR. OSMOND
          All those in favor say "Aye."

                    THE WHOLE CLUB
          AYE!

                    MR. OSMOND
          Opposed?

                    THE WHOLE CLUB
                (With equal force)
          NAY!

                    MR. OSMOND
                (Pounding on the bar)
          Motion carried... ooook!

DISSOLVE TO:

D-16   THE TRACKS - AT NIGHT

The train whistles and roars PAST US.

DISSOLVE TO:

D-17   A STATEROOM - FROM THE WINDOW SIDE - IN THE CLUB CAR

Mr. Hinch appears in the corridor, turns on the light
and leads Gerry into the room. Mr. Hinch is now more
chivalrous than ever.

                    MR. HINCH
          There you are, my dear; you'll be
          as snug as a rug... as snug as a
          rug in a... it's funny, I just
          can't remember what the rug is snug
          in. Well, it's of no importance...
          Would it be a mug? No, well, never
          mind...anyway, I just want to tell
          you how flattered we all are to have
          you with us as our guest...

11-21-41   (Continued)

142

D-17 (Cont'd)

                    MR. HINCH (Cont'd)
                (Suddenly; triumphantly)
          It's a thug in a mug!... No.
          Well, as I was saying...

                    GERRY
                (Recognizing an after-
                  dinner speaker)
          You've all been so very kind, I
          don't know what to say except
          good night and thank you.
                (She wishes him to the
                  door but he remains
                  planted)

                    MR. HINCH
          I don't want you to get an idea
          just because the boys got a lit-
          tle wild that there's anything
          rough about them or that anyone
          of them wouldn't treat you like
          his sister.

                    GERRY
          I am sure of that and believe
          me, I appreciate it deeply.

                    MR. HINCH
          Osmond is a pillar of the church...
          ook!... Asweld has seven daughters...

                    GERRY
          Poor man.

                    MR. HINCH
          Dr. Kuck is a world famous psy --
          kila - psy - physician --
                (He holds up a finger)
          ... A BUG IN A RUG, THANK HEAVEN!

                    GERRY
          Now we can both relax.

                    MR. HINCH
          And even I myself... if I do say
          so myself... am a man not without
          some... pretensions, let us say...
          to those deeper qualities of
          American honor, steadfastness and
          integrity... without which our
          founding fathers... how about a
          little night cap before we turn
          in?

11-21-41   (Continued)

D-17 (Cont'd)

                    GERRY
          I've really had enough, Mr. Finch;
          thank you very much.

                    MR. HINCH
                    (Gently)
          Hinch... Hinch's Emulsion.

                    GERRY
          Of course... I'm so sorry... our
          cook used to use it... I mean my
          grandmother.

                    MR. HINCH
                    (Laughing from one side
                    of his face only)
          Well, I'm not quite that old but
          it's all right. Good night...and
          if there is the slightest trouble
          ... just knock...
                    (He does so)
          ... on my wall.

                    GERRY
                    (Pushing him out in the
                    corridor)
          Thank you very much.

                    MR. HINCH
                    (With his foot in the
                    door)
          Don't give it a thought... as I
          have so often said at dinners and
          our little gatherings... where's
          your baggage?

                    GERRY
          What?

                    MR. HINCH
                    (Coming back into the
                    stateroom)
          Where's your luggage? What are
          you going to sleep in?

                    GERRY
          Why, that's perfectly all right,
          I'll just... you see I left rather
          hurriedly.

                    MR. HINCH
          Why bless my soul... you stay right
          there... I'll have you a pair of
          pajamas before you can say...what
          size do you wear?

-11-21-41   (Continued)

D-17 (Cont'd)

> MR. HINCH (Cont'd)
> Well, I guess you'll have to
> take my size... they may be a
> little big.

    DISSOLVE TO:

D-18   GERRY - IN MR. HINCH'S PAJAMAS

    The sleeves are a foot too long and so are the pants.
    She rinses her mouth with water from a glass and gets
    into bed and looks rather despondent.

D-19   CLOSE SHOT - GERRY

    She switches out the light. She sniffles once.

    DISSOLVE TO:

D-20   TOM - IN HIS SEAT IN AN AIRPLANE

    He looks very sore.

    DISSOLVE BACK TO:

D-21   GERRY

    Her eyes are moist with tears. Now there is a knock
    at her door. Gerry turns and scowls at the door.

> GERRY
> What is it?

    Four voices say something unintelligible.

> GERRY
> What did you say?

    The four voices speak again and we hear: "Open the
    door." Gerry gets out of bed and opens the door a
    crack. It flies open the rest of the way and Messrs.
    Asweld, McKeewie, Kuck and another member enter.

> MR. ASWELD
> I want you to hear something.

> GERRY
> But I've already gone to bed.

> DR. KUCK
> That's perfectly all right.

D-21   (Cont'd)

MR. McKEEWIE
Go back to bed. We'll put you to
sleep.

Gerry gets into bed. Mr. Asweld starts beating time
and the quartet breaks into a vociferous "Sweet
Adeline."

D-22   CLOSE SHOT - GERRY

She winces, then looks toward the door.

D-23   FULL SHOT - OF THE STATEROOM

As the moth to the flame, so are the gentlemen attracted by the music. They come in one by one and
join their voices to the singing. Gerry looks very
desperate.

D-24   THE FIRST AND SECOND MEMBER - IN THE CLUB CAR

The bartender is taking this opportunity to clean up
a little in the background. The Second Member is
practically asleep. The First is listening sourly to
the music, toying with a shotgun the while.

THE FIRST MEMBER
(Disgustedly)
Bunch o' sissies... supposed to   (Protect for
be a gun club... not a blasted   England
singing society.   "Fatheads")

THE SECOND MEMBER
(Opening his eyes)
Make mine with plain water, never
mind the ice.

THE FIRST MEMBER
Ought to expel 'em all from the   (Protect for
club... bunch o' co-eds...   England)
Sweet Adeline... phooey!
(He pretends to shoot
some imaginary birds)

THE SECOND MEMBER
Never mind the ice. Just with
plain water.

The First Member looks at him disgustedly, then picks
up an empty glass and puts it between his hands.

D-24   (Cont'd)
> THE SECOND MEMBER
> Thank you very much.

He looks at the glass nearsightedly then takes a deep
drink of it, smacks his lips, wipes his mustache,
then starts taking a deep interest in the First Member's imaginary shooting.

> THE FIRST MEMBER
> Bang bang!

The Second Member laughs in a superior manner.

> THE FIRST MEMBER
> What are you laughing about?

> THE SECOND MEMBER
> (Taking a sip of his
> drink)
> Never touched 'em.

> THE FIRST MEMBER
> (Belligerently)
> Is that so.

He shoots at two more imaginary birds.

> THE FIRST MEMBER
> Bang bang... I suppose I never
> touched 'em that time.

> THE SECOND MEMBER
> The left one got away.

> THE FIRST MEMBER
> (Disgustedly)
> The left one got away... you
> oughta have your eyes examined.
> (He turns to the
> bartender)
> Throw up some crackers, George.

> THE BARTENDER
> (Just faintly worried)
> Yassuh.

He throws two crackers into the car.

> THE FIRST MEMBER
> Bang bang!

The crackers fall on the carpet.

> THE FIRST MEMBER
> I supposed I missed 'em that time.

11-21-41   (Continued)

                    THE SECOND MEMBER
            Both of 'em.

The strains of "Moonlight Bay" drift out of Gerry's
stateroom.

                    THE FIRST MEMBER
            I suppose you could do better.

                    THE SECOND MEMBER
            For fifty bucks.

                    THE FIRST MEMBER
            Who's goin' to be the judge?

                    THE SECOND MEMBER
            You be the judge.

A look of greedy pleasure comes over the First Member's face. Now he offers the Second Member his gun.

                    THE FIRST MEMBER
            All right, go ahead.

                    THE SECOND MEMBER
                (Cunningly)
            Ah no, no, no, no, no, not with
            that old blunderbuss....I'll use
            my own.

He takes a gun down from a hook, breaks it, slips
two cartridges in it, closes the breech and turns
to the First Member.

                    THE SECOND MEMBER
            Fifty bucks.

                    THE FIRST MEMBER
            Fifty bucks.

                    THE SECOND MEMBER
            You be the judge.

                    THE FIRST MEMBER
            I'll be the judge.

                    THE SECOND MEMBER
                (Coolly)
            All right, go ahead.

                    THE FIRST MEMBER
                (To the bartender)
            All right, toss 'em up, George.

D-24   (Cont'd)

The Bartender does so and the Second Member blows the
crackers to pieces, at the same time blowing two windows out of the side of the car. The Bartender ducks
behind the bar. The First Member turns and stares
solemnly at the Second Member.

                    THE SECOND MEMBER
                    (Quietly)
               That's fifty bucks.

The First Member blinks at him in surprise, then looks
frowningly at the carpet.

D-25   GERRY - IN THE MIDST OF THE TROUBADOURS

                         GERRY
               What was that noise?

One of the singers moves out into the corridor.

D-26   THE FIRST AND SECOND MEMBERS

                    THE FIRST MEMBER
               Bet you can't do it again.

                    THE SECOND MEMBER
               You're on.

He breaks his gun and the shells jump out. As he
reaches for two more shells...

                    THE FIRST MEMBER
               Wait a minute... you're using
               real shells.

                    THE SECOND MEMBER
               Well, what do you think I was
               using, bird seed?
                    (He reloads his gun)

                    THE FIRST MEMBER
                    (Breaking his gun)
               Well, wait a minute... two can
               play at that game.
                    (He loads his gun and
                     closes it)
               Fifty dollars?

                    THE SECOND MEMBER
               You're on.

                    THE FIRST MEMBER
               Toss 'em up, George.

11-21-41

149

D-27   THE BARTENDER - PEEKING OVER <u>THE BAR</u>

> THE BARTENDER
> I wouldn't do that if I was you, gen-
> tlemen... Conductor's apt to get lil
> bit irritated.

D-28   FULL SHOT - THE CAR

> THE FIRST MEMBER
> (Threateningly)
> Will you toss those biscuits up?

> THE BARTENDER
> (Ducking very low)
> Y-yassuh.

He tosses two biscuits in the air and the two members
fire simultaneously, shooting a lighting fixture off
the ceiling and another window out of the car.

D-29   A DELIGHTED MEMBER - LOOKING IN FROM <u>THE ENTRANCE TO
THE CORRIDOR</u>

He turns and runs back to Gerry's stateroom.

D-30   THE FIRST AND SECOND MEMBERS

> THE FIRST MEMBER
> (Indignantly)
> Well, wait a minute... you weren't
> supposed to shoot that time.

> THE SECOND MEMBER
> All right, it's my turn this time.

> THE FIRST MEMBER
> All right... fifty dollars.
> (He reloads his gun)

> THE FIRST MEMBER
> Fifty dollars. Toss 'em up, George.

D-31   CLOSE SHOT - THE BARTENDER

> THE BARTENDER
> I wouldn't do that if I was you
> gents... You apt to do some
> damage.

-11-21-41

D-32 THE FIRST AND SECOND MEMBERS

         THE FIRST MEMBER
         (Belligerently)
     You gonna toss 'em up or am I
     gonna toss you up?

D-33 THE BARTENDER

         THE BARTENDER
     Y-yassuh.

With a shaking hand he tosses a handful of crackers
in the air and ducks behind the bar. We hear four
shots.

D-34 GERRY - IN THE MIDST OF THE TROUBADOURS

As she turns her head toward the corridor, the delighted member rushes in, more delighted than ever.

         THE DELIGHTED MEMBER
     Hey, fellas... trap shooting!...
     come on.

He turns and runs out and the others run after him.
Left alone, Gerry gets out of bed, puts a blanket
around her and very nervously goes into the corridor.

D-35 FULL SHOT - THE CLUB CAR

         ONE MEMBER
     What do you mean, fifty?... I'll
     bet you a hundred.

         ANOTHER MEMBER
     I'll take half of that.

         MR. HINCH
     Now, wait a minute, boys.

D-36 THE BARTENDER

         THE BARTENDER
     I wouldn't do that if I was you,
     gentlemen.

D-37 THE GROUP

         A MEMBER
     Quiet!

11-21-41

D-38   GERRY - LOOKING IN

                              GERRY
                        (Rather frightened)
                  Gentlemen, if I were you... why
                  don't you wait till you get to
                  ... gentlemen, I wouldn't...

          Now some terrific firing starts. Smoke drifts in
          front of Gerry and she gets genuinely panicky.
          A light fixture is shot off the wall over her head.
          She sticks her fingers in her ears and runs away.

D-39   THE VESTIBULE OF THE CAR

          Gerry comes into this, pauses in indecision, opens the
          door back into the car, listens to the shooting and
          the barking of the dogs again for an instant, then
          crosses through the dining car and into the next car.

D-40   INT. A PULLMAN CAR WITH THE BERTHS MADE UP

          Gerry appears, looking for refuge. She peeks into a
          lower berth, then a second one, then a third one,
          then a fourth one. Now she peeks into an upper
          berth. This seems to be empty so she begins to try to
          get into it. She steps a few times on the edge of the
          lower berth, then puts one foot on the arm of the s t
          across the way, hangs onto the curtain bar of her
          chosen berth and starts to get one knee up.

D-41   INT. OF THE LOWER BERTH

          John D. Hackensacker III, a near-sighted but person-
          able young man, turns on the light, and adjusts his
          pince-nez the better to notice all these kickings
          against his curtain. Now he sticks his head out
          through the opening.

D-42   GERRY - TRYING TO GET INTO THE UPPER BERTH

          As she kicks her legs, the CAMERA SLIDES DOWN them
          ONTO John D.'s face. As he looks up near-sightedly,
          Gerry's foot, encased in the long pajama leg, steps
          squarely on the bridge of his nose.

D-43   LOW CAMERA SHOT - CLOSE UP AT GERRY

          She looks down and seems to see what she has done.
          She lets herself down.

-11-21-41

D-44   CLOSE SHOT - GERRY'S AND JOHN D.'S HEADS

        John D.'s eyes are tightly closed but the remains of
        his pince-nez are on them,

                            GERRY
                I'm terribly sorry... I hope I
                didn't hurt you.

                            JOHN D.
                        (Trying to blow the
                         glass away)
                That's quite all right. Just pick
                off any little pieces you see,
                Will you?

                            GERRY
                        (Doing so)
                There... and I can't tell you how
                sorry I am.

                            JOHN D.
                Don't mention it.... I break them
                all the time. Were you climbing
                upstairs there?

                            GERRY
                Well, I was, yes.

                            JOHN D.
                Just a minute; I'll help you.

                            GERRY
                That's very kind of you.

                            A VOICE
                Quiet!

        John D. disappears inside the curtain.

D-45   INT. JOHN D.'S BERTH

        He removes the nose pincer of his pince-nez, wipes
        his eyes, snaps a new pince-nez on from the window
        sill, then swings his feet out and sits up.

D-46   GERRY - IN THE CORRIDOR

        John D. pokes his head through the curtain.

11-21-41   (Continued)

                              153

D-46 (Cont'd)

                    JOHN D.
          Now you put one foot here...
               (He indicates one
               arm of the seat)
          and one foot there...
               (He indicates the
               other arm)
          ...and you'll be up in a jiffy
          ...I'd gladly trade berths with
          you but mine has already been...

                    GERRY
          I wouldn't think of it. You've
          been much too kind already.
          Thank you very much.

D-47   AN IRATE PASSENGER - STICKING HIS HEAD OUT THROUGH
       THE CURTAINS

                    IRATE PASSENGER
          Quiet!

D-48   GERRY AND JOHN D.

                    GERRY
               (Putting one foot on the
               arm of the seat)
          Is that right?

                    JOHN D.
          Well, you're standing on my hand,
          but otherwise it's...perfect.

                    GERRY
               (Getting down)
          Oh, I'm so sorry.

                    JOHN D.
               (Shaking his hand)
          Don't mention it...you're as
          light as a feather.

                    GERRY
          Thank you. Good night.

                    JOHN D.
          Good night.

D-49   THE IRATE PASSENGER - BETWEEN THE CURTAINS

                    IRATE PASSENGER
          Good night!

-11-21-41

D-50   GERRY AND JOHN D.

She gives this man a look, then puts one foot on
one arm, the other foot on the other, one knee on
the upper berth and there she's stuck.

D-51   CLOSE SHOT - GERRY

                     GERRY
          Just push my other leg up a
          little, will you?

D-52   CLOSE SHOT - JOHN D.

                     JOHN D.
          Why certainly.

He grabs her leg in both his hands and lifts it
over his head.
                     JOHN D.
          There.

Slowly the leg slips through his hands and the heel
comes gently to rest on his pince-nez. There is a
slight crunch.

D-53   GERRY

She leaps into the upper berth, then sticks her head
out.

D-54   CLOSE SHOT - GERRY - THROUGH THE CURTAINS

                     GERRY
          That's fine, thank you very
          much.
             (Now she frowns)
          Is there something the matter?

D-55   CLOSE SHOT - JOHN D.

He is shaking off the remains of his pince-nez.

                     JOHN D.
          Nothing at all...everything is
          fine, thank you.

D-56   CLOSE SHOT - GERRY

                     GERRY
          Then good night.

-11-21-41   (Continued)

D-56 (Cont'd)

                         JOHN D.'S VOICE
          Good night.

She disappears inside the curtains.

D-57   THE IRATE PASSENGER - <u>THROUGH THE CURTAINS</u>

                       IRATE PASSENGER
          Good night!

D-58   JOHN D. - <u>INSIDE HIS BERTH</u>

He pulls his head in, removes the wreckage of his
pince-nez, wipes his eyes, puts on a new pince-nez
from the window sill and snaps out the light.

D-59   THE DOGS - BARKING VIOLENTLY <u>IN THE CLUB CAR</u>
<u>COMPARTMENT</u>

We hear the sound of shooting and yelling.

D-60   THE BARTENDER - <u>BEHIND THE BAR</u>

He peers over fearfully, then ducks below as a shot
smashes the bottles behind him. He reappears with a
flag of truce, made with a towel and muddler. Again
he ducks just in time as more bottles are smashed
behind him.

D-61   MR. HINCH - IN THE MIDST OF THE SHOOTERS

He is in his pajamas and thoroughly indignant.

                       MR. HINCH
                    (Hollering)
        Gentlemen...GENTLEMEN...IF I MAY
        CALL YOU THAT...remember that we
        have a guest... a lady is partaking
        of our hospitality...we must not
        frighten her...I will take her your
        apologies.

He turns and starts for Gerry's room. The members
look at each other, then for want of something
better to do, start singing "Sweet Adeline."

D-62   <u>GERRY'S STATEROOM</u>

Mr. Hinch appears, discovers Gerry's absence and
hurries out.

-11-21-41

D-63   THE GENTLEMEN - SINGING "SWEET ADELINE"

> MR. HINCH
> (Rushing in)
> Gentlemen, she's gone!

> A MEMBER
> Gone!

> MR. HINCH
> Gone.

> MR. ASWELD
> But that's terrible.

> DR. KUCK
> We must find her at once.

> MR. McKEEWIE
> (Raising a finger)
> Kidnapers!

Mr. Osmond raises a finger and opens his mouth.

> MR. OSMOND
> (After a moment)
> Oik!

He removes his handkerchief and presses it to his lips.

> THE FIRST MEMBER
> Less organize a posse.

> SEVERAL DIZZY MEMBERS
> Hurray!

> THE SECOND MEMBER
> (With difficulty)
> Where th' dogs?...You can't
> have a posse without the dogs.

> THE FIRST MEMBER
> Who says you can't?

> THE SECOND MEMBER
> For fifty dollars.

> SEVERAL DIZZY MEMBERS
> Hurray!

DISSOLVE TO:

11/21/41

157

D-64   THE DINING CAR

We hear the noise of the approaching hoodlums and
the yarking of dogs. Some colored waiters stick
their heads out of their quarters. Now the posse
appears in full cry. It is led by the eight dogs on
leashes, followed by the eleven members singing:
Ahunting We Will Go," followed in turn by Mr. Hinch
who is trying to stop them, who is followed by the
Bartender who nearly faints into the arms of some of
the waiters. At the end of a musical phrase a member fires his gun, which keeps the dogs brisk.

                     A MEMBER
                (Presenting one of
                Gerry's shoes for the
                dogs' inspection)
          There, now where is she?

Now they start singing again.

D-65   THE CAR THAT CONTAINS JOHN D. AND GERRY

We hear the end of the hunting refrain and the bang
of the shotgun.

D-66   GERRY - IN THE UPPER BERTH

Petrified, she pulls the covers around her and the
pillow over her head.

D-67   TRUCKING SHOT - AHEAD OF THE POSSE

As frightened passengers stick their heads out, the
dogs lick them in the face.

                     THE MEMBERS
                   (In unison)
          We want our mascot! We want
          our mascot!

A shotgun goes off and the ladies in the car scream.
As the posse moves forward -

D-68   JOHN D. - IN HIS BERTH

He slops over with a start and turns on the light.
Now he opens his curtains to see where the barking
is coming from and his berth immediately fills with
dogs. As they bark and lick his face --

11/21/41

D-69   THE MEMBERS - IN THE CORRIDOR

                        ONE OF THE MEMBERS
            Well, they found something.

                        ANOTHER MEMBER
                Hurray!

A gun is fired and women scream again.

D-70   GERRY - IN HER BERTH

She disappears under her pillow.

D-71   THE CONDUCTOR, THE PULLMAN CONDUCTOR AND THE BRAKEMAN

They are in a men's washroom.

                        A PORTER
                    (Rushing in)
            Mr. Ed, they's a posse goin'
            through the train!

                        THE CONDUCTOR
                    (Threateningly)
            What?
                    (He gets up)
            Come on, Al.

They start out.

D-72   JOHN D. - IN HIS BERTH

He is trying to kick the dogs out of the berth.
They knock his pince-nez off and look for titbits
under his pillow and under the blankets.

D-73   THE MEMBERS - HOLDING THE DOGS

                        A MEMBER
            Whoa, boys, we've got the wrong
            pew...that's a gentleman.

Now he looks into the opposite curtains and is
rewarded by a shriek.

11/21/41

D-74   THE OTHER END OF THE CAR

The Conductor, the Pullman Conductor and the Brakeman
appear. THE LENS IS ABOUT EIGHT FEET HIGH SO THAT IT
CAN PAN THE APPROACHING MEN INTO THE SHOT WITH THE
A & Q. MEMBERS.

                         THE CONDUCTOR
              What's going on here? Go back.
              in your car.

                         THE FIRST MEMBER
                         (Belligerently)
              Who are you? You're expelled.

                         THE CONDUCTOR
              Go on, get back in your car be-
              fore I get the engine crew and
              have you all locked up.

D-75   AN OBSCURE MEMBER

                         THE MEMBER
              Yippee!

He fires his gun.

D-76   THE CONDUCTOR - PAST THE MEMBERS

                         THE CONDUCTOR
                         (Frothing)
              Who fired that gun? Don't you
              know that's a misdemeanor? If
              you don't get back in your car
              I'll wire ahead and have the
              whole bunch of you locked up...
              Go on now, get back in your car
              ...go on.

Suddenly the members turn about-face and start singing "Ahunting We Will Go," and march off toward their
own car.

D-77   JOHN D. - IN HIS BERTH

He wipes his nose, locates his pince-nez with difficulty, puts it on his nose and looks out at the retreating hunters. He throws a bone out of his bed.
Suddenly a flea gets him.

11/21/41

D-78   GERRY - IN HER UPPER BERTH

She comes out from under the pillow and breathes more
easily. Now she sticks her head out through the
curtains.

D-79   CLOSE SHOT - GERRY'S HEAD - THROUGH THE CURTAINS

GERRY
(Looking down)
Are you all right?

The CAMERA PANS DOWN.

JOHN D.
(Poking his head out)
I'm f-f-fine, thank-thank-thank...

His head disappears and the curtain moves around as
if he were landing a sailfish. Now his bare foot
sticks through the curtain. The CAMERA PANS UP TO
Gerry who looks a little surprised at this nonsense.

D-80   THE CLUB CAR

We hear the singing hunters as they appear, followed
by the two Conductors and the Brakeman. Suddenly the
Conductor gets a look at the interior of the car.

THE CONDUCTOR
Well, I'll be...Oh you will,
will you!...Well I'll show you...
this is one trip you'll remember...

A MEMBER
Oskeewow-wow!

He fires both barrels.

DISSOLVE TO:

D-81   THE BRAKEMAN - AT A HAND SWITCH

He is waving the train back. As the Club car goes
PAST US --

DISSOLVE TO:

D-82   A BIG COUPLING BEING DISCONNECTED

We hear a whistle and the jerk of a train.

11/21/41

D-83   TRUCKING SHOT AWAY FROM THE ALE AND QUAIL CLUB

They are on the front of their club car, Some of
them are on the ground. They look a little indignant.

ONE OF THE MEMBERS
Hey!

D-84   THE DEPARTING TRAIN

On the rear of it we see the Conductor, the Pullman
Conductor and the Brakeman. As it pulls away --

D-85   PULL-AWAY SHOT FROM THE ALE AND QUAIL CLUB

The music reprises "Ahunting We Will Go" and they
all fire their guns in the air.

DISSOLVE TO:

D-86   GERRY - IN HER BERTH

We begin to hear the rail clicks. She pulls the
covers a little more tightly around her.

DISSOLVE TO:

D-87   TOM - IN HIS PLANE SEAT

He turns up his coat collar.

DISSOLVE TO:

D-88   GERRY - IN HER BERTH

She pulls the blankets a little more snugly around
her, looks rather forlorn, shrugs and closes her
eyes and prepares to sleep. The music reprises the
"Hunting Song."

FADE OUT:

END OF SEQUENCE "D"

11/21/41

FADE IN:

E-1 A PRETTY STRETCH OF TRACK IN THE SUNLIGHT

    The streamliner roars toward us.

    DISSOLVE TO:

E-2 JOHN D. - IN THE MEN'S WASHROOM

    He is shaving with a straight razor.

E-3 A PORTER - IN THE AISLE OF THE PULLMAN CAR

    He looks worried and apologetic.

         THE PORTER
     No, m'am.

E-4 CLOSE SHOT - GERRY - PAST THE PORTER

         GERRY
     What do you mean, my clothes
     aren't there? They're in
     Stateroom "B" in the private
     car right behind the diner...
     the club car and my ticket and
     my handbag and my lipstick and
     everything.

         THE PORTER
     No, m'am.

         GERRY
     Don't stand there saying "no,
     m'am"... You looked in the
     wrong room. It's Stateroom "B".

         THE PORTER
     No, m'am.

    As Gerry opens her mouth, the Porter continues:

         THE PORTER
     Maybe in Stateroom "B" all
     right... but they ain't in
     the car behind the diner
     'cause there ain't no car
     behind the diner.

11-21-41   (Continued)

E-4 (Cont'd)

                        GERRY
                  (Narrowing her eyes)
There ain't no car behind the
diner.

                    THE PORTER
No, m'am.

                        GERRY
                  (At patience's end)
There isn't a car with twelve
old toss-pots and eight dogs
that looks like a cyclone
struck it.

                    THE PORTER
No, m'am.

                        GERRY
You just didn't look.

                    THE PORTER
                  (Doggedly)
Yes, m'am, I looked but I didn't
see it 'cause it warn't there...
that's why I didn't see it.

                        GERRY
I suppose it just blew up.

                    THE PORTER
No, m'am...We set it out - we uncouple it!

                        GERRY
                  (Horrified)
You uncoupled it!

                    THE PORTER
Yassum....Conductor got kinda
riled with 'em...so he
just left 'em on a siding in
Rockingham Hamlet... to cool
off... very pretty little city.

                        GERRY
With my clothes in it. Where's
the Conductor?

                    THE PORTER
Oh, he get off at Rawley...
that's where he live... just a
little ways out... very pretty
countryside there...

                        GERRY
You don't seem to understand
that my clothes are lost.

11-21-41   (Continued)

E-4   (Cont'd)

          THE PORTER
They ain't lost. Nothin' ever
gets lost on a Pullman... they's
safe all right... I recollect
one time a lady leave a whole
pile o' diamonds right on the
window sill...

          GERRY
I want to get into my clothes.

          THE PORTER
You can't do that.

          GERRY
Well, what do I go around in...
a blanket like an Indian?

          THE PORTER
I got a brown overcoat.

          GERRY
That's very kind of you... Do
you suppose the new conductor
carries something for an emergency?

          THE PORTER
You mean clothes?

          GERRY
Yes.

          THE PORTER
He usually bring his other suit
... the blue serge.

As Gerry looks around helplessly she sees somebody.

          GERRY
Oh, hello.

E-5   JOHN D. - APPROACHING

          JOHN D.
       (Cheerfully)
Oh, hello... What are you doing
for breakfast.

The CAMERA PANS him INTO THE GROUP.

          GERRY
Well, if you don't invite me I
won't be doing much... and if
you do invite me it might make
quite a scandal.

11-21-41   (Continued)

E-5   (Cont'd)
                    JOHN D.
         Hunh?

                    THE PORTER
         Lady lose her clothes.

                    JOHN D.
                 (Horrified)
         You lost your clothes; why
         that's terrible!

                    GERRY
         And my ticket and my bag and
         my make-up and my shoes and my
         toothbrush... only I don't think
         I had one.

                    THE PORTER
                 (Taking it out of
                  his pocket)
         This might be one of your shoes
         ... found it in the dining car.

                    GERRY
         That'll be a big help... I can
         play hopscotch.

                    JOHN D.
                 (Indignantly)
         But this is disgraceful... I'll
         certainly write to the president
         of the company... How could such
         a thing happen?

                    GERRY
                 (Evasively)
         I don't know... my things got into
         a car back there somewhere, somehow,
         and now the car just doesn't....
         seem to be there.

                    JOHN D.
         Not that car full of drunks, I
         hope, that they had to disconnect.

                    GERRY
         Perish the thought.

                    JOHN D.
                 (Thinking hard)
         Well... as soon as we come to a
         town... I could jump over to a
         store and jump back...

11-21-41   (Continued)

                        166

E-5 (Cont'd)

                     GERRY
With a Mother Hubbard. That's
really terribly kind of you...
in the meantime I suppose
I'll have to lie here in this hatrack...

                     JOHN D.
              (Thinking hard)
Maybe we could make you something out of a blanket...

                     GERRY
You and Schiaparelli.

                     JOHN D.
Well...

                     GERRY
Anyway, I haven't got any money
for you to jump over to the
store and back with.

                     JOHN D.
Oh, I have money.

                     GERRY
Have you?

                     JOHN D.
Oh yes, now if you could just get
over to the store to pick out what
you need.

                    THE PORTER
We got a stretcher in the baggage
car up ahead!

                     JOHN D.
              (Inspired)
Wouldn't that be stretching it
a little? Ha, ha, ha!

Gerry freezes him with a look.

                     JOHN D.
My sister has piles of clothes...

                     GERRY
In Poughkeepsie, I suppose.

                     JOHN D.
No, Palm Beach.
              (Inspired)
Wait a minute: maybe we could
borrow some odd pieces here
and there among the lady passengers.

11-21-41   (Continued)

E-5 (Cont'd)
>   GERRY
>   (Seeing herself
>   as in a vision)
>   Oh, unspeakable word!

She puts her hand to her head.

>   JOHN D.
>   (Delighted)
>   That's a wonderful idea...
>   (He turns to
>   the Porter)
>   You take that side and I'll take
>   this side.

>   THE PORTER
>   Yassuh!

>   GERRY
>   And I'll take the neck.

DISSOLVE TO:

E-6   JOHN D. AND THE PORTER - <u>OUTSIDE THE LADIES'</u>
<u>RETIRING ROOM</u>

They each have an armful of clothes. The door is
ajar.

>   JOHN D.
>   Here... we've got some more
>   ... or are you satisfied?

E-7   GERRY - <u>IN THE LADIES' ROOM</u> - <u>IN FRONT OF A MIRROR</u>

A colored maid is peering over her shoulder. Gerry
is wearing quite an outfit; it starts at the ground
with some button shoes with pearl gray tops and ends
in a hat with roses on it. In between there is a
long black satin evening dress and a knee-length
blue serge dressmaker coat. Shyly the colored maid
puts a feather boa around her neck.

>   GERRY
>   (Throwing the boa
>   on the floor)
>   Satisfied!

E-8   JOHN D. AND THE PORTER - <u>IN THE HALL</u>

>   JOHN D.
>   (Passing in a hat)
>   How about this one?

E-8 (Cont'd)

    There is a second's pause and a pile of clothes
    hits him in the face and drapes over his head.

E-9   GERRY AND THE MAID - IN THE LADIES' ROOM

    Gerry slams the door, examines the blanket and the
    pajamas, then turns to the maid.

                GERRY
        Get me a pair of scissors.

    DISSOLVE TO:

E-10   JOHN D. - IN THE DINING CAR

    He pauses in the act of eating a grapefruit, looks
    up, then smiles delightedly.

                JOHN D.
            (Looking up)
      Why, that's lovely. Now you
      won't _need_ anything else.

                GERRY
      That's what _you_ think.

    The CAMERA PANS DOWN to her shoes as she takes her
    place at the table.

E-11   THE WAITER WHO IS PUSHING HER CHAIR IN

    He reacts to Gerry's stern.

E-12   GERRY - SITTING DOWN

    Across her beam we read: "THE PULLMAN COMPANY."

E-13   JOHN D. - PAST GERRY

    He looks at her admiringly.

                JOHN D.
      If there's one thing I admire,
      it's a woman who can whip up
      something out of nothing.

                GERRY
      You should taste my popovers.

11-21-41   (Continued)

E-13 (Cont'd)
                              JOHN D.
            I'd love to. The homely virtues
            are so hard to find these days
            ... a woman who can sew and cook
            and bake, even if she doesn't
            have to, and knit and... and...

                              GERRY
                         (Helping him out)
            And weave.

                              JOHN D.
            You're joking but I mean seriously:
            that is a woman.

                              GERRY
            Were you going to buy me some break-
            fast, or would you like me to bake
            you something right here at the
            table?
                              JOHN D.
            I like a witty woman, too.
                         (He picks up the
                          bill of fare)
            Now what will you have? The
            thirty-five cent breakfast seems
            the best at first glance, but if
            you analyze it for solid value,
            the fifty-five center is the one.

                              GERRY
            I wouldn't want to impose.

                              JOHN D.
            No, no, feel free to choose what
            you like... there's even a seventy-
            five cent breakfast, if it appeals
            to you.

                              GERRY
            We might share one.

                              JOHN D.
                         (Suddenly interested
                          in the menu)
            Wait a minute... with two eggs,
            toast and choice of fruit thrown
            in, I'm not sure the seventy-five
            cent breakfast isn't the best
            value after all.

                              GERRY
                         (Mockingly)
            Do we dare?

    -11-21-41   (Continued)

E-13 (Cont'd)

JOHN D.
(Laughing suddenly as
he understands her)
I'm not really the way you think
I am... it's just my upbringing.
(Now he looks up
at the waiter)
Two seventy-five cent breakfasts.

GERRY
I'll start with a prairie oyster.

THE WAITER
Uh... yes, m'am.
(Now he adds with
a smile)
Very tempting choice in the dollar
ten breakfast.

JOHN D.
(Firmly)
Two seventy-five cent breakfasts,
and I'll start with a prairie
oyster also... whatever it is.
Make mine on the halfshell.

THE WAITER
(Surprised)
Yassuh, but de prairie oysters is
a la carte.

JOHN D.
All right, all right... they always
get the best of you somehow... Now,
you say you have no ticket?

GERRY
That's right.

JOHN D.
That presents quite a problem.

GERRY
I can't think of any solution.

JOHN D.
Naturally I can't buy you a ticket
... I mean, a perfectly strange
young woman.

GERRY
Naturally.

JOHN D.
In the first place you wouldn't
accept it, and in the second
place...

-11-21-41   (Continued)

E-13 (Cont'd)

> GERRY
> There's the expense.

> JOHN D.
> I wasn't actually thinking of that
> ... now I get off at Jacksonville...

> GERRY
> I guess I do too... unless they
> throw me off sooner.

> JOHN D.
> That presents quite a problem.

> GERRY
> It would take an Einstein.

> JOHN D.
> Did you say you were going to
> Palm Beach, or did I dream it?

> GERRY
> Yes.

> JOHN D.
> That presents quite a problem
> ... or does it?

> GERRY
> Don't tell me you found a way out.

> JOHN D.
> Suppose we go to a little store
> in Jacksonville and buy you the
> few little things you need, and
> then you come the rest of the
> way with me by boat? You won't
> have had to accept a ticket from
> somebody you don't know, but you'll
> still get to where you're going...
> how's that?

> GERRY
> I don't have to row, do I?

> THE WAITER
> (Putting them on the
> table)
> Two prairie oysters.

John D. rears at his, then scowls at the waiter.

DISSOLVE TO:

11-21-41

E-14   A VERY FASHIONABLE SALESMAN - IN THE LADIES' FOOTWEAR
        DEPARTMENT OF A VERY FASHIONABLE DEPARTMENT STORE IN
        JACKSONVILLE

                        THE SALESMAN
                    (Lifting up the button
                    shoes)
                And where shall I send these, madam?

        DISSOLVE TO:

E-15   JOHN D. SITTING IN A CHAIR - IN THE LADIES' DRESS
        DEPARTMENT

        He is writing in a little black book with a pencil.
        Now he looks up and smiles.

                        JOHN D.
                Very nice... let's have that one
                too... How much is it?

E-16   GERRY - IN FRONT OF A MIRROR

        Behind her we see a saleslady, a girl with an armful
        of dresses and a man taking the paper off some new
        suitcases. There is also evident a shoe trunk full
        of shoes and a pile of handbags. Gerry is looking
        around at all this a little fearfully.

                        THE SALESLADY
                    (Enthusiastically)
                Two hundred and twelve fifty,
                monsieur.

                        JOHN D.'S VOICE
                That's fine.

        Gerry crosses to him and the CAMERA PULLS BACK TO
        INCLUDE HIS HEAD AND MAKE A BIG TWO SHOT

                        GERRY
                    (Worried)
                I really didn't expect you to
                buy all this stuff... I really
                don't think I can accept it...
                if you'd just get me a dress
                and a pair of shoes and a...
                hat... really more in the nature
                of a loan.

                        JOHN D.
                    (Confidentially)
                Nonsense. It is cheaper in the
                end to buy good quality... and
                enough of them so that you don't

-11-21-41   (Continued)

E-16 (Cont'd)

                    JOHN D. (Cont'd)
          wear them out. They last longer,
          they look better, and there's a
          certain pleasure to having a change.

                    GERRY
          It's very kind of you...but are
          you sure you can afford all this?

                    JOHN D.
          Oh, I think so...We haven't
          done anything very extravagant
          yet.

                    GERRY
          I wouldn't want you to end up
          on a chain g ang.

                    JOHN D.
          I think we're still perfectly
          safe.

He looks at his little book. Gerry walks away and
starts taking off the dress.

E-17   INSERT: THE LITTLE BOOK

We read:	2 breakfasts	$ 1.50
	2 prairie oysters	.50
	Tip	.10
	Taxi	.60
	12 pairs of stockings	19.98
	12 pairs of shoes	104.65
	1 shoe trunk	49.00
	4 suitcases	168.50
	8 handbags	212.50
	6 slips	96.00
(This is "corsets"	3 ~~corsets~~ girdles	30.00
with a line	3 brassiers (fancy)	24.60
through it)	1 doz. pants (fancy)	60.00
	6 nightgowns	150.00
	1 bathrobe	49.95
	2 doz. handkerchiefs	36.00
	1 tooth brush	.35
	Tooth paste	.20
	Perfumery	196.00
	Hats	160.00
	Gloves	36.75
	1 dress	39.50
	1 dress	59.50
	1 dress	79.50
	1 dress	99.50
	1 dress	149.75
	1 dress	212.50

11-21-41

174

E-18   JOHN D. - LOOKING UP FROM HIS BOOK

E-19   GERRY AND THE OTHERS

       Gerry is now trying on another dress in which the
       sleeves come halfway between the elbow and the wrist.
       Gerry crosses to John D. again and once more they end
       up in TWO BIG HEADS.

                     GERRY
          You're really sure it's all right.

                     JOHN D.
          Oh, certainly.

                     GERRY
          You're not a burglar or something.

                     JOHN D.
              (Laughing)
          No, no, that was my grandfather ....
          at least that's what they called
          him.

                     GERRY
              (After giving him
               a long look)
       Oh.

E-20   THE PROPRIETOR AND TWO STORE DICKS - PEERING AROUND
       A COLUMN

       They exchange a look.

E-21   GERRY AND JOHN D.

       She walks away from him, then turns around and
       models the dress for him.

                     GERRY
          Do you like this one?

E-22   JOHN D. - BOOK IN HAND

                     JOHN D.
              (Frowning slightly)
          Aren't the sleeves a little short?

11-21-41

175

E-23   GERRY AND THE OTHERS - PAST JOHN D.

> THE SALESLADY
> Zat iss for a bracelette, monsieur
> ...zat iss what iss call zee
> bracelette lenx.

E-24   JOHN D.

> JOHN D.
> Oh...would you like a bracelet?

E-25   GERRY AND THE SALESLADY

> GERRY
> What kind of a bracelet do you
> mean?

> JOHN D.
> Any kind you like.

> GERRY
> (After a pause)
> You mean with stones?

> THE SALESLADY
> (Quickly)
> Certainlee wid stones...zay are
> all zee rage.

E-26   JOHN D.

> JOHN D.
> (Innocently)
> Why not? What kind of stones
> do you like?

E-27   GERRY AND THE SALESLADY

> GERRY
> (Undecided)
> Well...

> THE SALESLADY
> (Quickly)
> Rad!
> (She turns and
> speaks meaningly
> to Gerry)
> Zay are all zee rage.

11-21-41

E-28   JOHN D.

> JOHN D.
> (Innocently)
> You mean like garnets?

E-29   GERRY AND THE SALESLADY

> THE SALESLADY
> (As if she had been
> slapped in the face
> with a fish)
> Garnets! Garnets is for cutting
> glatz!

> GERRY
> (Timidly, but watching
> John D. like a falcon)
> Don't you think garnets are a little
> lifeless?

DISSOLVE TO:

E-30   CLOSE SHOT - A RUBY BRACELET AND THEN SOME

E-31   GERRY, JOHN D., THE JEWELRY SALESMAN AND THE SALES-
LADY AND THE OWNER OF THE DEPARTMENT STORE -- IN THE
JEWELRY DEPARTMENT

> JOHN D.
> (Pleasantly)
> Why certainly...this is great
> fun...I've never bought things
> for a girl before...I mean in
> any such quantities.

> THE SALESLADY
> You have been denying yourself
> one of zee basic pleasures of
> life.

> JOHN D.
> I guess I have.

Now he lifts the ticket on the bracelet and peers
at it near-sightedly. He whistles silently, then
looks around and chuckles.

> JOHN D.
> All right.
> (He starts writing
> in his book.)

11-21-41   (Continued)

E-31 (Cont'd)

> THE JEWELRY SALESMAN
> Plus tax.

>> JOHN D.
> Yes, it's these taxes that get
> you down.

>> GERRY
>> (After exchanging a
>> slight look with
>> the others)
> I keep feeling that two men
> with butterfly nets are going
> to creep up behind you and lead
> you away.

>> JOHN D.
>> (Laughing)
> You're thinking of my Uncle...
> I'm not the crazy one in the
> family...I'm perfectly normal.

>> GERRY
> Then, why do you travel in a
> lower berth?

>> JOHN D.
> I find it a little stuffy in an
> upper...Oh, you mean, who don't
> I take a stateroom?

>> GERRY
> Yes.

>> JOHN D.
> Staterooms are un-American.

>> GERRY
>> (Looking at
>> the bracelet)
> Well, thank you very much, anyway.

>> JOHN D.
> Don't mention it...and now, if
> you can't think of anything else
> you need, we'd better get started.
>> (He turns to the
>> Proprietor of
>> the store)
> Just charge everything, please,
> and have it put in the taxi...
> good day.

He nods pleasantly and starts for the door. The
agonized Proprietor touches John D. on the shoulder.

E-31 (Cont'd)
                            JOHN D.
                      (Turning in surprise)
          Yes?

                        THE PROPRIETOR
                      (Miserably)
          Uh... excuse me...

     John D. looks at him a moment, then at the nervous
     staff. Then he chuckles.

                            JOHN D.
          I'm so sorry...
                      (He reaches for
                       his billfold)
          ... forgive me...
                      (He takes a card
                       from the billfold
                       and hands it to
                       the Proprietor)
          ... I'm so used to buying in
          stores where I'm known that it
          totally slipped my mind...

                        THE PROPRIETOR
                      (Electrified as he reads
                       the card)
          Mister Ha...
                      (The rest of the word
                       trails off to nothing)
          Excuse me that I didn't...

                            JOHN D.
          That's all right, don't mention
          it.

     Gerry looks at him in puzzlement as he
     takes her arm and pushes her out the door.

                        THE PROPRIETOR
                      (Ferociously to his employees)
          Well, what are you standing there?
          Where are the packages? How about
          some service? I have to do every-
          thing yet!

          DISSOLVE TO:

E-32   WATER-LEVEL SHOT - A MAGNIFICENT DIESEL YACHT COMING
        TOWARD US

E-33   THE NAME OF YACHT - "THE ERL KING - New York"

          DISSOLVE TO:

11-21-41

                               179

E-34   GERRY AND JOHN D. - <u>ON THE AFTER DECK OF THE YACHT</u>

John D. is writing in his little book. Gerry wears a
sports outfit with a hood. John D. is dressed as before except he has put on rubber-soled shoes. A
glittering tea set is on a low table before them.

                    GERRY
              (After a long look
               around)
          Is this yours?

                    JOHN D.
          Oh, yes. Actually it was my grand-
          father's but he didn't like it...he
          only used it once. Do you happen
          to remember how much tip I gave
          that taxi driver?

                    GERRY
          I didn't see the coin, but from his
          face I think it was ten cents.

                    JOHN D.
              (Writing in his book)
          Tipping is un-American.

                    GERRY
          What's your name?

                    JOHN D.
              (Looking up in surprise)
          Hackensacker.

                    GERRY
              (Rigidly)
          Not...John D. Hackensacker.

                    JOHN D.
          I'm not my grandfather, of course...
          he's dead anyway. I'm John D. the
          Third.

                    GERRY
          You're the richest man in the world,
          then.

                    JOHN D.
              (Embarrassed)
          Well...yes...I suppose so.

                    GERRY
          I <u>would</u> step on your face.

11-21-41   (Continued)

E-34   (Cont'd)

>   JOHN D.
>   (Laughing)
>   Oh, that's all right...I rather en-
>   joyed it.

>   GERRY
>   Twice.

>   JOHN D.
>   You made quite an impression.

He laughs at his joke, removes his pince-nez and
wipes it.

>   THE STEWARD
>   (Entering THE SHOT)
>   May I get you a rug, madam?

>   GERRY
>   No, thank you.

>   THE STEWARD
>   Will you dine on deck, Mr. Hacken-
>   sacker, or in the saloon?

>   JOHN D.
>   (To Gerry)
>   We can have it on deck if you like,
>   but it blows everything all over
>   the place. There are a lot of in-
>   conveniences to yachting that most
>   people don't know anything about.
>   Give me the peaceful train.

>   GERRY
>   In the saloon, please.

>   THE STEWARD
>   (Departing)
>   Very good, madam.

He lurches and nearly falls down.

>   JOHN D.
>   (Indicating)
>   You see what I mean. I just hap-
>   pen to own this thing or I'd never
>   go near it.

>   GERRY
>   Did you say you were John D. the
>   Third or the Fourth?

>   JOHN D.
>   The Third...the Fourth will be my
>   son...when I marry.

11-21-41   (Continued)

                          GERRY
                  (Fingering her bracelet)
                  Then it didn't really mean anything
                  to you at all...to buy me all those
                  things...did it?

                          JOHN D.
                  I can't pretend that it was a great
                  sacrifice, but it gave me a great
                  deal of pleasure.

                          GERRY
                  You like to write in your little book.

                          JOHN D.
                  It used to please my grandfather...
                  it's just a habit. It's nonsense,
                  really...I write things down but I
                  never add them up...where are you
                  staying in Palm Beach?

                          GERRY
                  No place...yet.

                          JOHN D.
                  Oh.

                          GERRY
                  Where are you staying?

                          JOHN D.
                  At my sister's.

                          GERRY
                  Oh, yes...the Princess...or is it
                  the Duchess?

                          JOHN D.
                  The Princess Centimillia...

                          GERRY
                  Of course.

                          JOHN D.
                  What are you going to Palm Beach
                  for?

                          GERRY
                  A divorce.

                          JOHN D.
                  Oh.

11-21-41   (Continued)

E-34   (Cont'd)

                     GERRY
Well, you don't have to look so sour
about it...your sister's been divorced seven times, hasn't she?

                     JOHN D.
No, no, five...she was annulled twice.

                     GERRY
I've never been divorced before.

                     JOHN D.
Good. By the way, what is your name?

                     GERRY
Jeffers. Geraldine Jeffers.

                     JOHN D.
Was he brutal to you?

                     GERRY
Not... particularly.

                     JOHN D.
A drunkard, hunh?

                     GERRY
                (Shrugging her
                  shoulders)
Oh... not congenital or anything like
that.

                     JOHN D.
Women always protect the man they've
been married to.

                     GERRY
I suppose it's human nature.

                     JOHN D.
Did he beat you?

                     GERRY
                (Shrugging)
Oh...not...often.

                     JOHN D.
The hound.

11-21-41   (Continued)

E-34   (Cont'd)

                   GERRY
                (Nobly)
A man is a man...I suppose they're
all tarred with the same brush.

                   JOHN D.
How brave you are...when I marry
there will be no divorce...that's
why I've been a little cautious.

                   GERRY
You're afraid somebody will marry
you for your money.

                   JOHN D.
I expect that...when money reaches
certain proportions you can't ignore it any more than you can a...
a...

                   GERRY
                (Helping him out)
A horse in the bedroom.

                   JOHN D.
I wasn't thinking exactly of that
...but it will serve. No, I mean
that the person who marries me,
the lady, for my money...would
still have to be the right person.
She'd have to be able to spend
like a drunken Indian, of course,
but at the same time...

                   GERRY
Write it in the book.

                   JOHN D.
Something like that. And when we
traveled...

                   GERRY
You take the upper...I'll take the
chair car.

                   JOHN D.
                (After a little laugh)
No, I see marriage as a...a...

-11-21-41   (Continued)

E-34   (Cont'd)

>   JOHN D. (Cont'd)
>   (He helps out with
>   hand movements)
>   ...sort of permanent welding...a
>   growing together of two trees, in
>   spite of anything my sister can
>   demonstrate to the contrary, into
>   a sort of permanent mess -- mass,
>   like the grafting of two trees
>   into a permanent...graft.

>   GERRY
>   (Straight-faced)
>   That one is too easy.

>   JOHN D.
>   Oh, you mean...
>   (He starts to laugh)
>   ...a permanent graft...
>   (He laughs again)
>   I get it.

The laugh falls off his face like a hot towel.

>   JOHN D.
>   But it doesn't have to be...it
>   can be very nice...I'm sure.

>   GERRY
>   It can be.

>   JOHN D.
>   (After a pause)
>   And after the divorce...you have...
>   plans?

>   GERRY
>   Oh, yes.

>   JOHN D.
>   Anybody I know? I know almost
>   everybody in Palm Beach.

>   GERRY
>   Oh, I haven't picked him out yet...
>   just some...very rich man.

>   JOHN D.
>   Oh.

>   GERRY
>   (In defense of herself)
>   I'm not really suited to being a
>   poor man's wife...I tried it and
>   it just didn't work out...it's

11-21-41   (Continued)

E-34 (Cont'd)

        GERRY (Cont'd)
.like you have one kind of horse
for a beer wagon and another
kind of horse for the derby...you
change them around and they'd both
be flops.
    (She laughs dryly)
Funny.

        JOHN D.
    (After giving her a
    long, pensive, almost
    embarrassing look)
You say you're looking for a rich
man.

        GERRY
    (After a pause)
I wasn't thinking of anybody as
rich as you...that might get to
be annoying.

        JOHN D.
It is.

        GERRY
    (With an airy motion)
I just meant somebody who's...
well fixed...
    (Now an idea comes
    into her eyes)
...and who could spare the ninety-
nine thousand dollars without
missing it too much.

        JOHN D.
I'm not sure I understand about
the ninety-nine thousand dollars.

        GERRY
    (A little nervously)
Well, he just happens to need
ninety-nine thousand dollars,
that's all...and I don't see
why he shouldn't get it...if I'm
throwing it out the windows.

        JOHN D.
    (A little stiffly)
This is your last husband you're
talking about.

        GERRY
Yes.

        JOHN D.
He wants to sell you for ninety-
nine thousand dollars!

11-21-41   (Continued)

E-34 (Cont'd)

> GERRY
> (Startled)
> Oh, no, I don't think he had
> any such idea at all.

> JOHN D.
> Well, what do _you_ call it?

> GERRY
> Well, I mean, after all, he's
> entitled to something...I mean
> he did protect me and give me
> food, such as it was, and
> clothes, such as they were, for
> a few years, and now if I can
> repay...

> JOHN D.
> (Indignantly)
> But the man is a vermin! No
> court of law would even consider...
> I mean you read things like that
> in the Sunday magazine section
> but you don't run up against them
> in real life.

> GERRY
> (Innocently)
> Don't you think I'm worth ninety-
> nine thousand dollars?

> JOHN D.
> (Fuming)
> That has nothing to...you're
> probably worth that and...twice
> that...three times....but even
> so, the days of serfdom, I mean
> bondage...I mean the days you
> bought a wife for a cow are over.
> I've never heard of such a thing,
> I....chivalry is not only dead...
> it's decomposed!

> GERRY
> How much did this yacht cost you?

> JOHN D.
> (Severely)
> That is entirely beside the point
> ...a woman is not a vessel...I
> mean with all the filthy things
> I've heard in my life, I still...
> how does he want it?

> GERRY
> In cash maybe.

-11-21-41   (Continued)

E-34 (Cont'd)

                     JOHN D.
               (Glaring at the
               horizon)
In cash!
               (He laughs
               vitriolicly)
So I won't stop the check,..I
mean, so that whoever...

                     GERRY
Oh, I don't suppose he'll ever
get it...it was just an idea...
I'm all he ever had...and if he
doesn't get anything out of me...
he'll probably never get anything
out of anything.

                     JOHN D.
               (Raising a finger)
There is a name for such reptiles...
but I won't sully this sweet ocean
breeze by mentioning it...
               (He clenches his fists)
I'm not exactly in shape, but if
ever I meet this Mr...Jeffers...
I'll thrash him within an inch
of his life.

                     GERRY
Then I hope you never meet him.

                     JOHN D.
I suppose he's...large.

                     GERRY
Well, he's not...small.

                     JOHN D.
That's one of the tragedies of
this life...that the men who
are most in need of a beating
up...are always enormous.

FADE OUT:

                   END OF SEQUENCE "E"

11-21-41

GB   THE PALM BEACH STORY   F-1
Preston Sturges   (106)
                      SEQUENCE "F"

FADE IN:

F-1   THE STREAMLINER - PULLING INTO WEST PALM BEACH

F-2   A RAILROAD SIGN THAT SAYS: "WEST PALM BEACH -
         Elev. 1 ft."

         The CAMERA PANS DOWN ONTO Tom. He moves forward
         slowly and the CAMERA PANS WITH HIM. He stops in
         front of a car and looks searchingly as passengers
         go by him.

         DISSOLVE TO:

F-3   THE PORTER WHO HELPED BORROW THE CLOTHES FOR GERRY

         He has his hat on and is going home.

                     THE PORTER
             Yassuh, I know who you talkin'
             about.. you mean de young lady
             who lose all her clothes.

F-4   CLOSE SHOT - TOM

                     TOM
             She lost all her clothes!

F-5   THE PORTER - PAST TOM

                     THE PORTER
             Yassuh, but we fix her up wid
             a blanket when she get off at
             Jacksonville.

                     TOM
             Oh, she got off at Jacksonville.

                     THE PORTER
             Yassuh.

                     TOM
                (Swallowing)
             Alone?

                     THE PORTER
             You might practically say she
             was alone... gentleman she get

11-21-41   (Continued)

F-5   (Cont'd)

> THE PORTER (Cont'd)
> off wid gimme ten cents from
> New York to Jacksonville...
> she's alone but she don't know
> it.

> TOM
> Then she's in Jacksonville.

> THE PORTER
> Nawsir... she say he say he takin'
> her down here on his boat, yassuh,
> I suppose she mean a yachet, but
> I don't see where no gentleman
> who come up wid ten cents from
> New York to Jacksonville get off
> to have a yachet... more like a
> bicycle... or a canoe... yassuh.

DISSOLVE TO:

F-6   THE BOW OF THE YACHT - (DAY)

We hear a whistle, the anchor hits the water with a
splash and the chain rattles through the hawse pipe.

F-7   TOM - ON A BENCH - ON A QUAI

He looks at the arriving yacht with very little
thought that this is the one. Now he raises some
rented binoculars to his eyes and suddenly becomes
rigid.

F-8   GERRY AND JOHN D. - AT THE RAIL OF THE YACHT -
MATTE SHOT

They are surrounded by the traditional binocular-
shaped matte. Gerry wears another outfit and is
laughing and talking with John D. Stewards stand by
with luggage while sailors and a quartermaster adjust
the boarding ladder.

F-9   TOM

Looking very grim, he rises and gives the binoculars
back to a guy in a twenty-five cent yachting cap.

> TOM
> Thanks.

Now he stands by the railing.

11-21-41

F-10   GERRY AND JOHN D. - <u>AT THE RAILING OF THE YACHT</u>

> THE PRINCESS' VOICE
> Yoo-hoo!

> GERRY
> (Looking out into
> the water)
> Who's that?

> JOHN D.
> (Disapprovingly)
> Oh, that's my sister... the
> Princess... Hello, Maude.

F-11   HIGH CAMERA SHOT - DOWN ON A GLISTENING MOTOR BOAT
COMING ALONG SIDE

A man in uniform is at the wheel. Sitting high on
the mahogany we see the Princess and a small foreign
gentleman called "Toto."

> THE PRINCESS
> Hello, Snoodles... where did
> you get the pretty girl?

> TOTO
> (Waving limply)
> Grittinks.

A sailor hooks the motor boat.

F-12   JOHN D. AND GERRY - <u>ON THE DECK</u>

> JOHN D.
> She calls me Snoodles.

> GERRY
> Is that the Prince?

> JOHN D.
> No, the Prince is all washed
> up... this is something new.

> GERRY
> It might be a duke.

> JOHN D.
> It might be her tailor, too;
> she goes out with anything.

11-21-41   (Continued)

F-13   THE PRINCESS AND TOTO - COMING UP <u>THE BOARDING LADDER</u>

> THE PRINCESS
> Hello, darling, what a perfectly
> beautiful dame... Where you sea-
> sick on the way down... Wherever
> did you find her... this is Toto;
> say "How do you do," Toto.

> TOTO
> Grittinks.

> THE PRINCESS
> Toto is a refugee... from his
> creditors, I think... aren't
> you, Toto?

> TOTO
> Grittinks.

> THE PRINCESS
> (Stamping onto
> the deck)
> Glad to be aboard, sir.
> (Now she takes
> Gerry's hand)
> How do you do. Glad to see you
> aboard... you get prettier as
> one gets nearer.... However did
> you manage it?... He's stiff as
> a plank... this must have done
> him a power of good.

> JOHN D.
> (Formally)
> This is my sister Maude, Mrs.
> uh..uh..Mrs...

Before Gerry can say her name, the Princess cuts in
with a whoop of delight.

> THE PRINCESS
> Don't tell me he doesn't even
> know your name... this is per-
> fectly marvelous... Now just
> tell me that he picked you up on
> the train and you will make me a
> happy woman.

> TOTO
> Grittinks.

> THE PRINCESS
> All right, Toto, you've said
> how do you do... Wait till I
> tell the papers!

11-21-41   (Continued)

F-13 (Cont'd)
                          JOHN D.
              Really, Maude, you know somebody
              meeting you for the first time
              who didn't know you were cracked
              might get the wrong impression
              of you.

                        THE PRINCESS
                          (Delightedly)
              Did he really pick you up on the
              train?

                          GERRY
              I was in awful trouble...until he
              came very nobly to the rescue.

                        THE PRINCESS
              Now you've spoiled everything...I
              hoped for once he hadn't done any-
              thing noble...that he was really
              cooking with gas...What a lovely
              dress.

                          GERRY
              He got it for me.

                        THE PRINCESS
                          (Delighted)
              Why, Snoodles, you rat! We'll
              work this into something yet!...
              this is perfectly electrifying;
              you must come and stay with us
              and we'll warm this up...You're
              divorced, of course.

                          GERRY
              Not quite.

                        THE PRINCESS
              That's marvelous. I don't think
              I'm quite through with the Prince
              yet, either...We'll look for new
              husbands together...
                   (She winks toward
                    John D.)
              We can swap private info and have
              a wonderful time. I'm thinking
              of an American -- at the moment,
              it seems more patriotic.

                          TOTO
              Grittinks.

                        THE PRINCESS
              No, no, Toto...his English is a
              little elementary.

                          TOTO
-11-21-41   Yitz.   (Continued)

                            193

F-13 (Cont'd)

                    THE PRINCESS
              (Shaking her head)
          Nitz.

                    TOTO
              (Shrugging)
          Spegoglu.

                    GERRY
          What language does he speak.

                    THE PRINCESS
          I don't know...I think it's
          Beluchistan, but it's impossible
          to tell.

                    TOTO
              (Beaming)
          Grittinks.

                    THE PRINCESS
              (Leading the way)
          Now let's go ashore. I'll put
          you in the blue suite...and we'll
          have a marvelous time...I suppose
          you're perfectly respectable but
          of course. So long as we don't
          roll on the floor and give the
          butler hysterics, we'll be cooking
          on the front burner...I talk a lot,
          don't I?

                    GERRY
              (Politely)
          Why, no, I hadn't noti....

                    JOHN D.
          Yes.

                    THE PRINCESS
          Ah, Snoodles, you snake in the
          grass!...Get in and help the lady,
          Toto.

     After Toto doesn't get in --

                    THE PRINCESS
          He doesn't understand anything.

     They get in and the motor boat pulls away. As the
     motor roars away --

11-21-41

                         194

F-14   TOM - LEANING ON <u>THE RAILING</u>

We hear the motor getting louder as it gets nearer.

F-15   THE GROUP - <u>IN THE MOVING MOTOR BOAT</u>

                    THE PRINCESS
                 (Taking Gerry's wrist)
            What a lovely bracelet you have
            there.

                    GERRY
            Well, it...

                    THE PRINCESS
                 (Enraptured)
            <u>Not</u> from Snoodles! My dear, how
            <u>perfectly</u> marvelous! He's tighter
            than a titmouse and twice as wary...
            how <u>perfectly glorious</u>! Did you
            have to get him drunk...or how did
            you do it?...You must tell me all
            about it later...Look at that <u>very</u>
            handsome man...I wonder who he <u>is</u>...
            I haven't seen him around before...
            I thought I knew all the handsome
            men in this village...We can use
            some new faces.

F-16   CLOSE SHOT - TOM

He looks stonily back at us.

F-17   THE GROUP - <u>IN THE MOVING MOTOR BOAT</u>

                    GERRY
                 (Yammering)
            It isn't possible...

                    THE PRINCESS
            What isn't possible?

                    GERRY
            I think I...know that man...
            in fact, I'm sure of it.

                    THE PRINCESS
            Well, introduce me to him will you
            ...I'd like to cut a carpet with him.

Gerry clamps her jaw shut and glares at Tom.

11/21/41

F-18   TOM - WATCHING <u>AT THE RAIL</u>

F-19   HIGH CAMERA SHOT - DOWN ON THE MOTOR BOAT <u>AT THE</u>
<u>FLOAT</u>

       The group gets out, Gerry seems to say "Excuse me,"
       to the others, then hurries up the gangplank. The
       CAMERA PANS her INTO A TWO SHOT WITH TOM.

                    GERRY
                  (Quickly)
      What did you follow me down here
      for anyway? That isn't fair.

                    TOM
      What do you mean, what did I follow
      you down here for... you're my wife;
      you're making an ass of yourself...
      you're exposing yourself to all sorts
      of dangers... that I swore to love,
      honor and protect you from.

                    GERRY
               (After a quick look
                over her shoulder)
      Look - you have to be fair... you
      know I'm fond of you... but I want
      to do everything for you that I can.

                    TOM
               (Irritably)
      I don't want you to do any more.

                    GERRY
      But you've got to understand that
      I've left you... that I'm not your
      wife any more... that you're not my
      husband.

                    TOM
      But Gerry!

      He throws his arms around her and holds her tight.

                    GERRY
               (Breathlessly)
      Stop it, you idiot; you've got to
      be a sport; you're just going to ....

              THE PRINCESS
            (Arriving by her side)
      Well, I should say you <u>do</u> know him.

11-21-41   (Continued)

F-19 (Cont'd)

GERRY
(Releasing herself)
The Princess Centimillia...this
is my brother...Captain McGlue.

THE PRINCESS
(Taking his hand)
Captain...we should have met
sooner...and if I'd seen you
around, we would have.
(She turns)
This is my brother, Captain
Hackensacker...Captain McGlue...
that's an odd name.

TOM
Yes, isn't it. How do you do,
Captain.

JOHN D.
(Amiably)
I'm not a Captain...that's just my
sister's joke because I own a yacht.

TOM
It's my sister's joke because I
don't own one.

JOHN D.
I'm very glad to meet you. Your
sister didn't tell me she had a
brother here.

TOM
I just dropped over and...

THE PRINCESS
You're staying with us of course.

TOM
(Quickly)
No, no, I think we'll go to a hotel...
We wouldn't want to inconvenience you.

GERRY
(To Tom)
But Mac.

THE PRINCESS
Inconvenience us! Bumble puppy!
We practically run a hotel anyway...
except the museum where Grandfather
lives...this will give the servants
some exercise...I won't take no for
an answer.

(Continued)

11-21-41

F-19 (Cont'd)

        She takes Gerry's arm and moves away.

                    THE PRINCESS (Cont'd)
        Your brother's a very fine looking
        man...you look exactly alike...I
        suppose he's married.

                    GERRY
        He's entirely free.

                    THE PRINCESS
          (Looking around at Tom)
        You don't tell me.

                    TOM
    Now look...

                    JOHN D.
          (Putting his hand on
           Tom's shoulder)
        Don't pay any attention to her,
        Captain, her bark is worse than
        her bite.

                    THE PRINCESS
        That's what _you_ think.
          (Now she frowns slightly)
        Oh, dear, I wish I hadn't brought
        Toto today...somebody think of an
        errand to send him on.

                    TOTO
    Hello.

                    THE PRINCESS
          (To Toto)
        This is Captain McGlue, Toto...
        I'm going to see more of him and
        less of you from now on.

                    TOTO
    Hello.

                    THE PRINCESS
        Listen to me carefully, dear. I
        left my handkerchief...mouchoir...
        taschentuch....on the yacht...
          (She makes a swimming
          motion)
        You go fetch it, see.

                    TOTO
    Nitz.

11-21-41   (Continued)

F-19 (Cont'd)

               THE PRINCESS
      Yitz, Toto.

               TOTO
      Nitz.

               THE PRINCESS
         (Threateningly)
      It will be nitz to you, Toto.

               TOTO
         (Shrugging)
      Grittinks.

He bows from the waist and goes back down the gangplank.

               THE PRINCESS
      And now, Captain, you may take my
      arm. By the way, what did you say
      you were a captain of?

               TOM
         (Frigidly)
      I didn't say a word about it.

               THE PRINCESS
         (Looking up into his eyes)
      How wonderful it is to meet a silent
      American again...my husbands were
      all foreigners...and such chatterboxes.
      I could hardly get a word in edgeways.
      Let's move ahead, they probably want
      to be alone.

As Tom opens his mouth she drags him OUT OF THE SHOT.
The CAMERA PANS ONTO John D. and Gerry followed by
Stewards and chauffeurs with bags.

               JOHN D.
      They make a very handsome couple,
      don't they?

               GERRY
      Hunh?

               JOHN D.
      My sister and your brother...it would
      be nice if something came of it.

               GERRY
      Yes...wouldn't it...it would be
      wonderful for him.

11-21-41   (Continued)

F-19 (Cont'd)

                          JOHN D.
            Of course she's no bargain...but
            it might happen very easily...
            she's a woman of iron determination...
            once her mind is made up...you might
            as well yield.

                          GERRY
            I can see what you mean.

                          JOHN D.
            I'm very glad that you are going
            to stay with us...and your brother,
            too.

                          GERRY
            Are you?

                          JOHN D.
            I don't know why I didn't think
            of it...or maybe I did think of
            it...but it took somebody with my
            sister's courage to make it come
            true.

                          GERRY
            You're very sweet.

                          JOHN D.
            Thank you very much...the Captain's
            a big fellow, isn't he?

                          GERRY
            Yes, isn't he.

                          JOHN D.
            You look exactly alike.

                          GERRY
            Yes, don't we...People always
            remark on it.

        FADE OUT:

                     END OF SEQUENCE "F"

11-21-41

Preston Sturges

FADE IN:

G-1   AN ENORMOUS HOUSE - IN PALM BEACH - (DAY)

        DISSOLVE TO:

G-2   THE PRINCESS' DRESSING ROOM

        This is something. She is making up at an extraor-
        dinary dressing table and watching her brother in the
        mirror.

                        THE PRINCESS
             Why don't you marry her, she's lovely?

                        JOHN D.
             Well, in the first place she isn't
             free yet, and in the second place you
             don't marry somebody you just met the
             day before... at least I don't.

                        THE PRINCESS
             That's the only way... if you get to
             know too much about them and never
             marry them... I'd marry Captain McGlue
             tomorrow... even with that name.

                        JOHN D.
             And divorce him next month.

                        THE PRINCESS
             It isn't how long it was, dear... it's
             how nice it was, - at least that's my
             philosophy. Nothing is permanent
             except Roosevelt.

                        JOHN D.
                  (With some embarrassment)
             As a matter of fact, Maude, I'm very
             much attracted to this young woman...
             more so than I have ever been to any-
             one... I had known for the same length
             of time, of course, but I want to know
             how she is early in the morning, late
             at night, rain or shine, under trying
             circumstances as when the servants
             leave in a body... how she is with
             children...

                        THE PRINCESS
             What are you going to do, rent some?

11-21-41   (Continued)

201

JOHN D.

Why not?...or we might be able to
borrow some.

THE PRINCESS

You mean a mock marriage.

JOHN D.

I certainly do not. I revere
marriage. I...unlike some people
I could mention...

THE PRINCESS

You're just going to keep on being
cautious Charlie until you shrivel
up and land in a home somewhere.
Don't you know that no woman can
stand that much inspection? You
either take them at face value or
give up the idea. You're perfectly
priceless, Snoodles. You should
be pinned on a card and let other
people examine you...you'll be the
death of me yet.

JOHN D.

I don't see anything very funny
about it. When I marry it's going
to be for always...I see it as the
forging together of two beings who
are suitable in every respect...
even of two families...I feel already
as if Captain McGlue were my brother.

THE PRINCESS
(Wincing)

That name...even so I may make him
your brother...the Princess McGlue!

G-3 TOM AND GERRY - IN THE BLUE SUITE

TOM

But why "Captain McGlue?"
Of all the idiotic names...

GERRY

Because I want him to build your
airport for you. He seems to
have something against my husband...but as my brother.

11-21-41 (Continued)

G-3 (Cont'd)

>   TOM
> Apart from the fact that I wouldn't
> let him build a chicken coop for me,
> I'd still like to know why I'm
> called Captain McGlue! Of all the
> nincompoopish...

>   GERRY
> Wasn't that your mother's name?

>   TOM
> What, Captain McGlue? Her name was
> McGrew, M-o-G-r-e-w.

>   GERRY
> I'm sorry, darling, I remembered it
> as McGlue.

>   TOM
> Well, I guess I'm stuck with it now.
> Captain McGlue! And what am I sup-
> posed to be the captain of...a gar-
> bage scow?

>   GERRY
> I just put that in to make it more
> dignified...couldn't you have been
> a captain in the last war?

>   TOM
> Sure, I was eleven years old when it
> finished. A captain in short breeches!

>   GERRY
> How about the Boy Scouts?

>   TOM
> Wonderful. I'll make bonfires on
> the drawing room carpet...why not
> the Salvation Army. I'll go around
> with a tambourine!

They both laugh.

>   GERRY
> I'm sorry, darling. I really meant
> it for the best.

>   TOM
> I know you did...that's what's so
> irritating about it.
> > (He puts his hands on
> > her shoulders)
> Where did you get that brother idea?

-11-21-41   (Continued)

GERRY
Because you had your arms around
me.

TOM
I suppose nobody's ever had his
arms around you except your brother
...only you haven't got one... I
don't suppose Captain Hackensacker
put his arms around you.

GERRY
Of course not.

TOM
Of course not. Yachts must have
changed since the last time I
was on one. That's what they
build yachts for.

GERRY
Naturally he will put his arms
around me...when and if we're
engaged...and you'll just have to
get used to it.

TOM
Oh, we're engaged now, are we?

GERRY
Is there anything wrong in being
engaged?

TOM
     (Indignantly)
You ought to know. Where did you
get that dress?

GERRY
     (Archly)
Oh, you're beginning to notice
them now are you?

TOM
And what's that on your wrist?

GERRY
Just what you think it is, dear.

TOM
What kind of stones are those?

GERRY
Exactly what they look like.

                              TOM
                        (Grabbing her suddenly)
                    You know how it feels to be strangled
                    with the bare hands?

Gerry looks at him quietly until he releases her,
then looks around and picks up a little Staffordshire
group that might be called "Innocence"...a boy and a
girl and a lamb...or a young girl with an armful of
lillies... or a bride and groom looking away from
each other.

                              GERRY
                    Tom....I'll put this here on the
                    mantelpiece...so long as it's there
                    you won't have the slightest, small-
                    est thing to be unhappy about...it
                    will be a signal and we'll never have
                    to mention the subject...so long as
                    it's there...
                        (She shrugs, then adds in
                        a voice considerably harder)
                    ...and that goes for you too.

                              TOM
                    Hunh?

                              GERRY
                    And your friend, the Princess, you
                    seem to be cutting such a groove with.
                        (Then suddenly)
                    Where did you get the money to fly
                    down here?

                              TOM
                    The same place you got yours only
                    I didn't kiss him goodbye.

                              GERRY
                        (Tenderly)
                    The Wienie King.

                              TOM
                    Yes. He wanted to see us get back
                    together, I guess...don't you think
                    we owe it to him? Look: why don't
                    you let me go out and punch this
                    guy in the nose and then...

                              GERRY
                        (Gently)
                    Because I've left you, darling...
                    for both our good...just because
                    I don't hate you doesn't mean I

G-3 (Cont'd)

> GERRY (Cont'd)
> haven't left you...I have the
> right to do that, and if you'll
> just be sensible...and sweet...

> TOM
> And brotherly.

> GERRY
> ...everything is bound to come
> out all right.

> TOM
> Don't you think as your brother
> I could punch him in the nose
> for that bracelet?

As Gerry opens her mouth to answer, there is a knock
at the door.

> GERRY
> Come in.

G-4   JOHN D. ENTERING

> JOHN D.
> Excuse me.

The CAMERA PANS him INTO THE SHOT with the others.

> JOHN D.
> Mac, did you happen to, you don't
> mind if I call you Mac...your bags
> seemed rather small, did you happen
> to bring a tuxedo with you?

> TOM
> I did not. The business I came
> here to do didn't call for one.

> JOHN D.
> That's all right. In a pinch
> you can wear one of mine.
> (He laughs)

> GERRY
> In a pinch...very funny.

> TOM
> I don't think I'll be here that
> long.

> GERRY
> Why Mac!

                           JOHN D.
              That's too bad, old man. I'd hoped
              you'd spend the season with us...I
              wanted to get to know you better...
              in any case, there's something I
              want to talk to you about before you
              go. I'm very glad you showed up just
              when you did.

                           TOM
              So am I.

                           JOHN D.
              Good. I needed the male member of
              Gerry's family.

                           TOM
              You have him.

                           JOHN D.
                        (In some embarrassment)
              Fine. Uh...I have a certain thought...

                           TOM
              So have I. And what I'm thinking
              about at the moment is that bracelet.

                           GERRY
              Mac.

                           JOHN D.
              I'm very glad you brought that up.

                           GERRY
                        (Quickly)
              Mac is delighted with it, Snoodles.

                           JOHN D.
              He shouldn't be.

                           TOM
              He isn't.

                           JOHN D.
              Fine. The first bracelet my sister
              got...I punched the fellow right in
              the nose...fellow by the name of
              Wallace.

                           TOM
              Good. I can see that we understand
              each other.

11-21-41   (Continued)

G-4   (Cont'd)

JOHN D.
I didn't like it any more than you
like this.

TOM
You are reading my mind.

JOHN D.
Splendid. But there's a difference between Wallace and me. Wallace was a man who threw bracelets
in all directions....I am not.

TOM
I believe that too.

JOHN D.
Wallace was the type of hound...

TOM
I am not interested in Wallace.

JOHN D.
There's no reason why you should
be. Now I, on the other hand...

GERRY
If I could trust you two boys not
to slug each other, I'd like to
make an exit about here. I feel
like a bone between two dogs.

JOHN D.
(Chuckling)
Oh, we're going to get along all
right...there's nothing the matter with my intentions...as Mac
will be the first to admit. The
only thing that could embarrass
you would be the lovely things I
want to say to him about you...
your face...your figure...things
a brother is naturally blind to,
your future and this little plan
I have...which I'd better discuss
with Mac before...springing it on
you.

GERRY
Yes, well I absolutely <u>hate</u> to
have anything sprung on me...any
form of practical joke I consider
the very lowest form of...

11-21-41

G-5   THE PRINCESS - <u>COMING IN THE DOOR</u>

         The CAMERA PANS her INTO THE GROUP with the others.

                         THE PRINCESS
                 What's buzzin', cousins...what's
                 the dirt?

         Toto wanders in behind her.

                         JOHN D.
                     (Frowning at her)
                 Now never mind, Maude. It's just
                 a little something I want to dis-
                 cuss with Mac.

                         THE PRINCESS
                     (Busting out laughing
                      ... to Gerry)
                 Ho-ho-ho! My dear, you'll simply
                 expire when you hear what it is.

                         JOHN D.
                     (Desperately)
                 Maude!

                         THE PRINCESS
                     (Licking her lips)
                 It is too, too excruciating!

                         JOHN D.
                 Maude!... Please!

                         THE PRINCESS
                     (Leaning against the
                      mantelpiece to keep
                      from falling down)
                 He wants a miniature marriage with
                 you...

         Toto joins the group, full of curiosity.

                         THE PRINCESS
                 Go away, Toto, this is not for
                 children.
                     (Then to Gerry)
                 You know, everything up to the
                 dissolve, and then...
                     (She puts her hand
                      on her heart, then
                      warbles very nobly)
                 Good night, sweetheart... I'll
                 see you in the morning.

                         TOM
                     (Frigidly)
                 What's this?

11-21-41   (Continued)

                         209

G-5   (Cont'd)
                          THE PRINCESS
                           (Happily)
                 The boy wants to bundle!

                          JOHN D.
                 Maude!

                          THE PRINCESS
                           (Fiendishly)
                 And then he's going to make you
                 cook and sew and wash the windows
                 and then...
                          (She is nearly over-
                           come by mirth)
                 ...and then he's going to get
                 some little brats to see if you
                 know how to change them!

                          GERRY
                           (On the verge of
                            breaking down)
                 But how?

                          THE PRINCESS
                           (Triumphantly)
                 He's going to rent them!

        The two ladies fall into each other's arms and scream.

G-6   CLOSE SHOT - TOM

       He is glaring at John D.

G-7   THE MISERABLE JOHN D.

       He removes his pince-nez and polishes the lenses.

G-8   THE GROUP

       The ladies separate.

                          THE PRINCESS
                           (Seizing Tom's arm)
                 Come on, let's you and I go some
                 place... they probably want to be
                 alone.

                          TOM
                           (Holding back)
                 Just a minute...

11-21-41   (Continued)

G-8   (Cont'd)
                         THE PRINCESS
                Oh, don't take it so seriously...
                they want to bake a cake...dear.
                Come on.

Tom opens his mouth to say something but is dragged
out of the room. John D. looks the picture of morti-
fication. Gerry avoids his eye and eventually gets
control of her features. Now she trusts herself to
look at him but immediately falls howling into a
chair.

                         JOHN D.
                    (Helplessly)
                I don't know what to say, I...
                didn't realize it was so humorous.

                         GERRY
                    (Struggling with
                     her features)
                Did you really want to... put me
                through all that?
                    (She starts to
                     laugh again and
                     puts her handker-
                     chief over her
                     mouth)

                         JOHN D.
                I'm afraid I'm... there's no use
                trying to conceal it now...
                    (He sinks on one
                     knee and takes her
                     hand in both of his)
                I might have guessed it on the
                train... I certainly should have
                known it in Jacksonville... and
                on the yacht... the trial was as
                much for you as for me...and how-
                ever ridiculous I may seem...
                there's nothing ridiculous about
                the way I feel in my heart... I'm
                madly in love with you.
                    (He kisses her hand)

Gerry reaches out her hand to touch his hair, then
looks quickly to the door.

G-9   TOM - IN THE DOORWAY

       Lightning is flashing from his eyes.

11-21-41   (Continued)

                              211

G-9 (Cont'd)

                    THE PRINCESS
                (Coming in quickly)
        Oh, isn't that pretty!
                (Now, scoldingly
                 to Tom)
        What are you bothering them
        for all the time?

                    TOM
                (Through clenched teeth)
        My hat.

                    THE PRINCESS
                (Picking it up and
                 putting it on his
                 head)
        There's your hat, now leave them
        alone.

She drags him out but he grabs the door handle.

                    THE PRINCESS
                (Pulling him out)
        If you want to bother somebody...
        bother me.

Tom slams the door like an explosion of dynamite.

G-10   GERRY AND JOHN D.

They bounce slightly at the door slam.

                    JOHN D.
        You know, I'm not sure that Mac
        likes me.

                    GERRY
        Oh, nonsense...he's always like
        that...He just doesn't think
        anybody's good enough for me.

                    JOHN D.
                (Smiling)
        Well, he's <u>right</u> there.

DISSOLVE TO:

G-11   TOTO - ALONE <u>AT A TABLE</u> - <u>IN THE EVERGLADES CLUB</u> -
        (NIGHT)

He wears a dinner jacket and a paper hat. We see
Chinese lanterns swinging behind him and the shadows

G-11 (Cont'd)

         of the dancers pass in front of him to the swing of
         the lilting music. He looks around sourly, starts
         to fill a champagne glass, then fills a highball
         glass with it instead. As he raises it to his lips
         he has a slight reaction.

G-12   CLOSE SHOT - THE PRINCESS AND TOM - DANCING

         She is glistening in jewels, draped across his chest.

                   THE PRINCESS
         You don't care for me much, do
         you?

                   TOM
         Why certainly.

                   THE PRINCESS
         Then, why do you let me flop
         around?

                   TOM
             (Tightening his
              grip a little)
         I'm sorry, I...

                   THE PRINCESS
         You will care for me, though, I
         grow on people...like moss.
             (Then to Toto who
             tries to cut in)
         Oh, sit down, Toto, and stop fol-
         lowing me around. Couche -- platz --
         sitz.

                   TOTO
         Nitz.

                   THE PRINCESS
             (Threateningly)
         Yitz -- Toto!

G-13   GERRY AND JOHN D. - DANCING

         She looks very beautiful. By a fortunate happen-
         stance, the orchestra is playing a tune owned by
         Paramount and John D. is singing the words in her
         ear.

                   GERRY
         You have a nice little voice.

                   JOHN
         Thank you. I used to sing in college.

-11-21-41   (Continued)

G-13 (Cont'd)

                    GERRY
         With a mandolin?

                    JOHN D.
         I wouldn't play it around the
         house.

                    GERRY
         Would you be around the house
         much?

                    JOHN D.
         Not any more than you wanted me
         ...I have an office...not that
         I do much in it...
                    (Suddenly getting
                     an idea)
         Say, maybe Mac could come and
         help me.

                    GERRY
         That would be wonderful...you
         could plan the airport together.

                    JOHN D.
         What airport is that?

                    GERRY
         It's the most remarkable invention
         you've ever heard of...it's a sus-
         pended airport right in the middle
         of the city...you know, stretched
         like a tennis racket...

                    JOHN D.
         But would that be strong enough...
         I mean, after all, a tennis
         racket...

                    GERRY
         Made of steel cables, of course...
         about so far apart....the light
         and air can go through...it's
         almost invisible from below...
         but planes can land and take off...
         right in the middle of the city...
         isn't that wonderful?

                    JOHN D.
                    (Seriously)
         It's perfectly remarkable, as
         a matter of fact...if those cables
         are strong enough.

11-21-41   (Continued)

G-13 (Cont'd)

> GERRY
> That's what holds up the Brooklyn
> Bridge.

> JOHN D.
> That's very interesting...I might
> be able to help him...in fact I
> will be able to help him...in
> fact I'll help him...why not?

> GERRY
> (Delighted)
> Will you really?

> JOHN D.
> Of course I will...I mean up to
> a certain point, of course...
> how much would a working model
> cost?

> GERRY
> (Quickly)
> Ninety-nine thou...I mean about
> a hundred thousand dollars...
> in that neighborhood.

> JOHN D.
> (Smiling)
> Well, that isn't a difficult
> neighborhood to find...I think
> that could be done all right.

> GERRY
> Really? Oh, that makes me so
> happy...you have no idea how much
> trouble he's had.

> JOHN D.
> (Sympathetically)
> Is that so?
> (Now he looks across
> the room)
> Of course he won't know what
> trouble really is until he tangles
> up with Maude...that's rather un-
> kind, isn't it?...I'm sorry I said
> it...you say about a hundred
> thousand dollars?

> GERRY
> Exactly.

> JOHN D.
> It's built --

11-21-41   (Continued)

G-14   THE PRINCESS AND TOM - DANCING

THE PRINCESS
What is Gerry's husband like?

TOM
Who?... Oh... just a flop.

THE PRINCESS
A big flop?

TOM
Yes...·any way you take it.

THE PRINCESS
(Philosophically)
Well, he won't be such a flop
with his ninety-nine thousand
dollars... Snoodles will give
it to him all right... and why
not? What I ought to do is
marry him and get the money back
in the family; that would be a
big joke... Of course I'm crazy,
I'll marry anybody.

TOM
(In a dead voice)
What about ninety-nine thousand
dollars?

THE PRINCESS
(Alarmed)
Oh, dear, have I let the cat out
of the bag again?... I'm awfully
sorry... I naturally thought you
knew all about it... I'll never
learn to keep my kisser closed.

TOM
(Doggedly)
What about this ninety-nine
thousand dollars?

THE PRINCESS
(Airily)
Oh, it's just the usual holdup...
before they give you a divorce...
it's dirt cheap, as a matter of
fact... mine always asked a
positive fortune... the rats.

G-14 (Cont'd)

> TOM
> (Through clenched teeth)
> You say her husband wants ninety-
> nine thousand dollars before he'll
> give her a divorce?
> (He holds her fiercely)

> THE PRINCESS
> Oh, I love you like this...with
> lightning flashing out of your eyes.

> TOM
> Did she tell you that story?

> THE PRINCESS
> (With half-closed eyes)
> Why should we talk about that
> heel when you're here?

> TOM
> (Shaking her)
> Did she tell you that?

> THE PRINCESS
> Do that again, I love it.

> TOM
> Now listen.

> THE PRINCESS
> Well, she told Snoodles, and I
> swore not to mention a word of
> it. Naturally, you being her
> brother...

> TOM
> Naturally.

G-15   TOTO - AT THE TABLE

He looks bored.

G-16   GERRY AND JOHN D. - REACHING THE TABLE

As John D. pulls a chair out for her, Tom and the
Princess arrive.

> GERRY
> Darling, I have the most wonder-
> ful news for you. Snoodles is
> going to build your airport.

> THE PRINCESS
> Why should Snoodles build it?
> I'll build it.

11-21-41   (Continued)

G-16 (Cont'd)

        JOHN D.
You don't even know what it
is, Maude.

       THE PRINCESS
Well, neither do you, probably...
you just looked in her eyes and
said, "Of course."
   (She laughs)
I love men.

        JOHN D.
No, that's a very interesting
thing, Mac...if the cables are
strong enough, of course. I
can see it with one great terminal
building: the beacon tower, the
elevators, the waiting rooms...

       THE PRINCESS
And a little bar in the back.

        JOHN D.
The Air Terminal Building... we
own a block on Fifty-First Street..

       THE PRINCESS
We own eight... he's being modest.

        JOHN D.
Very interesting.

        TOTO
   (In double talk)
....
.............................!

       THE PRINCESS
Quiet, Toto.

        JOHN D.
Well that gives us a lot to look
forward to, doesn't it? I don't
know whether I told you or not,
Mac, but your sister and I have
progressed considerably since
this afternoon.

        TOM
Is that so?
   (Now he turns to Gerry)
What's this business of your hus-
band wanting ninety-nine thousand
dollars before he sets you free?

11-21-41   (Continued)

G-16 (Cont'd)

>   GERRY
>   (Nervously)
> Oh, that was just a little idea
> he had...you know how people are
> when they're upset. I'm not sure
> he actually meant it. Let's not
> even talk about it.

>   JOHN D.
> No, let's face it. Gerry natur-
> ally wants to defend this human
> bacterium...I suppose that's only
> natural and gallant...but the fact
> of the matter is he asked her for
> it, and as soon as my name comes
> into it we're doomed.

>   THE PRINCESS
> Broiled.

>   JOHN D.
> As a Hackensacker, I find it cheaper
> to pay than to fight. Ninety-nine
> thousand dollars isn't a small
> amount...on the other hand it isn't
> large.

>   THE PRINCESS
> I should say not...when I think of
> Stefan...not even mentioning Serge
> or...that big one with the scar...
> what was his name?

>   JOHN D.
> Itsk.

>   THE PRINCESS
> Baron Itsk...Lucius.

>   TOTO
>   (Happily)
> Itsk!

>   THE PRINCESS
> Nitsk.

>   TOM
> Well, I'm awfully sorry to hear
> that about Tom. I knew he was a
> failure and a dreamer, I guess,
> but I didn't know he was a skunk.
>   (He turns to John D.)
> It's very kind of you to want to
> build the airport...I mean the
> model of it...I guess I was a
> little too...stunned to say thank

-11-21-41   (Continued)

G-16 (Cont'd)
              TOM (Cont'd)
you...you know how it is when
you've been waiting for something
a long time...there's only one
trouble with the whole set-up...
something Gerry forgot to tell
you...and that is that I'm not
alone in this invention...that
human bacterium we were talking
about, her husband, has had
exactly as much to do with it as
I have, so that if you help me
you'd be helping him too, you see,
and I'm sure that nothing could be
further from your wish...I just
thought you'd better understand
that.
      (He turns to Gerry)
How about dancing with your brother.

She rises without smiling and they dance away.

          TOTO
      (In double talk)
....
....

        THE PRINCESS
    (Without looking around)
Shut up, my brother is thinking.

G-17   TOM AND GERRY DANCING
          GERRY
What did you have to do that
for, you fat-head? Don't you
ever get tired of being noble?
Everything I build up for you
you knock down. I've got you the
money twice already and...

          TOM
Look, darling...

          GERRY
I don't want to listen to anything
that begins with "look, darling"
so that you can get off another
noble saying. Can't you ever
learn to be practical? Don't you
know that the greatest men in the
world, the founders of our country
have told lies and let things be
misunderstood if it was useful to
them? Didn't you ever hear of a
campaign promise?
         (Continued)

220

G-17 (Cont'd)
                              TOM
                The way you are is the way you've
                got to be, honey. That's how I
                am and if I'm supposed to be a
                flop...

                              GERRY
                Well you're not going to be a
                flop. Nobody who's been married
                to me for five years is going to
                come out of it a flop. You're go-
                ing to get your airport if I have
                to build it for you myself...
                after I'm married.

                              TOM
                You know how much of that money
                I'm going to touch.

                              GERRY
                You'll never know whose money you're
                touching. Some day an old investor
                from Arkansas will appear, or maybe
                it will be a young one from New
                Jersey, or maybe a rich Indian or an
                oil man from Texas...you'll never
                know; and then you'll get rich and
                successful, because you really have
                something on the ball, and one day
                you'll be driving up Fifth Avenue in
                a big shiny car and I'll be in an-
                other big shiny car and we'll come
                to a stop signal, and we'll see each
                other and smile a little, and then
                I'll say: "You know that rich Indian
                who started you off to making all
                these millions?" and you'll frown and
                say: "Yes," and I'll say: "Well,
                that was me," and your mouth will
                fall open and I'll laugh at you, and
                then the lights will change and you'll
                go on straight up the avenue and I'll
                turn off west.

        John D. and the Princess dance INTO THE SHOT.

                              JOHN D.
                        (Tapping Tom on the
                         shoulder)
                I've got it! I'll build it and his
                share will be more than ninety-nine
                thousand so he'll have to release
                her.

                              221

                          THE PRINCESS
                Isn't that brilliant?   It's
                the first bright thought he's
                ever had.

                          GERRY
                It's marvelous.

                          JOHN D.
                It was really very simple. Now
                shall we change partners? It
                seems a shame to waste such a
                beautiful sister on a brother
                who doesn't appreciate her.

                          THE PRINCESS
                You said it.

                          GERRY
                     (To Tom)
                I told you you'd get someplace
                some day.

                          THE PRINCESS
                He can get there tonight if he
                likes -- I understand there's a
                preacher in Arcadia who stays open
                very late...

          DISSOLVE TO:

G-18   EXT. OF THE PRINCESS'S MANSION - (NIGHT)

        A shiny open car drives INTO THE SHOT and Tom and the
        Princess descend.

                          THE PRINCESS
                Thank you so much...it was de-
                lightful...oh, dear!

                          TOM
                What's the matter?

                          THE PRINCESS
                We must have forgotten Toto some-
                where...I suppose he'll show up,
                though...he's very hard to lose.

        She turns and looks back at the sound of a yawn.

G-19   TOTO - IN THE RUMBLE SEAT

                          TOTO
                     (Stretching himself)
                Grittinks.
-11-21-41

                                222

G-20   TOM AND THE PRINCESS

> THE PRINCESS
> Wouldn't he be awful to be married
> to...always hanging around.

She takes Tom's arm and goes into the house.

G-21   <u>TOM AND GERRY'S SITTING ROOM</u>

Through the hall door Tom and the Princess appear.

> THE PRINCESS
> Goodnight, Captain. You have
> renewed my faith in mankind.

> TOM
> You're a very embarrassing lady.
> If I weren't a little bit mixed up
> at the moment I'd take you up on a
> few of your dares and make you say
> papa.

> THE PRINCESS
> Papa.
> (She smiles and then
> continues)
> How would you like to drive over to
> Fort Meyers tomorrow...there's noth-
> ing there, but the ride would be nice
> ...we might put Toto in the Army.

> TOM
> I may not be here tomorrow.

> THE PRINCESS
> What do you mean, you may not be
> here tomorrow?

> TOM
> Well, I'm...a little bit mixed up...
> I have a sort of an appointment in
> New York.

> THE PRINCESS
> Oh, let her wait, whoever she is...
> she's no good for you...while I, on
> the other hand...

> TOM
> You never think of anything but
> topic "A" do you?

11-21-41   (Continued)

G-21 (Cont'd)

                    THE PRINCESS
            Is there anything else? Topic "A"
            Is here to stay. I'll leave you
            with that thought, Captain...bon-
            soir, drip-drap.

        She undulates away from the door. Her hand is the
        last we see of her, trucking. Tom closes the door
        and glares around the room. He walks up and down
        a couple of times, then stops and looks at the
        statuette.

G-22   THE STATUETTE

        It winks an eye at us.

G-23   GERRY AND JOHN D. APPROACHING - IN THE HALL OUTSIDE

                    JOHN D.
            I think this is the happiest
            night in my life.

                    GERRY
            Really, Snoodles?

                    JOHN D.
            Yes. You've freed me of a cer-
            tain timidity from which I've
            always suffered...and now with
            you...and Mac...and the airport
            ...I see great days ahead full
            of fun...and everything.

                    GERRY
                (Leaning against
                the door)
            I'm sure of it, Snoodles.

                    JOHN D.
                (Laughing inwardly)
            By the way, I'll have a little
            surprise for you...in a few
            minutes...so don't be surprised.

                    GERRY
                (With a nervous
                backward look)
            What is it?

                    JOHN D.
            Well, if I told you what it was it
            wouldn't be a surprise any more.
11-21-41   (Continued)

G-23 (Cont'd)
                    GERRY
              (With another nervous
              glance at the door)
          I wouldn't do anything too sur-
          prising, if I were you, Snoodles
          ...You never can tell how those
          things are going to work out.
              (She laughs nervously)

                    JOHN D.
          I'm persuaded you will be de-
          lighted.

                    GERRY
          I certainly hope I will be.

                    JOHN D.
          If you'll just leave your window
          open...onto the balcony...

As Gerry looks at him very nervously --

G-24   TOM - INSIDE THE SITTING ROOM

He is staring in a fury at the door. Now he turns
to the mantelpiece, seizes the statuette of virtue
and hurls it to the floor.

G-25   GERRY AND JOHN D. - OUTSIDE THE DOOR

They bounce.

                    JOHN D.
          What was that?

                    GERRY
              (Brightly)
          I didn't hear anything...good
          night.

She opens the door behind her.

                    JOHN D.
              (Confidentially)
          I'll see you in a little while,
          then.

                    GERRY
              (Very nervously)
          Good night, Snoodles.

                    JOHN D.
          I'll see you in my dreams.
-21-41   (Continued)

225

G-25   (Cont'd)
                              GERRY
                    That's a good place.

She backs into the room.

G-26   TOM - IN THE LIVING ROOM

He is watching the door.

G-27   GERRY - PAST TOM

She closes the door behind her, looks at Tom a moment, then crosses to a place near him and looks down
at the floor.
                              GERRY
                    I got your message...you're a fast
                    worker, aren't you?

                              TOM
                    You have your nerve to talk.

                              GERRY
                         (With rising fire)
                    So you couldn't even wait...a
                    decent interval...you and your
                    Princess...I hope you're very proud
                    of yourself...Captain McGlue.

She starts for her room.

                              TOM
                         (Putting his hand
                          on her shoulder)
                    Wait a minute.

Gerry freeing herself.

                              GERRY
                    Let me go! You big pull-over!

                              TOM
                         (Looking at the floor)
                    No, no... I just broke that because
                    it was handy.

                              GERRY
                    Well then, you ought to be ashamed
                    of yourself.
                         (She starts to cry)

11-21-41   (Continued)

G-27   (Cont'd)

                    TOM
               (Indignantly)
Look - I'm the one who has the right
to...

                   GERRY
              (Shaking herself out
               of it)
I know I'm an idiot... I suppose it's
when you've been fond of somebody for
a long time...
              (Then accusingly)
You shouldn't have come down here...
You had no right to come down here
like this...you should have given me
a little time to get used to the
idea.

                    TOM
              (Holding her elbow)
Maybe I should... but you can't blame
a man for trying to hold onto something that he loves...that he always
has loved...that he always will love.

                   GERRY
You're just going to make me cry
again.

                    TOM
Gerry.

                   GERRY
You're forgetting the airport...
you're forgetting everything that
counts.

                    TOM
              (Still closer to her)
Gerry.

                   GERRY
              (Holding him off)
No... it's all finished... When you
make a decision you have to stand
by it... and you can't let champagne
... or tree toads... or night flowers
... or memories get in the way of it.
It's all over... and I know it's for
the best... He'll have to find out
who you are some day... but by then
he'll like you so much he won't
care... Listen to me just this once,

G-27 (Cont'd)
         GERRY (Cont'd)
     will you?... I've always done what
     you wanted...and it's always turned
     out a disaster... Good night, darling
     ... sleep tight.

  She turns out the light.

         TOM
     It'll be funny, sleeping with the
     sitting room between us...

         GERRY
     And the doors locked.

         TOM
     You won't have to worry about that.

         GERRY
     Good night, dear.

         TOM
     Don't you kiss your brother good
     night?

         GERRY
     I don't know - I never had a brother.

         TOM
     You have one now.

         GERRY
       (Laughing)
     You fool.

  She lifts her lips up to be kissed. As if the touching of their lips were a cue, which it is, the
  strains of a glorious orchestra drift up from the
  lawn below. Tom and Gerry separate slowly, look at
  each other, slowly discover the source of the music
  and walk to the window and look down.

G-28 HIGH CAMERA SHOT - DOWN ON THE ORCHESTRA FROM THE
    EVERGLADES CLUB - ARRANGED ON THE LAWN

    Like many another amateur conductor, John D. is lead-
    ing it with his hand. Now the music reaches the
    place for singing.

G-29 TOM AND GERRY - IN THE WINDOW

11-21-41

G-30   HIGH CAMERA SHOT - DOWN ON THE ORCHESTRA AND JOHN D.

John D. starts to sing. He sings the number with
great distinction.

G-31   TOM AND GERRY - <u>IN THE WINDOW</u>

                          GERRY
          He has no right to do things like
          that on a night like this... good
          night!

She hurries into her room and closes the door. Tom
watches her go.

G-32   <u>GERRY'S ROOM</u>

She comes in, closes the door behind and leans on it
for a moment. Then she goes quickly to her window
and closes it... the music still comes in. She undoes her dress, then slowly starts to refasten it.

G-33   TOM - <u>IN HIS BEDROOM</u>

He undoes his tie and looks out the window at the
singing.

G-34   THE ORCHESTRA AND JOHN D. - <u>ON THE LAWN</u>

G-35   TOM - <u>IN HIS BEDROOM</u>

He flops in a low-armed chair. Suddenly he looks up.

G-36   GERRY - <u>IN THE DOORWAY</u>

She comes past the window, then the CAMERA PANS HER
INTO THE SHOT with Tom.

                          GERRY
                  (Resignedly)
          I can't open this blasted dress.

                          TOM
          Come over here to the light.

As he works on her dress she sits on his lap to make
it easier for him. He admires her back for a moment.

11-21-41   (Continued)

G-36   (Cont'd)
                              GERRY
                         (After a while)
                    Can you get it?

Tom undoes one hook, then two, then three. Suddenly
Gerry turns and throws her arms around his neck. Now
she pulls his head down and crushes his lips against
hers.

                              GERRY
                    Oh, darling, darling, darling,
                    darling...
                         (She kisses him again)

G-37   CLOSE SHOT - JOHN D.

He is getting near the end of the song.

G-38   GERRY - ON TOM'S LAP

                              GERRY
                         (After a kiss)
                    I hope you realize this is cost-
                    ing us millions.

He kisses her again.

G-39   JOHN D. - ON THE LAWN

He hits the high note that finishes the song.

FADE OUT:

                    END OF SEQUENCE "G"

11-21-41

Preston Sturges

<u>SEQUENCE "H"</u>

FADE IN:

H-1   A CAGED CANARY BIRD - SINGING IN THE SUNLIGHT

By another fortunate happenstance, he is singing
the same tune as was played on the lawn.

H-2   THE PRINCESS - IN <u>SOME</u> BED - (MORNING)

A trim maid is putting a Lucite breakfast tray in
front of her.

> THE PRINCESS
> (Looking at the bird)
> Is there a law against shooting
> those things?...Good morning, Toto.

H-3   TOTO - <u>IN THE DOORWAY</u>

He comes forward with a rose in his hand.

> TOTO
> Grittinks.

H-4   THE PRINCESS

> THE PRINCESS
> It doesn't seem to matter how
> much champagne you soak up, you
> always feel great the next morning.

> TOTO
> (Cheerfully, as he
> COMES INTO THE SHOT)
> Hello.

He places the rose in the Princess' hands.

> THE PRINCESS
> Thank you, dear. I suppose it
> takes an iron constitution to
> be a house guest.

At this Toto bursts into a flood of double talk.

11-21-41   (Continued)

H-4 (Cont'd)
                    THE PRINCESS
                 (At last able to
                  get a line in)
          Why don't you go away some place?

Toto says another long, amiable piece.

                    THE PRINCESS
          There must be somebody else who
          can use a house guest...I can't
          be the only sucker in the world...
          Why don't you go to Havana...
          that's a nice place...and I'd treat
          you to a nice one-way ticket.

                    TOTO
          Havanag?...youg?... meeg?....
          Havanag?

                    THE PRINCESS
          Nogue, Toto. Youg Havanag, meeg
          here.

                    TOTO
          Nitz.

                    THE PRINCESS
          I was afraid of that.

                    JOHN D.
                 (Entering hurriedly)
          Say, Maude, is this all right?
                 (He takes a jeweler's
                  box out of his pocket)
          You have to work fast in these
          matters, so I just slid down to
          Margetsons...and slid back with
          this.

The Princess opens the box and closes one eye and
rears backwards as she reveals the dazzling jewel.

                    THE PRINCESS
          What is it, the Hope Blue?

                    JOHN D.
          No, no; it's just a chip from it.

                    THE PRINCESS
          Boy, when you fall you fall, don't
          you?

11-21-41   (Continued)

H-4 (Cont'd)
                        THE PRINCESS (Cont'd)
                      (Then to Toto, who
                       is leaning near)
                  Go away, Toto...this might give
                  you ideas...

                          JOHN D.
                      (Taking the ring)
                  It's all right, then.

                        THE PRINCESS
                  I think she'll know what you
                  mean.

                          JOHN D.
                  Good.
                      (He starts to turn)

                        THE PRINCESS
                      (Lifting a startling
                       watch, chain, and
                       pen knife from a
                       jewelry box on her
                       breakfast tray)
                  And how do you think this would
                  look on the Captain's vest?

                          JOHN D.
                      (Departing)
                  You're really incorrigible.
                      (He leaves)

                            TOTO
                      (Beaming happily
                       as he sees the
                       watch)
                  Ha!
                        THE PRINCESS
                      (Putting it away)
                  No, no, Toto; naughty-naughty.

                  She hands him a breakfast roll instead.

H-5   THE SITTING ROOM OF TOM AND GERRY'S SUITE

       There is a knock on the door, then John D. enters.
       He looks around, then comes forward, takes the ring
       box out of his pocket and holds his hands behind him.
       As he gets to the line between Tom's and Gerry's
       room he glances into Tom's room.

H-6   LONG SHOT - TOM - PACKING HIS SUITCASE

       He does not see us.
-11-21-41

H-7   CLOSE SHOT - JOHN D.

        He loosk surprised at this, then turns and looks into
        Gerry's room.

H-8   LONG SHOT - GERRY - PACKING HER THINGS

        Her back is to us.

H-9   JOHN D.

        He watches in amazement, then moves slowly to the
        doorway of her room. The CAMERA PANS him over.

H-10   CLOSE SHOT - GERRY - PACKING

        Now she picks up the bracelet, looks at it longingly,
        then hollers over her shoulder.
                              GERRY
                I suppose I'll have to give the
                bracelet back, won't I?

H-11   JOHN D. - IN THE DOORWAY
                              JOHN D.
                Why?

H-12   GERRY

        She looks startled for a moment.
                              GERRY
                Oh, dear.

        She starts forward slowly with the bracelet. The
        CAMERA PANS her INTO THE SHOT with John D.
                              JOHN D.
                        (With his hand still
                        behind his back)
                What are you talking about?

                              GERRY
                        (Closing her eyes)
                Snoodles, I'm so very fond of you...
                You're such a lovely, generous,
                good-natured man...you're really a
                woman's ideal...only you shouldn't
                have sung last night.

11-21-41   (Continued)

                              234

H-12 (Cont'd)

                    JOHN D.
             (Dropping his hands
             to his sides which
             reveals the jewelry
             box)
What?

                    GERRY
             (Pressing it into
             his hand)
Here's your bracelet; I'm going
back to my husband.

                    JOHN D.
             (Stupefied)
That skunk?

                    GERRY
He isn't, really. I let you
think worse about him than he
is...much worse...you know how
a woman likes sympathy.

                    JOHN D.
But the ninety-nine thousand
dollars!

                    GERRY
He didn't want that. I wanted
it for him.

                    JOHN D.
But, but...
             (He opens the box
             with the phenom-
             enal solitaire)

                    GERRY
             (Getting a gander
             at it)
Put it away.

                    JOHN D.
But, darling.

                    GERRY
I'll just look at it once more,
then put it away forever...
there's a limit to what a woman
can stand, you know.

At this point Tom drops a heavy hand on John D.'s
shoulder.

11-21-41   (Continued)

H-12   (Cont'd)

                         TOM
                      (Heartily)
           Hello, there, Snoodles, how's every
           little thing?

                       JOHN D.
           I'm very unhappy, as a matter of
           fact.

                         TOM
                      (Seriously)
           You'll get over it.

                       JOHN D.
           You know about Gerry's decision.

                       TOM
       Yes.

                       JOHN D.
           I'll never get over it as long as I
           live...I...I had such hopes...such
           plans.

                       GERRY
           I'm going to cry, Snoodles.

       John D. puts his arm around Tom.

                       JOHN D.
                      (Smiling bravely)
           Anyway...we still have the airport
           ...that'll keep us busy.

       A long silence follows this into which sweeps the
       Princess in a breath-taking lace negligee. In her
       hand she carries the jewelry box containing the
       watch and chain. Behind her hovers Toto who keeps
       an eye on the watches.

                    THE PRINCESS
                      (Happily)
         What's knittin' kittens?

                       JOHN D.
           Gerry is going back to her hus-
           band.

                    THE PRINCESS
                      (Dismayed)
           Oh, you poor dumb thing...I know
           just how it is...I'll bet he's a
           knock-out.

H-12   (Cont'd)

          GERRY
I'm awfully sorry about....

      THE PRINCESS
    (Turning to John D.)
Anyway, darling, you still have
your airport...and you and the
Captain and I will keep as busy
as bird dogs...won't we, Captain?

         TOM
I'm afraid that isn't possible,
either.

       JOHN D.
Why not?
    (Now he turns to
    Gerry)
I still have...I always will have...
the deepest affection for you...
certainly nothing has happened to
spoil my friendship with your
brother...being with him...will
remind me of you.

Another silence descends upon the group.

         GERRY
    (Looking down)
Well, you see...

       JOHN D.
    (Miserably)
What now?

         GERRY
    (In a very small
    voice)
He isn't exactly my brother.

       JOHN D.
    (Repeating
    mechanically)
He isn't exactly your brother?

         TOTO
    (Into the silence)
Hello.

      THE PRINCESS
Shut up.

         GERRY
He's my husband.

11-21-41   (Continued)

H-12   (Cont'd)

JOHN D. AND
THE PRINCESS
(Together...electrified)
Your husband!

THE PRINCESS
Well, no wonder! I thought I was
losing my grip.

JOHN D.
(Belligerently)
You mean that vermin who...who...
who...
(Then relaxing)
That's right, you said he didn't.

THE PRINCESS
(Suddenly)
Then, who is McGlue?

TOM
(Firmly)
There is no McGlue.

THE PRINCESS
Well, thank heaven for something
...that name!

JOHN D.
Then, it's the...Jeffers Airport
...that's it, isn't it?

THE PRINCESS
Are you still talking about that
airport? You really take it on
the chin, don't you?

JOHN D.
Why not? If an idea has merit, it
has merit...sentiment and business
don't belong in the same bed...
After all grandfather loathed oil,
you know...it made his eyes water
but that didn't stop him from making billions out of it.

THE PRINCESS
Bless his oily old heart!

TOM
You still want to go through with
the airport?

11-21-41   (Continued)

                     JOHN D.
                     (Violently)
Why not... on a purely business
basis, you understand... Right now
I don't like you... although I may
get over it later... Right now I
need something to occupy my mind...
the airport is something... if not
exactly what I hoped for...

                     THE PRINCESS
You might have some little air-
ports some day.

John D. just looks at her.

                     THE PRINCESS
I'm sorry.

                     JOHN D.
I'll be lonely without you, Gerry.

Gerry puts a handkerchief to her mouth but doesn't
answer.

                     THE PRINCESS
                     (Looking up at Tom)
Oh, Captain... and thou!

                     JOHN D.
I don't suppose you have a sister...

                     GERRY
                     (Looking down)
Only a twin sister.

                     JOHN D.
                     (Coming to life)
A twin sister!

                     GERRY
Oh, didn't you know about that?...
that's how we got married in the
beginning...both being twins... of
course that was another plot entirely.

                     THE PRINCESS
                     (Happily)
Both twins! What are they doing?

                     TOM
                     (Seriously)
Well, nothing... you see...

We hear the crash of the Wedding March and we
DISSOLVE TO:

239

H-13   THE SAME CHURCH WE SAW AT THE BEGINNING OF THE
        PICTURE

        We come in on a CLOSE SHOT of Tom and Gerry stand-
        ing in the marriage line. They are dressed to the
        teeth. The CAMERA PULLS BACK and next to Gerry we
        see John D. as a bridegroom. Next to him stands
        Gerry's twin sister as the bride. Next to her
        stands Tom's twin brother as the groom. Next to
        him stands the Princess smothered in bridal veils.
        Last, but not least, we find Toto looking very sour.

H-14   CLOSE SHOT - TOTO

                            TOTO
                 Schnitz!

H-15   THE SEVEN PEOPLE - PAST THE PREACHER

        The CAMERA PULLS BACK RAPIDLY, through flowers and
        vegetation until we find ourselves looking through
        the grill with the nice Valentine lettering. It
        reads:

                    AND THEY LIVED HAPPILY
                       EVER AFTER

        The CAMERA PULLS STILL FURTHER BACK and on another
        grill we read:

                    OR DID THEY?

                       THE END

11-21-41

240

Triumph over Pain/
The Great Moment

What is called *The Great Moment* is the only uncharted star in the Sturges constellation, if not, indeed, its black hole. Coming to be in shining company—*Sullivan's Travels* and *The Palm Beach Story* before it, *The Miracle of Morgan's Creek* and *Hail the Conquering Hero* after—the film has gravitational force but not visibility.[1] This has thrown more than one Sturges-watcher considerably off course.

What is irreducible is that, due to Paramount's abridgment and reediting, *The Great Moment* is not the film that Sturges wrote, shot, and edited—a film which he called *Triumph over Pain*. That film is lost; fortunately its final script, reprinted below, is not.

Sturges's *Triumph over Pain* was based upon the book of the same name by the Hungarian writer René Fülöp-Miller.[2] Appearing in English translation in 1938, it concerns, according to its jacket,

a little Boston dentist [who] discovered how to use ether practically for the relief of surgical pain. His name was Dr. William T. G. Morton [1819–1868] and Europe reveres him as America's greatest scientist next to Benjamin Franklin. Now anesthetical surgery is a commonplace, yet Americans have almost completely forgotten the man who made possible the triumph over pain.

Whether Sturges read the book in 1938 is uncertain; that someone at Paramount did is likely—the studio bought the rights before publication. "A motion picture is to be made from [the author's] account of Morton," says the jacket. According to James Curtis, it was to be directed by Henry Hathaway with Gary Cooper as Morton—both were under contract to Paramount and the two had worked together before.[3] The project got as far as the writing of a script, or extended treatment, by Samuel Hoffenstein, but Cooper and Hathaway undertook obligations to other studios. Sturges, who was then a screenwriter under contract to Paramount, became interested in the project and obtained permission from studio chief William LeBaron to proceed with a script.

Sturges took his first note on the project on March 15, 1939, four days before finishing his script for *Remember the Night* (1940). He took his last note (of 1939) on December 19, eight days after shooting had begun on his first directorial effort, *The Great McGinty*. In the nine months between, he had put *Triumph over Pain*—the title of all his script versions as well as his preferred title for the film—through one partial draft, dated July 13, and three complete ones, dated August 2, September 13, and December 15. During this period, Sturges also worked on rewrites for *Remember the Night,* signed contracts to direct his first film—something he had ardently sought at least since 1933—and, between September 28 and November 28, completely rewrote his 1933 script *Down Went McGinty.* Further revision resulted in a December 5 script and shooting began—on what was later called *The Great McGinty*—on December 10. That Sturges continued to work on *Triumph over Pain* while engaged in an enterprise so crucial to his aspirations is remarkable. Perhaps he planned *Triumph over Pain* as his second film.

As it happened, Sturges followed *The Great McGinty* (1940) with *Christmas in July* (1940) and that in turn with *The Lady Eve* (1941), both of them based, like *McGinty,* on earlier scripts by him that he thoroughly rewrote before shooting. The scripts for his next two films—*Sullivan's Travels* (1941) and *The Palm Beach Story* (1942)—were entirely new, in each case written from first to last, and directed, in six months. Sturges may have sought relief at this point from the pressure to write and direct another entirely new screenplay in the next six months. If so, *Triumph over Pain,* the only unfilmed script in his files, was the only relief available.

Sturges finished shooting *The Palm Beach Story* in late January 1942. A rough cut was assembled and a dialogue continuity prepared by February 7, with little work required after this date. During the rest of February and March, Sturges rewrote *Triumph over Pain* in preparation for filming, basing his rewrite on his August 2, 1939, script version rather than that of September 13 or December 15. The cover of the rewritten script is dated March 30, its individual pages as late as April 3. Shooting was to begin on April 8 but Sturges, as usual, continued to revise, producing a final script, still with March 30 on the cover page, on April 27. (This is the script reprinted below.)

The shooting process, which concluded in early June, brought further changes, which are reflected in the dialogue continuity of June 10. Paramount production chief Buddy DeSylva asked Sturges to clarify a point in the film and Sturges accordingly did a bit of reshooting. Once this new bit was edited in, the film stood as Sturges wished it to stand.

I

Sturges did not question Fülöp-Miller's book—it remained the limit, the horizon of all his work on the project. A summary of the book is necessary if we wish to follow the evolution of, and evaluate, Sturges's screenplay. To trace what he selected, what he left out, what he altered, and what he imagined, will also help us to understand what engaged Sturges in the material in the first place.

Despite its jacket claims, *Triumph over Pain* is not in any usual sense a biography of Morton. It does not mention his name until page 107 and continues for 91 pages after his death. Even the 228 pages of the book devoted to Morton are shared with other participants in the discovery of anesthesia: Dr. Crawford Long of Georgia (1815–1878); Dr. Horace Wells of Hartford (1815–1848); and Dr. Charles Thomas Jackson of Boston. Also, with the exception of a brief paragraph, Morton's early life is entirely ignored: he is already a dentist when he first appears and already in search of a method of painless extraction. Morton's misfortunes in the years after his discovery are recounted, but they are limited mainly to the public sphere; their effects on Morton himself and his family are scarcely mentioned. Fülöp-Miller's true subject is the history of humanity's "arduous struggle against the mighty forces of pain." He begins with a consideration of magical, ritualistic, and other methods of pain relief used in the centuries before the nineteenth, and continues, after the account of Morton, with the chloroform experiments of James Young Simpson (1811–1870), and still later developments.

Morton wished to become a doctor, according to Fülöp-Miller, but his father could not afford to support him during the years of training required, so Morton took a dental diploma. With the aid of a one thousand dollar loan from a mutual friend, he and his friend Horace Wells set up a dental practice in Boston in 1842 but did not do well at first. Wells "soon lost courage" and returned to Hartford. Morton, "being more of a sticker," persisted and eventually succeeded: within a year he repaid the loan. Morton fell in love with Elizabeth Whitman in the spring of 1844 but his attentions, according to an article she wrote after his death, "were not well-received by my family, he being regarded as a poor young man with an undesirable profession." Nevertheless, William and Elizabeth were married in May 1844, and a son was born the following year. Searching for a specialty that would give him an edge over his competitors, Morton became interested in crowns. He knew he lacked technical competence so, in exchange for five hundred dollars, the vice-president of the Dental Society opened the doors of his laboratory to Morton, who was thereby able to learn from the experience of older dentists. Morton discovered a device with the aid of which crowns could be attached to the stumps of old teeth, but the procedure was painful and few patients lasted the course of treatment.

At this time, Fülöp-Miller reports, Morton's income was about ten thousand dollars a year; but "he could easily triple this were he to make free use of his new discovery, and would then become the leading dentist in Boston." "In those days," the author continues, "a dentist who made a discovery would, in defiance of the spirit of modern science, treat it as his own property and conceal it as far as he could from his colleagues. No friendship, no corporate ties, could overcome this commercialism."

Morton's crown technique could not be employed unless a way could be found to deaden the severe pain it caused. However, painless dentistry had been sought in vain by so many for so long that it seemed a will-o'-the-wisp. Finding no other way to proceed, Morton wrote to the medical faculty of Harvard proposing to resume his medical studies. At Harvard, Morton met the well-known scientist Dr. Charles Thomas Jackson, who was a physician, a chemist with his own laboratory, and a geologist whose researches had won considerable renown. Morton attended Jackson's lectures at Harvard and—hoping to learn more from him—roomed with Elizabeth at Jackson's house, where they also took meals. Fülöp-Miller notes that Morton learned from Jackson a good deal about sulfuric ether, the legitimate medical use of which was then mainly confined to the treatment of asthma. When Jackson mentioned in passing that ether sprinkled on the skin could relieve pain, Morton asked if ether could be used with advantage in his dental practice. "Why not?" Fülöp-Miller has Jackson respond. "I will give you a drop bottle of it to try."

Morton tried the drops with some success but the ether was so volatile that the insensibility produced was of very brief duration. Around this time Morton's former partner, Wells, made a demonstration at Harvard Medical School of a method of painless extraction on which he had been working. It was based upon the patient's inhalation of nitrous oxide, known widely as "laughing gas." Wells had administered the gas to himself and had a colleague pull one of his teeth; he felt no pain. At the Harvard demonstration, however, the patient cried out with pain, and Wells was booed and hissed. Wells was convinced he had used too little of the gas at Harvard, but the fact seems to be that he had not experimented long enough to know the right dosage. Back in Hartford, Wells gave another demonstration, this time using too much of the gas; a too profound insensibility resulted and the patient nearly died. Wells gave up his experiments and, indeed, left dentistry altogether.

Morton had acted as Wells's assistant at Harvard, although not before advising him to see Jackson, who cautioned against the experiment, which he regarded as dangerous. Wells's demonstration was a fiasco but it served to turn Morton's thoughts from drops to inhalation as a way to produce insensibility. Morton would probably have consulted Jackson about gas inhalation, but the two had had a falling-out: Morton had arrived late for dinner several times and Jackson, a stickler for punctuality, at last exploded and insulted Morton in the presence of Elizabeth. The Mortons promptly moved out.

A number of books were of some use to Morton, particularly Michael Faraday's monograph of 1818 comparing the anesthetic effects of ether and laughing gas. Morton also asked his friends about any experiences with ether they might have had. One told of ether parties he had attended where large quantities were inhaled apparently without ill effect; but another told of a man who had lain insensible for thirty hours after inhaling ether.

Wells's experience led Morton to considerable caution—he resolved to experiment with his method thoroughly before making it public. In order to continue his experiments without interruption, he asked a colleague to take over his dental practice for a time and moved with Elizabeth and their expanding family to a country house they had built in West Needham.

Morton obtained a large supply of ether from Burnett's drugstore and worked every day for months from early in the morning to after midnight. He experimented with ether on the family dog, Nig, on the family goldfish, on larger fish he caught in a brook, on insects, caterpillars, worms, and other creatures. Sometimes the experimentee died but most often an unarousable insensibility was followed by total recovery. Once Morton upset a flask of ether while pursuing a twice-shy Nig; lest it go to waste he soaked up some of the spill in a handkerchief and administered the gas to himself. His wife found him unconscious but he too soon revived. Having extended his absence from Boston longer than announced, Morton now hurried back with his family, not to resume his dental practice—as Elizabeth hoped and expected—but, asking his colleague to stay on as his replacement, to experiment with ether on human subjects.

Preparing to try the substance on two dental assistants, Morton purchased a half-gallon of ether from a wholesale druggist firm, Brewer, Stephens, and Cushing. At their first breath, his subjects passed into a condition of intense excitement, thrashing their arms, upsetting tables and chairs. Both refused to take part in further experiments, whatever they might be paid to do so. (One thought it over but his outraged parents threatened to prosecute Morton should he again put their son under ether.) Morton went down to the docks and offered laborers and sailors he met there five dollars to extract a tooth without pain, but he found no takers. Morton consulted an instrument maker he knew for advice but the latter regarded himself as incompetent on the subject and suggested Morton consult Dr. Jackson, whom he called the leading chemical authority in the city.

In describing Morton's reluctance to ask Jackson for advice, Fülöp-Miller invokes—besides the two men's earlier dispute—an anxiety that he plausibly but unverifiably attributes to Morton: "A more serious matter was that Morton did not trust Jackson, but rather feared him as a possible rival." The author here recalls an incident from Jackson's earlier career that might have given pause to any advice seeker. While returning by ship from Europe in 1832, Samuel F. B. Morse had worked on his telegraph apparatus. Jackson, also on board, showed Morse and others a new electromagnet that he had bought in France, and talked a number of times with Morse about the future of electricity. Morse later perfected his invention, Congress adopted it, and he became wealthy. At some later point, to his astonishment, Morse came across an item in a Boston paper that credited the discovery of the telegraph to Charles T. Jackson. Morse protested this lie, calling Jackson a "lunatic" and an "intolerable nuisance," but so obstinately did Jackson press his case that it took Morse seven years to persuade the world that Jackson's claim was false.

Morton's problem, according to Fülöp-Miller, was to get the information he needed without putting Jackson onto his discovery. The scene between the two men that the book presents is novelistic, even though Fülöp-Miller presents it in a documentary fashion as occurring on September 30, 1846. Morton visits Jackson on the pretext of borrowing an airtight gasbag in order to administer a pain-allaying gas to a patient in need of an extraction. Still thinking of Wells, Jackson warns Morton against nitrous oxide and suggests instead ether vapor. The word ether gives Morton "a great shock" but he keeps his composure and remarks "in an indifferent tone" about the ether drops that Jackson had once recommended to him that had failed. Jackson replies that the drops were chloric ether (ethyl chloride) whereas "for inhalation you must use sulfuric ether, highly rectified, and you can only get it from Burnett. Impure ether will produce most uncertain effects." "Sulfuric ether!" exclaims Morton, with well-simulated astonishment . . . "What is that? Is it a gas? . . . Have you ever watched the effect of that kind of ether on human beings?" "Watched it?" says Jackson lustily. "That would not do much good, but I have inhaled it myself."

Jackson, "who was by nature garrulous," then recounts to Morton an incident in which he needed oil for his stove to make tea but his friend Burnett brought him a bottle of ether by mistake—both passed out and were found on the floor the next morning by Jackson's assistant. On another occasion, Jackson continues, he had inhaled chlorine and almost choked; he reached for a bottle of ammonia but then, changing his mind, reached for a bottle of ether, which is an antidote for chlorine poisoning, and felt easier at once. As Morton is about to leave, Jackson tells him there is something better than a gasbag for the administration of the ether and takes from his shelf "a flask with a glass tube thrust through the cork."

Morton secured some highly rectified ether, which is what he used in his experiments at West Needham, and promptly administered it to himself, carefully noting the spreading of insensibility throughout his body. Morton then told Dr. Hayden, the colleague who had taken over his practice, about his discovery. Hayden was delighted and the two looked over the next day's patients for a likely prospect for the new procedure. Impatient, Morton wished Hayden to pull out one of his own teeth under ether. Toward evening, however, a man came in in great pain and asked to have a tooth extracted. He wished to be mesmerized but agreed to try the new method. He became unconscious almost immediately and, awakening after the extraction, averred that he had felt no pain. This was September 30, 1846, and the man, Eben Frost, became a loyal and persistent spokesman for Morton and his discovery—living testimony that it worked.

Morton took some immediate steps to secure the credit and the financial rewards of his discovery. The very night of the operation he brought Frost and Hayden to the editorial office of the Boston *Daily Journal,* which the next day printed the following notice:

Last evening, as we were informed by a gentleman who witnessed the operation, an ulcerated tooth was extracted from the mouth of an individual without giving him the slightest pain. He was put into a kind of sleep, by inhaling a preparation, the effects of which lasted for about three-quarters of a minute, just long enough to extract the tooth.

On the morning of October 1, Morton appeared at the Boston Patent Office before the arrival of its director, Richard E. Eddy. What Eddy knew, Fülöp-Miller says, was made known on the same day to the chemist, the doctor, and the merchant, that is, among others, to Burnett, Drs. Gould and Dana, "and naturally to Dr. Jackson as well." To all who brought news to Jackson of Morton's success Jackson replied that the dentist would never have made his discovery without his advice. To friends who urged him to seek publicity for his contribution he said that he would have nothing to do with the matter. He declared that ether was dangerous—prolonged use might injure the brain, and if too much were inhaled at one time, asphyxia, coma, or death might ensue. "Morton is a reckless, dare-devil fellow," Jackson is quoted as saying, "and will kill somebody yet. He is sure to have a mishap of some sort. Well, let him go on with it, if he don't bring my name in with it."

However, when Gould and Burnett spoke of the large sums of money that Morton was likely to make, Jackson wrote Morton asking for a compensation of five hundred dollars. Morton was surprised but agreed to meet at Eddy's the next day and sign a document to that effect. Jackson arrived first, and Eddy urged him to go beyond his request for five hundred dollars and join the patent itself, asking for at least 10 percent. As "an ethical physician of high standing," however, Jackson knew he was forbidden to make a secret of any remedy he discovered. When Morton arrived with two witnesses, Jackson raised objections and the matter was postponed to the next day. When he heard of the demand for 10 percent, Morton strongly denied that Jackson had had any share in the discovery—he had only consulted Jackson as an expert chemist. Eddy advised him that patents were delayed and sometimes dismissed due to disputes over priority; also Jackson's reputation in the scientific world would help him. Finding that Dr. Gould was also of the same opinion, Morton agreed.

In the meantime, Morton's dental business had rapidly doubled, but rival dentists in the city had formed a committee to fight the new discovery. Both developments led Jackson to increase his claim to 25 percent, but Morton was unperturbed by the hostility of his colleagues and ignored Jackson's veiled threats.

At this point something unexpected occurred. At the height of his success, Morton withdrew from the public sphere and devoted himself entirely to extending the use of ether to general surgery. Allowing Hayden to take over his practice once again, he retired to his study to conduct experiment after experiment, to develop—if he could—longer periods of ether insensibility. Morton's assistants, his friends, and his wife were puzzled and made anxious by his

247

behavior. Moreover, Morton was frequently the subject of his own investigations, taking ever larger and more dangerous doses of ether.

His experiments showed Morton that his drenched handkerchief method of administration was not sufficient to control either the desired dosage or the length of time the patient remained unconscious, both being necessary for general surgery. To overcome this problem, Morton designed an inhaler, a small two-necked glass globe. Into one of the necks was inserted a wooden tube controlled by taps, while the other permitted the free ingress of air. Putting the wooden tube in his mouth, the patient inhaled air across the surface of ether in the middle and the air became charged with ether vapor. Morton brought his design to an instrument maker named Chamberlain and spent hours with him explaining the details. Once he was sure of his ground, Morton visited a number of prominent surgeons and demonstrated his new procedure, always taking Eben Frost along to verify his claims.

No surgeon would adopt Morton's method in an operation until he approached Dr. John Collins Warren, senior surgeon of Massachusetts General Hospital. It was difficult to see Warren, but Morton finally accosted him on his way out of the hospital building and explained his procedure nonstop to avoid being cut off. Warren was skeptical but nevertheless agreed to give the method a try. "Ever since I performed my first operation," said Warren, "I have been longing for some such means as you describe. I will let you know as soon as I have a suitable case." Warren decided to try the method on a man named Gilbert Abbott, who had a vascular tumor on the right side of his neck. The operation was set for October 16, 1846—only sixteen days after the extraction of Frost's tooth—and Morton was alerted. Waiting for an improved version of his inhaler from Chamberlain, Morton was late for the operation. Warren was about to begin to operate in the old way when Morton burst in. The ether was applied, the patient failed to respond to a pin prick, and Morton turned the patient over to Warren. The operation was performed, the wound was stitched, and the patient awakened. He had felt no pain. "Gentlemen, this is no humbug!" Warren announced to the assembled spectators.

Dr. W. J. Bigelow, a leading physician and a respected Harvard professor, shared Warren's enthusiasm: "We have today witnessed something of the utmost importance to the art of surgery. Our craft has, once and for all, been robbed of its terrors." Two other operations were conducted the next day, another tumor removal and a cauterization performed on an old woman's face. Morton employed his method successfully in both cases.

An issue arose, however, when Warren asked one of his assistants to call upon Chamberlain in order to purchase inhalers for the hospital. Chamberlain informed him that the apparatus was invented by Dr. Morton, who had applied for a patent; therefore the hospital was obliged to secure an authorization from him. Warren believed the cost to be well justified by its value to patients and saw no reason why the inventor should not make something out of his discovery. He asked Morton to call the next day to discuss terms, but the

Massachusetts Medical Society protested. Several doctors learned of the impending arrangement and argued that any scheme of compensation would be unethical. As a dentist, they said, Morton had been beyond the ethics of the medical profession. However, working as he now did in the medical profession, he could not use his invention for private profit-making. Medical ethics required that the discoveries of science be made freely available for the whole of mankind.

At a meeting the next day, the Medical Society resolved that as long as Morton insisted on the use of his invention as a means for private profit, Boston medical practitioners were to have nothing to do with the matter. Warren was greatly disappointed, especially as he had a far more difficult case in view for the next painless operation—the amputation of the leg of twenty-one-year-old Alice Mohan. "The high position attained by the medical profession in the United States, and the general adhesion to ethical standards of practice, were largely his work," says Fülöp-Miller of Warren. But he also felt that such standards should not be allowed to stand in the way of using such a discovery as Morton's to relieve the pain of patients. At the same time, he felt bound by the judgment of the Medical Society. So informed, Morton wrote Warren offering Massachusetts General Hospital the free use of his preparation for all of the hospital's operations. The next time the two men met, Morton asked Warren to supply him with as complete a list as possible of the hospitals and charitable institutions in the country, in order to grant them free license to use his discovery.

The operation on Alice Mohan was set for November 7. A large crowd had gathered in front of the hospital and the operating theater was filled to capacity with physicians, students, and other visitors. As the crowd waited for an hour and more, and began drumming their feet on the floor, the Medical Society was meeting with Dr. Warren. "Are you acquainted with the composition of the remedy with the air of which you intend to perform this operation?" the Society's vice-president asked Warren. The latter admitted that he was not. The vice-president replied that for Morton to forgo a profit was not enough, that medical men must know the composition of any remedy which they propose to introduce into general practice. "The use of secret remedies is a device of quacks, with which responsible medical practitioners can have nothing to do." Bigelow and Warren spoke up passionately for sparing patients from needless pain, but the vice-president insisted that the fault was Morton's, who, simply from avarice, was keeping his remedy secret, and thus withholding it from general use.

Morton told Bigelow he would be glad to disclose the nature of his remedy if only his patent had already been granted. "If I disclose my secret now, the patent will be invalidated." Bigelow replied that the matter could not wait—the patient was waiting for her operation. He continued: "Consider carefully, Morton, whether the preservation of your secret and all the advantages you may hope to derive from it can justify you in allowing a fellow

249

creature to suffer needlessly. Your discovery is far too important to remain any man's private property, even if that man be the discoverer himself." After careful consideration, Morton responded: "If the only question which remains at issue is that I should sacrifice my secret, then you can rest assured that Alice Mohan will be spared needless pain." Proceeding with Bigelow to the assembled Medical Society, Morton said: "Gentlemen, to remove any objection to the use of my remedy, I have the honor to inform you that it is nothing more or less than pure rectified sulfuric ether." There was an astonished silence, Fülöp-Miller reports, and then Dr. Warren issued orders for the patient to be taken into the theater.

Alice Mohan's operation took place on November 7, 1846. Morton died on July 15, 1868, at the age of forty-nine. Fülöp-Miller's account of this long period focuses not on Morton alone but also on Wells and Jackson and, to a lesser extent, on Crawford Long; hence he frequently doubles back over time periods already covered to present the activities of one or another of these figures.

In October 1846, Morton had written to Wells suggesting that they might work together again; he had wanted to know if Wells could promote the ether method in New York. Wells came to Boston and the two men visited Eddy in the patent office. Wells considered the patent application to be in its early stages and chose instead to pursue two other projects—a Scientific Panorama Exhibition he had planned and what he hoped would be a big business in the resale of French prints and engravings. The exhibition, held in Hartford, was a failure and Wells prepared to leave for Paris to buy prints and engravings at low prices. Before he set sail, however, newspaper accounts appeared extolling the Alice Mohan operation and hailing Morton as a great discoverer. Fülöp-Miller asserts novelistically, but not implausibly, that in Wells's mind "I could have done it" became "I ought to have done it" and then, "The discovery was really mine, and Morton merely filched it from me." The day before his ship left, Wells published a letter in a Hartford paper claiming the discovery for himself, arguing that the choice of the "exhilarating agent," whether nitrous oxide or sulfuric ether, did not matter.

Paris too was "buzzing" with news of the discovery of ether; "seething with indignation," Wells told his version of the story to a man named Brewster, a friend who lived in Paris. Also indignant, Brewster advised Wells to return to America to collect proofs of his claim, and then return to Paris. Wells agreed but, before sailing home, published an article in *Galignani's Messenger* claiming priority in the great discovery. The article contained an important error that was later used to discredit Wells: the less air admitted to the lungs with the gas, the better, he said, a principle that would have produced asphyxia and, in some cases, death. Back in Boston, Wells presented his claim to Dr. Hayward, Dr. Warren's assistant, who asked Wells whether he had ever himself inhaled sulfuric ether, or performed an operation or made a patient insensitive to pain under it. Wells had either to reply no or remain silent to each question; Hayward then reported his claim to Morton, who showed him the letter Wells had written in response to Morton's offer that they work together again. It failed to make any claim to the discovery or to the patent. Fülöp-Miller comments: "The sometime partners were henceforward irredeemable foes."

Wells had heard of Simpson's use of chloroform and decided to experiment with it as an alternative to ether. He procured a large quantity and went to New York to try to convince hospitals, dentists, and doctors to use it. Having no success, he decided to experiment on himself. He inhaled chloroform day after day to determine the correct dosages for use in surgery, but in time became addicted to the chemical. His lucid moments became fewer and he wandered aimlessly, talking to anyone who would listen, including streetwalkers, who tended to ignore the penniless dentist. One night Wells spoke with a derelict who told him of a prostitute who, from pure malice, had spoiled his only decent suit, so that he could not go out among respectable people. He hoped to take his revenge on her. Wells had the derelict point the woman out to him and the next day he bought a bottle of sulfuric acid. That night he found the woman again and threw the acid at her and another woman. He was arrested and, when he could provide no coherent explanation for his action, was put in jail. Two days later, Wells wrote a letter intended for publication and another to his wife and then, inhaling some chloroform from a bottle that had not been found by the police, he opened the femoral artery in his left thigh and bled to death. Here Fülöp-Miller comments: "Morton might easily have held his ground against the claims and allegations of a living Wells, for he could have produced facts to the contrary. Now he had to face the shade of a dead man, one to whom the affection of survivors had given a martyr's rank. This martyr needed no proofs, since Death spoke for him."

Jackson, Morton's other colleague-turned-rival, was more formidable than Wells could ever have been, alive or dead. Jackson carefully dissociated himself from Morton's method until it was proven undoubtedly successful then just as carefully claimed that the discovery was his. On October 27, 1846, eleven days after the Gilbert Abbott operation, he put on a frock coat and called upon Dr. Warren at Massachusetts General Hospital. "Sir," he said, "I have the honor to inform you that the use of ether in surgical operations was my idea. William Thomas Green Morton was no more than a pupil of mine, acting on my instructions." Warren knew Jackson's claim was false but could not afford to offend him. He therefore suggested that Jackson instead of Morton administer the ether in an upcoming operation. Jackson evaded the issue by saying he had soon to depart on a geological investigation.

Jackson had a considerable reputation and had also travelled widely—he knew and was known by scientists around the world. On November 13, six days after the Alice Mohan operation, Jackson wrote of his alleged discovery of ether to a fellow geologist named Elie de Beaumont, a prominent member of the French Academy of Sciences. Jackson made up a chronicle of his early awareness of ether, true in relation to his reading perhaps, false in its suggestion of sustained investigation, let alone experimentation. He even made his inadvertent experiences with the gas—the Burnett incident and the chlorine incident—sound like stages of an investigation. Jackson had never witnessed an operation under ether but made a clever case that he had by reading medical books. His letter asserted further that "I have latterly put [my discovery] to use by inducing a dentist of this city to administer the vapours of ether to persons from whom he was to extract teeth. I then requested this dentist to go to the General Hospital of Massachusetts and administer the vapour of ether to a patient about to undergo a painful surgical operation." Jackson lied and lied, on this and many other occasions over the next twenty-five years.

Soon after Jackson had sent his report, Dr. Bigelow addressed the Boston Academy of Arts and Science extolling Morton's discovery and describing the recent operations. This was published in a Boston medical periodical on November 19 and was sent to Europe and the rest of the world by a Cunard steamer which sailed on December 19. Moreover, having secured his patent, Morton was sending specimens of his apparatus, with instructions for use, to various kings and governments. Jackson hurriedly wrote to Beaumont asking him to open the sealed report and present it to the French Academy of the Sciences. Jackson also wrote Alexander von Humboldt, widely regarded as the greatest scientist of his day, and renowned figures in the Ottoman Empire, the Scandinavian countries, and other places. These communiqués, and others affirming Morton as the discoverer, left for Europe on the same ship.

In the meantime, Beaumont presented Jackson's case to the French Academy, where it was accepted along with its claim that Morton played only a minor role in the discovery. Hearing the result from a friend in Paris, Morton was incredulous; he confronted Jackson in his laboratory, saying "You have cheated me." Jackson pretended to be as surprised by the news as Morton was, saying that his friend Beaumont must have made a mistake out of good-heartedness. Jackson assured Morton he would write to Beaumont by the next mail to make clear Morton's primary role in the discovery. After further thought, Jackson said he would publish an article in the *Daily Advertiser* giving a full account of the importance of Morton's discovery. It was to appear on the following Monday and on that day also the mail was to leave for Europe. But by the time a stunned Morton read that article—which claimed full credit for Jackson—it was on its way in the mail to Europe. Morton, fooled into making no protest on his own, had lost a crucial four weeks—the length of time that would pass before the next steamer left for Europe.

This time Morton did not confront Jackson, whom he now understood to be his implacable enemy. Worrying perhaps about what Morton might be up to, Jackson proposed to address the Massachusetts Medical Society. The meeting was set for March 2, but the steamer was departing for Europe on March 1. So Jackson wrote a "report" of the meeting—including the text of his speech and the implied approval of his audience—before the meeting had taken place, and gave the "account" to the *Daily Advertiser*. Once it was ready, he got hundreds of advance copies of the newspaper and sent them on the steamer to his contacts in Europe.

After that Morton went to see Warren, who was "greatly enraged by Jackson's artifice." Some of the hospital's staff urged Morton to collect documentary evidence of his claim and send this to the Academy of Sciences in Paris, accompanied by a protest against Jackson's misstatements; others, however, urged moderation. Dr. Gould, in particular, disapproved of the plan, arguing that the unknown Morton would not be believed against Jackson in Europe and must instead come to an understanding with Jackson in Boston. To Gould, who was acting as mediator, Jackson said he had always hoped for an understanding with Morton, that he desired an unbiased judgment between them. Fülöp-Miller comments, "This plan would keep Morton from protesting in Europe. He [Jackson] would gain time." Novelistic, but again plausible: Jackson dragged out the negotiations until both the April steamer and the May steamer had left.

Taking action at last, Morton sent a provisional report to the French Academy of the Sciences by the June steamer and promised detailed proofs to be sent a month later. Morton filled twelve cases with the detailed interviews and other documents he had compiled and sent nearly as much documentation to von Humboldt as well. Morton's two friends in Paris had left; hearing nothing from them, he wrote directly to the Academy but received no answer. After eight months, he learned that his materials had been held up by French customs. He found an agent, to whom he paid a considerable sum, but still needed someone to take charge of the papers and see that they reached their destination. Someone suggested an American named Brewster living in Paris. Morton sent Brewster money but heard nothing for two years. Finally, Brewster wrote Morton that he did not have room for the cases; he advised selling them as old paper. Finally Morton discovered that Brewster was Wells's agent in Paris and, in conjunction with the dentist's widow, was trying to get his claims recognized.

"Benefactor of Mankind," Fülöp-Miller's next chapter, points out that, while physicians and surgeons adopted anesthesia quickly, "the scientific societies were less easy to convert . . . only, at long last, over months or years, will anything so novel as anesthesia be passed to the credit account." A French philanthropist named Montyon had left the Academy of the Sciences a sum of money intended for anyone whom the academy should consider a "Benefactor of Mankind." The 1847–1848 prize was to go to the discoverer of anesthesia, but whether to Morton or to Jackson was a matter of considerable debate. Morton had made the apparatus and sent instructions as to its use; the reports from Boston, from Dr. Bott in London, and Dr. Simpson in Edinburgh all named him as the discoverer of ether anesthesia. Beaumont argued powerfully for Jackson, cleverly calling him the Columbus of the new surgical world and Morton the lookout man who called "Land ho!" So a commission was established to study the matter. (Wells's claim was considered briefly and rejected.) Three years elapsed in which no decision was made. Finally, on February 25, 1850, the following resolution was adopted: "Mr. Jackson and Mr. Morton were both indispensable. Had it not been for the persistency, the far-reaching vision, the courage, nay the audacity of Mr. Morton, Mr. Jackson's observations would probably have passed unnoticed and unapplied; but for the observations of Mr. Jackson, on the other hand, it is likely that Mr. Morton's ideas would never have been crowned with success."

The Commission accordingly recommended dividing the prize between the two men, twenty-five hundred francs apiece. "But the enmity between Morton and Jackson had by now exceeded all bounds," says the author. Gravely disappointed, or pretending to be, Jackson accepted the prize. Morton protested the decision and rejected the prize, saying that sharing it with an unrightful claimant would be an insult. The unclaimed prize made the Commission uneasy, particularly as the Academy had since received "a great deal more evidence which spoke convincingly in favor of Morton's claim to be the 'only genuine discoverer.'" The Commission decided to strike a gold medal, exactly worth his share of the prize, honoring Morton as a Benefactor of Mankind.

Jackson was "rabid": he had only a sum of money, whereas Morton had a gold medal with his name on it surrounded by a laurel crown. Jackson spread the rumor in Boston that Morton had had the medal struck himself and forged the document that came with it. Certain other prizes, notably one in London for ten thousand pounds, were not awarded at all due to the debate about who deserved credit. Other countries gave awards to one or the other of the two men.

Jackson recognized that in Boston he had to use different tactics to undermine his opponent than the ones he had used with the scientific societies and courts of the world. "In Boston he would get the better of the adversary by undermining Morton's moral standing, and try to cut Morton's financial resources. Then, when he had been successful in these matters, he would be able to push his own claims without fear."

Morton had neglected his practice for so long that it declined and his income fell off. To support himself he had drafted a plan for licenses to be granted under his patent; hospitals, benevolent institutions, and doctors who could not pay would have free use, doctors in small towns would pay much less than those in populous areas, et cetera. In May 1846, however, when war with Mexico broke out, Morton offered to supply inhalers to the Army and Navy wholesale and to instruct Army surgeons in their use. The services accepted his offer but refused to pay for the requisite licenses, a decision which was reported in the *New York Herald*. Jackson, whom Fülöp-Miller seems to see behind or around each of Morton's reverses, "was quick to grasp the full significance of the decision"—if the government was going to use the inhalers without compensating the inventor, then anyone could do so. With this in mind, Jackson asked Eddy if he would ever get any money from the patent and, when Eddy said he thought not, Jackson had his name removed from it. Subsequently, Jackson spoke before the Massachusetts Medical Society, claiming to have been duped by Morton into participating in the patent and expressing his wish that his discovery be used freely by anyone who was interested. He said he did not seek to make money from the suffering of others "after the shameless manner of a certain dentist of this town." If the government's action had lessened the value of the patent, Jackson's declaration destroyed its effects altogether. The doctors present at the meeting loudly applauded Jackson's decision: Morton had been stigmatized as "an avaricious rascal."

Jackson then told those who had bought licenses—both individual doctors and investors who had bought rights to market the inhalers—that they had been cheated: they had paid cash for what could be had for free. Morton was now besieged by doctors and agents demanding their money back and threatening to prosecute. Morton used his savings to satisfy some of these claims, then borrowed money to pay others. Jackson also convinced the manufacturer of the inhalers that he would lose his investment, with the result that he became Morton's relentless creditor. According to Fülöp-Miller, "Morton was unceasingly harassed with prosecutions. His life became one of unending vexation. Behind all this, Jackson had his part to play, stirring up the discontented. Morton, at his wits' end for money, harassed day and night, could not be a dangerous rival. Jackson was well-to-do and carefree. These advantages gave him an almost invincible superiority."

Resuming his dental practice, Morton worked from morning to night to pay off creditors and to support his family on the remainder. A creditor appeared and would not leave without a bill of sale on Morton's dental instruments and library, which he received. As if all this were not enough, suddenly his patients began appearing at his office in great agitation at having been sent bills for services for which they had already paid. "By degrees, Morton realized what had happened. Someone had been prying into his account books, and had managed to get judgment summonses sent to all his patients, whether they had paid their bills or not."

With this, even his assistants left him. One went into business for himself on the floor above Morton's office. Through these events, and Jackson's further rumormongering, an anti-Morton atmosphere was created and eventually Morton had a complete nervous breakdown. His doctor ordered absolute rest and avoidance of anything that might vex him. But "Jackson had composed a scandalous memorial about him, running to many hundred pages. It had been manifolded, and one of the copies would certainly go to Washington. Morton must compose a counterblast, must leave no stone unturned to defeat Jackson's calumnies." Morton moved with his family to their country house in West Needham. Soon, however, even that house was seized by his creditors.

However, Morton's fortunes began to improve somewhat, "precisely because of the poverty into which Jackson's intrigues had plunged him." Morton was practically penniless at West Needham, his family's possessions packed for removal. "Hatred miscalculates, forgetting compassion," Fülöp-Miller observes near the beginning of his next chapter, "The Conscience of the Nation." At this point delegates from Massachusetts General Hospital arrived in West Needham with an award of one thousand dollars they had voted him. A wave of sympathy for Morton and a sense of the injustice done him began to spread. "Everyone in Washington was talking about the scandalous way in which Morton had been treated." The government had infringed Morton's patent but a national grant could be made in compensation. A resolution to award him one hundred thousand dollars was under consideration. Summoned to Washington, Morton was received as a national hero; there he was acclaimed and widely entertained.

Reading of these developments, Jackson went to Washington to see what he could do to prevent the award. To discredit Morton, he had secured the signatures of 143 dentists and doctors in support of his own claims. Jackson reconsidered his strategy, however, for now Morton was a man "whose name was revered by a whole nation." He waited until Congress was about to vote the award and then announced his own claim, with the supporting affidavits. The decision on the award was postponed while a committee considered Jackson's claim. To Jackson's annoyance, however, the committee immediately applied to Massachusetts General Hospital; Warren, Bigelow, and the other physicians there replied that they had not heard of ether by inhalation until October 1846 when it was suggested by Dr. Morton. The committee decided that what Jackson's claim amounted to was that he made Morton certain proposals which the latter was able to use in furtherance of earlier successful experiments and laboratory work. The discovery was ruled exclusively Morton's because the real discoverer is a man who openly demonstrates practical use. Before Jenner many milkmaids knew that exposure to cowpox would safeguard them against smallpox, but it is not they who are honored for the discovery of vaccination. "The results of the investigation which took place on Jackson's own initiative were fatal to Jackson's claims . . . [even more] a formidable indictment of Jackson."

Jackson fought on, renouncing all financial awards, claiming the honor of the nation was at stake and the staff of Massachusetts General Hospital was in league with Morton. Therefore, the opinion of foreign experts should be consulted. Jackson's renunciation rang false and his argument was rejected. The House overwhelmingly decided that Morton was the discoverer of anesthesia and was entitled to the reward, upon receipt of which he would surrender his patent.

Jackson's next move was unpredictable and, judged in relation to his goal—the defeat of Morton—brilliant. Proceeding to Hartford, he approached the widow of Horace Wells. He told her that her husband and himself, not

Morton, were the true discoverers of anesthesia. Jackson said he needed and desired no financial reward but he could not abide the poor widow of a co-discoverer to be cheated out of her rightful reward. She gave Jackson her approval and he set to work collecting materials, interviewing the Hartford doctors and patients who had been most interested in the matter. He compiled an exhaustive report and engaged a lawyer named Truman Smith, who was also a senator from Connecticut.

The day came when the grant for Morton was to be considered by the Senate. Smith rose and his "voice quivered with indignation, and his whole body shook" as he denounced the attempt to steal money from the Treasury for an impostor who had robbed a poor widow and defenseless children of the benefits of Wells's discovery.

Smith convinced the Senate to postpone action on the matter until it was looked into. "Every delay would strengthen Jackson's position and weaken Morton's," comments Fülöp-Miller. A month had passed when, on January 21, 1852, Smith presented his materials to the subcommittee two weeks before the congressional session was to close. The "Mortonists" produced Wells's letter to Morton and Dr. Hayward's report that Wells was not the discoverer. It still seemed likely at this point that Congress would make the award to Morton in the following session.

Even so, Smith assured Jackson they would win, but Jackson decided that no more was to be gained by his own support of Wells's claim. For years Jackson had clipped and cross-referenced journals in medicine, chemistry, and geology. He remembered a notice about a doctor who had claimed to be the first ever to administer ether to a patient and pursued it. It turned out to be an 1849 notice about an operation performed in 1842 by Dr. Crawford Long of Athens, Georgia. Long had not published his results at the time. Pretending to his friends to be doing geological research in another part of Georgia, Jackson stopped in Athens to call upon Dr. Long.

There Jackson learned that Long, having attended ether parties and himself inhaled the drug, had cut out a tumor from one patient and amputated the finger of another under ether. Long and a number of observers felt that the painlessness of the first operation was due to mesmerism as much as ether. But when a black boy, who was a slave, had badly burned two fingers, Long had used ether to amputate the first finger, painlessly, but not to remove the second, at which the boy screamed with pain.

Long's experiments with ether had made him suspect in the town in which he practiced. "His practice was falling off, for people were afraid to consult him. He was cold-shouldered in the streets. The well-to-do planters refused any longer to bid him good morning. One day some of the elders of the village called on him [and] advised the young doctor to abandon his follies, for, they said, if he should have a mishap and kill someone with ether, there was not a doubt that he would be lynched." Long stopped using ether and did not publish his results until Morton's operations had become world famous. Of all persons concerned with the discovery of anesthesia, Fülöp-Miller observes, Long was the only one "whose life was unperturbed by vexatious disputes about priority . . . at least until March 8, 1854." That was the day Jackson called on him, stating as his business "to have a talk with the man who was the first to use ether during a surgical operation. . . . I want to help you to your rights." Jackson proposed that, since his own work with ether went back to 1838 but, unlike Long, he had never used it in a surgical case, they were codiscoverers. Long politely made Jackson understand that if what Jackson had said about him were true, he had no intention of sharing his discovery with anyone. Jackson agreed, Fülöp-Miller observes, "because the annihilation of Morton was nearer to his heart than even his own (unfounded) claim to priority." With Jackson coordinating the campaign, Long's assistants, his wife, and his patients wrote to Washington. At the opening of the new congressional session, Senator Smith was ready to press Horace Wells's claims and Senator Dawson of Georgia rose to present the claim of Dr. Crawford Long. The result of the Long claim was further committee work and postponement after postponement of a vote on the measure.

Sick of it all, Morton returned to West Needham. What few funds he had were invested in farming: he raised fowl and pigs, grew fruits, vegetables, and flowers, and engaged in dairy farming. The farm thrived—indeed he won $128 in prizes from the Norfolk County Fair in nearly every category: best dairy produce, important economic improvements, having the finest pair of farm horses and the best breeding sow, and "for his admirable geese."

Morton's farming idyll was interrupted by a letter from Senator Shields of Illinois saying that a motion to buy Morton's patent rights was before the Congress and that he must come to Washington immediately. "Never again was he to know another peaceful morning," the author notes. President Pierce, averring his sympathy for Morton, nevertheless wished to be sure of his ground. He asked the Smithsonian Institution for its opinion on the scientific value of Morton's patent and also consulted Army and Navy authorities. During the delay, Morton incurred enormous debts to moneylenders who advanced him funds for his expenses in Washington. Pierce himself granted Morton an interview in which he asked Morton why he had never brought suit to defend his patent from infringement. Morton replied that he did not wish to deny anyone the benefits of anesthesia. Pierce said that was all very well but Morton should now bring suit against the government to establish his claim.

While deciding whether or not to sue, Morton returned to West Needham. There he found his wife in tears—all of their furniture, livestock, and other possessions had been attached and were to be sold at auction to pay his debts. A Mr. Stone, his chief creditor, believed in Morton's cause so he bought the other notes of hand, took the farm and the other attached items in pledge, and advanced Morton an additional sum to begin his lawsuit.

Morton's attorney in the matter decided to sue a Navy surgeon. Jackson

"Believe me, I'd rather be you than President, any day."
Porter Hall as Franklin Pierce reassures Joel McCrea as
Morton in TRIUMPH OVER PAIN/THE GREAT MOMENT.

learned of the lawsuit and called on the surgeon, arguing that Morton was not the first to use anesthesia, that Crawford Long was, and Long would testify that he wished all doctors to use anesthesia without a licensing charge. While the suit was pending the opinion of the medical profession, that of newspapers and with them the public, turned against Morton. "The harvest season had come for Jackson's schemes," Fülöp-Miller observes. "The slanders he had for years been busily spreading about Morton now bore abundant fruit."

Back in West Needham, in front of his own house, which in fact he no longer owned, Morton was hanged and burned in effigy by his neighbors. As Elizabeth Morton later reported, "He was criticized on all sides for taking out the patent. Abuse and ridicule were showered upon him by the public press, from the pulpit, and also by prominent medical journals."

Physically and emotionally exhausted, Morton had another nervous breakdown. On December 1, 1862, Judge Shipman held that the patent, granted to Morton sixteen years earlier, was invalid. "A discovery is not patentable," he wrote. "It is only where the explorer has gone beyond the domain of mere discovery and has laid hold of the new principle, force, or law, and connected it with some particular medium or mechanical contrivance through which it acts on the material world that he can secure the exclusive control of it under the patent laws."

One by one, Morton pawned his medals to get food for his wife and children. An agricultural implement salesman later reported that in winter 1863 he had seen "a remarkable-looking broken-down man, with threadbare clothing and wasted features, standing beside a small handcart laden with wood. He was arguing with the baker's wife, trying to get some bread in exchange for his wood, which had been gathered in the forest. His children had had nothing to eat for days." The salesman learned that the man's name was Dr. Morton and that his friends had bought his house back for him when it was sold at auction.

In 1864–1865, Morton volunteered his services in the administration of anesthesia to the Northern Army. A witness reported that General Grant denied a civilian doctor's request for an ambulance to visit field hospitals—until he learned that the man was Morton. Grant ordered that Morton get his ambulance and anything else he needed and that he receive also tent and mess privileges at headquarters and a servant.

After the war, Morton returned to a life at West Needham no less gloomy than before. He was ignored for three years by everyone except his creditors. On the morning of July 5, 1868, he received a copy of a magazine with an article advocating the claims of Jackson to the great discovery and denouncing Morton. After twenty years, Jackson was still campaigning and making fraudulent accusations. Morton, whose health had been failing, became extremely agitated and insisted on going to New York to combat Jackson's attacks. In New York he had a serious attack and Elizabeth was sent for. After the couple's ride through Central Park, Morton dropped the reins, jumped to the ground and stared into the dark. Then he collapsed and soon afterward died. It was July 15, 1868.

As often happens, Morton was a more formidable adversary in death than he had been in life. Jackson kept up the fight with endless letters and other means, but Morton had begun to be almost universally recognized and acclaimed as the discoverer of anesthesia. Jackson took to drink and was eventually fired as the state geological surveyor because of alcoholism. In mid-1873, having finished yet another anti-Morton pamphlet, Jackson suffered the first of several bouts of insanity. Fülöp-Miller places this event in front of the Morton monument in Mount Auburn Cemetery in Boston, which bears the inscription:

William T. G. Morton

Inventor and revealer of anesthetic inhalation,
By whom pain in surgery was averted and annulled;
Before whom in all time surgery was agony,
Since whom Science has control of Pain.

According to Fülöp-Miller, "Jackson began to scream, to thrash with his arms, fighting shadows . . . the more he became aware of his impotence, the louder did he scream, and the more hopelessly did he fling his arms about and trample the earth. . . . It was the madness which, year after year, had worn the semblance of the chemist and physicist Charles Thomas Jackson. . . . Now this madness had broken loose from the enveloping shell . . . to stand before the Morton monument in its crude, naked, elemental energy." Jackson was eventually placed in McLean Asylum, where he survived for several years until his death in 1880.

*   *   *

Sturges's first note on *Triumph over Pain* was a three-page scene draft written March 18, 1939, in which Morton consults Jackson, his former teacher, in search of a way to neutralize the pain of his dental patients. The draft begins with Jackson's line, "Oh, yes! Morton. Of course I remember you . . . you were rather a dull student." Morton replies, "Yes, well, you didn't keep us doubled up with laughter, either." Coming to the point of his visit, Morton says,

MORTON
I'm looking for something to minimize pain . . .

JACKSON
(Interrupting)
Aren't we all!

MORTON
I don't mean generally I mean specifically: people get in my chair
and start to yell . . .

JACKSON
(Interrupting again)
What do you mean, your chair?
(He laughs)
Have you become a barber?

Jackson's line becomes, in the August 2 script, "Are you a barber now?" This is both a sharper taunt than its predecessor and, at least as spoken by Julius Tannen in the film, considerably more humorous.

MORTON
(Bitterly)
I'm a dentist! I didn't have enough money to finish medicine.

261

JACKSON
(Without sympathy)
Then you shouldn't have gone in for it in the first place! One of
the cankers of the profession is the number of youths without
funds or proper background who try to worm their way in for the
rich rewards they imagine it promises.

Sturges here strikes several notes that will echo through all subsequent phases
of the project: Morton's frustrated medical aspirations; the class barriers to
entering the professions that existed in Morton's era; and the low estate of
dentists in that time, a condition which later weakens Morton's claim to have
discovered the anesthetic properties of ether, especially vis-à-vis the eminent
Jackson. In regard to the pain problem, Jackson jokes, why not subdue the
patient's cries with a small orchestra, or freeze a tooth by filling the patient
with ice? Morton persists, however, until he gets Jackson to suggest something he might use.

JACKSON
(Getting an idea)
All right! There's another way of producing cold: try ethyl
chloride.

MORTON
What's that?

JACKSON
(to high heaven)
What's that! You are a credit to my classes and the living proof
that plowboys should stay behind the horse! Ethyl chloride . . .
what's that! IT'S ETHER, MY FRIEND, CHLORIC ETHER! DO
YOU THINK YOU CAN REMEMBER THAT?

The draft ends with the setting of a scene that does not take place.

DISSOLVE TO:

BURNETT'S DRUG STORE
This is a Boston drug store, 1846.

[END OF DRAFT]

On March 22, Sturges wrote a five-page draft of the film's opening. Preparations for a modern operation are shown during the main titles, after which
there is a scene between a little boy who is about to be operated on and his
parents who tell him that, thanks to ether, the operation will be painless and,
it is strongly implied, the boy will recover.

A-2   CLOSE SHOT – THE LITTLE BOY BEING ANESTHETIZED

THE ANESTHETIST (Slowly)
Now just one more deep one . . . and away we go . . . and there
we are.

262

He reaches for a valve and the CAMERA MOVES IN TO A
CLOSEUP OF THE LABEL ON THE ETHER TANK. We hear
a loud hissing as we --

DISSOLVE VERY SLOWLY TO:

A-3   A LARGE GOLD MEDAL IN A MAN'S HAND

It is from the Paris Academy of Sciences, inscribed in French
to "Dr. William Thomas Green Morton, The Benefactor of
Mankind" for his discovery of anesthesia. The CAMERA
TRUCKS BACK and Frederick T. Johnson, the pawnbroker,
tests the gold with aqua fortis. Now he looks suspiciously
through his wicket.

JOHNSON
Where'd you get this?

A-4   MORTON – FRAMED IN THE WICKET

He is only forty-four but illness, injustice, and privation make
him appear much more.

MORTON
(Pointing a shaking finger)
It says right there on the edge of the medal. That's the one from
the Paris Academy, isn't it?

A-5   THE PAWNBROKER – PAST MORTON

JOHNSON
I didn't ask you where it came from I asked where you got it.
This is enscribed to "Dr. William Thomas Green Morton, the
Benefactor of Mankind . . . with the gratitude of humanity."

A-6   MORTON – THROUGH THE WICKET

MORTON
Well, give me as much as you can for it . . . I'm Dr. Morton.

DISSOLVE TO:

A-7   THE MODERN OPERATING ROOM

The surgeon is handed a scalpel. He bends over the child.

A-8   THE SURGEON'S HANDS

They make a quick incision then exchange instruments.

A-9   CLOSE SHOT – THE LITTLE BOY'S FACE

A smile flickers on his lips. He is dreaming . . . possibly about
baseball.

DISSOLVE TO:

A-10   A WINDOW LABELED: "W. T. G. MORTON – DENTIST"

We hear the blood-curdling yell of a man in pain.

The first part of the draft reveals that Sturges had a flashback structure in mind from the outset of the project. Here the scene of the modern operation comprises a framing story that negotiates the return to different periods of Morton's life, notably the abject poverty of his postdiscovery years and the much earlier events that led up to the discovery itself. Was the modern operation to have served as a framing story for the whole film and, if so, how might it have been expanded to do so satisfactorily? A difficulty in this respect is that the characters of the framing story have only an abstract relationship to the story of Morton: they have benefited from his discovery. They are also composed of the thinnest cardboard.

The Morton-pawnbroker scene has difficulties also. Why is Morton pawning his medals? How much will he get and what will he do with the money? In fact there are vast omissions on either side of this slim scene: everything that happened to Morton between his discovery and his appearance at the pawnshop, and everything that happened to him after he pawned his medals. One almost expects a second framing story to open here, with flashbacks and flash-forwards to fill in these gaps.

Having arrived at the dental office of young Dr. Morton, the draft continues:

A-11   HIGH CAMERA SHOT DOWN ON EBEN FROST ACROSS
        THE STREET

He stands in front of the swinging doors of a saloon clutching a swollen jaw. Now he starts timidly across the street.

A-12   THE WINDOW LABELED: "W. T. G. MORTON – DENTIST"

There is another blood-curdling yell.

A-13   HIGH CAMERA ANGLE DOWN ON FROST

He turns hastily and hurries through the swinging doors of the saloon.

A-14   DR. MORTON – IN HIS OFFICE

His back IS TO US as he bends over the patient. Suddenly both men tense their muscles, there is a horrible gargling groan, then Morton straightens up and a tooth clanks into a metal pan. Now Morton turns TOWARD US and we see that he is in his twenties. His face is beaded with sweat. He pours a glass of whiskey and gives it to the fainting patient in the chair. The latter is almost too weak to hold the glass.

MORTON

Come on now, pull yourself together, it's all over.

264

He helps the man down the whiskey. Some of it slobbers out.

THE PATIENT
Oh, God!

MORTON
You don't think I enjoyed it, do you?

He turns, pours himself a drink and tosses it off quickly.

THE PATIENT
(Staggering to his feet)
How much do I owe you?

MORTON
How've you been doing lately?

THE PATIENT
Not so well. With this administration a man hasn't got much of a chance.

MORTON
What do you expect with Polk for President? Call it a dollar.

THE PATIENT
Thanks, Doc.

MORTON
S'all right.

The patient exits. Morton throws the dollar in a drawer and lifts out a day-book.

A-15 MORTON'S HAND WRITING

He draws a line under the preceding day's business, then writes:

"August 29th, 1846
1 – Extraction (Second Molar L.L.)"

A-16 MORTON WITH THE BOOK IN HIS HANDS

He blots what he has written, puts the book back in the drawer, takes the dollar out and bounces it on marble for genuineness, then puts it back in the drawer and goes over to the window to watch for business. Suddenly his look becomes intent.

A-17 HIGH CAMERA SHOT DOWN ON EBEN FROST

He is pretty drunk by now. He starts to weave across the street. Suddenly he stops and looks up suspiciously.

A-18 CLOSE LOW CAMERA SHOT – MORTON THROUGH THE WINDOW

He looks down at us intently.

265

A-19   CLOSE HIGH CAMERA SHOT – EBEN FROST

He looks up at us in horror and feels of his jaw.

A-20   CLOSE LOW CAMERA SHOT – MORTON THROUGH THE
WINDOW

He remembers to smile pleasantly.

A-21   HIGH CAMERA SHOT – DOWN ON EBEN FROST

Galvanized into action by the smile he turns and staggers back
into the saloon.

A-22   CLOSE SHOT – MORTON – THROUGH HIS WINDOW

He looks very sour.

[END OF DRAFT]

Sturges's portrait of the dentist as a young man is charming. Sturges uses
the figure of Eben Frost to build suspense in the scene: will he summon the
courage to put himself in Morton's care? This is suspense of the back-to-the-
future sort since it concerns whether or not Frost will make his rendezvous
with destiny by climbing the stairs of his local dentist. Morton, for his part, is
presumably ready for the rendezvous with a flask of ether up his sleeve and
some prior experience in using it. The scene suggests nothing of this, however. The entire process of Morton's discovery and experiments with ether
has been elided.

It is unlikely that Sturges had an overall plan for the film when he wrote
this draft scene, but that fact itself is noteworthy. Sturges's practice was not to
decide upon a flashback structure and a framing story in advance and then
to revise it as the project's main story developed. Rather, he recast the flashbacks and the framing story at the same time as he was recasting and revising
the main story. They were all being developed simultaneously or, more correctly, in fits and starts along several axes of advance. As the draft scenes for
Triumph over Pain show, he worked forward from his framing story drafts to
consider possible scenes and, indeed, possible plots in the main story. Inversely, his work on the main story led him at various times to consider new
kinds of framing stories and flashback structures.

The draft scene of March 22 was the last work Sturges did on the project
until April 16, almost a month later. On that day he wrote two pages which
built on the first page of the March 22 draft and took it in a different direction. The first of the two pages begins with the shot of the anesthesia apparatus in the modern operation and makes only slight changes. Instead of the
label on the ether tank, the camera now moves into a close-up of what is described as "the big gas machine." On the sound track "we hear the rhythmic
breathing of the re-breathing bag," and then the camera moves in closer for a
shot of the label on the ether container. Morton now "clutches a thin overcoat

around his throat." This time the pawnbroker asks for a translation of the medal, "which is in French or Italian or something," which Morton provides.

> MORTON
> It says: From the French Academy of the Sciences, to Dr. William Thomas Green Morton, the Benefactor of Mankind . . . with the Gratitude of Humanity.

> JOHNSON
> (Suspiciously)
> Who's that supposed to be?

> MORTON
> (After a slight pause)
> That's supposed to be me.

> JOHNSON
> Can you prove it?

> MORTON
> (Anxiously)
> Oh, yes. You see . . .

He pulls some more medals out of his pocket and puts them on the wicket ledge.

> MORTON
> Here's the Cross of the Order of St. Vladimir, that's from the Tsar; here's the Cross of the Order of Vasa, that's from the King of Sweden; I can't read this one . . . anyway, they're all inscribed to me. I'll spend them in Washington as I need them. I may not have to pawn them all.
> (He drums nervously on the ledge of the wicket.)

A-7   JOHNSON – PAST MORTON

Johnson fingers the medal and gives Morton a long suspicious look.

> JOHNSON
> What are you going to Washington for?

A-8   MORTON – PAST JOHNSON

[END OF DRAFT]

The April 16 scene fragment begins with a defeated, ill Morton. It is possible that Sturges planned to cut, or dissolve, at some point to Morton's early life and the stages that led up to the discovery. When and how he planned to do so—whether or not he had a plan at all at this stage—is unclear. The pawnbroker's final question seems to imply a scene or scenes in Washington—where Morton's hopes for recognition were finally dashed—and perhaps even scenes of the debt, poverty, and early death that followed.

267

These notes—comprising ten pages in all—were all that Sturges did on the project between March 18, when he took his first note, and April 24, a little over five weeks later. Between April 25 and May 17, Sturges worked steadily, completing, among other things, a long outline of the events leading up to the discovery, a much shorter outline (and a few scene drafts) of the events following the discovery, and three more versions of the flashback/framing story structure.

Starting April 25 and concluding May 3, Sturges wrote a twenty-three-page plot outline called "THE SEQUENCE OF EVENTS THAT LED UP TO THE DISCOVERY." Consisting of twenty-five numbered paragraphs, this outline did for what became the second half of the film something like what his "original stories" did for his fiction films. It furnished a detailed story summary that provided the basis for writing his first screenplay draft. Indeed, once the outline was finished, Sturges did no more on this part of the film until he began to write his first full screenplay draft in mid-July, over two months later.

The sequence of events leading up to and including Morton's discovery and public demonstration of anesthesia is, quantitatively speaking, the mainspring of all of Sturges's script versions and of the film that he shot. Even in the mutilated film that Paramount released, the discovery sequence suffers least—DeSylva's editors primarily altered the film's first part, which treats Morton's later years, and the framing story. Sturges's outline begins, as does Fülöp-Miller's account, with Horace Wells.

> 1. Posters advertising Colton's laughing gas exhibition for refined ladies and gentlemen . . . the soirée itself at which we see the eight strong men engaged to protect the audience from the violence of the entertainers. Here we meet [Horace] Wells, the Hartford dentist, who notices that one of the inhalers has injured himself BUT NOT FELT IT.
> 2. Wells calls on Colton and arranges for the latter to give him gas while a third party shall pull one of Wells' teeth . . . the extraction is enormously successful. Wells feels no pain whatsoever. He is exultant. He prophesies great things including a monopoly for himself and Colton in "Painless extraction."

As described by Fülöp-Miller, these events were reasonably sedate. In Sturges's hands, they sound lurid, even—the posters, the soirée, the eight strong men, the wound that is not felt, the devil's pact between the sideshow charlatan and the knowledge-mad, power-mad dentist—*Caligari*-like.

Perhaps it is perilous to begin a biographical film with a character other than one's subject, particularly one who is a claimant to his achievements. So, in any case, Hollywood wisdom instructs. It is also hard to imagine a framing story that would flash back to Wells rather than Morton. In the event, Sturges dropped the Wells sequence in all his screenplay versions, beginning the story of the discovery process with the events of paragraph 3. The genre marriage of biopic and expressionist film was not to be.

3. We see Dr. W. T. G. Morton's office window and through it hear the yells of a suffering patient. Inside the office we see Morton telling his patient to pipe down. Morton crosses to the waiting room door and catches two patients exiting. He manages to save one of them . . . Morton yanks the tooth, wipes the sweat off his brow then hurries to the waiting room. The last patient is just slipping out the door. Disgusted, Morton returns to his operating room, collects a dollar and marks the fee and the date in his cash book. Suddenly he puts on his hat and walks out of the office.

4. The laboratory of Dr. Charles Thomas Jackson, a remarkable if somewhat eccentric scientist. Morton is announced and Jackson recognizes him as one of his former medical pupils, and a rather dull one. In answer to Morton's request for something, anything, to prevent patients from yelling so loud, Jackson tells him to try dropping ethyl chloride (chloric ether) on painful teeth.

5. Burnett's drug store. Morton hurries in and asks for some ether. "Chloric or sulfuric?" says Burnett. "Chloric," says Morton, but while the druggist is preparing it for him he asks about sulfuric ether and eventually decides to take a little of that too.

In Fülöp-Miller's book Morton was not a beginning dentist but a successful one, making ten thousand dollars a year, when he returned to medical school to begin his search for dentistry without pain. The Morton of Sturges's outline cannot afford to return to medical school: he pursues painless dentistry, on his own, to save a failing practice. Fülöp-Miller's Jackson did recommend chloric ether drops for dental pain but he also discussed, on at least one later occasion, the properties of sulfuric ether, which at the time was used mainly as a treatment for asthma. Sturges's omission of this fact makes his protagonist more single-handedly the discoverer of ether anesthesia—although not quite in the way one might suppose.

In the outline Morton asks the druggist for chloric ether but buys a bottle of sulfuric ether also as a kind of afterthought—this is intelligent curiosity on Morton's part since he remembers quite well that Jackson had recommended chloric ether. In the screenplay versions that follow, however, Morton orders both kinds of ether because he cannot remember which Jackson told him to buy. Once home he confuses the two bottles and thereby discovers the anesthetic effects of sulfuric ether only accidentally. Reducing the scope of Jackson's advice does not increase Morton's scientific mastery: it creates room for him to stumble onto the truth. Sturges thereby shows what he later called "thought coming in through the backdoor." Indeed, Sturges makes Morton less astute, less intelligent, and less systematic than he actually was.

6. Morton hurries back to his office and finds his ex-partner Wells waiting for him. The latter is full of his tremendous discovery. "That's funny," says Morton. "I was just trying to do the same thing." Almost reluctantly he puts down his bottles of ether. "You don't have to bother about it," says Wells, "I've already done it." And he tells Morton about the experiments he has made and the successes he has had in fifty per cent of the cases. "Why didn't you have a hundred per

cent success?" says Morton. "If it works with one it ought to work with all." "How do I know?" says Wells. "One out of two is already a lot better than none." "Did it make your patients sick?" says Morton. "No," says Wells, looking away uneasily. Then he decides to tell the truth. "Well, one or two of them, but they got over it." "You'd better find out a little more about it," says Morton. "Come on, I'll take you over and introduce you to Dr. Jackson . . ."

7. Dr. Jackson is dead against the idea and advises the young men to give it up. He tells them about Davy, Faraday, Beddoes and others who tried it and tells them they cannot hope to succeed where science has failed. Morton does not see the point of this argument and Wells refuses to give up the idea. "Well don't say I didn't warn you," says Dr. Jackson.

8. Wells' experiment at Harvard Medical School. Morton assists. At the first yank the patient comes to, drunk and fighting. The students yell gleefully then become angry and Wells and Morton are thrown out bodily.

Once paragraphs 1 and 2 are eliminated, we no longer know who Wells is or what his method of painkilling is. This information must then be introduced when the character himself first appears. As he often managed to do, Sturges here skillfully fuses expository necessity with the dramatic need to move the action forward. In the outline, Wells seems to have come to Boston only to present his ideas in general and Jackson evaluates them on that basis. In the August 2 screenplay and later versions, Wells is in Boston to give his demonstration at Harvard Medical School the very morning of his visit to Morton. Hence the ideas he spouts, and Jackson's evaluation of them, have much sharper dramatic focus. Wells's confession of only 50 percent success rate with his method also has more significance if he is to make a public demonstration that day. It makes Wells seem reckless, if not unstable.

The outline continues:

9. Morton's office. The young men return disconsolately and Morton picks up his ether bottle and looks at it. "Why bother with that stuff?" says Wells angrily. "I tell you my invention works perfectly. I just didn't give that fellow enough, that's all." As they argue, a patient arrives. Morton insists upon trying the ether drops. They are not of much help although they minimize the pain slightly. "Let me try the gas," says Wells in a whisper. Reluctantly Morton consents. Wells administers the gas and, anxious to avoid a repetition of the afternoon's fiasco, he gives a great deal too much of it. Morton extracts the tooth. [Later in the outline] He feels the patient's pulse then yells at Wells. "Go and get a doctor quick, there's one at the end of the hall! This man is either dead or so close to it that . . ." They are still working on the patient at midnight. Wells is hysterical with fear and swears that if the man lives he, Wells, will never experiment again with human life. Presently the patient regains consciousness . . . Now the patient discovers that his tooth is out, smiles weakly and says: "Why that's wonderful, doctor, I never felt a thing." Wells says goodbye and hurries out into the night. Morton looks very pensive.

By having them occur on the same day, Sturges telescopes the later experiment in Hartford, in which Wells used too much nitrous oxide and the patient almost died, with the failure of his Harvard demonstration. When Wells says he will never again experiment with human life he effectively removes himself from the race to find a painkiller, as was indeed the case after the Hartford incident. In paragraph 9, Morton has a bottle of chloric ether on hand and wishes to try it on a patient. In actuality, Morton had tried chloric ether drops in May 1844 but had not as yet experimented with, or even considered, sulfuric ether. Wells's experiments with nitrous oxide seem to have suggested the idea of inhalation to Morton, an influence Sturges diminishes by placing a bottle of sulfuric ether in Morton's possession at the time of Wells's visit.

> 10. Morton's home. He comes in to the great relief of his bride who has been worrying about him. He answers her briefly then gets into a long white nightgown and hops into bed. She asks him what the matter is and begins to weep when he answers her shortly. He comes to and tells her that he loves her then blows out the candle. A ray of moonlight, however, shows us that he is not sleeping . . . we see his sleeping wife. Drowsily she feels for Morton then comes to as she discovers he is gone. She lights the candle and gets out of bed . . . we discover Morton on top of a ladder in his library. By the light of a candle stuck to the edge of a shelf he is reading Faraday's monograph of 1818 in Pereira's Materia Medica. His wife enters and reproaches him but Morton merely says: "Listen to this." Trembling with excitement he reads her the part about ether.

This is the outline's first mention of Mrs. Morton, who as yet has no name of her own. At this point, Elizabeth has virtually no role in the events that led to her husband's discovery. Her growing importance as a character and her increasing participation in the action are principal features of the revision process as a whole.

Even in the outline it is only after Wells's fiasco at Harvard that Morton begins consciously to experiment with ether. This accords with the historical facts; indeed, Wells's demonstration took place in 1844, before Morton and Elizabeth were married. Even in the screenplay drafts, however, Morton marries first, experiences difficulty in setting up a dental practice, experiments—unknowingly—with sulfuric ether, and then assists Wells at Harvard. In later versions of the screenplay, Morton is shown to be a responsible researcher if not exactly a systematic one. He does not try sulfuric ether on a patient until he has tested it thoroughly, this having been the lesson provided by Wells's unfortunate experience.

The next several paragraphs have Morton experimenting with sulfuric ether on the family cat, dog, and goldfish, and then on himself—he accidentally but painlessly impales his hand on a spike, which proves to Morton that he is on the right track. (Why and when Morton had abandoned ethyl chloride and began experimenting instead with sulfuric ether are not explained in the outline.)

Morton puts out a sign offering painless dentistry and Eben Frost, "a small man with a big toothache," crosses the street to Morton's office. The operation on Frost is a fiasco, however. He "goes completely insane from the ether, almost breaks up the office" and, tearing outside, assaults a policeman and lands in jail. Then Morton tries a small dose on himself with proportionately small but ill effects—sufficient to confirm a problem with the method. Consulting Jackson, Morton learns that what he had obtained from his other source was cleaning fluid; what he needs is highly rectified sulfuric ether, available only at Burnett's pharmacy. Still angry over the ordeal of the previous day, Frost returns to Morton's office to retrieve his fiddle. Morton cajoles him into sniffing an ether-soaked handkerchief and, once he is out, pulls his sore tooth. Frost admits upon waking that he felt nothing. A notice of the operation appears in the next day's newspaper and Morton's office now swarms with customers.

In Fülöp-Miller's account, it was not Frost who had a violent reaction to the impure ether but Morton's two assistants. After consulting Jackson, Morton secured some highly rectified ether and used it successfully on Frost the same day. Making Frost the patient in both cases allows Sturges to create several absorbing and amusing scenes. It also increases Frost's participation in the action and gives William Demarest—the Sturges regular who plays the character—additional screen time.

Next the outline has Jackson visit Morton and observe his prosperity. As a result he demands five hundred dollars for the expert advice he gave to Morton. Morton agrees, whereupon Jackson increases his demand to 10 percent of any profit from the discovery; when Morton agrees to this, Jackson demands 25 percent. Bristling, Morton tells Jackson he has no rights in the matter because he merely told Morton what Faraday and Davy had done. Elizabeth comes in with a large wrapped bottle and lets slip that Burnett's won't have any more of what's in her parcel until tomorrow noon. Jackson smiles at this confirmation of his suspicion and repeats his demand for 25 percent; Morton again offers him 10 percent and Jackson refuses the offer. Morton and Frost try to persuade a surgeon to try ether but he refuses, saying he would only do so if Dr. Jackson were to recommend the substance. Morton offers Jackson his 25 percent if he will endorse the use of ether in general surgery but Jackson refuses.

At dinner with Elizabeth, Morton and Frost are despondent until Morton has an idea. If they can't use the method on the rich, he says they'll try it on the poor, whereupon Morton and Frost head to Massachusetts General Hospital. Once there, an assistant tells them that Dr. Warren is operating and tries to get rid of them. They persist and finally catch up with Warren. Morton hurriedly makes his case and Warren agrees to try the method during an operation. Morton has an instrument maker create an inhaler after his own design and uses it in administering the anesthetic to Dr. Warren's patient. When the unspecified operation is successfully completed without pain, Warren says to the assembled guests: "Gentlemen, this is no humbug." The spectators roar, Morton smiles weakly, and Frost faints. Here the outline ends.

Appended to this long outline of events leading up to Morton's discovery are four pages of notes on the events that followed the discovery. The first three pages, written on May 4, were rearranged and revised on May 8 in a one-page outline:

1. 1846—Morton discovers anesthesia and is granted a U.S. patent.
2. Jackson and Wells contest his claims (but not his patent) and a controversy rages. In the meanwhile all doctors, dentists and all governments infringe his patent by using ether anesthesia.
3. 1852–53–54–55 movements are set on foot in Congress and the Senate to reward Morton, now practically a pauper, for his discovery. This intention invariably winds up in oratory and nothing is done.
4. 1854—Morton is advised (possibly by the President) to start a test case against some physician in the Government employ for the purposes of getting a decision so that the Government will be justified in giving him damages. Morton starts suit and the entire world turns upon him. Editors gird their loins and denounce him gleefully as an avaricious little dentist trying to snatch the solace of ether away from suffering mankind. He is treated as a pariah and finally burned in effigy in view of his front windows. His suit does not progress and his family becomes more and more destitute until . . .
5. In 1862 he is reduced to selling his medals. In this year he also sues the New York Eye Infirmary which was making his inhaler for export. Judge Shipman ruled that this patent was invalid and this was the end of his hopes. He volunteered his services during the Civil War and seems to have done good work as an anesthetist.
6. By 1868 he was pretty well recognized as the discoverer of anesthesia but there was no longer any way to reward him. Someone sent him a magazine article by Jackson attacking again his claims. He became violently ill, then hurried to New York to refute Jackson's statements. He died.

Sturges's work on Morton's later years, which comprise the first part of the script, is obviously far less developed at this point than his work on the discovery events, which comprise the second part of the script. He is not sure as yet what he is going to include in this part or how he is going to present it. Indeed, this developmental imbalance continued through all of the work Sturges did on the project in 1939. There is a larger number of versions of the first part of the script and they exhibit far more variation than do those of the second part. One cause of this disproportion is that Morton lived for twenty-two years after his discovery, whereas the discovery process itself took only a few months; even if the discovery part of the film is deemed to begin with the courtship between William and Elizabeth, it comprises only a few years.

On May 10 Sturges wrote a one-page draft of Morton's encounter with a glass manufacturer, in which he "upsets the whole table of inhalers," which he regarded as unlawfully copied from the inhaler he designed. A brief note the next day reconsiders the problem of the framing story.

Hypotheses:

Morton hocks medal for the purpose of:

1. Eating
2. Going to Washington
3. Buying a dress for his daughter
4. Having an operation which he needs
5. Buying a revolver with which to shoot Jackson

This note indicates that Sturges still planned to begin the film with the pawnshop scene that he had drafted on March 22 and revised on April 16. This note shifts the emphasis, however, from Morton's interactions with the pawnbroker to the possible reasons for his having to pawn his medals in the first place. The note also shows that Sturges's ideas about the film's framing story were closely linked to his ideas about the overall plot of the film and particularly that of its first part. To consider different framing stories was to consider different plots.

A half-page draft on May 15 pursues the Washington option. Morton tells the pawnbroker that he'd rather borrow on his French medal than sell it, "because you see Congress has voted me a hundred thousand dollars, for my patent, that is, and the President is going to sign the bill . . . that's why I need the money to go to Washington. . . . I've been waiting twenty years for it . . . it's been a long time." Below this brief draft are six asterisks, under which is another, longer scene draft. It begins:

First they said it didn't work, then they said I didn't do it, then they said anyway I shouldn't get anything for it and I was a scoundrel to try to, then the Government said it was going to give me a hundred thousand dollars because they'd infringed my patent, and then they said they shouldn't ever have given me a patent in the first place because I hadn't invented anything, all I'd made was a discovery or something . . . sometimes I wonder if I ever lived at all . . . and then I get hungry and I know I'm alive all right.
(He chuckles)

The last point, of a sort usually called Brechtian, cuts against the long recital of society's moral failures that preceded it with a final stress on the material needs of the complainant's body. The need for bread is more urgent than the need for justice; and, paradoxically, Morton's hunger constitutes a more effective indictment of his era than his list of the wrongs done him. How the passage would fit into an actual scene, however, and exactly where it would be placed, are unclear. Equally troublesome is that in this speech Morton summarizes virtually the entire plot of the postdiscovery years. If he does this early in the film, the summary will undermine many of the upcoming scenes; if he does it after those scenes have occurred, his summary will seem repetitious, if not superfluous.

Morton's speech on the crosses he has had to bear gives way to yet one more variation on his exchange with the pawnbroker.

> PAWNBROKER
> (Perplexed)
> Yes, but this is enscribed to the benefactor of mankind with the gratitude of humanity. Who's that supposed to be.

> MORTON
> That's supposed to be me. I'm supposed to have discovered the use of ether.

> PAWNBROKER
> (Astonished)
> Well did you?

> MORTON
> (Smiling wryly)
> You promise not to tell anybody?

> PAWNBROKER
> (Surprised)
> Why certainly.

> MORTON
> (After looking around)
> I did.

He looks at the pawnbroker with amusement as we
DISSOLVE TO:

THE DISCOVERY OF ANESTHESIA

Morton becomes here, and in a few other notes and drafts later on, a kind of mole, a grotesque character whom suffering and injustice have disfigured. For this one moment only, perhaps, the spirit of Gogol and Dostoyevsky enters Sturges's writing. Will there be a return to the older Morton after the "discovery of anesthesia" scenes? Showing his disappointments in Washington and later would be anticlimactic after the discovery half of the film, particularly since we have already seen him reduced to pawning his medals. But neither can the older Morton just be left stranded in the pawnshop, like Cégeste abandoned in La Zone at the end of Cocteau's *Orphée*.

On May 17, Sturges proceeded in a much lighter vein by sketching a new beginning for the film as a whole.

TITLES-1 THE PARAMOUNT TRADE MARK WITH "PARAMOUNT
           PICTURES PRESENTS"

           DISSOLVE TO:

TITLES-2 "THE GREATEST DISCOVERY OF MODERN TIMES"

DISSOLVE TO:

TITLES-3   THE WORKBENCH OF A THIRTEENTH-CENTURY ALCHEMIST

Raymondus Lullius, played by the Managing Director of Production, discovers sweet vitriol and almost passes out from inhaling it.

DISSOLVE TO:

TITLES-4   "TRIUMPH OVER PAIN"

This rolls up onto the cast.

TITLES-5   A SIXTEENTH-CENTURY WORKBENCH

Theophrastus Bombastus Paracelsus von Hohenheim, played by the scenarist, gives ether to a chicken which clucks itself to sleep.

DISSOLVE TO:

TITLES-6   CREDIT FOR SCREEN PLAY

which rolls past onto technical credits.

DISSOLVE TO:

TITLES-7   AN ENGLISH DOCTOR'S BACK ROOM, 1798

Humphrey Davy, played by the producer, takes a whiff of nitrous oxide and nearly explodes with laughter.

DISSOLVE TO:

TITLES-8   THE DIRECTOR'S CREDIT

DISSOLVE TO:

Whether or not, even for a moment, Sturges planned to open his script this way, the drollery of the passage is revealing. Sturges writes himself into the history of the struggle to defeat pain; in fact he's there before Morton. He includes a credit for the director but, by denying him a role in the discovery of anesthesia, he also denies him a name—to be filled perhaps, at least in fantasy, with his own name.

After a half-page space, to be filled in by the "modern operation" perhaps, Sturges sketched yet another version of the pawnbroker scene. This time he pursued, for the first and last time, the revolver option in his menu of possible plots issuing from the framing story.

DISSOLVE VERY SLOWLY TO:

INT. 1868 BOSTON PAWNSHOP – NIGHT

The pawnbroker, Frederick C. Johnson, is selling a revolver to a poorly dressed man whose back is to us.

JOHNSON

. . . and when you have fired one it turns by itself to the next one
and all you have to do is pull the trigger. A really great invention.

Morton says he'll take the revolver but he hasn't any money. Instead he
reaches into his pocket and pulls out a medal. When Johnson asks Morton,
after exchanges identical to the versions quoted earlier, "Who's that supposed
to be?" Morton "sticks the gun in his pocket" then replies, "That's supposed
to be me . . . you can laugh after I've gone." After Morton leaves, Johnson
picks up the medal and examines it again. In nearly all his variations of this
scene, Sturges makes a final shot of the "Benefactor of Humanity" medal
(whoever happens to be holding it in his or her hand) the trigger that brings in
the past, and hence the pivot that moves the film from one time frame to another. The idea for the scene is puzzling in that Morton did not in fact ever
shoot Jackson or anyone else, including himself. If he trades his medals for a
gun only later to change his mind, a great deal of time has been wasted and
the precious medals have been sacrificed for no reason.

Sturges did nothing whatever on the project between May 18 and June 18,
1939. From June 19 through 29, however, he worked steadily on a treatment
for Morton's later years and the framing story, drafting—in all—six more
outlines of the former and three more versions of the latter. Both matters had
to be resolved before a screenplay could be started.

On June 19 he wrote a three-page, three-point outline of the events immediately following the Alice Mohan operation. Point 1, headed "Morton the
World's Greatest Hero," mentions the medals and the "Gratitude of Humanity" Morton received for "REVEALING HIS SECRET," then considers some
consequences of his having done so, notably an argument with Elizabeth.

His wife, resentfully: "You'd give your head away if anybody asked for it." Morton,
looking at her sideways: "I gave my heart away once, but I'm not always so sure you
wanted it." His wife, putting her arm around him: "Don't talk like a fool. All I say is
that when a man has a wife and small children he ought to think about *them* and let
humanity take care of itself, or the first thing you know you'll wind up with a medal
and nothing else."

Point 2, headed "Morton's Big Offices," briefly describes Morton arriving
at his offices to find them empty. Eben Frost tells him that his dentists have
quit to work for themselves. "With my invention!" Morton says angrily, adding, "Well, we'll see about that." In point 3, "We See Morton Consulting a
Lawyer," where Morton is told that every dentist in Boston is using ether but
that he need only sue one of them and get an injunction against the others.
Morton says "sheepishly" that he doesn't care much for the idea but he'll
think it over. The outline continues:

On the way back they pass the window of a glass manufacturer which is full of his
patented inhalers. Play this scene as written ending in Morton's arrest for smashing

the manufacturer's stock. Possibly we see him sentenced by the judge. His wife walks home with him and tells him he had better forget his ether invention and pay more attention to his dental business. Morton mentions the coming law suit and explains to his wife that he plans to sue a government doctor because the government itself is infringing on his patent.

[END OF OUTLINE]

On June 21, Sturges wrote a paragraph under the title "THE STORY":

They called him a money-grubber, an avaricious little dentist, a man without ethics and a shame to his profession: they said his honors were fictitious or undeserved, they withdrew the titles they had conferred upon him, they refused him their greeting and their practice, they burned him in effigy, dishonored his name, took away his property and brought his family and himself to the verge of starvation. Their jibes and especially their injustice broke down his strength and finally killed him. And what had this monster done? He had given the world ether anesthesia. His name: Dr. W. T. G. Morton. And who were they? The recipients of this supreme gift, the inhabitants of that selfsame world, distinguished from the lower animals by their many virtues.

This is less a story summary in the usual sense than a kind of editorial statement protesting the treatment that Morton received. The statement's perspective is that of the present and it looks back on Morton's life as a whole. The paragraph is in fact an early draft of what became the prologue in the final script (page A-1), and was itself anticipated by two earlier passages, both speeches by Morton and both written on May 15. The first, beginning "First they said it didn't work, then they said I didn't do it . . . ," was quoted earlier; the second is a brief fragment standing by itself: "Well, I used to feel pretty bad about it and then I began to inquire into what happened to the other fellows who did something . . . for people . . ." (An early version of the prologue to *Sullivan's Travels* likewise appeared first in one of Sullivan's speeches, albeit as the prologue he intends to attach to a film he wishes to make.)[4]

In a three-page outline dated June 23, Sturges begins with a fragment of the pawnbroker scene, then—at a new place in the scene—makes a transition to the past.

THE PAWNBROKER
But this was to the "Benefactor of Mankind," who's that supposed to be?

MORTON
That's supposed to be me . . . of course it was some time ago . . . when I didn't know as much about the gratitude of humanity as I do now.

During the last few words WE HAVE DISSOLVED TO Morton's home in 1846. His wife is putting the baby to bed or something when she hears the door slam. She rushes downstairs to greet the home-coming young Morton.

HIS WIFE
Did it work?

MORTON
(Wearily)
Of course it worked.
(Now with a little more cheerfulness)
It always did and it always will.

HIS WIFE
Then we're rich. We'll be able to etc., etc., etc.

MORTON
Sure, etc., etc., etc.

Despite this lapse into blanks, the scene continues. "HIS WIFE" asks if there's a chance others will find out about Letheon, as Morton apparently now calls his substance. Morton tells her, haltingly, that the secret is already out. The Massachusetts Medical Association had demanded to know what Letheon was if the substance was to be allowed in the amputation scheduled for that day. "Otherwise they were going to take her leg off without anything at all." "HIS WIFE" responds:

What of it? Millions of people have had it done that way . . . it was always done that way until you came along with the greatest discovery the world has ever known . . . AND NOW YOU'VE THROWN IT AWAY! YOU'LL NEVER GET ANYTHING FOR IT! YOU'LL BE A CHEAP DENTIST TO THE END OF YOUR DAYS AND WE'LL NEVER GO TO EUROPE AND WE'LL NEVER HAVE A HORSE AND CARRIAGE AND TOMMY WON'T GO TO COLLEGE . . .

MORTON
(Putting his arm around her)
I happen to have a patent, granted by the Government of the United States of America, etc., etc.

[End of Note]

On June 27, Sturges wrote an eight-page, ten-point outline of the first part of the film. Its first sentence—"Morton reveals his secret to the world"—had been the implicit starting point of much of Sturges's prior work on the film's first part. (It is also, of course, the final point of the film's second part, hence the ending of the film itself.) In this version, Mrs. Morton's protestations are all but eliminated and what remains occurs offstage: "His wife voices her fears but he reminds her that he has a patent about to be granted." Dr. Jackson, who has a 10 percent share in Morton's patent, confronts him at his dental office and berates him for giving up the patent's secret for nothing. Morton replies that Jackson has no rights in the matter, saying, "I gave you ten per

279

cent because you helped me a little bit but any other chemist could have done the same thing." Jackson responds that he's known about ether narcosis for years; in which case, replies Morton, it was reprehensible to keep it secret. The next paragraph, "MORTON AT HIS INSTRUMENT MAKER'S" has Morton show his patent to an instrument maker, proposing that they manufacture inhalers. The manufacturer is pleased but resists Morton's idea that charitable institutions receive them free. You can charge for the inhalers, Morton tells him, my license will be free. A very large order will be forthcoming from the U.S. Government, Morton tells the manufacturer, noting that the country is at war with Mexico. "Say, do you think they'll buy these?" asks the instrument maker. "Well, they buy guns, don't they?" replies Morton.

The paragraph that follows is a "SCENE BETWEEN MORTON AND A U.S. ARMY OFFICER." In it Morton is well received and learns that both the Army and the Navy will use his invention. When he asks how many will be needed, the officer answers, "We don't need any at all. The order was placed last week." Further, he tells Morton, no licensing fee will be paid and "you can't sue the Government." Morton asks to know the name of the firm that sold them, and then:

4. WE SEE THE EXTERIOR OF A BOTTLE FACTORY. Scene in which Morton smashes the bottles and is arrested for it.
5. NEWSPAPER REPORT OF THE FACT THAT ETHER ANESTHESIA is to be used in the army and the navy in the war with Mexico. What a boon to mankind! What gratitude we owe Dr. Morton for his altruism in giving the discovery to the world . . . free!
6. MORTON IN JAIL — His wife and Eben Frost come to bail him out. He is furious at the injustice. His wife advises him to forget the whole thing and go back to his dentistry. "There isn't much of that to go back to," says Eben Frost and explains how Morton's associates have gone in business for themselves.

In paragraph 7 Morton finds his dental offices empty. "A patient arrives but Morton is still too angry to be very polite or grateful." The patient leaves saying, "I can get painless treatment from any dentist in town." "Not for long you won't," Morton responds. "I happen to have a patent." At this point Jackson arrives with a patent attorney, demanding to know why the government is getting the inhalers free when he owns 10 percent of the patent. Morton explains and the attorney says, "That's the end of your patent . . . if the Government won't pay . . . don't imagine anybody else is going to pay." Jackson then asks that his name be struck from the patent, for he refuses "to charge suffering humanity for any consolation I may have brought them." "Especially when they won't pay anyway," says Morton, who adds later, "You're very free with things that don't belong to you, aren't you?" "Posterity will discover whose it was to give away," answers Jackson. "Don't worry about posterity," says Morton, "because it isn't going to worry about you." Then he adds, "That faker," as Jackson exits.

In paragraph 8, "MORTON, HIS WIFE AND CHILD AT BREAKFAST NEXT MORNING," Mrs. Morton reads a newspaper

which contains Jackson's free gift to the world and also a notice from Horace Wells claiming priority in the discovery. Morton holds his head.

He refutes both claims. Jackson's is "a dirty lie" and Wells never used ether in his life. Mrs. Morton then sees a notice about Dr. W. Crawford Long of Georgia, who claims to have used ether in 1842.

Morton gets to his feet hysterically. "It's a lie! Don't you see it *has* to be a lie! He may have used ether in 1842 but he can't have done it successfully or we would have heard about it. Even a monster couldn't keep a discovery like that to himself. I only found out how to do it six weeks ago AND THE WHOLE WORLD IS USING IT!" Now his attention is distracted by his child who is sniffing a waterglass and lying back as if she were asleep. Morton, to his wife: "What's she doing?" The child, giggling: "Taking ether."

Paragraph 9 begins with a "DISSOLVE THROUGH THE WHITE HOUSE AT WASHINGTON TO MORTON SPEAKING TO PRESIDENT PIERCE." Pierce is sympathetic to Morton's cause but advises him to sue a government doctor in order to establish a precedent so that Congress will award him damages. This is followed by the last paragraph of the outline, which begins:

10. SERIES OF HEADLINES:

"MORTON SUES GOVERNMENT PHYSICIAN" then editorials about the money grubbing little dentist. Now the judge throws the case out of court on the grounds that Morton's patent is not valid. As Morton and his wife and Frost leave the courtroom, he is hissed by the spectators. They return to a poor apartment. A man is waiting inside having been let in by the little girl. Morton: "You're from the landlord, I presume, I'm terribly sorry I know it's only a question of a few days and then everything will be all right and I'll be able to . . . " Mr. Renavent rises in some embarrassment and with a slight French accent he says: "I am afraid you confound me with somebody else . . . "

The visitor turns out to be "Viscount XYZ, attached to the French Embassy" and his mission is to present Morton with the medal inscribed to him as "the Benefactor of Mankind with the Gratitude of Humanity." When the medal has changed hands,

Morton looks away for a second then more closely at the medal. "Pretty, isn't it?" We CUT TO A CLOSE SHOT OF THE MEDAL, THEN TRUCK AWAY. IT IS HELD IN THE HAND OF THE OLDER MORTON, STANDING IN THE PAWN-BROKERS.

[End of Outline]

281

Why is there a flash-forward at this point, just when the narrative of Morton's later years seems about to conclude? Perhaps Sturges felt no need to follow Morton's story to its end—his patent is invalid, his reputation is ruined, he is about to be evicted; his life is effectively over, even if not actually so. However, as long as the screen Morton is alive, a restoration of his fortunes is possible and viewers may be stirred to hope.

Another difficulty is that the pawnshop scene comprises both the framing story and an event in Morton's life. The divergent pressures of these two demands perhaps account for the large number of variations that Sturges put the scene through. Sometimes the scene is placed before the main story scenes and sometimes at their end; sometimes it leads to the first part of the film and sometimes the second, and so on. The temporal coordinates of the scene are different in a number of versions also. In the May 8 outline, for instance, Morton sues the government doctor in 1854 and sells his medals in 1862. But in the final script, as we shall see, Morton pawns his medals in 1868, when, according to Mrs. Morton's account after his death, he needed money to go to New York in order to refute Jackson's latest attack on him. It was there, as we have seen, that Morton died.

Although unfinished, the outline of the postdiscovery years was now sufficiently detailed for Sturges to begin a screenplay draft. Indeed everything was now in place for that effort except the framing story that would launch and link the two extended flashbacks.

On June 28, the day after he wrote the long outline, Sturges wrote a less complete, four-page version, with a new framing story.

1. Eben Frost swaps his violin for Morton's medal, gets Morton's address from pawnbroker and starts to leave. "Is he a friend of yours?" says the pawnbroker. "Yes," says Frost, "only he's dead now."

2. THE HOUSE IN THE COUNTRY WHERE MORTON'S WIDOW AND CHILDREN LIVE. Frost arrives and presents her with the medal. She describes his last trip to New York and his death. She looks at the medal and says: "He must have sold it to go to New York. And for all he did, this is all he had left . . . only he didn't even have it. He depended too much on human gratitude . . . I guess." Frost, pointing to the medal: "Sure, the gratitude of humanity. They're a fine bunch." Mrs. Morton: "Just think what that man did: before him in all time since the beginning of the world surgery . . . and there must always have been some . . . was agony . . . he conquered pain." Frost: "And the world doesn't know it . . . that's what makes me boil." Mrs. Morton, gently: "Oh, they will in time. Truth will out. Dr. Jackson says *he* did it. [Frost: "In a pig's eye he did."] . . . that he'd known about it for years." She laughs softly. "Can you imagine anybody discovering anesthesia and keeping it a secret?" Frost: "He claimed he invented the telegraph too only Samuel F. B. Morse stole it from him." Mrs. Morton: "I know. Then they said Horace Wells discovered it first [Frost: "In a pig's nose."] and then that Dr. Crawford Long discovered it *four* years before! Well, if they did, it was pretty mean of them to let people go on suffering all

that time." She pauses before concluding: "Six weeks after my husband discovered anesthesia . . . THE WHOLE WORLD WAS USING IT!" Frost: "And what a wonderful world it was."

DISSOLVE TO:

3. MORTON'S DENTAL OFFICES . . .
4. MORTON CONSULTING A LAWYER . . .
5. SCENE BETWEEN MORTON AND U.S. ARMY OFFICER . . .
6. SCENE AT THE BOTTLE FACTORY . . .
7. SCENE IN MORTON'S OFFICES . . .

Sturges had struggled with the framing story and flashback structure since March 22. On June 28, over three months later, he finally solved it. As long as Sturges had tried to put Morton at both ends of both flashbacks, he ran into problems that he could not solve. If Morton is in the framing story as well as in both flashbacks, then neither framing story nor flashbacks can ever conclude: coming or going, we always come back to him. As a consequence, there is no way to enclose, or comment on, Morton's life as a whole. This suggests a modern, or postmodern, biopic form, in which the impossibility of closure—at the beginning and/or the end of the life represented—is affirmed. Such a form might also suggest the infernal nature of the biographical subject: who is intolerably inexhaustible; who is met with anew at every turn of a work; who is bounded here only to become, once again, unbound there; who in fact can never be got rid of or finally have done with.

In the new framing story, it is Mrs. Morton who now reviews the other claims to the discovery, as Morton had done in paragraph 8 of the June 27 outline. She concludes with the line "Six weeks after my husband discovered anesthesia . . . THE WHOLE WORLD WAS USING IT!" How much softer yet firmer is her recital than his, and how much more persuasive, free as it is of his paranoia and rant. To rage against the dying of the light is fine, if the dissolve comes quickly; otherwise the audience gets restless and asks, "Is that all there was—that one note of outrage?" Frost then says, somewhat incongruously after his denunciation of humanity, "And what a wonderful world it was." This is followed by a dissolve to Morton's busy dental offices, where a newspaper arrives telling of Morton's revelation of the secret of Letheon. "Why won't everyone now use it?" his assistant dentists want to know. Because he has a patent, says Morton. Subsequent paragraphs mainly summarize the earlier outline: Morton consults a lawyer; he meets with a U.S. Army officer; he goes to the bottle factory, "where Morton smashes infringing inhalers and gets arrested for it"; and, finally, the scene in Morton's offices, which "are much quieter than before."

On the next day, June 29, Sturges wrote another incomplete three-page outline, this time beginning with a "PROLOGUE: Child being operated on" and then cutting to "MEDAL IN HOCKSHOP WINDOW." Frost returns the medal to Mrs. Morton who then "tells him of Morton's death in a scene ending with the line: 'And what a world it was.'" In the next scene, as before, Morton's business is brisk but, instead of a newspaper arriving, announcing his disclosure of the secret of his discovery, he tells Mrs. Morton that he made the disclosure to the surgeons at the hospital.

> "Otherwise they couldn't use it . . . they were going to take her leg off without it." "Whose leg?" says Mrs. Morton. "I don't know," says Morton . . . "some girl."

The final paragraph of the outline is a long account, mainly dialogue, of Morton and his wife at breakfast the next day. She is worried about his business. He says he has a patent for his discovery and, in any case, business is fine. Frost then comes in with the news that Morton's dentists have gone into business for themselves. Morton says that at least he has the credit for the great discovery. Then a reporter comes with a copy of Jackson's speech to be delivered that evening, in which he claims for himself all credit for the discovery. Morton, who is here more easygoing than in any other version, "laughs and says 'you have to expect things like that.'" Morton tells the reporter that Jackson had also claimed invention of the telegraph.

> "Is that the same Jackson?" says the amused reporter. "Sure it is," says Morton. "Enough said," says the reporter.

The reporter then mentions Horace Wells's claim to have "discovered what you discovered." A still philosophical Morton says that he guesses there will be many such claims. "It's funny they always come after the discovery. You'd think they'd say something about it sooner. I worked with Wells. He tried laughing gas. He never even heard of ether."

Everything was now in place for the composition of a screenplay but, as was often the case with Sturges, he took one last stab at something else—in a rather wild direction—before settling down to write his script. On July 11, he wrote three pages addressing a flaw he had evidently noticed in the otherwise satisfactory new arrangement: if Morton pawns his medals in 1868, then how does he get to Washington in the 1850s? In the July 11 scene outline, Morton hurries to tell his wife of the movement in Congress to secure him a reward. "During this scene we see the little country dental office he has rigged up." Mrs. Morton wonders if it mightn't be better "to forget about the ether. It's never brought you any luck and I don't think it ever will." Morton's thoughts are "already elsewhere," however, and he asks her how much it costs to go to Washington. The answer is thirty dollars and they have twenty-seven dollars, sixty-five cents saved. Just then a father enters with "a fat boy whose jaw is very much distended." Morton says it will cost—"He pauses, looks at the ceiling and with some difficulty subtracts twenty-seven sixty-five from thirty." "Two dollars and thirty-five cents!" he says and the father agrees. There is then a

DISSOLVE TO:

THE WINDBAGS IN WASHINGTON. We see high camera shots of the orating. At the mention of a hundred thousand dollars it seems that everyone in the world discovered ether. They orate and orate [no period in the original]

Fortunately, Sturges never returned to the country extraction scene that here gets Morton to Washington. Hackneyed devices of this sort were especially abundant in thirties films, but by no means ended with that decade. However, Sturges and other good writers usually avoided them and, if they happened to sneak in, managed to write them out before the final draft.

Beginning July 13, Sturges worked steadily through August 2, 1939. What he finished on that date was the first complete screenplay version of *Triumph over Pain*. An incomplete draft of this screenplay—entirely a transitional work—is preserved in the Sturges papers. Having no sequence "A," it begins with the scene of "MORTON AND HIS WIFE AT BREAKFAST," which begins sequence "B." Also lacking an ending, this script draft breaks off at the pandemonium that greets Dr. Warren's, "Gentlemen . . . THIS IS NO HUMBUG!" at the first successful demonstration of ether anesthesia in surgery. The draft ends with a "DISSOLVE TO," although what is being dissolved to is unspecified. A revised and completed version of this draft was typed at the studio on August 2 and 3.

The August 2 script was followed by two other complete screenplays— one dated September 13, the other December 15. Limitations of space require that I skip over the two later screenplays—it was the August 2 script that Sturges returned to in 1942, and on which he based the final script reprinted below.

The August 2 script has nine sequences: "A," "B," and "C" are devoted to the initial framing story and Morton's postdiscovery years; "D," "E," "F," "G," "H," and "J" cover the second part of the framing story and Morton's discovery years. Sequences "A" through "C" comprise 56 pages, "D" through "J" 129 pages—185 pages in all. Appearing in the August 2 script for the first time is the "Foreword," which appears, with a few changes, on page A-1 of the final script, reprinted below.

The Foreword is followed by the modern scene of the little boy on the operating table, which is followed in turn by a close-up of a silver medal which Eben Frost redeems from a pawnshop. Frost travels to Morton's house, where Mrs. Morton tells him the circumstances of Morton's death. A dissolve—on "And what a wonderful world it was!"—shows Morton's moment of triumph amidst cheering crowds following the Alice Mohan operation. In the next scene he tells his wife at bedtime that he disclosed the secret of ether anesthesia to prevent the pain of a young girl undergoing surgery. Sequence "B" begins as Morton reads favorable newspaper accounts to Mrs. Morton at breakfast the following morning; then Frost arrives to say that Morton's assistant dentists have left. An inset shot shows Burnett the pharmacist tell "a crowd of anxious dentists" that there is no more ether in the city. Taking a carriage ride to his office, the Mortons notice ether signs over the offices of several other dentists. Except for the cashier, Morton's waiting room is empty. A reporter arrives asking Morton's reaction to Dr. Jackson's statement that he discovered anesthesia. Morton is surprised but answers calmly that this is untrue. An inset shot of a newspaper Morton is reading adds Horace Wells to the list of claimants to the discovery. When a representative of his landlord arrives, Morton tells him that he will not need all of the offices he is renting but is told that the landlord "is a stickler for signed papers." The reporter returns with a question about Wells and yet another claimant to the discovery of ether, Dr. Crawford Long of Georgia. Wells, Morton says, "doesn't know the difference between ether and dish water"; Long he has not heard of. In the next scene, which takes place in THE BEAUTIFUL DRAWING ROOM OF THE MANSION, Mrs. Morton says,

> It doesn't *matter,* dear. We just went a little too fast, that's all. Naturally I liked it. Any woman would . . . but nobody *needs* a house as big as this . . . and all those . . . silly servants . . . eating their heads off! I'll really be glad to get your meals again . . . like I used to. And I'm sure it isn't really . . . healthy for children . . . to be brought up in such . . . lavishness . . . governesses . . . and g-goat carts and . . . and
> (She buries her face in her hands)

Morton, who stands at the window, holding a newspaper behind him, does not seem to be listening. He tells his wife "dully" that Wells has committed suicide in New York and the papers say it was on account of Morton. Next there is a scene of Morton in his operating room in which a woman leaves indignant at his fee of five dollars for an extraction. She can get it done for three dollars from another dentist, she says. Dr. Warren comes in with a loose filling, which Morton repairs; Warren, suspecting that Morton's nerves are in bad shape, examines him and insists he get "a good solid rest," which Morton says he cannot afford. So Warren suggests Morton sell his inhalers to the Army, which is currently engaged in the Mexican War, and gives him his card on which he writes an introduction to an Army colonel. The colonel tells Morton that they have already bought their inhalers from a glassmaker whose name he provides. Morton visits the glassmaker and, being rebuffed, he upsets two tables of glassware and hurls heavy bottles at him, some of which smash through the showcase window. Then "he is almost foaming at the mouth as he tries to throttle [him]." The police are sent for—an inset newspaper carries the story—and Morton is next seen in bed while Frost, Mrs. Morton, and Dr. Warren look on. Warren tells Morton that now he must get rest and then presents him with one thousand dollars, voted by the trustees of Massachusetts General Hospital, with a dedication in praise of Morton's dis-

*Morton, Lizzie (Betty Field), and their children read a
letter from Washington in* Triumph over Pain/
The Great Moment.

covery. Sequence "C" begins with Mrs. Morton and the couple's three children surprising Morton, now an amateur farmer, as he hoes a field. They bring
a letter that has arrived from Washington informing Morton of a motion in
Congress to vote him a one hundred thousand dollar award. It also requests
that he come to Washington. Mrs. Morton, "smiling ruefully," asks him how
he is going to do it. When Morton responds that they will have to borrow on
the place, Mrs. Morton says, "I did want to hold on to this for the children . . .
they're so helpless." Once in Washington, Morton is informed by a Senator

287

*A publicity still of the "Mr. Stone" scene, cut
from THE GREAT MOMENT.*

Davis that a number of other claimants to the discovery have also come
forth—a number besides those Morton is already aware of. Davis urges him,
at the suggestion of someone who does not wish to be quoted any more than
Davis does, to sue some government doctor to establish infringement of his
patent. A reluctant Morton does so and a wave of indignation in the press
greets his attempt. Finally a judge rules the patent invalid. Morton returns
home to find a banker named Stone about to foreclose on his property. Surprisingly, Stone says that he will hold off foreclosure if Morton farms the
land for profit. An astonished Morton agrees. Just then the "Benefactor of
Humanity" medal arrives from France and Sturges cuts from a close-up of it
to a close-up of the medal in Mrs. Morton's hand in the framing story, as her
tear falls upon it.

Frost and Mrs. Morton go into the kitchen for dinner as sequence "C"
ends. Sequence "D" begins with a close shot of "THE REMAINS OF THE
PIE." Mrs. Morton recalls how Morton loved pie, saying that he had eaten so
much of it when he was a boarder that her mother had wanted to throw him
out. In the final script, that reminiscence is the trigger to the second flashback. However, in this version Mrs. Morton goes on to tell of an article she is
writing on Morton for *McClure's Magazine* and, as Frost reads the manuscript, the flashback—as though illustrating the article—begins.

In the selection and ordering of events from the discovery years, the August 2 script follows the June 27 outline closely. Since only the 1942 revisions made changes in this part of the script, those revisions are considered below. Worth noting now, however, is that the August 2 script concludes, as does the final script, with a last instance of Morton's comic ignorance, which is followed by the briefest return to the framing story.

J-50   MORTON – PAST WARREN

> Both men stop. Now Morton places the package in Warren's hands.

> MORTON
> Professor Warren, it's called . . . sulfuric ether . . . highly rectified.

J-51   PROF. WARREN – PAST MORTON

> PROF. WARREN
> (Stupefied)
> You mean plain $C_2H_5OC_2H_5$?

J-52   MORTON – PAST WARREN

> He lifts his arms helplessly.

> MORTON
> I don't know . . . I guess so.

> WARREN
> (Seizing his hands)
> Oh, my boy . . . my boy.

> The music swells to a triumphant paean. The scene

> DISSOLVES SLOWLY TO:

J-53   MRS. MORTON AND FROST SITTING <u>IN THE PARLOR OF THE FARMHOUSE 1868</u>

> Frost gets slowly to his feet, and ON THE SCREEN APPEAR THE WORDS:

> THE END

In early 1942 Sturges returned to *Triumph over Pain* for the first time since having put the project aside in December 1939. A contract screenwriter then, Sturges was now a successful writer-director and—beginning with *Triumph over Pain*—his own producer. He was free for the first time to film this project, which the studio had never liked, and, of course, to base his final script on whichever of the 1939 versions he chose. In fact, although he had completed two later script versions on the subject, he returned to the August 2 script—the earliest—which he had abandoned, possibly under studio pressure, for the more compromised and accessible scripts of September 13 and December 15.

No notes or drafts for Sturges's 1942 revisions have survived, so it is unclear just when he took up the project again. Editing *The Palm Beach Story* occupied him at least until early February of that year, but since few changes seem to have been needed, that process was perhaps finished by the middle of the month. By early April, in any case, Sturges had completed a revised script for *Triumph over Pain*. Its cover page is dated March 30, 1942, but individual pages are dated as late as April 3. Shooting was scheduled to begin on April 8 but Sturges, as usual, continued to revise, producing a final script on April 27. That is the script that is reprinted below even though, as the reader can see, it retains the March 30 cover page (and thus the date) of its predecessor. To avoid confusion, I will refer to these as the April 27 and the April 3 scripts, respectively.

The most important of the April 3 changes—in relation to the August 2, 1939, script—was an entirely new beginning for the film's second part, which presents the discovery events. The April 3 script, like the August 2, 1939, script before it, begins sequence "D" with a brief return to the framing story, from which it then flashes back to Morton's early years. Rather than begin the flashback with the kitchen scene of the August 2 script, however, the April 3 script begins it with an ether party scene that Sturges borrowed from his September 13 script.

D-4   THE WHITMAN PARLOR

> This contains about twelve young folks, a few parents, Dr. and Mrs. Whitman. On a table in the background a light collation has been put out: punch, cookies and cakes. Dr. Whitman holds a bottle of ether and a handkerchief. All are laughing, and the girls are screaming at a young man who seems to be suffering the blind-staggers. He is talking dipsy-doodle talk and carrying on very crazily. After a moment Dr. Whitman puts his arm around the young man's shoulders and shakes him.

The young man comes out of the ether and says, "Where was I?" The other young people comment on his performance and laugh and Dr. Whitman asks who is next. "Billy Morton" is the answer, but he is nowhere to be found. One of the girls lets it slip that he is on the porch with Lizzie, the Whitmans' daughter, and Mrs. Whitman goes to find her.

D-5   THE MOONLIGHT PORCH

> Mrs. Whitman appears but finds nobody.

D-6   MORTON AND LIZZIE – IN A SUMMER HOUSE AT THE FOOT OF THE GARDEN

"They are looking at each other miserably," Sturges notes, as Morton tells Lizzie he hasn't got the money to finish his studies and won't become a doctor. He is going to become a dentist, he tells Lizzie, who is "aghast." "But they work in wagons at country fairs," she says, to which Morton replies,

> Not the better type, Miss Elizabeth. They have offices . . . and office hours . . . Of course it isn't like being a doctor, but then it isn't like being a corn doctor either. It's kinda half way in between.

Lizzie looks away without replying. Morton says that he is sorry she feels that way about it. There follows a page or so of dialogue in which Morton tries to tell Lizzie how he feels about her but he loses heart and stammers when he does so. He keeps trying, however, and she encourages him, but he cannot quite get it out. The scene is reminiscent of one in *The Power and the Glory* in which Tom Garner cannot tell his wife-to-be that he loves her and, as a stalling device, takes her ever higher up a mountain, and finally to its peak, in his search for the requisite courage.

Morton and Lizzie rejoin the others; Morton goes off to the parlor to try the ether while Lizzie tells her mother he is going to be a dentist. "Oh, my gracious!" she says, adding after Lizzie defends Morton that she doesn't really care, but Mr. Whitman will. Lizzie then goes into the parlor and she takes ether, too.

> Suddenly Morton stiffens and bursts into laughter. At the same time Lizzie dissolves in boo-hoos. This strikes the guests as very funny. Now Morton notices Lizzie. Suddenly he takes her in his arms and kisses her passionately. At this Lizzie begins to laugh hysterically and it is Morton who weeps. Everybody roars with laughter.

"Locked happily in each other's arms," the two are "oblivious to the laughter." Sturges links the conclusion of the ether party scene to the beginning of the next scene and thereby bridges a five-year gap in the story.

LIZZIE
(Oblivious to her father's voice)
I love you, Doctor Morton.

MORTON
I worship you, Miss Elizabeth.

The two lovers kiss passionately.

DISSOLVE TO:

D-12   LIZZIE IN DR. MORTON'S ARMS – DAY

> I repeat, it is day instead of night, and the clothes they wear are different. The position, however, is exactly the same.

291

LIZZIE

I love you, Doctor Morton.

MORTON

I worship you, Mrs. Morton.

The CAMERA TRUCKS BACK SLOWLY and we see that they are standing in a dental office.

LIZZIE

I'm so happy.

MORTON
(Indicating something PAST THE CAMERA)
It's pretty from here, isn't it?

LIZZIE

Beautiful!

D-13   THE LATEST DENTAL CHAIR AND STAND, MODEL 1840

The chair is a very graceful number with lions' heads, ball-and-claw feet and a little skirt around the bottom of it. The stand is elegantly simple, being merely a sort of plush-covered table with a water fountain above it and a plain brass spittoon below it.

The April 27 script involves rewrites of only 18 of the April 3 script's 160 pages—10 in sequence "D," 8 in sequence "E"—but the impact of these changes is greater than the numbers suggest. Most important, the April 27 script drops the ether party sequence altogether and reinstates the "Large Kitchen in 1840" opening from the August 2, 1939, script. As the kitchen scene begins, Lizzie's mother exclaims about her boarder's appetite: "I do declare, Lizzie, I'm going to ask that young Mr. Morton to leave!" This opening makes the Whitmans appear considerably less affluent and socially prominent than they did as hosts of the ether party. They now take in boarders and Mrs. Whitman worries aloud about how much they eat. This opening also explains, as the April 3 version does not, how Morton and Lizzie met in the first place. Both script versions show Lizzie and Morton in love and both show the opposition of her parents to the match on the grounds that Morton is poor, socially obscure, and, above all, a dentist.

The April 27 script eliminates the ether party scene but preserves, unrevised, the dental office scene that followed it in the April 3 version. The scene itself still makes sense, but Sturges's accompanying remarks no longer do: "I repeat, it is day instead of night, and the clothes they wear are different. The position, however, is exactly the same" (page 47). Without the ether party scene, the camera movement back to reveal a dental office behind the enraptured couple does not make sense either. To avoid this confusion, Sturges cut during shooting both the young couple's embrace and the "I love you" and "I worship you" lines that accompany it, which accords with the somewhat deromanticized ambience of the April 27 script. This is a courtship based on genuine affinity but it takes place in a harsh world and in a context of compromise. Lizzie loves Morton and promises to wait for him but she does not like the fact that he is poor and going to be a dentist. A sense of regret and sadness hangs over the rewritten scene of their declaration of love. When they are next seen—in the dental office—the emphasis is no longer on young love but on the newness of the office and the young couple's hopes for success. The scene as Sturges actually shot it partially cuts and rearranges the script's dialogue to strike immediately, but ironically, the note of Lizzie's hope for success.

> And I know you're going to be rich and famous, and I'm going to be so proud of you, Darling, and Father won't be able to talk against dentists any more, and we'll have a big house, and while you're at the office, I'll be at home taking care of my end of things.

Given what we already know from the film's first part, these hopeful words have a somber effect—if one knew where one's life was going, would one have the courage to live it? Much of the script, perhaps all of it, must be read in the double register of its two parts: the poverty and disappointments of the couple's later years and their optimistic, oblivious early years, which result in brief success.

On April 13, 1942, Sturges rewrote pages 54–55 of the April 3 script, expanding them into three and a half pages (see pages 54, 55, 55a, and 55b below). These pages include a brief dinner scene between Dr. and Mrs. Morton that is situated between two longer scenes: the dental office scene with fleeing patients (page 53) and Morton's visit to Dr. Jackson to ask him about pain-deadening techniques (page 56). The version of the scene in the April 3 script had been as follows:

D-22   MORTON AND HIS WIFE AT DINNER

> The dining room is modestly furnished and lit by a whale oil lamp or candles. Mrs. Morton is clearing the dishes off the table on which half a pie remains. Morton, preoccupied, looks off into space.

MRS. MORTON
(in surprise)
Don't you want another piece of pie, dear?

MORTON
What? Oh . . . no thank you, Lizzie.

MRS. MORTON
Are you worried about something?

293

MORTON

Hunh?

MRS. MORTON

What are you frowning about?

As if in answer we hear the wail of a small baby.

MORTON
(Pointing in the direction of the sound)

That.

MRS. MORTON

Why William!

D-23   NEW SCENE in which Morton decides to visit his old pro-
        fessor, Dr. Jackson. He seems to remember that Jackson said
        something once about desensitizing a tooth. He leaves.

It is not clear what relation this scene has with the dental office scene that precedes it and the scene of the visit to Jackson that follows. This might be an everyday dinner, in which Morton is preoccupied because his practice is suffering, or for some other reason. Sturges puts Morton's reason for going out after dinner in a shot description, to which the viewer has no access, rather than integrating this information into the dinner scene itself.

The scene's presentation of the young couple's relationship is also odd. Just four pages earlier the April 3 script had Lizzie and Morton say to each other "I love you" and "I worship you" and had them repeat these declarations after their marriage. This repetition was separated/linked, moreover, by a dissolve, which, in this context, indicates the persistence of their rapture through time. Here they are but a few years later, however, barely communicating. The viewer cannot square this scene with the script's later, and earlier, emphasis on the strong bond of love and loyalty between them—which, on her part, outlasts his death.

The revised script deftly solves both problems (pages 54–55a). Morton is preoccupied with the day's reverses but when his wife questions him about his mood, he answers candidly. She suggests that since Morton cannot recall the remedy Professor Jackson recommended when Horace Wells had a toothache, Morton should go to see Jackson and ask him directly. The revised scene emphasizes the couple's cooperation and also stresses Morton's reluctance to see Jackson—"because I despise him so, that sarcastic old bastard." Also in this version, Morton does not refer negatively to his baby's crying, it is Mrs. Morton who does, jokingly.

The sequence "E" changes realized by the April 27 script are slighter than those of sequence "D," but worth noting. At the bottom of E-5 in the April 3 script, Horace Wells asks Morton,

> You remember when we were students we used to try to figure out some way of pulling a tooth without pain?

MORTON
(Ruefully)
I'm <u>still</u> trying to figure it out.
(He pulls the bottle out of his pocket.)
I just bought a bottle of chloric ether to see if . . .

The April 27 script puts the ellipsis marks after "a bottle of . . ." This change makes Morton appear less open with his friend than before; he no longer discloses the identity of the substance on which he has begun, however preliminarily, to experiment. Were he too easily to reveal his great secret, however, we might sympathize less fully with him in the second half of the film than we did in the first half because he would be shown to have been partially to blame for letting others know his method. Also, the second part of the film—in a sense both parts—move toward the illumination of Morton's great moment of sacrifice in disclosing the substance of his method. This moment and the long process that leads up to it are undermined, or confused, if Morton casually mentions its name to Wells at this early point. During shooting, the speech became: "I'm still trying to. I just bought a bottle of . . ." In the released print of the film, however, the bottle line is cut altogether, and with it all reference to Morton's own experiments besides the vague "I'm still trying to." Again, did Sturges cut this or did Paramount? It certainly seems Sturges-like in its intelligence and gradual improvement of a script until its parts interrelated as logically and effectively as possible. The Paramount cuts, on the contrary, were mainly unintelligent. However, there is no way to decide the point with certainty.

The other changes on this page are general improvements in the framing and flow of the dialogue. In the April 3 script Wells admits that the substance he uses is so well known that it cannot be considered his secret. He then adds: "I'll just have to be the father of painless dentistry and let it go at that." (He cannot claim, as he would like to do, discovery of a new substance or new properties of a known one, let alone discovery of a general anesthetic, although it is not clear whether or not he aspired to the last.) In the April 27 script this line is cut, but Sturges restored it during shooting and Paramount did not cut it, so it appears in the released film.

Page E-8 improves the dialogue of its predecessor in a number of ways, none of which alters the logic or function of the scene. In both scripts Sturges begins the scene in which the two dentists confront Dr. Jackson with the concluding line of Wells's presentation to their former teacher—"in extracting teeth without any pain whatsoever." Jackson's response, of course, is "Poppycock!" In shooting the film, Sturges expanded the conclusion of Wells's speech to a full sentence: "I can extract teeth or fill them or do anything I like with them without any pain whatsoever!" This line is crossed out in the dialogue continuity, however, and indeed it does not appear in the film. The scene begins with Jackson's response "Poppycock!" Wells's method has just been explained to us in the scene before, so why repeat any of it? (Many screen-writers, nevertheless, do repeat such lines.) This is an example of Sturges's tendency to bounce his audience into the heart of a scene without elaborate, if any, preparation and buildup. What is revealed by this example and many others in Sturges scripts is that he only achieved such effects by careful revision through many drafts.

In the April 27 script, Sturges rewrote pages E-18(84)–E-21(87) of the April 3 script and added a new half-page: E-21a(87a). These are more important than the earlier sequence "E" changes discussed above. In the April 3 script, Morton and Wells discuss briefly what happened in the latter's demonstration at Harvard Medical School earlier that day, then

> Suddenly Morton puts his hand on Wells' shoulder for silence. He looks toward the reception room.

E-54   THE DOOR FROM THE HALL TO THE RECEPTION ROOM

> A very nice looking old lady comes in. Her face is drawn with pain. As she stands waiting --

E-55   MORTON – PAST THE OLD LADY

> MORTON
> (Quietly)
> Yes, madam?

E-56   THE OLD LADY – PAST MORTON

> THE OLD LADY
> I'm in terrible pain . . . a dentist . . . broke my tooth and . . .

> Her eyes roll up and she starts to faint. Morton helps her to a chair and the CAMERA PANS WITH THEM.

> THE OLD LADY
> Thank you . . . I'm sorry.

> MORTON
> I hope I have something that will help you . . . just a minute.

> He goes into his operating room.

E-57   WELLS IN THE OPERATING ROOM

> He had overheard the conversation. As Morton enters, Wells speaks excitedly.

> WELLS
> I've got another gas bag, let me go out and get some ammonium nitrate and . . .

> MORTON
> (Roughly)
> Oh, shut up!

He picks up his bottle of chloric ether and hands it to Wells.

> MORTON
>
> Put some of this in a drop-bottle for me.

> WELLS
>
> (Desperately)
> I tell you, Bill . . .

> MORTON
>
> Quiet.
> (Now he turns toward the reception room.)
> Will you come in, please, madam.

DISSOLVE TO:

E-58   MORTON'S RECEPTION ROOM

Wells sits dejectedly in a chair. Now he gets up, walks around,
then sits down again. He is the prey of vast irritation. Suddenly
we hear a woman's moan which has nothing funny about it. A
moment later Morton appears in the door of the operating room.
He seems utterly dejected. Now he comes in and closes the door
after him.

> MORTON
>
> (Wearily)
> It's no good! That stuff is about as much use as sheepdip! And
> that poor old woman . . .
> (He shrugs his shoulders)

> WELLS
>
> (Quickly)
> Then <u>why</u> don't you try my system? We can make it in ten
> minutes . . . and this time I'll <u>guarantee</u> it will work! I'll put
> her under if it's the last thing I ever do!

Morton thinks for a moment, then gets to his feet.

> MORTON
>
> (Quietly)
> Go and get your stuff.

> WELLS
>
> (Happily)
> You'll see.

From this point the scene plays basically the same in the April 3 and in the
April 27 scripts. In the April 3 script, both men agree to try Wells's method.
As the old lady finally shows vital signs and begins to come to, it is Morton,
not Wells, who "starts to laugh. He tries not to but he can't help himself. He
puts his hand over his face and laughs almost hysterically."

In the April 27 script, however, the initial discussion between Morton and Wells is extended for the better part of a page. In this discussion and in the events that follow, it is made clear that the differences between Morton and Wells have to do with more than their methods of anesthesia. Wells does not merely protest the constraints imposed on him at the Harvard demonstration, he rants and raves. Morton silences him not because he hears a patient outside but because Wells seems out of control. Morton urges him "to experiment, and try it out little by little" and offers to go out and get a rabbit for him to experiment on. It is while Morton is away on this errand that the woman with a toothache comes into the office. This time, however, she is "a streetwalker . . . in her middle years, poor and pathetically flamboyant." Wells invites her in and, "swallowing nervously," tells her his treatment won't hurt, obviously intending to try his nitrous oxide on her. When Morton returns and sees what has happened he tells Wells that he shouldn't have done it and is alarmed at the "funny color" of the woman, who is still unconscious. Morton summons a doctor, who, after some effort, is able to revive her.

Like its predecessor, the April 27 script specifies that it is then Morton who laughs hysterically but, as the prior pages have been rewritten, this no longer makes sense. The dialogue continuity indicates that it is Wells who laughs at this point and, of course, this is what happens in the print of the film that Paramount released. In the rewritten version, Morton is not at all amused by Wells's recklessness, which, had a fatality resulted, would have incriminated him too and ruined his career.

Since Morton is not now complicit in the dangerous experiment, the focus of the rewritten scene shifts to Wells, which serves to heighten the contrast between the two men. In the April 3 script, Morton and Wells are shown to be like-minded, each willing to try insufficiently tested substances on an unwarned patient. In the April 27 script, only Wells is willing to do so: Morton is shown throughout as a man of conscience and impeccable medical ethics. Morton experiments on animals and then himself. Only when sure of his method does he try it on other humans. This not only accords with the known facts, it is a dramatic necessity if Morton is later to sacrifice his career for the good of humanity. It would be inconsistent to have Morton laugh hysterically with relief, even though the danger to him was real enough. Even Sturges's less-than-brilliant Morton must exhibit some nobility perhaps. Wells, on the contrary, is shown to be rash and erratic as a scientist and unstable as a man.

This is reinforced in the film by casting. Played by Louis Jean Heydt (1905–1960), Wells's instability is predetermined, perhaps overdetermined. Heydt specialized in intelligent but unstable characters. He had played two such roles in prior Sturges projects: the clean-cut American hero who turns out to be a cad in *Strictly Dishonorable,* Sturges's hit play of 1929; and Thompson, the man who tries to kill himself at the opening of *The Great McGinty.*

The rewritten scene also incorporates, by allusion, a number of features of the actual life and tragic destiny of Horace Wells: his instability, his delusions, his calamitous encounter with a streetwalker. Here too he holds her life cheap by using her for a dangerous experiment. "I'll never experiment with human life again," he says, but he did later experiment on himself and, becoming addicted to chloroform, lost his reason.

*   *   *

Shooting began on April 8, 1942, and was scheduled to run for fifty days and one holiday; due to finish on June 5, Sturges actually concluded, according to James Curtis, one day early.[5] The dialogue continuity, prepared on June 10, reveals the changes Sturges made during shooting. As usual with Sturges, there were innumerable small dialogue changes, far too many to address here. Among the other changes were a number of deletions, additions, and rearrangements of script elements. The deletions include the scene between Frost and the livery stable man (pages A-4 to A-5) and the shots of the Morton daughter in the kitchen and Mrs. Morton writing at a desk in the parlor (page A-5). There was also an important change in Mrs. Morton's long speech about Morton's death (pages A-9 and A-10). Omitted from the speech were these lines:

> We thought he was all through worrying about things . . . that he
> was happy with the farm, you know he won all the prizes one
> year, best kept farm, most improvements, best sow, "three dollars
> for his admirable geese." He won a hundred and thirteen dollars
> that kept us through the winter . . .

Note that Sturges had repeated these words exactly in the briefer speech by Mrs. Morton that occurs at the end of the flashback presenting the postdiscovery years (page 41). One of the speeches had to be cut but Sturges was obviously not sure when he wrote the final script which it would be. In Mrs. Morton's long speech (pages A-9 and A-10), the passage is confusing. Having begun by saying that it was the trip to New York that killed Morton, she interrupts herself to speak of his happy years as a farmer and the prizes he won before she gets back to the reasons why Morton went to New York and what happened there. The remarks about farming seem more appropriate when they follow the scene in which Mr. Stone agrees to let Morton farm the land adjacent to his house—although this leads to some ambiguity also. Since sequence "C" begins with Morton farming before he hurries off to Washington to pursue his award, we do not know which farming period was happy— the one at the beginning of sequence "C" or that which follows Mr. Stone's offer? Situating the speech just after the scene with Stone seems unmistakably to refer to the later period. Spending his late thirties and forties farming may seem a poor reward for Morton's discovery, but compared to Morton's actual fate it is a pastoral dream. The real Morton never escaped the debts he

Elizabeth Morton writes on Morton's discovery for
McClure's Magazine, *a scene cut from* THE GREAT
MOMENT. *Had she been composing a love letter or a
thank-you note, the scene might have survived.*

incurred in Washington, says Fülöp-Miller; a pauper until his death, Morton never farmed again.

One of the lines added on page A-13 puts an aspect of the script as a whole in question. The addition comes after the celebration that follows the operation on Alice Mohan. Morton orders champagne for everybody and Frost gets drunk and follows Morton home. Once there he starts to talk again about his famous painless extraction ("It was the evening of September thirtieth . . ."), and Mrs. Morton cuts him off in a line added during shooting: "Yes, Eben, that was five weeks ago." Fülöp-Miller's Morton is a successful dentist making ten thousand dollars a year for some time before his discovery of ether anesthesia, so he might plausibly live in a mansion with servants, have a goat cart for his children, et cetera. But Sturges has Morton living in a modest house with furniture donated by his in-laws and enjoying little success in his practice until his discovery gives him an edge on his competitors. Since he cannot have used ether on his dental patients until after the successful procedure on Frost, this means that he has gained a fortune, which he is now about to lose, in five weeks!

The first part of sequence "B" (pages 17–20) was comprehensively reorganized during shooting. The entirety of this section of the script, including the scene with the reporter, takes place in the Morton breakfast room. Frost's entry (page 18) interrupts the Mortons' discussion with the news that Morton's dentists have all quit and that the whole town is giving ether. This leads plausibly to Lizzie's "Then we are ruined . . ."—a line cut during shooting—and her speech that begins, "It doesn't really matter. I suppose nobody really needs a house like this . . ." (page 19). But Frost's first line (page 18)—"You'd better come down to the office right away"—which seems a clear cue to action, inexplicably elicits no response. Despite Frost's news, which is followed by news from the reporter of other claims to the discovery (page 19), Morton just sits in his breakfast room until, puzzlingly, he appears in the next scene at the desk of an Army officer (page 20). As Sturges reworked the scene during shooting, Lizzie's "It doesn't matter" speech—and Morton's attempt to reassure her—are moved up to precede Frost's entrance. Following Frost's "The whole town's giving . . . ether," there is a dissolve to a scene in the dental office.

RECEPTIONIST: Good morning, Dr. Morton.

1ST DENTIST: Dr. Morton, I --

RECEPTIONIST: I don't know what to say. The world just seemed to drop out from under us.

MORTON: Well, advertise in the paper for some more dentists right away.

RECEPTIONIST: Oh, I beg your pardon.

MORTON: Who are you?

REPORTER: Say, Doc, the old man wants a statement from you. I

2ND DENTIST: Doctor --

MORTON: I --

REPORTER: I'm from the Daily Advertiser -- about a story just come through.

MORTON: What story is that?

3RD DENTIST: Goodbye, Dr. Morton.

REPORTER: Did you invent ether?

MORTON: Of course not. Ether was discovered in the Thirteenth Century. I discovered the use of it for ana -- ana -- for putting people to sleep.

The reporter then lists the other claimants to the discovery, and Morton responds, very much as appears in the script (pages 19–20). By virtue of changes made during shooting, Morton now takes what action he can by rushing to his dental office to limit the damage. Instead, he unexpectedly confronts the even worse news of other claimants to the discovery. Having mentioned his patent to the reporter, he now proceeds plausibly to the office of a quartermaster colonel in order to assert it (pages 20–22).

A minor rearrangement occurs in the Presidential Office scene in sequence "C": the brief conversation between Senator Borland and Morton (page 29) now occurs first and a trimmed version of the "Whackpot" scene on the same page follows. A major addition occurs following the series of newspaper headlines specified on pages 34–35. The script calls for a most interesting transition from the last of the headline series to a close-up of Morton at his patent trial: Morton's face is to appear superimposed on the last few shots of the newspapers in which he is being pilloried.

> THROUGH THE LAST FEW SHOTS A CLOSEUP of Morton has started to FADE IN.

> C-23   CLOSEUP – MORTON – IN COURT

> He looks harassed and miserable.

During shooting, Sturges added a scene in a newspaper office with an editor, identified later in the scene as Horace Greeley, who is in the midst of dictating an editorial to an employee.

GREELEY: -- and it is with a sense of scalding shame that the citizens of Boston watch the progress of this trial. Villified by every newspaper in the country and abroad, expelled from the American Medical Association, disowned by his fellow dentists, burned in effigy by his fellow townsmen, this avaricious little dentist, this money-grubbing little opportunist, walks in shame – alone – unhailed. Period. Whatever the result of the trial, and we pray that Morton will lose hands down, let this be a lesson to the future --

ARTIST: How's this, sir?

GREELEY: (LAUGHS) Not bad. I think I'd make his fingers a little longer -- more clawlike -- more vulturesque.

ARTIST: Yes, Mr. Greeley.

GREELEY: Now where was I? Oh, yes. Whatever the results of this trial, and we hope that Morton will lose hands down, let this be a lesson to the future shylocks who attempt to prey upon the misery of man. Exclamation point. Read that back to me.

SECRETARY: Yes, Mr. Greeley.

The dialogue continuity reveals that Sturges also made a fundamental change in the "trigger" that leads to the first flashback. Some of the material in D-3 (pages 43–44)—Frost's halting question about money and Mrs. Morton's response about the article she is writing about Morton for *McClure's Magazine*—is moved up to the beginning of sequence "D." However, everything after her line "He lived too long" (page 44) is cut. Frost does not then read her manuscript so his reading about Morton's past is no longer the trigger of the flashback. Instead, Mrs. Morton follows "He lived too long" with a question to Frost, "Won't you have still another piece of pie, Eben?" This leads her to remember how much Morton loved pie—"He ate so much, Mother wanted to throw him right out of the house. Oh, dear, I do declare!" That last line, added during shooting, is also the first line spoken, by her mother, in the flashback. The repetition smooths the new transition, which is preferable to the somewhat hackneyed article-reading transition that it replaces.

The speech by Lizzie's mother that begins "Why honey child!" does not make perfect sense as written (page 45), apparently because a phrase was omitted in one of the lines. With the critical phrase restored during shooting, the remainder of her speech became: "I had no idea you *were fond of him,* and you know I don't mean half the things I say. I wouldn't send him away if he ate twice as much, heaven forbid, unless you wanted me to."

The young couple's scene in Morton's new dental office, already truncated (the condensed pages 47–50 and page 51), was rearranged during shooting. In the script, Lizzie's hopeful speech about their future is placed at the end of the scene, so that her remark "and while you're at the office, I'll be taking care of my end of things," is followed by a shot of her giving a toddler—not two children, as the script specifies—a bath. In the dialogue continuity, Lizzie's speech is placed at the beginning of the scene, so that it follows her father's shocked response to the news of the impending match: "A dentist! Jumping Jehosophat!"—which was itself added during shooting. The beginning of Lizzie's speech, although set a few months later, seems a response to her father's exclamation: "And I know you're going to make a big success. You're going to be rich and famous, and I'll be so proud of you, and Father won't be able to talk against dentists any more." The humorous material about Morton's new dental chair now follows Lizzie's speech and in turn dissolves to the brief child-bathing scene. The program outlined in Elizabeth's speech— you in office, me at home—should not, for reasons of pacing, be realized too quickly, or literally, by an immediate dissolve to a child. Especially given the terrible years that are coming, the couple should be shown having a little fun while young and, relatively, carefree. Their playfulness around the dental chair—particularly when Lizzie falls all the way back in the chair with a scream/laugh and Morton kisses her—accomplishes this and perhaps stands in for sex itself. The next scene, at the bath at home, shows that years have gone by and also, given Lizzie's proposed division of labor, creates viewer expectation of an office scene, which indeed follows.

In that scene, Morton says to his waiting patients, who are frightened by the screams of the patient in the chair, "Don't be in a hurry, I'll be with you in just a moment" (page 52). The rest of the dialogue (page 53) is cut, however, in favor of some pleasing visual narrative: we see on his office door the silhouettes of the departing patients and, as Morton's eye follows their departure down the stairway, the shadows of their descending figures. A sentence in Morton's subsequent complaint to Lizzie about dental patients (page 54) has a phrase missing, which was supplied during shooting: "You can't put in *a nice inlay* like you did in dental college with somebody screaming bloodymurder in your face or trying to bite you."

To explain how Morton comes to find Dr. Jackson at a saloon, Sturges added to the script a brief scene at the doorway to Dr. Jackson's house (page 55a): "He's not at home," the butler says, "but you might try Costello's, sir." The scene between Jackson and the bartender (pages 55a–b and 56), including Jackson's careful construction of a layer drink, is eliminated. In the film Jackson seems to be mixing a much simpler drink from two bottles when Morton, who enters and greets Jackson, accidentally jostles him. "Why don't you look what you're doing?" says Jackson, to which Morton replies: "Say, do you remember what you gave Horace Wells the night he had a tooth-ache?" "Do I know you?" says Jackson, and the scene then plays, small changes aside, as written. Morton's earlier line, "I didn't recognize you at first," was eliminated in shooting; since Morton has come in search of Jackson, it is either dissembling on his part or is part of some discarded scene in which Morton wanders into a saloon and fortuitously finds Jackson.

Morton's arrival at Burnett's pharmacy (page 61) was changed during shooting to coincide with the store's closing time, which makes the timing more appropriate to a postsaloon visit and also makes for a more dramatic, he-almost-missed-destiny scene. When the script's Morton returns to the pharmacy in the morning—to find out why he passed out the night before—Burnett explains and offers him another bottle of sulfuric ether. Having accidentally inhaled the substance and appeared drunk to his scolding wife, Morton tells the pharmacist that it is the other (chloric) ether he wanted, and still has, and he leaves. In the dialogue continuity he says no to the sulfuric ether at first but then changes his mind saying, "Wait a minute—give me a bottle of that." This puts him solidly on the sulfuric ether track for the next scene, in which Horace Wells arrives for his nitrous oxide demonstration at Harvard Medical School. (The script mistakenly says Howard Medical School [page 76].)

In the next scene in the dialogue continuity, Morton tells a sign painter to underline the word "double" before the phrase "your money back" in the new sign over his office, but the rest of their conversation (pages 96–97) is cut. The scene of Frost's first visit to Morton's office (pages 100–102) is rearranged somewhat without altering its meaning and has also been expanded.

Frost, for instance, repeatedly asks the question "Double my money back [if I feel anything]?" to which Morton reassuringly replies each time, "Double your money back." Much of Frost's deranged dialogue under the "bad" ether—which Jackson calls "cleaning fluid"—is dropped in favor of what the dialogue continuity twice refers to as Frost's (that is, Demarest's) "AD LIB."

At the end of the meeting between Morton and Jackson (page 109), an amused Jackson asks Morton if he wouldn't care to settle for fifty dollars cash for the advice he has just given Morton. "Thank you just the same, Doctor," Morton says earnestly. Cut during shooting is the part in which Jackson takes a second whiff of the "bad" ether Morton has brought him and says "Phew!" as he pours it down his sink. On the right track again—with highly rectified ether from Burnett's—Morton tricks an angry Frost into inhaling it and he passes out. Morton then removes Frost's tooth and immediately after envisions the use of ether for medical surgery. Something that is not in the script but does appear in the film is the date of the Frost operation—"September 30th, 1846"—printed large across what appears to be a freeze-frame but which begins, at least, as a motionless tableau of the three players (McCrea, Field, Demarest).

Sequence "G" begins with:

G-1 A MONTAGE OF MORTON'S SUCCESS:

THE CAMERA STARTS ACROSS a line of windows. Each marked: "W. T. G. Morton." Below this each has a different slogan:

"The Painless Dentist" -- "The Discoverer of Letheon" -- "The Man Who Made Dentistry a Pleasure" -- "Come Up and Be Convinced" -- "The Conqueror of Pain" -- "The Pain Killer" "Pulls Them Out With a Smile"

While the CAMERA IS MOVING SIDEWAYS PAST the windows the FOLLOWING SHOTS DISSOLVE IN AND OUT:

[Patients running up his stairs at Morton's offices; the receptionist sending dentist applicants to an interview room; Frost telling his story to a male patient; more patients running up the stairs; the perspiring cashier; the Mortons getting out of a carriage to see their new house, followed by a shot of their mansion; a dentist with an empty inhaler asking for more Letheon; Frost telling his story to a lady patient; Mrs. Morton on the porch of the new house with her three children blindfolded—they yank off the handkerchiefs and run to "a shiny little carriage with two goats hitched to it"; people coming up the stairs of Morton's office; a Letheon bottle emptying rapidly; the cashier counting piles of money.]

OVER THIS AND THE LAST OF THE WINDOWS COMES
A THIRD EXPOSURE:

A CLOSE SHOT OF DR. JACKSON who looks faintly sinister.
NOW THE MONTAGE ENDS, LEAVING --

G-2   DR. JACKSON – IN THE RECEPTION ROOM

What a curious, fascinating passage—and how difficult for the reader to visualize! Not including the final shot of Jackson, which begins the first of a series of dialogue scenes, the passage has thirteen shots. Five of these have dialogue, however brief, eight do not. Was the passage in fact shot? It may be impossible to say. Dialogue continuities record dialogue only, with brief notations of the setting at the beginning of each dialogue scene and occasional indications that a character "LAUGHS" or a player "AD LIBS": visual material is omitted. In the dialogue continuity in this case, the sequence begins in the Hall outside Morton's dental offices with Morton, perhaps walking down that hall, saying "Good morning—good morning." Next is a series of remarks by the receptionist, comprising a kind of de facto monologue:

At the end of the hall, Madam, and number four for you, Madam. No, no, new dentists are interviewed in room seven from eight to five—Yes, the doctor will see you now. You can go right in. What is it? I'm sorry, you'll have to wait. I'm sorry, I can't do anything. I'm sorry, ladies and gentlemen—one moment, please—one at a time—

This is followed by two slightly different descriptions of Frost telling the story of his extraction, followed in turn by the entry of Dr. Jackson. (Once Jackson enters, script and dialogue continuity proceed almost identically to the end of the sequence.)

There is no way to know whether the receptionist is on screen during the whole of her remarks or any part of them; perhaps her speech underlies and links the thirteen shots, or some of them, perhaps not. In *The Great Moment,* the receptionist's monologue is dropped. Instead there is a modified, reduced version of the passage the script describes: nine shots, with music but without dialogue, comprising approximately fifty-five seconds of screen time. The first shot shows a sign with an arrow pointing toward Dr. Morton's office, with a number of shadows of people passing across it in the direction of the arrow. The camera turns and we see dozens of people tramping up the stairs to see Dr. Morton, while at the same time others, who have presumably seen one of Morton's dentists, are heading downstairs. This shot is the reverse of the earlier shot in which people are leaving Morton's office from fear of pain before he has seen them; it is followed by a dissolve to Frost miming his story to a group of ladies. This gives way to a shot of Morton striding happily down a hallway—the happiest he will appear in the entire film—and looking in through the row of windows that line his office, each decorated with a slogan. Then comes a second shot of Frost miming his story to the group of

306

ladies, this one shot through the office glass. It is followed by a shot from the hallway through the office windows of Morton walking the length of his office and receiving the adulation of his patients. After that there is a shot of the busy cashier, which is set up by a movement of the camera along the office glass but not itself shot through the glass. Next we see Mrs. Morton, presumably at home, watching her three children, who are attended by two servants, riding in a goat cart. The next shot shows us Frost for the third time miming his operation to a group of ladies. This is followed by the last shot in the series, which is of a number of people queued up at the cashier's window to pay for painless services rendered. (Only four of the shots, 3 through 6, are linked by the camera's sideways movement past the windows. So, while this is certainly a montage, it is not the one called for on pages G–1 and G–2.)

Both the script and dialogue continuity include a brief scene in which Jackson comes to the office and demands to see Morton. Told that Morton is busy, he temporarily departs, or seems to, only to barge in later as Morton is on his way to Massachusetts General Hospital—whereupon an extended confrontation between the men ensues. *The Great Moment* cuts Jackson's first visit and comes directly from the montage to the scene in which Lizzie learns from the butler that Morton will not attend the formal dinner party she has arranged for that evening. Without the initial Jackson scene, his forcible entry and intense anger a little later may seem undermotivated. Such near-motiveless malignancy may call to mind the actual Jackson, but it seems inadequately prepared for in the film, particularly since the last time we saw Jackson he was jovially skeptical of Morton's research efforts. At the same time, the brief scene that is dropped also shows him to be angry already. Implicit here is that Jackson is angered by and jealous of Morton's success itself, and, even more so, of the discovery that has made it possible.

Next, Morton and Frost proceed to Massachusetts General Hospital where they are rebuffed by a Dr. Haywood, Dr. Warren's assistant, but sneak in anyway to watch—from seats in the back of the amphitheater—Warren perform an amputation. When Frost faints Morton carries him outside. Dr. Warren appears and looks at Frost. Seizing this opportunity, Morton gives Warren a pitch about Letheon and Warren invites him to try his method at an operation that will take place that very week. When Morton gets home, Lizzie scolds him for missing the dinner party and, told of his news, she questions the advisability of applying his method to medical surgery, a move which might jeopardize his secret.

Sequence "H," in which script and dialogue continuity are virtually identical, focuses on perhaps the most famous operation in medical history—on Gilbert Abbott—and ends with Warren's line, "Gentlemen, this is no humbug!" In sequence "J," the script and dialogue continuity diverge at a small number of places. (Perhaps because "I" is both a letter and a Roman numeral—and therefore ambiguous—there were no sequence "I"s in Paramount scripts.) The press interview with Morton (pages 149–152) is the same in

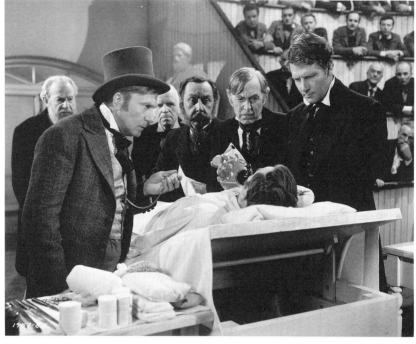

*Morton performing the first public demonstration of
ether anesthesia—October 16, 1846—in a scene from*
Triumph over Pain/The Great Moment.

both texts. When the scene shifts to Massachusetts General Hospital (page
152), Sturges added during shooting the following lines before Jackson says
"No, no, it's [the discovery is] mine . . ."

DELEGATE: It's perfectly preposterous.

VICE-PRES: They'll find out how preposterous it is before I'm
through with them.

ATTENDANT: Cards, please. Cards -- no admission without a card --
(ETC)

JACKSON: Some lunkhead put it in my alcohol burner by mistake.

BIGELOW: Then as I understand it, Morton worked for you.

JACKSON: No, no, etc.

The scene in and around Warren's office (pages 154–158) was shot as
written with a few minor exceptions. One of Warren's lines was cut: "Al-

A sketch-op: Morton briefly famous in TRIUMPH
OVER PAIN/THE GREAT MOMENT.

though as a surgeon my professional forebears were bargers, I am bound to
the ethics of my superiors" (page 156). When the Vice-President accuses
Morton of delaying disclosure of the ingredients of his method in order to
make money (page 157), the dialogue that follows was amended during shooting to be more interactive:

MORTON: What! You stuffy little --

WARREN: Morton!

MORTON: You've been splitting fees --

WARREN: Morton!

MORTON: -- and robbing your patients for so long --

The film is now rapidly on the move to its climax or, one might say, it is
returning to the climax with which the story of Morton began. After Warren says to his attendant, "I shall operate in the . . . usual way" (page 157),
Sturges inserted the following brief scene during shooting:

INT. OPERATING THEATER

SOUND: (APPLAUSE)

WARREN: I'm sorry to disappoint you, gentlemen, but this opera-
                tion will be performed in the old way.

SPECTATORS: (AD LIB)

INT. CORRIDOR OUTSIDE OPERATING THEATER

This inset scene of Warren in the operating theater makes vivid to the viewer what will now happen without ether. It also recalls the scene of amputation that Morton and Frost observed—in this room by this surgeon—earlier in the film. This intensifies the drama and emotion of the decision Morton faces at this point. Back in the corridor, Morton encounters a priest—whose prayer in the dialogue continuity is unchanged from the final script—and Alice Mohan, the "servant girl" who is to have her leg amputated—whose conversation with Morton is also unchanged. New in the dialogue continuity is that Morton's final words to her—"That's right. It doesn't hurt anymore — NOW OR EVER AGAIN!"—are also the last words of the film. Morton walks toward Warren, who knows that Morton has decided to divulge his secret. Warren is ecstatic, and there the film ends. Cut entirely are the remaining dialogue and action on page 160 and, as mentioned above, the brief return to the framing story. This modification keeps the focus where it should be—on Morton's momentous decision. In the script version, the final exchange with Warren shifted the focus, in part at least, to Warren and inappropriately emphasized Morton's scientific ignorance at the moment of his great sacrifice.

The completed version of the film that Sturges made was previewed at the Alexandra Theatre in Glendale, California, on August 13, 1942, and at the Academy Theater in Hollywood on August 27. These were the film's only public screenings: those audiences were the only viewers, outside of Paramount professionals, who ever saw it.

Sturges's film is not available for viewing, but his final script, reprinted below, is now at hand, as is documentation of the changes he made during shooting. (For the sake of simplicity, the script-as-amended by the filming process will be referred to in what follows simply as "the script.")

A conspicuous feature of the script is its presentation of Morton's life in two chronologically reversed parts. Basing their accounts on *The Great Moment,* many of Sturges's critics and biographers have mistaken this feature for the structural principle of the film Sturges made. The script reveals a compositional structure that is far bolder and more complex than the studio re-edited film—less an arrangement of "parts" in the usual sense, than a series of distinct, interrelated texts.

Foreword
Title
Modern Operation
Framing story
    Frost buys medal
    Frost visits Mrs. Morton
    Mrs. Morton's narrative of Morton's last days, death, funeral, and public
        response
Morton Story, Part II
Framing story
    Mrs. Morton's memory of farming
    Mrs. Morton and Frost go into dinner
    End of dinner, the two remember the early years
Morton Story, Part I

Many of the texts are clustered toward the beginning of the film. All of them either precede or immediately follow the narration of the second part of Morton's life. No text of any kind follows the narration of the first part of Morton's life. The immediate function of the text series as a whole is to negotiate the viewer's access to the events of Morton's life; but they also develop a series of perspectives on that life, particularly on Morton's discovery and its aftermath. The events of Morton's life are set up as an "in itself" that the other texts seek to understand or interpret.

The foreword has a primarily didactic function: "humanity" is to blame for the deplorable treatment Morton and other benefactors have received. But it also has a narrative one: despite, or because of, the greatness and universality of Morton's discovery, he was reviled and hounded almost literally to death. The title that Sturges used for the script and film—*Triumph over Pain*—is at once an acknowledgment of its source text, an emblem of the film itself, and a summary of its narrative. It is also an important item in interpretation. It strongly suggests, contra Fülöp-Miller, that it was Morton's work by itself which accomplished the triumph over pain. The modern operation demonstrates that modern medicine still utilizes Morton's discovery and that people still benefit from it. It also shows the realization of Morton's prediction in the film that as a result of his discovery surgeons can take their time and perform procedures unthinkable before anesthesia. The modern operation is itself a brief narrative, but it has only an abstract relationship to the narrative of Morton's life itself, hence its function is entirely didactic: this is the contemporary meaning and consequence of Morton's discovery and, as the film reveals, of his enormous sacrifice.

The framing story narrates Frost's redemption of Morton's medal, but it also provides narrative information about Morton's life: he is dead now; Frost had been his friend; and, at some point in his life, Morton was obliged to pawn this treasured medal. Presenting the medal to Mrs. Morton is the occasion for Frost's visit to her house. That visit, and the medal itself, is the occasion for

311

the two flashbacks to the main story itself. The presentation of the initial remeeting of Mrs. Morton and Frost is conventional; but her proceeding to narrate at length Morton's last days, his death, funeral, and the notice that newspapers took of his death is extraordinary. This is precisely the kind of information a surviving spouse would fill in for an old friend but also precisely what classical cinema, Hollywood and European, almost never did. Thus the main story of Morton's life is told backwards not just in two, but in three main arcs or movements. First Mrs. Morton tells us of his last days and his death; then the film shows events from the twenty years that preceded his death and, finally, the events from his earlier life that led up to the discovery of ether anesthesia and its immediate aftermath.

In addition to its narrative function, the film's presentation of Part II of Morton's story also provides perspective on Part I of that story and especially on the film's climax, Morton's "great moment" of sacrifice. It demonstrates, among other things, what Morton's sacrifice cost him—his practice, his health, his savings, his family's well-being, and his reputation. At the return to the framing story following Part II, Mrs. Morton remembers "how happy we were" when Morton was successful at his farming, when it and the prizes he won "kept us through the winter." This is some solace in the account of Morton's dismal later years that we have just seen and heard. However, it also prepares us for the longer recalling of the mainly happy years that will follow in Part I of Morton's story.

After her "kept us through the winter" speech, Mrs. Morton and Frost go into dinner, whereupon the film fades out. It fades in again on "THE RE- MAINS OF THE PIE" at dinner's end; this scene leads in turn to a dissolve to "A LARGE KITCHEN IN 1840," which begins Part I of Morton's story. Sturges might have elided the framing story dinner with a dissolve. Why did he use instead a fade out/fade in, which is a far more emphatic break? Traditionally, a dissolve is obligatory, as he knew, for the movement from a framing story to a flashback, such as was soon to occur at the end of this scene. Dissolves tend to link scenes that are separate in time but closely related in some other way. But back-to-back dissolves of such very different kinds and functions might have been confusing to viewers. At the same time, Sturges also knew, or sensed, that viewers needed a firm separation between Parts II and I of Morton's story, to bound the darkness of Morton's later years and thereby to clear the viewer's perception—although not the viewer's memory—for the brighter tones of Part I. Here the fade out/fade in technique accomplishes this.

All the other texts mentioned provide perspectives on the text of the Part I events. Within Part I itself, however, the earlier events depicted may be read as providing perspectives on the later ones, and particularly on Morton's discovery and his pivotal "great moment" sacrifice. These include: Lizzie's role in Morton's life; Morton's medical aspirations; his desire to find a method of painless dentistry (apparently) to make a go of his practice and to support his family; his experimental process of trial and error; his vision of painless surgery at the moment he achieves painless dentistry; his patent application; his relations with the doctors of the medical society, who clearly look down on dentists; et cetera.

A dimension of the series of texts that we have not discussed is voice. The script's series of texts is also a play of voices, what Mikhail Bakhtin calls dialogism and what Roland Barthes calls a polyphony of voices. Indeed, the film literally begins with a voice, the "clear, pleasant" voice that, over a shot of Morton's grave, speaks the foreword. In this extraordinary text the voice, which is anonymous, speaks to the audience about the film before the title of the film, or any other credit, has been shown. This voice speaks not on its writer-director's behalf, but on behalf of the maker-owner of the film in a commercial sense:

> Paramount Pictures, Incorporated, has the honor to bring you
> the true biography of an American of supreme achievement,
> Dr. W. T. G. Morton of Boston, Massachusetts in a motion
> picture called --
>
> During and between the MAIN TITLES we see the preparations for
> a modern operation. At the conclusion of the MAIN TITLES --

The presentation of the modern operation has no voice-over but someone is showing us this scene, which is so distant from the time zone of the film's main story. This "someone" is not the actual Preston Sturges but what Wayne Booth has called "the implied author," which is an entity created by the text itself. The foreword and the modern operation are the strongest assertions of an implied authorial voice in all of Sturges's work. In this respect—and, of course, in others—*Triumph over Pain* is the farthest thing from screwball comedy, the effects of which depend upon the suppression of the authorial voice.[6]

The events of Morton's last days are narrated by the voice of a character— Mrs. Morton—who is on camera while she speaks. Parts II and I of Morton's life are by implication told or remembered by Frost and Mrs. Morton, but there is no voice-over in either part, or even a spoken narration in the framing story before either part begins. Mrs. Morton's final lines before the beginning of Part I—"He (Morton) ate so much, Mother wanted to throw him right out of the house. Oh, dear, I do declare!"—anticipate the first line of the flashback itself—Mrs. Morton's mother's "Oh, dear, I do declare!" (It might also be said that the first line of the flashback echoes Mrs. Morton's line.)

I have discussed above Morton's "great moment" sacrifice which is presented on the very last page of the script. In a sense, all of the film's texts and all of its voices bear upon, and finally converge at, this moment. Surprisingly, however, none of the texts or voices mentions or otherwise refers to Morton's sacrifice itself. In a number of ways, Morton's "great moment" sacrifice in *Triumph over Pain* plays something of the role that "rosebud" plays in *Citizen Kane*. Both have a problematic meaning that may or may not be resolved by what each work shows us at its very end. In each case, moreover, the item of problematic meaning both launches the narrative and closes it—is at once its earliest point of departure and its latest point of arrival. *Kane* begins with the word "rosebud" and proceeds to the revelation of its meaning at the end of the film. The main story of *Triumph over Pain* begins with the immediate aftermath of Morton's sacrifice, including his confession of it to his wife, and moves to the revelation of the meaning of that sacrifice at its end. Most interesting of all, perhaps, is that in both cases the meaning of the problematic item eludes all the intermediate entities of the film—all the voices, perspectives, and characters of the work. The meaning revealed at the conclusion of each work is the result of a direct communication between the implied author and the viewer—which strikes with the force of revelation. This is the godlike effect in film: the setting up of an elaborate system of intermediaries and emissaries, whose authority is short-circuited at the last possible moment in favor of a direct authorial voice and vision.

Let us return to the script's conclusion for a closer look. The presentation of Morton's sacrifice—on the script's last page—has been discussed in several places. Easily lost in focusing on the "great moment" itself, however, are the script's extraordinary descriptions of the decision-making process (pages 158–159) that leads up to that moment. They follow immediately Dr. Warren's statement, made in his office, that without knowledge of Letheon's ingredients, he will have to operate in the usual way:

J-40 MORTON – STANDING BY THE DOOR

He seems completely lost. He makes slight movements with his hands as if he were about to speak, then drops them hopelessly to his side and shifts his weight from foot to foot. Now he turns slowly, opens the door, looks back once more, then hurries out.

J-41 A LONG DARK VAULTED CORRIDOR

Morton is walking slowly toward us, the picture of dejection. He makes a helpless gesture, retraces a few steps, stops, then comes toward us again. The man is lost. The problem is too great for him. The CAMERA TRUCKS SLOWLY AHEAD OF HIM as he walks: angry, disgusted, stung with injustice, broken-hearted. Suddenly he walks into a ray of sunlight which hits him shoulder high. He turns and looks stupidly toward the light.

J-42 A SMALL ALCOVE OFF THE CORRIDOR

On one side doors lead off to the operating room. In the back a window has taken the form of the arched corridor. It is a Gothic window. In the pool of sun streaming through this we see the operating cart. A young Irish woman lies on it. An old priest kneels beside her praying.

J-43   MORTON – PAST THE OPERATING CART

He stands looking at it, his head in shadow, the white package
under his arm in the bright sunlight . . . Now Morton shuffles
forward, further into the light until now only his eyes are still
dark . . .

J-45   MORTON – PAST ALICE AND THE PRIEST

MORTON
(Having difficulty in talking)
I'm . . . terribly . . . terribly . . . sorry . . .

J-47   MORTON – PAST ALICE AND THE OLD PRIEST

Morton's face begins to work with emotion. Now he steps forward until he is entirely in the light . . . We hear the triumphant
peel of a trumpet. The doors from the operating room swing
wide and let in much light as the attendants appear. Morton turns
and looks through the doors.

J-48   LONG SHOT – THE OPERATING THEATRE – PAST
MORTON

We see Warren, his assistants and the attendants waiting on the
platform. The background is black with spectators. Morton starts
forward slowly, then increases his speed till he is almost running. As he gets halfway to the platform --

J-52   . . . The music swells to a triumphant paean.

Sturges's description of his hero's immersion in darkness and gradual
emergence into the light recalls, to my ear, the epilogue from St. John's Gos-
pel at the end of Martin Scorsese's *Raging Bull* (1980), which discusses the
blindness that precedes the seeing of salvation, presumably of its own lost
hero.[7] Thus there might be the unlikeliest of links between arguably the most
extraordinary biopic project of the forties and the most extraordinary biopic
of the eighties.

"He turns and looks stupidly toward the light." One reads the line again,
indeed several times, to make sure it is there. It is there and so are its implications: Morton's sacrifice is explicitly presented as his emergence into and
comprehension of the light, that is, of salvation. A skeptic might say that,
since Morton was denied reward in this world, his biographer can only suggest that he will receive it in the next. One then recalls the bitter cynicism of
Sturges's own foreword to this script—the alpha that seems to fit so oddly with
the omega of this conclusion. (A little less oddly, perhaps, if one considers
Sturges's literary formation in New York in the twenties, in which cynicism
and sentimentality, or cynicism and redemptive uplift, so often went together.
The writings associated with the Algonquin Round Table often exhibited one

or the other of these dualities.) That cynicism is often a protection against strong feeling may be a cliché, but it illuminates the foreword/conclusion divergence in *Triumph over Pain.*

Despite its powerful conclusion, the mixed voices, mixed perspectives, and mixed emotions of the script never resolve themselves. In this respect alone, *Triumph over Pain* directly challenges the hundreds of homogenized biopics that Hollywood turned out in the thirties, forties, and fifties.

II

Sturges's progress in shooting *Triumph over Pain* had been monitored closely by B. G. "Buddy" DeSylva, Paramount's head of production. He sent Sturges a hurry-up memo on May 14, 1942, which was day thirty-two of the film's fifty-day schedule. At some point, the memo indicates, the title of the prospective film had been changed from *Triumph over Pain* to *Great Without Glory,* in DeSylva's mind if not in Sturges's.

Dear Preston:

You are a man of your word, so don't be too alarmed if I remind you of a statement you made some weeks ago.

You said that you had been allotted more than ample time for GREAT WITHOUT GLORY, and undoubtedly would come in several days ahead of schedule. I think if you bear this statement of yours in mind, you can level just a little harder and start to pick up some of the time. Today's three-shot which was played by capable actors and was certainly simple enough, required twenty-one takes. I am sure that at that rate you will not pick up much ground – even, perhaps *lose* some ground.

I suspect your answer will be that you are doing your level best at present. I am sure that you sincerely feel that way. But even persons who are doing their best can put a little pressure on and do a little more than their best. I am sure you will try. Any cost that can be eliminated on this project will help its chance to be a sound commercial venture. As you must know, at $750.000 [*sic*] it is not, as Mr. Freeman pointed out, the best gamble in the world. So see what you can do!

DeSylva's tone is civil, even routine-sounding, but no such communication may be found in the files on earlier Sturges films. However, the files on his film that followed this one—*The Miracle of Morgan's Creek*—contain several such communications, which lends support to James Curtis's view that *Triumph over Pain* soured Sturges's friendly relations with Paramount and led ultimately to his departure from the studio.[8] Paramount had been dubious about letting Sturges develop a script in 1939 and again about making the film in 1942; he was allowed to proceed in both cases, says Curtis, only because the studio valued, and wanted more of, Sturges's comedy work.[9] The available documents—which are only part of the story—suggest that the studio's explicit objections to the film were voiced only after it was shot, and even then developed gradually. Things seemed rosy enough at first. Sturges finished shooting on schedule, or even a day early, and Y. Frank Freeman, head of Paramount's West Coast Studios, sent him a note of congratulations.

[Undated]

Dear Preston—

Thanks for every effort made to reduce the cost of "Great Without Glory." It is now down to the figure we first discussed—and I know you did your part. Thanks.

But on June 5, the same day or the day after his note of thanks, Freeman sent a memo to DeSylva, relayed by the latter to Sturges, that the director must have found less welcome.

In GREAT WITHOUT GLORY, Preston Sturges has written the following prologue:

"One of the most charming characteristics of Homo Sapiens, the wise guy on your right, is the consistency with which he has stoned, crucified, burned at the stake, and otherwise rid himself of those who consecrated their lives to his further comfort and well-being so that all his strength and cunning might be preserved for the erection of ever larger monuments, memorial shafts, triumphal arches, pyramids and obelisks <u>to the eternal glory of generals on horseback, tyrants, usurpers, dictators, politicians and other heroes who led him, usually from the rear, to dismemberment and death</u> . . ."

Please note very carefully the lines which have been underscored. I am sure you will agree with me, and I feel sure that when Preston Sturges thinks this through, that in view of the situation today it would be most inadvisable to present a great motion picture such as he has just finished, with a prologue which would create immediate unfavorable reaction. We are at war, and whether we like the restrictions imposed on us or not, we have to accept them. And this is an instance where we would definitely subject ourselves to adverse criticism.

I am writing this memorandum so you will have my views and I would like to know whether you agree with me or not; and if you do, you can then discuss the matter with Preston Sturges and see how we can rearrange this prologue so as to eliminate the objectionable part.

Penciled at the top of Freeman's memo is a note from DeSylva to Sturges: "Preston S.—Will discuss with you. B. G. DeS." If Sturges and DeSylva did in fact discuss the memo, there is no record of what they said. In any case, the matter was not resolved, or perhaps even seriously engaged by Sturges, until much later.

A dialogue continuity for the film was prepared on June 10, the title *Great Without Glory* appearing on its cover page. The film was screened without music, which had not yet been put on the sound track, on June 22. After that screening, DeSylva evidently made it known that he wanted a better transition between Morton's first operation and his confrontation with the Medical Society on the morning of his second operation, which is the film's climax. Sturges responded to DeSylva in the following undated note:

317

Dear Buddy:

I am sorry that I did not know that you had a conference this morning. Herewith are two versions I propose shooting. If they are all right will you tell Miss Brecker so. If they are not, will you indicate on the back of this what you would like?

CLOSE SHOT. THE MEMBERS OF THE MEDICAL SOCIETY.

THE PRESIDENT
What do you suppose that stuff is?

THE VICE PRESIDENT
That is what we are going to find out.

SECOND VERSION:

THE PRESIDENT
Very pretty . . .

THE VICE PRESIDENT
Yes, but I think Professor Warren has forgotten a little rule of the medical society.

Replying on the note itself, DeSylva crossed out the first version, including Sturges's paragraph of apology, and put a check by the second version, which he evidently preferred. He also wrote a brief note at the bottom of the page: "Pres: Perhaps you could add a line about their seeing Prof. Warren about it. Buddy." Sturges obliged with the following brief scene, which he then shot and edited into the film.

THE PRESIDENT
Very pretty . . .

THE VICE PRESIDENT
Very pretty indeed, but I think that Professor Warren has forgotten a little rule of the medical society.

THE PRESIDENT
Of course. That we shall see him and remind him of.

This addition does improve the film's concluding passage; without it, the doctors' objections on the morning of the second operation would have struck audiences as sudden and inexplicable. As a result, the viewer would have been inadequately prepared for the film's crucial moment, in which Morton makes his decision and his fate is sealed. That the triumph of the first operation is undercut by the scheming doctors who have just observed it enhances the film's dark theme.

On June 23, Sturges received thirteen numbered suggestions for improving the film from Chas. P. West, who seems to have been the head of Paramount's editing department at this time. Since these advisories bear directly on what Paramount later did to the film Sturges made, they will be considered below.

What is notable here is that West's suggestions apparently created no imme-diate stir; no action was taken in the short run. In retrospect, however, West's remarks sound the first ominous note of what was to be the film's fate.

Sturges began taking notes on *The Miracle of Morgan's Creek* on July 8. On July 27, Freeman received a telegram from Russell Holman, a Paramount executive based in New York.

AT MEETING ATTENDED BY MESSRS BALABAN ZUKOR AGNEW GOLDEN-SON REAGAN RAIBORN AND MYSELF ALL TITLE SUGGESTIONS FOR TRI-UMPH OVER PAIN WERE CAREFULLY REVIEWED. UNANIMOUS OPINION OF ABOVE EXECUTIVES WAS THAT GREAT WITHOUT GLORY WAS UN-QUESTIONABLY BEST TITLE FOR PICTURE

Freeman wrote a memo to Sturges the same day attaching a copy of the tele-gram and noting: "I insisted today in my telephone conversation with the New York executives that we were going to reach a final decision on a title for this picture today." He continues:

I presented all arguments in connection to going back to the original thought of using TRIUMPH OVER PAIN. The New York executives, without exception, are opposed to this title and feel it will definitely have an adverse influence on the public when the picture is presented. They are satisfied with the title GREAT WITHOUT GLORY and feel it is one which can be sold and properly exploited in connection with the picture.

Since that part of the organization who must now deal with the picture and sell it to the public are satisfied with the title and feel it is one out of which they can get the greatest value, I think we ought to accept it and call it a day.

I have done my best to overcome all the difficulties in connection with the proper title and seem to have failed. Therefore feeling that the matter must be brought to a close I believe you and I should accept this decision and go ahead with the title GREAT WITHOUT GLORY.

DeSylva had referred to the film as *Great Without Glory* in his May 14 memo to Sturges, while shooting was still under way. One assumes that Sturges had not accepted the change then; otherwise, no further communication re-garding it would have been necessary. Sturges apparently appealed DeSylva's decision to Freeman, who referred the question in turn—in what terms we don't know—to the company's New York executives. Sturges's decision to go over DeSylva's head was probably a tactical error, particularly in that he knew, or should have known, that he could not win by doing so. Studio exec-utives tended to close ranks in such cases. The incident reveals, however, the depth of Sturges's attachment to the original title and his determination to retain it.

As mentioned above, the completed version of the film that Sturges made was previewed under the title *Great Without Glory* on August 13 and 27. Ac-cording to James Curtis, the audience preview cards were a mixture of favor-able and unfavorable but, he notes,

319

his colleagues were used to raves at Sturges previews and this reaction was something new and quite different. DeSylva pointed to the indifferent and negative cards and said something definitely was going to have to be done.[10]

Sturges pointed in turn to the favorable cards—there were a few, Curtis says— but DeSylva was so opposed to the film that he threw even positive cards on a pile of negative ones. He then said to Sturges, according to one eyewitness, "I'll see you at Lucey's [a popular restaurant/bar near the Paramount studios] for the next six days!"[11] If such meetings did take place, later events make clear, the two men failed to reach agreement.

On August 17 Sturges received a memo from DeSylva, which indicates that the title question had been resolved in the studio's favor and that DeSylva had turned his attention once again to the problem of the prologue.

The following is no attempt at final phraseology – only a suggestion for the proposed new introduction to GREAT WITHOUT GLORY:

In these days of war, we think it an opportune time to reveal the life story of the Boston dentist who gave you ether: before whom in all time surgery was agony, since whom science has control of pain. Ridiculed, reviled, burned in effigy and eventually driven to despair and death, he yet lives in every hospital – on every battlefield – in the world.

Paramount Pictures, Incorporated has the honor of bringing you the true biography of an American of supreme achievement: W. T. G. Morton, of Boston, Mass. in a motion picture called . . .

There is no record of a response to this communiqué in the Sturges papers. An answer of another kind came in a September 1, 1942, letter to columnist Sid Skolsky, c/o Warner Brothers Studio, which is signed Jean (La Vell)— Sturges's secretary at the time. It makes clear that Sturges had still not capitulated on either the film's title or, beyond a few concessions, its prologue.

My dear Sidney:

I am sending you a copy of the foreword on TRIUMPH OVER PAIN, which we were telling you about at luncheon today.

If you notice, at the end there is a line which reads "in a motion picture called . . . what?" This is because we have not a definite title on the picture.

As soon as I get some dirt I'll call you.

As ever,

Jean

The accompanying document, referred to in La Vell's note, is Sturges's revision of the prologue according to his own, not DeSylva's, lights.

One of the most charming characteristics of Homo Sapiens, the talking gorilla on your right, is the consistency with which he has stoned, crucified, burned at the stake, boiled in oil and otherwise rid himself of those who consecrated their lives to his further comfort and well-being, in order to preserve all of his strength and cunning for the erection of ever larger monuments, obelisks, triumphal arches, statues on horseback and further hocus-pocus to the eternal glory of the Tyrants, Usurpers, Dictators and others who led him from the rear to dismemberment and death.

This is the story of the Boston dentist who gave you Ether, before whom in all Time surgery was agony, since whom Science has control of Pain.

It should be almost unnecessary then to tell you that this man whose contribution to human welfare is unparalleled in the history of the world, was ridiculed, reviled, burned in effigy and eventually driven to despair and death . . . from which refuge his charitable shadow continues to stalk the battlefields, the hospitals, the corridors of pain.

Paramount Pictures Incorporated has the honor of bringing you the true biography of an American of supreme achievement: W. T. G. Morton of Boston, Massachusetts, in a motion picture called . . . what?

Hindsight fails, quite often, to grasp the context in which an action is taken. That said, Sturges's protracted insistences on his preferred title and the exact wording of his foreword seem to have been tactical blunders, particularly his move to outflank Paramount through Skolsky. What does it finally matter what a film is called if it is otherwise released the way it was made? (My favorite example of this kind is the "angel series": *Street Angel* [1928], *Fallen Angel* [1945], *The Tarnished Angels* [1957]—in each case a wretched title for a superb film.)[12] The elimination of the phrases Freeman underlined alters the meaning of Sturges's foreword, but Sturges must have known that those phrases would never have been allowed in wartime. The rules of the Hollywood survival game were not the same for all, but entailed, most often, acquiescence in a host of lesser matters. This made resistance, when it was necessary, much more effective—the tantrum of a reasonable, cooperative person is terrifying. The ability to distinguish a closed door from a partially open one was also crucial. But, whatever Sturges did or didn't do after the film was made, the fate of *Triumph over Pain* would likely have been the same.

The writing and shooting of *The Miracle of Morgan's Creek* occupied Sturges full-time, and DeSylva and Freeman part-time, until December 28, 1942. The editing stage that followed was complicated by the unprecedented attention devoted to the film by the Hays Office and the Office of War Information. In late February of 1943 Sturges shot several days of retakes to mollify the censors. It was only at this point, at the end of February and early March 1943, that he turned once again to the foreword for *Triumph over Pain,* as he still insisted on calling it. In drafts dated February 27 and March 2, 9, 11, and 13, we can see taking shape the revised foreword that appears in *The Great Moment*:

It does not seem to be generally understood that before ether there was nothing. The patient was strapped down . . . *that was all.* This is the story of W. T. G. Morton of Boston, Mass., before whom *in all time surgery was agony,* since whom surgery has control of pain.

Of all things in nature great men alone reverse the laws of perspective and grow smaller as one approaches them. Dwarfed by the magnitude of his revelation, reviled, hated by his fellow men, forgotten before he was remembered, Morton seems very small indeed until the incandescent moment he ruined himself for a servant girl and gained immortality.

Why did Sturges compromise at last on the foreword issue? Surely it was that by the time he did so, the film had already been abridged and reedited under Buddy DeSylva's instructions. Precisely when that deed was done, we do not know. Approximate dates are suggested by the man who did the job— Stuart Gilmore, the editor of six of the eight films that Sturges directed for Paramount (all except *The Great McGinty* and *Christmas in July* [both 1940]). James Ursini, who interviewed Gilmore about *The Great Moment* in 1971, summarizes his testimony as follows:

Although Sturges argued for the film's immediate release in its original form, Paramount hedged and finally refused outright to distribute it without significant changes. Declining to become bogged down in a futile battle with the "powers" and more than ever disenchanted with the studio system, Sturges embarked on his next project [*The Miracle of Morgan's Creek*]. In the meantime, Gilmore was assigned the job of re-editing.[13]

Sturges "embarked" on *The Miracle of Morgan's Creek* on July 8, 1942. Had the reedit of *Triumph over Pain* taken place before September 1, however, it would surely have been mentioned in one of his communications on the film and also, one supposes, in Jean La Vell's note of September 1 to Sid Skolsky. Sturges was most immersed in *The Miracle of Morgan's Creek* from the beginning of September to the end of December 1942, during which time he completed the script and shot the film. Thus the reedit of *Triumph over Pain* probably took place between September 1 and December 28, 1942.

Most of Chas. P. West's June 23 suggestions to Sturges had to do either with shortening scenes or with somewhat technical editing matters. His comments reveal a well-developed sense of conventional editing and a resolve to impose that sense on a film to which it is, for the most part, inappropriate. He does not perceive the special editing requirements of *Triumph over Pain,* let alone its originality. Two of West's points (numbers one and three) bear directly on what Paramount later did to the film.

MR. STURGES:

The following comments may be of some value in further editing. It is quite probable that you already planned to make changes suggested here, but I am listing all the points that I noticed at yesterday's screening.

322

1. Interior of the Parlor—scene between Mrs. Morton and Frost. This scene seemed very long to me. Would it be possible, after the insert of the medal, to come back on Mrs. Morton's lines later in the scene—possibly with her dialogue "The papers spoke of him as the man who claimed to have discovered the use of ether"?

3. As I mentioned yesterday, the scene in the bedroom in which Morton tells his wife that he has given away the secret of ether, detracts from the finish of the picture. You might consider eliminating this dialogue in order to protect the audience's interest in the finish.

West's third point became a prime part of the studio's plan—to avoid any mention whatsoever of Morton's sacrifice until the very end of the film. Corroboration of this view is provided by James Ursini's interview with Stuart Gilmore:

The goal of the studio was, as Gilmore explains, to place the final act (or the sacrifice and its aftermath) in its "rightful" position. [Skipping the modern operation, the film proceeds directly to Frost and Mrs. Morton.] Then, as in the original, we flashback to the period following Morton's sacrifice. But there again the similarity ends. More than half of many original scenes were deleted, while others were transposed to a later position in the film (except for a parade sequence which now, quite perplexingly, is the background for the titles). The cumulative effect is one of monumental confusion.[14]

At least as important as the studio's goal of "protecting the finish"—more so, in my view—was its opposition to the entire first part of the film, which shows in detail the painful events of Morton's later years. Indeed, what the studio finally did to the film resulted in a far more radical abridgment and rearrangement than all of West's suggestions combined. West's most important contribution to this "surgery" was the method he proposes under his first point: to use inserts of the medal to cover a new set of transitions.

Another major goal of the studio was to smooth out the narrative as much as possible (not revealing the finish prematurely was only a part of this). To protect the finish one had only to eliminate the bedroom scene in which Morton discloses his sacrifice. Hostility toward Part II itself and a desire to resolve Sturges's complex structure into simple linearity—these were far more radical goals, and far more inimical to the project.

Using the script reprinted below as a guide is the best way to grasp what, under the studio's instructions, the studio cutters did to the film. A print or VHS tape of *The Great Moment* is also essential. The first shot after the new foreword is the silver medal in the pawnshop window (shot A-3), which is followed by the pawnshop scene (shot A-6). This dissolves to a very brief shot of the farmhouse (A-7), which dissolves in turn to Mrs. Morton and Frost talking as they walk toward seats in the parlor (shot A-14). After some preliminary talk, Frost presents Mrs. Morton with the medal and she says, "How very kind of you, Eben. This was the last one, you know. He hated to part with it." At this point there is a cut to a shot of the medal in Mrs. Morton's hands, which we know from the tear that splashes on it is shot C-35 on page 41—that is, the return to the framing story after the whole of the first flashback. Over this shot of the medal we hear Mrs. Morton reading its dedication (the last sentence of her speech is in shot C-34), which is followed by Frost's apology for stirring up painful memories and Mrs. Morton's recollection of how happy they were when William was farming—a speech which now ends with "his admirable geese." This is followed by a cut to the beginning of sequence "C" on page 27 wherein Elizabeth and the children bring Morton the letter from Washington as he is plowing their field. Morton's speech about the money he'll receive and his gratitude for his wife's patience is followed by a scene in which two senators are presenting an anti-Morton resolution to the President's secretary (shot C-5), who then asks Morton and Senator Borland to come in to see the President. Next comes a cut to the final part of their interview with the President: Senator Borland's brief appeal on Morton's behalf in C-16, which is followed in turn by C-19 and C-20, in which Morton agrees reluctantly to establish his patent by suing an Army or Navy doctor. After that there is the montage of newspapers called for in C-22 and the Horace Greeley scene that was added during shooting. This is followed by a very fast dissolve to C-24, in which a judge announces the decision that invalidates Morton's patent. This dissolve is so fast that we hear the last few sentences of Greely's diatribe over the first shot in the courtroom! The cutters were in such a hurry to get through Morton's later life that they stumbled onto the overlapping of scenes technique that is sometimes thought to be a New Wave invention.

The scene in which Morton rises and starts out wearily from the courtroom (C-25) is followed by the scene with the glassmaker (B-7), which occurs in the script thirteen pages earlier! We are to believe that, informed he has no legal rights to his discovery, Morton destroys a glassmaker's shop out of spite. (In the script he believes his patent valid and the glassmaker has committed an outrageous infringement.) The glassmaker scene is followed by an abridged version of the scene of the exhausted Morton in bed (D-16). Here Dr. Warren says that Morton must rest and Morton says that he can't afford to because his practice is gone and he is assailed by claims that he stole other people's ideas. Morton asks Warren. "You know I discovered the use of ether, don't you?" and Warren says, "Of course I know it." The film now cuts back to A-9 for an abridged version of Mrs. Morton's account of Morton's last days and death, which is followed by the whole of the rest of her speech concerning the other claimants to the discovery of ether and the fact that it was Morton's discovery that led to the whole world's use of ether. In the script, Mrs. Morton remarks at one point in her long speech that Jackson's article has brought back all the misery of twenty years. *The Great Moment*'s reedited, abridged Part II suggests a vastly shorter period; particularly with overlapped cause-and-effect editing that leaves no room for ellipses or a sense of time going by. After a dizzying series of overlapping fragments, we see a shot of Morton in bed and then there is a cut to the scene in which Elizabeth tells us that he got up in the middle of the night to sort his papers, went to New York, and later died. After her mother's speech, the Morton daughter Betty comes in to announce dinner and there is a brief dissolve to the end of the dinner, whereupon Mrs. Morton begins to reminisce about the early days of her and Morton's relationship.

If feature film editing could be evaluated outside of its narrative context, then many of Paramount's edits are rather clever. As it is, the narrative of *The Great Moment* is incoherent and the editing, more than any other factor, makes that incoherence possible. (The editing of *The Great Moment* may be read as a deconstruction of classical Hollywood editing.) Considered the other way around, the footage available to the editors of *The Great Moment* did not support the editing scheme the studio had decided on. Even if the footage had been available, moreover, the exercise would have served no more purpose than it now serves: to turn a very interesting structure into a very boring one. Another important factor is the absurdly fast, heavily overlapped editing whereby *The Great Moment* races through even the fragments it retains of Morton's later years. This pacing lessens comprehension of those fragments themselves but may have been designed to distract viewer attention from the incoherence of this part of the film and/or to abridge still further the "painful" part of the film. When the second flashback begins, showing the discovery years and Morton's sacrifice, the editing shows down considerably and the film seems, for the first time, to breathe.

Abridging and reediting was only part of the process the studio went through to refashion *Triumph over Pain*. Sturges's new foreword had to be shot and the musical score, originally recorded on August 6, 1942, had to be remixed to synchronize with the reedited film. At some point the title of the film had been changed to *The Great Moment,* which of course entailed a reworked credit sequence. All of these things were completed, and the film itself was ready for release, on April 28, 1943. This is the date of the Release Dialogue Script, a document prepared for the Paramount Exchanges, which were regional film depots to which prints of a film were sent by the studio and from which they were returned. The Exchanges checked each print against the Release Dialogue Script when it arrived from the studio and again when it was returned by the theaters served by the Exchange after the film's run. The Release Dialogue Script for *The Miracle of Morgan's Creek* is dated April 23, 1943, five days earlier than the one for *The Great Moment.* Yet another Sturges film, *Hail the Conquering Hero* (1944), began shooting on July 14 and was completed in early September 1943. When two previews of that film— the second on December 9—received mixed audience responses, DeSylva threatened cuts and rearrangements of the kind he had already done on *The Great Moment.* To complicate matters even further, Sturges's contract was to expire on December 10, 1943. Sturges and Paramount tried to find terms for a mutually satisfactory renewal but a meeting of the minds did not take place, so Sturges left Paramount with three films unreleased.

The Miracle of Morgan's Creek, the only one of the three films never recut, was released in January 1944 to an immediate and prodigious box office success—nine million dollars in its first year. A heavily reedited version of *Hail the Conquering Hero,* in which the "talkier" passages had been eliminated, was previewed in New York in February with disastrous results. Sturges then offered to return to Paramount without salary to adjust *Hail* and *Great Without Glory* "to everyone's satisfaction." He wrote a new ending for *Hail* in late March and shot four days of retakes in early April, spending the rest of that month restoring the film to the way he had shot it and harmonizing it with the new material he had shot.[15] The film was scheduled for release in August 1944.

DeSylva refused to let Sturges restore *Great Without Glory,* however, so on June 22, 1944, Sturges appealed, as he had done almost two years earlier, to Y. Frank Freeman.

Dear Frank:

While there's Life, there's Hope . . . at least in my breast. With the present postponement of "Hail the Conquering Hero" there should still be time to save "The Great Moment" from the mediocre and shameful career it is going to have in its present form and under its present title. The majority of reviews in the trade papers should be enough of a foretaste, the handwriting is on the wall, and I don't see what Paramount, its stockholders, you, Balaban, Reagan and myself are going to gain by putting out a picture in the form of a guaranteed, gilt-edged disaster, when, by the expenditure of less than fifty thousand dollars and some of my time which I will give for nothing you are nearly certain to have a picture of dignity and merit which will reflect credit on all of us and do a great deal more business. Our recent adventures with "Hail the Conquering Hero" and its New York preview should, I believe, at least give me the benefit of the doubt. I don't think I came through the adventure as a complete idiot and when I tell you that "The Great Moment" should be called "Triumph Over Pain" and that it should not be cut in its present streamlined form, you ought to listen to me, Mr. Reagan to the contrary notwithstanding. I urge that you do so.

Cordially yours,

Hail the Conquering Hero had originally been readied for previews in mid-December 1943. The recut studio version was previewed—unfavorably—in February 1944, so the film was still basically on hold. When Sturges returned to the film in March 1944, the original sound and visual materials were at hand and the actors and sets were available for retakes. The case of *The Great Moment* was different. The studio had not only reedited the film, it had remixed the sound track and made all final preparations for release. That the cut footage was preserved seems unlikely, but there is no way to know for sure. The studio had been certain, and probably remained so, that the Sturges version would never bring in audiences. If its own recut version did no better, nothing was lost. About a film like *Hail the Conquering Hero,* which was of a kind in which Sturges excelled, no producer could be sure he knew more than the director, especially after the success of *The Miracle of Morgan's Creek.*

Just what Sturges wanted fifty thousand dollars for is not clear. Perhaps he had in mind a few days' retakes of the sort he had just done for *Hail the Conquering Hero.* If so, no evidence has survived of what the new material was to consist. On the other hand, if Paramount had discarded the footage that it cut from *Great Without Glory,* fifty thousand dollars would hardly begin to cover the costs of reshooting it. Even without the fifty thousand dollars one supposes that Sturges would still have wanted both to restore the cut footage—if it existed—and to restore the original order of the film's scenes. He does not mention this possibility in his letter, however, or, failing to get the money requested, propose it in a follow-up letter. Sturges did not write to Freeman again either because Freeman replied to his letter and closed all doors or never replied at all. No letter from Freeman to Sturges on this matter may be found in the Sturges papers.

In later 1944, Sturges remarks on *The Great Moment* in a number of letters, some of them to old friends and colleagues, others to viewers who had written him about the film. The fate of the film having been sealed, Sturges was free to say, perhaps for the first time, how he viewed what had happened to the film and what it was he had tried to do in the first place. On July 6, 1944, for instance, he wrote to Ben De Casseres, a New York columnist who was also an old family friend. Sturges begins by bringing his correspondent up to date on his activities since they last met:

I had started as a playwright a little before my Mother's death, with some success, and I have recently been making pictures. You were extremely kind to my last one, "The Miracle of Morgan's Creek," and this letter is partly to thank you for that, partly to tell you that I have just read your excellent column on W. T. G. Morton—and that I thought you might like to know that I made a picture about him which will be out some time in October. It is called "The Great Moment."

I had a spoken foreword on it which my studio objected to. As you will not hear it in the picture, if you see the picture, and as it expressed very much the same sentiments you did in your article (on Morton), I thought it might amuse you to read it. One saw a vast plain, dotted with the wreckage of war: half a cannon, half a triumphal arch, half an equestrian statue . . . the rear half. There was no sign of life, the only movements coming from swirls of poison gas. Over this one heard a cheerful voice. It said: [complete text of the foreword]. My studio felt this was not the moment to say such things and, for all I know, they may be right.

Cordially yours,

On August 3, Sturges wrote again, this time addressing his correspondent as "Benjamin De Casseres, Esquire."

By all means use anything I wrote for your column. Incidentally, when people attack motion pictures they should sometimes attack something else than Hollywood. I have just received an English trade paper containing a full page ad about "The Great Moment" as "Triumph Over Pain" is now, over my dead body, called. You are familiar with Fulop-Miller's book and although I put in as much fun as I could, the story of Morton is still serious, thrilling and a little sad. The advertisement bills it as: "Paramount's escapist laugh tonic! Hilarious as a whiff of laughing gas."

Cordially yours,

On August 5, two days after writing the foregoing, Sturges wrote De Casseres again:

I don't want to snow you under with correspondence but after writing to you the other day it occurred to me that it would be better if that part of my letter commenting on the way in which The Great Moment is advertised in England were not published, if you had any such intention.

This, because, although I have fought bitterly against stupidities in this particular branch of the theatre, and with some good result. I have kept the quarrels within the family walls and never yelled out my accusations for the edification of the neighbors. Each shameful thing that has happened to me has really been a proof of my own weakness. I believe I will soon be strong enough to correct this matter. I would rather do that than yelp about it.

Cordially yours,

Sturges's references to his present and former weakness and his anticipated strength have surely to do with the agreement that he was about to conclude with Howard Hughes. Having been negotiated for months, the contracts were finally signed on August 24, 1944, less than three weeks after he wrote this letter. (The signing coincided with the release of *Hail the Conquering Hero,* Sturges's second commercial and critical success within eight months. Hughes took few chances.) The momentous event of this day may also have had something to do with the note that Sturges wrote Buddy DeSylva on the next, August 25:

Dear Buddy:

I just called Harrison Carroll to tell him the The Great Moment had *not* been cut since I left Paramount and discovered that you had already called him. He will print the item and that should close the matter.

My personal opinion of the picture in its present form, after seeing it again, was stated with some clarity in a letter to Frank Freeman dated June 22, 1944. I will be very glad to send you a copy of the letter if you have not seen it but all this is water under the bridge and I say The Hell with it. With all good wishes for your new enterprise, I remain

Cordially yours,

Harrison Carroll was evidently a Hollywood journalist. What he had printed initially, and whether or not Sturges or an associate had "planted" it, is not clear. It seems unlikely that Sturges did because, as he correctly observes to DeSylva, *The Great Moment* had been "cut" before he left Paramount. DeSylva wrote back the next day:

Dear Preston:

Many thanks for your gracious letter.

Perhaps I was a little touchy. The only time that "Paramount" (or by implication, DeSylva) was mentioned in one of your reviews was, in this case, by Harrison Carroll. God knows Paramount (and I) have contributed little enough to your movies. But somehow or another, I got a little bit burned at being blamed by inference when one of them turned out not quite so good as all the others. I am sure you are convinced that I never had the slightest notion that Harrison Carroll's comment was inspired by you.

As I told you in the commissary, we unit men must stick together. I shall always be rooting for your success.

As ever,

The principle of keeping quarrels within the family walls was often honored by Sturges but not always. Indeed, on August 25, the day he wrote DeSylva his note of reconciliation, he also wrote letters to two servicemen who had written to him. They reveal that "water under the bridge . . . The Hell with it" was by no means his unequivocal attitude toward the fate of *The Great Moment*. They also reveal, as do his letters to De Casseres and others, that what he wrote about the film varied quite a bit according to the person he was addressing and the views that he or she had already expressed. To Captain Jud Allen, he wrote:

Thank you very much for your interesting letter of August 18th. I appreciate your criticism although I do not agree with it.

It is true that in The Great Moment you saw a mutilated version of a bitter story which I intended to sweeten a little with some funny moments. The studio, which I have since left, decided that the picture must be cut for comedy. As a result, the unpleasant part of the story was cut to a minimum, the story was not told, and the balance of the picture was upset.

To Mr. Frank M. Flack, who was serving with the First Guard Company at Ft. Leavenworth, Kansas, Sturges wrote:

Thank you very much indeed for your courteous and encouraging letter anent The Great Moment. I am glad that you liked the method. I wish there were more of you. Unfortunately for me many people believe in the hand-in-the-bosom-prematurely-turned-to-marble form of biography, and these people are outraged at the idea of anything funny being shown in the foreground of a picture which has a serious background. Many of the reviews have been bad and many more will be. However, as I believe Oscar Wilde said: "When the world begins to agree with me, I start to suspect that I am wrong." Thank you again.

Three months later, on November 25, Sturges wrote De Casseres again:

Thank you very much indeed for the nice things you said about Eddie Bracken and me in your column. The picture "The Great Moment" ("Triumph Over Pain") is playing at the Globe Theatre at the moment and whereas it got slapped around by some of the critics it received 3 1/2 stars in The News and excellent reviews in The Times and The Mirror. I hope that you will publish that foreword some day. It would do my soul a lot of good.

His letter to Flack indicates that Sturges had been expecting bad reviews for *The Great Moment* and that, as a result, both his critical reputation and his bankability as a director would suffer. Led by Bosley Crowther of the *Times,* the New York critics—many of them Sturges partisans—did not allow this to happen. When the braced-for disaster did not occur, Sturges seems to have been elated. And yet, Sturges's last two sentences to De Casseres sound a note of regret. That the regret, and the anger, persisted is indicated by a letter Sturges wrote a year and a half later, on May 7, 1946, to a viewer named Syril Cosner who had written him about several of his films.

I am surprised that in your dislike of "The Great Moment," a dislike justified by the form in which it was cut and released (over my dead body, incidentally), you were blinded to the many unusual things it contained. How lightly you waive away a year of my life with the glib and insulting conclusion that the picture looked as if it had taken five minutes to write and five minutes to direct. How blandly you ignore the effort to bring to the screen a worthy subject presented in a contemporary manner.

You probably prefer the Pasteur manner, where every character knows already his place in History and acts as if carved in marble. How blind you are to have missed the symbol of thought coming through the backdoor to get past traditional smugness . . .

The mixing of humor and seriousness in *The Great Moment* is a topic that a number of Sturges commentators have discussed. Since we do not have the film that Sturges directed and edited, we do not know what the balance of humor and seriousness in it was. Reading the script takes us only so far in this respect since how a written scene is directed is crucial to the balance of humor and seriousness in it. Part I of the script, which deals with the second part of Morton's life, seems to have little humor, as Sturges's remarks to Captain Allen tend to confirm. In cutting to a minimum "the unpleasant part of the story" (i.e., Part I), Paramount thereby "cut the film for comedy." The only apparent exception in Part I—the bitterly satiric portrait of President Franklin Pierce—proves the rule: the weasel-like and indecisive Pierce, who dashes Morton's hopes, is no laughing matter. Part II of the script certainly has humor but, without a coherent Part I, its humorous effect is off-balance and hard to read.

330

Even in Part II of *The Great Moment,* some recutting was done. A scene in which Eben Frost jumps out a window after inhaling bad ether is a case in point. Chas. P. West's editing suggestion number 10 was implemented in the reedit:

Interior of Office Building — I question whether the comedy of Frost's running around the balcony will justify the amount of footage given to it in the present cutting. It probably is wise to preview in this length, but if it does not hold, I believe you could easily take Frost out of the window without letting him make a complete circuit of the balcony.

As Sturges evidently shot the scene, Frost leaps from the dental chair then runs and shouts madly around the balcony, before he plunges through the window and, according to the script, "slides down [an] awning [and] lands unharmed" (page 103). Without complete and continuous footage of Frost's actions, the scene is confusing and therefore probably much less funny than it was in the film that Sturges shot and edited. Narratively, the scene lacks proper preparation as it is: we learn only later, at the same time that Morton learns it, the reason for Frost's reaction.

Sturges's brief discussions of the issue in the three letters quoted above, while hardly a substitute for seeing the unseeable film, shed some small light on the matter. Interestingly, while not logically inconsistent, the letters to Allen and Flack emphasize nearly opposite points. The letter to Allen stresses the seriousness of the film Sturges wrote and shot, which Paramount undermined by omitting most of the serious material and thereby cutting the film for comedy. In the letter to Flack, however, Sturges defends the introduction of humor as something that he himself did.

Brief passages in the letters to Flack and Cosner make a more interesting point, which is that Sturges used humor in the film "to get past [the] traditional smugness" of biopics, the "prematurely-turned-to-marble form of biography." To Flack he contrasts this, intriguingly, with showing funny things "in the foreground of a picture which has a serious background," as he understands himself to do. Whether he means foreground/background in a figurative sense or literally in terms of the frame itself is not clear. In his letter to Cosner he criticized the marbleized protagonists of most biopics in which "every character knows already his place in history." Humor, slapstick, and accident are Sturges's ways of projecting characters who are unaware of their place in history, as is "the symbol of thought coming through the backdoor." Each of these devices has the effect of diminishing the control that biopic protagonists have over the achievements for which they are known, and, one might add, alters the relation of the viewer to them. Sturges is here concerned with the dramaturgy of biography, that is, with how past events should be presented by filmmakers and experienced by viewers. Sturges clearly felt that one of the great pitfalls of biography is to attribute to the protagonists our knowledge of them, whether of the later events of their lives or of posterity's understanding of them. Showing "thought coming through the backdoor," which Sturges manages to do in *The Great Moment,* must be extremely difficult—one can scarcely think of another example.

*   *   *

Sturges obviously admired Fülöp-Miller's book. As we have seen, he did everything he could to retain the author's title for his film. But Sturges's actual view of Morton differs in fundamental respects from Fülöp-Miller's. The latter, taking a lofty view, criticizes Morton for wanting to make money from his discovery and seems unconcerned that Morton's fortunes, and those of his family, were ruined by that discovery. Regarding Morton's surprising withdrawal to his study to refine his discovery for general surgery, Fülöp-Miller says:

> Dr. Morton, the Boston dentist, had undergone a transformation which was beyond the comprehension of those of his own household—the transformation to greatness.
> Destiny works in accordance with laws of her own when she picks a man out from among the crowd to make of him something very different from the others. Morton, the dentist, was a little man with a little mind whom petty motives had led to make a discovery. But his discovery was overwhelmingly important. Thereupon the miracle was worked. The great discovery took charge of the little man. Its greatness snatched him out of the sphere of little things, imposed greatness upon him, so that, by the caprice of fate, the petty dentist of Boston became one of the supreme benefactors of mankind.
> Discarding practice, money, health and family life, Morton lived henceforward for his idea.[16]

If there are idealisms pleasant and unpleasant, then Fülöp-Miller's is very unpleasant. He is all too ready to sacrifice Morton's material needs and comfort for the "idea." To affirm the vastness of difference between the person of "greatness," however arrived at, and "the crowd" is never welcome—in 1938 even less so than at other times. Sturges, on the contrary, does not begrudge Morton any rewards that might have resulted from his discovery; indeed he bemoans their absence. And he rails at the other humiliations and discomforts of Morton's life with bitter invective. Nothing could be farther from Fülöp-Miller's viewpoint than the savage indignation of Sturges's original foreword. (His revised foreword—which, as we have seen, was written under duress— is less far from Fülöp-Miller's view of Morton.) Even here, however, there is an important difference. What Sturges says is that Morton "*seems* very small indeed until the incandescent moment he ruined himself for a servant girl and gained immortality [my emphasis]." Sturges's Morton responds to a fellow creature in pain, not to the demands of living for an idea.

Instead of empathetic understanding of his subject's plight, Fülöp-Miller indulges in irony, a remote sense of the tragic, and bemused talk about the "curse" afflicting participants in the discovery of anesthesia. Indeed he even seems to blame Morton for any hesitation whatever in disclosing his secret before the operation on Alice Mohan:

> The moment had come in which Morton would have to make a great decision. Would he prove equal to the test? Was the discoverer worthy of his discovery?
>
> Unquestionably the man with whom Dr. Bigelow was now to talk things over was very different from the Morton who . . . had . . . applied for a patent in the hope of making money out of the new method. Yet less than six weeks had passed. That had been October 1st; it was now November 7th. Thirty-seven days seem a brief period in which to transform a money-making dentist into an unselfish benefactor of the human race. Morton [however] had not completely put off the old Adam.[17]

The old Adam is the desire for money in general and the "Protestant ethic" in particular. (Sociologists Max Weber and R. H. Tawney have analyzed this phenomenon and its relation to the rise of capitalism, at length.) Says Fülöp-Miller:

> The puritan conscience had entered into an alliance with economic advance, and piety sanctified money-making. Business success and wealth were henceforth regarded as tangible evidence of God's approval. . . . Thus was money-making declared a virtue. Morton was devoted to this virtue.[18]

Neither Sturges's Morton nor what we know of the actual Morton fits this description. Had Morton been devoted to moneymaking, he might have continued his lucrative dental practice for forty or fifty years. Having discovered a painkiller, he might have kept it secret and made even more money.

By 1846, the views of Emerson—who began as a reformer against the worship of money—prevailed among educated people, particularly in New England. Morton may perhaps best be regarded as an Emersonian adventurer, hitching his wagon to a star. If he wished to make money also, that was Emersonian as well, as the great transcendentalist's essay on wealth makes clear. (Kenneth Burke referred to an early Emerson essay as "a Happiness Pill" and refers to the philosopher as "a highly respectable vendor of uplift.")[19]

Following the Emersonian formula, Morton had built "a better mousetrap"—his discovery is considered by some the most important single development in the history of medicine—but few indeed beat a path to his door, though he built his house in Boston.[20] Sturges's Morton—and what we know of the actual Morton—may be regarded as a living contradiction of the optimistic philosophy that Emerson had advanced so successfully. In this respect, Morton's life may be understood as what critic Glauco Cambon calls, writing of Emily Dickinson's work, "downward transcendence."[21] A stanza by the poet, suppressed by her early editors, recalls the unhappy discoverer also.[22]

And then a Plank in Reason, broke,
And I dropped down, and down –
And hit a World, at every plunge,
and Finished knowing – then –

NOTES

1. See Stephen W. Hawking, *A Brief History of Time: From the Big Bang to Black Holes* (New York: Bantam, 1988).

A star that was sufficiently massive and compact would have such a strong gravitational field that light could not escape: any light emitted from the surface of the star would be dragged back by the star's gravitational attraction before it could get very far. . . . Although we would not be able to see them because the light from them would not reach us, we would still feel their gravitational attraction. Such objects are what we now call black holes, because that is what they are: black voids in space. (81–82)

2. René Fülöp-Miller, *Triumph over Pain,* translated by Eden Paul and Cedar Paul (New York: Literary Guild of America, 1938).

3. James Curtis, *Between Flops: A Biography of Preston Sturges* (New York: Harcourt Brace Jovanovich, 1982), 168.

4. Brian Henderson, ed., *Five Screenplays by Preston Sturges* (Berkeley: University of California Press, 1985), 518–520.

5. Curtis, *Between Flops,* 172.

6. See Brian Henderson, "Romantic Comedy Today: Semi-Tough or Impossible?" *Film Quarterly* 31, no. 4 (Summer 1978): 20–21.

7. The epilogue to *Raging Bull* (1980) is as follows:

> So, for the Second time, [The Pharisees]
> Summoned the man who had been blind and said:
>
> "Speak the truth before God.
> We know this fellow is a sinner."
>
> "Whether or not he is a sinner,
> I do not know." The man replied.
>
> "All I know is this:
> once I was blind and now I can see."
>
> John, IX: 24–26
> The New English Bible

8. Curtis, *Between Flops,* 167–177, 182–193.

9. Ibid., 124–125.

10. Ibid., 173–174.

11. Ibid., 173.

12. *Street Angel* (1928) was directed by Frank Borzage, *Fallen Angel* (1945) by Otto Preminger, and *The Tarnished Angels* (1957) by Douglas Sirk.

13. James Ursini, *Preston Sturges: An American Dreamer* (New York: Curtis Books, 1973), 118–119.

14. Ibid., 119.

15. Ibid., 190.

16. Fülöp-Miller, *Triumph over Pain,* 138.

17. Ibid., 158–159.

18. Ibid., 131.

19. Kenneth Burke, "I,Eye,Ay—Emerson's Early Essay 'Nature': Thoughts on the Machinery of Transcendence," in Myron Simon and Thornton H. Parsons, eds., *Transcendentalism and Its Legacy* (Ann Arbor: University of Michigan Press, 1966), 3, 7. "Hitch your wagon to a star" is a phrase from Emerson's essay "Civilization," which appeared in his 1870 book, *Society and Solitude.* Emerson was born in 1803 and died in 1882.

20. "If a man write a better book, preach a better sermon, or make a better mousetrap than his neighbour, tho' he build his house in the woods, the world will make a beaten path to his door." The origin of this ultra-Emersonian formula was, and perhaps still is, a matter of dispute. Mrs. Sarah S. B. Yule (1856–1916) credited the quotation to Emerson in her *Borrowings* (1889), saying in a 1912 article that she copied it from a lecture delivered by Emerson. But Elbert Hubbard (1859–1915) claimed that he authored the much-quoted lines.

21. Glauco Cambon, "Emily Dickinson and the Crisis of Self-Reliance," in Simon and Parsons, *Transcendentalism,* 127.

22. The complete poem is as follows:

> I felt a Funeral, in my Brain,
> And Mourners to and fro
> Kept treading – treading – till it seemed
> That Sense was breaking through –
>
> And when they all were seated,
> A Service, like a Drum –
> Kept beating – beating – till I thought
> My Mind was going numb –
>
> And then I heard them lift a Box
> And creak across my Soul
> With those same Boots of Lead, again
> Then Space - began to toll
>
> As all the Heavens were a Bell,
> And Being, but an Ear,
> And I, and Silence, some strange Race
> Wrecked, solitary, here –
>
> And then a Plank in Reason, broke,
> And I dropped down, and down –
> And hit a World, at every plunge,
> And Finished knowing – then –

This is Poem No. 280, written circa 1861, in Thomas H. Johnson, ed., *The Complete Poems of Emily Dickinson* (Boston: Little, Brown and Company, 1960). Cambon reports that the early editors lopped off the fifth stanza from the body of the poem: "They could not accept this downward transcendence, especially since it supervenes as a sudden rupture of the trance-like quiet on which Stanza 4 had come to rest." (In Simon and Parsons, *Transcendentalism,* 127.)

APPENDIX

The footage that Paramount cut from *Triumph over Pain* has disappeared, although not without leaving a trace. Among the Sturges papers devoted to *Triumph over Pain/The Great Moment* is "Production Script #1337." This is in fact Sturges's final script, dated March 30, 1942, which is reprinted below. What sets the production script apart from other copies of the final script, indeed from all other script versions of *Triumph over Pain,* is that it contains a single positive 35mm frame from every shot of the film, in some cases several frames from a single shot. There is only one other such script in the Sturges papers—that for *The Lady Eve.* The positive 35mm frames from *The Lady Eve* provide traces of a few scenes that Sturges himself chose to cut from the film—a matter of relatively minor interest. On the contrary, the frames from *Triumph over Pain* comprise our only evidence—besides the final script itself—of what the scenes excised from the film looked like.

Printed below are forty-two frame enlargements from the single frames of Production Script #1337. The less-than-perfect quality of the enlargements is due to the poor quality of the frames themselves. The principal factors are that fifty-two years of neglect have taken their toll and that individual frames deteriorate more rapidly than film on reels. Originally, the frames had been arranged in chronological order and taped into the pages of the script according to the shots and scenes they illustrated. But the decay of the tape over time has caused most of the frames to fall into a heap at the inside margin of the pages to which they had been attached. This worsened their condition and also required re-sorting them into what seemed to be their original order. Nevertheless, for anyone interested in *Triumph over Pain,* the existence of frames from Sturges's lost film is a major discovery.

The frame enlargements printed below have to do with the following scenes:

1. The Modern Operation scene (6 frames), script page A-2.
2. The Preparing for Bed scene (10 frames), script pages A-15 to A-16.
3. The Breakfast and Dental Office scenes (12 frames), script pages 17–20.
4. The Army Colonel scene (3 frames), script page 21.

5. The Letter from Washington scene (5 frames), script pages 27–28.
6. The Visit to President Pierce scene (4 frames), script pages 28–31.
7. The Patent Court scene (2 frames), script pages 35–36.

The first three sequences—the modern operation, preparing for bed, and breakfast and dental office—are crucial passages that were cut entirely from *The Great Moment*. For this reason, frame enlargements from these sequences are provided as fully as the available frames allow. The Army colonel scene was also cut from the film but, because it serves primarily as an expository scene, is incompletely illustrated. The letter from Washington, the visit to President Pierce, and the patent court scenes are all included—in a more or less abridged form—in *The Great Moment*. Because shots have been omitted from each of these scenes, the frame enlargements printed below fill important gaps.

The modern operation scene is one of several texts in the final script that provide perspective on both parts of the film, that is, on the whole of Morton's life and work. It immediately follows the script's "Foreword" (page A-1) and immediately precedes its dissolve to the silver medal in the pawnshop window—"To Dr. W. T. G. Morton, the Benefactor of Mankind with the gratitude of Humanity" (page A-3). The point of the modern operation is evidently that, thanks to Morton's discovery of 1846, a little boy in 1942 can undergo a surgical procedure—unspecified—that will enable him to walk, run, swim, and play sports. On page A-2, as the reader can see, the script calls for presentation of the scene in two shots. The only exception to this scheme is that, during shooting, Sturges felt it necessary to shoot and cut in a close-up of the little boy (frame 2). Frames 1a, 1b, and 1c are successive phases of a single shot—a trucking shot of the gurney being wheeled to the operating room. The third shot, represented by frames 3a and 3b, moves from the anesthetist administering ether to the boy to what Sturges calls "the big gas machine." What is unusual about the shot is its inexplicable menace: the eyeless nurse and doctor and the looming shadows of nurse, doctor, and IV stand of 3a; and the horrible entanglement of metal, rubber, chemical tanks, and disembodied hand in the anesthesia apparatus of 3b.

The manifold changes worked by Paramount's cutters in the framing story, including its long first part (pages A-3 to A-10), are discussed in the introduction above. The framing story flashes back to a number of scenes (pages A-10 to A-16) that take place just following the Alice Mohan operation, the first painless amputation in medical history, on November 1, 1846. A large crowd has assembled to hail Morton upon his emergence from Massachusetts General Hospital. The cheering throng, including two brass bands loudly playing different numbers, accompanies Morton's carriage down an avenue that passes by his dental offices and finally arrives at his stately home, whereupon the triumphant dentist orders champagne for all. A slow dissolve (page A-12) is followed by a shot of Morton waving good-bye to the departing celebrants; getting rid of a tipsy Eben Frost takes another script page. Mrs. Morton tells

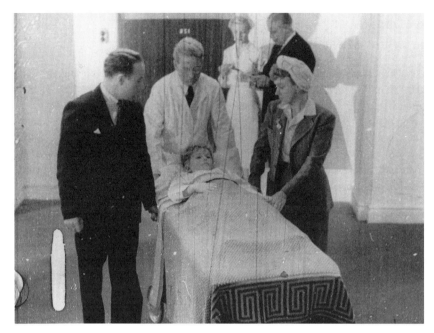

Frame 1a

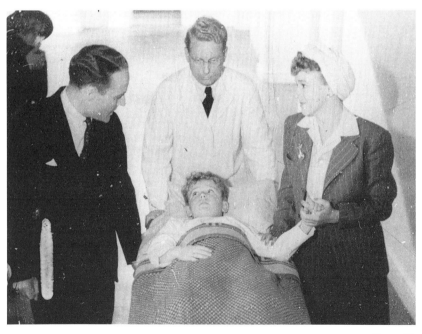

Frame 1b

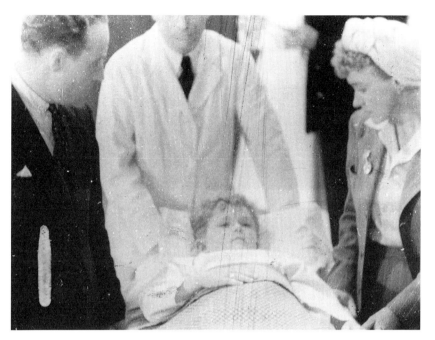

Frame 1c

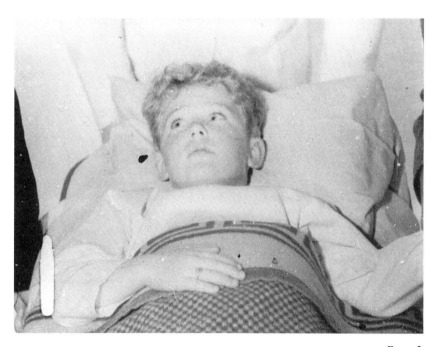

Frame 2

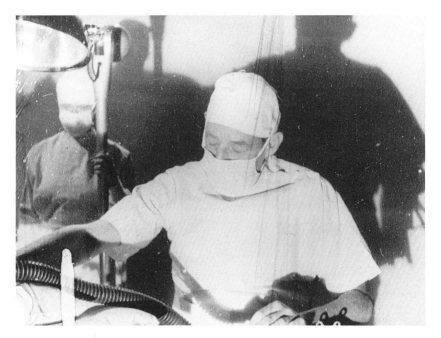

Frame 3a

Frame 3b

her husband how proud of him she is and asks his forgiveness if she hasn't always appreciated what he was doing. He replies that it is he who needs forgiveness for reeking of chemicals, working all night, and forgetting social events. After they climb the steps to the second floor, Mrs. Morton pauses for a moment to look down and say how proud she is of their house.

The Mortons walk down the hall (frame 4) and enter the bedroom (frame 5), and, as they get ready for bed, have an extended conversation. Morton's undressing motions provide a continuity that allows us to order the frames in a fairly reliable way. What cannot be determined reliably is which lines of dialogue occur in a given shot. A character's mouth may be open in one of the frames, but that does not mean that the other character may not have spoken already and/or may speak again in the same shot. Hence the response to a line of dialogue may occur in the same shot or in the next shot. As a result, the assignment of shots that follows has a sizable component of guesswork.

When Morton "sighs heavily" (frame 5?) a surprised Mrs. Morton asks if he is worried about something (frame 6). He denies it, but she admits that she herself is worried that all of their success is too good to be true; she has a horrible fear that somebody will find out what Letheon is (frame 6). Morton asks if it would make such a difference (frame 7), and Mrs. Morton replies at length that it would make all the difference in the world—that is why she was nervous about trying the substance at the hospital where there are such fine scientists and chemists who could analyze it (frames 7 and 8). Morton replies that she need never worry about that again (frame 9a). Has he found some way to disguise the substance, she asks. He replies that he had to disclose the secret of Letheon—his name for sulfuric ether—or the Medical Society would not let it be used (frame 9b). Mrs. Morton's stunned reaction, which may in fact begin in frame 9b, is traced in frames 10a, 10b, and 10c: "But you didn't tell them! I mean you weren't such a fool as to tell them the most valuable secret in the world, just for the asking!" Morton replies that they were going to take her leg off without anything. "Whose leg?" Mrs. Morton demands, to which Morton replies, "I don't know—some servant girl!"

It is this scene, above all, that Paramount wished to excise, in the name of "protecting the finish" of the film. If Morton's sacrifice were revealed this early in the film, they felt, there would be no suspense, and the audience would lose interest. Although this argument should have some force, it has none; indeed, it makes us appreciate more fully the subtlety of Sturges's script and the lost film based on it. Under pressure from his wife, whom he did not consult before making his decision, Morton admits, in a manner at once defensive, offhand, and stumbling, that he has disclosed his secret to the doctors who otherwise would have operated without anesthesia. As a result, the viewer knows what Morton did but not why he did it or what he felt as he did so. The viewer has information but not understanding. Some of the facts of Morton's sacrifice now lie on the surface of the film, but in a way that makes them unreadable. The sacrifice will be readable only at the end of the film.

Frame 4

Frame 5

Frame 6

Frame 7

343

Frame 8

Frame 9a

344

Frame 9b

Frame 10a

Frame 10b

Frame 10c

Sequence "A" concludes with the preparation for bed scene; the breakfast and dental office scenes begin sequence "B." As explained in the introduction, above, these scenes were altered during shooting, as the dialogue continuity—prepared after shooting—reveals. As the breakfast scene opens, Dr. Morton is reading a passage from the newspaper: "It says here that I did a very generous thing—giving my secret to the world—that there's going to be a new era in surgery" (frame 11). In the dialogue continuity, Morton is reading the passage to his butler; as he does so, Mrs. Morton appears, and the butler pours her a cup of coffee (frame 12). For her benefit, Morton reads the passage from the newspaper again. Beginning here, the available frames do not support the extended conversation between Mr. and Mrs. Morton that the script and dialogue continuity indicate. Again, similar to the preparation for bed scene, it is unclear which lines of dialogue correspond to which frames. In frame 13, for instance, Mrs. Morton might be saying, "I was wondering how we were going to send the children to college," or she might be speaking her later remark, "It would be a wonderful satisfaction to have this house paid for, too." As for Morton's extended justifications, they are not covered by frames at all.

In the script, there is no scene in the dental office; the entire scene, including the intrusion of the reporter, takes place in the Morton breakfast room. Frost walks into the scene and announces his news that Morton's dentists have gone in business for themselves and that the whole town is giving ether. This seems to be a cue to action, but Morton just sits there. As Sturges shot the scene, however, Frost runs up the stairs, yelling, "Hey!" (frame 14) and excitedly conveys his news (frame 15). The three characters then take a fast carriage ride to the dental office (frame 16), enter the office (frame 17), and confront the receptionist (frame 18), who says, "I don't know what to say. The world just seemed to drop out from under us." Morton replies, "Well, advertise in the paper for some more dentists right away" (frame 19). Just then the reporter, glimpsed approaching in frame 18, confronts Morton with a question: "Say, Doc, the old man wants a statement from you—I'm from the Daily Advertiser—about a story just come through." The story he summarizes (frames 20 and 21) concerns the other claimants to the discovery of ether anesthesia—Dr. Charles T. Jackson, Horace Wells, and Crawford Long. Frame 22 shows the reaction of the Mortons.

The Army colonel scene is a brief connective scene between two longer ones. As the breakfast/dental office scene draws to a close, Morton tells the reporter, "Anyway, I've still got a patent . . . I think." The jovial colonel informs Morton that the government has not ordered the ether inhaler that Morton designed and patented, and later discloses the name of the glassmaker who did get the order—whom Morton regards as the infringer of his patent. The scene with the colonel is followed by the scene of Morton's glass-breaking rampage in the display room of E. Gruber & Sons, the firm that got the Army order.

Frame 11

Frame 12

Frame 13

Frame 14

Frame 15

Frame 16

Frame 17

Frame 18

351

Frame 19

Frame 20

Frame 21

Frame 22

353

The Army colonel scene is no more than a dramatic convenience, but it has one interesting twist. The colonel opens a drawer in his desk to find the Gruber inhaler but his eye comes to rest instead on some horrible weapons that are also in the drawer—a revolving pistol and what the script calls a "horrendous-looking saw-toothed bayonet" and "a bullet that opens out like a small umbrella." Of the two latter devices the colonel says, "Nasty little things these are. We don't believe in them. Of course if the other side should start using them . . ." Three frames from this *Strangelove*-like moment show the drawer the colonel has opened (frame 23), the colonel himself commenting on its contents to Morton (frame 24), and a half-empty drawer with part of its contents on the edge of the desk and the colonel apparently in the process of putting yet another weapon on the desk (frame 25). The tone of the scene is light, but its emphasis on destruction recalls the foreword's denunciation of "generals . . . tyrants, usurpers, dictators, politicians and other heroes [who lead Homo Sapiens], usually from the rear, to dismemberment, and death."

The letter from Washington scene is rendered in some detail in *The Great Moment* but, as argued above, is so out of context as to be unreadable. Frames 26 and 28, which show Mrs. Morton and her three children hurrying across the field with a letter to Morton from Washington, may be seen in *The Great Moment.* The older girl, who is carrying the letter, stumbles and falls, "shooting the letter to one side," whereupon the boy picks it up without helping her and carries it to Morton. Frame 27 shows Morton pausing in his farming the field to mop his brow with a handkerchief—an action which is not mentioned in the script. In *The Great Moment,* Morton reaches into his pocket for a handkerchief, but the film cuts before he can raise his arm to his face. Actual labor and its physical consequences—such as profuse perspiration—were rarely shown in classical Hollywood films. Frame 29—the arrival of Mrs. Morton in the shot—may also be seen in *The Great Moment,* but frame 30, an overhead shot of Morton reading the letter with his family gathered around, is not. Frame 30 is pleasing in its abrupt change of angle from frame 29 and, in a number of respects, pleasing in itself. One also sees, in retrospect, the difficulty of including all the Mortons in one shot (frame 29), particularly with the bulky dresses that women in Mrs. Morton's time were obliged to wear. On the contrary, the overhead shot shows the entire family in a manner that is both casual and inventive. The overhead shot also allows us to see that Morton is still strapped to his horses and plow and that the older Morton girl is seated on the plow itself. We also see the plow ruts in the earth, which make dynamic, Eisenstein-like diagonals in the composition as a whole.

One is tempted to speculate what the shot represented by frame 30 might have meant. This is partly because overhead shots are extremely rare in the films that Sturges directed. He uses an overhead shot for Charles's shipboarding in *The Lady Eve,* but this is understood by the viewer as corresponding to Jean's point of view—indeed, she drops an apple on his head before the scene

Frame 23

Frame 24

Frame 25

Frame 26

Frame 27

Frame 28

Frame 29

Frame 30

is over. There is no conceivable character who looks down on the Mortons in this shot, so the viewer understands the film itself to be doing so. Why it does so—what the shot might mean—is not easy to formulate. A starting point might be that we see the attentive faces of Mrs. Morton and the three children but not that of Morton, who, turned away from us in the shot, is totally absorbed by the letter. The letter's news is good (Morton might get a $100,000 award from Congress), but its urgent advice is less so (he must come to Washington immediately), and his plan to raise money for the trip (to borrow on the farm) proves to be disastrous for himself and his family. As Mrs. Morton says, "I did so want to hold on to this—for the children's sake. They're so helpless." The script views Morton as a victim, indeed as a prime example of humanity's ingratitude to its benefactors. Perhaps in this one moment, however, the film's Morton gambles needlessly with his family's welfare. His desire to improve their lot is sincere, but he is also preoccupied with his own struggle for recognition.

The visit to President Pierce is set in the antechamber and the office of the President of the United States (who at that time was Franklin Pierce). The scene begins with a brief exchange between a "Whackpot" and the antechamber secretary (frame 31), whom the dialogue continuity refers to as a "receptionist," probably to differentiate him from the President's secretary. The Whackpot is played by Sig Arno, who earlier played Toto, the hanger-on who speaks an imaginary language in *The Palm Beach Story*. During shooting, two additional "speeches" were written for the Whackpot—both of them referred to in the dialogue continuity as "double talk." Indeed, the only words the Whackpot manages to say in the scene are "Universal Peace Movement." The receptionist says he's sorry but "you will have to take that up with the War Department," to which the Whackpot replies, "Hein?"

In frame 32 the President's secretary enters the anteroom through the door to the president's office, in order to take Morton and Borland inside. Also waiting in the antechamber are two Georgians, a "Gentleman" and Senator Smith, who carries a memorial from twenty senators who oppose the award to Morton. Smith tries to give the memorial to the secretary, who declines it, saying, "One at a time, please." Smith presumably gives the memorial to the receptionist, however, for it is delivered to Pierce during his meeting with Morton.

Morton's scene with the President is five pages long, nearly all of which was retained during shooting. *The Great Moment* cuts most of it—everything from the secretary's instructions to Morton on how to address the President (page 30) to an abbreviated version of Borland's remarks (page 33): "This bill has passed both houses, it requires only your signature . . . this man has been waiting for years." This is followed by a cut to Pierce's line, added during shooting: "I can't sign this yet." This, in turn, is followed by his speech which begins, "Now don't look as if you'd just lost your best friend . . ." (page 33).

The Pierce passage as a whole paints him as many kinds of fool and also as a coward, afraid to trust his own judgment. As he begins to sign the amendment awarding Morton one hundred thousand dollars (frame 33), his quill pen "breaks and makes a big splotch on the document" (frame 34). "Goldern it!" he says, "I must be the sloppiest President we ever had." He whittles a new point on the pen, slits it, and tries it—it breaks at once. He calls in his secretary to fix the pen, and the secretary drops off a memorial that has just arrived. Pierce says he'll look at it later but sees that it concerns the award to Morton and reads it. He decides not to sign Morton's award—the President must conduct himself like "Cautious Charlie . . . for that he was elected." Instead he urges Morton to sue an Army or Navy surgeon for infringement of his patent—he will surely win the suit and silence his critics.

In the film that Sturges shot, this scene brings Morton and the viewer to the brink of a long-dreamed fulfillment, only to pull them back—by virtue of a faulty pen and a memorial that just happens to catch the presidential eye— at the last moment. In Fülöp-Miller and in Sturges alike, Morton's particular hell was not only the externally determined decline of his fortunes. It was also the recurring illusion of hope that, again and again, elicited from him precisely those actions that sealed his fate beyond repair.

The suit that Morton files against an Army or Navy doctor—the script never specifies which it is—brings him to his lowest point. He is expelled from the American Medical Association, disowned by his fellow dentists, and excoriated by newspapers in every major city. The patent court scene in the script— in which Morton's patent is declared invalid—is a brief half-page. Sturges shot it verbatim, but *The Great Moment* eliminated the last two lines of the judge's speech; even his praise of Morton as "among the greatest benefactors of mankind" trails off into the noise of the spectators delighted with the decision. Frame 35a may be seen in *The Great Moment,* but frame 35b, which shows Morton exiting a row of hostile spectators, is cut. Frame 35b is interesting because it shows the doors that lead out of the courtroom and into the life that now awaits him. Morton is the only one facing those doors in frame 35b; everyone else, turned toward the judge's bench, is glaring at Morton.

Frame 31

Frame 32

Frame 33

Frame 34

Frame 35a

Frame 35b

TRIUMPH OVER PAIN

Preston Sturges
March 30, 1942

SEQUENCE "A"

FADE IN:

A VERY BEAUTIFUL CLOUDED SKY

The word   "FOREWORD"

DISSOLVES INTO THE MIDDLE OF THE SCREEN and -

Two things begin simultaneously:

Number 1:   THE CAMERA ANGLES DOWN very slowly bringing into
            view first the horizon; then some pretty trees;
            then a little valley; then a little fence and
            the small, forgotten graveyard it encloses, and
            finally directly beneath us, the headstone of
            W.T.G. MORTON - BORN 1819 - DIED 1868, partly
            covered by weeds.

Number 2:   A clear, pleasant voice says the following:

            One of the most charming characteristics
            of Homo Sapiens, the wise guy on your right,
            is the consistency with which he has stoned,
            crucified, burned at the stake, and other-
            wise rid himself of those who consecrated
            their lives to his further comfort and well-
            being so that all his strength and cunning
            might be preserved for the erection of ever
            larger monuments, memorial shafts, triumphal
            arches, pyramids and obelisks to the eternal
            glory of generals on horseback, tyrants,
            usurpers, dictators, politicians and other
            heroes who led him, usually from the rear,
            to dismemberment and death.

            We bring you the story of the Boston dentist
            who gave you ether. Before whom in all time
            surgery was agony. Since whom Science has
            control of pain. It is almost needless to
            tell you that this man, whose contribution
            to human welfare is unparalleled in the
            history of the world, was himself ridiculed,
            burned in effigy, ruined and eventually
            driven to despair and death by the bene-
            ficiaries of his revelation.

            Paramount Pictures, Incorporated, has the
            honor to bring you the true biography of
            an American of supreme achievement, Dr.
            W.T.G. Morton of Boston, Massachusetts,
            in a motion picture called --

During and between the MAIN TITLES we see the preparations
for a modern operation. At the conclusion of the MAIN
TITLES --

A-1   A MODERN HOSPITAL CORRIDOR

We TRUCK AHEAD of a cart on which a nervous little boy is
being wheeled to the operating room. His parents walk on
either side.

                    THE LITTLE BOY
          Is it going to hurt?

                    THE FATHER
          Why of course it isn't going to hurt!
          You'll just go to sleep and then bye
          and bye...bye and bye...

                    THE LITTLE BOY
          Then will I be able to walk?...like
          the other little boys?

                    THE MOTHER
                (Emotionally)
          Why, of course you'll be able to
          walk, my angel. You'll be able to
          walk and run and...and...

                    THE LITTLE BOY
          Will I be able to play baseball?

                    THE FATHER
                (Scornfully)
          Baseball! You'll be able to play
          football and hockey and tennis and...

                    THE LITTLE BOY
          And swim?

                    THE FATHER
          Like a fish!

                    THE LITTLE BOY
          Gee whiz!

He smiles at his mother who wipes away a tear than kisses
him.

DISSOLVE TO:

A-2   CLOSE SHOT - THE LITTLE BOY ON THE OPERATING TABLE

                    THE ANESTHETIST
                (Slowly and soothingly)
          Now just one more deep one.....
          and one more.....and away we go...
          and there we are, doctor.

He reaches for a valve and the CAMERA MOVES INTO A CLOSEUP
of the big gas machine. We hear the rhythmic breathing of
the re-breathing bag as we MOVE IN STILL CLOSER ONTO A label
on the glass ether container.

DISSOLVE VERY SLOWLY TO:

A-3   CLOSE SHOT - A SILVER MEDAL INSCRIBED IN FRENCH

It is from the Academy of the Sciences of the Institute of
France inscribed "To Dr. W. T. G. Morton, the Benefactor
of Mankind with the gratitude of Humanity."

A-4   LOW CAMERA SHOT - UP AT EBEN FROST

We are SHOOTING FROM THE APPROXIMATE POSITION OF the medal
UP THROUGH THE WINDOW, so that BEYOND Frost's head WE SEE
the three balls of a hock shop. Frost is poorly dressed for
the winter of 1868. He carries a fiddle case. Now he starts
for the door and the CAMERA FOLLOWS HIM part way PASSING OVER
mandolins, banjos, and the usual pawnshop window decoration.

A-5   THE PAWNBROKER: FREDERICK T. JOHNSON

He is repairing a watch. A bell jangles, he looks up sourly,
then removes the lupe from his eye.

A-6   EBEN FROST - PAST JOHNSON

He comes up to the counter, puts down his fiddle case, blows
on his fingers, then speaks.

> FROST
> How much do you want for that medal
> in the window?

> JOHNSON
> That's solid silver.

> FROST
> I know all about it. What do you want
> for it?

> JOHNSON
> I'll take its weight and a dollar over.

> FROST
> Get it out.

He watches the pawnbroker walk OUT OF THE SHOT then RETURN.

> JOHNSON
> (Weighing the medal)
> Fourteen dollars and sixty cents
> plus a dollar is fifteen sixty.

> FROST
> Where's the case?

> JOHNSON
> I'll have to charge you two bits more
> for that.

3-31-42   (Continued)

A-6 (Cont'd)   FROST
                                  (Counting out the money)
                          One bit is plenty.

                                         JOHNSON
                          Oh, all right, I won't bargain with
                          you.

                                         FROST
                          Now give me the address of the man who
                          hocked it.

                                         JOHNSON
                          Is he a friend of yours?

                                         FROST
                          Yes, only he's dead now.

          DISSOLVE TO:

A-7   MEDIUM LONG SHOT - A SMALL FARMHOUSE - (NIGHT)

      It is fairly ramshackle but has still white paint on it,
      and that together with the moonlight and the vines make it
      attractive. We hear treetoads.

A-8   FROST AND A LIVERY STABLE MAN IN A BUGGY

                                    THE LIVERY STABLE MAN
                                  (Pointing with his whip)
                          There y'are.
                                  (He spits a squirt
                                   of tobacco juice)
                          That'll be fifty cents.

                                         FROST
                                  (Giving him a coin from his
                                   purse)
                          Thanks.

      He gets down from the buggy, fiddle case in hand. The livery
      stable man looks at the single coin and spits again.

                                    THE LIVERY STABLE MAN
                          How are you going to get back?

                                         FROST
                                  (Indicating the house)
                          They probably have a rig.

                                    THE LIVERY STABLE MAN
                          No they ain't...I'll tell you what I'll
                          do...you stayin' for supper?

                                         FROST
                          I suppose so...although.....
3-31-42   (Continued)

A-8 (Cont'd)   THE LIVERY STABLE MAN
                        Well, I'm goin' to the Oddfellows tonight
                        and I'll mozy by here on my way home.

                                        FROST
                        Thanks.

                                   THE LIVERY STABLE MAN
                        I may be a little high.

                                        FROST
                        That's all right.

                                   THE LIVERY STABLE MAN
                        That'll be fifty cents.

                                        FROST
                        In advance?

                                   THE LIVERY STABLE MAN
                              (After spitting)
                        I'll trust you.

                                        FROST
                        I'll do the same for you.

             He starts toward the house.

A-9   THE FARMHOUSE KITCHEN

        A pretty young girl is making a pie. We hear a distant
        knock. The young girl goes to a door and calls not too
        loudly.

                                   THE YOUNG GIRL
                        There's somebody at the door, Mamma.

A-10   MRS. MORTON - AT A DESK IN THE PARLOR

        She is an attractive woman in her middle forties, writing
        loose pages of manuscript.

                                   MRS. MORTON
                              (Sighing)
                        I suppose it's another creditor... oh
                        well.

        She rises and crosses the room.

A-11   FROST WITH HIS BACK TO US - FACING THE FRONT DOOR

        The door opens and Mrs. Morton appears, squinting into the
        darkness.

                                   MRS. MORTON
                              (Faintly worried)
                        What is it, please?

3-31-42   (Continued)

A-11 (Cont'd)

Now she beams as she recognizes her visitor.

     MRS. MORTON
Why Eben Frost! I'm so happy to see you.
  (She takes both his hands)
Come in. You must stay and have supper
with us.

     FROST
Why that isn't necessary, Mrs. Morton.
I just came by to bring you...

     MRS. MORTON
  (Interrupting him)
Nonsense. Betty's making a pie. She's
the only one with me. The others are at
my sister's. Come in.

A-12 THE PARLOR - SHOOTING AT THE FRONT DOOR

     MRS. MORTON
  (Closing the door after
  Frost)
Let me take your hat and your fiddle.
  (She chuckles)
You remember the day you came back for it.

     FROST
  (Holding his jaw as if
  in pain)
September thirtieth, 1846. I was in excruciating pain.

     MRS. MORTON
  (Shutting him off)
I know. It seems more like yesterday
than twenty years ago.

     FROST
It was the great day of my life.

     MRS. MORTON
  (Gently)
His too.
  (Pause)
Come and see Betty.

She leads him toward the kitchen.

A-13 THE KITCHEN - SHOOTING PAST BETTY

Mrs. Morton comes in followed by Frost.

3-31-42   (Continued)

A-13 (Cont'd)   MRS. MORTON
Betty, this is Mr. Eben Frost who is
staying to supper with us.

                                BETTY
                    (Starting to hold out her
                    hand, then drawing it back
                    because it is covered with
                    flour)
How do you do, Mr. Frost.

                                MRS. MORTON
Does that name mean anything to you, dear?

                                BETTY
                    (Frowning slightly)
It's very familiar....

                                FROST
I used to hold you on my lap when you were
a baby.

                                MRS. MORTON
                    (Almost reverently)
Mr. Frost was the first man that your
father operated on, dear.... the first man
to whom he gave ether.

                                FROST
I was in excruciating pain. It was the
night of September thirtieth, eighteen
hundred and....

                                MRS. MORTON
                    (Gently)
Come in the parlor, Eben.

She pushes him before her.

                                MRS. MORTON
                    (In a whisper to Betty)
Have we got enough for three?

                                BETTY
                    (In a whisper)
I'll put in some more potatoes.

Her Mother smiles at her and exits.

A-14   THE PARLOR

Mrs. Morton and Frost finish entering.

                                MRS. MORTON
                    (Holding out her hands to Frost)
It's so good to see you, Eben.... So good...
now that it's all over.
                    (She smiles at him)
3-31-42   (Continued)

                                372

A-14 (Cont'd)

                          FROST
          I'm sorry I couldn't be there. By the
          time I heard about it....it was too late.

                       MRS. MORTON
          It didn't matter, Eben. Nobody was there
          but the children and me.

                          FROST
                       (Angrily)
          You'd think the Medical Society would
          have had the decency....

                       MRS. MORTON
                       (Gently)
          They probably didn't know about it. Any-
          way, none of that matters now. When he
          was still alive we hoped he'd get justice
          --I mean for his sake, you know how we
          felt about him--but now it's only a ques-
          tion of how long it takes the world to ac-
          cord him the honor he deserved during his
          life.

                          FROST
                       (With fire)
          He ought to have a monument in every city
          and a park called after him and a Morton
          boulevard...

                       MRS. MORTON
                       (Gently)
          That might be a little too much... Maybe
          one hospital ... sometime ...

                          FROST
                       (Snorting)
          One hospital! Every hospital oughta be
          called after him.

Now he reaches into his pocket, takes out the medal case and
gives it to her.

                          FROST
          This is what I came to bring you.

                       MRS. MORTON
                       (Opening the case)
          Oh.

She blinks as if she were about to cry for a second then
regains her composure.

A-14 (Cont'd)   MRS. MORTON
                      How terribly kind of you, Eben. This was
                      the last one, you know. He hated to part
                      with it. Wherever did you find it?

                                  FROST
                      In a...shop.

                                  MRS. MORTON
                      Oh, yes. He must have pawned it to go to
                      New York. You must let me pay you for it
                      ....some day.

                                  FROST
                            (Belligerently)
                      Just try to!

                                  MRS. MORTON
                            (Looking into the shadows)
                      That's what killed him, --- the trip to
                      New York... We thought he was all through
                      worrying about things.... that he was
                      happy with the farm, you know he won all
                      the prizes one year, best kept farm, most
                      improvements, best sow, "three dollars for
                      his admirable geese." He won a hundred
                      and thirteen dollars that kept us through
                      the winter....it was that last article of
                      Dr. Jackson's saying he was a charlatan,
                      saying he'd stolen his discovery, bringing
                      back all the misery of twenty years....re-
                      opening the wounds....he said, "I've got
                      to go to New York at once, Lizzie....pack
                      my things"...and then he fainted dead
                      away. We got him to bed, but in the mid-
                      dle of the night he got up again and
                      started sorting his papers; to prove that
                      Jackson was a liar. His hands trembled
                      so that he could hardly hold the papers.
                      Then he told Bill to hitch the rig....
                      that not a moment was to be wasted....we
                      begged him to wait but he was like a
                      maniac....it had started up again....
                      they wired for me on July eleventh. He
                      had had another collapse. By the fif-
                      teenth he seemed better. It was very hot.
                      I took him for a drive in Central Park.
                      He insisted on holding the reins himself
                      although he said they were very heavy.
                      Suddenly he pulled up the horses, got
                      to the ground and looked into the dark-
                      ness. I said, "What's the matter, dear?"
                      I said, "William, answer me!" He smiled
                      as if suddenly he'd understood something...
                      at long last... then he pitched forward
                      on his face.
                            (She pauses for a moment, then
                            continues levelly)

3-31-42   (Continued)

A-14 (Cont'd)   MRS. MORTON (Cont'd)
The papers spoke of him as the man who
CLAIMED to have discovered the use of
ether. They dug up the whole dirty
business: that Dr. Jackson told him how
to do it, that he, Jackson, had known
about it for years -- can you imagine
anyone keeping a secret like that? --
then they brought in poor Horace Wells'
claim that he did it first, and then Dr.
Crawford Long's claim that he did it
four years before! Well, maybe they all
did do it first, maybe they all did
discover the use of ether before him --
I guess they did all right -- why should
they lie about it....only it seems cruel
of them to have let people go on suffering
so long...after they knew how to stop it...
All I know is that --
            (She pauses before
            concluding)
three months after my husband discovered
anesthesia...THE WHOLE WORLD WAS USING IT!

                      FROST
And what a world it was!

We hear the gay music of a brass band as we --

DISSOLVE TO:

A-15   THE EXTERIOR OF THE MASSACHUSETTS GENERAL HOSPITAL -
       PLAINLY LABELED - (DAY)

There is a large crowd of medical students, Harvard boys
and plain onlookers. Morton's open carriage is waiting
in front of the steps, and the coachman, assisted by some
students, is unhitching the horses. Two large brass bands
are present, their instruments gleaming. There are also
a lot of banners ready to be lifted labeled variously:

         "Hurray for Morton!"   "Honor to
         W. T. G. Morton"   "The Conqueror
         of Pain"   "Who's All Right? - Morton"

In the midst of all this we see Eben Frost in frock-coat
and silk hat running around as master of ceremonies.

A-16   CLOSE SHOT - FROST, HOMER QUINBY AND SOME OTHER BOYS

                      FROST
            (Excitedly)
Now keep cool...there's plenty of
time...we can have as many rehearsals...
                  HOMER QUINBY
            (Piercingly)
3-31-42   Here he comes NOW!

A-17   MORTON COMING OUT THE DOOR

He looks worried and preoccupied, a man actually twenty-six
but appearing more. There is a wild yell. Morton smiles
and lifts his silk hat. He is immediately surrounded by a
crowd of medical students.

A-18   EBEN FROST

He is waving his arms wildly and screeching to be heard
above the roar of the crowd.

                            FROST
                        (Desperately)
                    Start playing!

A-19   THE FIRST BRASS BAND

Taken entirely by surprise, the leader gets it going as
well as he can. It is at least very loud.

A-20   FROST

He turns and waves violently at the second brass band. It
begins an entirely different number, also very loud.

A-21   THE STUDENTS SURROUNDING MORTON

The CAMERA PANS WITH THEM as they push through the crowd
and deposit him in his carriage. Now they pull and push
the carriage to get it started. Morton laughs. The first
band hurries to a position in front of the carriage, the
second band gets behind it, the banners are raised and the
procession forms. Morton's coachman brings up the rear
with the two horses.

A-22   THE PARADE PASSING BY

Morton smiles from right to left and raises his hat.

A-23   MOVING SHOT - FROST RUNNING ALONGSIDE THE CARRIAGE

Morton helps him in and thereafter Frost bows and raises
his hat in unison with Morton.

        DISSOLVE TO:

A-24   MOVING SHOT - UP AT SECOND STORY WINDOWS - BOSTON STREET,
        1846

We hear the blare of the bands which are playing together
now. All sorts of people come to the windows and wave and
cheer.

A-25   HIGH CAMERA SHOT - DOWN ON MORTON AND FROST

They are waving their hats.

3-31-42

A-26   MOVING CAMERA SHOT - AT THE SECOND-STORY WINDOWS

Now we MOVE ONTO Morton's own offices. The excitement is
intense as his own dentists and patients wave down at us.
The front of the window is plastered with Morton's adver-
tisements. We read:

> "The Painless Dentist" -- "The Dis-
> coverer of Letheon" -- "The Man Who
> Made Dentistry a Pleasure" -- "Come
> Up and Be Convinced" -- "The Conqueror
> of Pain" -- "The Pain Killer" -- "Pulls
> Them Out With a Smile"

A-27   HIGH CAMERA SHOT - MORTON AND FROST WAVING BACK

A-28   SHOT DOWN THE STREET

The parade moves PAST AND AWAY FROM US and disappears
around the corner, Morton's horses still at the end of it.

DISSOLVE TO:

A-29   THE PORTICO OF MORTON'S BEAUTIFUL MANSION

The young Mrs. Morton stands here with the baby boy and
two small girls. Behind her stand the nurse, the butler
and the other household servants, perhaps ten in all. The
music of the bands is already upon us. Suddenly the
children recognize their father.

                        THE CHILDREN
                    (Dancing up and down)
            Daddy! Daddy!

A-30   THE PARADE ENTERING THE DRIVEWAY - PAST THE GROUP ON THE
        PORTICO

Morton's carriage is pulled up to the steps and he descends
happily. There are wild yells as he kisses each of his
children in turn and short band concert as he kisses his
wife.

                        MORTON
                (Yelling to his butler)
        Champagne for everybody!
                (Now he turns and
                hails the crowd)
        Come on! Champagne for everybody!

There is a wild yell and some hats are thrown in the air.

SLOW DISSOLVE TO:

3-31-42

A-31   MORTON IN HIS FRONT DOORWAY - NIGHT

                            MORTON
                          (Waving)
                Goodbye...goodbye...thank you all.

        A bass tuba says "Goodbye." Morton chuckles, waves once
        more, then enters the house and closes the door.

A-32   THE HALLWAY - PAST MRS. MORTON WHO IS IN THE DRAWING ROOM
        WITH FROST

        We see Morton closing the door. Now he comes in TO US.
        He chuckles ruefully and mops his head.

                            MORTON
                That was quite an ordeal.

A-33   FROST - PAST MORTON AND MRS. MORTON

        He holds a glass in his hand.

                            FROST
                        (A little tipsily)
                I've got to go too, Doctor...I just
                wanted to shay: I'm proud of you! and
                ...it's an honor to have been on the
                same world with you.

        He finishes his champagne and bows deeply to Mrs. Morton.

                            FROST
                Madam.

        He nearly loses his balance.

                            MORTON
                          (Gently)
                Thank you, Eben.

        He puts his arm around Frost to steady him.

                            FROST
                        (As they start out)
                Never will I forget...it was the
                evening of September thirtieth...

A-34   MRS. MORTON

        She smiles after the two men.

                            FROST'S VOICE
                ...I was in excruciating pain...

                            MORTON'S VOICE
                Thank you, Eben. I'll see you tomorrow.

3-31-42   (Continued)

A-34   (Cont'd)

We hear the great door close. Mrs. Morton smiles more
brightly as she sees her husband coming back towards her.
Now he comes INTO THE SHOT and faces her.

> MRS. MORTON
> I'm proud of you too, William....more than
> you will ever know.
> (Now she looks contrite)
> If I haven't always appreciated exactly
> what you were doing...it's because I
> didn't understand. I hope you'll forgive
> me.

A-35   MORTON - PAST HIS WIFE

He comes forward and puts his hands on her arms.

> MORTON
> (Gently)
> But there's nothing to forgive, Lizzie.
> I'm the one who needs forgiveness. It
> can't have been much fun to have a hus-
> band who always reeks of chemicals, who
> works all night, who never comes home,
> who forgets dinner parties and birthdays
> and everything else a husband ought to
> remember.

A-36   MRS. MORTON - PAST MORTON

> MRS. MORTON
> (Putting her arms around
> his neck)
> As if any of that mattered.

A-37   MORTON - PAST MRS. MORTON

> MORTON
> Thank you, Lizzie....anyway, it's all
> over now....they've got their pain-
> less operations.....and I can get back
> to work.

> MRS. MORTON
> (Facing us as she takes
> his arm)
> The first thing you need is a good night's
> sleep.

> MORTON
> I think that's a very noble thought.

She blows out the candles in the drawing room, having first
lit a solitary candlestick. Now she takes his arm, smiles
at him, and they go PAST THE CAMERA.

3-31-42

A-38   THE GREAT STAIRWAY OF THE MORTON MANSION

Morton and his wife are coming up the last steps. As they
reach the top step Mrs. Morton pauses and looks down at the
rich curve of the baluster.

                          MRS. MORTON
              I'm so proud of this house.

                          MORTON
              I'm glad.

They go PAST US.

A-39   THE BEDROOM OF THE MORTON MANSION

The Morton's enter and Mrs. Morton lights some wall sconces
with her candle. Morton sighs heavily.

                          MRS. MORTON
                     (Surprised)
              Are you worried about something, dear?

                          MORTON
                     (With bravado)
              Oh no.

                          MRS. MORTON
                     (Confidentially)
              I worry. It all seems too good to be true...
              I suppose anything does that happens so
              quickly...I guess I just haven't had time to
              get used to it...But ever since you dis-
              covered..Letheon, I've had this horrible
              fear somebody would find out what it was.

                          MORTON
                     (Poo-pooing the idea)
              Do you think it would make such a difference?

                          MRS. MORTON
              A difference! But Darling!...it would make
              all the difference in the world! You're the
              only man on earth who can perform painless
              dentistry! You're the only man who can per-
              form painless operations. They have to come
              to you!

Morton sits on the edge of the bed and looks a little worried.

                          MRS. MORTON
              That's why I was so nervous about your let-
              ting them try it at the hospital where they
              have such fine scientists and chemists....
              they might analyze it...

                          MORTON
                     (More worried)
              Well, I'll tell you about that, Lizzie..
3-31-42   (Continued)

A-39   (Cont'd)   MRS. MORTON
                              (Interrupting him)
        Oh, I know! It's a very fine thing, William,
        and I'm just as proud about it as you are....
        but if only you could add something to it so
        they couldn't possibly recognize the odor...
        it's that odor you can't forget once you've
        smelled it.... and if they ever found out
        that Letheon was just plain old suphuric ether...
                              (Here she lowers her voice and
                              looks around nervously)
        ...that they could get at any old pharmacy...
                              (She makes a helpless gesture)

                                   MORTON
                              (Looking away)
        Well, if that's all you're worried about, Liz-
        zie, you'll never have to worry about it again.

                                   MRS. MORTON
                              (Hopefully)
        Have you found some way to disguise it?

                                   MORTON
                              (Looking at the rug)
        Well, not exactly....but you see today at the
        hospital....the Medical Society wouldn't let
        them use the Letheon....unless they knew what
        it was....so they asked me what it was.

                                   MRS. MORTON
                              (Staccato and smiling, on the
                              verge of hysteria)
        But you didn't tell them....
                              (She twists her hands)
        ....I mean you weren't such a fool as to tell
        them the most valuable secret in the world,
        JUST FOR THE ASKING?

                                   MORTON
                              (Miserably)
        But Lizzie: they were going to take her leg
        off without it....without anything!
                              (He seems on the verge of
                              hysteria himself)
        They were just going to strap her down and
        hack it off!

                                   MRS. MORTON
                              (Vehemently)
        Whose leg?

                                   MORTON
                              (With a trace of exasperation)
        I don't know....some servant girl!

His wife makes a hopeless gesture. He starts to unlace his
shoes.

FADE OUT
                              END OF SEQUENCE "A"

                                   381

FADE IN:

B-1   MORTON AND HIS WIFE - AT THE BREAKFAST TABLE

The table is covered with newspapers and mail.

                        MORTON
                (Looking at a paper)
        It says that I did a very generous thing...
        giving my secret to the world...that there's
        going to be a new era in surgery.

                        MRS. MORTON
        I was wondering how we're going to send the
        children to college.

                        MORTON
                (Irritated)
        Oh, don't be silly, Lizzie, will you? I've
        got the biggest dental business in Boston.
        I could send a hundred children to col-
        lege...and their parents with them!

                        MRS. MORTON
        It was the Letheon that made the business
        big.

                        MORTON
        Well, Letheon or ether, I'll still use it,
        won't I?

                        MRS. MORTON
        Yes, but you won't be the only one.

                        MORTON
        What of it?
                (Then after a pause)
        Even if my business wasn't quite as big,
        don't you realize what wonderful satisfac-
        tion there is in the honor of having done
        something for your fellow men?

                        MRS. MORTON
        There'd be wonderful satisfaction in hav-
        ing this house paid for, too!

                        MORTON
                (Dismissing this with a shrug)
        They'll say Samuel F. B. Morse invented
        the telegraph...William T. G. Morton dis-
        covered...wait a minute...
                (He finds a letter on the table)

3-31-42   (Continued)

                            382

B-1   (Cont'd)   MORTON
               (Struggling with the word)
...anesthet--anesthic...
               (He shakes his head and chuckles)
This is from Mr. Oliver Wendell Holmes, he's
a patient of mine, he wants me to call it...
               (He closes one eye, then pro-
               nounces the word laboriously)
...an-es-the-sia! Try that on your clarinet.
               (He chuckles again)
Anyway, they can't take that away from me.
I discovered...anes...
               (He points to the letter)
...this.
               (Then seeing his wife is not
               joining in the joke he adds:)
And I'll pay for the house too!

Now he looks around at the sound of a footstep. Frost
enters looking greatly disturbed.

               MORTON
               (Gaily)
Hello, Eben, what's the matter, you got the
toothache?

               FROST
               (Gravely)
You'd better come down to the office right
away.

               MORTON
               (Amused at Frost's gravity)
Why? The place on fire?

               FROST
No...but your dentists have all quit.

               MORTON
               (Genuinely alarmed)
Whatever for?

               FROST
They've gone into business for themselves...
the whole town's giving letheon...ether.

               MRS. MORTON
Then we are ruined...

               MORTON
               (Irritably)
What are you talking about, Lizzie? I got a
United States patent on my inhaler...at
least I have applied for it...it's basic
and they will have to give it to me...why
the Army alone will need...I don't know how

3-31-42   (Continued)

B-1   (Cont'd)   MORTON (Cont'd)
many of them...and that's in peace times...
why in War time...only I don't suppose I'd
like to make money out of that.

                              MRS. MORTON
It doesn't matter...nobody really needs a
house like this...with all of these silly
servants...and foolish luxury...I'm sure
it isn't really healthy for children to be
brought up in such lavishness...with governesses and...and...goatcarts and...and...

                              MORTON
                    (Taking her in his arms)
But you're going to keep your house and
your governesses and your goatcarts...noth-
ing has happened nothing can happen...I
have a basic...who are you?
                    (The last is to a reporter who
                    just came in)

                              REPORTER
Say, Doc, the old man wants a statement
from you. I'm from the Daily Advertiser...
about a story just come through.

                              MORTON
What story is that?

                              REPORTER
Did you invent ether?

                              MORTON
Of course not. I discovered the use of
it for ana...ana...anast...for putting
people to sleep.

                              REPORTER
Yeah. Well now there is a Dr. Charles
T. Jackson just come to the office and
says he told you how to do it and then
there is a Dr. Horace Wells, says he
showed you how to do it, and then there
is a Dr. Crawford Long down in Jefferson,
Georgia who claims he has been doing it
for years only there is a doctor P. G.
Wilhite who says he done it ahead of him
over in Athens, then the old man dug up
a Robert G. Collyer who done something
on the Island of Jersey and Doctor Henry
Hill Hickman who done something in Edinburgh, Scotland and Doctor James Estelle
who done it in England and Doctor E. E.
Marcy of Hartford, Connecticut who also
done it. Now all the old man wants to
know is where you fit in.

3-31-42   (Continued)

B-1 (Cont'd)   MORTON
                 I don't know, I...Nobody's even
                 seemed to have heard about ether till
                 yesterday... and now...everybody seems
                 to know all about it...
                           (Now he concludes more
                            brightly)
                 Anyway, I've still got a patent... I
                 think.

                                  FROST
                           (Roughly to the reporter)
                 Go peddle your papers, who do you think
                 you are?

        DISSOLVE TO:

B-2   MORTON AT THE DESK OF A UNITED STATES ARMY OFFICER - THE SHOT
      IS PAST MORTON - ON THE OFFICER

      The latter wears the insignia of a Colonel in the Quarter-
      master Corps, 1846.

                               THE COLONEL
                           (Cheerfully)
                 I esteem it an honor to have met you,
                 Dr. Morton. I know for certain your
                 discovery is going to be used in the
                 army and I believe, although I can't
                 guarantee this, you understand, I be-
                 lieve it's going to be used in the
                 navy, too.

      His eyes twinkle.

B-3   MORTON - PAST THE COLONEL

      He looks much cheered up.

                                 MORTON
                           (Beaming)
                 Well, that's certainly good news, Colonel.
                           (Now he unwraps an inhaler)
                 About how many of these would you need?
                 I might as well take the order while I'm
                 here and pass it on to the instrument maker.

B-4   THE COLONEL - PAST MORTON

                               THE COLONEL
                 How many what?

      He frowns slightly as Morton unwraps his package.

                               THE COLONEL
                 Oh, the inhalers; we already have those.
                 They were ordered several weeks ago.

4-1-42

B-5   MORTON - PAST THE COLONEL

> MORTON
> (Scowling)
> Well, that's funny...my instrument maker
> didn't tell me anything about it.

The Colonel picks up the inhaler.

B-6   THE COLONEL - PAST MORTON

> THE COLONEL
> (Examining the inhaler)
> They were a little smaller, I think...
> wait a minute, I may have the sample.

He puts down the inhaler and opens a drawer from which he
takes an assortment of samples. The first thing he produce
is an early revolver.

> THE COLONEL
> (Picking it up)
> Ever see one of these? A revolving
> pistol.
> (He demonstrates)
> You fire it, turn the barrel and there
> you are all ready to fire again. Neat,
> eh?

He pulls out a few horrendous-looking saw-toothed bayonets.
He picks up a bullet that opens out like a small umbrella.

> THE COLONEL
> Nasty little things these are. We don't
> believe in them. Of course if the other
> side should start using them... here we
> are.

He pulls out an inhaler and examines a label pasted to it.

> THE COLONEL
> We ordered them on the seventh or the
> twelfth. How do they work, anyway?

He tries to blow through the hole.

B-7   MORTON - PAST THE COLONEL

> MORTON
> (Controlling his anger)
> May I see that, please?

He receives the inhaler from the Colonel and compares it with
his own.

4-1-42   (Continued)

B-7   (Cont'd)   MORTON
(His voice shaking)
This is a fake! It's a copy of my invention. They have no right to make
these.

B-8   THE COLONEL - PAST MORTON

                      THE COLONEL
(Mildly interested)
Well, bless my soul, I'm sorry I didn't
know about it before... of course
there's nothing we can do now we've accepted them...
(His voice trails off)

B-9   MORTON - PAST THE COLONEL

He wraps up his inhaler.

                      MORTON
(Coldly)
Thank you.
(He gets to his feet)
Would you give me the name of the firm
that sold those to you?

B-10   COLONEL - PAST MORTON

He also rises..

                      THE COLONEL
We don't give out such information as
a rule, but I'll make an exception in
your case.
(He opens a large book)
Now let me see, that would be under uh-
er..."Medical Supplies"... uh-h-h...
(He runs his finger down a list)
...oh, yes...

DISSOLVE TO:

B-11   A CURVED BRASS SIGN BELOW A SHOW WINDOW

It is labeled:

                 "E. GRUBER & SONS
           GLASS OF EVERY DESCRIPTION
             Wholesale & Retail"

The CAMERA ANGLES UP, and through a window full of samples
we see Morton talking to a fairly old man who looks as if
his name might be Gruber.

QUICK DISSOLVE TO:

4-1-42

B-12 MORTON AND MR. GRUBER - <u>IN THE DISPLAY ROOM</u>

The stock tables are covered with glassware and there are
cases of it in the BACKGROUND. The table in front of them
is covered with inhalers.

        GRUBER
     (Holding up an inhaler)
Yes, sir, it's the same as we sell to the
government, guaranteed in every respect.

        MORTON
Is this the same as Doctor Morton's?

        GRUBER
     (Uneasily)
This is an ether inhaler guaranteed to
work perfect. Whether it's the same as
Doctor What's-his-name's I wouldn't know.

        MORTON
     (Harshly)
Well I would, because I happen to be Dr.
What's-his-name and these happen to be
my invention.

        GRUBER
     (Sarcastically)
So you invented bottles, hunh? People
have been using them a long time and
they'll be very glad to know you invented
them at last. Maybe you invented the
wheel, too, and the needle and thread.

        MORTON
     (Angrily)
You know what I'm talking about!
     (Now he adds suddenly)
What's that hole for?

        GRUBER
     (Acidly)
To stick flowers in. Look: I sell bottles. People can keep in them schnapps
or hair oil or maple syrup and see if I
care.

        MORTON
     (Very angry)
You'll care when I get through with you,
you dirty swindler!

He starts for Gruber who jumps behind a table of inhalers.
Morton starts around the table, then reverses his direction
as Gruber starts in the same way. Morton seizes the edge

                  (Continued)

B-12   (Cont'd)

of the table and turns it over. Gruber yells "Help!" as
the inhalers crash to the floor. He runs behind another
display table and Morton turns that one over. Gruber
starts for the offices at the back and Morton pursues him,
hurling heavy bottles after him. Some of them crash through
showcases in the back. A woman cashier hurries out, sees
what is happening and screams piercingly. As Gruber is
about to reach the safety of the offices he stumbles and
falls against a table. Morton catches him, seizes him by
the throat, bends him back on the crashing glassware and
starts to strangle him.

B-13   CLOSE SHOT - LOW CAMERA SHOT - UP AT MORTON

He is almost foaming at the mouth as he tries to throttle
Gruber.

                        MORTON
                    (Breathlessly)
            You would, would you...you invented it,
            hunh? You want to rob me, do you?...
            Well, you're not going to! I did it,
            you understand? It was ME! And nobody
            else! You...dirty...

B-14   TWO SHOT - MORTON AND GRUBER

The bookkeeper creeps behind Morton and hits him with a
heavy vase. Morton crashes to the floor.

                        THE BOOKKEEPER
            I'll get the police.

DISSOLVE TO:

B-15   NEWSPAPER READING:

                "PAINKILLER ARRESTED FOR
                ASSAULT AND BATTERY --

                In a scandalous attack on
                one of our leading merchants
                yesterday afternoon, Dr. W.T.G.
                Morton, self-styled discoverer
                of anesthesia..."

DISSOLVE TO:

D-16   MORTON'S BEDROOM

Beyond Mrs. Morton and Eben Frost we see Morton in bed. On
the far side of the bed is Dr. Warren.

4-1-42   (Continued)

B-16   (Cont'd)   WARREN

Well, you're going to get it whether you
want it or not. You MUST rest...both for
yourself and for your family.

                      MORTON
                   (Desperately)
I tell you I can't afford it, Doctor. My
business has gone all to pieces. I
neglected it when it was good, and now my
assistants have gone and taken all the
patients with them. I got too wrapped up
in this ether thing...I'm so mad most of
the time...I mean all those people saying
I stole their ideas...you know I discovered
the use of ether, don't you?

                      WARREN
Of course I know it.

                      FROST
And how he knows it. It was the night of
September Thirtieth. I was in excruciat-
ing pa...

Mrs. Morton puts a hand on his shoulder.

                      WARREN
Hold your hand out as rigidly as you can.

Morton does so and the hand shakes violently.

                      WARREN
It isn't very healthy to be angry all the
time.

                      MORTON
I'll get over it.

                      MRS. MORTON
                   (Gently)
Of course he will.

                      FROST
                   (Belligerently)
Why should he?

                      WARREN
You worked very hard on your discovery,
didn't you?

                      MORTON
I guess so.

                      WARREN
And you experimented considerably on yourself.

4-1-42   (Continued)

B-16   (Cont'd)   FROST
                    And on me...I hardly got a...
                    (He sticks his finger in his mouth)

                              WARREN
            Look at the third button on my waistcoat.

Quickly he lifts Morton's eyelids and peers at the eyes.

                              WARREN
            Yes, sir, a nice long rest.

                              MORTON
            There's nothing the matter with me, I'm just
            so angry.

                              WARREN
            No, that's why you're angry...your nerves
            are gone...you're...

                              MORTON
            I tell you I can't do it. I haven't got the
            time, I haven't got the...

                              WARREN
                    (Holding his wrist)
            Mrs. Morton tells me you have a little place
            in the country...

                              MORTON
            Yes, but I haven't got any money...we're los-
            ing this house, I lost my offices, I..I...

Now he pauses and looks to see what Warren is doing.

                              WARREN
                    (Opening a package containing a
                    silver box)
            You have money...and friends who respect you
            and believe in you. This was sent by the
            trustees of the Massachusetts General Hospi-
            tal...I have nothing to do with it.
                    (He clears his throat of this lie
                    before proceeding)
            It contains one thousand dollars in gold and
            is inscribed: "For William Thomas Green Mor-
            ton...before whom in all time surgery was agony,
            since whom science has control of pain."

He opens the box so that Morton may see the contents. Morton
licks his lips, then closes the box to see the inscription.

                              MORTON
            Yes...but it's the outside...

The CAMERA PANS ONTO Mrs. Morton and Frost. The tears are
running down both their cheeks. He hands her his handkerchief.

FADE OUT:
                    END OF SEQUENCE "B"

391

FADE IN:

C-1   A LITTLE GIRL AND A LITTLE BOY

       They are running toward us across a field as fast as their
       short legs will permit and screaming. The little girl car-
       ries a letter.

                          THE LITTLE GIRL
                          WITH THE LETTER
                    Daddy...here's a letter for you!

       At this she stumbles and falls in a heap, shooting the let-
       ter to one side. The little boy picks it up like a flash
       and continues running, paying no attention to his sister who
       rises and hobbles after him.

C-2   MORTON - HOEING

       He is bronzed and healthy-looking. The little boy bursts
       INTO THE SHOT.

                          THE LITTLE BOY
                    Letter.

       Now the little girl runs INTO THE SHOT and jumps up and down
       disappointedly.

                          FIRST LITTLE GIRL
                    I carried it all the way and then I tripped
                    and...

                          THE LITTLE BOY
                    I got it.

                          MORTON
                    (Putting the little boy down)
                    Now what do you suppose this can be?
                    (He looks at the postmark)
                    Washington, D.C.

                          THE FIRST LITTLE GIRL
                    (Piercingly)
                    That's where the President lives!

                          THE LITTLE BOY
                    Washington crossed the Delaware.

                          MORTON
                    (Turning the letter over)
                    United States Senate...

       He tears the letter open and reads it. His hands start to
       shake and the children watch him round-eyed. Now he turns
       and runs toward the house. The children run after him.

4-3-42

C-3   MRS. MORTON - BEHIND THE HOUSE

She is churning butter. Morton runs INTO THE SHOT, followed by the children.

>   MORTON
>   (Exultantly)
>   Lizzie, listen to this! Dr. Warren and the
>   staff of the Massachusetts General addressed
>   a memorial to Congress, Daniel Webster sup-
>   ported it, and now they're going to vote me
>   a hundred thousand dollars award...

>   MRS. MORTON
>   (Throwing her arms around his
>   neck)
>   Oh, how wonderful, William! Thank God...at
>   last!

>   MORTON
>   I'll have to go to Washington right away...

>   MRS. MORTON
>   (Smiling ruefully)
>   How are you going to do it?

>   MORTON
>   We'll have to borrow on the place.

>   MRS. MORTON
>   (Worried)
>   I did want to hold on to this...for the
>   children...they're so helpless.

>   MORTON
>   But Lizzie, you don't seem to understand.
>   It's already passed Congress and only has
>   to be ratified by the Senate. The money's
>   as good as in the bank...and the years of
>   waiting are behind us. Everything I've
>   ever promised you...will be yours with in-
>   terest...and love and gratitude for the
>   patience you've displayed.

>   MRS. MORTON
>   You poor lamb...it's you who've been patient.

FADE OUT:

FADE IN:

C-4   THE ANTE-CHAMBER OF THE PRESIDENT OF THE UNITED STATES

This is full of politicians, men in uniform, and whackpots.

4-3-42

C-5   A WHACKPOT ADDRESSING A SECRETARY

> WHACKPOT
> I am Johnson of the Universal Perpetual
> Peace Movement and I desire to see
> President Pierce personally.

> SECRETARY
> I'm sorry, Mr. Johnson, you will have
> to take that up with the War Department...
> Next please.

Senator Smith moves into the shot.

> SMITH
> (Handing over a large
> envelope)
> This is a memorial to the President,
> signed by twenty United States Senators
> and...

> GENTLEMAN FROM GEORGIA
> It must be delivered to him at once...
> before he signs....what he's about to
> sign...

He looks over his shoulder -

C-6   SENATOR BORLAND AND DR. MORTON - <u>NEAR THE DOOR TO THE</u>
<u>PRESIDENT'S OFFICE</u>

They both look very cheerful.

> BORLAND
> He's signing it at once as a great
> favor, because you've waited so long.
> Sometimes it takes <u>months</u>...Sometimes
> he never signs it.

> MORTON
> I don't know how to thank you, Senator.

> BORLAND
> You don't have to...My wife had an
> operation last month...I thank <u>you</u>.

The door to the President's office opens and a quiet-voiced
secretary appears and speaks to Borland.

> SECRETARY
> (To Borland)
> Will you come in, please?

Morton and Borland rise hastily.

> MORTON
> (Nervously)
> Do you say "Mr. Pierce," or "Mr.
> President Pierce?"

4-3-42   (Continued)

C-6 (Cont'd)

As Borland turns to answer, the Secretary says it for him.
                          SECRETARY
                          (Smiling)
            "Mr. President."

Borland chuckles and leads the way into the room.

C-7   BORLAND AND MORTON - ENTER THE PRESIDENTIAL OFFICE

They stop and the secretary closes the door behind them.
                          BORLAND
            Good morning, Mr. President.

C-8   PRESIDENT PIERCE - AT A GREAT DESK - PAST MORTON AND BORLAND

We see this from three-quarters rear and the President is
entirely hidden in the depths of a great swivel chair.
                      THE PRESIDENT'S VOICE
                          (Very Yankee)
            Good morning, good morning!

He swings around in his chair and we see he has been reading
the amendment which he holds in his lap.
                        THE PRESIDENT
                  (Looking over his glasses)
            Hello, Borland, I suppose this is Dr.
            Morton a great honor to meet you Sir
            when kings and presidents are forgotten
            your name will go echoing down the
            halls of time. You're a credit to your
            country. Come around to the other side
            of the desk.

He swivels his chair around and disappears.

Morton and Borland cross to a place in front of the desk.
                          MORTON
            Thank you, Mr. President.

C-9   THE PRESIDENT - PAST MORTON AND BORLAND

                        THE PRESIDENT
            Nonsense.
                  (He indicates the amendment)
            I've looked through this very carefully
            and I don't see any reason why I shouldn't
            sign it.
                  (He picks up a quill pen -
                   looks up with his eyes twinkling)
            Do you know any reason why I shouldn't
            sign it?

4-3-42

C-10   MORTON AND BORLAND - PAST THE PRESIDENT

> MORTON
> (Chuckling)
> I guess I might be a little bit prejudiced.

Borland laughs cheerfully.

C-11   THE PRESIDENT - PAST MORTON AND BORLAND

> THE PRESIDENT
> (Dipping the quill pen in
> a big inkwell)
> You might at that.
> (He riffles the pages)
> Now, let me see, a hundred thousand
> dollars - now, where do I sign?...
> They usually put an "x" for me...There
> we are!

He dips the pen in the ink again and signs the first two
letters of his name before the point breaks and makes a big
splotch on the document.

> THE PRESIDENT
> Goldern it!...I'm probably the sloppiest
> President we ever had.

He shakes some black sand over the splotch, takes out his
penknife, detaches it from the end of his watch-chain and
starts whittling a new point on the pen.

> THE PRESIDENT
> (To Morton)
> I wish it were proper for the President
> to use a steel pen...a good painless steel
> pen...instead of these blasted quills.

He slits the quill, moistens it in his mouth, dips it in
the ink and tries it on a piece of paper. It breaks at
once. With some irritation the President rings a small
dinner bell. A secretary appears at once, bearing a document.

> THE PRESIDENT
> Fix this up for me, will you? This
> goose must have had rickets.

> SECRETARY
> Yes, Mr. President...And this memorial
> just arrived.

He puts it in front of the President and picks up the quill
and starts working on it.

> THE PRESIDENT
> I'll look at it later.

C-11 (Cont'd)

        He picks it up to put it aside. In doing so, a few words
        catch his eye.

                              THE PRESIDENT
                              (Pausing)
                    Oh...It's about your amendment.

C-12   MORTON AND BORLAND - PAST THE PRESIDENT AND SECRETARY

        Morton looks uneasily at Borland but the latter smiles re-
        assuringly. Now he stops smiling and both watch the
        President anxiously.

C-13   THE PRESIDENT - PAST MORTON AND BORLAND

        We see the Secretary's hand sharpening the quill.

                              THE PRESIDENT
                              (Still reading the memorial)
                    The opposition wants to know...and not
                    without some justice...why, since you
                    had a patent, you never sued those who
                    invaded it.

        He looks up slowly at Morton.

C-14   MORTON AND BORLAND - PAST THE PRESIDENT AND SECRETARY

                              BORLAND
                              (Quickly)
                    Mr. President...

                              MORTON
                              (Interrupting him)
                    Mr. President, I don't know how you
                    feel about it, but I'd sooner have the
                    smallpox than go to court.

C-15   THE PRESIDENT - PAST MORTON AND BORLAND

                              THE PRESIDENT
                              (Chuckling)
                    Very natural in a. layman, my friend,
                    but you must remember that our country
                    is run by laws which are passed by lawyers
                    and interpreted by other lawyers. Whether
                    you like it or not I'm a lawyer, Borland's
                    a lawyer, your bill was voted in by twenty-
                    one lawyers over the objections of twenty
                    other lawyers who ask...
                              (He indicates the memorial)
                    ...and, I repeat, not without some justice,
                    why you did not establish your claim by a
                    simple law suit.

4-3-42

C-16 MORTON AND BORLAND - PAST THE PRESIDENT

                        MORTON
            But Mr. President...

                        BORLAND
                (Interrupting him, pleadingly)
            But Mr. President, this bill has passed
            both houses, it requires only your signa-
            ture..this man has been waiting for years..

C-17 THE PRESIDENT - PAST MORTON AND BORLAND

                        THE PRESIDENT
            My dear Senator, you must remember that I
            represent both sides. Why does a bill
            require the President's signature? Because
            he is in honor bound to exercise the utmost
            caution: he is dealing with the people's
            money; he is not swayed by oratory, because
            he has not heard the debate.

C-18 MORTON AND BORLAND - PAST THE PRESIDENT

                        BORLAND
            But Mr. President...

C-19 THE PRESIDENT AND THE SECRETARY - PAST MORTON AND BORLAND

                        THE SECRETARY
                (Handing him the pen)
            I think you'll find that all right, Mr.
            President.

                        THE PRESIDENT
                (Taking the pen)
            Thank you.
                (Now he looks up and laughs)
            Now don't look as if you'd just lost your
            last friend, gentlemen. As a man, I am
            entirely for you. As a lawyer I must grant
            your opponents some merit. As the President
            I am forced to lean over backwards. How-
            ever he may feel personally, the President
            of the United States must always conduct
            himself like an old fossil. That is his
            mission... for that he was elected.
                (He picks up the amendment
                and looks at it)
            Now I'm going to sign this amendment of
            course, but first I want you to do one thing:
            I want you to bring a little suit against
            some army or navy surgeon for invading your
            patent. He's bound to lose, that will give
            us a precedent and these gentlemen..
                (He indicates the memorial)
            ..will have to quit hollering.

4-3-42   (Continued)

C-19 (Cont'd)

He smiles and puts the amendment on a pile of other papers.

                         THE PRESIDENT
                I'm not even going to put this away
                in a drawer. I'm going to keep it
                right here on top of the pile until
                you come back with a judgment.... it
                will only take a few days.... a few
                weeks at the outside. I won't wish
                you luck, you won't need it. You're
                a fine man, Doctor. Believe me, I'd
                rather be you than President, any day.

C-20   MORTON AND BORLAND - PAST THE PRESIDENT

                         BORLAND
                    (Heavily)
                Thank you, Mr. President.

                         MORTON
                    (Depressed)
                All right, Mr. President, I'll do it..
                but I certainly hate to have it look as
                if I were making the Government pay to
                relieve wounded soldiers from - from

C-21   THE PRESIDENT - PAST MORTON AND BORLAND

                         THE PRESIDENT
                    (Snappishly)
                Government pays for the guns, don't it?

       DISSOLVE:

C-22   NEWSPAPER HEADLINES:

       1. Baltimore Herald --

           MORTON SUES NAVY DOCTOR

       2. New York Herald --

           ETHER MONOPOLY SOUGHT BY BOSTONIAN

       3. An editorial page --

           MERCY vs. GREED

           With scalding shame, the citizens
           of Boston learned today of the
           efforts of their fellow townsman,
           Dr. W. T. G. Morton, to coerce...

4-3-42   (Continued)

C-22 (Cont'd)

    4. The Boston Courant --

        MORTON EXPELLED FROM A.M.A.

        The American Medical Association, at
        its meeting today, condemned as un-
        ethical and outside the pale of...

    5. A Washington paper --

        DENTISTS DISOWN DISCOVERER

    6. Now we see a badly drawn cartoon of Morton
        snatching a bottle labeled "Ether" from a
        kindly doctor about to operate on a child.
        Morton's pockets are stuffed with dollar
        bills and he is carefully labeled. The
        caption says: "SHAME!!!"

THROUGH THE LAST FEW SHOTS A CLOSEUP of Morton has started
to FADE IN.

C-23 CLOSEUP - MORTON - IN COURT

He looks harassed and miserable.

                      THE JUDGE'S VOICE
          A discovery is not patentable.

There is a "Hurray!" from the spectators. Morton does not
move. We hear the Judge's gavel pound.

C-24 THE JUDGE ON THE BENCH

                        THE JUDGE
              (Pounding once more)
          Any more demonstrations of this kind
          and I will clear the courtroom.
              (He waits for silence,
                then continues)
          A discovery is not patentable. It
          is only where the explorer has gone
          beyond the domain of mere discovery
          and has laid hold of the new principle
          and connected it with some mechanical
          contrivance by which it acts on the
          material world that he can secure the
          exclusive control of it under the
          patent laws.

The audience starts to cheer and the Judge whangs his gavel.

4-3-42   (Continued)

C-24 (Cont'd)   THE JUDGE
          The patent is invalid but its dis-
          coverer is entitled to be classed
          among the greatest benefactors of man-
          kind. The beneficent and imposing
          character of the discovery, however,
          cannot change the legal principles on
          which the law of patents is founded.
          Case dismissed.

C-25 MORTON - IN THE COURTROOM

He rises and starts out wearily. The spectators near him
begin to hiss. He looks at them levelly, then continues on
his way.

FADE OUT:

FADE IN:

C-26 MRS. MORTON, THE CHILDREN AND STONE, THE BANKER ON THE PORCH
OF THE FARMHOUSE

                             STONE
                       (Argumentatively)
          Why shouldn't he lose the case? I
          think he was a blockhead to bring
          suit in the first place. Anybody
          could have told him he'd lose.

                          MRS. MORTON
          He must have had a good reason...
          I know he never wanted to sue....
          Anyway he lost it, he didn't get
          anything from Congress, I don't know
          how he's going to pay you... and I
          should think you could give him at
          least one day of peace with his
          family before you brought the matter
          up.

                             STONE
                         (Smiling)
          Mrs. Morton, it's been my experience
          that when you have something to settle,
          the sooner you face the music, the
          better you feel. When I was young in
          this business I used to beat around
          the bush and in the end we all felt
          terrible. I'm doing your husband a
          favor by coming here today.
                       (He snickers)

                          MRS. MORTON
                       (Indignantly)
          That's extremely kind of you.

4-3-42   (Continued)

401

C-26   (Cont'd)   THE LITTLE BOY
(Piercingly)
There's Daddy!

He hops off the porch and falls flat on his face. The little girls gallop over him.

C-27   A RIG COMING TO A STOP - AT THE FRONT GATE

Morton sits beside the driver. The little girls rush PAST THE CAMERA.

                     THE LITTLE GIRLS
         Daddy!   Daddy!

C-28   MRS. MORTON PICKING UP THE LITTLE BOY

He opens his mouth to howl.

                     MRS. MORTON
            (Pretending to be surprised)
      On the day that Daddy's coming home!

Now the little boy grins and rushes after his sisters yelling: "Daddy!" Mrs. Morton hurries after him.

C-29   MORTON GETTING DOWN FROM THE RIG

He lifts two suitcases to the ground and the little girls rush into his arms. He lifts them into the air as the little boy enters THE SHOT and makes a flying leap at his sisters' backs. He gets part of the lift.

C-30   MR. STONE - SITTING ON THE PORCH RAIL

He watches this touching group for a moment, then spits into the flower-bed.

C-31   MORTON, HIS WIFE AND THE CHILDREN APPROACHING

Mrs. Morton whispers in her husband's ear. Morton starts nervously, then sees Stone. He pauses a moment.

C-32   MR. STONE - SITTING ON THE RAILING

                     MR. STONE
         Hello.

C-33   MORTON, HIS WIFE AND THE CHILDREN

                     MORTON
         Hello.

He comes forward, climbs the steps and puts down his suitcases.

C-33   (Cont'd)   MORTON
                 (To his wife)
        Have the children go and play for a few
        minutes.

He walks toward Stone.

C-34   MR. STONE - <u>SITTING ON THE RAILING</u>

Morton COMES INTO THE SHOT.

                 MORTON
       You didn't waste any time, did you?

                 MR. STONE
      Nope. Time is my business.

He spits over the rail.

                 MORTON
             (Not knowing what to say)
     Well... I suppose you know what happened.

                 MR. STONE
     Yep.

                 MORTON
    I guess I'll never get anything... now.

                 MR. STONE
             (Chuckling)
     I guess not.

                 MORTON
    So there you are.

                 MR. STONE
             (Amiably)
    I've been there before.

                 MORTON
   Of course, if I could just get my dental
   business going again...

                 MR. STONE
            (Pulling his lower lip)
   That might take quite a little while...
            (He smiles)
   ...the way everybody seems to feel about
   you and all...that Mr. Horace Greeley
   certainly took a fall outa you.
            (He laughs out loud)
   You didn't make yourself very popular, did
   you?

C-34   (Cont'd)   MR. STONE (Continued)
                        (He cackles gleefully)
              I know how that feels too.
                        (He chuckles)
              Certainly done me a power of good to
              have 'em say something against somebody
              besides money lenders...ah...ha.
                        (He wipes his eyes)

Mrs. Morton COMES INTO THE SHOT with a small package
bearing French stamps.

                        MRS. MORTON
                        (Nervously)
              This came while you were away, dear.
              I was going to forward it, but then
              I thought you'd be home soon...

                        MORTON
                      (Taking the package)
              Thank you.
                      (He looks at it without seeing it
                      while speaking)

                        MR. STONE
                      (After spitting)
              You ever think of farming?

                        MORTON
                      (Surprised)
              You mean farming...like a farmer?

                        MR. STONE
              It ain't so bad. Pretty good soil here,
              too. That's why I made you the loan.
              You can take a lot of stuff outa this
              soil...good for the kids, too.
                      (He spits)

                        MORTON
                      (With the first ray of hope)
              You mean you'd be willing to wait?

                        MR. STONE
              That's what I come to tell ya. Time don't
              mean nothin' to me...It's my business.
                      (He gets to his feet and in a
                      very hard tone concludes)
              Well...think it over. So long.

He starts off the porch. Morton stares at him for a second
then steps forward and grips his hand.

                        MR. STONE
              Aw, shucks.

C-34   (Cont'd)

He goes down the steps.

                        MRS. MORTON
                    (Taking Morton's hand)
        I'm so glad, William, so very glad.

The children rush back into the scene.

                        A LITTLE GIRL
            Can we stay, now?

                        MORTON
                    (Misunderstanding)
            It looks that way.

His eyes blink and he looks down at his hands which hold
the foreign package.

                        THE LITTLE BOY
            What's that, Daddy?

                        MORTON
            I don't know, son. We'll open it and
            find out.

The children crowd around as Morton opens the box with
fingers that tremble somewhat. From inside the box he
removes first a letter sealed with sealing wax.

                        MORTON
                    (Reading)
            "Monsewer Le Doctor Gwillome T.G. Morton"...
            Maybe it's for somebody else.

                        MRS. MORTON
                    (Wiping her eyes)
            No, Gwillome is French for William.

                        MORTON
            Oh...isn't that silly.

Now he opens the envelope and takes out a letter.

                        MORTON
                    (After looking at it helplessly)
            I guess it's in French, all right.

He hands the letter to his wife, separates some cotton in
the box, removes a case wrapped in tissue paper, opens it
and reveals the beautiful medal from the Academy of
the Sciences.

                        ONE OF THE LITTLE GIRLS
                    (Delightedly)
            Look: money!
                        THE LITTLE BOY
            Let me see!

                                    MORTON
C-34   (Cont'd)   (Turning it over)
                        It's a medal, I guess.
                        (He hands it to his wife)
                        Can you read it, Lizzie?

                                  MRS. MORTON
                              (Taking the medal)
                        It's from the Academy of the Sciences
                        of the National Institute of France.

                                  A LITTLE GIRL
                              (Piercingly)
                        What's that, Mamma?

                                  MRS. MORTON
                        Sh. It's inscribed to Dr. William T.G.
                        Morton, the Benefactor of Mankind...
                        with the gratitude of Humanity.

                                    MORTON
                              (Smiling over her shoulder)
                        Pretty, isn't it?

C-35   CLOSE SHOT - THE MEDAL IN MRS. MORTON'S HANDS

        A tear splashes on it. The CAMERA DRAWS BACK VERY SLOWLY
        and we see Mrs. Morton sitting next to Frost in the little
        parlor of the Prologue.

                                    FROST
                              (Contrite)
                        I'm sorry I stirred everything up.
                              (He pats her shoulder)

                                  MRS. MORTON
                              (Smiling)
                        I was just thinking how happy we were...
                        it was really the only happy time of his
                        life. We thought he was all through
                        worrying about things...that he was happy
                        with the farm, you know he won all the
                        prizes one year, best kept farm, most
                        improvements, best sow, "three dollars
                        for his admirable geese." He won a
                        hundred and thirteen dollars that kept
                        us through the winter...
                              (Now she shakes herself and rises)
                        My gracious, I'd better see how that
                        pie's coming.
                                    BETTY
                              (Sticking her head in the door)
                        Supper's ready, Mamma.
4-3-42   (Continued)

C-35   (Cont'd)

                     MRS. MORTON
           Oh...well...then come in, Eben.

She takes his arm and they go into the kitchen. Through
the door we see an attractive table set for three.

<u>FADE OUT</u>

            <u>END OF SEQUENCE "C"</u>

4-3-42

<u>SEQUENCE "D"</u>

FADE IN:

D-1   CLOSE SHOT - THE REMAINS OF THE PIE

                  MRS. MORTON'S VOICE
         Will you have another piece of pie,
         Eben?

D-2   FROST - PAST MRS. MORTON AND BETTY

His napkin is tied around his neck like a bib and shows
evidences of pie as does his chin.

                  FROST
             (Politely)
     Why...urp...no thank you.
             (He smiles at Betty)
     You're going to make some man very
     happy some day...urp!

Mrs. Morton and Betty burst out laughing.

                  MRS. MORTON
     My, how your father loved pie! I really
     think that's why he married me.

                  BETTY
     Oh, Mamma.

                  MRS. MORTON
     He ate so much, Mother wanted to throw
     him out of the house...

She starts for the parlour. Betty clears the table.

CUT TO:

D-3   <u>THE PARLOUR</u>

Mrs. Morton and Frost enter.

                  FROST
            (In some embarrassment)
     How are you getting along with...I mean
     about...well...you know...money?

                  MRS. MORTON
            (Cheerfully)
     We're all right, Eben. It doesn't take
     very much to be happy...when you <u>had</u>
     everything. You don't have to envy
     anybody...you just think back.

                      (Continued)

D-3 (Cont'd)

                     FROST
I feel a little bit that way, too.

                   MRS. MORTON
There's beginning to be a little bit of
interest in William's life. McClure's
Magazine has asked me to write the story
for September....that will mean a little
something. I don't know how to write, of
course, and then his life would be hard
to tell, I think, even for an experienced
writer. Those glorious three months...
and then twenty years of increasing bitter-
ness. He lived too long.

                     FROST
            (Picking up some manuscript)
Is this it?

                   MRS. MORTON
That's the beginning of it.

                     FROST
            (Hopefully)
Am I in it?

                   MRS. MORTON
            (Surprised)
But of course you are, Eben.

                     FROST
Can I look at it?

                   MRS. MORTON
I don't spell very well.

                     FROST
I don't either.

He moves to a position near a lamp.

                     FROST
            (After reading a paragraph)
I think Columbine has two l's in it.

                   MRS. MORTON
            Probably.

She watches anxiously as Frost reads.

DISSOLVE TO:

D-4   <u>A LARGE KITCHEN IN 1840</u>

We see Mrs. Morton as a young girl drying dishes. Her mother
is washing dishes and expostulating.

                                   (Continued)

D-4 (Cont'd)

              MRS. WHITMAN
I do declare, Lizzie, I'm going to ask
that young Mr. Morton to leave! He
pays his board regularly but he's just
eating us out of house and home! Tonight
he had three plates of soup, twelve slices
of bread not that I counted them, four
helpings of roast beef, six potatoes, almost
a whole bunch of sparrowgrass, a hatful of
peas, and beets and turnips and three
wedges of pie! Now how can I do that
on three dollars a week?

In reply, Lizzie snuffles.

              MRS. WHITMAN
           (Unheeding)
Mrs. Biden charges four dollars a week
and doesn't give...

Now she becomes conscious of the fact that her daughter has
snuffled. She pauses with her mouth open and looks at the
back of her daughter's neck. Lizzie snuffles again, wipes
her eyes on the back of her hand and then goes on wiping
the dish. Mrs. Whitman looks at her in amazement and walks
over behind her. Lizzie sniffles once more.

              MRS. WHITMAN
           (Astonished)
Why Lizzie!

Suddenly a look of tremendous dawning comes over her face.

              MRS. WHITMAN
Why honey child! I had no idea that you
and...you know I don't mean anything I
say. I wouldn't send him away if he ate
twice as much, God forbid...if you didn't
want me to.

              LIZZIE
           (Miserably)
He's leaving anyway.

              MRS. WHITMAN
           (Indignantly)
Why? Don't tell me that I indicated by so
much as a single look or gesture the fact
that I...

              LIZZIE
His money's all gone. He can't be a
m-m-m-medical student any more.

She collapses and sobs on her mother's breast.

                              (Continued)

D-4 (Cont'd)   MRS. WHITMAN
                              (Genuinely sorry)
                    Why the poor lamb!...Well, there are plenty
                    of other businesses. Maybe he'd do well
                    in the...meat business. He seems to like it.

                                    LIZZIE
                              (Wailing)
                    He's going to be a d-d-d-dentist!

She bursts into tears.

                                 MRS. WHITMAN
                              (Patting her on the back)
                    Oh...and he was such a nice young man.

DISSOLVE TO:

D-5   MORTON AND LIZZIE - ON THE PORCH IN THE MOONLIGHT

The porch has columbines, woodturnings and considerable
fretwork.

                                    MORTON
                              (Miserably)
                    I'm certainly going to miss you, Miss
                    Lizzie.

                                    LIZZIE
                              (Miserably)
                    I'm certainly going to miss you, Mr.
                    Morton.

                                    MORTON
                    It won't be very cheerful..in Boston.

                                    LIZZIE
                    It certainly won't be very cheerful here.

                                    MORTON
                              (Taking her hand)
                    You mean that, Miss Lizzie?

                                    LIZZIE
                    Unhunh.
                              (She snuffles)

                                    MORTON
                              (Distressed)
                    Now don't do that.

                                    LIZZIE
                    I can't help it.

                                                   (Continued)

D-5 (Cont'd)　　　　　　　MORTON
(Putting his arm around her)
Miss Lizzie, if I thought that you'd
wait for me, I'd work so hard that...
in almost...no time at all, I venture
to say, I'd be in a position to support a
...a...not in luxury, maybe, but nevertheless, to support a....a...

LIZZIE
(Swooning in his arms)
William!

MORTON
Lizzie!

He crushes her to him.

D-6　MRS. WHITMAN STANDING JUST INSIDE THE DOOR TO THE PORCH

She is faintly lit from the parlor light. Now she turns and
tiptoes to the parlor. The CAMERA SWINGS WITH HER AND BRINGS
INTO VIEW Mr. Whitman who is reading the evening paper. He
looks up.

MRS. WHITMAN
(Forcefully)
You may not like the idea, but you're
going to have a dentist in the family
just the same!

She walks on down the hall and Mr. Whitman looks after her with
his funny face.

DISSOLVE TO:

D-7　OMITTED
8
9
10
11

D-12　LIZZIE IN DR. MORTON'S ARMS - (DAY)

I repeat, it is day instead of night, and the clothes they
wear are different. The position, however, is exactly the
same.

LIZZIE
I love you, Doctor Morton.

MORTON
I worship you, Mrs. Morton.

The CAMERA TRUCKS BACK SLOWLY and we see that they are standing in a dental office.

(Continued)

D-12   (Cont'd)   LIZZIE
            I'm so happy.

                              MORTON
                    (Indicating something PAST THE
                    CAMERA)
            It's pretty from here, isn't it?

                              LIZZIE
            Beautiful!

D-13   THE LATEST DENTAL CHAIR AND STAND, MODEL 1840

       The chair is a very graceful number with lions' heads, ball-
       and-claw feet and a little skirt around the bottom of it.
       The stand is elegantly simple, being merely a sort of plush-
       covered table with a water fountain above it and a plain
       brass spittoon below it. Morton and his wife ENTER THE SHOT.

                              LIZZIE
                    (Hopping into the chair)
            It's deliciously comfortable, William.
            One would be reluctant to leave it.

                                        (Continued)

D-13 (Cont'd)   MORTON
                      I hope the patients feel the same way
                      about it. You see, you tip it like this...

He steps on some kind of a pedal, there is a loud ratchet
noise, the chair flops backwards, the footrest comes up and
tosses Lizzie's legs in the air and she screams slightly.

                                     MORTON
                      I'm sorry, dear.

He steps on another pedal and Lizzie is compressed in and up
as if she were caught between the halves of a closing dictionary. She starts to laugh.

                                     MORTON
                                (Sheepishly)
                      I'll get the hang of it afterwhile.

                                     LIZZIE
                                (Tenderly)
                      Of course you will, darling, and you're
                      going to make a big success...I know it.
                      You're going to be rich and famous...
                      and I'll be so proud of you...and father
                      won't be able to talk against dentists
                      any more...and we'll live in a big house...
                      and while you're running your big office...
                      I'll be taking care of my end of it...

She kisses Morton gently on the cheek.

DISSOLVE TO:

D-14   MRS. MORTON WASHING TWO CHILDREN IN A BATHTUB

She seems a little hot and there is no great evidence of
wealth present. There is one little girl and a very small
little boy. There is much gurgling and splashing.

DISSOLVE:

D-15   A WINDOW PAINTED: "DR. W. T. G. MORTON"

Beneath this it says:

                      "Dental Parlor."

Suddenly we are startled by a male voice yelling in anguish.

D-16   MORTON AND A PATIENT - IN THE OPERATING ROOM, STYLE 1846
        AND NOT TOO RICH

Morton wears a moustache and seems about five years older
than we last saw him. The patient holds his jaw and scowls
at Morton. The latter holds a horrifying tool in his hand
and looks disgustedly at the patient.

4-3-42
                                              (Continued)

                              414

D-16 (Cont'd)   MORTON
                  (Angrily)
What are you trying to do, ruin my
business?

                 THE PATIENT
                 (Furiously)
What are _you_ trying to do, ruin me?

                 MORTON
I've taken bigger teeth out of children
and they smile while I did it.

                 THE PATIENT
They must have been half-wits.

                 MORTON
                 (Stepping nearer)
Now open your mouth and keep your trap
shut.

                 THE PATIENT
                 (Indignantly)
What?

                 MORTON
Try to show a little courage. This isn't
going to hurt a bit.

                 THE PATIENT
If I could lie like you I'd take up
fortune telling.

                 MORTON
Now open your mouth.

The patient thinks this over, then suddenly shuts his eyes
and opens his mouth wide. The instant Morton inserts his
instrument the patient roars like a lion. Morton hurls his
instrument to the floor, turns to tell his patient what he
thinks of him when he sees a shadow on the ground glass door.
He hurries toward this.

D-17   MORTON'S WAITING ROOM

A woman is passing out the door and two men are tip-toeing
toward it. Now the glass door behind them flies open and
Morton comes in anxiously.

                 MORTON
Don't be in a hurry, I'll be with
you in just a moment.

4-3-42   (Continued)

D-17 (Cont'd)   THE FIRST PATIENT
                                   WITH A VERY SWOLLEN
                                   FACE
                    You don't have to worry about me, Doc,
                    I don't know how it happened but the
                    pain just...disappeared...like magic.

He starts out the door.

                              MORTON
                         (Pointing to his face)
                    Yes, but that swelling...

                              THE PATIENT
                    I was born that way.

He disappears. Morton turns and blocks the other patients'
egress.

                              MORTON
                         (Soothingly)
                    Now just sit down quietly for a minute.
                    Don't be frightened.

                              PATIENT
                         (Pointing toward the
                          operating room)
                    I'm not frightened...I just don't like
                    to hear people suffer.

                              MORTON
                         (Indignantly)
                    He's not suffering! He's a nervous
                    wreck! He was yelling when he came
                    in. Now you sit down and I'll be with
                    you in a moment.

                              THE PATIENT
                         (Frightened to death)
                    All right.

He sits on the very edge of a chair. As Morton starts for
the operating room the patient starts to rise. Morton turns
and looks at him from the door. The patient reseats himself
guiltily.

D-18   THE DOOR FROM THE OPERATING ROOM SIDE

         Morton enters energetically, closes the door behind him,
         scowls toward the chair and says:

                              MORTON
                    Now...

         His expression hardens at what he sees.

4-3-42

416

D-19   THE EMPTY CHAIR FROM MORTON'S POSITION

The CAMERA PANS OVER to another door which is ajar.

D-20   MORTON - LOOKING AT THIS

He reaches for his keys, crosses to the door and locks it.
While doing this he seems to hear something. He looks quickly
back over his shoulder at the ground glass door. There is
no shadow on it. Morton turns back and finishes locking the
door.

D-21   THE PATIENT IN THE WAITING ROOM

He is on his hands and knees just passing under the ground
glass. Now he hurries out. An instant later Morton opens
the ground glass door. He looks angrily at the empty room.

DISSOLVE TO:

D-22   MORTON AND HIS WIFE AT DINNER
(New
Scene) Mrs. Morton is clearing the table on which half a pie remains.

MRS. MORTON
(In surprise)
Aren't you going to have another piece
of pie, dear?

MORTON
(Preoccupied)
What? Oh. No thank you, Lizzie.

MRS. MORTON
Are you sick?

MORTON
Hunh? What?

MRS. MORTON
What are you frowning about?

MORTON
Oh, the dental profession.

MRS. MORTON
I'm sorry, dear.

MORTON
(Shrugging)
It can't be helped...but they YELL
so, Lizzie, it's blood-curdling, it
gets on your nerves. You can't do
like you did in dental college with
somebody screaming bloody-murder...

(Continued)

D-22 (Cont'd)   MORTON (Cont'd)
...and trying to bite you...it just
isn't possible...you'd have to be deaf
or a demon or something, who <u>liked</u> to
see people suffer.

                    MRS. MORTON
Could you stuff something in your ears?

                    MORTON
          (Not hearing her)
If there were just some way to...to...
like your leg goes to sleep sometimes...
from resting your elbow on it, only it
would be pretty hard to put your head
to sleep, I guess. There ought to be
some way to desensitize a nerve...didn't
Jackson say something about that one night
when we boarded there?

                    MRS. MORTON
I don't remember, dear.

                    MORTON
Somebody had a toothache...

                    MRS. MORTON
          (Brightly)
That's right, it was Horace Wells.

                    MORTON
That's right, and Jackson said the only
way to desensitize a tooth was...what?

                    MRS. MORTON
I don't remember.

                    MORTON
It was some kind of drops or something, and
he said that sometimes they were of some
help.

                    MRS. MORTON
Why don't you go and ask him?

                    MORTON
Because I despise him so, that sarcastic
old blow-hard!

                    MRS. MORTON
It would be better than hearing people yell.

                    MORTON
I don't think it worked anyway...I think
Horace said...

                                        (Continued)

418

D-22 (Cont'd)   MRS. MORTON
           You're not sure.

We hear the wail of a baby.

                 MRS. MORTON
                 (Smiling)
           You might try to find something for
           that too.

DISSOLVE TO:

D-23   THE DOORWAY OF DR. JACKSON'S HOUSE

Morton has rung the bell and is waiting.

DISSOLVE TO:

D-24   ELIMINATED

D-25   FULL SHOT - A FASHIONABLE SALOON - (NIGHT)

After a little atmosphere --

D-26   CLOSE SHOT - THE BARTENDER - PAST DR. JACKSON

The latter is JUST TIPPED INTO THE SHOT. The Bartender, whose
hair is neatly greased, is watching what Dr. Jackson is doing
with intense interest.

                 DR. JACKSON
           Now the mint...

                 THE BARTENDER
           Yes, sir, Doctor.

He reaches behind him and hands Dr. Jackson a bottle.

D-27   DR. JACKSON - PAST THE BARTENDER

In this case the Bartender is JUST TIPPED IN and we see all
of Dr. Jackson (above the bar, of course) and the empty space
next to him. Dr. Jackson is in the act of constructing in a
large goblet one of those layer drinks in which the different
ingredients, of contrasting colors, float one on top of the
other but do not mix. He is surrounded with bottles. As we
CUT INTO THIS SHOT, he completes the act of receiving the
mint from the Bartender. Now, with a surprisingly steady
hand, for such an eccentric looking old gentleman, he floats
some mint on the other layers. Having succeeded with this,
he says:

                 DR. JACKSON
           Now the brandy.

                       (Continued)

D-27 (Cont'd)
                          THE BARTENDER
                        (Handing it to him)
                  Yes, sir, Doctor...but what I can't
                  figure out is why don't they mix?

                          DR. JACKSON
                       (Picking up the brandy)
                  If I told you it was the specific gravity
                  you wouldn't know any more than you do now.
                  I saw this done in Paris.

He raises the brandy which forces him to stick his elbow out
into the vacant place next to Jackson, jostles his elbow
slightly.

                                        (Continued)

D-27 (Cont'd)   MORTON
                            (Still irritated from the
                             crying scene)
                      Straight rye.

                                    JACKSON
                            (Roughly)
                      Look out!

                                    MORTON
                            (After a quick look)
                      Sorry.

He looks straight ahead while the Bartender fills his drink.
Jackson gives him a dirty look, then floats the brandy on top
of the mint. This catches Morton's attention. He receives
his drink from the Bartender but does not down it at once,
as he is watching Jackson's hands.

                                    JACKSON
                            (With satisfaction)
                      There.

He puts down the brandy bottle and admires his concoction.

                                    MORTON
                            (With superior amusement)
                      What are you going to do with it now?

                                    JACKSON
                            (With irritation)
                      What do you think I'm going to do with it,
                      throw it in the spittoon?

He picks up the goblet and downs it at one gulp.

                                    MORTON
                            (With a smile of recognition)
                      Why hello, Professor Jackson, I didn't
                      recognize you at first, here's to you.

He downs his rye and takes a swallow of the chaser.

                                    JACKSON
                            (After a slight belch)
                      Do I know you?

                                    MORTON
                      Don't you remember: W.T.G. Morton?
                      I was a pupil of yours at Harvard Medical.

                                    JACKSON
                            (In the professor-to-student
                             tone)
                      Oh, yes, Morton, of course... you were
                      rather a dull student as I remember.
                            (He cackles dryly)
4-3-42   (Continued)

                                    421

                              MORTON
                         (With a slight frown)
              Yes, well you didn't keep us in stitches,
              either.

                              JACKSON
                         (After a mirthless cackle)
              I suppose you are now a <u>successful</u> physi-
              cian!
                         (He sighs)

                              MORTON
                         (Almost harshly)
              I didn't finish. I didn't have enough
              money.

                              JACKSON
                         (Warming to a pet subject)
              Then you shouldn't have gone in for
              medicine in the first place! One of
              the cankers of our profession is the
              number of youths without funds or proper
              background who try to worm their way in-
              to it for the rich rewards they imagine
              it holds.

     He glares at Morton.

                              MORTON
                         (Dryly)
              Thanks. I'm glad to see the years haven't
              changed you.

                              JACKSON
                         (Deciding to be a little
                          more amiable)
              How are you getting along?

                              MORTON
                         (Without enthusiasm)
              Pretty fair.

                              JACKSON
              Can I buy you a drink?

                              MORTON
              Thanks.

     Catching the Bartender's eye Jackson points to Morton's glass
     and adds:

                                422

D-27 (Cont'd)
JACKSON
And a rum punch for me.

MORTON
(Thinking of his problems)
Of course it could be a lot better ...
if there were just some way of deaden-
ing the pain a little ... they get in
my chair and start to yell and the first
thing you know...

Dr. Jackson interrupts him by pointing a finger at him.

JACKSON
(Perplexed and faintly
disgusted)
You say your chair... are you a <u>barber</u>
now?

MORTON
No, no, I'm a dentist.

JACKSON
Oh!
(He chuckles at his
mistake)
And you say your patients yell?

MORTON
(With feeling)
They certainly do!

JACKSON
(Airily)
Well, the remedy for that is very simple.
It's been known since the fifteenth
century! They still do it at county
fairs. You merely provide a small orchestra and when the patient screeches, you
out-screech him.

He roars with laughter and pounds on the bar.

MORTON
(Sourly)
I suppose you think that's very funny.

JACKSON
I see your sense of humor hasn't improved
any.

4-3-42   (Continued)

423

D-27 (Cont'd)   MORTON
                     (Levelly)
Neither have your jokes.

                   JACKSON
                  (Ruefully)
I thought that was a pretty good one...
ah, well.

He drinks of his rum punch, and as his guest, Morton has to
drink with him. Jackson wipes his mouth, then becomes
serious.

                   JACKSON
I suppose you've tried oil of cloves?

                   MORTON
               (With exasperation)
I've tried oil of cloves, I've tried pep-
permint, I've tried camphor, I've tried
whisky, I've tried brandy, I've tried
gin...

                   JACKSON
None of those things are any good. There's
only one way to de-sensitize a nerve and
that's to freeze it. You might fill your
patient full of ice...

                   MORTON
               (Frowning)
What with?

                   JACKSON
               (Irascibly)
How do I know? A funnel!

                   MORTON
I thought you were serious.

                   JACKSON
Well, there's another way of producing
cold... and that's by evaporation...
you might try something with a low boil-
ing point...
               (Now he scowls)
... but I didn't come here to deliver
a lecture on chemistry. Give me a drink,
bartender.

                   MORTON
Let me buy you one.

                   JACKSON
Well, unaccustomed as I am to imbibing
with dentists...

4-3-42   (Continued)

D-27   (Cont'd)   MORTON
                       (Containing his temper)
           What has a low boiling point?

                    JACKSON
           Oh, one of the ethers I suppose. You
           might get yourself some ethyl chloride
           drops...and that's all the shop I care
           to talk!

                    MORTON
           What's ethyl chloride?

                    JACKSON
                 (To high heaven)
           What's ethyl chloride?
                 (Then to the bartender)
           He studies with me for years and then
           he doesn't know what ethyl chloride is.
                 (He turns back to Morton)
           You are the living proof that plowboys
           belong behind the horse.

                    MORTON
                 (Doggedly)
           Well, what is it?

                    JACKSON
                 (A little tipsily)
           What's what?

                    MORTON
            Ethyl chloride.

                    JACKSON
                 (Promptly)
           C_2H_5Cl...known to corn doctors as
           chloric ether.

                    MORTON
           Oh. Where can I get some?

                    JACKSON
                 (With heavy sarcasm)
           Well, you might try a feed store and then
           if they didn't have it you could try
           Burnett's Pharmacy.

He jerks his thumb at Morton and leans over to the bartender.
                    JACKSON
          My pupil!

The bartender laughs in embarrassment, then puts out two
drinks.

D-27   (Cont'd)   MORTON
                          (Slapping a silver dollar on the
                           bar)
                       Here's to you, Professor.

                                   JACKSON
                          The same to you...DOCTOR!

He catches the bartender's eye and roars with laughter.

DISSOLVE TO:

D-28   EXT. BURNETT'S PHARMACY - (NIGHT)

Mr. Burnett, aided by an assistant, is putting up the wooden
shutters. Morton goes BY THE CAMERA and starts to enter the
shop. A bell jangles.

                                MR. BURNETT
                          (Sharply)
                       Yes?

                                   MORTON
                          (Turning and seeing him for the
                           first time)
                       I want to get some ether, please.

                                MR. BURNETT
                       Do you have to have it tonight?

                                   MORTON
                       Well, I'd like to.

                                MR. BURNETT
                          (Making a great concession)
                       Oh, well.
                          (He turns to his assistant)
                       Hold it, Charlie.

He crosses and precedes Morton into the shop.

D-29   INT. OF THE OLD-FASHIONED PHARMACY

The whale oil lamps are out. A candle burns on the counter.
Burnett and Morton enter. Burnett goes behind the counter.

                                  BURNETT
                          (Rapidly as he is in a hurry)
                       Do you want chloric or sulphuric?

                                   MORTON
                          (Who does not hear him very
                           distinctly)
                       What?

4-3-42   (Continued)

                                  426

D-29   (Cont'd)   BURNETT
                              (Impatiently)
                    C H Cl or C H OC H ?
                     2 5   2 5 2 5

                                    MORTON
                              (Confused)
                    Now wait a minute.

                                    BURNETT
                    (Almost at the end of his patience)
                    Do you want it for corns or asthma?

As Morton looks at him blankly, he reaches the end of his
patience.

                                    BURNETT
                    Why don't you come in in the morning?

                                    MORTON
                              (Beginning to be angry)
                    Give me a bottle of each.

                                    BURNETT
                    An ounce?

                                    MORTON
                              (Shouting him down)
                    A pint!

Burnett blinks at him for a moment, then disappears behind
the counter.

DISSOLVE TO:

D-30   MORTON'S FRONT HALL - NIGHT

He enters quietly, removes the two bottles from his overcoat, hangs the coat and hat on a hat tree and goes into
the parlor.

D-31   THE PARLOR

The lamp has been turned very low. Morton enters, turns the
lamp up, unwraps his bottles of ether and examines them.
One is labeled "Chloric Ether," and the other "Sulphuric
Ether." He takes a good smell of the chloric ether, then
replaces the cork. He takes a long smell of the sulphuric,
reacts slightly, then corks it, puts it down and starts
across the room. He bumps into a chair which falls to the
floor. He looks back at the ether bottle in surprise,
then picks up the chair.

4-3-42

D-32   MRS. MORTON - IN BED

We see her in the moonlight. She sits up.

                  MRS. MORTON
      Is that you, William?

D-33   MORTON - IN THE PARLOR

He looks up at the ceiling.

                  MORTON
      Yes, dear, I'll be up in a little
      while.

He crosses to the bookcase, removes Pereira's "Materia
Medica" and carries it to the table. Now he looks in
the index, then turns to the proper page.

D-34   INSERT: THE HEADING "ETHER"

Under a sub-heading: "CHLORIC ETHER" we see the
beginning of a chapter about its use.

D-35   MORTON READING

                  MORTON
           (Understanding suddenly)
      Oh.

He pushes the sulphuric ether away, takes up the chloric
ether bottle and with the cork puts some on the back of
his hand. Now he takes a pin from his lapel and tries
the sensitivity of the spot. He repeats the experiment,
then corks the bottle and goes back to his reading. The
CAMERA PANS ONTO the bottle of sulphuric ether and MOVES
INTO A VERY CLOSE SHOT of it. We realize now that when
Morton moved it away, he placed it in close proximity
to the chimney of the whale oil lamp. Bubbles are rising
from the bottom of the bottle. They leak past the cork
and bubbles around the cork. Now with a soft plop the
cork pops out onto the table. The ether now reaches
95°F. and really boils.

DISSOLVE TO:

D-36   MRS. MORTON - IN BED

She feels sleepily for her husband, then sits up.

                  MRS. MORTON
         William!

Now she lights a match and looks at her watch on the
nightstand. It is 12:00.

4-3-42   (Continued)

D-36 (Cont'd)   MRS. MORTON
                      (Thoroughly alarmed)
          WILL-YUM!

The match goes out. She lights another one, lights a
candle with it, then puts on slippers and a wraparound,
picks up the candle and goes out of the room.

D-37 THE WINDING STAIRS

Mrs. Morton comes down very prettily in the candle light.
She pauses halfway down and calls fearfully.

                      MRS. MORTON
          Will-yum!

She comes down the last steps very slowly. At the bottom
she stops in astonishment. Now her face hardens into the
standard indignant-wife look. She draws herself up in
disgust and starts forward.

D-38 POINT-OF-VIEW SHOT - FROM MRS. MORTON'S POSITION

We see Morton in the parlor. He has sprawled off his chair,
his book has fallen to the floor and he is snoring drunken-
ly with his head on the seat of the chair. The CAMERA
MOVES TOWARD Morton at the speed of Mrs. Morton walking.
As it COMES INTO A CLOSE SHOT, Mrs. Morton's hand goes
PAST THE LENS and touches Morton on the shoulder.

                  MRS. MORTON'S VOICE
                      (Horrified)
          William!

Morton stirs slightly and mutters some gibberish through
flopping lips.

                  MRS. MORTON'S VOICE
                      (Louder)
          William!

Her hand shakes him again. Again he mutters gibberish.

D-39 MRS. MORTON SHAKING HER HUSBAND

She puts her candle down on the table and reacts to something she sees.

D-40 THE HALF EMPTY SULPHURIC ETHER BOTTLE

The cork lies beside it and the label is turned away from
us.

D-41 CLOSE SHOT - MRS. MORTON AND MORTON

                      MRS. MORTON
                      (Indignantly)
          I should think you'd be ashamed of
          yourself!
4-3-42   (Continued)

D-41 (Cont'd)

Morton chews his lips for a moment, mutters incoherently,
then blinks his eyes open. After a second he closes one
eye to see better.

D-42 LOW CAMERA SHOT UP AT MRS. MORTON

She is out of focus and her outline wallows around like a
reflection in the water.

D-43 CLOSE SHOT - MRS. MORTON AND MORTON

MRS. MORTON
(Indignantly)
You're drunk!

MORTON
(Trying to scowl)
Whooje drunk?

He tries to sit up and succeeds partially.

MORTON
Whayoumean...I'm drunk?...
(He holds up
two fingers)
I h-had two dringje....
(He drops one
finger and repeats)
...two.

He sees that this is not right so he puts the second finger
up again.

MORTON
Two...no more...no lesh.

MRS. MORTON
(Catching him under the
armpits)
You're not going to make things any
better by lying about it. You reek of
cheap liquor - Now get up...I'll help you.

MORTON
(Struggling to release
himself)
Who ashed you for any help....
whashamatter wi' you Lijjie, you
crajy?

MRS. MORTON
(Impatiently)
Get up.

D-43 (Cont'd)   MORTON
                     Whdo I wanta get up for? I',
                     not down anyplash!

                                  MRS. MORTON
                     Then what are you doing on the floor?

                                   MORTON
                                 (Furiously)
                     Whoje ona floor? Whereja floor?
                                 (He twists his neck
                                 around, feels the floor
                                 with surprise then says:)
                     Thass funny.

                                  MRS. MORTON
                                 (Yanking him to his
                                 feet)
                     Now get up.

                                   MORTON
                                 (Weaving back and forth on
                                 his feet, indignantly)
                     Lijjie, I tell you I have not been
                     dringing...I had...
                                 (He holds up two fingers)
                     TWO dringjes...two shmall dringjes.
                     Why should I lie to you? If I had
                     three dringjes...or four dringjes...
                     or even...oop!...FIVE dringjes...
                     wulp! I'd jesh ash shoon...gloop!

He claps one hand to his stomach, the other over his mouth
and makes a headlong dive out of the room. Mrs. Morton
glares after him. Her lips begin to tremble.

FADE OUT:

                     END OF SEQUENCE "D"

4-3-42

FADE IN:

E-1   THE DOORWAY OF MORTON'S HOUSE - (MORNING)

The door is fairly ugly and has some beveled glasswork in the
top of it.

                          MORTON'S VOICE
              I...WAS...NOT!

The door opens and Morton appears, looking very angry. He
buttons his overcoat. Now he replies to something we do not
hear.

                          MORTON
                      (Exasperatedly)
              I don't know, but I tell you... I...
              WAS...NOT...DRUNK!

He steps out on the stoop and slams the door so hard the
beveled glass crashes on the stoop beside him, then tinkles
onto the sidewalk. Morton gives the door a look, then starts
toward us.

DISSOLVE TO:

E-2   INT. BURNETT'S PHARMACY

Mr. Burnett is occupied at the moment in making a pyramid of
jars under a sign. The top of the sign shows a hand-painted
gent with his hair and moustache parted in the middle and
well slicked. Beneath this we read:

                   "For That Well-Groomed Look
                   BURNETT'S FRESH BEAR GREASE
                    Distilled from Healthy Bears"

Now he hears a step and looks up.

                          MR. BURNETT
              Good morning, sir.

E-3   MORTON - PAST BURNETT

                          MORTON
                      (Scowling)
              Good morning. Tell me something: was
              I drunk when I came in here last night?

E-4   BURNETT - PAST MORTON

                          BURNETT
              Oh, you're the young man who wanted
              the ether.

4-3-42

432

E-5   MORTON - PAST BURNETT

> MORTON
>
> That's right. Would you say that I
> was drunk at the time?

E-6   BURNETT - PAST MORTON

> BURNETT
> (After a moment's recol-
> lection, cautiously)
> Not particularly.

E-7   MORTON - PAST BURNETT

> MORTON
> (Indignantly)
> What do you mean, "not particularly!"
> I had two drinks...
> (He holds up two fingers)
> ...two, with Professor Jackson down
> at Costello's, I came in here <u>cold</u>
> sober, I went <u>straight</u> home... but
> at midnight my wife found me <u>rolling</u>
> on the floor!

E-8   BURNETT - PAST MORTON

> BURNETT
>
> Well...
> (He pulls his lower lip and
> looks toward the ceiling
> through his glasses)
> ...your liver must be torpid. You
> see, the poisons are normally dissi-
> pated through the liver, but when this
> organ becomes congested... now I have
> here...

He turns and reaches for a bottle on the shelf.

E-9   MORTON - PAST BURNETT

> MORTON
> (Interrupting him)
> Yes, well I happen to have been a
> medical student myself and I'm a
> practicing dental surgeon now.

E-10   BURNETT - PAST MORTON

> BURNETT
>
> Oh.

4-3-42

E-11   MORTON - PAST BURNETT

                              MORTON
                    My liver works like a buttered eagle
                    and if there was anybody drunk in
                    here last night, it wasn't me.

       He gives Burnett a defiant look.

                              MORTON
                    Now...two things are possible:
                    either I had a stroke which I don't
                    appear to have had, or in some way
                    that bottle of ether, which my wife
                    found half empty...

E-12   BURNETT - PAST MORTON

                              BURNETT
                         (Quickly)
                    How did it get half empty?

E-13   MORTON - PAST BURNETT

                              MORTON
                    The cork got out of it somehow.

E-14   BURNETT - PAST MORTON

                              BURNETT
                         (Laughing)
                    Well there's your answer. You don't
                    have to go any further. The fumes of
                    sulphuric ether are extremely noxious.
                    We have to keep it tightly sealed and
                    I'm always telling my assistant, if
                    I've told him once I've told him a
                    thousand times, I've said, "Charlie..."

E-15   MORTON - PAST BURNETT

                              MORTON
                         (Cutting him off)
                    I see.
                         (Now he chuckles)
                    Well, that mystery is cleared up,
                    though I don't suppose my wife will
                    ever believe it.
                         (He turns to go)
                    Thank you.

E-16   BURNETT - PAST MORTON

                              BURNETT
                    Do you need any more of it, to take
                    the place of...

4-3-42

                                434

E-17   MORTON - PAST BURNETT

> MORTON
>
> I should say not. It was the other
> I wanted anyway.
> > (He half pulls it out of
> > his pocket)
>
> I just couldn't remember last night.
> Good morning.

> BURNETT
>
> Good morning, call again.

> MORTON
>
> Thanks.

He exits.

DISSOLVE TO:

E-18   THE HALLWAY OUTSIDE MORTON'S OFFICES

It is wide and lit by a skylight. The other doors are labeled
variously:

> THE NUGGET GOLD MINING CO.
> DR. GRENVILLE G. HAYDEN, DENTIST
> DR. ORESTES PARKS, DENTIST
> DR. SILAS WYNDHAM, DENTIST
> ALPHONSE P. DE LAVAL & DANIEL O'LEARY
> > Attorneys at Law
> THE ELECTRIC OIL COMPANY
> > (Guaranteed to Grow Hair)
> THE NE PLUS ULTRA EMPLOYMENT AGENCY
> DR. THEODORE DAHLMEYER, M.D.

Waiting restlessly we see a young man of Morton's age: Dr.
Horace Wells, Dentist. His satchel stands before Morton's
door. He looks at his watch with irritation as the building
comes to life and tenants enter their various offices. As
Dr. Hayden enters his office, Wells accosts him.

> WELLS
>
> What time does Mr. Morton get here
> as a rule?

> DR. HAYDEN
>
> He doesn't seem to get here as early
> as the rest of us, does he?
> > (He opens his door
> > invitingly)
>
> Are you in pain?

> WELLS
> > (Quickly)
>
> No, no, I'm a dentist myself.

4-3-42   (Continued)

E-18 (Cont'd)   DR. HAYDEN
                       (Briefly)
    Oh. Good morning.

He enters his office and closes the door after him. A mother
and child now go into another dental office and a completely
bald-headed gentleman enters the Electric Oil Company. Two
men in checked suits enter the Nugget Gold Mining Company,
and a man on crutches goes into Dr. Dahlmeyer's offices.
Wells becomes more and more impatient. He whips out his
watch, consults it for a moment, then decides he can't wait
any longer. He puts the watch back in his pocket and picks
up his satchel. At this moment he sees Morton approaching.

                       WELLS
                       (Accusingly)
             Well, at last!

E-19   MORTON - PAST WELLS

                     MORTON
                 (Surprised and pleased)
    Why Horace Wells! How are you?

The men shake hands.

                     MORTON
    What are you doing in Boston?...Come in.

He sticks his key in the lock.

                     WELLS
                 (Picking up his satchel)
    I came down from Hartford this morning.
    I have something very interesting to
    tell you.

E-20   MORTON'S WAITING ROOM - SHOT FROM OPERATING ROOM

    The men enter and come directly into the operating room.

                     MORTON
                 (Removing his hat)
    What is it?

                     WELLS
    You remember when we were students we used
    to try to figure out some way of pulling
    a tooth without pain?

                     MORTON
                 (Ruefully)
    I'm still trying to figure it out.
         (He pulls the bottle out
          of his pocket)
    I just bought a bottle of...

                                   (Continued)

E-20   (Cont'd)   WELLS
                          (Taking the bottle and
                           examining it)
Forget it. That's what I came to tell you
about.
                          (Now with rising enthusiasm)
I have made the most important discovery in
the world! I CAN EXTRACT TEETH, OR FILL
THEM OR DO ANYTHING I LIKE WITH THEM WITHOUT
ANY PAIN WHATSOEVER!

                                  MORTON
                          (Thunderstruck)
No!

                                  WELLS
                          (Proudly)
Absolutely. That's what I'm here for.
                          (He looks at his watch)
I'm giving a demonstration at Harvard Medical
at ten thirty. I want you to lend me a key
and act as my assistant.

                                  MORTON
But that's wonderful. How do you do it...
or is that your secret?

                                  WELLS
I wish it were my secret...but the stuff is
so well known you can't stop them from recognizing it.

                                  MORTON
What is it?

                                  WELLS
Laughing gas...nitrous oxide.

                                  MORTON
                          (In astonishment)
Laughing gas! You mean like they use at
county fairs?

                                  WELLS
That's right...for the amusement of the
yokels. That's where I got the idea. I
saw this lout dancing around and making a
fool of himself and laughing his head off...
and all the time he had a gash that long
in his shin he'd got falling off the platform. He didn't even know it. He hadn't
felt it.

                                          (Continued)

MORTON
(Completely perplexed)
That's very interesting, but how can
you work on them while they're laughing?

WELLS
Because they're not laughing! I give
them a little more and they go to sleep.

MORTON
But they must be half asphyxiated, and
that isn't very healthy. I had an experience just last night...

WELLS
(Interrupting)
Naturally you have to be careful...

MORTON
How many times have you done it?

WELLS
Four times.

MORTON
Then I don't think you're ready to give
any demonstrations at Harvard Medical...
if the stuff didn't happen to work...

WELLS
(Almost crossly)
It has to work! And I'm not going to
wait around till somebody else hears
what I'm doing, then steals it from me
and says he invented it! If you don't
want to help me, I'll borrow a forceps
somewhere else and...

MORTON
(Quietly)
I'll help you... on one condition:
that we go by Dr. Jackson's first, and
that he says it isn't dangerous.

(Continued)

438

E-20 (Cont'd)
                              WELLS
              What's that old moss-head got to do with
              it? He doesn't know any more about it
              than I do. He'll just try to steal it
              from me and say he invented it -- like he
              did with Morse and the telegraph. He never
              liked me anyway when I was his pupil and I
              feel the same way about him only double.

                             MORTON
                    (Shrugging his shoulders)
              Then...good luck to you, Horace.

                              WELLS
                    (Hurt)
              You won't come along?

                             MORTON
              I will not. I haven't got much of a
              reputation...but what I've got I'm going
              to hang onto, and not risk any fly-by-
              night....

                              WELLS
                    (Giving in)
              All right...we'll see Jackson...
                    (Now he raises a warning
                     finger)
              ...but if that old pickle-head says any-
              thing I don't like the sound of I'll punch
              him right in the snoot.

        DISSOLVE TO:

E-21   DR. JACKSON - IN HIS LABORATORY

        He wears a long white chemist's coat and listens with
        extreme displeasure.

                            WELLS' VOICE
              ...in extracting teeth without any pain
              whatsoever!

                            JACKSON
              Poppycock!

E-22   WELLS AND MORTON - PAST JACKSON

                                   WELLS
                         (Angrily)
                         What do you mean, "poppycock!"
                         I tell you I've done it!

E-23   JACKSON - PAST THE OTHER TWO

                                  JACKSON
                         (Exasperatedly)
                         And I tell you you're endangering
                         the lives of the fools who trust
                         you! Certainly you can render a
                         man unconscious: by asphyxiating
                         him or drowning him or hitting him
                         on the head with a dornick! That's
                         no discovery. Henry Hill Hickman
                         went all through that. Priestley
                         found laughing gas and Humphry Davy
                         tried all this stuff fifty years ago.
                         Faraday experimented with every type
                         of inhalant he could lay his hands
                         on. In the end all these men
                         abandoned the idea. Do you expect
                         to succeed WHERE THE GREATEST
                         SCIENTISTS IN THE WORLD HAVE FAILED?

E-24   WELLS AND MORTON - PAST JACKSON

                                   WELLS
                         (Defiantly)
                         Well...discoveries are still made,
                         aren't they?

E-25   JACKSON - PAST THE OTHER TWO

                                  JACKSON
                         (Irascibly)
                         Yes, but they're not made by half-
                         educated schoolboys. You'd better
                         give up this nonsense before you
                         kill somebody! And that goes for
                         you too, Morton! Go back to your
                         tooth yanking and leave Science to
                         the scientists.

4-3-42

E-26   WELLS AND MORTON - PAST JACKSON

WELLS

Thanks.
(He pauses a moment then
consults his watch)
Nevertheless, at ten-thirty this morning,
at the Howard Medical School, I will extract a tooth totally without pain by
using the Wells Method. Good morning.

He turns and starts out. Morton hesitates for a moment,
looks from one man to the other, then follows Wells.

E-27   JACKSON

He glares after the young men.

JACKSON
(With fine sarcasm)
The Wells Method!...the half-asphyxiation
method!

Now he consults his own watch. Suddenly he jams it back
into his pocket, tears off his chemist's coat and reaches
for his hat which he puts on sideways.

E-28   HIGH CAMERA SHOT - <u>DOWN ON A BOSTON STREET - 1846</u>

Wells walks rapidly beneath us. A few feet behind him and
overtaking him quickly comes Morton. In the background and
hurrying to catch up is Jackson.

DISSOLVE TO:

E-29   PROF. WARREN - PAST THE STUDENTS - <u>IN A CLASSROOM AT HARVARD</u>
<u>MEDICAL SCHOOL</u>

He stands on the platform addressing the students.

(NOTE: Actually this room was a lecture-theatre but a
classroom will do just as well and I would like to save the
operating-theatre for the first Morton-Warren experiment.)

PROF. WARREN
And now, young gentlemen, we are to assist
at a very interesting experiment.

E-30   <u>A TABLE NEAR THE PLATFORM</u>

It is covered with chemical apparatus, the main articles
being; an alcohol heater, a retort containing ammonium
nitrate, some tubes leading to a flask of sulphuric acid,
a gas bag to collect the resultant nitrous oxide, and some

4-3-42   (Continued)

forceps loaned by Dr. Morton. With Morton's assistance
Wells is busy making the laughing gas.

                    PROF. WARREN'S VOICE
            Dr. Horace Wells of Hartford, Connecticut...

Wells turns and smiles.

                    PROF. WARREN'S VOICE (Cont'd)
            ...and his assistant...

Morton nods sheepishly.

                    PROF. WARREN'S VOICE (Cont'd)
            ...are about to demonstrate the "Wells
            Method"...

E-31   DR. JACKSON AND A STUDENT - IN THE FIRST ROW

They sit together at a double desk. Dr. Jackson's face is
twisted into a sneer. The round-faced young man next to
him has one cheek slightly swollen and looks a little
nervous. He mops his forehead.

                    PROF. WARREN'S VOICE
            ...of painless extraction on your fellow
            student, Homer Quinby...

The round-faced student half turns and half smiles.

                    PROF. WARREN'S VOICE
            ...who has volunteered to be the subject.

Homer wipes his brow again.

                    PROF. WARREN'S VOICE
            We have as our honored guest Dr. Charles
            T. Jackson...

Jackson waves sourly.

E-32   PROF. WARREN - PAST THE STUDENTS

                    PROF. WARREN
            ...whose courses you have all enjoyed and
            profited from.

He smiles perfunctorily, then clasps his hands behind his
back and crosses to the edge of the platform where Wells
and Morton are completing their preparations. Morton holds
the gas bag which is swelling up like a balloon.

4-3-42   (Continued)

E-32   (Cont'd)   PROF. WARREN
                    Are we nearly ready?

                                      WELLS
                    Yes, sir.
                        (Then to Morton)
                    That's enough.

He folds over the mouthpiece of the gas bag and extinguishes
the alcohol lamp.

                                  PROF. WARREN
                        (Looking out into the room)
                    Then if you will kindly step up here,
                    Homer...

E-33   JACKSON AND HOMER QUINBY

                                      HOMER
                        (Miserably)
                    Yes, sir, Dr. Warren.

He starts slowly to rise.

                                     JACKSON
                        (In a whisper)
                    Don't let them give you too much of it.

                                      HOMER
                        (After registering fright)
                    N-no, sir.

He steps into the aisle, mops his brow one last time and
starts for the platform.

E-34   PROF. WARREN, WELLS AND MORTON - WAITING ON THE PLATFORM

They stand behind a wooden armchair. Morton holds the gas
bag. Wells holds the folded mouthpiece in one hand and a
shining forceps in the other.
                                  PROF. WARREN
                    Sit right here, Homer.

Homer ENTERS THE SHOT and sits nervously.

                                      WELLS
                        (Taking charge in a
                         boisterous way)
                    Now this isn't going to hurt you a
                    bit, Homer. Just sit back and....

4-3-42   (Continued)

E-34 (Cont'd)

                    HOMER

                  (Scowling)

Don't you give me too much of that

stuff.

                    WELLS

Don't you worry about that. Now I

think we're all ready.

He brings the mouthpiece nearer Homer's face, then remembers
something.

                    WELLS

By the way, which tooth is it?

At Homer's horrified expression the entire classroom howls
with laughter. This includes Warren, Wells and Morton.
Everybody except Homer who glares at Wells and puts his index
finger on the tooth.

                PROF. WARREN

                (Looking out)

That's all right, now quiet, please.

E-35 JACKSON - IN FRONT OF SOME STUDENTS

With an effort the students stop laughing. Jackson turns
back to them slightly and speaks sourly.

                    JACKSON

It's all very funny but they're apt

to kill him.

              A ROUND-EYED STUDENT

              NEAR HIM

No!

                    JACKSON

Yes!

Several of the students now frown as they watch the platform.

E-36 PROF WARREN, WELLS, MORTON AND HOMER

                    WELLS

            (Bringing the mouthpiece

            down to Homer's face)

Now I just want you to put this in

your mouth and breathe deeply.

                    HOMER

Don't you give me too much of it,

now.

4-3-42   (Continued)

E-36 (Cont'd)
                         WELLS
                       (Nervously)
         You leave that part to me. Now:

Homer rolls his eyes toward Prof. Warren.

                      PROF. WARREN
                        (Gently)
             Open your mouth.

Slowly Homer does so. Wells unfolds the mouthpiece of the
bag and puts it in Homer's mouth.

                         WELLS
             Now breathe deeply.

Homer takes a deep breath, then looks at Prof. Warren.

                      PROF. WARREN
             Keep on breathing, Homer.

Homer closes his eyes and takes another deep breath. Suddenly he explodes in giggles.

E-37 JACKSON AND THE STUPEFIED STUDENTS

E-38 WARREN, MORTON, WELLS AND HOMER

                         WELLS
             Now keep on breathing.

Homer explodes into wild guffaws, he slaps his knees, stamps
his feet with merriment and Wells has a lot of trouble keeping the end of the gas bag in his mouth.

E-39 JACKSON AND THE STUDENTS

The students are roaring with laughter and slapping each
other on the back. Jackson watches quietly.

E-40 WARREN, MORTON, WELLS AND HOMER

Now Homer's laughter gets weaker. It subsides into stupid
chuckles, then he lies back, inert.

                         WELLS
                       (To Morton)
             Now hold his mouth open.

Morton seizes Homer's chin and Wells squeezes the gas bag
roughly as he forces nitrous oxide into Homer's mouth in
rhythm with his breathing. There is a deathly silence broken
only by the heavy breathing of the subject. The tension becomes quite great and Morton begins to frown with anxiety.
Prof. Warren frowns slightly. Wells alone is unafraid and
continues to pump the gas bag enthusiastically.

4-3-42

                          445

E-41   JACKSON AND THE STUDENTS

Fear has spread throughout the classroom.   All look worried
and several students mop their foreheads.   Suddenly Jackson'
voice shatters the silence.

                            JACKSON
                What are you trying to do, kill
                that boy?

Half the students get to their feet in their excitement.

E-42   WARREN, MORTON, WELLS AND HOMER

                            WELLS
                        (Turning savagely)
                I know what I'm doing!

                            PROF. WARREN
                        (Gently)
                Maybe that's enough, Doctor.

                            WELLS
                        (Nervously)
                Well...

He removes the gas bag, folds over the mouthpiece and hands
it to Morton.

                            WELLS
                All right.

He takes the forceps from his coat pocket and tries to open
Homer's mouth. The teeth are tightly clenched. With considerable effort he gets the mouth open, then reaches inside
and closes the forceps firmly on the tooth.

                            WELLS
                Hold his head, please.

Morton holds Homer's head. Now Wells seizes the forceps
with both hands, puts one knee on the arm of the chair and
starts to pull. Like the explosion of a bomb, Homer comes
to life yelling. He scrambles to his feet.

E-43   JACKSON AND THE STUDENTS

For the first time Jackson throws his head back and howls
with merriment. Very few of the students are laughing,
however. Most of them look very indignant. There are
mutters of "Faker!" "Humbug!" and "Dirty Swindler!" and
some of them move forward menacingly. As they move PAST
THE CAMERA --

4-3-42

E-44   WARREN, MORTON, WELLS AND HOMER

Homer is on his feet waving his arms drunkenly. Now he claps
one hand to his jaw.

> HOMER
> (At the top of his lungs)
> If that's what you call painless...

There is a yell from the students.

> WELLS
> (Turning exasperatedly
> to Warren)
> I knew that wasn't enough!

> HOMER
> (Furiously)
> I'll show you how painless it is...

He takes a wild swing at Wells and happens to catch him in
the eye. Morton seizes Homer's wrist and Homer tries to
hit him.

> PROF. WARREN
> Stop that immediately! Quiet!

E-45   A STUDENT IN THE BACK OF THE CLASSROOM

He picks up a book and hurls it PAST THE CAMERA.

E-46   WARREN, MORTON, WELLS AND HOMER

By now some students are milling IN THE EDGE OF THE SHOT.
The book crashes against the blackboard, missing Wells by
inches.

E-47   CLOSE SHOT - JACKSON

He is yelling with joy. Now a book clunks him on the head
and he stops laughing.

E-48   MORTON AND WELLS STRUGGLING IN A MELEE OF STUDENTS

E-49   PROF. WARREN ON THE EDGE OF A BUNCH OF STUDENTS

Their backs are to him. They are trying to reach Wells and
Morton.

> WARREN
> Gentlemen! Gentlemen! Stop it
> immediately!

E-50   THE TABLE WITH THE CHEMICAL APPARATUS

Pushed by milling students it crashes to the floor.

4-3-42

E-51 THE HALLWAY OUTSIDE THE CLASSROOM

      Students, professors and janitors are hurrying toward the
      riot. Suddenly the door to the classroom bursts open and a
      fighting mob appears. Now Wells is hurled out into the hall
      As he is helped to his feet Morton is thrown out also. The
      following students are blocked, however, by Prof. Warren who
      spreads his arms across the doorway.

E-52 CLOSE SHOT - PROF. WARREN - PAST THE STUDENTS

      In the hallway outside we see Morton and Wells.

                              WARREN
                           (Loudly)
                  Any man who goes by me will be expelled
                  immediately! I know every one of you
                  and I have a perfect memory. I am
                  astounded and disgusted at your behavior
                  and your reception of a sincere and
                  worthwhile effort.

      SLOW DISSOLVE TO:

E-53 MORTON AND WELLS - IN MORTON'S OPERATING ROOM

      Morton is bathing Wells' injured eye.

                              MORTON
                           (Putting the cotton away)
                  There... it's going to be a little blue..
                  but that will pass.

                              WELLS
                           (Seething)
                  Thanks.

      His jaw muscles swell out a couple of times before he con-
      tinues.

                              WELLS
                  If they wouldn't hang me for it I
                  think I could get a great deal of
                  pleasure out of strangling Jackson
                  to death.

                              MORTON
                           (Angrily)
                  Don't talk like a child! I told you
                  you weren't ready for a public experi-
                  ment, but you couldn't wait.

                              WELLS
                           (Desperately)
                  You can see that it works, can't you?

4-3-42   (Continued)

E-53 (Cont'd)

MORTON
I didn't see it work.

WELLS
(Shouting)
THAT'S BECAUSE HE DIDN'T GET ENOUGH OF IT!
I was going to give him more until that
old mealymouth...I tell you this is the
greatest discovery in the world! I am the
father of painless dentistry! I can extract teeth or fill them, or do anything I
like with them without any pain whatsoever.
You've got to believe me, Morton. This is
the greatest...

MORTON
(Soothingly)
Take it easy, will you. Maybe it's everything you say, but you still have to experiment, and try it out little by little and
creep before you walk and...

WELLS
(Excitedly)
I tell you I have done it four times with-
out a failure. I...

Now he subsides quickly.

WELLS
All right. I'll make up some of the stuff
...you go get me a cat, or a dog, or a
horse, or a lion...

MORTON
(Smiling)
I'll get you a rabbit.

WELLS
(Truculently)
And then you'll learn something.

MORTON
I'll be glad to, Horace...believe me.

Wells watches him go and lights an alcohol flame and starts
the preparation of nitrous oxide.

CUT TO:

E-54   THE MORTON WAITING ROOM

A streetwalker enters. She is in her middle years, poor
and pathetically flamboyant. She holds a handkerchief to
her cheek.

THE WOMAN
Is anybody in?

(Continued)

CUT TO:

E-55 WELLS NEAR THE SINK

He turns.

CUT TO:

E-56 THE DOOR FROM THE WAITING ROOM

The woman stands there.

                              THE WOMAN
                    I'm in terrible pain, dearie...some faker
                    broke my tooth and then..couldn't yank it
                    ...could you do anything for me?
CUT TO:

E-57 WELLS

He examines the woman for a moment, swallows nervously, then
comes forward. The CAMERA PANS him into the shot with her.

                         WELLS
          Sit down.

                              THE WOMAN
                         (Starting to whimper)
                    I s'pose it's going to hurt...something
                    terrible.

Wells crosses and closes the door before replying.

                              WELLS
                    No...it isn't going to hurt a bit.

He smiles triumphantly.

FADE OUT:

FADE IN:

E-58 MORTON COMING INTO THE WAITING ROOM WITH A RABBIT UNDER HIS
      ARM
                              MORTON
                         (Gaily)
                    He says there's really nothing the matter
                    with his teeth, but...

His voice trails off and he scowls as he looks past the
CAMERA.

CUT TO:

E-59 WELLS IN THE DOORWAY OF THE OPERATING ROOM

Behind him we see the figure in the chair.

                              WELLS
                    Come in, I want to show you something.

TG   TRIUMPH OVER PAIN   4-27-42   E-20
                                                            (86)
      CUT TO:

E-60 MORTON

      He comes slowly past the camera.

      CUT TO:

E-61 WELLS IN THE DOORWAY - FROM THE BACK

      Morton comes into the shot. The CAMERA PULLS BACK, and the
      two men look at the woman in the chair.

                            WELLS
                        (Triumphantly)
                  There you are! No pain! The tooth is
                  gone... she never moved a muscle.

                            MORTON
                        (Rigidly)
                  You shouldn't have done it, Horace.

                            WELLS
                        (Angrily)
                  What are you talking about? I tell you
                  this is the greatest...

                            MORTON
                  She's a mighty funny color.

                            WELLS
                  That doesn't mean anything. They turn
                  all kinds of colors...she'll be all
                  right. I tell you this is the greatest..

                            MORTON
                  How long has that woman been unconscious?

                            WELLS
                  I didn't watch the time, I....

                            MORTON
                        (Staccato)
                  Grab her feet! Help me put her on the
                  floor! This woman is either dead or so
                  close to it... get a doctor quick! Get
                  Dahlmeyer at the end of the hall. Bring
                  some smelling salts and some brandy...
                  bring anything you can, and hurry up
                  about it!

                            WELLS
                  But...

                                              (Continued)

                            451

Now he turns and flies out of the room. Morton raises and
lowers the woman's arms rhythmically.

                    MORTON
                  (Pleadingly)
Come on now...come on now, old girl...you
wouldn't play us...a trick like that.

DISSOLVE TO:

E-62 CLOSE SHOT - THE RABBIT

He is crouching in a corner, watching. The shadows of the
men move over him.

                    DR. DAHLMEYER'S VOICE
          And now the salts again.

                              MORTON'S VOICE
          Yes, doctor.

DISSOLVE TO:

E-63 OUT

E-64 WELLS CROUCHED ON A CHAIR

His face is ghastly. On the wall behind him we see the
shadows of Morton and Dr. Dahlmeyer. Wells passes his
hand over his forehead and speaks in a low voice.

                              WELLS
          How is she?

                    DR. DAHLMEYER'S VOICE
          I don't know yet.

                              WELLS
                  (Brokenly)
          If she lives...I'll never.... experiment
          again...with a human life...so help me, God.
                  (He passes his hand over
                  his eyes)
          If she doesn't live...

E-65 DR. DAHLMEYER, MORTON AND THE OLD WOMAN

Dr. Dahlmeyer stands with his back to us but has turned
his head to speak to Wells. Morton, on the far side of
the patient, is clearly outlined in the candlelight.

                    DR. DAHLMEYER
                  (Angrily)
You won't get the chance to! I'll put
you both in jail! The idea of a couple
of half-baked dentists...   (Continued)

E-65 (Cont'd)

Morton has been watching the patient. Now he grabs Dahlmeyer's
shoulder roughly.

                   MORTON
        Just a minute!

He points to the patient, then quickly passes some smelling salts under her nose.

E-66   CLOSE SHOT - THE OLD LADY

Slowly she opens her eyes, blinks, and then smiles. Morton
comes INTO THE SHOT as he puts his arm around her and helps
her to sit up.

E-67   WELLS - ON THE CHAIR

He starts to get up, then falls back again weakly.

E-68   CLOSE SHOT - MORTON AND THE OLD LADY - PAST DAHLMEYER

The old lady moves her tongue around inside her mouth,
with some difficulty puts her finger in her mouth,
then starts to smile.

                         THE OLD LADY
            Why...it's OUT!   That's simply wonderful,
            doctor...I NEVER FELT A THING! It didn't
            take a second, did it?

Morton starts to laugh. He tries not to but he can't
help himself. He puts his hand over his face and laughs
almost hysterically.

DISSOLVE TO:

E-69   MORTON'S PARLOR - NIGHT

The light is turned low. The clock points to nearly 1:00.
We hear a key clicking in the door and immediately
afterwards a low growl.

E-70   CLOSE SHOT - "NIG" THE SPANIEL IN A CHAIR NEAR THE TABLE

He growls for a moment, then wags his tail.

E-71   MORTON - PAST THE TABLE

He stands in the doorway of the room. He looks terribly
tired and his necktie is askew. We see him remove his
coat and hat before entering. The little dog jumps off
the chair and crosses to him.

                         MORTON
                 (Quietly)
            Hello, "Nig."

Now he drops into the chair, passes his hand over his
forehead and thinks over the events of the day. After
a moment he rises and crosses to a table on the other
side of the room.

E-72   CLOSE SHOT - THE TABLE

On it we see Pereira's "Materia Medica"; behind this
in the fairly deep shadow the half bottle of ether.

E-73   MORTON - PICKING UP THE BOOK

He is about to return to his chair when he sees the ether
bottle. He reaches over as if to pick it up, but instead
presses the cork more firmly into the bottle, then crosses
to the chair and sits down.

4-3-42

E-74   CLOSE SHOT - MORTON SITTING INTO THE CHAIR

       He looks at the volume for a moment, then turns to the
       index.

E-75   THE BOOK AND MORTON'S FINGER LOOKING FOR "NITROUS OXIDE"

       He finds it and it says: "See oxide, Nitrous". Morton's
       hands turn the pages and at "Oxide, nitrous," it says;
       "See vapors, inhalation of".

E-76   CLOSE SHOT - MORTON

       He gives the book an exasperated look, then turns the
       pages, finds "Inhalation of vapors" and starts to read
       without much interest. After a moment his attention
       is drawn to the floor beside his chair. He smiles,
       then lifts "Nig" into the chair with him and continues
       his reading.

E-77   MRS. MORTON - IN BED

       Half asleep she feels to see if Morton is home. Finding
       him absent she rolls herself angrily into the blankets.

E-78   MORTON READING

       His expression is one of great boredom. Now he takes the
       page between his fingers, preparatory to turning it,
       sighs and gets the page half turned before his eye is
       caught by something on the bottom line. He turns the
       page back again, re-reads the last line, then flips the
       page over and reads the top paragraph. Now he looks
       off into space for a moment, then turns the page back
       quickly and starts to read it again.

E-79   INSERT: THE BOTTOM OF THE PAGE

               "In his monograph of 1818 Faraday
               also issued the following warning:
               'When the vapour of ether is mixed
               with common air and inhaled, it
               produces effects very similar to
               those occasioned by nitrous oxide...

E-80   LOW CAMERA SHOT - UP AT MORTON

       "Nig" has his nose on the book. Morton scowls at what
       he has read for a moment, then turns the page over. As
       he reads --

E-81   INSERT: THE TOP OF THE NEXT PAGE

               "By the incautious breathing of
               ether vapour a man was thrown into
               a lethargic condition which, with
               a few interruptions, lasted for
4-3-42   thirty hours."

E-82   CLOSE SHOT - MORTON AND "NIG"

Morton looks up from the book and into space. He puts
his hand to his face and twists his lower lip. Now he
turns his head slowly and his eyes focus across the room.

E-83   LONG SHOT AT THE ETHER BOTTLE

SLOWLY THE CAMERA MOVES CLOSE TO IT, THEN HOLDS IT
for a moment.

E-84   LOW CAMERA SHOT - UP AT MORTON - PAST THE ETHER BOTTLE

He looks at it for a moment, then picks it up and
scrutinizes it as if he had never seen it before.
Slowly he returns to his chair.

E-85   MORTON - NEAR THE CHAIR

"Nig" has moved over into the warm center of the seat.
Morton reaches down to push him to one side, then stops
with his hand in mid-air and gives "Nig" a long
speculative look. After a moment he comes to a
decision. First he reaches down and gives "Nig"
a good patting.

> MORTON
> (In a low voice)
> There's a good old boy....we're not
> afraid of a little experiment, are we?
> (He takes his handkerchief
> out of his pocket and adds
> soothingly)
> Of course we're not.

Now he pulls the cork out of the ether bottle with his
teeth, takes a smell of it, then saturates his handkerchief
After putting the bottle back on the table and corking it
he gets into a squatting position, pats "Nig" soothingly
with his left hand and with his right hand brings the
saturated handkerchief close up under the dog's nose.
"Nig" sneezes at once, then draws back in alarm. Morton
pats him on the back, then starts to close his grip on
the back of the dog's neck.

> MORTON
> (Soothingly)
> Quiet, "Nig"...there's a good old
> man...this isn't going to hurt a...

With one bound "Nig" gets out of the chair and disappears.
Still in a squatting position Morton looks around for him.
Now he sees him.

4-3-42

E-86 CLOSE SHOT - "NIG" - UNDER A CHINA CABINET

He looks out at us suspiciously.

E-87 MORTON - NEAR THE CHAIR

He feels of the handkerchief, wets it again with ether, re-stoppers the bottle and, still doubled over, starts across the room.

E-88 CLOSE SHOT - "NIG" - UNDER THE CHINA CABINET

                    MORTON'S VOICE
              (Coming closer)
     There's a good old "Nig" ... We're not
     afraid of anything, are we?

Morton's left hand shoots INTO THE PICTURE and "Nig" vanishes.

E-89 MORTON - SQUATTING BY THE CHINA CABINET

He looks around, finally sees "Nig" and scowls at him.

E-90 "NIG" - UNDER THE PIANO

By now he thinks it's a game. He pants happily and wags the stump of his tail.

E-91 MORTON - BY THE CHINA CABINET

He gets on his hands and knees and goes PAST THE CAMERA.

                    MORTON
     Come on, now.

E-92 PART OF THE PIANO AND A PEDESTAL WHICH SUPPORTS A SMALL STATUARY GROUP ENTITLED "A VISIT TO THE DENTIST'S"

We hear a yelp and "Nig" flies out from under the piano. Morton dives after him and "A Visit to the Dentist's" comes down with a crash.

E-93 MRS. MORTON - SITTING UP IN BED

She lights a candle and her expression tells us she fears the worst. Now she draws her wraparound about her, picks up her candle and starts for the stairs.

E-94 THE WINDING STAIRWAY

Mrs. Morton comes down the steps, pauses in disgust and holds the candle high.

E-95 HIGH CAMERA SHOT - MORTON ON HIS KNEES ON THE FLOOR

He is half under the piano and he is whispering to "Nig"

who skitters about beyond the remains of "A Visit to the
Dentist's."

                        MORTON
                     (In a whisper)
                  Come on, old boy.

E-96 MRS. MORTON - <u>ON THE STEPS</u>

                      MRS. MORTON
                  Drunk again, I suppose...

Her chin begins to shimmy.

E-97 HIGH CAMERA SHOT - DOWN ON MORTON

Morton comes out from under the piano.

                        MORTON
                  (On his hands and knees)
                  For heaven's sake, Lizzie, what's the mat-
                  ter with you?

He glares up at her.

E-98 LOW CAMERA SHOT - UP AT MRS. MORTON

                      MRS. MORTON
                  (Between tears and indignation)
                  What's the matter with <u>you</u> would be more
                  to the point. You stay away from dinner
                  ... you don't even send word! ... It was
                  the baby's birthday and you didn't even
                  remember it... and now... in the middle
                  of the night... I find you groveling...

E-99 MORTON - <u>NEAR THE PIANO</u>

He gets to his feet angrily.

                        MORTON
                  Lizzie, I've had enough irritations to-
                  day without standing for any more from
                  you when I come home tired and weary.
                  I just wanted to catch that ... blasted
                  dog...

Now he stops suddenly and looks guilty.

E-100 MRS. MORTON - <u>ON THE STEPS</u> - PAST MORTON

Mrs. Morton descends like an avenging angel. She hurries
to Morton and confronts him.

4-3-42   (Continued)

E-100   MRS. MORTON
            What were you doing to that dog? What
            have you on that handkerchief? William
            Thomas Green Morton, if you harm a hair
            of that dog's head -- that's my dog, you
            know, I'll go straight home to Mother!

                               MORTON
                          (Angrily)
            Is that a promise?

                               MRS. MORTON
                          (Outraged)
            Oh! You brute! Talking that way to the
            m-mother of your ch-children!
                          (She sobs, then speaks
                           brokenly)
            C-come here, "N-nig" ... I'll protect you!

        She sweeps "Nig" into her arms and hurries to the stairs.
        Halfway up the stairs she pauses dramatically.

                               MRS. MORTON
            You may regret this night...William
            T-thomas G-green M-morton!

        Bursting into tears she climbs out of sight.

E-101 HIGH CAMERA SHOT - DOWN ON MORTON

        The CAMERA MOVES IN CLOSE as he looks after his wife in ex-
        asperation. Now he sighs, then looks at the handkerchief in
        his hand. He smells of it, then looks around hopelessly.
        Suddenly his eyes fix on something.

E-102 A GOLDFISH GLOBE - ON THE WINDOWSILL

        Three little fish swim around amiably.

        DISSOLVE TO:

E-103 THE GOLDFISH GLOBE - ON THE TABLE NEAR THE LAMP

        It contains two little fish. The CAMERA TRUCKS BACK and we
        see Morton crouched over the table looking at a goldfish on
        a piece of blotting paper. Morton replaces the cork in the
        ether bottle, then prods the fish gently with the dull end
        of a penholder. The fish seems quite dead. Morton turns
        it over and gives it a slight poke with the nib of the pen.
        The fish remains quite unconscious. Now Morton picks the
        fish up by the tail, blows on it, then drops it back into
        the aquarium. The little fish floats on its side.

4-3-42

E-104   CLOSE SHOT - MORTON WATCHING ANXIOUSLY

        Suddenly he leans forward in excitement. Now he smiles
        exultantly.

E-105   CLOSE SHOT - THE GOLDFISH GLOBE

        The three little fish are swimming happily.

E-106   MORTON - PAST THE GOLDFISH GLOBE

        He rises triumphantly and pauses with his clenched fists res
        ing on the table. Now he looks down at the ether bottle,
        considers it a moment, then looks at something else on the
        table.

E-107   CLOSE SHOT - AN OLD-FASHIONED SPIKE

        This is the type on which bills and memoranda used to be kep

E-108   MORTON - LOOKING AT THE SPIKE

        Now he looks back at the ether bottle, then slowly removes
        his handkerchief.

        DISSOLVE TO:

E-109   MRS. MORTON - IN BED WITH "NIG"

        She is lit by the guttering candle. She holds the little do
        to her breast as she mutters against her husband.

                            MRS. MORTON
                        (Between snuffles)
                ...and we'll show him...(sniff)
                we'll take the babies (sniff)...
                and we'll take you (sniff, sniff)
                and we'll take the furniture...

        She takes three long sniffs and looks around the room to see
        where the smell is coming from.

                            MRS. MORTON
                ...because Father gave it to me after all...

        Now she takes a long whiff, looks worried and gets to her
        feet. The CAMERA PANS her to the door. She opens it and
        takes another smell.

                            MRS. MORTON
                        (In faint alarm)
                William!

        As there is no answer, she raises her voice slightly.

                            MRS. MORTON
                Will-yum!

4-3-42   (Continued)

E-109 (Cont'd)

As there is still no answer, she pulls the wrap-around tight
and starts down the stairs, having forgotten her candle.

E-110   THE DARK WINDING STAIRS

Mrs. Morton descends and comes to a stop where we can see her
in the light from the lamp.

                          MRS. MORTON
                       (Starting at once)
               William, all I can say is...

Now she screams blood-curdlingly, then, almost paralyzed
with fear, comes down the remaining steps and walks stiffly
toward us. Her eyes are staring. The CAMERA MOVES SLOWLY
AHEAD of her until Morton's chair IS BROUGHT INTO THE FORE-
GROUND. He lies back, inert, a handkerchief over his face.
We see everything except his left hand. Suddenly Mrs.
Morton's eyes widen still further. She points to his left
hand which is OUT OF THE SHOT, starts to yammer, then lets
out a scream compared to which the first one was a violin
note. Morton shivers at this and the handkerchief slips off
his face. His eyes open and he looks down at his left hand.
Now he grins stupidly.

E-111   MORTON'S LEFT HAND

The spike has come through the back of it and a little
trickle of blood has run onto the chair.

E-112   MORTON AND HIS WIFE - LOOKING DOWN AT THE HAND WHICH WE DO
         NOT SEE

                          MORTON
                    (Grinning at the hand
                     drunkenly)
               Never felt it...went through by itshelf
               when I wash...shleeping. Take a good
               look at that, Lijjie...you've just seen
               the first....
                    (He reaches out of sight
                     and makes an effort)
               ...the first....

A spasm of pain crosses his face and he topples over in his
chair.

FADE OUT:

                        END OF SEQUENCE "E"

4-3-42

SEQUENCE "F"

FADE IN:

F-1   DR. MORTON'S WAITING ROOM

A sign-painter is putting the finishing touches on a stretched canvas sign. Morton, with a bandage on his left hand, watches over his shoulder anxiously.

> THE SIGNPAINTER
> How's that?

> MORTON
> Underline the word "double".

> THE SIGNPAINTER
> All right.

He dips his brush in a pot, then reaches for the sign.

F-2   THE SIGN - WITH MORTON TIPPED IN THE FOREGROUND

It says:

> Dr. W. T. G. MORTON, DENTIST
> Completely Painless Extractions
> Guaranteed or
> Double Your Money Back

While we read, the painter's hand underlines the word "Double".

F-3   MORTON AND THE SIGNPAINTER LOOKING AT THE SIGN

> MORTON
> That's fine. Now hang it right outside the window there.

> THE SIGNPAINTER
> You got a hammer?

> MORTON
> Right in here.

He leads the way into his operating room.

F-4   THE OPERATING ROOM

Morton and the signpainter enter. From the bottom of a dental stand Morton takes a hammer and an old can of nails which he gives to the painter.

> THE SIGNPAINTER
> Fine.

4-3-42   (Continued)

F-4   (Cont'd)

He starts for the waiting room, then steps back and to one
side as Mrs. Morton hurries in with a wrapped gallon jug
under her arm.

                         THE SIGNPAINTER
              Excuse me.

He exits.

                         MORTON
                    (Taking the jug)
              Good.

He closes the door after the painter, puts the jug on a
table and starts to unwrap it.

                         MORTON
                    (Anxiously)
              You didn't go to Burnett's?

                         MRS. MORTON
              No, I got it from Brewer, Stevens & Cushing
              on Washington Street.

                         MORTON
              You didn't mention my name.

                         MRS. MORTON
              No, dear.

                         MORTON
              Good.

The signpainter starts to hammer in the next room.

                         MRS. MORTON
                    (Startled)
              What's that?

                         MORTON
              The new sign.

                         MRS. MORTON
              Oh.

Morton examines the gallon jug which is labeled "Sulphuric
Ether", and starts scratching the label off it with a penknife.

                         MORTON
              We'll keep buying it at different places
              till I get the patent. Because this is
              bound to make a lot of talk, Lizzie.
              Every dentist in town will try to find
              out what I'm using...

4-3-42   (Continued)

                            463

F-4   (Cont'd)   MRS. MORTON
                  What are you going to tell them if they ask
                  you?

                            MORTON
                  (Polishing the place where the
                  label had been)
                  I figured out a pretty good name.

        He cuts a label with a pair of scissors, then dips a pen in
        an inkwell and starts to print.

                            MORTON
                  (Printing)
                  Did you ever hear of the River Lethe...
                  in mythology?

                            MRS. MORTON
                  No. I never even heard of mythology.

                            MORTON
                  (Finishing his label)
                  It was the stream...of oblivion...that
                  banished all earthly sorrows.
                  (He holds up the label and
                  reads it)
                  LETHEON!

        DISSOLVE TO:

F-5   LOW CAMERA SHOT - UP AT MORTON'S SIGN OUTSIDE THE BUILDING

F-6   BOOM SHOT - DOWN ON EBEN FROST - ACROSS THE STREET

        Fiddle case in hand, the little man is looking up at us woe-
        fully. The CAMERA SLIDES DOWN to a CLOSE SHOT of him. His
        cheek is swollen and he looks very miserable. He also
        looks undecided. Now he frowns disbelievingly at the sign.

                            FROST
                  That's what you say!

        He starts away and the CAMERA MOVES WITH HIM. After a
        moment he comes to a stop again and looks back up at the
        sign.

F-7   INSERT: PART OF THE SIGN

        We see only the part which says:

                        Guaranteed or
                    Double Your Money Back

F-8   CLOSE BOOM SHOT - DOWN ON FROST

        Suddenly he makes up his mind, steps off the curb and
        starts across the street. The CAMERA ROTATES WITH HIM so
        4-3-42   (Continued)

that we see him from the front, from above and then from
the rear as he enters the building.

F-9   MORTON AND HIS WIFE - IN THE OPERATING ROOM

Morton holds an ordinary chemical flask with two bent tubes
passing through the cork.

                         MORTON
                 (Explaining with his finger)
          The air comes in through here, you see,
          passes over the Letheon...
                 (He smiles)
          ...then out here and into the patient.

                         MRS. MORTON
                 (Anxiously)
          Are you sure it will work, William?

                         MORTON
                 (Almost with irritation)
          It has to work, Lizzie! I've tried it on
          myself I don't know how many times, on
          the gold fish, on a cat, on another cat,
          on...

                         MRS. MORTON
          But not on "Nig."

                         MORTON
                 (Chuckling)
          No, not on "Nig." But if I'd been able
          to catch him...

                         MRS. MORTON
                 (Smiling)
          Then do you really think we're going to
          be rich?

                         MORTON
                 (Enthusiastically)
          How can we help it? I've got the dental
          business right by the...forceps!
                 (He pulls a document out
                  of his pocket)
          Here's my application for a patent. They'll
          either buy a license from me or go out of
          business! I can do things in dentistry that
          have never been known! There's a way of
          crowning teeth with a lute which is wonder-
          ful...only it's so painful nobody's ever
          been able to stand it...all right! I CAN
          USE A LUTE! Then consider impactions: the
          horror of the business, well...

4-3-42   (Continued)

                              465

F-9   (Cont'd)   MRS. MORTON
                  (Warningly)
William...

                   MORTON
                  (Vaguely)
Hunh?

Mrs. Morton jerks her thumb toward the waiting room.

                   MORTON
                  (Seeing Frost)
Oh.

Now he beams a professional smile and calls heartily.

                   MORTON
Come right in, sir!

F-10   FROST HALF IN AND HALF OUT THE DOOR

He seems poised for flight.

                   FROST
You guarantee twice the money back if I
feel anything?
              (He points to his cheek)

F-11   MORTON - THROUGH THE DOOR OF THE WAITING ROOM

Mrs. Morton peers anxiously over his shoulder.

                   MORTON
                  (Proudly)
I do, sir! Come right in!

F-12   FROST - IN THE DOORWAY OF THE WAITING ROOM

Frost thinks it over carefully then looks at Morton with
mild defiance.
                   FROST
             (Reaching into his pocket)
I'll take ten dollars of that bet.

DISSOLVE TO:

F-13   FROST IN THE DENTAL CHAIR

His fiddle case is on his lap. Morton and his wife are at
the stand behind him. Morton is pouring the ether into the
flask held by Mrs. Morton. Frost looks extremely nervous.

                   FROST
What's that...pew...stink?

                   MORTON
             (Putting the cork in the flask)
That is the Letheon, my friend...that is
what kills the pain.

He comes close to Frost. Mrs. Morton watches anxiously
in the background.

                    FROST
          I don't like the smell of it.

                    MORTON
               (With fine assurance)
          Nevertheless you will be grateful
          for it. Now: I want you to put
          this end in your mouth and breathe in
          deeply for a few moments.

                    FROST
          What happens then?

                    MORTON
          You will then sink into a gentle
          slumber...a sort of catnap...
          from which you will arise without
          pain...and without the tooth.

                    FROST
               (Beginning to be
                impressed)
          Really?

                    MORTON
          Really...a little invention of my own.
          Hold this, please.

He tries to put the flask in the hands of Frost who seems
loath to take them off his fiddle case.

                    MORTON
               (Taking hold of the
                fiddle case)
          Would you mind...

                    FROST
               (Anxiously)
          Look out, that's a very delicate fiddle.

                    MORTON
               (Getting it away from him)
          I'll take the best care of it.
               (He puts it on the dental
                stand)
          There.

He returns to Frost who holds the flask gingerly.

                    MORTON
          Now let me see the tooth, please.

He looks in Frost's mouth and puts his finger in it.

F-13 (Cont'd)
                        MORTON
        Is that it?

                        FROST
        Wow!

                        MORTON
                (Chuckling)
        In a few moments it will be only a
        memory. Put the tube in your mouth.

Frost does so fearfully.

                        MORTON
        Now inhale deeply...now once more..
        Do you begin to feel drowsy?

Frost scowls at him.

                        MORTON
        Then take another one...

Frost looks at him with wild eyes.

                        MORTON
                (Soothingly)
        Don't you begin to feel a little bit...

At this moment Frost leaps from the chair like a wild
man and begins to wave the flask around. He is in the
throes of insane excitement.

                        FROST
                (At the top of his lungs)
        Here they come, boys, here they
        come! They're coming in the
        window! Ready aim fire!

He hurls the flask of ether through the window.

                        MORTON
                (Trying to grab him)
        Stop that! What's the matter with you?

                        FROST
                (Escaping him and knocking
                over the dental stand)
        Avast! Lay but one finger on yon
        silver head!...

He snatches up his fiddle case and threatens Morton with it

                        FROST
        Here they come, boys? You would
        would you?

4-3-42   (Continued)

F-13   (Cont'd)

He crashes the case on Morton's head. It flies open and
the fiddle sails across the room.

                        MORTON
                 (Making a dive for him)
              Come here, you....

                        FROST
                 (Snatching up the fiddle
                  by the neck)
              Give me liberty or give me death!

He busts the fiddle over Morton's head, then as Morton
staggers back...

                        FROST
              Sound the retreat! Follow me, boys!

To Morton's horror he jumps through the remains of the window.

F-14   EXT. OF THE BUILDING

Frost slides down the awning. As he slips off the edge of
it --

F-15   THE STREET IN FRONT OF MORTON'S BUILDING

Frost lands unharmed. To the startled passersby he yells:

                        FROST
              The Hessians are coming!' Sound the tocsin!
              Follow me, boys!

He gets up speed and runs straight into the arms of an
enormous policeman.

F-16   CLOSE SHOT - FROST AND THE POLICEMAN

                        FROST
              So there you are, general! I've been look-
              ing for you all over the battlefield.

                        THE POLICEMAN
                 (Menacingly)
              Well you won't have to look any further...
              you've found me.

He gets a good grip on the back of Frost's collar.

4-3-42

F-17   MORTON AND HIS WIFE - IN THE WRECKAGE OF THE OPERATING ROOM

They are looking out the window. Now they turn and look at
the mess. Still too dazed to speak, Morton picks up the
limp fiddle and places it on a chair. Mrs. Morton looks
at him then looks away.

                        MORTON
                    (After a while)
            Do you think maybe he was crazy?

                        MRS. MORTON
            He didn't seem crazy when he first
            came in.
                    (Then after a moment)
            Do you suppose maybe it affects people
            in different ways?

                        MORTON
                    (Ignoring her question)
            You're sure you got ether....sulphuric
            ether!

                        MRS. MORTON
            Of course I did, dear.
                    (She reaches for
                    her handbag)
            Here's the bill.

She hands Morton the bill.

F-18   INSERT: AN INVOICE FROM --

                    "BREWER, STEVENS & CUSHING
                        Wholesale Druggists
                        208 Washington Street"

In a fine handwriting we see the date:

                        "September 30th, 1846"

Below this:

            1 gallon Sulphuric Ether.......$4.75

F-19   MORTON AND HIS WIFE - IN THE OPERATING ROOM

Morton drops the invoice on the table and pulls the jug of
ether closer to him. He looks at it helplessly before speaking.

                        MORTON
            The only way to find out if it acts
            differently on different people...is
            to try it.

He takes out his handkerchief. He saturates the handkerchie
4-3-42   (Continued)

F-19 (Cont'd)
MORTON
I want you to watch me closely, Lizzie,
and tell me if I do anything peculiar.

He picks up a chair, then saturates the handkerchief again.
Now he seats himself on the chair.

MORTON
It ought to put me quietly to sleep
for a few minutes...and that's all.

He throws his head back, puts the handkerchief over his nose
and inhales deeply.

MRS. MORTON
Don't take too much, William. It always
make me a little frightened and...

She screams as Morton leaps to his feet laughing like a
maniac.

MORTON
Ha-ha-ha-ha-ha-ha-ha-ha-ha-ha !

He waves his arms, then picks up the chair and hurls it
through the ground glass into the waiting room. Now he
picks up the heavy jug of ether and starts pursuing his
wife.

MRS. MORTON
William!...please...William, stop!

He backs her into a corner and gets ready to crash the
heavy jug on her head. She opens her mouth to scream.

F-20   CLOSE SHOT - MORTON

He holds the heavy bottle aloft. His expression is maniacal.
Now he blinks his eyes and slowly puts the jug on the table.
After this he passes his hand over his face and looks per-
plexed.

F-21   MRS. MORTON - PAST MORTON

She watches him open-mouthed.

F-22   MORTON - PAST MRS. MORTON

MORTON
Lizzie...did I do anything peculiar
then?

F-23   MRS. MORTON - PAST MORTON

As she looks at him in stupefaction

DISSOLVE TO:

4-3-42

F-24   PROF. JACKSON - IN HIS LABORATORY

He stands in front of the apparatus for some experiment
talking to a maid.

                    THE MAID
          And he said he'd like to see you, sir,
          if you could spare the time.

                    JACKSON
                 (Roughly)
          Bring him in, bring him in!
                 (Now he turns and
                 shouts PAST THE
                 CAMERA)
          COME IN, MORTON!

F-25   THE DOORWAY TO THE LABORATORY

Morton appears and hesitates a moment. He has a small
bottle of ether in his coat pocket. He looks somewhat
crestfallen.

                    MORTON
          Good morning, Professor Jackson.

F-26   JACKSON AND THE MAID - PAST MORTON

The maid goes OUT OF THE SHOT.

                    JACKSON
          Good morning...Doctor.
                 (He cackles)

Morton crosses to him slowly and the CAMERA FOLLOWS.

                    JACKSON
          How is everything in the scientific
          world today? Any more great dis-
          coveries? I hear Wells is going
          into some other line...

F-27   MORTON - PAST JACKSON

                    MORTON
                 (Quietly)
          When you told me to try ether the
          other night, I got a bottle of sul-
          phuric ether...

F-28   JACKSON - PAST MORTON

                    JACKSON
                 (Explosively)
          I told you to try chloric ether!
          Haven't you got any memory at all!
          You go fooling around with sulphuric

4-3-42   (Continued)

F-28 (Cont'd)   JACKSON (Cont'd)
ether and you'll blow your head off
or wind up in another magnificent
exhibition like you two scientists
put on the other day! Let me know
when you do it...I want to be there.

F-29   TWO SHOT - MORTON AND JACKSON

> MORTON
> Listen! I can put myself to sleep
> with sulphuric ether.

> JACKSON
> What about it? That's nothing new!
> I was unconscious from it for fifteen
> minutes once. Some lunkhead put it
> in my alcohol burner by mistake.

> MORTON
> (Taken aback a little)
> Well, anyway...I've put myself under
> time and time again.

> JACKSON
> What for...how'd you do it?

> MORTON
> By inhaling it. I wanted to see if
> I could extract teeth with it. I was
> sure I could...I'm still sure I can...
> I know it's just around the corner...
> but I'm stuck...something went wrong...
> If you'll help me out, I'll pay you
> for your help.

> JACKSON
> (Cackling)
> My regular fee is five hundred dollars.

He enjoys Morton's discomfiture at this.

> MORTON
> (Uneasily)
> Well, I haven't got five hundred dollars
> but I'll tell you what I'll do... I'll
> give you ten per cent of my patent...if
> it's worth anything.

> JACKSON
> What are you patenting?

> MORTON
> (A little sheepishly)
> The use of...Letheon. That's what I'm
> calling it, you see, so people won't
> find out the secret.

4-3-42   (Continued)

Morton pulls the document out of his pocket, picks up a pen
and writes and says the following:

> MORTON
> I hereby assign to Dr. Charles T.
> Jackson one-tenth of my interest
> in this discovery for his assistance
> in its perfection...now you sign it
> to show you accept it.

> JACKSON
> Suppose I can't perfect it?

> MORTON
> Then it may not be worth anything anyway.

Jackson shrugs his shoulders and signs rapidly.

> JACKSON
> If I make five hundred dollars on this
> I'll die of a syncope. Now what is
> this deep problem, professor?

> MORTON
> Well, the ether's been working perfectly
> ever since I started, and then... this
> morning... I tried it out on a patient..
> and he jumped out of the window.

> JACKSON
> (Roaring with delight)
> There goes my five hundred!
> (Then regaining his com-
> posure he barks at Morton)
> You have a sample of your ether?

> MORTON
> (Handing it over)
> Yes, sir.

> JACKSON
> (Smelling it)
> Where'd you get it?

> MORTON
> Brewer, Stevens & Cushing on Washington
> Street.

> JACKSON
> (In mock dismay)
> The only trouble with you is you can't
> remember anything. I told you to go to
> Burnett's. It's the only place in town
> you can get highly rectified ether.....

4-3-42   (Continued)

F-29 (Cont'd)   JACKSON (Cont·d)
                         HIGHLY RECTIFIED! Write that in your
                         hat...
                                  (He holds up the bottle)
                         This is cleaning fluid!

                                  MORTON
                                  (Stunned)
                         You mean that was... the trouble?

                                  JACKSON
                         That was the problem, professor.

Suddenly Morton seizes Jackson's hand.

                                  MORTON
                         Thank you, doctor!... you're going to
                         be a rich man for this.

                                  JACKSON
                                  (Amused)
                         You wouldn't care to settle for fifty
                         dollars cash, would you?

                                  MORTON
                                  (Ignoring this thrust)
                         Thank you.

He hurries out. Jackson watches him go, then takes another
smell of the ether.

                                  JACKSON
                         Phew!

He pours it down the sink.

DISSOLVE TO:

F-30   MORTON IN HIS OPERATING ROOM

He is pouring the gallon jug down the sink. In the background Mrs. Morton is putting the place to rights with the
assistance of the janitor. Now Morton rinses the jug out
and starts filling it with a bottle from Burnett's.

                                  MRS. MORTON
                                  (To the janitor)
                         Thank you very much, and if you can get
                         the glazier here right away...

                                  THE JANITOR
                         Yes, ma'am, I'll go right now.

                                  MRS. MORTON
                         Thank you.

4-3-42   (Continued)

                                  475

F-30 (Cont'd)

The janitor exits and she crosses to Morton.

       MRS. MORTON
    Are you sure this time?

       MORTON
     (Happily)
    I'm as sure as....

He stops and looks toward the waiting room.

F-31 EBEN FROST HALF IN AND HALF OUT OF THE WAITING ROOM DOOR

He seems on the point of flight.

       FROST
    I'll have my fiddle, please... and
    no shenanigans.

F-32 MORTON - VIEWED FROM THE WAITING ROOM

       MORTON
     (Coming forward)
    I'm so glad you came back. I want
    to explain something to you.

F-33 FROST - POISED IN THE DOORWAY

       FROST
    I'll have no explanations, thank you.
    Just give me my instrument.

F-34 MORTON - IN THE DOORWAY

He looks over at the fiddle.

F-35 CLOSE SHOT - THE FIDDLE

It is hanging over the edge of a table like a bath towel.

F-36 MORTON - IN THE DOORWAY

He looks back at Frost.

       MORTON
     (Gently)
    Won't you even let me have it repaired
    for you?

F-37 FROST - IN THE DOORWAY

He comes forward angrily.

       FROST
    What are you talking about? What did
    you do to that fiddle? I think I'll
    have you arrested.

4-3-42

F-38   MORTON - IN THE DOORWAY

> MORTON
> Won't you come in and talk it over?

F-39   FROST - IN THE DOORWAY

> FROST
> (Indignantly)
> I will not. You know where I've been
> for the last eight hours? In the
> jug! Charged with drunkenness!
> (He takes a step forward)
> I who have never touched anything
> stronger than sassafarilla! Now give
> me my violin and don't try any pranks.

F-40   MORTON - PAST FROST

> MORTON
> How's your tooth?

> FROST
> I'll take care of that.

> MORTON
> Will you listen to me a minute?

> FROST
> No.

> MORTON
> All right. Your fiddle is right over
> there.

He jerks his thumb toward it and retires into the corner
near the Letheon bottle.

F-41   FROST - PAST MORTON

Morton pretends to be ignoring Frost but actually he watches
him. Frost comes in slowly, stops in horror as he sees the
remains of his fiddle, then crosses to it quickly and picks
it up like a mother. Now Morton saturates a handkerchief
with Letheon and moves to a place between Frost and the door.
Frost turns quickly, reacts violently to the sight of the
handkerchief and steps back.

> FROST
> You keep away from me, now! I'm going
> to put you in jail for this fiddle and..
> you keep away from me now!

> MORTON
> (Stepping closer)
> I just want you to smell this...Just
> to convince you... you see, I sent my

4-3-42   (Continued)

F-41 (Cont'd)   FROST (Cont'd)
wife out for some Letheon this morning
and by mistake she got something
<u>entirely</u> different.

                 FROST
Well you try it on somebody else.

                 MORTON
I don't want to try it on you. I
just want you to smell it so I can be
sure it isn't the same.

He comes a step nearer and holds the handkerchief out.

                 MORTON
Do you remember what it smelled like
this morning?

                 FROST
I'll remember it till the day I die.

                 MORTON
       (Coming another step nearer)
Is this anything like it?

He sticks the handkerchief toward Frost who leans forward a
little and smells it reluctantly.

                 FROST
      Exactly.

                 MORTON
       (Smelling it himself)
That must be because it's drying off.
Actually there's no similarity at all.

He crosses to the Letheon jug and soaks the handkerchief
again, then returns to Frost in a business-like manner.

                 MORTON
      Smell it now.

                 FROST
       (After two inhalations)
It smells the same to me.

                 MORTON
       (Pretending to be angry)
How can you say it smells the same?

He holds it close under Frost's nose.

                 MORTON
Don't you notice that faint odor of
peaches?

4-3-42   (Continued)

F-41 (Cont'd)

Frost is beginning to look a little strange. Morton holds
the handkerchief close to him.

                    FROST
          Peashej? I don't notish any peashej..
          shmells more like....like...

                    MORTON
          Why don't you sit down for a minute?

                    FROST
              (Sitting into the chair)
          Don't you shtart anything, now.

                    MORTON
          You are the most suspicious man I
          ever met.

                    FROST
              (Indignantly)
          Whosh shushpishush?

                    MORTON
              (Soaking the handkerchief
               for the last time)
          You are! If you think I care anything
          about your tooth you're crazy.

He comes back to Frost and sticks the handkerchief under
his nose.

                    MORTON
          All I want to know is does this smell
          like peaches...or more like pears?
          Now give me your answer like a man.

Frost takes a terrific smell and mutters:

                    FROST
          Peashej.

He takes another whiff and mutters:

                    FROST
          Pearje.

He looks around dizzily and has another whiff.

                    FROST
          Peashej!

Now his head falls back.

                    MORTON
              (To his wife)
          There you are....

F-41 (Cont'd)

He slaps Frost's face a couple of times gently to see if there
is any feeling in him, then picks up a forceps and steps
BETWEEN FROST AND THE CAMERA. He bends slightly, tenses his
muscles, then straightens up and puts the forceps back on the
stand.

>MORTON
>(Completing his sentence)
>...as simple as falling off a roof!
>(He indicates Frost)
>Why, Lizzie, I could have...sawed...his
>leg off without his feeling...
>(Suddenly he yells in
>excitement)
>Lizzie!

>MRS. MORTON
>(Worried)
>What is it, dear?

>MORTON
>(Putting his hand on
>Frost's shoulder)
>If I could make this sleep last a little
>longer - say ten or fifteen minutes.. No
>...that would be too much to hope for...
>no it isn't! Lizzie...I TELL YOU I CAN
>DO IT.

>MRS. MORTON
>You mean fill teeth in some---

>MORTON
>(Interrupting)
>Nothing to do with teeth....

He stares off into space. At this moment Frost's face begins
to wiggle. Now he opens his eyes and smiles stupidly. A
second later he remembers where he is and sniffs.

>FROST
>(Raising a finger happily)
>I got it.... pershimmons!

Morton looks at him vaguely and chuckles. Suddenly Frost
scowls and sticks his finger in his mouth.

>FROST
>(Indignantly)
>Hey!

Morton hands him his tooth absently and turns to his wife
and raises a positive finger.

>MORTON
>I can!... I'm sure of it!

FADE OUT:

-4-3-42   END OF SEQUENCE "F"

TRIUMPH OVER PAIN   G-1
                                    SEQUENCE "G"   (115)

FADE IN:

G-1   A MONTAGE OF MORTON'S SUCCESS:

       THE CAMERA STARTS ACROSS a line of windows. Each is marked:
       "W. T. G. MORTON." Below this each has a different slogan:

                    "The Painless Dentist" - "The Discoverer
                    of Letheon" -- "The Man Who Made Dentistry
                    a Pleasure" -- "Come Up and Be Convinced" -
                    "The Conqueror of Pain" -- "The Pain Killer"
                    "Pulls Them Out With a Smile."

       While the CAMERA IS MOVING SIDEWAYS PAST the windows the
       FOLLOWING SHOTS DISSOLVE IN AND OUT:

       HIGH CAMERA SHOT OF PATIENTS RUNNING UP THE STAIRS PAST US

       A RECEPTIONIST IN A LARGE WAITING ROOM

                                  THE RECEPTIONIST
                    New dentists are interviewed in room two
                    twenty-one from eight to...

       FROST TALKING TO A MALE PATIENT

                                  FROST
                    (With his finger in his mouth)
                    It was on the night of September thirtieth...

       MORE PATIENTS RUNNING UP THE STAIRS

       THE PERSPIRING CASHIER

       He throws money in a drawer, makes change, receipts the bill
       and passes it out the wicket.

       MORTON HELPING HIS WIFE OUT OF A CARRIAGE

       He points out the new house to her. Mrs. Morton looks at it
       unbelievingly.

       SHOT OF A BEAUTIFUL MANSION

       Mrs. Morton throws her arms around her husband's neck.

       A DENTIST WITH AN EMPTY INHALER

                                  DENTIST
                    Some more Letheon, please.

4-3-42   (Continued)

G-1 (Cont'd)

FROST WITH A LADY PATIENT

                 FROST
            (With his. finger in his
            mouth)
       It was on the night of September thirtieth....

MRS. MORTON ON THE PORCH OF THE NEW HOUSE WITH THE THREE
CHILDREN WHO ARE BLINDFOLDED.

                 MRS. MORTON
            (Counting)
         ...THREE!

The children yank off the handkerchiefs, scream with delight
and the CAMERA DRAWS BACK as they rush down and clamber onto
a shiny little carriage with two goats hitched to it.

PEOPLE COMING UP THE STAIRS OF MORTON'S OFFICE

A LETHEON BOTTLE EMPTYING RAPIDLY

THE CASHIER COUNTING PILES OF MONEY

OVER THIS AND THE LAST OF THE WINDOWS COMES A THIRD EXPOSURE:

A CLOSE SHOT OF DR. JACKSON who looks faintly sinister. NOW
THE MONTAGE ENDS, LEAVING --

G-2   DR. JACKSON - IN THE RECEPTION ROOM

The CAMERA TRUCKS BACK SO AS to bring the receptionist INTO
THE SHOT.

                 DR. JACKSON
            (Sourly)
       Well, when can I see him?

                 THE RECEPTIONIST
            (Doubtfully)
       Perhaps in the morning some time. He is
       working on a new discovery and cannot be
       disturbed in the afternoon.

                 DR. JACKSON
            (Derisively)
       Ha!

He stamps out of the reception room.

DISSOLVE TO:

4-3-42

G-3   MRS. MORTON IN THE SUPERB DINING ROOM OF THE MORTON
MANSION - (NIGHT)

The table is set for sixteen and is loaded with fruit, flowers and fine silver. Mrs. Morton in a fashionable evening
gown is setting place-cards. We hear the crunching of horses'
hoofs in the driveway. Mrs. Morton pulls a curtain aside.

G-4   A CARRIAGE COMING TO A STOP

G-5   MRS. MORTON - IN THE DINING ROOM

Now a butler hurries through from the pantry.

> MRS. MORTON
> (Gaily)
> Tell the doctor to hurry and dress... he's
> late.

She continues with the place-cards. We hear a door close. A
second later the butler re-enters.

> THE BUTLER
> The doctor is extremely sorry, madam,
> but he won't be home for dinner.

> MRS. MORTON
> But I thought he just came.

> THE BUTLER
> He sent word, madam, through the coachman.

> MRS. MORTON
> (Pointing hopelessly to the
> table)
> But...

Now she swallows her disappointment.

> MRS. MORTON
> (With dignity)
> Thank you, Roberts.

> THE BUTLER
> Very good, madam.

He returns to the kitchen. Mrs. Morton's lips tremble
slightly as she removes one card from the table and tears it
up.

DISSOLVE TO:

G-6   THE CASHIER COUNTING HIS MONEY THE FINAL TIME - (NIGHT)

He makes an entry in a book, ties the wad of money neatly with
a piece of tape, then goes out into the reception room.

4-3-42

G-7   THE CASHIER CROSSING THE EMPTY DIMLY LIT RECEPTION
      ROOM

      He goes down a long hall and disappears from view.

G-8   THE CASHIER COMING AROUND A BEND IN A HALL

      He stops, straightens his tie, then knocks on a door.

                              MORTON'S VOICE
                         (Roughly)
                    What is it?

                              THE CASHIER
                         (After clearing his
                         throat)
                    The day's receipts, Dr. Morton.

      The door opens a foot and Morton appears in his shirt
      sleeves. He sticks his right hand out.

                              MORTON
                    Let me have it.

                              THE CASHIER
                         (Placing the wad of money
                         in Morton's hand)
                    Would you be so kind as to count it,
                    Doctor? I always say, however much one
                    trusts....

                              MORTON
                         (Impatiently)
                    Go away, will you?

      He slams the door.

                              THE CASHIER
                         (Loosening his collar)
                    Yes, Doctor.

      He clears his throat and starts away.

G-9   MORTON - INSIDE THE DOOR

      This is the same old operating room he started with. He is
      in his shirt sleeves and holds a watch in his left hand
      and the wad of money in his right. He looks at the money
      vaguely, then stuffs it in his pocket. Now he looks PAST
      THE CAMERA.

                              MORTON
                    How do you feel now?

4-3-42

                              484

G-10   FROST - PAST MORTON

        He lies back in the dental chair and looks very much the
        worse for wear.

                            FROST
                        (With difficulty)
                    I feel terrible, and I'll tell you
                    shumping elsh....

G-11   MORTON - PAST FROST

                                    MORTON
                        (Gleefully)
                    Do you know how long you were under?

G-12   FROST - PAST MORTON

                                    FROST
                    I don't....really.....care.

G-13   MORTON - PAST FROST

                                    MORTON
                        (Triumphantly)
                    Nineteen minutes. And every fifteen
                    seconds I jabbed you with this.

        He picks up a large darning needle.

G-14   FROST - PAST MORTON

        He shifts slightly on his base, then claps his hand to
        his hip and scowls at Morton.

                                    FROST
                    I'm getting to feel like a pin cushion.

G-15   MORTON - PAST FROST

                                    MORTON
                        (Decisively)
                    Come on, we'll go right down and see
                    him now. We'll get a bite to eat
                    on the way.

        He reaches for his coat. There is a loud knock on the
        door.

                                    MORTON
                        (Roughly)
                    What is it now?

        The door opens and Jackson stalks into   the room.

4-3-42   (Continued)

G-15   (Cont'd)

                JACKSON
       (Pointing a finger at Morton)
       You've been dodging me as long as
       you're going to..you and your new
       discoveries!

Morton looks at Jackson for a moment then turns to Frost.

                MORTON
       Get a cab and wait for me downstairs.
       I'll be with you in a minute.

He waits for Frost to exit and close the door after him.

Now he turns and glares at Jackson.

                MORTON
       (Roughly)
       Now what is it? I've never dodged
       anybody in my life.

                JACKSON
       (Shaking an angry finger at him)
       You've swindled me!

                MORTON
       (Menacingly)
       I'd be a little more careful of my
       verbs if I were you, Professor.

                JACKSON
       (Violently)
       I'll use any verbs I like and that
       goes. for adverbs and adjectives!
       You swandangled me into accepting
       ten percent of this...Lethoon or
       whatever you call it...

                MORTON
       You wanted five hundred dollars,
       you're going to get much more.
       What are you complaining about?

                JACKSON
       You didn't reveal its possibilities
       to me. You pretended you were just
       a poor little dentist trying to get
       along, so that when I suggested
       ether to you.....

                MORTON
       (Interrupting)
       You suggested chloric ether...drops,
       that didn't work.

4-3-42   (Continued)

G-15   (Cont'd)
                         JACKSON
              Maybe I did, but that's what gave
              you the idea.

                         MORTON
              Did it give you the idea?

                         JACKSON
                 (Taken aback for a moment)
              I've known all about sulphuric ether
              for years....and why you should come
              along and profit by my discovery...

                         MORTON
                 (Interrupting)
              Look: I've known all about you for
              years, Professor Jackson. The only
              trouble with you is that you're a
              little bit cracked in the head. Let
              me tell you something for your own
              good: you did not discover the
              electric telegraph. That was Samuel
              F.B. Morse.

                         JACKSON
                 (Almost exploding)
              You miserable little...

                         MORTON
                 (Cutting him off)
              And you did not discover ether
              narcosis...I did. Now is there
              anything else?

                         JACKSON
              I'll have twenty-five percent of
              that patent I signed, or by Joseph
              I'll...

                         MORTON
                 (Coolly)
              I'm afraid you'll have to take that up with
              Joseph, because as far as I'm concerned
              you're getting more than you deserve. I
              could have gone to any chemist in the city
              to find out what I wanted to know. I
              happened to go to you....

                         JACKSON
              That is your ultimatum?

                         MORTON
              If that means what I think it means it is.

                         JACKSON
              Very well, sir!

                         MORTON
4-3-42   Yes, sir.   (Continued)

                              487

G-15 (Cont'd)   JACKSON
We shall see.

          MORTON
We certainly shall...this could
go on all night, you know. I'm
going down to Massachusetts General
to ask Professor Warren to try the
Letheon. You want to come along?

          JACKSON
       (Horrified)
You mean in a surgical case?

          MORTON
Certainly, why not?

          JACKSON
WHY NOT! Don't you know the
difference between a serious operation and yanking a tooth? You'll
kill somebody yet with this murderous
nonsense as sure as my name is
Jackson!

          MORTON
Then I take it you don't want to come
along.

          JACKSON
Come along! If you even mention my
name to Professor Warren as co-discoverer...

          MORTON
Well make up your mind! Are you in...
or out... or on the fence?

          JACKSON
       (Menacingly)
You'll find out, young man.

          MORTON
All right.

          JACKSON
You'll see.

          MORTON
All right, I'll see.

          JACKSON
And it won't take long.

          MORTON
It's taking too long right now. I'm
paying a dollar an hour for a cab and
I want to get some use out of it.
Goodnight!

4-3-42   (Continued)

G-15   (Cont'd)

He puts on his hat and walks out. Jackson looks at him
angrily, then starts to follow him. Now he turns back and
blows out the lamp.

DISSOLVE TO:

G-16   A DOORWAY WHICH SAYS: "THE MASSACHUSETTS GENERAL HOSPITAL" -
        (NIGHT)

G-17   THE OFFICE OF THE HOUSE SURGEON - DR. C. F. HEYWOOD

We see him behind his desk PAST Morton and Frost.

                        DR. HEYWOOD
                    (Exasperatedly)
            But Professor Warren is performing an
            emergency operation!

                        MORTON
            Then I'll wait for him.

                        DR. HEYWOOD
            You don't seem to understand that after
            an operation a surgeon is completely
            enervated...exhausted.

                        MORTON
            All the more reason.

                        DR. HEYWOOD
                    (Reluctantly)
            My dear Dr. Morton, as Professor Warren's
            assistant, part of my duty is to shield
            him to the best of my ability from the
            many well-meaning, I won't say cranks but
            let me say, amateur inventors who come
            here every day with every kind of gew-gaw
            and gimcrack for every purpose imaginable.
            Why only yesterday...

                        MORTON
                    (Interrupting him)
            You don't seem to understand that my method
            is being used by all of my assistants on
            hundreds of people all day long.

                        DR. HEYWOOD
            In dentistry, my dear sir. What has
            dentistry to do with medicine?

                        MORTON
                    (Grabbing Frost)
            But here is the living proof...

4-3-42   (Continued)

G-17   (Cont'd)   FROST
                    (At once)
            It was on the night of September thirtieth...
                    (He sticks his finger in his
                    mouth)
            ...I was in excruciating agony...

                        DR. HEYWOOD
                    (Wincing)
            You told me all about that when you first
            came in.
                    (He turns to Morton)
            If you will be so good as to write to Prof.
            Warren I am persuaded that within due
            course you will very probably receive an
            answer.

He opens the door and follows Morton and Frost into the
lobby.

G-18   THE LOBBY OF THE MASSACHUSETTS GENERAL HOSPITAL

We see a porter at his desk IN THE BACKGROUND. Morton,
Frost and Heywood come out.

                        MORTON
                    (Icily)
            Thank you.

                        DR. HEYWOOD
                    (Faintly amused)
            You are entirely welcome...and now if you
            will excuse me...

He starts to turn. Frost points to the cavity in his teeth.

                        DR. HEYWOOD
            Very interesting.

He hurries away down a long vaulted corridor. Morton and
Frost stand hopelessly for a moment. Now Frost, after a
look toward the porter, stretches up and whispers in
Morton's ear. Morton also looks at the porter, then back
at Frost. Now both men turn and tiptoe off in the direction taken by Dr. Heywood.

G-19   THE INTERSECTION OF TWO CORRIDORS - DIMLY LIT

Morton and Frost come INTO THE SHOT and look hopelessly at
the three alleys offered them. Suddenly there is a horrible groan and a clank of metal on metal. Frost grabs
Morton's arm in horror. Morton looks off to the right and
walks off that way dragging Frost after him.

4-3-42

G-20   MORTON AND FROST - <u>IN FRONT OF SOME BIG SWINGING DOORS</u>

As they hesitate we hear the muffled scream of a man, the
clank of metal and the doctors' voices. Frost sways on his
feet.

MORTON
(Without noticing Frost's
condition)
Come on.

He opens the door very carefully.

G-21   <u>INT. OPERATING THEATRE</u> - HIGH CAMERA SHOT - DOWN ON MORTON
AND FROST

They climb up a steep little stairs which curves up from the
entrance to the aisle between the massed tiers of empty
benches. As they reach the aisle the CAMERA TRUCKS AHEAD
of them. Morton walks slowly, looking down into the theatre.
Frost tries not to look. Now Morton indicates an opening
between the iron railings. They go through it and sit on a
bench.

G-22   LOW CAMERA SHOT - UP AT MORTON AND FROST

Morton looks down PAST US with great interest. Frost has
his head half turned away and is watching out of the corners
of his eyes.

G-23   HIGH CAMERA BOOM SHOT - <u>DOWN ON THE OPERATING THEATRE</u> - PAST
MORTON AND FROST

NOTE: "Silent in the corners of the room stood Egyptian
mummies. To right and to left were human skeletons, and
glass cases containing surgical instruments of polished
steel. Ropes and pulleys hung from the ceiling. The operating table stood upon a low dais. Facing it, tier upon
tier, were rails behind which the spectators would sit."

The CAMERA MOVES IN CLOSE DURING THE SCENE. A patient is
strapped to the operating table. Masking one of his legs
stand some male attendants with buckets, sponges, bandages
and other unpleasant paraphernalia. (Trained nurses did not
appear for another twenty-six years.) On the far side of
the patient we recognize Professor Warren, Dr. Heywood, and
we see two doctors we do not know, one of whom is the vice-
president of the Massachusetts Medical Society. Prof. Warren wears a frock-coat and over this an apron with a bib.
Half of the bib has been folded on the diagonal so that one
point only goes to the right breast where it is buttoned to
the top button of the coat. The group is lit by hanging
whale oil lamps but one of the attendants holds a candela-
brum wherever more light is required. AS WE COME IN ON THE
SHOT Warren is bending over the patient's hidden leg. We
hear gaspings from the patient, clinkings of instruments
and low-voiced directions from Warren.

4-3-42   (Continued)

G-23   (Cont'd)   PROF. WARREN
                            (Not too clearly)
                   Now pinch that one off...not that one, the
                   big one...now a pad...all right, pinch it...
                   a sponge...there.

         By now the CAMERA IS CLOSE on Prof. Warren. He straightens
         up, wiping his hands on a towel. He mops his forehead with
         the same towel, then throws it to one of the attendants.

                              WARREN
                         (Turning to the patient's
                          head)
                   How do you feel, old man?

G-24   CLOSE SHOT - THE PATIENT'S HEAD

         His face is streaming with sweat.

                              THE PATIENT
                   I...I...
                            (He starts to sob)

         An attendant's hand comes INTO THE SHOT and mops him off.

G-25   LOW CAMERA SHOT - MORTON AND FROST

         Morton grips the rail in front of him till his knuckles are
         white. Frost seems about ready to pass out. His head
         swims from side to side, his mouth droops stupidly and his
         eyes do not look focused.

G-26   CLOSE SHOT - WARREN

                              WARREN
                   The next part is the bad part, old man.
                   I'll do it as fast as I can.
                            (He turns to an attendant)
                   Give me a wedge.

         An attendant hands him a small wedge-shaped block of wood.

                              WARREN
                         (Handing it to the patient
                          who is out of sight)
                   Try biting on it...it helps a little some-
                   times.

         He looks at the patient for a long moment, then holds his
         right hand toward an attendant. A saw is placed in it.
         Suddenly Warren is galvanized into action.

                              WARREN
                         (Staccato)
                   All right.

4-3-42   (Continued)

G-26 (Cont'd)

He pulls up his right sleeve slightly and steps to one side.
We hear the first shrieking rasp of the saw.

G-27 LOW CAMERA SHOT - MORTON AND FROST

Morton claps his hand over his eyes and Frost falls right
over backwards. Morton hears a clunk, turns toward Frost
and finds that he has disappeared. As he rises in alarm --

DISSOLVE TO:

G-28 THE VAULTED CORRIDOR OUTSIDE THE OPERATING THEATRE

The door bumps open and Morton emerges, half carrying, half
dragging the inert Frost. He skids him across the corridor
and sits him up against the wall. Now Morton straightens
up and looks around for help. Frost immediately falls over
sideways. Morton gets on his knees and starts to loosen
Frost's collar.

                         MORTON
                      (Angrily)
          Come on, now...this is no time to behave
          like a woman.
                      (He slaps his face)
          Come on.

G-29 WARREN - AT THE EDGE OF THE OPERATING GROUP

He is wiping his hands on a towel.

                         WARREN
                      (To the unidentified surgeon)
          Will you finish up for me, please.

                    THE UNIDENTIFIED SURGEON
          Certainly, Professor Warren.

He bends over the patient.

                         WARREN
                      (Passing his hand over
                       his eyes)
          Thank you.

He unbuttons the bib of his apron and an attendant unties
and removes it. Looking distressed and ill Warren moves
OUT OF THE SHOT.

G-30 THE SWINGING DOORS OF THE OPERATING THEATRE - FROM THE
CORRIDOR SIDE

Warren comes through and starts down the corridor when he
sees Morton and Frost.

4-3-42   (Continued)

G-30 (Cont'd)   WARREN
                        (Pausing, with irritation)
                        Now what's all this?

G-31   MORTON AND FROST - PAST WARREN

        Frost is still sitting against the wall, out to the world.
        Morton is still on his knees. He half turns to Professor
        Warren without recognizing him at first.

                                 MORTON
                        It was the noise of the saw... Oh!
                        Professor Warren!

        He gets up hastily and Frost topples over like a sack of
        flour.

G-32   WARREN - PAST FROST AND MORTON

                                 WARREN
                        (Hurrying toward Frost)
                        Stretch him out...let the blood get
                        to his head.

        He kneels beside Frost and Morton gets down on his knees
        also.

                                 MORTON
                        He'll be all right.

        Now Dr. Heywood hurries into the corridor following Prof.
        Warren. He stops in surprise, looks distressed, then
        addresses Prof. Warren.

                                 DR. HEYWOOD
                        Oh, I'm so sorry, Professor Warren, I
                        tried to keep these people away from
                        you, but now they seem to have...
                        (He scowls at Frost)
                        ...attracted your attention by...

                                 WARREN
                        (Briefly)
                        Go get some smelling salts.

                                 DR. HEYWOOD
                        (Surprised)
                        I beg your pardon?

                                 WARREN
                        (Roughly)
                        Smelling salts! Ammonium carbonate!

        Looking very much displeased, Heywood hurries back into the
        operating room.

4-3-42   (Continued)

G-32 (Cont'd)   MORTON
(Desperately)
I was waiting to see you, Professor
Warren. If you'll listen to me, never
again will you have to go through what
you've just gone through in there. As
God is my judge, I swear by all that's
holy, you can operate without pain. I
do it every day. For any length of time
you want.
(He points to Frost)
Just tonight I had this man out for
nineteen minutes.

WARREN
(With a flicker of a smile)
He's still out.

MORTON
(Without humor)
No, that was the...

WARREN
(Interrupting)
What's your name?

MORTON
W. T. G. Morton, the dentist.

WARREN
Oh, yes. Didn't you take part in that
fiasco at Harvard Medical School?

MORTON
I did.

WARREN
Are you proposing that I try that same
remedy?

MORTON
(Forcefully)
What I propose is entirely different.
It has been thoroughly tried out, tested
and proved. It cannot fail and it will
not fail!

As Warren looks at him speculatively, Heywood hurries INTO
THE SHOT with the smelling salts.

HEYWOOD
I'm sorry it took a moment, they were
using it on the patient.

4-3-42   (Continued)

G-32 (Cont'd)

Warren takes the salts from Dr. Heywood.

WARREN

(To Morton)
Hold his head up.

Morton does so.

WARREN

(Passing the salts under
Frost's nose)
Be here Friday morning at ten o'clock
and bring your bag of tricks.

MORTON

(Exultantly)
You mean you'll try it?

WARREN

(Levelly)
I'll try it on my first operation.

Now he sees signs of life in Frost. He holds the salts
away and slaps his face gently.

WARREN

Come on, now, old man.

Frost's face begins to work spasmodically.

MORTON

(Simply)
I don't know how to thank you, Professor
Warren.

Frost opens his eyes and looks stupidly at Warren.

WARREN

(Soothingly to Frost)
That's better, old man.
(Now he turns sharply
to Morton)
Because I don't think it's going to
work...but SOMEDAY...SOMEBODY...IS
GOING TO FIND SOMETHING!...IT MUST
COME!
(Then looking at Frost)
Now sit him up.
(Now he turns back to
Morton and concludes
quietly)
And when that somebody comes along I'd
like to be there to open the door for
him.

Now he looks sharply at Frost who starts in at the top of
his lungs.

4-3-42   (Continued)

G-32 (Cont'd)   FROST
                        It was on the evening of September
                        thirtieth...I was in excruciating
                        pain...

He tries to stick his finger in his mouth, misses it the
first time but succeeds the second.

                                    WARREN
                              (With a slight smile)
                        So were a lot of other people...

SLOW DISSOLVE TO:

G-33   THE MORTON BEDROOM IN THE NEW MANSION

Morton sits in his shirt sleeves on the edge of the great
four-poster bed. His necktie is untied, his trousers are
dusty, he looks tired and he needs a shave. He is occupied
at the moment in unhooking the back of his wife's pretty
party dress.

                                 MRS. MORTON
                        (Between sniffles and indignation)
                        ...kept asking where you were and I just
                        didn't know what to say...then Mrs.
                        Burroughs leaned over and said, "I know
                        how it feels, dear," and of course every-
                        body knows her husband is the biggest soak
                        in Boston! I never had such an evening!

                                   MORTON
                              (Having trouble with the
                               hooks and eyes)
                        Don't move around so much.

                                 MRS. MORTON
                        I couldn't understand a thing the French
                        Consul said, the Mayor's wife kept look-
                        ing at the silver as if she thought it
                        was stolen, and then the sherbet came in
                        ahead of the fish!

                                   MORTON
                              (Dryly)
                        It must have been terrible.

                                 MRS. MORTON
                        And for the finale you really came in
                        looking as if you'd been rolling in the
                        gutter!

The top of her dress falls down revealing some very strong
foundations.

4-3-42   (Continued)

G-33 (Cont'd)   MORTON
                          (Yawning)
               I guess the hospital was kind of dusty.
               They're going to try it out Friday morn-
               ing at ten o'clock.
                          (He starts unlacing his shoe)

                               MRS. MORTON
                          (Stepping out of her dress)
               Try what out?

          Morton looks up from his shoe and gives her such a piercing
          look that she remembers.

                               MRS. MORTON
               Oh.
                          (Then after a moment)
               I'm sorry, dear.

                                 MORTON
                          (Looking through the walls)
               Just think, Lizzie, it won't hurt any
               more...surgeons will be able to take
               their time...they'll be able to do
               things, that have been impossible up to
               now...and people will choose operations
               willingly, WHEN THEY NEED THEM...in-
               stead of waiting till Death is standing
               in the corner.

                               MRS. MORTON
                          (Worried)
               But...suppose it doesn't work...and
               people hear about it...won't that hurt
               your business?

                                 MORTON
               It will work...anyway, that's the risk
               you have to take.

          He crosses his legs and starts untying the other shoe.

                               MRS. MORTON
                          (Moving closer to him)
               Why? Why do you have to take that risk?
               You've made a wonderful success...you've
               done a great deal for people already...
               why endanger all that?

          Morton finishes untying his shoe and sits up.

                                 MORTON
                          (Quietly)
               Did you ever see an amputation?

          FADE OUT:

                          END OF SEQUENCE "G"

4-3-42

FADE IN:

H-1   THE CALENDAR PAD OF FRIDAY, OCTOBER 16, 1846

        DISSOLVE TO:

H-2   THE OPERATING THEATRE OF THE MASSACHUSETTS GENERAL HOSPITAL

        A couple of porters finish mopping up the marble floor. Some
        groups of medical students are spotted around the front row
        benches, eating their breakfast. (These are the same stu-
        dents we saw at Harvard Medical School.) Now the porters
        lay a sheet over the operating table.

H-3   AN OLD PORTER LOOKING UP AT THE NEAREST MEDICAL STUDENT

                         THE OLD PORTER
          Something special today?

                         THE MEDICAL STUDENT
                 (After swallowing a
                 mouthful)
          The Old Man's going to try another
          painless operation.
                 (He takes a sip of
                 coffee from a can)

                         THE OLD PORTER
                 (Wisely)
          Oh.

                         THE MEDICAL STUDENT
          I'll give you two to one for four bits.

        As the porter feels in his pocket speculatively a student
        once removed from the first student cuts in.

                         THIS STUDENT
          I'll give you three to one.

                         THE FIRST STUDENT
                 (Indignantly)
          Who asked you to horn in?

                         HOMER QUINBY'S VOICE
          I'll give you ten to one !

        The porter and students turn quickly and look across the
        theatre.

                         THE PORTER
                 (Avariciously)
4-3-42   Who said that?

H-4   CLOSE SHOT - HOMER QUINBY

He is drinking from a can of coffee and we do not recognize
him until he puts it down.

                    HOMER
              (Wiping his mouth)
       I did. And I'll take all you've got.

H-5   MORTON AND FROST AT CHAMBERLAIN'S, THE INSTRUMENT MAKER

Mr. Chamberlain is grinding in the valve of the spigot on
the inhaler. Morton looks at his watch nervously.

                    MORTON
       Hurry up, it's ten after nine and you
       promised it by nine.

                    MR. CHAMBERLAIN
              (Soothingly)
       Now hold your horses.

He continues slowly to grind in the valve which has been
dipped in powdered pumice. Morton looks very nervous.

                    FROST
              (Consolingly after
               consulting his own watch)
       It's only nine after.

DISSOLVE TO:

H-6   MORTON'S MAIN WAITING ROOM

It is full of people as usual. Morton and Frost enter
hurriedly, Morton carrying the package which contains the
inhaler.

                    A DENTIST
       Oh, Doctor Morton.

                    MORTON
       Not now, please.

                    THE DENTIST
       It's a matter of great importance,
       Dr. Morton. About those lutes...do
       you want the cap...

                    MORTON
       Just a minute.

He turns to Frost and hands him the package.

                    MORTON
       Fill that half full of Letheon and
       also a quart bottle.

4-3-42   (Continued)

500

H-6 (Cont'd)   FROST
                 Right.

He hurries out.

                             MORTON
                    (Pulling out his watch
                    and turning to the
                    dentist)
                 Now...talk fast.

DISSOLVE TO:

H-7   MORTON'S OLD OPERATING ROOM

Frost is by the dental stand tying a package which contains
the quart bottle of Letheon. Next to it, already tied, is
the package containing the inhaler. Now we hear hurried
steps down the hall and Morton throws the door open.

                             MORTON
                 All ready? We have just thirty minutes!

                             FROST
                    (Apologetically)
                 Thirty-one.

                             MORTON
                    (Ignoring this)
                 The inhaler is in here?
                    (He touches the box)

                             FROST
                 Half full.

                             MORTON
                 Did you stopper it tightly? Because if
                 it should happen to leak on the way...

                             FROST
                    (With a trace of irritation)
                 Certainly I did.

                             MORTON
                 I'd better have a look.

He picks up a pair of scissors and to Frost's disgust opens
the package and finds that the inhaler is quite properly
stoppered with a cork and string.

                             MORTON
                    (Pointing to the other box)
                 Is that done the same way?

                             FROST
                    (Acidly)
                 Exactly.

4-3-42   (Continued)

                             501

H-7 (Cont'd)   MORTON
All right, then you can tie this one
up again.

As Frost starts to do so, there is a knock on the door.

               MORTON
             (Roughly)
What is it?

The door opens and the little cashier appears.

             THE CASHIER
             (Timidly)
Dr. Morton, there's a Doctor Horace
Wells to see you. He said he was a
friend of yours or I would never...

               MORTON
           (Exasperated)
YES, BUT NOT NOW! TELL HIM...

At this point Wells comes into view behind the cashier.
His face looks very stern.

               MORTON
Hello, Horace, glad to see you.
        (He looks at his watch)
I wrote to you because I want you to
do some field work for me. I think
you can make a lot of money. Will you
come back and see me in the morning?

               WELLS
             (Rigidly)
I was here yesterday.

               MORTON
Oh...I'm sorry...I've been so confoundedly
rushed...

               WELLS
           (Interrupting)
I came as a patient...I said I wanted
some work done and I asked them to give
me "The Morton Method."

               MORTON
          (Sensing trouble)
What about it?

               WELLS
You stole it from me! Lock, stock, and
barrel! You're just using it differently.

4-3-42   (Continued)

H-7 (Cont'd)   MORTON
                                (Scowling)
                    You're talking like a child, Horace.
                    I'm using something entirely differ-
                    ent...I'm sorry you feel this way.

                                  WELLS
                            (In a dead voice)
                    You'll be sorrier still.

                                 MORTON
                            (With sincerity)
                    I will never be sorrier than I am at
                    this moment, Horace.

Wells walks out of the room. Morton stands sadly for a
moment, then looks at his watch and reacts as to an electric
shock.

                                 MORTON
                                (Yelling)
                    Now let's get out of here!

He grabs the package which contains the quart bottle. Frost
picks up the newly tied inhaler, grabs for his hat and drops
the package which crashes on the floor in a wet mass.

                                 MORTON
                                (Coolly)
                    All right...it can't be helped. We'll
                    use the one I tried the other night
                    and fit the new mouthpiece into it...
                    that will still give us twenty minutes.

                                  FROST
                            (Lifting down an inhaler
                             with exaggerated care)
                    Twenty-one.

By now Morton is on the floor tearing the package apart.

DISSOLVE TO:

H-8   BOOM SHOT - CLOSE - A CLOCK IN THE OPERATING THEATRE OF
         MASSACHUSETTS GENERAL HOSPITAL

         It is one minute to ten. The CAMERA DRAWS AWAY and we see
         the operating theatre well filled with students and doctors.

H-9   HOMER QUINBY BEHIND SOME SEDATE LOOKING GENTLEMEN

         He is looking across at the opposite tier.

H-10   THE FIRST STUDENT
         He holds up two fingers then ten then one.

H-11   HOMER QUINBY

         He nods assent and writes something in a little book.

H-12 CLOSE OVERHEAD SHOT - DR. HEYWOOD AND SOME ATTENDANTS
AND THE PATIENT ON THE OPERATING TABLE

The patient is a long thin young man whose vascular tumor is
hidden by towels. His head is held slightly to one side.

>DR. HEYWOOD
>You understand the risks involved in this
>experiment, Mr. Abbott?

The patient nods weakly.

>DR. HEYWOOD
>And you give your full consent?

>THE PATIENT
>(In a low voice)
>I do.

>DR. HEYWOOD
>Thank you.

He moves away.

H-13 PROF. WARREN - BY A TABLE FULL OF INSTRUMENTS

An attendant is tying on his apron.

>DR. HEYWOOD
>(ENTERING THE SHOT)
>The patient is ready, Professor Warren...
>he fully consents to the new experiment.

The clock starts to strike ten. Warren looks up at it over
his shoulder, then sadly at Heywood.

>DR. WARREN
>Our Messiah doesn't seem to be here....

>DR. HEYWOOD
>(With a superior chuckle)
>No, he doesn't, does he?

He looks pleased.

>DR. WARREN
>(Undecided)
>Well....we'll give him a couple of
>minutes. Count the instruments.

>HEYWOOD
>(Outraged)
>I beg your pardon?

>WARREN
>I said, "Count the instruments."
>That will take you a couple of minutes.

4-3-42   (Continued)

H-13 (Cont'd)

Heywood moves away in vast displeasure. Warren looks at the
floor sadly.

H-14 AUTOMOBILE SHOT - AHEAD OF MORTON'S CARRIAGE

The horses are galloping madly. The coachman is standing on
the box whipping them.

H-15 MORTON AND FROST - INSIDE THE SWAYING CARRIAGE

                         MORTON
                   (Grimly, looking at his
                    watch)
              It's one minute past.

                         FROST
                   (Desperately)
              No, it isn't, it's only...

                         MORTON
                   (Interrupting him without
                    looking at him)
              Don't say it because I'm apt to strangle
              you.

H-16 AUTOMOBILE SHOT - BEHIND THE FLYING CARRIAGE

The carriage takes a corner on two wheels.

H-17 WARREN - LOOKING AT THE FLOOR

Heywood comes into the shot quickly.

                         HEYWOOD
                   (Waspishly)
              There are one hundred and seventeen instru-
              ments, Professor Warren...., the same number
              we brought in.

                         WARREN
                   (After a slight pause)
              All right....strap the patient down.

He straightens and sighs, then holds a hand up to the
audience.

H-18 LOW CAMERA SHOT - UP AT THE AUDIENCE

They are chattering volubly. Now one by one they see Warren's movement. We hear "Sh!" in various places and the
room becomes quiet.

4-3-42

H-19   CLOSE HIGH CAMERA SHOT ON WARREN, THE PATIENT AND PART
          OF HIS STAFF

                            WARREN
              We were gathered here today, you to
              witness, I to perform, an experiment
              in which I had, if not confidence, at
              least a grain of hope.
                  (He sighs)
              We were to try a method advocated by a
              young dentist of this city, Dr......
              Morton.
                  (Now with considerable
                    bitterness he adds)
              It seems that Dr. Morton is otherwise
              engaged!

          There is a high piercing yell from Homer Quinby followed by
          a thunder of laughter from the audience.

H-20   HOMER QUINBY - SURROUNDED BY SPECTATORS

          Having won all his bets instantly he is delirious with
          pleasure. People around him are laughing. A couple of gray-
          beards in front of him turn around just as he makes a foot-
          nose at his friends across the theatre.

H-21   THE BOYS WHO LOST THE BETS

          They look very sour indeed amongst the laughing spectators.

H-22   THE VICE-PRESIDENT OF THE MASSACHUSETTS MEDICAL SOCIETY
          AND DR. HEYWOOD

                       THE VICE-PRESIDENT
              Personally I'm just as glad. I don't
              care to see medicine invaded by dental
              practice.

                        DR. HEYWOOD
              I second your sentiments with enthusiasm.

H-23   PROFESSOR WARREN

          He holds up a hand for silence.

                        WARREN
                  (After silence has been
                    re-established)
              This is not a minstrelsy, gentlemen. I
              doubt that the patient is enjoying your
              laughter.

4-3-42   (Continued)

H-23 (Cont'd)

Behind Dr. Warren we see the attendants strapping the patient
down. Warren turns to his instrument table.

H-24 THE STEPS OF THE MASSACHUSETTS GENERAL HOSPITAL

Morton's carriage gallops INTO THE SHOT and comes to a grinding stop. The door flies open and Morton and Frost leap out,
each bearing his precious package. Morton flies up the steps.
Frost misses a step, then regains his balance and trails
after Morton as fast as he can.

H-25 LOW CAMERA SHOT AT PROFESSOR WARREN - PAST THE PATIENT'S HEAD

        PROFESSOR WARREN
    I will work as fast as I can, Mr. Abbott,
    the less you move, or jerk or scream...
    the better it will be for us both. I am
    going to hurt you...considerably. If I
    can give you any consolation it is that
    pain carries no memory. You will forget
    it. Hold his head, John.

Warren lifts a bistouri, brings it near the patient, then
scowls at it and hands it away.

        WARREN
    No, give me the Velpeau.

H-26 A LONG HOSPITAL CORRIDOR

Small at first but growing rapidly, Morton pounds TOWARD US.
He flashes PAST THE CAMERA. Frost staggers along, a bad
second.

H-27 A PART OF THE PATIENT AND WARREN'S HANDS

Beyond this we see the swinging doors leading into the operating theatre from the hall. Warren's hands receive the
Velpeau knife.

        WARREN'S VOICE
    Thank you.

His left hand forms a bridge and the shining instrument is
placed against the patient's neck.

        WARREN'S VOICE
    All ready, John?

        THE ATTENDANT'S VOICE
    Yes, sir.

At this instant the doors in the background fly open and
Morton staggers into the operating theatre.

4-3-42

H-28   CLOSE SHOT - MORTON - THE DOORS STILL SWINGING BEHIND
       HIM

                            MORTON
                        (Breathlessly)
                  Wait!

       Gripping his package, he leans against the wall and pants
       like a steam engine.

H-29   MEDIUM CLOSE SHOT - THE OPERATING STAGE

       Professor Warren turns quickly, his knife in mid-air. All
       the others turn.

H-30   MORTON AND THE DOORS BEHIND HIM

                            MORTON
                     (Fighting for breath)
                  Terribly sorry...had to get another one...
                  it broke!

       At this moment the doors fly open and Frost crashes into
       the room. Attempting to stop, he skids and loses his
       balance, his package flies straight into the air, Frost
       makes a dive for it, catches it and thuds to the floor in
       a sitting position, the package still safe.

H-31   FULL SHOT - THE OPERATING THEATRE - PAST MORTON AND FROST

       The entire room is howling with laughter.

H-32   PROFESSOR WARREN

       Even he is having trouble suppressing his chuckles.

H-33   THE PATIENT AND THE ATTENDANT, JOHN

                          THE PATIENT
                        (Hopefully)
                  What's the joke?

                            JOHN
                      (Pointing weakly)
                  He..he..he...
                      (He explodes in guffaws)

H-34   HOMER QUINBY

       He scowls down at Morton, sore as a pup.

H-35   HOMER'S FRIENDS

       They are delirious with laughter. They point Homer out to
       each other, then pound the people in front of them includ-
       ing some very solemn old gents.

4-3-42

508

H-36   CLOSE HIGH CAMERA SHOT - ON WARREN

He turns and once more holds up his hand for silence. Having regained it, he says:

                        WARREN
            This operation seems to be accompanied
            by an unusual amount of levity...
                (He smiles faintly and adds:)
            ...not that I blame you, exactly.

The laughter starts again but Warren holds up his hand at
once.

                        WARREN
                (When silence is re-established)
            Please, gentlemen...no more.

H-37   MORTON AND FROST

Morton is helping Frost to his feet. Now he comes forward,
tearing the wrapping off the inhaler. Frost follows, doing
the same with his package.

H-38   MOVING CAMERA - AIMED AT MORTON AND THE GROUP AROUND THE
        PATIENT

When the CAMERA GETS TO WARREN IT STOPS, and Morton, with
his BACK TO US, steps INTO THE CORNER OF THE SHOT.

                        WARREN
                (Severely)
            Well, sir, your patient is ready.

H-39   MORTON AND FROST - PAST WARREN

Morton holds the shining inhaler in his hand. Frost is
still struggling with his package.

                        MORTON
                (Gravely)
            Thank you, sir.

He looks at the inhaler, the cork of which is tied to the
lip of the neck.

                        MORTON
            May I have a scalpel? Anything will do.

Frost reaches into his pocket at once and humbly offers him
a pair of blunt-nosed scissors, the kind that are entrusted
to children.

                        MORTON
            Thank you.

4-3-42   (Continued)

                            509

H-39   (Cont'd)

He cuts the string, puts the cork and the scissors in his
pocket, turns the spigot, blows through the inhaler once,
then says:

> MORTON
> I'm ready.

H-40   WARREN - PAST MORTON AND FROST

> WARREN
> (To his assistants)
> Step back, please.

All step away, leaving the patient entirely alone as Morton
crosses to his head. After a moment's hesitation, and a
look around, Frost trots after him.

H-41   VERY CLOSE SHOT - MORTON AND THE PATIENT

The patient's neck has been re-covered.

> MORTON
> (Gently)
> Don't be afraid.

The patient rolls his eyes and turns slightly to answer.
At this moment Frost sticks his head in from the other side
and speaks in a vehement whisper.

> FROST
> You don't have a thing to worry about!

The patient turns weakly toward Frost.

> FROST
> It was on the night of September thirtieth
> ...I was in excruciating pain...but agoniz-
> ing!

Morton holds up his hand as he sees the patient is about to
speak.

> THE PATIENT
> (In a low voice)
> I'm not afraid.

> MORTON
> Then breathe in deeply.

He puts the mouthpiece in Abbott's mouth.

> MORTON
> (Quietly)
> That's all you have to do...just keep on
> breathing.

4-3-42   (Continued)

H-41   (Cont'd)

As we hear the rhythmic breathing --

H-42   SLOW PANNING SHOT - AROUND THE ENTIRE OPERATING THEATRE

Not a sound is heard except the ever deeper breathing of the patient. All eyes are riveted upon him, and the expressions become increasingly tense. At last the CAMERA COMES TO Homer Quinby. Alone of all those present he is looking at Morton. Now he is sure. He scowls and says to the student next to him.

> HOMER QUINBY
> (Disgustedly)
> Why that's the guy who helped the guy who almost ruined me!

> A GRAYBEARD IN FRONT OF HOMER
> Sh!

He turns and gives Homer a look.

H-43   MEDIUM CLOSE - MORTON, THE PATIENT AND FROST

Morton is still bending over the patient who babbles incoherently. Frost has his arms folded and is looking at his watch which is in the right hand. He looks proud.

> FROST
> (With dignity)
> Time.

Morton lets the patient inhale once more, then removes the inhaler and turns the spigot. He waits a moment till the patient stops babbling, then turns in the direction of Professor Warren.

> MORTON
> (With a slight bow)
> Dr. Warren, your patient is ready.

H-44   WARREN, HEYWOOD, THE VICE-PRESIDENT OF THE MEDICAL SOCIETY, SOME OTHER DOCTORS AND THE ATTENDANTS

Warren looks at Morton for a moment, then picks up a long darning needle from the instrument table and comes forward. The CAMERA MOVES BACK, TIPPING Morton and Frost INTO THE SHOT. Reaching the side of the patient, he holds up the shining needle.

> WARREN
> Will he feel this?

> FROST
> (Repressing a spontaneous
> chuckle)
> You ought to see my uh-hum!

4-3-42   (Continued)

H-44   (Cont'd)

Warren lowers the needle OUT OF THE SHOT, then clenches his jaw muscles as he drives it home. Now he bends over the patient.

H-45   CLOSE SHOT - THE PATIENT - PAST WARREN

He is sleeping like a child, smiling a little.

H-46   WARREN AND MORTON - PAST THE PATIENT

Warren straightens up, looks searchingly at Morton, then says:

> WARREN
> Shall we hold his head?

> MORTON
> (Quietly)
> That will not be necessary.

He bows slightly and steps back.

> WARREN
> (Holding up his right hand)
> The Velpeau.

The instrument is placed in his hand by an attendant and the other attendants and surgeons immediately crowd around the patient, blocking him from view.

H-47   MORTON - AT THE SIDE OF THE THEATRE

He places the inhaler on a table, leans back and folds his arms. Frost comes INTO THE SHOT, places his package next to the inhaler, then takes his place beside Morton. After a moment he folds his arms also. Now we hear the clanking of instruments, snipping noises and Warren's voice.

> WARREN'S VOICE
> Pinch it...another sponge...now the next one...

Frost's eyes begin to get out of control. He mops his head, then sinks onto a little stool.

H-48   SLOW PANNING SHOT - OF THE OPERATING THEATRE

The spectators are leaning forward in their seats. Many of them have their mouths open, excited whispers break out. As we near the completion of the CAMERA movement, these men are beginning to smile with hope. As we reach Homer Quinby, we find him half off the bench, his face working with excitement. He is as ready to cheer as the others.

4-3-42

H-49   CLOSE SHOT - PROFESSOR WARREN - PAST THE PATIENT

       His face is working with excitement. His mouth is twisted
       to one side, grinning. Now we hear him put down his instru-
       ments. He straightens up and looks into the patient's face.

H-50   THE PATIENT'S FACE - PAST DR. WARREN

       He is still smiling. Now he moves his lips and chuckles.

                              WARREN
                Can you hear me, Abbott?

                              THE PATIENT
                         (After a long pause)
                Yes, sir.

                              WARREN
                Did you feel any pain?

                              THE PATIENT
                         (Opening one eye)
                Hunh?

                              WARREN
                I said: "Did you feel any pain?"

       Abbott opens the other eye and blinks stupidly.

                              THE PATIENT
                When?

H-51   LOW CAMERA SHOT UP AT WARREN - PAST THE PATIENT

                              WARREN
                         (Stunned)
                When!

       Now he straightens up, raises both fists to high heaven and
       shouts exultantly.

                              WARREN
                Gentlemen...THIS IS NO HUMBUG!

       There is a roar from the spectators.

H-52   SHOTS OF DIFFERENT SECTIONS OF THE OPERATING THEATRE
to
H-62   Men are beside themselves with joy. They howl and shout and
       pound each other on the back and laugh incoherently. Gray-
       beards dance with students and students jump up and down
       like monkeys and throw their hats in the air.

H-63   HOMER QUINBY IN THE SEETHING MASS

       He is twice as excited and happy as the others. Now he

4-3-42   (Continued)

                              513

H-63 (Cont'd)

    starts to climb down toward Morton and manages to step on
    the old gentlemen in front of him.

H-64 WARREN, MORTON AND FROST

    They are surrounded by men eager to reach them. Morton and
    Frost are backed against the wall. Warren is pumping
    Morton's hand up and down. Now he takes him in his arms
    and hugs him. After a second he does the same to Frost.
    From now on Frost gets a fifty-percent share of the congratu
    lations. Morton, Frost and Warren disappear occasionally
    from view behind the enthusiastic spectators. Homer Quinby
    sppears over the top of the crowd. He almost dives into it.

H-65 CLOSE SHOT - MORTON AND QUINBY

    Quinby has Morton by the hand. He shouts piercingly to be
    heard above the tumult.

QUINBY
Don't you remember me, Doctor?

He loses his balance and Morton·saves him from a heavy fall.

FADE OUT

END OF SEQUENCE "H"

4-3-42

514

FADE IN:

J-1   MORTON'S MAIN WAITING ROOM

A bunch of patients are crowded around the glass door to the
private waiting room. They are given tidbits of information
by the Receptionist on one side and the Cashier on the other.
Through the glass door we see Morton posing for his portrait.
A lady newspaper artist is making a chalk engraving. Across
from him are the Reporter we have already seen and two others.
Behind Morton stands Frost, trying to get into the portrait.
The three reporters are making notes. Morton is talking.

                    ONE PATIENT
               (To another who is in a
                better position)
          Does it look like him?

                    THE OTHER PATIENT
          You can't tell, she hasn't put the
          hair on yet.

                    THE RECEPTIONIST
          No, it's called an interview. The fat
          one is from the New York Herald. He
          came all the way.

                    A THIRD PATIENT
          Is he going to raise his prices now?

                    THE CASHIER
          Certainly not. Dr. Morton's contribu-
          tion to science is purely on a
          dilettante basis.

                    A MALE PATIENT
          On a what?

                    THE CASHIER
          He isn't going to make nothing out of it.

                    A WOMAN PATIENT
          They say that poor man didn't feel a
          thing...and they almost cut his head off.

                    THE RECEPTIONIST
          He sang during most of the operation.

                    A VOICE
          Were you there?

                    THE CASHIER
               (Loudly)
          No, she wasn't.

4-3-42   (Continued)

515

                        THE RECEPTIONIST
                       (To the Cashier)
                    Well, you weren't either.

                         THE CASHIER
              Yes, but I didn't pretend that I was.

          Now we see Dr. Morton look at his watch.

J-2   CLOSE SHOT - MORTON - PAST THE LADY ARTIST INSIDE THE WAITING
      ROOM

                           MORTON
                    I'm sorry, I'll have to get back to
                    the hospital now. We're operating at
                    four.

                        THE LADY ARTIST
                    Just one more minute, please, Doctor.
                    I want to get that curl over your
                    forehead.

                           FROST
                    We must not be late.

          He holds the pose rigidly.

J-3   THE REPORTERS

                                    THE UNKNOWN REPORTER
                         Are you amputing the right or left
                         leg?

                                    THE NEW YORK HERALD
                         Amputating.

                                    THE UNKNOWN REPORTER
                              (Roughly)
                         What's the difference?

J-4   MORTON AND FROST - PAST THE OTHERS

                           MORTON
                    The right leg. Above the knee.

                        THE REPORTER WE KNOW
                    You are using the regular Letheon...
                    the same as you use in your office?

                           FROST
                    There is only one Letheon.

                        THE NEW YORK HERALD
                    Do you anticipate any pain, Doctor?

4-3-42   (Continued)

Morton opens his mouth to speak but Frost beats him to it.

            FROST
Where there is Letheon there can be
no pain.

        THE REPORTER WE KNOW
Do you expect a distinguished audience?

            MORTON
Well...

            FROST
Everybody will be there.

        THE NEW YORK HERALD
      (To Frost)
Are you the co-discoverer?

Frost pretends not to hear.

            MORTON
     (In mild amusement)
He's talking to you, Eben.

            FROST
     (Quietly)
I wish I were.

            MORTON
Mr. Frost's contribution has been
invaluable.

Frost begins to swell with pleasure.

            MORTON
He was the first patient on whom I
operated and he has offered himself
since for countless experiments. I
cannot thank him enough.

            FROST
It was on the night of September thirtieth...I was in excruciating pain...

            MORTON
     (Rising and looking at
     his watch)
We haven't the time, Eben. I really
have to go.
     (He turns to the reporters)
Thank you very much.
     (He turns to the lady artist)
And you, madam.

She turns the chalk engraving so that he can see it.

4-3-42

J-5   INSERT - THE CHALK ENGRAVING

       The resemblance is distant and the eyes are faintly crossed,
       but the hair is wonderfully curly.

J-6   MORTON LOOKING AT THE ENGRAVING

                              MORTON
                    Remarkable! Thank you again.

       He goes PAST THE CAMERA followed by Frost.

       DISSOLVE TO:

J-7   THE MASSACHUSETTS GENERAL HOSPITAL

       A large crowd is milling outside: solemn men of medicine,
       medical students, Harvard boys and plain idlers.

J-8   THE MAIN DOOR

       A queue is passing in.

                           AN ATTENDANT
                    Kindly show your cards... no admission
                    without a card.

J-9   A GROUP OF DOCTORS GETTING OUT OF A CAB

       In the middle of them Dr. Jackson is holding forth.

                             JACKSON
                          (Cheerfully)
                    No, no, it's mine...entirely mine...
                    I merely allow Morton to use it in his
                    dental business.

                      A SOLID LOOKING MAN
                          NEXT TO HIM
                    But the paper distinctly said...

                             JACKSON
                       (Interrupting him)
                    My dear Bigelow, you don't believe
                    what you read in the papers, do you?
                    I'll have something to say on that
                    subject!

       They PASS BY THE CAMERA.

J-10   THE OPERATING THEATRE

       It is full and more people are squeezing in. The attendants
       are placing the sheets on the table.

4-3-42

J-11 DR. WARREN - IN HIS OFFICE

He stands alone behind his desk. We see him PAST three men
facing him. Heywood is TIPPED IN to the SIDE OF THE SHOT.

> WARREN
> (Scowling)
> What does it matter, so long as it
> works?

J-12 THE DELEGATION FROM THE MEDICAL SOCIETY - PAST WARREN

The vice-president stands in the middle.

> THE VICE-PRESIDENT
> It matters very much indeed.

> THE SECOND DELEGATE
> Enormously.

> THE VICE-PRESIDENT
> The principle involved is basic.
> Permit this one exception and our
> doors are opened wide to every form
> of quackery and charlatanism.

> THE THIRD DELEGATE
> When we took our Hippocratic oathes...

J-13 WARREN - PAST THE OTHERS

> WARREN
> (Quickly)
> My dear sir, Morton is a dentist. He
> is not bound by the Hippocratic oath.
> He doesn't have to share his discover-
> ies with others. Dentists all have
> secrets and they don't share them.
> They're not obligated to.

J-14 THE OTHERS - PAST WARREN

> THE VICE-PRESIDENT
> (Gently)
> Nor are we obligated to use their
> secrets. This man wants our endorse-
> ment for the purpose of making money!
> Already he has received columns of free
> advertisement... on the front pages of
> every newspaper...where no dentist
> ever was before. Now he wants more
> limelight, a graver operation, more
> notoriety to further the sale of his
> patent remedy.

J-15 WARREN - PAST THE OTHERS
> WARREN
> (Quickly)
> I don't believe it!

4-3-42

J-16   THE CROWD IN FRONT OF THE HOSPITAL

Suddenly all heads turn. Now a shout goes up and we hear
the name "Morton!" on every side.

J-17   MORTON'S CARRIAGE - SURROUNDED BY THE CROWD

It is open. Morton raises his hat. The ovation grows louder
as Frost raises his hat. The door of the carriage is opened
and Morton, bearing a package, descends, followed by Frost,
bearing a package. As they come forward --

J-18   WARREN - PAST THE OTHERS - IN HIS OFFICE

                  WARREN
              (Quickly)
I don't believe it! He came to me of
his own free will...he ran the risk of
ridicule and injury to his business...

J-19   THE VICE-PRESIDENT

                THE VICE-PRESIDENT
And why not? Don't you think the odds
are worth it? From the pinnacle of your
generosity, Professor Warren, from the
loftiness of your own viewpoint, you are
apt to overlook the meanness and avari-
ciousness of these little people. The
Medical Society is trying only to protect
you.

J-20   WARREN - PAST THE OTHERS

He seems to vacillate for a moment, then shakes his head.

                  WARREN
I don't believe it. I don't believe
one particle of it.

J-21   THE OTHERS - PAST WARREN

                THE VICE-PRESIDENT
              (Icily)
You mean you intend to ignore the protest
of your colleagues in the Society? The
men who put you in charge of this hospital?

J-22   WARREN - PAST THE OTHERS

                  WARREN
You know very well that I can't...I wish
I could.
              (Then after a pause)
What do you want me to do, ask him what
the stuff is?

4-3-42

J-23   THE VICE-PRESIDENT

                           THE VICE-PRESIDENT
                         (Amiably)
                    That's all. Nothing more.

J-24   WARREN - PAST THE OTHERS

                              WARREN
                    And if he won't tell us?

J-25   THE VICE-PRESIDENT - PAST WARREN

                           THE VICE-PRESIDENT
                         (Philosophically)
                    In that case we will operate in the good
                    old-fashioned way. After all, people
                    have been operated on for centuries with-
                    out any assistance...from the dental
                    profession.

                           AN ATTENDANT
                         (Entering)
                    Dr. Morton is here, Professor Warren.

                              WARREN
                         (After a moment)
                    Show him in.

       All turn toward the door.

J-26   THE DOORWAY TO WARREN'S OFFICE - PAST THOSE INSIDE IT

       The attendant opens the door and we see Morton and Frost
       outside. Morton enters. As Frost starts to follow, the
       attendant closes the door on him.

                              MORTON
                         (Quietly)
                    Good afternoon, gentlemen.

J-27   WARREN AND THE OTHERS - PAST MORTON

                              WARREN
                    Good afternoon, sir.

       He comes forward and shakes Morton by the hand.

                              WARREN
                         (Without beating around
                          the bush)
                    A very disagreeable situation has arisen,
                    Dr. Morton. My colleagues of the Massa-
                    chusetts Medical Society have protested
                    against our operation this afternoon.
                    These gentlemen are their delegates.

J-28   MORTON - PAST WARREN

       He listens to Warren incredulously.   (Continued)

J-28 (Cont'd)   WARREN
                    As you probably know, physicians may
                    not use nor prescribe patent medicines,
                    the ingredients of which they ignore,

J-29   WARREN - PAST MORTON
                                WARREN
                    Although as a surgeon my professional
                    forebears were bargers, I am bound to
                    the ethics of my superiors. In other
                    words, they think you want to make money
                    out of your stuff. I don't care whether
                    you do or not. My only interest lies in
                    the fact that it works.

J-30   MORTON - PAST THE OTHERS

                                MORTON
                        (Laughing with relief)
                    You had me worried for a moment. Believe
                    me, gentlemen, I have never had the
                    slightest intention of making money out
                    of this. Letheon is yours, freely and
                    in perpetuity.
                        (He smiles)
                    Not only your property but that of all
                    other hospitals and charitable institutions
                    in this country and all other countries.

J-31   THE VICE-PRESIDENT OF THE MEDICAL SOCIETY - PAST MORTON

                            THE VICE-PRESIDENT
                        (Smiling politely)
                    That is very generous of you, Dr. Morton,
                    but I'm not sure you quite understood
                    what Professor Warren said.
                        (He smiles again, then
                         adds:)
                    "Physicians may not use nor prescribe
                    medicines, the ingredients of which they
                    ignore."...Unfortunately we still ignore
                    the ingredients of your mixture.

J-32   MORTON - PAST WARREN AND THE OTHERS

                    After an astonished look at the Vice-President, Morton turns
                    to Warren.

                                MORTON
                        (Quickly)
                    Of course you can understand why I can't
                    tell you that, can't you, Professor
                    Warren? It's the secret of my business.

4-3-42   (Continued)

J-32 (Cont'd)   MORTON (Cont'd)
                   The one advantage I have over my
                   rivals. If I told you what Letheon
                   was, why in no time at all...
                        (He makes a helpless
                        gesture)
                   ...everybody would be using it.

J-33   THE VICE-PRESIDENT - PAST MORTON

                             THE VICE-PRESIDENT
                        (Smiling sweetly)
                   Would that be such a dreadful catastrophe?

J-34   MORTON - PAST THE OTHERS

                             MORTON
                   I'm afraid it might be for me. You see,
                   my patent hasn't been granted yet...it's
                   still pending. Maybe if you'd use the
                   Letheon this way for a little while...
                   why...later...when the patent had been
                   granted...

J-35   THE VICE-PRESIDENT - PAST MORTON

                             THE VICE-PRESIDENT
                        (Silkily)
                   You could sell it for more money.

       He stops smiling and all his scorn shows in his face.

J-36   MORTON - PAST THE OTHERS

                             MORTON
                        (Outraged)
                   What!

       He steps forward belligerently, then stops.

                             MORTON
                   You miserable cur! You've been splitting
                   fees and robbing your patients so long
                   you judge others by yourself. Of all
                   the slimy...

J-37   WARREN - PAST THE OTHERS

                             WARREN
                        (Firmly)
                   That's enough, Morton. Stop it! The
                   ethics that govern our profession have
                   done much more good than harm. They
                   happen not to fit this case. It is
                   regrettable but there is nothing more
                   to be said.
                        (He holds out his hand)
                   Thank you for your good intention.

4-3-42

J-38   MORTON - PAST THE OTHERS

He makes no move to take Warren's hand.

                          MORTON
                    (Unable to believe
                    his ears)
               You mean you're going to continue to
               let people be tortured...when it isn't
               necessary?

J-39   WARREN AND THE OTHERS - PAST MORTON

                          THE VICE-PRESIDENT
                    (Angrily)
               That is a very high-handed interpre-
               tation of the matter, my friend.

                          WARREN
                    (Holding up a hand)
               No.
                    (He turns to Morton
                    and speaks gravely)
               We will share the blame, Dr. Morton...
               you and I.

He hits a bell on his desk and an attendant comes in.

                          WARREN
               Make the patient ready...I shall operate
               in the...usual way.

J-40   MORTON - STANDING BY THE DOOR

He seems completely lost. He makes slight movements with
his hands as if he were about to speak, then drops them
hopelessly to his side and shifts his weight from foot to
foot. Now he turns slowly, opens the door, looks back once
more, then hurries out.

J-41   A LONG DARK VAULTED CORRIDOR

Morton is walking slowly toward us, the picture of dejection. He makes a helpless gesture, retraces a few steps,
stops, then comes toward us again. The man is lost. The
problem is too great for him. The CAMERA TRUCKS SLOWLY
AHEAD OF HIM as he walks: angry, disgusted, stung with injustice, broken-hearted. Suddenly he walks into a ray of
sunlight which hits him shoulder high. He turns and looks
stupidly toward the light.

J-42   A SMALL ALCOVE OFF THE CORRIDOR

On one side doors lead off to the operating room. In the
back a window has taken the form of the arched corridor.
It is a Gothic window. In the pool of sun streaming through
this we see the operating cart. A young Irish woman lies
on it. An old priest kneels beside her praying.
4-3-42

                              524

J-43 MORTON - PAST THE OPERATING CART

He stands looking at it, his head in shadow, the white package under his arm in the bright sunlight.

                    THE PRIEST'S VOICE
          And the prayer of faith shall save the
          sick and the Lord shall raise him up; and
          if he have committed sins, they shall be
          forgiven him.

The old man gets to his feet and we see him IN THE FOREGROUND
OF THE SHOT

                    THE OLD PRIEST
              (Gently)
          Our Lady of Sorrows is watching down over
          you, Alice, and will send an angel to
          protect you.

                    ALICE
              (Quietly, with a slight
              brogue)
          Thank you, Father.

Now Morton shuffles forward, further into the light until
only his eyes are still dark.

                    MORTON
              (Haltingly)
          Are you...having the operation?

J-44 ALICE MOHAN AND THE OLD PRIEST - PAST MORTON

                    ALICE
          Yes, sir.

J-45 MORTON - PAST ALICE AND THE PRIEST

                    MORTON
              (Having difficulty in talking)
          I'm...terribly....terribly...sorry.

J-46 ALICE AND THE OLD PRIEST - PAST MORTON

                    ALICE
              (Smiling faintly)
          It isn't as bad as it sounds, sir... I
          understand some gentleman has made a new
          dis--discovery...and it doesn't hurt any
          more.

J-47 MORTON - PAST ALICE AND THE OLD PRIEST

Morton's face begins to work with emotion. Now he steps forward until he is entirely in the light.

4-3-42   (Continued)

525

J-47 (Cont'd)   MORTON
(Excitedly)
That's right...
(Now he starts to smile and
speaks more loudly)
...it isn't going to hurt a bit...NOW ...
OR EVER AGAIN!

We hear the triumphant peel of a trumpet. The doors from the
operating room swing wide and let in much light as the attendants appear. Morton turns and looks through the doors.

J-48   LONG SHOT - THE OPERATING THEATRE - PAST MORTON

We see Warren, his assistants and the attendants waiting on
the platform. The background is black with spectators. Morton
starts forward slowly, then increases his speed till he is
almost running. As he gets halfway to the platform --

J-49   TRUCKING SHOT - AHEAD OF PROF. WARREN

Seeing Morton approaching, his expression becomes hopeful.
Now he gets down off the platform and hurries toward Norton,
his arms stretched slightly forward.

J-50   MORTON - PAST WARREN

Both men stop. Now Morton places the package in Warren's
hands.
                   MORTON
Professor Warren, it's called...sulphuric
ether...highly rectified.

J-51   PROF. WARREN - PAST MORTON

                  PROF. WARREN
(Stupefied)
You mean plain $C_2H_5OC_2H_5$?

J-52   MORTON - PAST WARREN

He lifts his arms helplessly.

                  MORTON
I don't know...I guess so.

                  WARREN
(Seizing his hands)
Oh, my boy...my boy.

The music swells to a triumphant paean. The scene

DISSOLVES SLOWLY TO:-

J-53   MRS. MORTON AND FROST SITTING IN THE PARLOR OF THE FARMHOUSE
1868

Frost gets slowly to his feet, and ON THE SCREEN APPEAR THE
WORDS:

                  THE END
4-3-42

The Miracle
of Morgan's Creek

The first words Sturges wrote on this project were "The Miracle of Morgan's Creek," which appear at the top of a script fragment he drafted on July 8, 1942.* Below the title is "SEQUENCE 'A'" and below that is the following:

> During the main titles we see a succession of shots of young men being drafted into the military service: boys being weighed and examined, receiving outfits, being herded onto trains, then drilling as rookies to the sound of martial music. The last title comes over a group of youngsters dancing in a barn decorated for the occasion with bunting. We see a few shots of couples dancing, the male being always in uniform. We see some silhouetted couples hanging on to each other against the moonlight and then we go back to some boys and girls at the bar.

A-1   A BOY
          (Suddenly and slightly alcoholically)
   Say . . . I got a wunnerful idea . . . Oh boy.

As the others gather around him

DISSOLVE TO:

A-2   AN OLD GENTLEMAN IN A DOUBLE BED – Moonlight.
      His nightgowned wife is hanging out the window.

               THE WIFE
   Just a minute.
         (She crosses to the bed and shakes the old man.)
              [End of scene]

The boy's "idea" is, presumably, "Let's all get married," which the tipsy soldier in the final script actually says not once but three times. The dissolve

---

* *Sullivan's Travels* and *The Miracle of Morgan's Creek* are the only Sturges-directed films that were never called anything else; each of the others, including six more for Paramount and *Unfaithfully Yours,* had had at least one other title before the final one was adopted.

to the soon-to-be-wakened old gentleman—most likely a justice of the peace—does not appear in the film. Had it appeared, we would soon know, among other things, who Ratzkiwatzki[1] is and what Trudy's relationship to him is: a different movie. A defect of the fragment as a whole is that it begins the film with its pivotal scene—the farewell-to-the-boys party—before the characters who will be affected by the scene and who give it meaning have been introduced. Sturges began to remedy these problems the same day in a longer script fragment, which is identical to the first up through the phrase "the sound of martial music," but eliminates the party shots in order to follow the credits with a scene that occurs before the party.

After the main titles

A-1   INTERIOR OF A TEN-CENT STORE

The son of the proprietor, Edgar, is talking to a girl in the cosmetic department.

EDGAR
(Crossly)
Well, suppose they are going away . . . that's no reason to forget those who aren't going away. He also serves, you know, who only sits and whatever it is.

MINNIE
But Dr. Discus asked us to . . . the church is doing it . . . We've got to give them a going-away . . . something to remember us by.

EDGAR
Why doesn't the church mind its own business?

MINNIE
But that is the church's business.

EDGAR
What--to give barn dances?

MINNIE
It isn't a barn dance, it's a . . . it's a . . . Yes madam, I'll be right with you . . . Why don't you come, it's only fifty cents.

EDGAR
It isn't the fifty cents, it's the principle of the thing.

MINNIE
(Departing)
Maybe you could rent a uniform.

EDGAR
Now listen.

DISSOLVE TO: [End of scene]

The names Sturges gives his characters in this draft are intriguing. One imagines Dr. Discus as a minister-athlete, perpetually hurling a round object skyward. "Minnie" calls to mind Minnie Mouse and "Edgar," Edgar Bergen, the popular ventriloquist, and his dummies Charlie McCarthy and Mortimer Snerd. It is fascinating that this first incarnation of Trudy and Norval establishes them, particularly when they talk to each other, as a cartoon character and a dummy. While never ceasing to be cartoonlike, Trudy and Norval became more particularized, even perhaps more complex, with each stage of the revision process. This paradox—as fruitful as it is strange—is discussed elsewhere.[2] That Minnie works in the cosmetics department of a ten-cent store seems Trudy-like but that Edgar is the son of the store's proprietor seems unlike Norval. To be the son of a store owner may be a modest distinction, but it is more than the film's Norval—who is an orphan—can claim. Norval has a job in a bank but he has no prospects, no self-confidence, and no sense of belonging anywhere.

On July 15 Sturges wrote a note headed "Concerning the 'MIRACLE' story," which considered several ways in which "the little girl involved could arrive at the main situation":

1) She could get tight, get married, forget where she was married and the name of her husband, and presently be in the situation.

2) She could get married to a soldier on the spur of the moment and, through the medium of a slight automobile accident, get a conk on the head and find herself in the same situation as in 1).

Why Trudy forgets how she got in her predicament is the crucial question posed by these paragraphs. In the first, Trudy's judgment is alcohol-impaired when she gets married and has sex, and her memory of these events is impaired for the same reason. In the second, she marries consciously, if impetuously, but her memory of the event is impaired by a conk on the head—whether she has sex before or after the conk is unclear. These are very different premises but, unless the wedding scene of the second paragraph is shown, and with it Ratzkiwatzki, the two have similar consequences, as Sturges sees in the second paragraph—in neither case does Trudy remember what happened the night before. Because the two approaches have the same eventuation, Sturges did not have to resolve the question in order to continue working. The problem was finally solved—over three months later—by combining elements of the first and second paragraphs. Trudy conks her head on an overhead reflector when her jitterbug partner lifts her a little too high. Everything that happens after this event—including getting married and having sex—she does not remember.

To many viewers, Trudy's getting tight or deciding to marry someone she has known only a few hours makes her complicit in her fate. A viewer making this judgment might watch Trudy's worsening situation in a detached way as a kind of object lesson. The consequence is essentially to exclude such a viewer from the logic of the film. On the contrary, the conk on the head approach greatly increases the viewer's involvement in two ways. First, it requires the viewer to suspend judgment on Trudy; second, it focuses the viewer's curiosity on the question of what happened on the night of the military party—a question that the entire film revolves around. Both factors require the viewer's closest attention to the film.

There was a third approach, which Sturges did not pursue; but it reveals, like a photographic negative, aspects of Trudy and her plight that he did pursue.

3) She could get married secretly, fearing the wrath of her parents, intending to reveal the fact much later on. Finding herself pregnant, she would reveal the fact immediately, and needing proof, go to the county clerk's office only to find it had just burned to the ground. Next she would go to the army authorities to ask the whereabouts of her husband, but as we are at war, the whereabouts of her husband could not be revealed. (Some other element is needed, however, for the townspeople to believe that she is NOT married.)

Trudy does not marry secretly, which presumes conscious choice and planning. She has only one parent—Officer Kockenlocker, who seems wrathful about everything—but she does not fear him. She reveals she is pregnant only to her sister, Emmy, and, later, to the doctor and the lawyer. No record of her marriage can be found because she used a false name at the time, which she has forgotten. Because she has also forgotten her husband's name, she cannot search either for marriage records or for him. The townspeople, who presumably learn of Trudy's pregnancy only when it's apparent, can be counted on to believe the worst of her situation.

Later the same day, Sturges attempted to move forward by writing out what he here calls "Scene – Page 1."

GRADY

But what are you gonna do when your f-father f-finds out?

BETTY

(gaily)

That's all right. He won't find out . . . I used a false name.

GRADY

You used a f-false name? What name did you u-use?

BETTY

Oh, I dunno . . . just something. It seemed kind of funny at the moment.

GRADY

And it's gonna get f-funnier as the years go on . . . You ain't married at all.

BETTY

What do you mean I'm not married . . . I guess I ought to know.

GRADY

You ought to but you don't . . . you ain't married any more than a-a bird.

BETTY

(Indignantly)

I guess I ought to know.

GRADY

What was his name?

BETTY

Joe . . . no it wasn't, it was George . . . no, you're just trying to mix me up. It was Joe.

GRADY

Joe what?

BETTY

The last name was very hard to pronounce . . . the guy who married us had a terrible time.

GRADY

He had a terrible time.

BETTY

It was full of x's and z's like . . .

(She makes an xzcp noise)

He had a terrible time . . . everybody laughed.

GRADY

Whatever he had is going to be a picnic next to what you got waitin' for you.

BETTY

You're always making mountains out of mohills [*sic*].

GRADY

Where were you married?

BETTY

(Vaguely)

Out . . . that way a piece.

GRADY

(Doggedly)

Which way?

BETTY

We had a bottle of champagne--how do I know?

GRADY

Who was driving?

BETTY

George.

531

GRADY

Who's George?

BETTY

(Indignantly)

The fellow I'm married to . . . haven't you any memory at all?

GRADY

(Mops his brow and then starts slightly as a
customer comes up behind him, saying:

CUSTOMER

I'd like to hear "The End of a Perfect Day" please.

GRADY

Yes m'am. So would I.

Several features of the final screenplay appear here for the first time: the fact that the male lead stutters; the unpronounceable name of the unlocatable husband; and the setting of the first scene between the leads in a record store in which customers can listen to records. It appears from the customer who speaks to him that here it is Grady who works in the record store, and that Betty has come there to talk to him. Grady shows some of Norval's outrage at his friend's situation but, since he lacks Norval's devotion to Trudy, his skepticism seems a little like meanness—he gives Betty a relentlessly hard time about her poor memory of crucial events. Showing little sympathy for his friend, Grady receives little from the audience, despite his stutter. As for Betty, she is here an out-and-out airhead, even a heliumhead, not only because the details of her wedding night elude her but also because, unlike Trudy in the film, she is not in the least bothered by it.

In the July 8 scene fragment, Minnie had been rather callous about Edgar's civilian status and her preference for military men. This seesaw between the characters, in which now one, now the other has the upper hand, is a feature of the final film, although Norval's unquestioned devotion to Trudy makes his side of the exchange more a lover's complaint than true faultfinding. Intimate bickering between a man and woman, a Sturges specialty, requires a relationship of some mutuality, a situation which only develops in the film after Trudy is pregnant. It is unclear from the later fragment whether Grady is in love with Betty/Trudy or is just a friend; his disparaging skepticism about her story suggests the latter. In the final script and film, of course, the character who questions Trudy about her lost night and is alarmed by her answers is not Norval but Emmy, Trudy's younger sister, a character whom Sturges was not to introduce until some time later. In the film, when Norval is told about the lost night, he reacts like a stupefied lover—he takes Trudy's difficulties at face value and, as distressed as he is, does not really pass judgment on her. He cannot be both who he is in the final film—Trudy's slave and then her would-be rescuer—and the wise-guy questioner of her stupidity concerning the lost night. It would seem uncharacteristically harsh for Norval to do that, but Emmy is so young and so clearly loving toward her sister that she can carp and disparage and not seem hostile. Sturges understood that someone has to ask these questions, not only as an expositional device but also as a stand-in for the audience—itself skeptical and curious.

The four passages we've looked at so far are revealing in regard to Sturges's compositional method, particularly in the early stages of a project. Sturges often went back and forth between prose notes on a story and dramatized scenes or fragments of scenes. Once he had sketched a plot more or less to his satisfaction, he occasionally resorted to brief prose notes to alter or add details to his scheme or, as we saw above, to decide which of several pathways to follow to a preconceived end. Always, however, he wished to get a new story idea into script form as soon as possible, which, it seems, was the only way for him to test it. To put an idea into script form involved at least description and dialogue and, as soon as possible, sequence, scene, shot, and page numbers, which linked a new element to what had gone before and what was to come after. This was also one of the principal ways in which Sturges developed script ideas. In the passage above, for instance, did Sturges know before writing the scene that the male lead stuttered or that the missing husband's name was unpronounceable and had x's and z's in it, or did he discover these things in writing? Did he know in advance that the scene was set in a record store, or did this arise from the need to give the scene not only an ending but also what a critic has called "the sense of an ending" (the "End of a Perfect Day" gag)?[3] Sturges's prose notes were more than conveniences—they attempted to consolidate his ideas between scene drafts and to project where the script as a whole might go. For the most part, however, Sturges thinking is Sturges sketching scenes and scene fragments.

On July 20, he wrote a two-page outline that attempted to move the story further along. That outline was divided into four sections, the first two of which were as follows:

A. MAIN TITLES
   Introduction of characters and village. Arrangements to go to party.

B. Return from party, memory of marriage also that husband was to meet her somewhere to bring her record or have her sign something or other. Connection missed but somebody says, "There was a soldier here looking for you." Betty says, "Did you ask his name?" They say NO.

Section A seems to subsume under the main titles the introduction of the film's characters, their village, and their preparations to go to the party. But to make Betty's return from the party the first scene after the titles is to elide not only that fateful event itself but also what it means to Betty and Grady. This construction is really no better than the July 8 fragment—Sturges's first note on the project—which does not introduce characters or village but does provide shots of the party during its own main titles and then dissolves to a pivotal scene from the party's aftermath. In the July 20 outline, however, Sturges seems less interested in resolving the film's opening than in moving its plot forward. In this respect, Trudy's just missing a connection with her new husband seems to promise that she will eventually find him, or he her. Sturges considered many variations of this reunion before abandoning it definitively much later in the revision process.

> C. Three weeks later Betty still has not located the guy and now finds she is pregnant. Renews efforts to locate her husband but meets with no success. In desperation she decides to marry Grady but breaks down in the middle of the plot. At first indignant, he becomes twice as indignant when he realizes it was bigamy [she was plotting]. What are you trying to do to me anyway? He walks Betty home and then has an unexpected scene with her father who is cleaning his shotgun. The father tells Grady that he approves of him and is glad to see him keeping company with his daughter. "Where I come from they don't take those things lightly." Grady departs slipping slightly on the front steps.

Here Trudy searches for her husband for three weeks, then, finding she is pregnant, makes "renewed efforts" to find him. This too seems to promise a reunion of some kind with Ratzkiwatzki. Grady's character, which is different in each note and script draft, seems still unresolved. He is very indignant at Betty's scheme, even though she cannot go through with it and confesses everything to him. The shotgun scene with Betty's father—the nature and placement of which vary quite a bit from draft to draft—illluminates some differences between Grady and Norval. Grady seems a character for whom a shotgun scene is pertinent—if unjust in this case—because he does not want to marry Trudy in her current condition. With Norval, on the contrary, who is eager to marry Trudy under any circumstances, the shotgun scene is hilariously inappropriate, just one more undeserved tribulation heaped upon him. As such, of course, it takes its place in the black comedy that swirls around Norval and Trudy like a perpetual wind from Dante's hell.

Section D, the last of the four, is also by far the longest—it can only be paraphrased here. It presents Betty's visit to the doctor, from whose office she is "ushered out . . . rather rudely"; her consultation—about a "friend" of hers—with the lawyer, who laughs when Betty "staggers a little" on the way out and says, "Your friend doesn't seem to feel so good" ("Betty threatens him with the back of her hand and leaves"); and finally her visit to a clergyman, "who is not sympathetic." In the film the clergyman is left out—a demand of censorship—only to resurface under the same name—Reverend Upperman—in *Hail the Conquering Hero,* Sturges's next film. Also in the film the doctor and lawyer are quite sympathetic to Trudy, if unable to help her.

Following her visit to the clergyman, Betty goes to have a soda with Grady:

> He offers to marry her and let the troubles fall where they may. She thanks him, but won't let him do it. In the middle of this *one* of four things happen [*sic*]:

a. She thinks she recognizes the picture of her husband in the newspapers.

b. She thinks she recognizes the picture of her husband in the newspaper as just having been arrested for bigamy.

c. She remembers her husband's name. It was "Smith."

d. Her father comes looking for her, having just talked to the lawyer.

Grady's sudden offer to marry Trudy to help her out of her fix seems to re-create his character yet again, this time decisively in the direction of Norval. The July 20 outline seems to have shifted Sturges's attention from the question of how to begin the film to a consideration of where it was going. Thus the four things that might happen as Betty and Grady drink sodas are four plot pathways forward from this point in the script, none of which, it turns out, Sturges used in any further note or draft. Over the next several days (July 21–27), he wrote a number of short passages—and a few longer ones—that summarize possible story developments and focus in particular on po-tential endings to the film. His thinking during this phase of work was ex-perimental, straying quite far at times from his earlier work, which is more closely related to the film that we know.

On July 21, for instance, he wrote several brief paragraphs under the head-ing "Note on the MIRACLE story." The first, and most provocative, was this:

It must be established that to find the man that Betty married is like finding a needle in a haystack. However, the phenomenal publicity attendant upon the event makes the problem seem simple. The only trouble is that too many fathers show up. Everybody seems to have been at the party and they are all reasonably certain they are the one.

Up to this point Sturges had considered various ways in which Minnie/ Betty might find herself "in the situation" and what her initial reaction might be, as well as that of Edgar/Grady. Sturges here considers disclosing the iden-tity of the father. This would occur not as a result of Minnie/Betty's search for him, which, as before, is a failure, but in response to the publicity that fol-lows the birth of sextuplets. The fact that "too many fathers" show up implies that all of them had sex with *somebody* that night. That they are "reasonably certain they are the one" further implies that they are less than certain who that somebody was. It is also possible that Trudy had sex with more than one person on the night in question—an image that passes disturbingly across the viewer's conscious/unconscious mind during the course of watching the film. Exactly what, in this respect, does "Let's all get married" mean?

Another brief note written on July 21 considers yet another possibility and mentions for the first time the film's male star, Eddie Bracken: "Betty, forbid-den to marry Bracken, does so secretly, but to save Bracken from her father's wrath *says* she married a departing soldier." A July 27 variant of this, headed "One way of doing it," proposes that "Eddy [*sic*]" has followed Betty to a military party, where, he confesses at the end of the film, he married her himself in order to prevent her from doing something foolish. The first note credits Betty, the second Eddy, with more calculation, control, and intelligence than either Trudy or Norval—or both of them together—exhibits in the film. Indeed, one of the dark wonders of the film is the way that the two characters, by pooling their intelligence, create disaster after disaster—each greater and more calamitous than either could have created alone.

In these notes one sees first Betty, then Eddy, take advantage of the war situation—at least of the omnipresence of soldiers—for his or her own ends. Such courses of action reduce the war to a mere background for their individual goals. How much larger a conception—finally attaining the power of myth—to have Trudy and Norval swept away by the war. Against the forces that buffet them—sex, war, social power of many kinds—they have little, if any, resistance.

Still another note from July 21 has two dialogue exchanges, the exact context of which, let alone their relation to each other, is far from clear. The first, apparently to have been placed somewhere in the middle of the film, is this:

SOMEBODY
But suppose he blats it out somewhere?

TRUDY
He swore on his honor he'd never mention it.

"SOMEBODY" is Trudy's intimate interlocutor and confidante, a role later to be filled by Emmy, Trudy's younger sister. Sturges considered for some time Grady or Bracken or Eddy, and later Norval, as Betty or Trudy's confidante, but that was inconsistent both with Grady's lack of sympathy and later with Emmy and Trudy's selection of Bracken-Norval as Trudy's substitute husband, hence as the solution to her dilemma. (It is through this scheme, which Trudy's affection for him botches, that Norval learns the truth.)

In the second passage, evidently to have been placed near the end of the film, Trudy says to her husband, who has suddenly appeared:

Then why didn't you say so before? Why did you let me go through all this?

THE CHARACTER X
You made me swear I wouldn't tell.

"THE CHARACTER X" is an appropriate appellation. Many of the plots that Sturges tried out at this time were different solutions to the problem of X: who is the father of Trudy's children? Several such answers, each a plot in brief, were sketched by Sturges at various times. Two quite different story solutions, both written on July 22, received more extended treatment. The first was a three-page story summary that began as follows:

536

Under the influence of champagne and sentiment, a smalltown girl marries in the night. The next morning she can't remember who she married or where it happened. She knocks wood, hopes for the best and goes to work.

In a very wealthy country house the local mill-owner and his wife are upbraiding their son for his choice of friends. It appears that he and their guest that morning came in in quite a condition, leaving their car in the middle of the rosebed. The son apologizes for his guest and goes up to see how he is feeling. The guest is feeling none too well and keeps asking questions about the night before. He seems to have something on his mind and suddenly, with a start of horror, he thinks he remembers that he got married last night. "Again?" says his friend. It develops that this is a little habit of his that his father pays off for, albeit reluctantly.

"Did you give your right name?" says the son of the house. "How do I know?" says the guest. "I'm not even sure I . . . the whole thing might be a nightmare."

At lunch time the little girl goes over to the county clerk's office; while she is asking vague and hypothetical questions, the son of the family and his guest come in with their hats over their eyes. Suddenly the guest almost falls in a syncope. The son of the family says, "What's the matter?" and the guest says, "The nightmare." The little girl leaves, not having found anything and the two young men follow her.

Just before closing in the store the guest appears at the little girl's counter and says, "How about a drink?" "Go peddle your papers," says the girl, "what kind of store do you think this . . . is?" This last as he begins to look very familiar to her. "Haven't we met?" says the guest. In a trance Trudy puts on her hat and coat and follows him out.

The ensuing conversation establishes that neither Trudy nor the guest found any record of the marriage and, more surprisingly, that the guest has been married seven times before. "Always like this?" she asks, and he nods; "Fooey!" says Trudy, who suggests hopefully that maybe it wasn't written down. The guest replies, "They always remember everything down to the last detail. You're a pretty little thing." "Never mind the applesauce," says Trudy. At this moment Norval appears, angry at Trudy who was to have met him after work. She introduces him as her fiancé then asks him to wait outside. She tells the guest, "I'd be willing to forget the whole thing . . . if only I were sure that-that . . ." Trudy proposes he "come back in a month, and maybe we can have it annulled . . . if we're not sure it happened . . . in the meantime," she concludes, "keep your trap shut." "That you can depend on," says the guest. "I won't even tell *my* fiancée." At the end of the story summary, Sturges wrote this brief dialogue: "GUEST: Suppose I never showed up again?; TRUDY: If you were that much of a heel, I'd be lucky to be rid of you; GUEST: There's something in that."

Starting a new page, Sturges sketched an alternate version of the same story. As before, the guest and his friend see Trudy at the clerk's office; instead of following her, however, they go to a bar.

"There's nothing for it," says the guest, "We'll have to call the lawyer," and they call Osmond, Bergstahler, Zitz & Finkelstein. "The great thing in these cases," says the guest, "is to pay off quick or you never can tell what's going to happen."

"We now leap to the guest's father," continues Sturges, who shows him dictating an angry letter to his son: "Wherever you are, you bum, you can stay there. I enclose $500 and that's the end of it." He also instructs his lawyers, "Now pay the girl off and try to keep the whole thing quiet."

How this plot might resolve itself is difficult to see. Even if it were to lead to the birth of sextuplets, the ending that Sturges already had in mind, then what? Would Trudy become Bluebeard's eighth wife? If so, by what transformation of the guest's character? And what would become of Norval?

A different solution for X appeared in dialogue form, after an opening written in prose:

For the end of the picture:

The man responsible for the six little kids must somehow walk in at the very end, not having heard anything about it. All during this time he has been looking for the girl whom he knew he married. Now, happy to have found her again, he holds her hand and whispers sweet nothings to her and says, "Gee whiz, we might even have a kid someday."

In the ensuing dialogue, Benny, the name of the father *ex machina,* says,

"Well you remember me, don't you? I been dreamin' about cha every day . . . every night . . . I've been savin' my dough for ya, honey . . . I knew I'd find ya some day . . . I've been tryin' to get to this berg for a year, but we kept playin' further and further away from it and if it wasn't for this dame that had the . . ."

This tantalizing explanation-in-the-making is suspended in midsentence and not returned to. Trudy says, "Gee you're cute looking. Weren't you a little taller?" But Benny, it becomes clear, is not a soldier at all but a performer travelling with some kind of show. "Gee it's good to see you," says Trudy. Benny asks, "Say, you ain't sick are ya? What are you doin' in a hospital?" "You don't read the papers much, do you?" asks Trudy, in turn, since Benny knows nothing of the recent miracle in Morgan's Creek. "No, they're a waste of time," he says, "I read *Variety* though," which comes out on "Sat'day." The scene continues as Benny imagines a little house where they will live, with a little yard, and a little white nursery, and she responds to each item, "Not too little, honey." Finally he says, laughing:

You talk like we was gonna have sextuplets or something.

TRUDY

We have.

BENNY
(Clutching his chest)

You mean, I, I--

TRUDY

Well certainly you are, you dope.

Benny starts to collapse. Trudy catches him, swings him into her arms like a baby. Now looking straight into the lens she says:

TRUDY

What a man.

CUT TO:

THE BIG WHITE NURSERY full of doctors and nurses. Trudy enters laughing, carrying the unconscious Benny like an infant in her arms.

TRUDY

What a man.

Although Sturges did not return to this plot, either, he adapted Benny's gradual realization of what has happened for the final script and film. Shot from the inside of the hospital nursery, Norval, uniformed at last, pantomimes to Emmy "which of the babies is – mine?" Of course none of the babies is Norval's and Emmy knows this. This embarrassed quandary of reference so close to the film's end perhaps dictated a scene without dialogue and thereby led to the wonderful result with which we are familiar. Emmy counts out the six babies in the nursery shot and waves her hand to include them all. Norval doesn't faint when he finally understands so Trudy—who is in any case sleeping—doesn't carry him in her arms, but Norval's legs do go rubbery, he does start to stutter, and he does see "the spots" as, one quote from *Twelfth Night* aside, the film ends.[4]

The test plots were abandoned but they illuminate, in a variety of ways, the final script and film. An example is the question of social class in *The Miracle of Morgan's Creek*, particularly the question of the vantage point from which Trudy and Norval are observed. The "guest" plot summarized above first establishes a social framework of condescension, then turns it on its head by making the wealthy character morally and psychologically a ninny. This may be regarded as a brief, interesting reprise of a story situation that Sturges had charted in *The Lady Eve, The Palm Beach Story,* and other works. The three-page "guest" spin-off, precisely by reverting to old Sturges themes, only dramatizes in the end how different this project was from his earlier ones.

To take another example, Benny is a blithe spirit and Grady, in his first incarnation anyway, a dour one; but they share linguistic markers of lower-than-middle class. Benny's poor grammar and Grady's *ain'ts*—precisely what do they signify: The characters' lack of education? The narrow and unpleasant side of small-town life? The attempted social realism of these scene drafts? Or, on the contrary, their own implied social distance from these characters—that is to say, their own condescension? In any case, by the time of his first script draft, Sturges had decided to drop such socially specific linguistic behavior. One of the oddly touching qualities of Trudy and Norval in the film is their ability to speak lucidly about their thoughts and feelings, clichéd and/ or confused as they so often are. That they regularly converse in colloquial but grammatical English brings them no nearer to solving their problems.

Seeking an identity for the father of Trudy's children turned out to be a dead end for Sturges: it did not lead to a plot that he could securely move ahead with. Ultimately more fruitful in this respect was a line of inquiry that Sturges pursued simultaneously with his search for "Character X." On July 21, for instance, he had written: "The classic form for this type of comedy is to plunge the heroine into trouble and keep her in ever-increasing trouble until she triumphs over all by the very degree of her trouble." This is a fine, pithy formula for what happens in *The Miracle of Morgan's Creek,* even if it did not, in the short run anyway, move the project forward. The next day, however, Sturges made his general description of his character a little more specific, and also found her name:

Design for Story

It concerns itself with part of the life of a well-meaning but clumsy and impulsive kid in a small town: the type who tore the seat out of her dress at the high school graduation exercises, who spilled a gallon of ice cream over the governor's wife on the Fourth of July, who let the cat out of the bag every time a secret was to be kept, who refers to the Chinese as Japanese, who can't remember names, including the name of a departing soldier whom she marries impulsively, or the town in which it happened. All in all, Trudy Kockenlocker is quite a girl, but being innocent, she is also the elect of God and accordingly protected.

At this stage, Trudy has become a character who is not just plunged into trouble by the plot—she is herself trouble-prone. Sturges continues this vein in a handwritten note later the same day (July 22).

Betty in music store calls good customer by wrong name--is scolded for this by the manager--says: "I'm sorry, Mr. Souse." "My name happens to be Douse" says the manager--or Klaus – Louse.

Still later the same day, Sturges began to integrate his emergent sense of Trudy's character with his overall plot idea:

Maybe the extraordinary birth should be the climax of a series of mishaps that happen to a dumb little klunk. In other words, she always does everything wrong, is always making trouble for herself and those around her, but her greatest trouble brings her fame and fortune.

Sturges is still far from a story outline that might serve as the basis for a screenplay, but an important step toward that goal occurred in three pages of notes headed "MIRACLE Story" that he wrote on July 27.

What happens to the girl:

She loses her job
She is expulsed from the church
She is thrown out by her family
She steals money from her father and is nearly put in jail
She discovers that she is pregnant
She gets put off a train without ticket and loses her baggage
She is nearly attacked by a motorist and is then arrested when she beats him up
She is threatened with prosecution by the doctor to whom she goes
She is nearly sent to reform school
She actually commits bigamy and is in danger of going to the penitentiary when . . .
She triumphs over all.

What happens to the boy:

He nearly gets pneumonia waiting for her
He is threatened with a shotgun by her father
He is punched in the eye by her brother
He tears his best suit, helping her into the house
He is arrested as a prowler while coming to see her, after having a pot dropped on his
    head by her sister
He borrows a friend's car but forgets to leave word
He signs his draft registration falsely
He is threatened with Mann Act prosecution for taking her across the stateline
He is locked out somewhere without his clothes
He loses his job
He is held up and robbed of all his savings
He smashes up his boss's car
He is fired at by her father
He commits bigamy two or three times in two or three places and . . . becomes a
    national hero, with a commission and a medal.

"She" and "he," who were soon to be called Trudy and Norval, are put
here, for the first time, on the same footing. The events that befall each, although listed separately, are interlinked. Above all, they are now together in
all of their adventures; they sink together, sink further, and sink further still
until they rise together, triumphant, at the end. This mutuality is a hallmark of
the project as it developed from this point forward. Here for the first time, the
"he" is as trouble-prone as the "she," even if a number of his troubles are
caused by "she." In later stages of the project, including the film, it is Norval
who becomes the chronic bumbler while Trudy, who is far less eccentric,
stumbles only once.

Sturges had at least a rough idea of Trudy's character at this time but was
less certain of Norval's, as a second page of the "MIRACLE Story" notes
indicates:

One way of doing it:

Eddy has always been in love with her . . . always she has treated him like dirt. Once more she uses him like a welcome mat and makes him take her to a military party . . . When she finds she is pregnant she tries to get Eddy to marry her and he is willing to. Unable to play such a dirty trick, she confesses her plight and he is still willing to.

In the final analysis, he confesses his shameful action, that he followed her to the military party and to stop her from doing something foolish, he married her himself.

Here for the first time are two features of the final script and film: "Eddy has always been in love with her . . . always she has treated him like dirt," and "Unable to play such a dirty trick, she confesses her plight and he is still willing to." Eddy/Norval is not only not indignant at Trudy's aborted plot to snare him, as Grady had been, but deeply honored and even eager to go through with it. Sturges's add-on—that Norval follows her to the dance and marries her himself—is inconsistent with the character he has just sketched, in a sense discovered, in the paragraph above. He has not yet caught up with the new character of Norval—what he can do and what he cannot do—or indeed with the crucial story development he has just achieved, as this note, immediately following, reveals:

Ironic Story:

The husband returns from a trip and finds his wife pregnant. Not by any stretch of the imagination can he be the father. He refrains from shooting her, but promises to divorce her immediately after the birth of the children. Six little boys are born and he becomes the most famous and the most furious man in the world.

A third page, again identifying the principals as "she" and "he," seems once again to evoke Norval and Trudy. It is headed "The reasons for his irritation":

First, she lets him sit like a bump on a log until he nearly gets pneumonia, while she becomes pregnant from someone else; she then causes him to smash his car, tear his suit and nearly get shot while helping her home. He then narrowly misses being arrested as a prowler and has to walk home five miles. When she finds out she is pregnant she tries to trick him into marrying her and then lets it be understood that he is responsible for her condition. Narrowly averting being shot again, he commits bigamy to satisfy her brother and trigamy to satisfy her father, has his engagement broken off with the boss's daughter, is fired by his boss and eventually despised by the entire community. As she is now the only person in the town who will speak to him, he decides to help her have her child on condition that it be done with absolute secrecy and that she give him a divorce immediately afterward so that he can pick up his life where he left off. Her secret becomes one of the most widely known secrets of all time and he is given a medal and a commission in the home guard . . . such men are needed at home . . . he will lecture to other husbands. There is a final moment of tenderness. She says, "We've been through so much together . . . I don't think they'd give you a divorce anyway . . . it would be against the public veal . . . weal, whatever they call it." Almost in tears, he says, "But I can't stand it, honey . . . to have those six little b . . . oys . . . staring in my kisser and hollering 'Poppa' at me all day long . . . I mean if you had four, or five even . . . but *six*. . . . besides, I wanted to have children of my own." She says, "Well, you don't think I'm through, do you?" He says, "Huh?" She says, "If it makes you happy, I'll have eight the next time." He says, "No foolin'." She says, "How can I miss . . . with a start like this . . . octopuses."

Engaged to marry the boss's daughter, the "he" of this passage initially has a love life separate from "she," as "Eddy" or "Bracken" seems to have had in a few notes. "He" also marries "she" with a plan to divorce her afterward so he can later "pick up his life where he left off." Needless to say, Norval has no love life apart from Trudy. He plans to divorce Trudy after he marries her as Ratzkiwatzki, so that they can later marry as themselves. Norval has "reasons for his irritation," to be sure, but, despite a few contrary suggestions, his is a lover's complaint. Norval is not an antagonist to Trudy, as Grady seemed to have been, or a character who shifts from indifference to involvement— without motivation—as "he" does here.

Sturges had worked steadily on *Miracle*'s story outline from July 8 to July 27. Between July 28 and August 26, however, other tasks took him away from the project, notably his attempts to save *Triumph over Pain/The Great Moment* from changes threatened by the studio. Even so, Sturges did manage—between August 1 and 15—to write script fragments for three of *Miracle*'s early scenes—fourteen pages in all.

One draft scene placed the film's opening in a small-town church, in which Dr. Upperman tells his congregation

that wartime is a dangerous time and that in any large group of men there is a definite proportion of fools and scoundrels . . . uniforms or no uniforms . . . and against these I *warn* you. Beware of the spell cast by the military . . . beware of a hasty act, to be repented at great leisure. Do not confuse patriotism with promiscuity, nor loyalty with laxity, lest impulse turn to remorse . . . beware!

In the final script, Sturges relocates the church scene to the end of sequence "C" (pages 31–32), and accents the sermon's theme by filling the church with screaming babies. Trudy and Emmy hear the sermon—on the morning after the military party—when it is too late to do Trudy any good. Trudy's visit to church is followed by her visits to doctor and attorney (in sequence "D"), hence it takes its place as one of three American institutions that notably fail to help Trudy: organized religion, medicine, law.

According to Luigi Luraschi, Paramount's in-house censorship expert, the Hays Office insisted

that the preacher be cast as a dignified, sincere member of the cloth and that he deliver a dignified and sincere denunciation of hasty military weddings . . . Also, you are to eliminate the scene of all the babies in the church which has an unpleasant implication and gets us nothing.

Perhaps Sturges declined to alter the scene in this way; perhaps he decided to cut it on other grounds. In either case, the scene does not appear in the film, in which the warning is made in print by the editor of the local newspaper. However—in the final script—a trace of the minister, who is renamed "Rev. Doctor Thorndyke," survives in the editorial itself: "MILITARY MARRIAGES MENACE SAYS MINISTER" (page 6).

A second scene fragment begins with a shot of Trudy's legs. Her sister Emmy—mentioned here for the first time—answers the phone and calls upstairs to Trudy that she thinks "it's that jerk, Norval." Trudy tries to avoid the call, Emmy is caught between them, and the girls' father, Kockenlocker, just wants the matter settled. There is a cut back to Trudy's legs, then "we pan her legs to the door," after which:

UPPER HALLWAY

Trudy's legs come into the shot, one of them swings over the bannister and the young lady appears, en chemise, as she slides to the floor below. She lands and grabs the phone with one movement.

TRUDY

Oh, hello Norval.

MR. KOCKENLOCKER
(after a double take of his daughter's outfit)
Well, I'll be a fruit-eyed rinkydink.

Trudy tells Norval she'd love to do whatever it is he is asking but she has a date for the night—a military affair to kiss the boys good-bye. Hearing Trudy's plan, Kockenlocker "stiffens and then looks down at his newspaper." To appease Norval, Trudy offers him Emmy, saying, "she's a cute kid if you can get her to stand up straight." Emmy responds "violently": "You lay your own eggs, I'll take care of my end," which becomes in an alternative version, enclosed in parentheses, "you butter your own nest, I'll take care of *my* evenings." Asked by Norval if she is giving him "the whiskbroom," Trudy invokes civic duty and hangs up.

A third scene fragment sketches the scene of Norval and Trudy's return to the Kockenlocker house the morning after the military party (pages 22–25). Kockenlocker attacks Norval, Trudy attacks Kockenlocker, et cetera. Two more pages continue the scene with Norval's exit—a "Just Married" sign on his car—then segue into the conversation between Trudy and Emmy concerning what happened on the military party, which is sketched with a number of slightly revised pages, in six additional pages (pages 25–31).

On August 27 Sturges returned to full-time work on *The Miracle of Morgan's Creek*. So far he had worked on the basic story outline and written some scene drafts. The story outline was far from complete and the scene drafts were few in number and unsystematic. Nevertheless—based on his work habits on earlier projects—it was likely that he would now throw himself into writing a first script version. However, on August 19 Sturges had received a memo from William Dozier, writing on behalf of Y. Frank Freeman, who was then the Head of Production at Paramount.

Dear Preston:

Before Mr. Freeman went east, he mentioned something to me about your intending to prepare an outline of *The Miracle of Morgan's Creek* for Hays' Office approval. Would you please let me know whether this was your intention and if so whether it has ever been accomplished. The reason I am asking is because I would like to send through the authorization to purchase the story from you.

It is worth noting here that for the six Paramount films he had written and directed before *Miracle,* Sturges's practice had been, for Hays Office needs and story purchase alike, to bypass a formal story outline phase and to write instead a complete screenplay. For none of those projects was a story outline required. Why then, with shooting a full two months away, did Paramount want a story outline for *Miracle?* Perhaps the studio foresaw the serious problems the project would face with the censors. Or had the locking of horns over *Triumph over Pain/The Great Moment* soured the easygoing relationship between studio and director?

Whether or not he even answered Dozier is unclear but, in any case, Sturges did proceed at this point to work toward a screenplay draft. Between August 27 and September 8, he wrote an unfinished script of forty-nine pages, comprising sequences "A," "B," "C," "D," and an unfinished sequence "E." This draft stops near the end of the conversation between Trudy and Emmy that takes place later in the evening on which Trudy, having set out to get Norval to propose, has been moved by his devotion and tells him about her predicament. Rather than continue with this draft—which was evidently typed by his own secretary—Sturges turned it over to the Paramount secretaries for retyping in the studio's standardized format on September 10, which is the date that appears on the script's cover. On September 11, under what additional pressure is unclear—perhaps he just needed the money—Sturges wrote a two-page, single-spaced story summary, reprinted below, for which he was promptly paid his usual ten-thousand-dollar story fee.

"THE MIRACLE OF MORGAN'S CREEK"

An Original Story

by

Preston Sturges

Forbidden by her father to go to a "Kiss the boys goodbye" military farewell hoopla, Trudy Kockenlocker uses her homely friend and devoted admirer, Norval Jones, as a front to get her out of the house. Norval waits all night for her in the lobby of a picture theater, then takes her home at eight in the morning to the irritation of her father and the consternation of the neighbors. The next morning she remembers, as in a dream, that she married somebody with a "Z" in his name . . . something like Ratzkiwatzki. A moment later she remembers she took the precaution of using an assumed name . . . a name she has forgotten. The more she thinks about it the less she remembers. She is not even sure she got married at all until three weeks later when the doctor says there is no question about it. Efforts to locate Ratzkiwatzki are fruitless. In desperation she decides to marry Norval, but her good heart takes possession of her and instead of accepting him she breaks down and confesses her plight.

After a momentary shock, Norval becomes her slave again and bends every effort to save her from her situation. He would even resort to bigamy if necessary but this is the last resort. The one thing Trudy needs is a marriage certificate: this is the basis of everything, proof of her marriage, demand for annulment or suit for divorce . . . but neither Ratzkiwatzki nor the certificate can be found. Suddenly Norval gets an inspiration: Trudy will marry Ratzkiwatzki again and this time there will be a certificate. "But where is Ratzkiwatzki?" asks Trudy. "I am," says Norval.

On the appointed day they cross the State Line; Norval puts on a uniform and Trudy Kockenlocker is married to Private Ratzkiwatzki. All goes well and they return to the Kockenlocker residence. The evasiveness of their answers to Mr. Kockenlocker's questions concerning their whereabouts arouses the latter's suspicions.

A few days later Kockenlocker plays a little scene with Norval in which, while cleaning his shotgun he tells Norval it would look very bad if he didn't marry Trudy when they have been out together so much and so late, and all. "You gotta understand this is a small town," says Mr. Kockenlocker. "I've already asked her," says Norval, "but she won't have me . . . at least not yet." "You didn't ask her right," says her father. "You gotta ask 'em rough. Dames love to be bossed . . . Now you take the rooster." "You don't seem to understand," says Norval, "Nothing would make me happier, nothing would please me more than to marry Trudy." "You're in," says her father. "Maybe Trudy will have something to say about that," says Norval. "Not in my house," says Mr. Kockenlocker. "In my house the frails do like I tell 'em. You let 'em get the jump on you and you're a dead duck." Brought into the scene Trudy has to admit she is already married. "Who to?" says her infuriated father. "R-Ratzkiwatzki" says Trudy. "Who is R-R-Ratzkiwatzki?" bellows the father. "I don't know exactly," falters Trudy. "Where is he?" hollers the father. "We can't find him," says Norval. "Oh we can't," says the father. "Well, I'll find him . . . where do you fit into this anyway?"

But unfortunately Ratzkiwatzki is found . . . in the person of Norval – who is clapped into jail for perjury, the Mann Act, and impersonating a United States soldier. This leaves Trudy without a husband but in the sad condition she was in before. Her reputation is gone and the whole town believes the worst of her although different factions believe different stories. In any case she is the shame of the town. A few rocks are thrown through her windows, her father nearly kills a man for saying something about his daughter and is forced to leave the police force in consequence, Norval is lingering in the clink and everything is very lousy when . . . Trudy is rushed to the hospital and delivered of sextuplets. This puts a different complexion on the whole matter. The war is snatched off the front pages, the Governor of the State flies in and takes charge of everything, accompanied by the Director of Public Relations, and merely as a matter of public weal, if not of sentiment, Trudy's marriage to the original Mr. Ratzkiwatzki is annulled, her marriage to Norval is legalized, a long distance phone call from a soldier named Goraschi-Luraschi is received and he is told to never put his foot in the State again, Norval is flown out of the clink, a protest is received from the Premier of Canada and the usual excitement prevails as we fade out on the happy Trudy and Norval, the most famous father in the world. Very roughly, this is THE MIRACLE OF MORGAN'S CREEK.

Sturges seems to have put the story in writing not for himself but for others, either to get the studio off his back and/or to receive his fee. It is likely that Sturges had known for some time where the story was going, at least in general, and had written it down only on demand. One indication of this is that writing the story had no discernible impact on his scriptwriting. He did not go back to sequence "A" to begin the script anew, as he often did when the whole of a project's story line fell into place. Even on September 10 and 11—presumably the days on which he wrote the story—he continued to work on sequence "E" of the September 10 script. In the weeks that followed he wrote sequences "F," "G," and "H," which he completed on October 1.

Another revealing feature of the story is that it omits—perhaps for simplicity's sake and so as not to upset the studio—story developments he had achieved much earlier. The most notable omission is the character of Emmy, who serves as Trudy's confidante, foil, support, and prod in two of the script fragments which had been written in early August, and in all of the sequences ("A," "B," "C," "D," and the unfinished "E") of the script that Sturges had worked on before writing the story. Two more omissions are the introduction of the main characters and of Morgan's Creek, which occur in sequence "A."

As mentioned, the September 10 script was in fact written between August 27 and October 1. It was 103 pages long and unfinished, getting only as far as a brief version of Norval's arrest after he attempts to marry Trudy under an assumed name. Since shooting was to begin on October 21, Sturges, who usually worked quickly, apparently still had time to complete a first script version and all but finish a second. It was not uncommon for him to complete his final script a few days after filming had begun. However, on *Miracle,* for reasons that are not entirely clear, the work progressed very slowly. On October 8, 9, and 10, Sturges rewrote some of the last thirty-one pages of the September 10 script and added sixteen new pages. This version recast and expanded the presentation of the failed wedding and the uproar—now huge—that follows it. Then on October 14, Sturges began a new script version, which made changes in the early parts of the September 10 script. This version ends well before the October 8 version does, getting only as far as the middle of the scene with the justice of the peace. Dated October 14, 15, 16, and 19, these changes evidently responded to the barrage of censorship objections that had begun to descend on Sturges by that time. The principal censorship documents, which called for additional changes, were received on October 21, the very date, as it happened, of the first day of shooting. As a result of these pressures, internal and external, Sturges started shooting without even a first version of a finished script. This was the only time in his career that he did so. He attempted to finish the script at night while filming during the day. The final script, which is reprinted below, was finished on December 10, just eighteen days before the end of shooting. This remarkable document, a kind of palimpsest, contains pages written as early as October 19 and as late as December 10, a period of fifty-three days overall. Its 156 pages bear nineteen different dates and, instead of the progression from early to late that one might expect, there is a thorough intermixing.

As this survey suggests, the process of writing and revising the script for *The Miracle of Morgan's Creek* was by far the most complicated—and probably the most difficult—of all the films that Sturges wrote and directed. To consider, in turn, each of Sturges's partial scripts would result in a needlessly, perhaps hopelessly complicated exposition. To simplify the discussion, I will proceed instead by focusing on the sequences of the various scripts and their realization in the film.

Sequences "A" through "E" develop *Miracle*'s basic situation and define the problems that later sequences try to solve. Sequence "A" shows the Kockenlockers at their workplaces—Officer Kockenlocker directing traffic at the town's main intersection and Trudy at Rafferty's music store, where she is employed as a clerk. Sequence "A" also introduces us to the town of Morgan's Creek, its buildings and streets, its citizens going about their business, and—most important of all—the recent influx of soldiers from camps surrounding the town. Sequence "B" shows the Kockenlockers at home and Norval at his rooming house. Sequence "C" presents the military party, the scene between Trudy and Norval in front of the movie theater, the knockabout farce with Trudy, Norval, and Kockenlocker, in front of the house, and a scene in which Trudy tells Emmy what she remembers, and does not remember, of the night before. A brief sequence "D" shows Trudy visiting first the doctor and then the lawyer while Emmy waits, then, as the sisters walk through town toward the music store, a discussion between them in which they decide that Norval is the solution to Trudy's dilemma. Sequence "E" begins with Norval invited for dinner at the Kockenlockers, which is followed by a scene of Norval's proposing to Trudy on the porch. This is followed by the couple's long walk through the town in which Trudy gradually discloses to Norval the nature of her predicament. Finally, in a late-night conversation, Emmy berates Trudy for having spilled the beans to Norval.

The introductory and expository functions of sequences "A" and "B" are handled differently in the September 10 script, the final script, and the film itself. In all versions, as sequence "A" opens, Officer Kockenlocker is contending with traffic at the heart of town. In the September 10 version, like the final script, Kockenlocker is beeped at by a car and crosses to an Army jeep to investigate:

OFFICER KOCKENLOCKER:
What's all the hurry? . . . where's the fire?

THE SOLDIER AT THE WHEEL:
We gotta round up some dames for the party tonight . . . you know any numbers?

OFFICER KOCKENLOCKER:
Yeh well if I did . . .

He is almost run over by an Army jeep going in the other direction.

OFFICER KOCKENLOCKER:
Just a minute you . . . where do you think you're going? Who do you think you are?

THE MAN AT THE WHEEL:
Listen flatfoot.

OFFICER KOCKENLOCKER:
Listen you, don't give me that stuff. I was in France before your father got your mother in trouble . . . now beat it before I haul you outta there and show you a couple you don't know.

THE SOLDIER AT THE WHEEL:
O yeh.

He starts to rise.

OFFICER KOCKENLOCKER: (nose to nose with him)
Yeh.

The horns begin to sound impatiently. At this point Norval Jones rides into the intersection on a scooter.

NORVAL:
Good evening, Mr. Kockenlocker.

OFFICER KOCKENLOCKER:
Good evening, Norval . . . go ahead.

He waves him through. Horns get louder.

OFFICER KOCKENLOCKER:
Now beat it, you.

The jeeps shoot past him in both directions and traffic whizzes by for a moment then again Mr. Kockenlocker is displeased.

MR. KOCKENLOCKER: (stepping up to an Army truck)
Just a minute where do you think *you're* going?

THE SOLDIER AT THE WHEEL:
We're lookin' for some dames, buddy, you got any addresses?

MR. KOCKENLOCKER: (opens his mouth to speak, then shrugs)
Come on beat it, you.

A motorcycle and side car rides in with five soldiers on it.

THE BOY ASTRIDE:
Could you tell me the whereabouts of a girl called Eileen Bach?

MR. KOCKENLOCKER: (furiously)
A girl called Eileen Bach?
(now he threatens him with his hand)
Will you get outta here?

The soldiers are looking for girls who "lean back" all right (Eileen Bach = "I lean back"), but Sturges must have known this would not pass the censors. In the final script the soldiers' gag becomes the anodyne "Miss Issippi" (page A-2), which was itself cut before shooting or was shot and then cut in the final edit.[5] It happens not infrequently in script revision, and often in Sturges, that an element altered for censorship or some other reason is discovered to have lost its original point or humor and is cut. Such realizations rarely occur at once, however, the writer being aware at first only of a defect overcome; seeing the new passage for what it is and how it fits with the rest of the scene, and the script as a whole, usually takes time.

The Hays Office was preoccupied with sex, as always, in its rulings on *Morgan's Creek,* but the proper presentation of servicemen in films made in 1942–1943 was the concern of a new kind of censor, the Office of War Information.[6] O.W.I. did not comment on *Miracle* in writing until after the film was shot and edited, at which time it focused on the party sequence and on the role of the military in Trudy's pregnancy. That O.W.I. was known to be concerned with the treatment of servicemen, however, may have inclined the studio managers to be careful. Paramount, more than any other studio, questioned the authority of O.W.I., whose mission and scope of authority were indeed vague.[7] It refused to submit its scripts to O.W.I. for approval in advance of production, but may have worried that *Miracle* would lead to a direct confrontation. This is speculation, admittedly, but one can point to a number of changes in the presentation of the soldiers from the September 10 script to the final script and film. In the final script, as the reader can see, the soldiers do not "almost run over" Kockenlocker, or even "shoot past him" in one direction, let alone two; no soldier says "Listen, flatfoot" or any other insult, or rises to threaten a fight. Sturges cut the "Miss Issippi" gag because it was bad, but also perhaps because even so mild a put-on was disrespectful to civilians. Also, the soldiers in the September 10 script seem completely unsupervised, which might intimidate civilians. In the final script, a soldier in an Army truck says to the driver, "Watch your step now . . . and keep under thirty-five"; and the MPs are not just "cruising around," as the opening description now has it; they intervene promptly at even the hint of a problem. "What's all the trouble?" says one, at no more than a number of soldiers speaking to a policeman (page A-1).

These changes in the soldiers' behavior subtly alter the nature of Kocken-

"We do it different now, Ed. It's all done with kindness." MP Frank Moran instructs traffic cop and World War I veteran William Demarest in THE MIRACLE OF MORGAN'S CREEK.

locker's responses, which themselves change little from version to version, and thereby alter our sense of his character. In the September 10 script, Kockenlocker is genuinely put upon by the actions of the soldiers. His irritated responses to their provocations are plausible. In the final script, however, the soldiers merely ask where the church is that is holding the dance and, as politely as possible, where they can find girls to come to the party. It is Kockenlocker, in both cases, who strikes the wise-guy note. When he tells the inquiring MP, "I just don't like to be talked to by Rookies," he seems decidedly unsympathetic. Making the soldiers more decorous, whether or not in response to O.W.I. censorship, considerably sharpens the character of Kockenlocker in the opening scene, and prepares us for his actions later.

The September 10 script dissolves from the Eileen Bach joke to an exterior of Rafferty's music store with an Army jeep parked in front of it. Norval rides his scooter into the shot and parks behind the jeep. As Norval enters the store, there is a cut to "a bunch of soldiers" leaning over the counter, listening to a Crosby record. This is followed in turn by a shot of Trudy, "FROM THE BOYS' POINT OF VIEW," as she lip synchs to the record.[8] The final script preserves this staging but the film reverses it: we do not see the soldiers first and then Trudy, but her first and then the soldiers watching her perform.

Since Trudy's actions set the film in motion, it is inappropriate to see her first from the soldiers' point of view, as though their desires create her or she is their projection. Instead, Trudy is shown holding court, first for an attentive group of servicemen, and then, once she has dismissed them by saying, "You better buy something before Mr. Rafferty gets after me," for Norval, the humble petitioner who hovers in the background, waiting for his opportunity. When it comes, he approaches timidly with his request, which he knows will be rejected. Whereas the soldiers had an audience and a show for free, Norval has to pay for his by buying some phonograph needles he does not need (since he doesn't have a phonograph).

After the Crosby rendition, Trudy puts on an opera record and mimes "the quartet from Rigoletto or the sextet from Lucia." (Sturges drops his cultural references lightly.) Trudy then "finishes up her performance with a basso profundo rendition of ASLEEP IN THE DEEP." Trudy is "asleep in the deep," all right, as her behavior on the military party will soon show; she prepares for the party and maneuvers around her father's prohibition and Norval's objections like a sleepwalker. (The robotlike way in which Hutton turns around and walks away from Bracken at the movie theater is uncanny.)

As the soldiers leave the music store, "Norval is revealed standing behind them. One of them bumps him and another one steps on his foot, which he forgives in polite pantomime." Norval "comes forward" to speak to Trudy. After some preliminaries, he says,[9]

> Say, I just passed by the lobby and they got three pretty good pictures playing at the Regent tonight and it occurred to me that if you weren't doing anything, considering that I was also free, we--

TRUDY: I'm awfully sorry but I wouldn't be able to make it tonight. You see, I promised to go to the dance for the boys that are going away.

NORVAL: Oh, the soldiers.

TRUDY: That's right, Norval. I'm awful sorry.

NORVAL: You think they'd give a party sometime for those who have to stay behind. They also serve, you know, who only sit and--well, whatever they do, I forget.

TRUDY: I'm sure they do, Norval.

NORVAL: I don't get to see you quite as much as I used to, or as I'd like to, Trudy.

TRUDY: I'm awfully sorry, Norval. Naturally the camps and the canteens and everything take up quite a lot of your spare time.

"Naturally," says Norval without irony. Trudy suggests that Norval himself go to the military party—"It's only 50 cents." "It's not the 50 cents," Norval says,

I just wouldn't feel right not being there in uniform.

TRUDY: I guess nobody feels very good about that.

NORVAL: It isn't as if I hadn't tried. But every time they start to examine me I-I and then--

TRUDY: I know.

TRUDY:
        (in unison) The spots!
NORVAL:

Early in the exchange between Trudy and Norval, there is a cut to an exterior of the music store, where "the jeep crunches back over the scooter and pulls ahead gaily. Now another jeep drives into the shot and parks over the fallen scooter." Later, after his exchange with Trudy,

> Norval comes out, looks around in dismay for his scooter and sees it under the jeep. As he crawls down for it THE CAMERA DUCKS DOWN ON THE OTHER SIDE OF THE JEEP. We see Norval on the other side of the jeep as he tries to pull the scooter out.
>
> CUT TO:
>
> A-9   THE TOP SIDE OF THE JEEP
> Four soldiers enter it.
>
> CUT TO:
>
> A-10 NORVAL UNDER THE JEEP
> The jeep pulls away suddenly and leaves his scooter a little worse off than it was before.
>
> FADE OUT.

The Office of War Information would almost surely have questioned showing soldiers destroying civilian property in this way. The potentially offending passages were, in any case, removed. Any mention of Norval's scooter is completely eliminated in the film and all but eliminated in the final script. (A fragment from earlier script versions accidentally remains in the final script—shot A-6 on page A-3 below—which makes no sense without the preceding and succeeding shots that gave it meaning in those versions.) The symbolism of the soldiers trampling on Norval's scooter seems heavy-handed: their powerful vehicle crushes his weak one, just as a soldier will soon trample on Norval's dream of a life with Trudy. The incident thus "foreshadows" or "prefigures" what is to come later, but in a film of such fast-moving action as this there is no need for this sort of thing and, really, no place to put it.

That Norval tootles around on a motor scooter announces, or rather screams, that he is a nerd or what was then called a twerp, not just temporarily or by circumstance, but by nature. However, we know all we need to know in this respect from his first exchange with Trudy, and it will be reinforced abundantly in his stuttering, his stumbling, his pratfalls, and the "spots" he sees when he's under pressure. The scooter business amounts to overkill, especially in light of the fact that Norval changes—or our view of him does—as the film proceeds. His loyalty to Trudy, his generosity, his willingness to take risks for her and endure tribulations for her impress Trudy and audience alike. His driving a car rather than a scooter makes this transition more plausible.

The introduction of characters in the September 10 script proceeds from Kockenlocker to Norval to Trudy. Scootering through the intersection, Norval greets Officer Kockenlocker; proceeding from the intersection to the music store, he thereby leads us from Kockenlocker to Trudy. But the decision to eliminate the scooter severed this link and we are left wondering who this clowning young woman is and what her relation might be to the irascible cop at the intersection. Sturges might have suspended this information until we see the characters at home that evening, but he usually preferred to get his introductory cards on the table as soon as possible.

Also unanswered is the question of how the soldiers found their way to Trudy's record counter in the first place. Their kidding as they leave the store might suggest that Trudy is known to them already—actually or by reputation—and that is why they are there. Trudy's remark to Norval in the music store does refer to "the camps and the canteens and everything," but the role of camp follower does not accord with what we know of Trudy. She has gone to military parties before but has never before gotten married or gone to bed with a soldier—this she tells Emmy, in so many words, and we believe her. If the soldiers have sized up Trudy as "a hot number," they seem to have done so upon a first encounter, which leaves unexplained how they found her.

Sturges's odd solution to these problems, appearing in the final script for the first time, is the character of Cecelia (page A-2a). (In the fragment below, the brackets indicate a passage that does not appear in the film.)

A-2   THE THREE SOLDIERS AND CECELIA

She is a tall blonde girl in spectacles.

CECELIA: Oh, excuse me, were you looking for thome girlth?

FIRST SOLDIER: We thertainly were.

CECELIA: Well, I know of <u>one</u>.

SECOND SOLDIER: I'll bet you do, sugar.

CECELIA: (Pointing at Kockenlocker) Ith Mr. Kockenlocker's daughter.

SECOND SOLDIER: That crab?

CECELIA: The'th one of the prettieth girlth in town. The
                    workth in Rafferty'th Muthic Thore.

[FIRST SOLDIER: For heaven'th thake.

THIRD SOLDIER: (To Cecelia)
                    How about yourself, Babe?

CECELIA: I'll be there anyway.
                    (She flips a badge at him)
                    I'm one of the Thivilian Thervith Thitherth . . .
                    but it'th tho hard to thay.

THIRD SOLDIER: You thaid it.]

Cecelia is no more than a stage convenience, who actually serves two purposes: she provides expository information on the relationship of two principal characters (Trudy and Kockenlocker) and, more important, she points
one group of characters (the soldiers) in the direction of another (Trudy). Of
course a stage convenience is also a character and Cecelia's character is particularly difficult to grasp. Is Cecelia a friend of Trudy's? She does not say.
Why is she so impervious to the soldier who flirts with her? Why doesn't
Cecelia herself express anticipation or pleasure about the dance? In the final
script she says she is going as a member of a group that has sponsored the
event or agreed to help out but this is cut in the film, perhaps because the lisp
gag was wearing thin. (Sturges, like other dramatists, does his best to disguise
stage conveniences with particularizing qualities like the lisp here.) Cecelia's
remarks seem to combine envy (Trudy is sexual and I am not) and hostility
(there's what you want, you animals). She may also be said to combine the
roles of pander and voyeur. But before we are able to raise these questions,
Sturges cuts directly from Cecelia to Trudy's distorted face and body "singing" in a deep bass voice—an image striking enough to make us forget how
we got to it. (Something like Eisenstein's "montage of attractions" is at work
here.)[10] The transversion of sexual characteristics involved in Trudy's performance is more grotesque than piquant, and has the effect of wiping from our
minds any notion of her as a "hot number." Nevertheless, the soldiers sense a
willing partner, as their laughing comments on the way out of the store indicate: "So long, Trudy," "Save the first dance for me"; "Save the last one for
me," says another under his breath, which gets quite a laugh. These remarks
establish an equivalence between dancing and sex that will be seen, by film's
end, to have structured the party sequence.
    In every script version, some action following the interchange between
Trudy and Norval in the music store concludes sequence "A." In the final
script, the crushed scooter business of the September 10 script is replaced by
a return to the framing story, in which the Editor insists on reading his editorial to the Governor and Boss, both of whom—like the viewer—prefer that he
just get on with the story. The scene is boring in itself and the three passages

A curtain call from THE GREAT MCGINTY: *Akim Tamiroff as the Boss and Brian Donlevy as the Governor in the framing story of* THE MIRACLE OF MORGAN'S CREEK.

from the editorial that he reads add nothing to the film. In any case, in the next scene, Kockenlocker reads and reacts to that very editorial. In the final film, this return to the framing story is cut entirely.

The principal action of sequence "B" centers on Trudy's maneuverings to attend the dance for the departing soldiers. Her father forbids her to go so she turns to a reluctant Norval to cover for her. The newspaper editorial Kockenlocker is reading as the sequence opens—MILITARY MARRIAGES MENACE SAYS MINISTER—prompts him to what in others is thought but in him is immediate reflex aggression. (On the other hand, the cheap alliteration preferred by so many headline writers may provoke more violence than is generally realized.) Kockenlocker "bends a suspicious look" and "scowls" at his fourteen-year-old daughter, who is merely playing the piano on the other side of the room. "You wasn't thinking of getting married was you?" he says. Kockenlocker's challenge is so paranoid—mapping his present mental distress onto the reality around him—that Sturges added to the film, though not to the final script, some basis for his reaction in Emmy's behavior: she is playing "The Wedding March." To restore Kockenlocker's disequilibrium, lest he now appear too sane, the film has him get out of his chair and hover over Emmy, rather than just glare at her from across the room, as all the script ver-

"MILITARY MARRIAGES MENACE SAYS MINISTER,"
reads Kockenlocker (William Demarest) to his daughters
Trudy (Betty Hutton) and Emmy (Diana Lynn) in
THE MIRACLE OF MORGAN'S CREEK.

sions have it. This first glimpse at Kockenlocker's approach to fatherhood prepares us for his categorical refusal to allow Trudy to go to the party. It also serves to introduce us to Emmy and to establish that, unlike Trudy, she gives as good as she gets from the old man. There is little change here from the September 10 to the final script to the film, but a subtle dialogue improvement in one of Emmy's responses to her father deserves mention. In every version, her father asks her if she is thinking about getting married and Emmy responds that "anyone can think about it, it's only when you do it that it costs two dollars." In the September 10 script, the scene continues as follows:

KOCKENLOCKER: What costs two dollars? You seem to know a great
                deal about a subject far beyond your years. . . .

EMMY: Well, you brought it in . . . if you don't like it,
                leave it lay . . . it's your subject.

In the final script and film, Emmy's riposte becomes:

EMMY: It's your subject, Papa . . . You introduced it, if
                you don't like it . . . ignore it.

557

Emmy is not only precocious, she is intelligent. She sees that Kockenlocker has introduced a subject in order to beat her over the head with it. However, her command of English idiom has not yet caught up with the rapidity and subtlety of her thought. The idiom is: to change a subject one does not like; or to drop it. But to ignore a subject one does not like is to leave it hanging there, an embarrassment that will not go away. Like many a bright young person, Emmy makes things up as she goes along, which sometimes leaves her out on a limb, having to come up with a word or phrase that finishes her thought. As this particular limb nears its end, Emmy continues to return her father's stare, and says, "if you don't like it . . . [pause, then with a shrug] ignore it."

Another slight but telling change occurs when Trudy, having been grounded, blurts out "I wish Mama was here" (page 9). In the September 10 script, Kockenlocker replies, "So do I, but she ain't." In the final script he says, "So do I . . . believe me, but she ain't [Sturges's underlining]." In the film Demarest turns the line in a different direction. Instead of leaning on "believe me," he says the line as a whole, almost to himself, with eyes lowered, like a quick prayer of remembrance. This is our first glimpse of a human side to Kockenlocker. We may even suppose for the moment that his personality has been shaped by his loneliness and his dual parent role—"your father and mother combined"—for which he may dimly sense he is ill-equipped.

The setting for shot B-9 of the final script, "NORVAL ON THE FRONT PORCH OF THE JOHNSON HOUSE," has been changed from what is in the September 10 script. In the September version this shot, which in both scripts constitutes an entire scene, is identified as "NORVAL ON THE FRONT PORCH OF HIS HOUSE." The woman Norval talks to is not Mrs. Johnson, the lawyer's wife, but his own mother. In the final script and film, Mrs. Johnson and her husband rent a room in their house to Norval. Although Mrs. Johnson is not Norval's mother, she is so sympathetically concerned with his problems that she seems quite motherly. Indeed the dialogue between the two characters changes little from the September 10 to the final script—"Norval" substituting for "dear" in Mrs. Johnson's speech, but Norval calling both women "Ma'am." In the September 10 script Norval hurriedly kisses his mother good-bye not once but—evidence of his distraction—three times. In the final script and film, he kisses Mrs. Johnson good-bye only once—surely enough for a landlady—which reinforces the maternal sense that still hangs over the scene. Indeed we are not sure that Norval is an orphan until his talk with Trudy a short time later:

TRUDY: They didn't call off that military dance, Papa just called it
          off as far as I was concerned.

NORVAL: Oh . . . he did? Well, he probably had a good reason . . .
          That's what parents are for . . . to listen to their advice . . .
          That's why I always missed losing my parents.

[Later in the scene, concerning the soldiers coming to the dance:]

TRUDY: (W)e can't send them off maybe to be killed in the rockets [*sic*] red glare . . . bombs bursting in air . . . without anybody even to say goodbye to them, can we?

NORVAL: They've probably got their families.

TRUDY: Well, even if they have, they ought to have girls and dancing and . . . how about those who haven't got any families? How about the orphans? Who says goodbye to them? You ought to know about them.

NORVAL: The superintendent probably goes down from the asylum . . . for old times' sake.

TRUDY: Norval, I think you're perfectly heartless . . .

It is ironic that Trudy, who is bulldozing Norval in this scene—even using his orphanhood against him—here accuses him of heartlessness. Sturges's decision to make Norval an orphan probably had more to do with dramatic economy than anything else. If he had parents, surely they would be hovering around when he returns with Trudy the morning after the military party, as well as when he is in jail, when he leaves for six months to find Ratzkiwatzki, when he returns to Morgan's Creek at Christmas time, when he is jailed again, and so on. It would have slowed the pace of the film enormously if the reactions of an additional couple of characters had to be factored into each of these situations.

The script and film's attitude toward Norval's orphanhood, once it's there, is a more complex question. On the one hand, it should increase our sympathy for Norval, and to some degree it does; on the other hand, it undermines whatever social and psychological footing the character had, casting him further adrift and rendering him even more hapless than before, and perhaps even more a comic figure than he would otherwise be, at least in the film's early stages. Paradoxically, the film seems sympathetic and lampooning in approximately equal measure.[11] However, the oddest puzzle has to do with what Norval actually says on the subject to Trudy: "I always missed losing my parents." Is this humor, introduced by Sturges to deflect the potential sadness of Norval's orphanhood? Or is it to be read as a revealing slip of Norval's tongue and/or of Sturges's pen? Literally speaking, one can only miss losing one's parents if they are still alive. To misspeak oneself in this way perhaps suggests an unconscious fantasy that one would be better off in some way if one were free of one's parents. For an orphan figure to say this makes no sense—unless that figure has somehow been unconsciously fused with another.

The most crucial part of sequence "C" has to do with the presentation of the military party, which is the mainspring of *Miracle*'s plot. The description of the party itself underwent very few changes between the September 10 script and the December 10 final script (pages 17–19). In the September 10 script "THE SOLDIER" makes his provocative suggestion only once:

Say, I've got a great idea.

A GIRL

What:

THE SOLDIER

Let's all get married.

In the final script he makes it three times: first in the church basement, then at the country club, and finally at the roadhouse, by which time he says "Shay" for "say" and "Lesh" for "Let's." In the film the soldier makes the suggestion in the church basement, but at the country club he only gets as far as, "Say, I've got a great idea," and by the time the group is at the roadhouse, the line has been eliminated.

The issue of liquor consumption at the party became a huge one for the censors, not only where the soldiers were concerned but more important, for obvious reasons, as regarded Trudy. In the church basement phase of the party, both scripts specify lemonade without sugar as refreshment, sugar being one of the things that was rationed during wartime. Sturges comments, "The lemonade is so sour they look as if they were whistling," but the face Trudy makes might also suggest her reaction to an alcohol additive. ("Spiking" the punch on such occasions was virtually a soldierly duty.) In any case, the fact that alcohol is being consumed is unmistakable at the country club where a wealthy member, himself drunk in the film, orders champagne for everybody. (He is played by Jack Norton, the Sturges repertory company's perpetual drunk.) The party then moves on to a roadhouse, the kind of place that is virtually synonymous with liquor consumption, not to mention steamy dancing and sex in the environs.

That sequence "C" never describes Trudy herself as drinking was not enough for the censors. On October 21, 1942—the first day of *Miracle*'s shooting—Joseph I. Breen of the Hays Office sent Paramount a seven-page, single-spaced letter with objections and suggestions for corrections. Breen had apparently communicated on October 20 directly with Buddy DeSylva or, more likely, with Luigi Luraschi, Paramount's in-house censorship expert and liaison with the Hays Office. In any case, DeSylva wrote Sturges on the twenty-first:

We are all right, according to Breen, up til the time that Hutton goes on the party. The scene in the Country Club must be developed as follows: Civilian buys champagne. Hutton refuses champagne--she never drinks. In some comedy way she must be hit on the head and protests, when put on her feet, that she is perfectly all right. When someone is introduced to her she gives a different name than her own. Another girl on the party suggests that they all get married as before, but Hutton is definitely in a daze. This avoids the Hays' objection of a drunken marriage and must be done in this way.

She is consequently not drunk on her arrival at the theatre and of course not drunk on her arrival at the house. Both these scenes must be rewritten and approved as I never liked them anyway.

Breen's memo in fact said, "We understand from our discussion of yesterday that Trudy will, at no time, be shown to be drunk, nor will there be any reference to the fact that she was drunk. It is acceptable to indicate that she, along with others, did drink some champagne, but she should not be shown drunk." That is, Breen himself was less categorical than DeSylva and, unlike the latter, had no personal axes to grind. It appears that DeSylva took the opportunity to assert his own authority over Sturges, probably a consequence of battles the two fought over *Triumph over Pain/The Great Moment,* a film which DeSylva seems never to have wanted to make in the first place.

In any case, this was a battle Sturges knew he could not win so he added the incident in which Trudy bumps her head on the ceiling while jitterbugging at the roadhouse (page 18). (During shooting it was decided it would look more plausible if she hit her head on a light-reflecting globe.) Both the Hays Office and DeSylva evidently believed the changes would solve their problems. There is no record of what Sturges thought of all this. It can be argued that not very much was accomplished by the head-banging ruse. That Trudy hits her head on a low-lying object does not necessarily mean that she was not drunk when she did so. (Her exuberance on the party and her banging up Norval's car tell their own story.) If she has not touched a drop, moreover, then her dreamy ecstasy when she picks up Norval must have some other source. Not the least fascination of *Miracle,* of the myth that it at once happens on and creates, is that censorial pressure on any of its elements that are deemed troublesome brings closer to the surface other, even more forbidden ones.

The three-stage military party is far more important to the film than the two pages devoted to it in the final script suggest (pages 17–18). This is one of the rare cases in Sturges in which the dialogue of an extended passage is much less important than the visual realization of its described action; another such instance is the tour of the "lower depths" by Sullivan and The Girl in *Sullivan's Travels.* In both cases Sturges changed the script during shooting, as he often did. The more interesting point, however, is how sketchy these descriptions are in both scripts—little more than balloons to be filled in on the set.

The immediate challenge in shooting the military party was to show all that censorship allowed yet not rule out everything that the viewer could imagine or project about how Trudy got pregnant. First-time viewers no doubt watch the film differently from repeat viewers. Knowing how the film turns out, one tends to pay a different kind of attention to the early part of the film and especially to the party sequence. One tries to spot a possible Ratzkiwatzki but Trudy is shown with so many men that other possibilities, such as that of Trudy's multiple lovers, are also entertained, at least unconsciously.

*Trudy (Betty Hutton) and friends in a publicity still of
the party scene from THE MIRACLE OF MORGAN'S CREEK.*

Even in its initial (January 1944) release, says James Curtis, "*Miracle* drew
a tremendous amount of repeat business, as its defenders and champions
brought their friends to see it."[12]

The passage begins with a dissolve from Norval going into the movie theater to a scene of assorted soldiers and girls, including Trudy, walking down
the steps to a church basement. The camera turns to reveal, through a lattice-
work of windows, the party under way inside, Trudy's arrival, and her beginning to dance. There is a sudden cut inside to a decidedly unglamorous
woman vigorously playing a harp in front of a small, middle-aged women's
swing band. (There are some male members also.) After a cut to the dancing
young people, there is a sudden cut to another female band member, over-
dressed and overweight, who is playing jazz trombone with even more gusto.
Moreover, the sound track for each shot is "sweetened" to emphasize the sound
of the instrument being played, so both aurally and visually the "montage of
attractions" continues. Dancing is the primary activity shown in the church
basement, as it is later at the country club and the roadhouse. In the church
basement Trudy is shown dancing with five GIs, two of whose faces we do
not see, then a stocky fellow who sings (badly) in her ear, then a tall, handsome fellow whom she seems to like, and finally a bouncy little guy who
seems to amuse her. The last three, each of whom we will see again in the

shots of Norval's car, comprise a round robin during one dance number, the tall fellow cutting in on the singer and the short guy cutting in on him. There is a dissolve to a lemonade bowl and a cut to Trudy and the little guy taking a break for a glass of the sour stuff. This is followed by a shot of the dance floor, which dissolves to a shot of Trudy driving Norval's car packed with girls and soldiers, all of them singing "Row, Row, Row Your Boat." From this shot there is a dissolve to a large group of soldiers and girls dancing at the country club. After the "champagne for everyone" bit, we see Trudy dancing in turn with four soldiers—who, again, cut in rapidly on one another—none of whom we have seen before. Again a shot of the dance floor dissolves to what seems to be the identical shot of Trudy driving Norval's car packed with soldiers and girls singing "Row, Row, Row Your Boat." This shot dissolves in turn to a shot of the dance floor at the roadhouse, a rotating, light-reflecting chandelier at the center. Following this shot, there is a shot of the legs of the jitterbugging couples. Sturges cuts back several times to this shot, which emphasizes a woman's legs in low heels without nylons performing an intricate step in the foreground. In one of these shots the fishnet-stockinged legs of a cocktail waitress walk by. Then we see Trudy dancing again with one of the four soldiers we saw her with at the country club. When he does a lift-up step, she bangs her head on the chandelier and crumples to the floor. The soldier stoops to help her up and she seems to be all right. The shot in which they continue dancing is followed by a long shot of the dance floor and this dissolves to a shot of Norval waiting for Trudy in front of the movie theater. He rubs his behind (sore from watching three movies), watches a milk wagon go by, and looks at his watch. He curls up on the bench to sleep and there is a dissolve to Trudy driving up in his wrecked car.

What exactly does "Let's all get married" mean? In the final script, the increasingly tipsy soldier announces his idea in the church basement, at the country club, and at the roadhouse, by which time at least some of the people at the party may be willing to try it—whatever it is. What are we to make of Trudy's dancing with four soldiers in the church basement and with four more at the country club, especially given the film's equivalence—culturally overdetermined—between dancing and sex. What are we to make in this respect of the two sets of three soldiers each cutting in to dance with Trudy in rapid succession in the church basement and at the country club? Or that "Row, Row, Row Your Boat" is a song that requires each singer to come in at a different point? For that matter, what are we to make of Trudy's dancing with only one soldier at the roadhouse, which is also where she presumably loses her memory. Is he at long last Ratzkiwatzki?

The emphasis of the military party sequence is not on the men but on Trudy. Norval says to Trudy before she goes to the party, "You're not the only dame in town, you know." Of course Trudy is insulted by this, but the fact is that everyone in the film, including Trudy herself, acts precisely as if she *is* the only woman in town. The soldiers are looking for girls and Cecelia says,

"Well, I know of *one*." A throng of soldiers crowds around and attends Trudy at the music store as though other women were not to be found in every other store and on every street in town. Trudy herself feels personally obligated—impersonally obligated?—to attend the military party and will do whatever is necessary to be there. No one else but she will do for this particular job. At the party itself, the soldiers are lined up to cut in for a few moments of dancing with Trudy. In the final script, when Trudy hits her head, "a boy," who is, like all the other males present, a nameless soldier, praises Trudy's military spirit—"we don't know when we're licked"—and asks Trudy her name.

> Trudy looks at him vaguely, rubs her head.
>
> A GIRL: (Slightly squiffed)
> Don't give your right name.

At this point the tipsy soldier says, "Lesh all get married," which ends the military party sequence, since it is followed by a cut back to Norval at the movie theater. Anonymity seems to be necessary for all the participants in the group marriage. But at the level of the symbolic, Trudy's loss of her name and her memory is also her promotion from individual character to mythic figure—the bride of the armed forces perhaps. What she returns to the armed forces is precisely its regeneration—six boys.

The balance of sequence "C" shows that the September 10 script, written before the project was reviewed by the censors, is freer than the final script in a number of particulars—for instance, the way in which Trudy is shown arriving back at the theater in Norval's car. Thus, in the September 10 script, "Norval's car appears zigzagging. It seems to be following itself in a snake dance." Cut to Trudy at the wheel: "She tries to focus on her watch but can't quite make it." Cut to the car coming toward us down the street: "It makes a quick turn into the theater lobby and stops with a bang against the ticket kiosk." Trudy is described, quite plausibly, as "slightly swacked"; she describes her first encounter with champagne: "It's just like seven up . . . with something added . . . then you rise up and fly away . . . right over the trees and everything . . . you shoulda seen your car."

Despite the intervention of the censors, the final script is better than its predecessor in almost every respect; the dialogue is far more polished and the lines are "pointed" in the best Sturges manner. In the shooting process, Sturges improved his script even further by making a series of judicious cuts—for instance, the scene between Cecelia and her mother (page 25); Trudy and Emmy's discussion of their relatives (pages 27–29); and the church scene that ends sequence "C" (pages 31–32). Oddly enough, as noted above, this last cut was stipulated by the censors.

Sequence "D" begins, presumably some weeks later, with Trudy's visit to a doctor who confirms that she is pregnant. Then Trudy rejoins Emmy in the

"You shouldn't have kept me out so late!" says Trudy
(Betty Hutton) to Norval (Eddie Bracken) in
THE MIRACLE OF MORGAN'S CREEK.

doctor's outer office and "almost resentfully" tells her sister the news. After the two snuffle for a while, Emmy suggests they see Mr. Johnson, the lawyer, "to find out if you're really married." Trudy replies: "You're kind of hard to convince, aren't you?" This remark conveys her own sense of morality. In her mind, if she's pregnant now, she *must* have been married then no matter how impaired her judgment may have been. The remark may also be read, however, as a deconstruction of the censor's requirement that sexual intimacy and, of course, any pregnancy must follow marriage. If Trudy is pregnant, she must have been married is also the logic of censorship. Indeed the film as a whole may be read as a search for the censor-required marriage, and hence the groom, that will validate the project and save it from suppression. That search failing, only a miracle can save the film. The birth of sextuplets is that miracle, mooting or transcending censorial impasses and impossibilities at all levels. If, mythically speaking, Trudy transcends her individuality to become the bride of the armed forces, then the true source of her agony is to become an individual again and to carry her shame through small-town existence. Only the miraculous birth catapults her again—through the nexus of

Trudy (Betty Hutton) imagines herself "in the situation" in a publicity still, never used, for THE MIRACLE OF MORGAN'S CREEK.

international fame—to transcendence. The mythic power of motherhood itself, which is probably celebrated by every culture in the world, is also involved here. Sturges's more narrow notion of a "black nativity" was the project's generative idea. Setting the births at Christmas and placing the exiled Kockenlockers in a "little farmhouse in the snow," with a cow wandering in the kitchen, makes this explicit. Kockenlocker says to Trudy—"All right, it's almost Christmas . . . where was he born . . . in a cow shed!" This is a moment in which Sturges's sentimentality and cynicism, sincerity and subversion run together along the edge of a knife's blade. A black—that is to say, blasphemous—nativity story in fact regenerates the tradition inverted. However, this is not true of the banalization of a tradition, to which Kockenlocker's speech comes close.

Symbolically, Trudy pays back her debt to the armed forces by giving birth to a whole squad of boys. Reproduction of the military, and of the workforce generally, is the mission of the family under capitalism and other total systems. *The Miracle of Morgan's Creek* subtly ridicules this state of affairs. It is quite the opposite of the serious treatment of the theme by John Ford in *Fort Apache* (1948), in which, at the end of the film, an infant son is admiringly given his place in the tradition and continuity of the cavalry when his parents name him after soldiers of three generations (Michael Thursday York O'Rourke).

Following the sisters' visit to the lawyer, Emmy walks Trudy back to the music store. This entails their walking through town and Sturges's following them—in a single long take—with a "trucking shot." This is the conversation (pages 36–37) in which Emmy suggests for the first time that Trudy solve her problem by marrying Norval, and it ends sequence "D."

When sequence "E" begins, Norval is having dinner at the Kockenlockers. The film includes Kockenlocker's disquisition on daughters from the final script but cuts the end of the conversation, which concerns sons (pages 38–39). Trudy and Norval then go out on the front porch to talk. Their conversation, which the film divides into three parts, covers ten script pages. The first part (pages 39–41) comprises Trudy's hints to Norval that he propose marriage. As he gradually comprehends her meaning and thereby grasps the opportunity that may be his, Norval's stutter gets increasingly worse, his knees become more and more weak, and so on. When he does finally blurt out, "Trudy, will you marry me?" she says, "Norval, this is so sudden!" The script calls for no formal break of any kind after her line. After somehow "recovering himself," as the script describes it, Norval delivers, in greatly calmer fashion, a long speech. In filming, Sturges had Norval fall off the porch after his proposal and Trudy's exclamation. (Kockenlocker rushes out to ask, "What's going on here?") The porch business provides a natural break between the proposal and the second phase of Trudy's and Norval's conversation. The state of panic that the decision causes in Norval could hardly have subsided as quickly as the script indicates, but a small physical trauma serves nicely to shake it out of him.

When he climbs back onto the porch, Norval is much calmer and delivers a long monologue (pages 41–42) that begins, "What do you mean it's so sudden?" in which he reviews at length his devotion to Trudy since early childhood. By the time he finishes Trudy is sobbing and bursts out loudly, "I can't

Three gazes ensnare the offscreen Norval: Betty Hutton, William Demarest, and Diana Lynn in THE MIRACLE OF MORGAN'S CREEK.

do it to you, Norval." Norval asks what it is she can't do to him and—earlier than in the script—Kockenlocker comes running out again to demand of Norval what he's done to his daughter. With that, Kockenlocker thrusts the pair unceremoniously from the porch and onto the sidewalk.

Rather than get in Norval's car, as the final script specifies, Trudy and Norval have the balance of their conversation while walking through town. (This transition is simpler and allows page 44 and half of page 45 to be cut.) The series of shocks that Norval will undergo has just begun. Having the rest of the conversation take place in his car—the final script calls for a collision and several near misses (pages 45–49)—would distract the viewer from the reactions of the characters and impede the dynamic of their interaction. This would be particularly unfortunate because that conversation is an extremely clever piece of dialogue writing and construction.

All that is going on in the scene is that Trudy is filling Norval in on various aspects of her marital situation and physical condition—facts that the audience already knows. One has viewed scenes like this in countless plays and films, but very few indeed are as good as this. Norval's incomprehension of what Trudy is saying as she works up to, and makes, each of her revelations is both in character and very funny. Those revelations themselves take the form of a series of statements by Trudy, each of which Norval repeats first calmly then, when its meaning sinks in, apoplectically:

Trudy is married.
She was married the night she was out with Norval.
She does not know whom she married.
How does she know she was married? Trudy indicates by her expression how she knows. (She is pregnant.)
Who is Trudy's father going to blame? Again—this time by pointing to himself—Norval understands the answer without Trudy's having to speak.

All but the first of these bombshells causes Norval to complain of "the spots," the result of his high blood pressure, which is what has kept him out of the army. At the realization of who Trudy's father will blame, the film has Norval say, "THE SPOTS," which the script prints in capital letters, and Trudy, equally distraught, says she can almost see them herself. Just as the script indicates (page 49), the film dissolves from Trudy's line—"Norval, you'd better take me home"—to a shot of Trudy coming alone through the door of her house. Trudy tells Emmy she couldn't go through with their plot and has, instead, told Norval everything. Emmy is at first censorious, saying, "you ought to have your brains counted" but the two end up sobbing, as before, as sequence "E" ends.

Sequences "F" and "G" are transitional in nature. In that they take place entirely in Morgan's Creek, they belong with sequences "A" through "E" as the presentation of the characters' town life before the attempted wedding of sequence "H" involves them—irreversibly—in the larger world outside. Sequences "J," "K," and "L" (the final sequences) trace the consequences of the failed wedding to the end of the film. Sequences "F" and "G" may also be regarded as belonging to the final sequences because in them Trudy and Norval decide upon and prepare for the wedding attempt.

In sequence "F," various pressures are brought to bear on Norval to marry Trudy, with whom, in the eyes of the town, he was out all night after the farewell-to-the-boys party. Norval is eager to marry Trudy in any case, but she declines since, in her mind, she is already married and "I can't keep on marrying people . . . no matter how sweet they are." At the end of sequence "F," Norval hatches his plan to impersonate Ratzkiwatzki: "It's f-f-fool-proof and almost legal, Trudy. And when we get through you can divorce that gink and marry me." In the brief sequence "G," Norval buys a ring and a bouquet and an old World War I uniform—the only one he can find—and in the evening he and Trudy pretend to go to the movies, intending instead to cross the state line and get married. Trudy and Emmy, who is in on the plan, raise Kockenlocker's suspicions by their tearful farewells. "What's all this goodbyeing to see a couple of bum features?" he demands. As mentioned, sequence "H" presents the attempted wedding and the beginnings of the uproar that follows. Sequences "J," "K," and "L" move through a few ups and a great many downs to the delirium of the film's ending. It took Sturges six attempts—including the September 11 story, the final script, and the film itself—to draft a sequence "H" that he found satisfactory. Surely, the presentation of the failed wedding and its chaotic aftermath was difficult to achieve. There was also a bewildering number of ways to proceed, as Sturges's successive drafts show. But there were larger issues as well. The emergence of the private story of Trudy and Norval (sequences "A"–"G") into the public sphere (sequences "H"–"L") is, by far, the most important transition in the film. Because the two halves of the film are aligned here, the transition from private to public spheres is a kind of seam. Sturges devoted extraordinary efforts to join the two halves of the film in such a way that the stitching did not show. This was absolutely necessary if the extraordinary momentum of the first part of the film was to be sustained and, indeed, accelerated until it seemed all but out of control.

Since accomplishing this transition was the principal structural problem of Sturges's revision process, it is useful to examine in considerable detail his various versions of this part of the film. Such a consideration will also be helpful in tracing sequence "H" through sequence "L," which is the conclusion of the film. In the final script, as noted above, Norval's idea for the false wedding, and the process that leads to it, takes place in sequence "F" and his preparations for the departure take place in sequence "G." In consequence, these two sequences will be considered in relation to sequences "H" through "L."

Our examination of the versions of the false wedding and the events that followed it begins with the September 11 story. The story may not have been useful to Sturges but it is useful to us. It shows that Sturges knew precisely where his script drafts were headed but that, especially regarding the wedding and its aftermath, he did not know how to get there. In the story, Norval and Trudy cross the state line, get married—using the names of Ignatz Ratzkiwatzki and Gertrude Kockenlocker—and return home safely. Their evasiveness about where they have been leads, a few days later, to the little scene in which Kockenlocker talks with Norval while he cleans his shotgun. Norval says he wants to marry Trudy but that she won't have him, at least not yet. Brought into the scene, Trudy admits she is already married to a man named Ratzkiwatzki, but she doesn't know who or where he is. Kockenlocker vows he will find him. Eventually Ratzkiwatzki is found . . . in the person of Norval, "who is clapped into jail for perjury, the Mann Act, and impersonating a US soldier." While Norval lingers in jail, the Kockenlockers leave town, shamed by Trudy's pregnancy. "Everything is very lousy," Sturges says, until Trudy gives birth to sextuplets, an event that transforms everything.

Among the difficulties of the September 11 story is that the drama moves by fits and starts, when it should accelerate—dizzyingly if possible—toward its climax. Instead, the drama of the phony marriage is followed by a return to complete normality, as though nothing had happened. (Since their scheme has apparently worked, one expects Trudy and Norval to get on with the next phase of their plan—a divorce or annulment from Ratzkiwatzki and, presumably, remarriage to each other.) It is only the shotgun scene that starts the story up again by causing Trudy to admit to her father that she is already married. (Might she not say instead, truthfully, that she and Norval do plan to marry?) As a result, Kockenlocker pursues Ratzkiwatzki only to find that he is Norval, who is thrown in jail. Who arrests Norval is unclear, but Kockenlocker's intervention might have been avoided altogether if Trudy or Norval had told him about her pregnancy and their marriage-divorce-remarriage scheme—which makes the finding of the actual Ratzkiwatzki an embarrassment. Even were Kockenlocker not told the whole truth, he might have backed off once Norval, under any name, is shown to be married to Trudy. Otherwise he is cutting his daughter's throat—and his own. In any case, once in jail, Norval just sits there for seven or eight months until Trudy has her sextuplets. The deus ex machine descends on a flaccid scene.

In the September 11 story Norval has devised the false marriage idea to extricate Trudy from her dilemma and to make possible their own marriage. Kockenlocker stages a shotgun scene with Norval to convince him to marry Trudy because, having been out with her so much and so late, "it would look very bad if he didn't." One might say that in the September 11 story both characters act on their own judgment. In the September 10 script this is not so. That script—and all later versions—backs the chain of causes that leads to the phony marriage attempt up to the beginning of sequence "F." The first link in that causal chain is Mr. Tuerck, the president of the First National Bank. He informs Norval, who is a teller in the bank, that coming home early in the morning, drunk, while fathers fire off shotguns, may be none of his business, but it is the bank's business (page 52). (In the script's sequence "C," Kockenlocker greets the returning couple, "leaning against a shotgun," which later accidentally fires twice.) Having planted a bug in Norval's ear, Tuerck proceeds to plant another in Kockenlocker's, as the latter directs the town's version of rush hour traffic: "I heard a rumor one of your daughters was going to get married, any truth in it?" Next we see Norval going from the bank to Mr. Rafferty's music store where he meets Trudy and then walks her home. Kockenlocker, encountering them on his own way home, expresses a wish to have a little talk with Norval. While Trudy walks on ahead, Kockenlocker begins, "There's getting to be quite a little talk in the town," but he comes quickly to his main point: "When are you and Trudy getting hitched?" Norval answers that he wants to but Trudy won't have him. Kockenlocker gives him three days to change her mind or he will accept for her. Thus it is Kockenlocker's pressure that leads Norval and Trudy to their phony marriage plan. In all versions subsequent to the September 10 script, Kockenlocker's three-day deadline is dropped and his "little talk" with Norval takes place not on the couple's walk home but once the couple has arrived at the Kockenlocker's gate. There Kockenlocker, who is cleaning his six-shooter, calls

Norval to the porch. The final script retains this plot line with a few minor changes. (See pages 52–53 and 62–70.)

In the September 10 script, Sturges has fixed another problem one finds in the September 11 story. In this script (and in all later versions), Norval mistakenly signs his own name on the marriage certificate. When the justice of the peace sees this, he holds Norval at gunpoint while he calls the MPs, the county sheriff, and the F.B.I. Sturges cuts at this point to brief scenes of a pair of men from each agency getting into a car and driving away. He also shows the arrival of each of the groups at the motel where the justice of the peace is still holding Norval at gunpoint. Once all the officials have arrived, their squabble over jurisdiction degenerates into a fistfight. This allows Trudy and Norval to escape out a window and make a run for it in Norval's car. Trudy drives, so that Norval can take off his uniform and throw it out the window. A shot of the road behind them, however, shows all of the interested agencies in hot pursuit. A B.Y.M. (Brilliant Young Man) from the F.B.I. stops to pick up Norval's soldier hat before proceeding. Trudy and Norval pull off on a side road and watch, astounded, as the party of cars goes by. They find another motel and check into it just before their pursuers appear at the desk asking questions. A constable and the motel manager then appear at the motel room door announcing their intention to arrest the young pair. A dissolve from the door takes us back to Kockenlocker and Emmy on their front porch as the telephone rings. Kockenlocker, who is cleaning his gun yet again, asks Emmy, who is playing the piano, to answer the phone. "If it's the widow, I ain't in," he says as an afterthought.

> Suddenly Emmy comes out on the front porch. She is crying silently.
>
> KOCKENLOCKER: S'matter now?
>
> EMMY: (Through her tears)
> T-t-rudy.
> (She can't go on.)
>
> KOCKENLOCKER: (Leaping to his feet)
> What happened?
>
> EMMY: She's in jail . . . They're both in jail . . .
>
> KOCKENLOCKER: What has that fish-head done this time?

Kockenlocker gets on the phone and demands to know what the charge is. He is told that Trudy has not been charged, that "they're just holding her." As for "Razzlewhatzki," whom he later calls "Razzledazzle," Kockenlocker says he's never heard of him. Emmy, of course, knows that Ratzkiwatzki is Norval. Kockenlocker asks what the couple was doing in the county seat, and when the sheriff on the other end answers him, he "bellows into the telephone: A MOTEL, A MOTEL! What do you mean, you found them in a motel?" But, given the gravity of the situation, he soon moderates his tone.

KOCKENLOCKER: How much bail do you want for that . . .
Razzledazzle . . . Make it low, will you? The
whole thing is some kind of a mistake . . . just
harmless kids . . . you know.
(Then to Emmy)
Get your hat.
(Now indignantly into the telephone)
Five thousand dollars! What are you talking
about? Who do you think you caught . . . Hitler?
I'll be right over . . . if my tires hold out.
(He hangs up. Now he turns to Emmy)
You call Norval's mother and tell her we'll take
her with us, see?

EMMY: Couldn't you tell her?

KOCKENLOCKER: (Rough with emotion)
No, I could not . . . I got enough to worry about
without worrying whether <u>her</u> heart is broken . . .
Daughters . . . haha.

FADE OUT:

Considered in retrospect, the rewrites of October 8, 9, and 10 may be
regarded as a transitional stage on the way to the final script and film. The
changes they make in the last sixteen pages of the September script are for
the most part minor. A number of them make the script racier than before.
Perhaps Sturges was enjoying himself, knowing he was going to face trouble
with the censors. For the earlier sign, "Justice of the Peace. Marriages performed at all Hours," Sturges now substituted "The Honeymoon Motel – Hot
and Cold Running Water – Marriages Performed At Any Hour – See Us First
. . . Satisfaction guaranteed." When Trudy and Norval appear at the motel
desk, the justice of the peace, who is reading his newspaper and listening to
boogie woogie music in the back room, asks his wife, "They want a room or
a marriage?" Sally, a friend of the justice's wife, summoned to witness the
wedding, asks—as she does in the September 10 script—"Is she [Trudy]
pretty?" However, in this version the justice's wife replies, "They're always
pretty in that pink light." After the shots of men from the various agencies
jumping into their cars, the October 8–10 rewrites add a brief scene back at
the motel in which Sally sympathizes with Trudy, calling her a "poor misguided lamb." Trudy replies to Sally, "Why don't you give yourself up?"
which leads the justice's wife to observe: "They never want to be saved . . .
I've seen it time and time again."

However, the most important changes in the October 8–10 version had to
do with the squabbling MPs, Sheriff, State Police, and F.B.I. men. They still
dispute who has jurisdiction over Norval, but they do not physically fight

and, presumably for this reason, Trudy and Norval do not have the opportunity to escape. The jurisdictional stalemate is now resolved in a new way:

H-32   NORVAL AND TRUDY IN THE MIDDLE OF THE
       ARGUING MASS

       Norval is being held by the MPs, the Sheriff, the State Police
       and the FBI men, not to mention Trudy who is trying to pull him
       away from them. He is in imminent danger of being dismem-
       bered. Everybody is talking at once.

       CUT TO:

H-33   THE JUSTICE OF THE PEACE

       JUSTICE OF
       THE PEACE: (Yelling)
                         Gentlemen, gentlemen, may I make a sugges-
                         tion . . . gentlemen . . .

       THE CAMERA PANS HIM IN THE SHOT with the
       struggling mass.

       JUSTICE: (Continuing)
                         Why don't we nip over to Morgan's Creek and
                         find out whether he's a soldier or not, or a spy or
                         whatever he is . . . this is ruining my business.

Not wanting to be found out, Trudy says, "Oh, no, let's not go to Morgan's Creek . . . nobody knows him there." She even says to the MP, "Don't you let them take him . . . he's your prisoner," to which the MP replies: "You're too anxious, sister . . . you tipped your mit [sic]." Trudy starts to cry and Norval puts his arm around her, as sequence "H" ends.

As sequence "J" opens, Kockenlocker and Emmy are sitting on the porch debating whether what they hear is a tree toad or a police siren. This cut to the Kockenlocker porch occurs five pages earlier in the October 8–10 notes than it did in the September 10 script. The compression is accomplished by reducing the squabbling among the authorities and by eliminating the couple's escape by car and the chase that finally ends at another motel.

The final script, as noted above, was begun on October 14, which is the date on its cover page, and concluded on December 10. The final script made its own changes in the aftermath of the phony wedding, and some of them are surprising. For instance, it reinstates Trudy and Norval's escape from the justice of the peace (pages 77–99). As before, the justice of the peace holds Trudy and Norval at gunpoint while he waits for the representatives of the various agencies he has summoned to arrive. As "we hear the ROAR of the Jeep outside and a distant siren," the justice crosses to the door to let them in and Trudy and Norval "back into the corner." Trudy calls Norval's attention "to the light switch which is near them and the window beside it." She reaches

574

for the switch and plunges the room into darkness. The justice fires in the air, but Trudy and Norval are nowhere to be found.

Two M.P.'s are getting out, drawing their guns. We hear a SHOT from the inside and two women screaming. The State Police arrive on moaning motorcycles, immediately followed by the sheriff and Pete, the U.S. Marshal and the Secret Service men. We hear another SHOT and more SCREAMS from inside.

THE SHERIFF: Draw your gun, Pete.

FIRST M.P.:   There's a riot inside.

Pete immediately fires his gun twice in the air.

SHERIFF: Not out here.

FIRST M.P.:   Follow me, men.

They drive up the stairs. As they do so, THE CAMERA PANS over onto Trudy and Norval who run around the side of the house, jump into a car and beat it. (page 96)

Norval drives away but Trudy takes over the wheel so Norval can go to the back of the car to change out of his uniform. When he finds that his clothes are missing, he realizes they have inadvertently stolen someone else's car. Trudy, who is disturbed by this news, is informed by Norval that she is "going forty-five," evidently a high rate of speed in the forties. We then hear "the whine of a siren and the headlight of a motorcycle flickers in the back window" (page 99). There is a fade-out at this point and a fade-in on Kockenlocker and Emmy on the front porch. Before long, "flanked by State Motorcycle cops and an ever-increasing number of townspeople, the car Norval stole has just arrived." Gun in hand, the justice "gets to the street and ushers Trudy and Norval toward the Kockenlocker house" (page 101). Since Trudy and Norval are only now apprehended by the authorities, the jurisdictional debate is not renewed; it begins here for the first time. The controversy is also joined by Mr. Johnson, the town lawyer, who represents Norval, and is witnessed by a number of curious townspeople. (A second jurisdictional debate breaks out on pages 106–108, which was cut in shooting or editing.)

Precisely what is accomplished by having Norval and Trudy escape and therefore arrested twice, or by having two jurisdictional debates among the contending agencies? This is the question we might ask of the September 10 script and the final script. (The October 8–10 rewrites have one arrest and one jurisdictional debate.) The film superbly improves on all previous versions by dissolving from the justice of the peace holding a gun on Norval and Trudy (page 93) to Kockenlocker and Emmy on the front porch (page 100). As before, father and daughter hear vague sounds of sirens, which get gradually louder, until a gaggle of authorities from five agencies storm their front lawn with Norval and Trudy in tow. This eliminates the duplication of arrests and jurisdictional debates and also the futile escape of Trudy and Norval. The result is better drama: it allows the viewer to share the anticipation of Emmy and Kockenlocker as they hear noises in the night, and their astonishment at the throng that suddenly appears on their property. Had we already seen the squabbling captors—and Trudy and Norval either fleeing or not fleeing—the scene of waiting with the Kockenlockers would seem tedious and the mayhem that follows predictable and repetitious.

From this point in his work on the final script, Sturges did not have an earlier script to revise so he had to devise bridging events between the events already presented and the preordained ending that was coming. At Mr. Johnson's suggestion, Kockenlocker ends the jurisdictional debate by asserting local sovereignty and locking up Norval in the Morgan's Creek jail. He then berates Trudy for bringing disgrace on herself, her family, and Norval. All is not lost, however. Kockenlocker discloses that the justice of the peace had done him "a favor" by tearing up the marriage certificate in his presence. Emmy and Trudy groan. Trudy tells him she is going to have a baby, the circumstance of her unlocatable husband, and Norval's role in trying to help her.

Realizing what Norval has tried to do for Trudy, Kockenlocker tries in half a dozen ways, each less subtle than the one before, to convey to Norval the idea that he should escape. But Norval is too respectful—and dense—to understand the hint, let alone to take it. Trudy arrives and tells Norval to escape, but it is only when Kockenlocker suggests he search for Ratzkiwatzki—and Trudy concurs—that he agrees to escape. Norval goes into the bank to take out his money for his trip but, despite his assurances to the Kockenlockers that he knows what he's doing, the bank alarm goes off. At Kockenlocker's suggestion, Norval hurries away in Kockenlocker's old Dodge while Trudy and Emmy tie their father up and knock him unconscious to make it appear that Norval has escaped forcibly.

At this point—while Norval is painstakingly searching for Ratzkiwatzki and Trudy is slowly moving toward miraculous childbirth—we might pause to consider the film's "framing story," which is really an antiframing story. The film begins—barely before the Paramount logo has ended—with the Editor of the Morgan's Creek newspaper (Vic Potel) and Mr. Rafferty (Julius Tannen) running to the newspaper office.

THE EDITOR:	(coming to a Tom Mix stop) Hold the presses!
MR. RAFFERTY:	Hold everything.
THE EDITOR:	What'll we do next?
MR. RAFFERTY:	Call the President.
THE EDITOR:	Wouldn't he be a little hard to get?
MR. RAFFERTY:	All right, then the Governor of the State.

The film eliminates everything after "Hold everything." The Editor then says,

> Get me the state capital. I've got to talk to the Governor immediately. It's a matter of life and death.

While they are trying to get through to the Governor, the film's credits appear. After this, the connection is made and the Editor and Rafferty tell the story of the Morgan's Creek miracle to the Governor of the state (Brian Donlevy) and the Boss (Akim Tamiroff), the main characters (and actors) from Sturges's *The Great McGinty*. Many framing stories aim for distance and ironic detachment. Others provide an intimate voice and perspective from inside the story, to show the impact of its events on a sensitive participant. This framing story resembles no other in cinema; frenzied, hysterical, almost all shouting, it adds to the chaos rather than clarifies it. After the Editor and Rafferty scream at the Governor, and vice versa, the politicians demand again to know what happened and the Editor says, "What we've got, Mr. Governor is . . ." A cut to the response of the "suddenly electrified" Governor—"You got WHAT!"— covers the omission, for the viewer, of the information the Editor has conveyed. Also diverting the viewer at this point is the sudden entry of the Boss, who calls for a new dam over Morgan's Creek before he even knows what's going on there. Of course the viewer does not know what "WHAT" is until the end of the film. We know only that everyone is excited but not why. The Governor directs the Editor to "give me all the facts," and the Editor tells him that he started the whole thing by writing his midweek editorial. The Governor and Boss are furious at this digression—"He's going to tell us his life story?"—but they have no choice but to listen. In the film, the Editor continues as follows:

> And it occurred to me that the girls in the town and the soldiers around the town would make an excellent subject for my editorial.

> I was looking out the window . . . and there I saw Officer Kockenlocker, our town constable, directing traffic as usual.

The dissolve from the Editor to Kockenlocker directing traffic is, like nearly all of the film's dissolves, a rather quick one—by no means the "eight foot dissolve" called for in the script (Prologue 6). Also cut from the script are the Editor's offer to read his editorial and his listeners' quick refusals and—most interesting—the Editor's remark that the editorial in question appeared "nine months, four hours, and twenty-one minutes ago." If it has taken exactly nine months from conception to the delivery that Trudy accomplished just moments before the Editor placed his call, then Trudy must have conceived four hours and twenty minutes after the editorial appeared. Indeed, Kockenlocker quotes the editorial to an all-dressed-up Trudy when he refuses to let her go to the military party.

An early return to the framing story (pages A-4 to A-5), in which the Editor actually reads his editorial to the Governor and the Boss, was wisely cut. This means that the framing story does not come back until nearly 120 pages later (pages 125–127). Norval returns to Morgan's Creek after searching for Ratzkiwatzki for, presumably, seven or eight months. (The various script versions and the film are unclear as to how long he's been gone.) Before we see Norval's return, however, Sturges cuts back to the framing story. As this episode begins, the Governor breaks into the Editor's narrative—which has presumably been the story of the film we are watching—demanding to know whether or not Trudy is married. The Editor apologetically replies, "Nobody knows whether she's married or not." The Governor then asks where the father is and he is told that he is in jail. "I thought you said he escaped," says the Governor, who is told by the Editor that he came back and got caught again. The Governor asks when this occurred and the Editor replies,

> Yesterday. It must have been around six o'clock, I guess, because Mr. Tuerck was still in the bank for the Christmas Club and Mr. Rafferty was still in his store.

During the speech there is a dissolve to Norval pulling up to the front of the Kockenlocker house. The dissolve—which again is fairly quick—begins approximately at "It" and is concluded approximately at "Mr. Tuerck." This means that quite a few words of the speech are actually spoken over the scene from the main story that is dissolved to. Indeed Mr. Rafferty's correcting remark about the time of Norval's arrival—"It was closer to seven"—occurs well into the scene.

Norval gets out of "Kockenlocker's old Dodge" and walks up the stairs of the Kockenlocker house, which turns out to be deserted. Norval then seeks out Mr. Johnson, who tells him that Kockenlocker lost his job and that the family has moved to the country somewhere. Norval mentions to Johnson that he was "looking for someone I never found" (page 129). Although unavailing, Norval's quest is important to the film—it is necessary that someone at some point search carefully for Ratzkiwatzki. Nevertheless, the elision of Norval's search—he is the one we see leave and return—covers the more important elision of Trudy's pregnancy, which was literally unshowable in 1940s Hollywood. When we do see Trudy, she is sitting in a chair with her back to us—we occasionally see her face but never her body.

Norval seeks out Mr. Rafferty, Trudy's former boss, and is about to go with him to visit Trudy when Mr. Tuerck of the bank, seeing Norval, goes back to the bank to get a gun and makes a citizen's arrest—which puts Norval back in jail. Rafferty visits Trudy and lets her know, reluctantly, that Norval has returned and has been rejailed.

The next sequence—"L"—begins with a town council meeting in which the fate of Norval is being debated by, among others, Mr. Johnson, who wants leniency for his client, and Mr. Tuerck, who wants him punished severely.

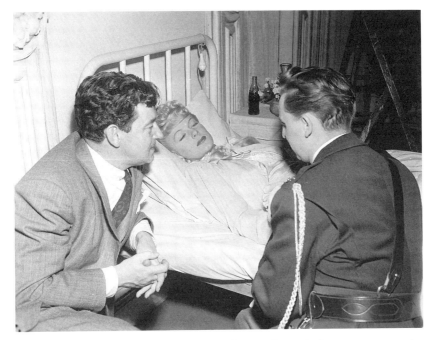

*Two proud papas in the postpartum scene that
concludes THE MIRACLE OF MORGAN'S CREEK:
Sturges, Betty Hutton, and Eddie Bracken.*

Kockenlocker and Rafferty break into the meeting to tell the assembled that
Trudy is downstairs in a car and wishes to speak to the council. She is invited
up, but Kockenlocker says the council will have to come down—"she don't
feel very good" (page 142). Just then Emmy runs up the stairs calling to her
father that Trudy is about to deliver.

In a finely dramatic scene—with low-register violin or cello sounds suggesting ticks on a clock—Trudy has her sextuplets. Needless to say this occurs offscreen, while Kockenlocker, Emmy, Rafferty, and, later, the Editor are
shown waiting in the hospital corridor. As the reader can see, the final script
notes the birth of Trudy's first boy but elides the rest. Sturges says in a note
at the bottom of page 145: "The rest of [Shot] L-16 (continuing onto page
L-8 [147]) is written, contains not one censorable line, has been sent to Mr.
DeSylva, and will be released at the proper time." Why Sturges wished to
keep his climax secret is not exactly clear. Perhaps he feared, or at least did
not wish to risk, that someone might lift the idea for inclusion in another film
before *Miracle* was released. Perhaps he wished to keep it out of the gossip
columns and newspaper reports. One recalls in this respect that Giuseppe
Verdi is said to have removed the aria "La donna mobile" from the score of
Rigoletto lest the song be leaked—and played throughout Italy—before the
opera's premiere.

579

The script's omitted section is described as the continuation of shot L-16, which, an early pan aside, is shot from the same angle—the camera pointed down "the upper hospital corridor"—as shots L-12, L-14, and L-15. What we see from this angle in L-16 is "the miserable group" of Kockenlocker, Emmy, Mr. Rafferty, and the Editor, waiting for Trudy's delivery. We also see the movements of a nurse walking and, later, running from the delivery room to a supply room where baby blankets are kept. (On one occasion the doctor runs for a blanket also.) The delivery room is located deep in the corridor and the supply room is located in the foreground. This means that the delivery team again and again hurries back and forth past "the miserable group," which is quite mystified. Despite what the script says, Sturges cuts away several times from L-16—the corridor shot—to brief insert shots. Among these are an interpolated shot of a clock on the wall, a brief dissolve to the doctor who is attending Trudy, and, when a nurse runs past holding up four fingers, a cut to a closer shot of the waiting group. What is surely the last shot of the omitted section is a later shot of the same nurse running through the corridor waving her arms like someone who has been "saved" at a revival meeting. Sturges cuts to a closer shot of the nurse for her line, "Six, all boys!"

The nurse's line is pivotal in that the project's conclusion begins here. As we shall see, there are considerable differences between the final script's conclusion and that of the film. Immediately following "Six, all boys!" the final script dissolves to:

L-17   A WESTERN UNION OPERATOR – PAST THE SHOULDER
       OF A TRAINED NURSE

       THE OPERATOR: WHAT!

       He sits down to his spider and the CAMERA WHIPS DOWN
       with him.

L-18   INSERT – THE SPIDER

       The operator's hand rattles it violently.

       DISSOLVE TO:

L-19   THE EDITOR'S OFFICE – OF A GREAT METROPOLITAN
       DAILY

       Through the partition in the back we see the city room. A boy
       runs in and hands a piece of paper to the editor. The editor does
       an enormous take-em, then files out into the city room holding
       the paper high and shouting at the top of his lungs.

       DISSOLVE TO:

L-20   THE SPIDER RATTLING AWAY

       DISSOLVE TO:

L-21   NEWSPAPER HEADLINE:

NOTE: INSERT TO BE RELEASED LATER

DISSOLVE TO:

L-22   THE SPIDER RATTLING AWAY

DISSOLVE TO:

L-23   MUSSOLINI'S OFFICE – <u>IN ROME</u>

LOW CAMERA SHOT. Some shiny boots run past us and end up in a tiny figure leaning over a great desk.

CUT TO:

L-24   MUSSOLINI READING A TELEGRAM

He slaps the desk a furious blow, then pops his fingers in his mouth and assumes an expression of pain.

L-25   THE SPIDER RATTLING AWAY

DISSOLVE TO:

L-26   HITLER'S TENT – <u>IN RUSSIA</u>

Hitler is handed a piece of paper and, as in the film, reacts apoplectically and "starts an epileptic oration." There is a dissolve to a newspaper headline, which in this case is indicated: "HITLER DEMANDS RECOUNT." Following this, there is a

SLOW DISSOLVE TO:

L-30   NORVAL – <u>IN HIS CELL</u>

He is shivering with cold. He rises and THE CAMERA PULLS BACK. He comes to the window and looks through the bars.

NORVAL: Hey . . . could somebody get me a bl-bl-blanket . . . I'm fr-freezing to death . . . Hey.

CUT TO:

L-31   <u>INT. OF THE FIRE STATION</u> – SHOOTING OUT PAST THE FIRE ENGINE

People are hurrying by, but nobody stops.

CUT TO:

L-32   NORVAL – BEHIND THE BARS

NORVAL: (Shivering)
            What's going on any-anyway?
                            (He blows on his fingers)

581

Following the brief scenes of Norval in jail, the final script cuts to the framing story. The Governor and the Boss yell orders to the Editor and Rafferty: drop the charges against Norval; cancel the charter of the banker and the justice of the peace; Norval was wearing a State Guard uniform—in fact he's commissioned as a Colonel in it; the marriage between Trudy and Norval is valid.

In the final script, as we have seen, news of the miraculous births in Morgan's Creek is flashed around the world by telegraph. No fewer than five shots are concerned with the telegraph apparatus itself. Three other shots show people reading telegrams—the editor of a large city newspaper, Mussolini, and Hitler. Moreover, by placing the newspaper headline of L-21 between two shots of an operating telegraph machine, the cutting makes clear that the news story itself is based on one or more telegrams. The film drops virtually all of this in favor of a series of newspaper headlines, many of them comic. This works better in every respect but one. In all versions, the Editor and Rafferty call the Governor immediately after the event, which explains, when telegraph is the medium in question, why he and the Boss do not already know about the miracle. However, when newspaper headlines are substituted for the telegraph, a problem arises. If newspaper accounts have appeared in various countries of the world, then why haven't the Governor and Boss already received the news? Indeed, since the Editor and Rafferty have run from the hospital to the newspaper office to call the Governor, how has there been time for newspapers to appear? Perhaps the viewer takes the newspaper headlines as gags or as momentary extensions into the future. In either case, the headlines are removed from the constraints of temporal logic. Perhaps it is simply that the passage works so well that the viewer does not think to ask these questions.

The film also eliminates the final script's scenes of Norval in jail. Showing Norval in jail accomplishes nothing and retards the film's acceleration toward its conclusion. A consequence of this omission is that we do not see Norval between his rearrest by Mr. Tuerck after his return to Morgan's Creek and his abrupt release from jail near the end of the film. At that point an ebullient, uniformed Kockenlocker, who is now chief of police, brings Norval the news of his freedom and a State Guard uniform. From the scene of Kockenlocker's appearance at the jail house until the end of the film, the final script and film tend to converge. (The film makes a number of brief, effective cuts in this part of the film also.) In script and film, Norval's bewilderment at his release and uniform—and at the thicket of reporters, photographers, and well-wishers at the hospital—is a fine comic set piece. Norval manages to back into Trudy's room and his intimate scene with the just-waking Trudy follows. He tells her he does not know why he is free or wearing a uniform; she says she does not know if she's had a boy or a girl. Norval tells her he will find out and Emmy takes him to the nursery for the revelation scene described above. When he realizes that all six babies are Trudy's—and his—Norval reverts to hysteria.

His legs become rubber, he sees spots, and he waves his finger and shakes his head at Trudy, while miming his protest of this last outrage: "No, no, no." He collapses on Trudy's bed as the rest of the throng outside enters Trudy's room and, on this final tableau of chaos, the final script and film end.

The film's most important revisions of the script we have yet to discuss. These consist in a number of trims and rearrangements that the film makes between the birth of sextuplets and Kockenlocker's appearance at the jail house. After the nurse shouts "Six! All boys," the film cuts to shots of newspapers being printed and then to a series of four shots of headlines, the last of which says "CANADA PROTESTS," with a subheadline, "'Possible but not probable,' says Premier." There is then a cut to a pared-down version of the first half of the scene with the Governor and the Boss, which includes several lines added during shooting:

THE GOVERNOR:	You mean he's still in jail, you dumb blockhead?
THE EDITOR:	Yes.
THE GOVERNOR:	Well get him out.
THE EDITOR:	But how can I Mr. Governor . . . with all those charges against him?
THE GOVERNOR:	By <u>dropping</u> the charges, you dumb cluck.
THE BOSS:	You weal head.
THE GOVERNOR:	Now get me that banker on the phone.
THE BOSS:	His charter is cancelled.
THE GOVERNOR:	And the Justice of the Peace.
THE BOSS:	His license is revoked and his motel is condemned.
THE EDITOR:	Do you want the M.P.s and the U.S. Men too?
THE GOVERNOR:	What have they got to do with it? That was a State Guard uniform.
THE BOSS:	I can see it from here.
THE GOVERNOR:	As a matter of fact he's a Colonel in it. I'm bringing him his commission tomorrow.
THE BOSS:	Retroactive as of last year . . .
THE GOVERNOR:	Go out and get him a uniform.

The Governor and the Boss have listened to the Editor for almost as long as it takes a feature-length film to run. The Editor's narration of what has happened ended, the question of what to do about it remains. At this point, the

Governor and the Boss seize control of the framing story and, barking orders and insults, make the Editor and Rafferty listen to them.

Sturges cuts at this point to a second series of newspaper headlines: a Los Angeles paper, a Russian paper, a Chinese paper, and an Italian paper. The last is followed by the scene with Mussolini mentioned above. This is followed in turn by a shot of an American newspaper announcing Mussolini's resignation—"'Enough is Sufficiency!' Screams Il Duce." This is followed by the second half of the scene with the Governor and the Boss, in which the Editor says,

	There's only one thing more, Mr. Governor: the marriage.
THE GOVERNOR:	(Roughly) What's the matter with the marriage? She's married to Norval Jones! She always has been. The guy married them, didn't he? The boy signed his right name, didn't he?
THE BOSS:	Sure.
THE EDITOR:	But he gave his name as Ratzkiwatzki.
THE GOVERNOR:	He was trying to say Jones . . . he stuttered.
THE BOSS:	What are you looking for, needles in a haystack?
THE EDITOR:	Then how about the first Ratzkiwatzki?
THE GOVERNOR:	He's annulled.
THE BOSS:	Schnook.
THE EDITOR:	Who annulled?
THE GOVERNOR:	The judge.
THE BOSS:	Retroactive . . .
THE GOVERNOR:	(to the Boss) Get (unintelligible) on the phone.
THE BOSS:	I'm getting it.
THE GOVERNOR:	He's out of the picture.
THE BOSS:	He was never in it.
THE GOVERNOR:	Now get me those guys on the phone.
THE BOSS:	Who do they think they are, anyway?
THE GOVERNOR:	Fooling with the honor of our fair-
THE BOSS:	(speaking over each other) (on two phones) Oh, hello-

Before the Governor or the Boss can finish his sentence, Sturges cuts to the brief scene of Hitler's receiving news of the birth and becoming apoplectic and the newspaper headline that follows: "HITLER DEMANDS RECOUNT."

The final script's construction is static. It goes through the entire telegraph series and then the entire scene with the Governor and the Boss and then it cuts back to Norval in jail for his deliverance. The final script divides the scene with the Governor and the Boss into two scenes and intersperses them with the headline series, which it divides into three parts. Thus its sequence is as follows: headlines I; Governor and the Boss I; headlines II; Governor and the Boss II; headlines III. The conclusion of the final script is static because it completes each scene or series before going on to the next. This leaves a dead space wherein one scene ends and another has to start up again. By rearranging these scenes and making judicious cuts, the film turns what follows the births into a masterful, even awe-inspiring comic crescendo.

The film's arrangement also redefines the Governor and the Boss themselves. By presenting all of the telegraph material first, the final script gives the Governor and the Boss enormous power over the narrative. They are truly *dei ex machina* who descend from heaven to sort out an ungodly mess. The film's arrangement projects the consequences of the miraculous birth as a whirlwind inexorably catching up and transforming everything in its path. The Governor and the Boss do not create the whirlwind; indeed, they are racing to catch it, if only to avoid being left behind.

The Governor and the Boss do not literally have the film's last word, but they do have the last word on what is perhaps the film's most troublesome element. Ratzkiwatzki, the Governor says, is "out of the picture." "He was never in it," adds the Boss (page 151). Which is more startling it is hard to say: that the film's ultimate self-reflexive statements are put in the mouths of these characters or that, perhaps for the first time in their lives, these two rascals have told the truth?

NOTES

1. How is *Ratzkiwatzki* spelled? In the September 11 story it is spelled *Ratziwatski*. This is also how it is spelled on pages 30 and 63 of the final script. However, on pages 79, 80, 87, 88, 108, 109, 121, 150, and 151 of the final script it is spelled *Ratzkiwatzki* and, to my ear, this is how it is usually pronounced in the film. (On page 60 it is spelled Ratzikiwatski, but this is surely a misprint.) Hence, for the sake of consistency, I have spelled the name *Ratzkiwatzki*.

2. See Brian Henderson, "Sturges at Work," *Film Quarterly* 39, no. 2 (Winter 1985–1986): 25–26; and Henderson, "Cartoon and Narrative in the Films of Frank Tashlin and Preston Sturges," in Andrew S. Horton, ed., *Comedy/Cinema/Theory* (Berkeley: University of California Press, 1991), 170–172.

3. Frank Kermode, *The Sense of an Ending: Studies in the Theory of Fiction* (New York: Oxford University Press, 1967).

4. The film's epilogue, held briefly on the screen, is from Shakespeare's *Twelfth Night* (II, iv): "Some men are born great, some achieve greatness, and some have greatness thrust upon them."

5. The Sturges papers in the Special Collections Department of the UCLA Graduate Research Library do not contain a dialogue continuity for *The Miracle of Morgan's Creek*. For this reason, it is impossible to know which scenes or fragments of scenes were cut before shooting and which were shot, then cut in the editing.

6. See Clayton R. Koppes and Gregory D. Black, *Hollywood Goes to War: How Politics, Profits, and Propaganda Shaped World War II Movies* (New York: Free Press, 1987), 48–328.

7. Ibid., 100–112.

8. Trudy's mime of the Crosby record and her opera rendition were either cut before shooting or shot and then cut in the editing phase. The Crosby record is not identified. In fact the singer had two hits that year, both Irving Berlin songs from the film *Holiday Inn*: "Be Careful! It's My Heart" (more Norval's lament than Trudy's), and "White Christmas." Sturges, as noted, associated *Miracle,* and hence Trudy's misbegotten deliveries, with his much-earlier-conceived "black nativity" idea. For Trudy to dream of Christmas, in the film's conscious/unconscious circuitry, is to dream of sex, perhaps of pregnancy itself; that the dream is white condenses it with her conscious desire to be respectable.

9. The Norval-Trudy dialogue in the record store, reproduced here, is taken from the film.

10. Eisenstein's theory of the montage of attractions is derived from the Petrograd-based Factory of the Eccentric Actor (FEKS), founded by Grigori Kosintsev, Leonid Trauberg, and Sergei Yutkevich. Kosintsev said on behalf of FEKS, "Life requires art that is *hyperbolically crude, dumbfounding, nerve-wracking, openly utilitarian, mechanically exact, momentary, rapid,* otherwise no one will hear, see or stop." Richard Taylor, ed. and trans., *S. M. Eisenstein: Selected Works, Volume I: Writings, 1922–1934* (London: BFI Publishing, 1988), 3. Eisenstein also borrowed the FEKS's interest in circus, from which his concept of "attractions" initially derived. Eisenstein defined attraction as "any aggressive moment in theatre . . . calculated to produce specific emotional shocks in the spectator in their proper order within the whole [work]" (*Eisenstein,* 34).

Regarding the montage of attraction in films, he said that "the American detective film and, to an even greater extent, the American comedy film (the method in its pure form) provide inexhaustible material for the study of these methods (admittedly on a purely formal level, ignoring content)" (*Eisenstein,* 44). Elsewhere he provided a list of basic premises of the method, including: "Breakdown of movement into its pseudo-primitive primary component elements for the audience—a system of shocks, rises, falls, spins, pirouettes, etc." (*Eisenstein,* 50).

11. The Victorian Era, and the Edwardian, in which Sturges himself was born, had mixed feelings about orphans: on the one hand, enormous sentimentality (Dickens), and on the other hand, perhaps as an antidote to this, satire, as in Wilde's *The Importance of Being Ernest*—"Losing both [one's] parents seems like carelessness"—and as in Gilbert and Sullivan's *The Pirates of Penzance*:

Recitative-GENERAL
Have pity on my lonely state,
I am an orphan boy!

KING and SAM	An orphan boy?
GEN.	An orphan boy!
PIRATES	How sad—an orphan boy . . .
ALL	The lonely orphan boy! Poor fellow!

Another aspect is that, in literature at least, orphans are sometimes lucky. They often end by succeeding quite famously, and of course Norval is no exception.

GEN.	And it sometimes is a useful thing To be an orphan boy.
CHORUS	It is! Hurrah for the orphan boy!

Indeed, is Norval less well-off than Woodrow in *Hail the Conquering Hero,* with his dead hero father and his mother, who worships at his father's shrine, hoping—along with the rest of the town—for another hero?

12. James Curtis, *Between Flops: A Biography of Preston Sturges* (New York: Harcourt Brace Jovanovich, 1982), 190.

*"Bye-bye;" or is it "Hello"? Betty Hutton
in an indeterminate publicity still for
THE MIRACLE OF MORGAN'S CREEK.*

APPENDIX
War Censorship of
The Miracle of Morgan's Creek

On February 18, 1943, J. H. Karp sent a night letter from New York to the studio in Hollywood:

Luraschi – War Dept. also screened MIRACLE OF MORGAN'S CREEK today and will not give approval until it hears from OWI because War Dept. slightly in doubt concerning one important aspect of picture. Therefore please straight wire when you have OWI reaction your screening this picture. War Dept. insists on elimination of approximately 4 feet of scene of soldier standing at bar with drink in hand, swaying slightly as if intoxicated. There is no talking in this footage. Will advise more exact description of footage to be eliminated when we get more details from War Department. Furthermore, War Dept. very concerned over doubt concerning paternity of children because all picture indicates is girl gets drunk on party with many soldiers, gets married and has children, but no indication as to who is father. War Dept. really would like picture to make clear that husband is father and no other soldiers involved, but perhaps if OWI approves picture we may be able to persuade War Dept. to approve picture as it is. However, you must understand that there is vigorous reaction on this point by War Dept. and they feel strongly that this aspect should be made crystal clear.

Handwritten at the bottom of the page of the night letter is the following notation, evidently added some time later: "Office of War Information saw film Friday Feb 19th and passed picture requesting elimination of 4 feet of film only in which soldier was drunk."

Some time later—probably no more than a day or two—Russell Holman sent the following undated wire (from Washington?) both to Luigi Luraschi at the studio and to J. H. Karp, who was presumably still in New York:

"Luraschi – Re MIRACLE OF MORGAN'S CREEK – Entire War Dept. Pictorial Board now has seen picture and after much vigorous discussion and argument concerning same War Dept. insists that following must be done to picture before it will approve picture which confidentially represents much less than War Dept. first demanded–

1. Re soldier drinking sequence at bar. Edge numbers given you previously for elimination this scene incorrect and War Dept. now states that scene to be eliminated begins at end of Reel 1-B with marginal number 24T23037 plus twelve frames before that number to marginal number 24T23040 plus three frames following that number, which sequence contains dialogue, "I've got an idea."

2. In Reel 1-B there are three separate sequences of Trudy and guests riding in open Ford touring car. The first sequence follows after lemonade drinking by party and is okay. The second sequence is after party leaves country club and contains much general noise and rollicking hubbub. War Dept. says this second sequence must be eliminated unless it can be made like first sequence that is more quiet and less rollicking drunkenness. War Dept. says the third sequence, which is very short and contains dialogue "We won't get home until morning," must be eliminated.

3. In sequence where Norval hunched up in corner in motion picture theatre lobby and there is crash off screen with shot of Trudy in Ford dishevelled and Ford banged up, Trudy acts drunk and Norval accuses her of being drunk. We know her condition due to blow on head but War Dept. insists this must be further clarified perhaps by insertion of line when Trudy puts hand to her head saying in effect "I must have been hit by something."

4. War Dept. insists that new short sequence be inserted to show soldiers on the morning after the all night party with Trudy. Sequence should be of three or four clean cut and fresh looking soldiers in uniforms in barracks saying in morning that they had swell time last night, but with no reference to drinking, and that now they are ready for duty and departure for war.

If above changes made War Dept. will approve picture but insist on seeing new print. Do you wish censorship print returned to studio or will you send us new print. If you send new print it will save time to air express same directly to Denton in Washington Exchange so he can expedite War Dept. screening and approval, but wire me shipping details. Cannot emphasize too strongly the vigorous reaction War Dept. had to this picture and extreme difficulty we had in reducing their objections to foregoing suggestions. Regards."*

In late February 1943, Sturges was authorized by the studio to shoot additional footage for the film, presumably to meet the O.W.I. demand, recounted in paragraph 4 above, for a brief scene showing soldiers who attended the party sober and ready for departure, and battle, the following morning. As it appears in the film, the passage begins with a shot of a road clogged with three columns of army transport trucks, only one column of which is moving. Following a brief dissolve, there are several shots of a number of soldiers throwing their gear onto a rack above a transport truck and clambering aboard. An officer walks by telling the men to move along and we see three soldiers com-

*In *Hollywood Goes to War: How Politics, Profits & Propaganda Shaped World War II Movies*, Clayton R. Koppes and Gregory D. Black elucidate the complex and shifting jurisdictional struggles between the civilian Office of War Information and the military, particularly the Army and Navy. Of the late 1942–early 1943 period, they say:

Elmer Davis [head of OWI] tried to lend whatever muscle he had. On December 3, 1942, he sent letters to the secretaries of War and the Navy asking them to channel all their contacts with Hollywood through OWI. Davis had sallied forth on a Quixotean tilt. His letter was passed down the chain of command to General Surles, the Army's PR chief, who said the close contact between the army and Hollywood dictated army involvement in every stage of production. "Only the Army can decide whether the proposed treatment is an appropriate depiction of the Army," he declared. OWI would be at best an intermediary, not "a useful collaborator." The agency suffered a similar rebuff from the Navy. This fruitless gambit reminded OWI that, unless the president intervened, civilian agencies in wartime were at the mercy of the military. (120–121)

ing up to say good-bye to the MP (Frank Moran) we've seen in several earlier scenes. The first soldier is the little guy who danced with Trudy at the party, the second is the burly fellow who sang in her ear, and the third—the victim of surgical censor strikes by the War Department and O.W.I.—is the soldier who said, "Let's all get married."

FIRST SOLDIER:	Ah so long Lefty, it's a swell town you got here. Take care of yourself.
SECOND SOLDIER:	Swell girls!
THIRD SOLDIER:	Swell party, Ho-ho!
MP:	How can you feel so good this morning?
FIRST SOLDIER:	What do you mean? I've never felt better in my life.
THIRD SOLDIER:	Why shouldn't we feel good?
MP:	If I'd drunk that much lemonade, I'd be sour for a week. [The three soldiers, whose turn it is to mount a truck, laugh at this then turn and go.] It puts my teeth on edge to think of it.
OFFICER:	Any prisoners, Sergeant?
MP:	Nothing, Sir. Sunday morning and not a stiff in the guardhouse.
OFFICER:	Fine. [The officer goes off to join his departing unit.]
MP:	[Pointing to his head] Psycholology.

Sturges managed to meet the demands placed upon him and to undermine them at the same time. None of the three soldiers who attended the party is the least bit hung over or still high from drinking. There must be some other reason that they are all feeling so good and, for the moment at least, unconcerned about where they are going.

Where might Sturges insert this passage, particularly in a film so chockablock with catastrophic incidents, multiplying perspectives, and torrents of dialogue? After the knockabout farce with Kockenlocker, a disheveled Norval drives his banged-up car home and, trying to get into his rooming house, encounters Mr. Shottish, his superrespectable neighbor who is escorting his family to church. Between this scene and the following scene—the morning-after-the-party conversation between Trudy and Emmy—Sturges inserts the scene of the departing soldiers. One might suppose that the soldier scene would undermine the Trudy-Emmy dialogue: with the soldiers gone, finding Ratzkiwatzki may be impossible. But so strongly does the viewer identify with Trudy—and her desire to find her husband—that the inset soldier scene does not in the least diminish her scene with Emmy.

P.1347
"SAVE FILM! HELP WIN THE WAR!"

THE MIRACLE OF MORGAN'S CREEK

Preston Sturges
October 14, 1942

593

THE MIRACLE OF MORGAN'S CREEK

CHARACTERS

NORVAL JONES...........................

TRUDY KOCKENLOCKER.....................

OFFICER KOCKENLOCKER..................

EMMY KOCKENLOCKER......................

MRS. JONES............................

GOVERNOR..............................

BOSS..................................

JUSTICE OF PEACE......................

JUSTICE WIFE..........................

SALLY.................................

SHERIFF...............................

PETE..................................

RAFFERTY..............................

1ST M.P...............................

2ND M.P...............................

1ST B.Y.M.............................

2ND B.Y.M.............................

1ST STATE POLICE......................

2ND STATE POLICE......................

MR. TUERCK............................

MR. JOHNSON...........................

* * *

After the Paramount Trade-mark:

DISSOLVE TO:

1. PROLOGUE 1 - THE MAIN STREET OF MORGAN'S CREEK - THROUGH THE
    GLASS DOOR OF THE BUGLE BUILDING

    About one hundred and fifty people are milling around talking
    excitedly. Suddenly they move back and look toward the door
    of the Morgan Memorial Hospital as it bursts open and the
    Editor of the Bugle and Mr. Rafferty come flying out. They
    take a wide turn, then hot-foot it toward us, knocking people
    right and left. As they get near the door of the Bugle, we
    PULL BACK to allow for their entrance.

    THE EDITOR: (Coming to a Tom Mix stop)
                      Hold the presses!

    MR. RAFFERTY: Hold everything.

    THE EDITOR: What'll we do next?

    MR. RAFFERTY: Call the President.

    THE EDITOR: Wouldn't he be a little hard to get?

    MR. RAFFERTY: All right, then the Governor of the State.
                      What are you standing there? This is a
                      matter of National veal....weal...whatever
                      it is.

    THE EDITOR: (Nervously)
                      You think it's all right to call the
                      Governor?

    MR. RAFFERTY: All right? What do you mean all right? I
                      voted for him...call him!

    They hurry to a phone.

    THE EDITOR: (Into a telephone)
                      Get me the State Capitol...I've got to
                      talk to the Governor immediately...It's a
                      matter of life and death.

    MR. RAFFERTY: (Correcting him)
                      No death...LIFE!

    THE EDITOR: All right, it's a matter of life and,
                      and...

    MR. RAFFERTY: Life, State honor and National pride.

                                          (Continued)

1.   (Cont'd)

    THE EDITOR: (Into the telephone)
                          That's right, that's right, the Governor
                          of the State. This is the Editor of the
                          Bugle...It's very important, I've got to
                          talk to him about...

MUSIC DROWNS OUT HIS VOICE and superimposed on the screen
we read: THE MIRACLE OF MORGAN'S CREEK. The Editor waits
for his connection during the rest of the titles and Mr.
Rafferty walks up and down nervously. After the last title,
THE MUSIC DIES DOWN.

    MR. RAFFERTY: What soivce!

    THE EDITOR: (Excitedly)
                          Hello...Mr. Governor?

    CUT TO:

    <u>PROLOGUE 2.</u>

2.   THE GOVERNOR

Three-quarters back to us. He leans on a great desk, telephone in hand. Beyond him we see the large Gubernatorial
office, its walls hung with paintings of former governors.
The afternoon sun slants in through the high windows.

    THE GOVERNOR: Yeah...the editor of what?...Oh the Bugle,
                          yeah...What was that town again?...
                          Morgan's Creek, yeah. Is it in my state?
                          I never heard of it.

He turns toward us and lights a cigarette with a match from
the rear or console desk.

    CUT TO:

3.   THE EDITOR, MR. RAFFERTY - <u>IN THE BUGLE OFFICE</u>

    THE EDITOR: (Indignantly)
                          You never heard of it, hunh? By tomorrow
                          morning Morgan's Creek will be the most
                          famous town in America.

    MR. RAFFERTY: (Indignantly)
                          The world, what are you talking?

    THE EDITOR: This is the last free phone in the town...
                          every room has been reserved for fifteen
                          miles around. A hundred newspaper men are
                          here already and five hundred more are ex-
                          pected in the morning.

                                          (Continued)

3.   (Cont'd)

    MR. RAFFERTY: A thousand.

    THE EDITOR: There's a shortage of food, telephones.

    MR. RAFFERTY: Milk.

    THE EDITOR: Telegraph wires.

    MR. RAFFERTY: Liquor.

    THE EDITOR: Transportation.

    RAFFERTY: Tents.

    THE EDITOR: Policemen and everything else. We need a
                      lot of help or they're going to tear this
                      town up by the roots.

    MR. RAFFERTY: And that's only the half of it.

    THE EDITOR: We need State Police, food, water, beds,
                      blankets.

    MR. RAFFERTY: Plumbing.

    CUT TO:

4.   THE GOVERNOR - AT HIS DESK

    GOVERNOR: Wait a minute. Take it easy, will you...
                      what happened down there...You got a flood
                      or did you strike oil, or something?

    CUT TO:

5.   THE EDITOR AND MR. RAFFERTY

    THE EDITOR: Did we strike oil or something!

    MR. RAFFERTY: Tell him!

    THE EDITOR: No, Mr. Governor, we did not strike oil!

    MR. RAFFERTY: Anybody can strike oil.

    THE EDITOR: We have not got a flood...

    MR. RAFFERTY: Anybody can have a flood.

    THE EDITOR: What we've got, Mr. Governor, is...

    CUT TO:

11-23-42

597

6.   THE GOVERNOR - AT HIS DESK

          GOVERNOR: (Suddenly electrified)
                            You got WHAT!
                                    (He leaps to his feet and
                                    presses several buzzer buttons)
                            Are you sure of your facts? This is terribly
                            important...I wish I could be there myself.
                            This is a matter of State policy, State
                            pride... National pride...hold the wire a
                            minute.
                                    (He turns to speak to two
                                    male secretaries who have
                                    just hurried in)
                            Get on this line and take everything down in
                            shorthand.
                                    (Then to the other one)
                            Get a map of the State and make sure Morgan's
                            Creek is in it... if it isn't we might be
                            able to...persuade them to move over or
                            something, oh boy!
                                    (Then to another secretary
                                    who hurries in)
                            Get me all the newspaper boys...and I want
                            to speak to the radio stations...things like
                            this have to be guided.

          CUT TO:

7.   A DOOR TO AN ADJOINING OFFICE

      It has just opened and the political boss of the state stands
      there, worried.

          THE BOSS: What happened?

          CUT TO:

8.   THE GOVERNOR - AT HIS DESK

      He talks to the Boss as the latter walks into the SHOT.

          THE GOVERNOR: You better get down to Morgan's Creek and
                         buy up a few choice corners, some hotel
                         sites maybe, they need some and the bus
                         franchises will be very valuable...

          THE BOSS: Morgan's what?

          THE GOVERNOR: (Impatiently)
                         Creek...Morgan's Creek...like a little river.

          THE BOSS: A little river should have a dam...a big dam.

                                                    (Continued)

8. (Cont'd)

    THE GOVERNOR: Why not?
                      (He turns to the telephone)
                      Now give me all the facts.
                      (Then to the Boss)
                      This is the biggest thing that's happened
                      to this state since we stole it from the
                      Indians.

    THE BOSS: Borrowed.

    Without asking permission the Boss picks up the phone and
    listens in.

    CUT TO:

9.   THE EDITOR AND MR. RAFFERTY

    MR. RAFFERTY: (Sharing the ear piece)
                     Who's excited now?

    THE EDITOR: (Into the phone)
                     I'll tell you all I know, Mister Governor.
                     As a matter of fact I started the whole
                     thing.

    MR. RAFFERTY: (Indignantly)
                     You started it, since whom?

    THE EDITOR: (Ignoring him)
                     I was writing my mid-week editorial, that is
                     to say I was looking for a subject for it,
                     I'm rather famous for my editorials in this
                     part of the State...

    CUT TO:

10.   THE GOVERNOR AND THE BOSS

    THE BOSS: (Putting his hand over
                      the mouthpiece)
                    He's going to tell us his life story?

    THE GOVERNOR: Shhh.

    CUT TO:

11.   THE EDITOR AND MR. RAFFERTY

    THE EDITOR: And I noticed that there were quite a few
                   soldiers in the town...

    MR. RAFFERTY: What an eye.

    THE EDITOR: Rounding up girls for a farewell dance.

                               (Continued)

11. (Cont'd)

  MR. RAFFERTY: And why not?

  THE EDITOR: And it occurred to me that the girls in the
         towns and the soldiers around the towns would
         make an excellent subject for my editorial.
           (He reaches for it)
         I'll be glad to read it to you, Mister
         Governor.

  CUT TO:

12. THE GOVERNOR AND THE BOSS

  THE BOSS: (Automatically into the phone)
        No.

  THE GOVERNOR: (Looking up at him)
        No.

  CUT TO:

13. THE EDITOR AND MR. RAFFERTY

  MR. RAFFERTY: No.

  THE EDITOR: (Hurt)
        Just as you say, Mister Governor. Anyway,
        that was nine months, four hours and twenty-
        one minutes ago.

  CUT TO:

14. THE GOVERNOR AND THE BOSS

  THE BOSS: (Looking to high heaven)
        What a bore!

  THE EDITOR: I was looking out the window...

  AN EIGHT FOOT DISSOLVE STARTS HERE:

  THE EDITOR: And there I saw Officer Kockenlocker, our
  (Cont'd)   town constable, directing traffic as usual.
        As I said before, there was a noticeable
        number of soldiers in the town...

  THE DISSOLVE IS NOW COMPLETE AND WE HAVE ARRIVED AT

A-1

11-23-42

THE MIRACLE OF MORGAN'S CREEK   10-16-42   A-1

SEQUENCE "A"

FADE IN:

A-1   A TRAFFIC COP AT THE MAIN INTERSECTION OF A SMALL TOWN - (DAY)

He directs the traffic expertly and importantly. He is a man
of forty-eight, roughly speaking. Some truck loads of soldiers are in evidence and there are quite a few on the side-
walks. A Jeep with some M.P.'s is cruising around.

OFFICER   Evening Henry... evening Mr. Dunbar...Watch
KOCKENLOCKER: your step Madam, stick between them white
                    lines or you won't get your insurance when
                    you get run over...who gimme that horn...
                    hold your horses you...what was that?

He crosses to an Army truck.

THE SOLDIER   Which Church is giving the dance tonight?
AT THE WHEEL:

KOCKENLOCKER: How many churches you think we got...it's
                    right behind you and no U turns.

SOLDIER AT   O.K. Sarge.
THE WHEEL:

KOCKENLOCKER: And you ain't kiddin'.
                         (Now he resumes his business)

THIRD   Watch your step now...and keep under thirty-
SOLDIER: five, you. What was that?

This last to a delegation of soldiers who have come out in
the middle of the street.

A SOLDIER: Say, we got to round up some more girls for
                    the dance tonight. You know any numbers?

KOCKENLOCKER: Try the telephone company...what do you
                    think I am?

FIRST SOLDIER: Oh, a tough guy, hunh?

KOCKENLOCKER: (Threateningly)
                    Tough enough, Rookie.

SECOND   Where do you get that Rookie stuff?
SOLDIER:

KOCKENLOCKER: Listen, cookie, I was in France before you
                    was housebroken...now get off the street
                    and behave yourself.

FIRST SOLDIER: What have we done?
(AN M.P.)   (Rolling up in a Jeep)
                    What's all the trouble?

                                        (Continued)

601

A-1 (Cont'd)

KOCKENLOCKER: There's no trouble I just don't like to
                be talked to by Rookies.

THE M.P.:   (With exaggerated courtesy)
                This is Mr. Kockenlocker, gentlemen, he
                was a sergeant in the other war.
                            (Then to Kockenlocker)
                We do it different now, Ed. It's all done
                with kindness.
                            (Now he turns to the three
                            soldiers)
                Come on, get off the street, quit blocking
                the traffic...please.

The soldiers hurry away.

M.P.:   (To Kockenlocker)
                You get the idea? It's more psychological.
                            (He raises his cap)
                Good afternoon.

He drives away in his Jeep. Kockenlocker laughs after him.
Two other soldiers approach him. The one is very innocent
looking and has a paper in his hand.

THE INNOCENT   I beg your pardon, could you direct me
ONE: to a family called Issippi....they have
                a daughter, I believe.

KOCKENLOCKER: (Suspicious of all rookies)
                A family called Issippi?

THE INNOCENT   Yes, we're looking for a Miss Issippi.
ONE:

KOCKENLOCKER: A Miss Issippi?

Then getting it suddenly.

KOCKENLOCKER: (Continued)
                Will you get outta here.

The boys jump.

KOCKENLOCKER: (After them)
                Please.

CUT TO:

A-2 THE THREE SOLDIERS AND CECELIA

She is a tall blonde girl in spectacles.

CECELIA: Were you looking for thome girlth?

FIRST SOLDIER: We thertainly were.

CECELIA: Well, I know of <u>one</u>.

FIRST SOLDIER: I'll bet you do, sugar.

CECELIA: (Pointing at
        Kockenlocker)
      Ith hith daughter. The'th one of the
      prettieth girlth in town.

SECOND SOLDIER: That crab?

CECELIA: She don't look anything like him. The
      workth in Rafferty'th Muthic Thore.

FIRST SOLDIER: For heaven'th thake.

THIRD SOLDIER: (To Cecelia)
      How about yourself, Babe?

CECELIA: I'll be there anyway.
       (She flips a badge at him)
      I'm one of the Thivilian Thervith
      Thithterth... but it'th tho hard
      to thay.

THIRD SOLDIER: You thaid it.

DISSOLVE TO:

A-3 A BUNCH OF SOLDIERS LEANING OVER <u>THE RECORD COUNTER</u> - (DAY)

They are listening enthusiastically and keeping time to a
Crosby record.

CUT TO:

A-4 TRUDY KOCKENLOCKER - FROM THE BOYS' POINT OF VIEW

Behind her we see the record cases and a playing phonograph.
It is she, however, who seems to be singing the Crosby
record.

              (Continued)

A-4 (Cont'd)

  Her lips are in perfect sync to the record and she seems to
  be doing the whole thing. She finishes in a blaze of glory

  SOME VOICES: Now do the opera again.

  Trudy takes the Crosby record off the machine, substitutes
  an opera record and proceeds to sing all by herself a quart
  from Rigoletto or the sextet from Lucia. She finishes up
  her performance by a basso profundo rendition of THE BELL I
  THE BAY, then gives her friends the brush.

  TRUDY: Come on now. You either gotta buy something
          or beat it before Mr. Rafferty gets after me

  A SOLDIER: Will you come tonight?

  TRUDY: Well...sure...I'll see you in church, so
          long.

  CUT TO:

A-5 THE DEPARTING SOLDIERS

  As they leave with "so long Trudy" and "save the first one
  for me," Norval is revealed standing behind them. One of
  them bumps him and another one steps on his foot, which he
  forgives in polite pantomime. As he comes forward THE
  CAMERA PANS to include Trudy.

  NORVAL: Good evening, Trudy.

  TRUDY: Oh good evening, Norval.

  NORVAL: I'd like a package of phonograph needles,
          please.

  TRUDY: Three indestructos or 36 Ragons?

  NORVAL: It doesn't really matter, Trudy --

  CUT TO:

A-6 EXT. MUSIC SHOP - (DAY)

  The jeep crunches back over the scooter and pulls ahead
  gaily. Now another jeep drives into the shot and parks
  over the fallen scooter.

  CUT TO:

A-7 NORVAL - RECEIVING THE PACKAGE OF NEEDLES

  NORVAL: Thank you, Trudy...Say, I just looked in the
          lobby and they've got three pretty good
          pictures at the Regent tonight and it
          occurred to me that if you weren't doing
          anything...considering that I was also free.

10-14-42   (Continued)

A-7 (Cont'd)

TRUDY: I'd be glad to, Norval.

NORVAL: Goodnight, Trudy.

TRUDY: You forgot your needles.

NORVAL: It doesn't matter, I haven't got a
                     phonograph anyway.

Trudy looks after him pitifully for a moment.

DISSOLVE TO:

A-8   THE EDITOR AND MR. RAFFERTY

THE EDITOR: (Editorial in hand)
                     Just let me read you the end of it,
                     Mister Governor.
                             (He wet his lips)

CUT TO:

A-9   THE GOVERNOR AND THE BOSS

THE BOSS: (Into the phone)
                     All right, let's have it...We're gonna
                     get it anyway.

We hear the Editor's voice faintly:

EDITOR'S   War time is a dangerous time...not only for
VOICE: the brave young men who sally forth to battle
                     but also for their sisters...who remain at
                     home. Let me be the last to urge a lack
                     of hospitality, but let me be the first to
                     remind you that all is not gold that glitters.

THE BOSS: A politician.

THE GOVERNOR: It ain't bad, I may use some of it.

THE EDITOR'S   (Faintly)
VOICE: That the young are scornful of danger, that
                     war time is an impetuous time.

THE BOSS: So what?

CUT TO:

A-10   THE EDITOR AND MR. RAFFERTY

THE EDITOR: (Ringingly)
                     ...And that in any large group of good men,
                     there are by necessity of the laws of
                     average, some scoundrels and some fools....
                             (Continued)

605

A-10 (Cont'd)

      THE EDITOR: It is against these that I warn you. Be-
      (Cont'd)   ware young woman, the spell of the jingling
                        spur...the spell of flags and marshal music,
                        of brass buttons, and short romances, of the
                        hasty act repented at long leisure, of
                        promiscuity confused with patriotism...or
                        loyalty with laxity...BEWARE!

      During the last of this speech we have DISSOLVED TO:

B-1

FADE IN:

B-1   NEWSPAPER INSERT - "MILITARY MARRIAGES MENACE SAYS MINISTER"
       "In an informal talk yesterday at the Ladies' Friday Luncheon
       Club the Rev. Doctor Thorndyke, local pastor, warned against
       hasty marriages. 'Act in haste,' he said, 'and repent at
       leisure.' Etc."

       CUT TO:

B-2   OFFICER KOCKENLOCKER - READING THE PAPER

       He looks up, considers what he has just read, then bends a
       suspicious look across the room.

       CUT TO:

B-3   EMMY - PLAYING THE PIANO

       She reacts to her father's scowl and looks at him suspicious-
       ly.

       EMMY: What are you looking at?

       CUT TO:

B-4   MR. KOCKENLOCKER - PAST EMMY

       KOCKENLOCKER: You wasn't thinking of getting married was
                        you?

       EMMY: At fourteen? I was thinking of going down
                        to the corner and having a soda.

       KOCKENLOCKER: (Irritably)
                        I didn't mean what you was thinkin' about
                        right now...I mean generally.

       EMMY: Generally, yes,

       KOCKENLOCKER: Generally yes, what?

       EMMY: Generally yes I think about marriage...
                        what else do you think I think about?

       KOCKENLOCKER: Oh, you do, do you?

       EMMY: Anybody can think about it, can't they...
                        It doesn't cost anything to think about
                        it... It's only when you do it that it
                        costs two dollars.

                                                    (Continued)

B-4   (Cont'd)

KOCKENLOCKER: What costs two dollars? You seem to know
                 a great deal about a subject far beyond
                 your years...like it says here in the
                 paper...

EMMY: (Placidly)
                 Well, it's your subject, Papa...You intro-
                 duced it, if you don't like it...ignore it.
                             (She goes back to her
                              piano playing)

Mr. Kockenlocker looks around hopelessly, then up at the
ceiling.

CUT TO:

B-5   TRUDY'S FEET

They do a little dance. Now THE CAMERA PANS UP ONTO Trudy
as she fastens her garters and gets ready to leave.

CUT TO:

B-6   MR. KOCKENLOCKER WITH EMMY IN THE BACKGROUND

He is still looking straight up and now receives a small
piece of plaster in his eye.

KOCKENLOCKER: Tell your sister the house ain't paid for,
                 will you?

EMMY: She knows that Papa, you tell her every
                 day.

KOCKENLOCKER: Every day ain't enough...What's she doing
                 up there anyway?

EMMY: Getting ready for the party.

KOCKENLOCKER: Oh...
                             (Then reacting suddenly)
                 Getting ready for what party?

EMMY: The dance, Papa...You've got to kiss the
                 boys goodbye...it's a farewell party...a
                 military affair.

KOCKENLOCKER: Again?...Where is this affair to be unfurled?

EMMY: I don't know Papa...I'm only fourteen.

KOCKENLOCKER: What kind of a answer is that?

CUT TO:

B-7   UPPER LANDING OF THE KOCKENLOCKER HOUSE

Trudy whisks out, puts one leg over the bannister and zips
down to the first floor.

TRUDY: So long Papa.

CUT TO:

B-8   KOCKENLOCKER AND EMMY - PAST TRUDY

KOCKENLOCKER: (Coming forward)
               Just a moment...What is this military kiss
               the boys goodbye business and where is it
               to be transacted?

TRUDY: Oh just like they always do...in the
               church basement and then at the country
               club and then kinda...like that.

KOCKENLOCKER: Like what?

TRUDY: (Edging away)
               That's all, goodnight, Papa.

KOCKENLOCKER: Just a moment, what happens after the
               Country Club?

TRUDY: (On the defensive)
               They bring you home.

KOCKENLOCKER: Yeh...by way of Cincinnati...with a side
               trip through Detroit. I was a soldier too,
               you know... in the last war.

TRUDY: But Papa...I've already promised, and I'm
               already dressed up...

KOCKENLOCKER: (A little bit lost)
               Yeh...well...you can get undressed... it
               says here in the paper:

TRUDY: (Pointing to her dress)
               But Papa...

EMMY: People aren't as evil-minded as they were
               when you were a soldier, Papa.

KOCKENLOCKER: (Threateningly)
               When I want any advice out of you, I'll
               ask for it.

EMMY: And you'll get it.

                                        (Continued)

KOCKENLOCKER: (Advancing)
                       Oh yes.

TRUDY: (Almost crying)
                       I wish Mama was here.

KOCKENLOCKER: (Stopping)
                       So do I...believe me, but she ain't.
                       Daughters! So as your father and mother
                       combined, I'm here to tell you that you
                       are not going on no more military parties.
                       Read what it says in the paper.

Trudy turns away and starts slowly for the stairs. Emmy
follows her.

EMMY: (Looking back)
                       If you don't mind my mentioning it, Father,
                       I think you have a mind like a swamp.

KOCKENLOCKER: (Whirling)
                       What!

He takes a flying kick at his youngest's southern exposure,
but unfortunately slips on a scatter rug. His daughters
come back and pick him up.

DISSOLVE TO:

B-9   NORVAL ON THE FRONT PORCH OF THE JOHNSON HOUSE

Mrs. Johnson is in a rocking-chair behind him, knitting.
In a window we see a sign: "Room To Let."

MRS. JOHNSON: Aren't you going out, Norval?

NORVAL: No, ma'am.

MRS, JOHNSON: I thought you were going to the picture.

NORVAL: I thought about it...and then I figured
                 I wouldn't.

MRS. JOHNSON: Oh.
                        (Then, after a pause)
                 Isn't there a dance or something tonight?

NORVAL: For the soldiers.

MRS. JOHNSON: Oh.
                        (Then after a pause)
                 I'm so sorry, Norval...

NORVAL: If they don't want me...They don't
                 want me.
                                        (Continued)

MRS. JOHNSON: Couldn't the doctor give you something to
                keep you calm just long enough for the
                examination...like some whiskey or something?

NORVAL: I'm perfectly calm...I'm as cool as ice,
                then I start to think maybe they won't
                take me, then some cold sweat runs down the
                middle of my back, then my head starts to
                buzz, then everything begins to swim in the
                middle of the room and I get black spots in
                front of my eyes, then they say I've got
                high blood pressure again and all the time
                I'm as cool as ice.

The PHONE RINGS inside the house and he jumps four feet
straight up in the air, nearly misses the step and rushes
into the house.

MRS. JOHNSON: Don't get so excited, Norval.

NORVAL: Who's excited?
                        (At the phone)
                Yes, yes...no foolin', well that's certainly
                swell Trudy...kind of lucky break, huh. Well
                I certainly appreciate your calling me right
                away...I'll be right over.

He hangs up and hurries out.

NORVAL: I changed my mind...I guess I'll go to the
                picture after all.

He kisses Mrs. Johnson happily.

MRS. JOHNSON: Aren't you going to take your hat, Norval?

NORVAL: Well...yes.

He starts for the door.

MRS. JOHNSON: Have you got money?

NORVAL: What?...Oh, money...What for, oh yes...
                I've got plenty. Goodbye. Goodbye.

MRS. JOHNSON: Your hat, Norval.

NORVAL: Oh, yes certainly.

He hurries up the steps, walks right through the screen
door, gets his hat, notices the door on the way out.

NORVAL: Something the matter with the door here.
                You ought to have it fixed. Goodbye.

10-15-42   (Continued)

Mr. Johnson appears, newspaper in hand.

MR. JOHNSON: What's going on here?

We hear a CAR DOOR SLAM, a MOTOR START, a BANG into the car
ahead, a BANG into the car behind, a fender being torn off
and the car pulling down the street.

DISSOLVE TO:

B-10   EXT. OF TRUDY'S HOUSE

We hear the squeal of BRAKES, the SOUND of skidding on
gravel, and Norval's car crashes into the shot and crunches
into Mr. Kockenlocker's sedan.

CUT TO:

B-11   KOCKENLOCKER PARLOR

Here we see Mr. Kockenlocker, Emmy and Trudy.

KOCKENLOCKER: (Rising to the crash)
                   ...What's that?

TRUDY: That must be Norval.

EMMY: It sounds like him.

They start out.

CUT TO:

B-12   EXT. KOCKENLOCKER HOUSE - (NIGHT)

Norval hurries toward us and THE CAMERA PANS him into the
group with the family which is coming out of the house.

NORVAL: Hello, Trudy, hello, Emmy...Good evening,
               Mr. Kockenlocker, well, I'm certainly glad
               you're going to the picture with me.

KOCKENLOCKER: Who me?

TRUDY: I'm very glad to go with you, Norval.

NORVAL: Fine. I don't want to sound unpatriotic,
               but I'm almost glad they called that dance
               off...for my sake I mean.

EMMY: It wasn't exactly for your sake.

                                              (Continued)

B-12 (Cont'd)

NORVAL: Oh, I didn't mean that.

KOCKENLOCKER: It was just called off.

NORVAL: (Pointing to Trudy's outfit)
Maybe I should have put on my tuxedo.

TRUDY: You look fine, Norval.
                (She takes his arm)
Come on. Goodnight, Papa, goodnight, Emmy.

EMMY: Don't do anything I wouldn't do.

KOCKENLOCKER: (To Emmy)
What kind of a joke is that?
                (Then to Trudy)
And be home right after the picture.

TRUDY: (With feigned indignation)
Where else could I _go_?

KOCKENLOCKER: I didn't ask you where else you could go,
I said...

EMMY: (Pointing into the distance)
There's a new little boogie-woogie joint
out...

KOCKENLOCKER: (Grabbing her by the back of
                    the neck)
Listen you.

TRUDY: Come on, Norval.

KOCKENLOCKER: And be home right after the picture.

TRUDY: Yes, Papa.

NORVAL: Yes, _sir_.

They go out of the SHOT.

KOCKENLOCKER: Now what do you know about this boogie
woogie joint?

EMMY: (Innocently)
Nothing, I just heard you were there...
digging quite a trench.

DISSOLVE:

10-15-42

B-13 TRUDY AND NORVAL IN CAR - (MOVING) - (NIGHT)

TRUDY: (With a tinge of nervousness)
It was certainly very sweet of you to come
and get me right away, Norval.

NORVAL: What are you talking about, Trudy. The
pleasure is all mine. Except to get into
the Army I can't hardly think of anything
that gives me as much pleasure as taking
you out.

TRUDY: That's certainly nice to hear, Norval. You
certainly helped me out by taking me out
tonight...when I was all dressed up like a
horse and everything.

NORVAL: The pleasure is mine, Trudy...Not that you
look anything like a horse.

TRUDY: Thank you, Norval...You certainly helped me
out.

NORVAL: Any time.

TRUDY: You really mean that, Norval?

NORVAL: Really mean what?

TRUDY: You'd help me out any time?

NORVAL: That's almost all I live for, Trudy. Except
maybe getting into the Army, nothing could
make me happier than helping you out. I
almost wish you'd be in a lot of trouble
sometime so I could prove it to you.

TRUDY: You can prove it tonight.

NORVAL: Hunh?

TRUDY: I am in a lot of trouble, Norval...They didn't
call off the military dance, Papa just called
it off as far as I was concerned.

NORVAL: Oh...he did? Well, he must have a good reason
then...That's what parents are for....to listen
to their advice...That's why I always missed
losing my parents.

TRUDY: I know, Norval...but he didn't have a good
reason. He's just old-fashioned...soldiers
aren't like they used to be when he was a
soldier...You know, all in France and like
that.

10-15-42   (Continued)

B-13 (Cont'd)

NORVAL: Aren't they?

TRUDY: Of course they're not. They're fine, clean
young boys from good homes and we can't send
them off maybe to be killed in the rockets
red glare...bombs bursting in air...without
anybody even to say goodbye to them, can we?

NORVAL: They've probably got their families.

TRUDY: Well, even if they have, they ought to have
girls and dancing and...how about those who
haven't got any families? How about the
orphans? Who says goodbye to them? You
ought to know about them.

NORVAL: The superintendent probably goes down from
the asylum...for old times' sake.

TRUDY: Norval, I think you're perfectly heartless...
I just hope you get into the Army some day
and the last thing that happens to you, the
last thing you get before you sail away,
the last thing you have to treasure while
you're fighting under foreign skies is a
kiss from the superintendent.

NORVAL: (Depressed)
Well...What do you want me to say?

TRUDY: I want you to say: 'Trudy, it's your bounden
duty to say goodbye to our boys, to dance
with them, and give them something to remember
and something to fight for! I won't take no
for an answer, so I'll drop you off at the
church basement, take in the movie, then
meet you and take you home like a chivalrous
gentleman so you don't get in wrong with
Papa', that's what I want you to say.

NORVAL: (After a slight pause)
I won't say it.

TRUDY: (Pathetically)
Oh, please, Norval.

NORVAL: I won't do it! I won't sit through three
features by myself.

TRUDY: Couldn't you sleep through a couple of them?

NORVAL: Besides, suppose you get caught, where
                       does that put me with your father?

TRUDY: Why should I get caught...Anyway I'm not
                       doing anything wrong...

NORVAL: Well, the whole idea sounds very cheesy to
                       me, Trudy, I don't want to be d-di-
                       disagreeable, but if all you want me for
                       is a kind of a f-f-false front, a kind of
                       d-d-decoy...I'd just as soon take you
                       home right, now, Trudy, and...say goodbye
                       to you.

Trudy sniffles.

NORVAL: (Noticing this)
                       That doesn't cut any ice with me.

Trudy sobs.

NORVAL: Go ahead...cry all you like...I've seen
                       you cry before.

Trudy snuffles.

NORVAL: Stop it, will you?

TRUDY: I'm not c-c-crying for me...I'm just
                       thinking of those p-p-poor boys going
                       away like p-p-poor little orphans.

NORVAL: Well, you're not the only...dame in
                       town, are you?

TRUDY: That's right, insult me.

NORVAL: I'm not insulting you, Trudy, I...where
                       would I meet you?

TRUDY: Oh, it doesn't matter now...that you
                       spoiled everything.

NORVAL: (Quickly)
                       Doesn't it?

TRUDY: (With snuffles)
                       What time is the third feature over?

                                          (Continued)

616

AL   Revised   THE MIRACLE OF MORGAN'S CREEK   10-26-42   B-11
                                                                                            (16)
B-13 (Cont'd)

NORVAL: (Gruesomely)
                     About 1:10...if my seat holds out.

TRUDY: (With snuffles)
                     All right, I'll drop you off at the theatre
                     and pick you up at 1:10.

NORVAL: (Indignantly)
                     Pick me up! What do you mean?

TRUDY: Well, don't you think I'd better take your
                     car? The boys mightn't have any.

NORVAL: (Outraged)
                     Take my car! First you get me out under
                     false pre - pre - pre...tenses which you
                     never even had the sl-slightest intentions
                     of, of, of ... then you want me to see three
                     f-f-features all by myself and now you want
                     to take my car into the bargain for a bunch
                     of, of, of all the confounded nerve I ever,
                     I ever, I ever...

Trudy bursts into sobs.

NORVAL: (At the top of his lungs)
                     ALL RIGHT...all right, you win. Do you want
                     anything else...Do you want my money and my
                     watch too...maybe one of the boys could use
                     it....WHAT A WAR!

FADE OUT.

END OF SEQUENCE "B"

SEQUENCE "C"

FADE IN:

C-1   THE BEGINNING OF THE PARTY IN THE CHURCH BASEMENT

It is refined and a little on the dull side.

CUT TO:

C-2   TRUDY DANCING WITH A SOLDIER 5'.

DISSOLVE TO:

C-3   TRUDY DANCING WITH A SOLDIER 6' 6"

DISSOLVE TO:

C-4   TRUDY DRINKING SOME LEMONADE WITH ANOTHER SOLDIER

The lemonade is so sour they look as if they were whistling.
There is a sign above the lemonade which says VICTORY
LEMONADE...SAVE SUGAR FOR VICTORY.

A SOLDIER: Say, I've got a great idea...

A GIRL: What?

A SOLDIER: Let's all get married.

DISSOLVE TO:

C-5   TRUDY DRIVING NORVAL'S CAR, WHICH IS LOADED WITH SOLDIERS AND
GIRLS

DISSOLVE TO:

C-6   THE DANCE AT THE COUNTRY CLUB

CUT TO:

C-7   A WEALTHY MEMBER OF THE COUNTRY CLUB

He orders champagne for everybody.

DISSOLVE TO:

C-8   SHOTS OF THE PARTY GETTING HOTTER
to
C-20   At the final episode it is hinted that they leave the country
club. Several times Trudy refuses champagne.

THE SOLDIER: Say, I've got a great idea.

A GIRL: What?

THE SOLDIER: Let's all get married.

THE GIRL: Don't give your right name.

DISSOLVE TO:

C-21   TRUDY DRIVING NORVAL'S CAR -

Which is packed jammed with soldiers and girls.

C-22   PARTY IN FULL SWING AT THE ROADHOUSE

Some jitterbug dancing begins. Trudy does a high one over her
partner's head, bumps her own head on the ceiling and lands on
the floor in a sitting position. When picked up she says she
is all right. A boy says, "That's the spirit that wins...we
don't know when we're licked. What's your name, sweetheart?"
Trudy looks at him vaguely, rubs her head.

A GIRL: (Slightly squiffed)
                 Don't give your right name.

C-23   THE SAME SOLDIER APPROACHING

SOLDIER: (To a girl)
                 Shay, I've got a wonderful idea.

THE GIRL   Well, don't keep it bottled up, pour it out.

THE SOLDIER: Lesh all get married.

TRUDY: 'Sa funny idea.

As they crowd around -

DISSOLVE TO:

C-24   NORVAL - IN THE LAST ROW OF THE PICTURE THEATRE

He is looking with glazed eyes at the third feature.

CUT TO:

C-25   THE SCREEN

We see the end of a picture in which a young military hero
receives not only the girl, but the congressional medal of
honor and also a million dollars in cash. As it fades out
CUT BACK TO NORVAL. He watches the screen dismally while the
lights come up, then massages his eyes, looks at his watch
and exits...the last one in the theatre.

CUT TO:

C-26   THE LOBBY OF A MOTION PICTURE THEATRE

Norval comes out and starts walking up and down. The manager,
the usher and the projectionist leave and bid him goodnight.
He walks up and down, and he looks at his watch. CUT TO
INSERT OF WATCH. It says 1:15.

DISSOLVE TO:

C-27   TRUDY DRIVING NORVAL'S CAR

It is full of soldiers, girls and paper hats.

FADE OUT.

FADE IN:

C-28   THE TOWN STREET - (DAWN)

The CAMERA PANS over to the lobby of the picture theatre.

CUT TO:

C-29   CLOSE SHOT OF NORVAL - (ASLEEP)

He is crouched in a corner like an Indian.

CUT TO:

C-30   LONG SHOT - DOWN THE STREET

Norval's car appears.

CUT TO:

C-31   TRUDY - AT THE WHEEL

CUT TO:

C-32   THE CAR COMING TOWARD US DOWN THE STREET

It makes a quick turn toward the theatre and stops with a
BANG against the curb.

CUT TO:

C-33   NORVAL SLEEPING

He jumps into the air like a jumping jack, then sneezes
violently.

CUT TO:

C-34   TRUDY - HANGING OUT THE WINDOW OF THE CAR

TRUDY: (Strangely excited)
Hello, Norval...How are you?...Gee it's nice
to see you...Did you enjoy the pictures...
Have you been waiting long?

CUT TO:

C-35   NORVAL APPROACHING

NORVAL: (Looking at the daylight)
Well, what do you think?
(Now he looks at his watch
and sneezes:)
Holy mackeral, you know what time it is?

THE CAMERA PANS him into the SHOT with Trudy. He looks from
his watch to her and back again.

NORVAL: What have you been doing until this hour.

(Continued)

TRUDY: We had a wonderful time, Norval. We sang
                    and then we danced and then we had some
                    lemonade, and then we sang some more, and
                    then we danced some more and then we had
                    some more lemonade and then we sang still
                    some more and then we danced some more...
                    and then I don't remember....isn't that
                    funny: the next thing I remember I was
                    driving down the street here and all of a
                    sudden I said 'Norval! Norval must be
                    waiting for me...I bet I'm a couple of
                    minutes late!'

NORVAL: You win.

TRUDY: I'm awfully sorry, Norval. If there's one
                    thing I despise it's people who - I mean if
                    there's one thing I love it's punctual...
                    punctualtu...people who are on time...and
                    to think that I let my little Norval wait
                    in...

NORVAL: You've been drinking.

TRUDY: (Indignantly)
                    Who's been drinking? I never had a drink
                    in my life! How dare you insinuate I've
                    been drinking?

NORVAL: Well, you certainly didn't get what you've
                    got on lemonade.

TRUDY: Well...I certainly did...

NORVAL: All right...what have you been using on
                    my car, a pickaxe?

He tries to straighten a fender.

TRUDY: (Happily)
                    Oh, is this your car? I just grabbed the
                    first jalopy I could find...Where do you
                    suppose I've been?

NORVAL: I don't know.

TRUDY: S' funny, I remember everything perfectly up
                    to...some place...and then I don't remember
                    anything.

NORVAL: What am I supposed to do now, take you home?

TRUDY: (Innocently)
                    Naturally, Norval, since I'm out with you.

NORVAL: What's your father going to say?
                                                    (Continued)

C-35 (Cont'd)

TRUDY: He's asleep, we don't have to worry about him.

NORVAL: I suppose you realize it's eight o'clock in
            the morning.

TRUDY: (With big eyes)
            Eight o'clock! Oh, Norval...You shouldn't
            have kept me out so late...Papa will be
            sorer than a boil.

NORVAL: (Crossly)
            I shouldn't have kept you out so late!

TRUDY: Papa will be very cross with you, Norval.
            He doesn't like me to be kept out so late...
            He'll say Norval, you're a naughty-naughty
            boy...whambo!
                       (She pretends to punch herself
                       on the nose and reacts.)

NORVAL: Oh, he will, will he! Suppose I just tell
            him I been waiting in a picture lobby for
            you all night.

TRUDY: (Hurt)
            That doesn't sound like you, Norval...I've
            heard lots of things against you, but I
            never heard anybody say you were a heel...
            at least not a total heel.

NORVAL: Thanks...well...maybe we could tell him we
            had an accident or something.

TRUDY: We'd have to wreck the car a little more.

NORVAL: It could pass the way it is...Maybe we just
            went for a ride after the movie and had a
            flat tire...That's old but it's reliable.

TRUDY: I don't think Papa goes for that one...he
            makes you show the patch.

NORVAL: Oh he does?

TRUDY: Yes...We might have fallen asleep in the
            movie and not waked up but the best thing
            I can think of is that Papa had better be
            asleep when we get there.

NORVAL: You said it.

TRUDY: Now, just tell me what the pictures were
            about and everything will be jake.

NORVAL: All three of them and the Newsreel, and the
            travelogue and the Popeye?
                                      (Continued)

622

C-35 (Cont'd)

TRUDY: Well, it isn't going to be any harder on
                    you than it is on me, Norval.

NORVAL: What a war!

The car backs into the street and, as it pulls away from us
we read, scrawled across the back of it: "JUST MARRIED".

DISSOLVE TO:

C-36 MR. KOCKENLOCKER SNORING IN HIS BED

Suddenly his alarm goes off. He makes a dive for it, misses
it and falls out of bed.

CUT TO:

C-37 THE STREET IN FRONT OF THE KOCKENLOCKER RESIDENCE - (EARLY
MORNING)

Norval's car arrives toward us and Trudy descends.

TRUDY: Thanks a million, Norval. I'll never for-
                    get your kindness tonight...I had a wunner-
                    ful time.
                            (In a whisper)
                    Even I can't remember anything about it.
                    And the pictures were just...lowvly.

NORVAL: (Slightly worried)
                    Can you get in all right?

TRUDY: (Striking a dignified attitude)
                    Can I get in all right...What's the matter
                    with you, Norval?...I never had a drink in
                    my life and you talk as if I was...swaffled
                    or something. Goodnight.

She catches her coat on the gate, falls the length of it
and falls flat. Norval scrambles out of his car and helps
her to her feet.

TRUDY: Now you stop that, Norval. You're playing
                    too rough.
CUT TO:

C-38 THE DOORWAY OF THE KOCKENLOCKER HOUSE

Mr. Kockenlocker stands here in his nightgown. His face
is covered with lather, and he holds the badger brush
in his hand.

KOCKENLOCKER: ...What kind of a game is this?

CUT TO:

C-39   TRUDY AND NORVAL - ON THE GROUND

TRUDY: (Very amiably)
Oh, hello, Papa. We were just kidding a
little before saying goodnight.

KOCKENLOCKER: (Frigidly)
I see...and what time do you say goodnight
as a rule?

NORVAL: (Scrambling to his feet)
Goodnight.

TRUDY: (Helping herself up by
                    hanging onto him)
Goodnight, Norval dear.

She kisses him on the cheek.

TRUDY: Thank you very much for taking me to
all those movies and everything...Good
night, Norval.

She gives him a little push.

KOCKENLOCKER: (Grabbing him by the shoulder)
Just a minute, Mr. Jones, where have you
been with my daughter till this hour of
the morning and I don't want to hear the
one about the little accident on the way
home, or the flat tire, or falling asleep
in the movies.

Norval opens his mouth but no sound issues therefrom.

TRUDY: It isn't late, Papa. Goodnight, Norval.

She tries to push him away from Kockenlocker, who holds onto
him.

KOCKENLOCKER: (With heavy sarcasm)
It may not be late where you come from,
but where I come from...

TRUDY: We come from the same place, Papa.

KOCKENLOCKER: (Loudly)
Shut up! We call eight o'clock in the
morning kinda late to be bringing a young
lady home.

Norval gestures no, no, no.

TRUDY: We were just fooling around a little
a little down the road a piece.

KOCKENLOCKER: (At the top of his lungs)
For eight hours?

                                         (Continued)

C-39 (Cont'd)

Norval opens his mouth and waves no, no, no.

KOCKENLOCKER: (At the top of his lungs)
                          Why don't you say something instead of
                          standing there like a stuffed ninny?

EMMY: (Hurrying out of the house)
                          Papa, don't make so much noise...you're
                          waking up the whole neighborhood.

KOCKENLOCKER: (To Emmy)
                          Will you get back in the house?
                          (Then to Norval)
                          Now I'll give you one more chance...

Norval feels of his temples, presses his cheeks with both
hands and tries unsuccessfully to speak.

TRUDY: He's going to explode.

NORVAL: (In a husky whisper)
                          Flat tire.

TRUDY: (Quickly)
                          We fell asleep in the movie.

NORVAL: (Gesturing no, no, no)
                          Flat tire.

TRUDY: (Gesturing no, no, no)
                        We fell asleep in the movie.

KOCKENLOCKER: (Menacingly)
                          That's all I wanted to know.
                        (He grabs Norval by the throat:)
                        I'll flat tire you, you...flat tire.

Trudy and Emmy now go to work to save Norval.

TRUDY: Stop it, Papa, beat it Norval, trip him
                up Emmy.

Norval is tripped flat on his face.

TRUDY: Not Norval....Help me with Papa. Now you
                stop it, Papa.
                        (She leaps on him:)
                Beat it, Norval. Trip him Emmy.

Emmy rubber-legs her father from the rear and the family
falls to the ground:

TRUDY: (From the ground)
                Now hang onto him, and beat it, Norval.

                                              (Continued)

C-39 (Cont'd)

KOCKENLOCKER: (Muffled)
                    Will you let go of me?

EMMY: (Triumphantly)
                    I've got a toe-hold.

KOCKENLOCKER: (Roaring like a lion)
                    WOW!

CUT TO:

C-40 A NEIGHBORING BEDROOM - OR KITCHEN

Cecelia in curlpapers is looking out of the window. The
mother is sitting up in bed - or at the stove.

THE MOTHER: What is it?

CECELIA: (Relishing the words)
                Norval Jones just brought Trudy Kockenlocker
                home and her father tried to beat him up.

THE MOTHER: You'd never think that of Norval to look at
                him.

CECELIA: Still waters run deep...as I always say.

She picks up a phone.

THE MOTHER: What are you doing at this hour?

CECELIA: (Putting the phone down)
                Oh nothing...I can always do it later.

DISSOLVE TO:

C-41 EMMY AND TRUDY - IN THE LATTER'S BEDROOM

Trudy is in bed, Emmy on the edge of it. A tray of bread,
butter, jam, tea and milk sits between them.

EMMY: But how could you stay out so late...no
                matter how much fun you had, Trudy?

CUT TO:

C-42 TRUDY - PAST EMMY

TRUDY: I can't figure it out either...I can remem-
                ber everything up to...up to....and the next
                thing I remember I was driving down Main
                Street...and Norval was waiting.

                                             (Continued)

C-42   (Cont'd)

EMMY: Did you go to sleep somewhere or something?

TRUDY: I don't think so...you know me I never get
                    tired...

EMMY: Do you remember anything about the party?

TRUDY: Oh, sure. We just laughed and danced and
                    had some lemonade, then we went some place
                    else and had some more lemonade.

EMMY: You didn't drink anything else?

TRUDY: Well of course I didn't...And some boob
                    kept saying 'Let's all get married..'

EMMY: (Aghast)
                    No!

TRUDY: Yes, and some of those poor dumb kids thought
                    that was a wonderful idea.
                              (She shakes her head in horror)
                    Can you imagine getting hitched in the middle
                    of the night to some boy who's going away
                    and you never even get to see him again,
                    maybe?

        CUT TO:

C-43   CLOSE SHOT - EMMY

EMMY: You don't suppose any of them...
                              (Now her expression becomes
                               horrified and she points to
                               Trudy's hand)
                    Trudy!

        CUT TO:

C-44   TRUDY - PAST EMMY

TRUDY: What's the matter?

EMMY: (Shaken)
                    What's that on your third finger?

        CUT TO

C-45   EMMY - PAST TRUDY

> EMMY: (Almost in tears)
>   You didn't... you didn't...oh, Trudy!
>   (She throws her arms around
>   her sister's neck)

Trudy looks from the ring to Emmy in amazement.

DISSOLVE TO:

C-46   THE STREET IN FRONT OF NORVAL'S HOUSE - (MORNING)

As Norval descends from his car, he sees the family next door
on their way to mass.

> THE FAMILY: Good morning, Norval.
>
> NORVAL: Good morning, Mr. Shottish.
>
> MR. SHOTTISH: Up early for you?
>
> NORVAL: Yes sir, well you know how it is.
>
> MR. SHOTTISH: I certainly do.

Norval crosses to his house and the Shottish family crosses
behind his car where they read "JUST MARRIED."

> MR. SHOTTISH: Well, for heaven's sake...Mr. Slyboots...
>   you'd never think that of Norval to look
>   at him, would you?

DISSOLVE TO:

C-47   TRUDY AND EMMY - IN HER BEDROOM

> TRUDY: But I can't be!
>
> EMMY: Then what does that mean?
>
> TRUDY: Well, if I'm married, I'm married. I guess
>   I shouldn't of but if I did, I did, and
>   maybe it will work out just as well as if I
>   spent nine years picking him out. You take like
>   Aunt Wilhelmina who thought it over for
>   sixteen years and sewed enough hope chests
>   to fill two box cars and then tried it for
>   one day...
>   (She makes a gesture)
>   she didn't like it.
>
> EMMY: Do you think he'll come and find you?
>
> TRUDY: (Indignantly)
>   Why shouldn't he?

(Continued)

EMMY: Well, maybe he didn't want to get married,
            maybe he's just waking up in some Army
            camp right now and saying 'holy Moses...
            it's a good thing I didn't give my right
            name!'..was it a Marine?

TRUDY: How do I know...and why do you have to
            dream up things like that...why should
            he be such a heel?

EMMY: How about Uncle Roscoe?

TRUDY: He isn't in the army is he?

EMMY: Are you sure you can't remember his name?

TRUDY: (Almost crossly)
            How can I remember his name when I can't
            even remember...wait a minute...

                          (Continued)

C-47 (Cont'd)

EMMY: (Rigidly)
              What?

TRUDY: I think he had curly hair.

EMMY: That's a big help. All we've gotta do
is get all the curly-haired men in the
Army and the Navy and the Marine Corps
and line them up and...

TRUDY: (Triumphantly)
       I think it had a "Z" in it.

EMMY: His hair?

TRUDY: His name, foolish...like Ratziwatski...
Private Ratziwatski, or was it...

EMMY: With a name like that I'd forget him.

TRUDY: ...Now you knocked it out of my head.

EMMY: Wait a minute, what's the matter with
us...if you got married you musta
given your name...all we've got to do
is find out where you got the license
and there you have your name and his
name and the date and everything and
there you are.

TRUDY: (In a small voice)
       I've just remembered something else.

EMMY: What?

TRUDY: (Avoiding her sister's
                 eye)
Somebody said don't give your right name.

EMMY: (In an icy voice)
But you didn't fall for it...you told
them to go suck a lemon...you weren't
such a corn-fed dope as to...
                 (her voice trails off)
what name did you give?

TRUDY: I don't remember.

EMMY: (After a pause)
Then the guy can't ever find you!...Even
if he comes looking for you.

Trudy looks at her then looks away.

C-47 (Cont'd)

EMMY: Then we'll never even know if you <u>got</u>
                   married.

TRUDY: I...hope not.

Emmy looks at her vaguely, then away, then looks back at her
violently. She puts her hand on her sister's wrist.

SLOW DISSOLVE TO:

C-48   LOW CAMERA SHOT - <u>UP AT THE STEEPLE OF A SMALL TOWN CHURCH</u>

We hear the WAILING of many babies and the voice of the
Sexton.

SEXTON'S   Here, here, here, now, now, now. Shut up,
VOICE: will you? There's a service going on inside.

BY NOW THE CAMERA HAS ANGLED down onto the sweating Sexton in
a rusty frock coat in a sea of baby carriages. (This may be a
small sea of about 29 baby carriages. Three practical babies
should be enough.)

THE SEXTON: (Picking up a milk bottle)
                   Look: Nice milky wilky...good.

He pretends to drink, rubs his stomach and smacks his lips.
The wails increase. He looks toward another crib, spills
milk down the front of his coat and pretends to laugh it off.

DISSOLVE TO:

C-49   <u>INTERIOR OF THE SMALL CHURCH</u> - MEDIUM CLOSE

DOCTOR   (Through the wails of the infants)
UPPERMAN: ...From the Book of Moses, called Genesis.
                               (He listens to the wail of the
                               infants for a moment:)
                   If some of the young mothers would be so kind
                   as to rise and lay soothing hands on their
                   offspring.
                               (Now in his other voice
                               he proceeds)
                   When the abominations we have committed seem
                   at last to have filled the cup till it over-
                   floweth, when the world is being destroyed,
                   when God seems to have abandoned us to our
                   own miserable devices and the race of men is
                   rapidly vanishing from this earth...it may
                   be particularly appropriate to talk about
                   creation, and particularly creation in war
                   time when it is so needful...for future wars...
                               (He looks down at the pulpit
                               and reads:)

C-49 (Cont'd)

DOCTOR
UPPERMAN:
(Cont'd)

and God bless them and God said unto them
'Be fruitful and multiply and replenish the
earth...and subdue it.
> (Now he looks up and removes
> his spectacles:)

War time is a dangerous time...not only for
the brave young men who sally forth to battle
...but also for their fathers and mothers...
and for their sisters...particularly for
their sisters. It is to these I speak today
...to these and to their parents. God said
be fruitful and multiply and replenish the
earth and it is a fact that during war the
earth is more fruitfully replenished than
during peace. The uniforms, the brass buttons, the bright colors, the helmets with
plumes and horses' tails, the music, all of
these have so captured the imagination,
electrified the emotions of all young women
from the beginning until now, that more little children, little boys especially, are
born in war time than any other time...which
is excellent in itself, but attended, as are
so many excellent things, with dangers. Our
homes are surrounded by camps...the camps
are full of lonely young men...let me be the
last to speak against them or urge a lack of
hospitality...but let me be the first to remind you that all is not gold that glitters,
that the young are impetuous, that war time
is a thoughtless time and that in any large
group of good men there are of necessity
some fools and scoundrels...and against these
I warn you. Beware of the spell cast by
jingling spurs...of the hasty act repented
at leisure...of confusing patriotism with
promiscuity, of interpreting loyalty as
laxity...beware young women.

He turns abruptly and the organ starts to play.

CUT TO:

C-50   TRUDY AND EMMY - IN THEIR SUNDAY BEST

They look around a little nervously, then Trudy leans close
to Emmy.

CUT TO:

C-51   TRUDY AND EMMY - TWO BIG HEADS

TRUDY: (Emotionally)
          We ought to come here more often.

EMMY: (Icily)
       And sooner.

FADE OUT.

END OF SEQUENCE "C"

FADE IN:

D-1   A SMALL TOWN DOCTOR - BEHIND HIS DESK

THE DOCTOR: (He rises, picks up a sheet
                               of paper and THE CAMERA PANS
                               HIM around the desk to Trudy
                               as he talks)
                    If you will just follow these instructions
                    and come in again in about a month.
                               (He reaches Trudy and pats
                               her on the shoulder)
                    There, there, there...you'll find your hus-
                    band, I'm sure of it...and if you shouldn't
                    find him...you will find him!

TRUDY: Thank you, Doctor.
                               (Now she gets to her feet)
                    You don't have to tell anybody - I mean you
                    won't tell anybody until I do find him?

DOCTOR: Of course I won't, Trudy - I'm a doctor, not
                    a column conductor.

TRUDY: (Folding up the instructions)
                    Thank you, Doctor.

CUT TO:

D-2   EMMY - IN THE OUTER OFFICE

She gets up stiffly and crosses to her sister.

EMMY: Well?

TRUDY: (Almost resentfully)
                    Well, what?

EMMY: How are we doing?

TRUDY: Great.

                                                    (Continued)

EMMY: (Sympathetically)
                        ...Then we're really in a mess.

TRUDY: (Sniffling)
                        Not you...just me.

EMMY: ...So what? You don't have to cry about
                        it...
                             (She snuffles herself)
                        You're not the first dumb cluck who couldn't
                        find her husband...What with the war and
                        all there'll probably be millions of them.
                             (She snuffles)
                        They say they have much the prettiest babies,
                        too.

TRUDY: He'll come back...He has to come back...
                        What are you laughing about?

EMMY: I was just wondering if I'm going to be an
                        aunt or an uncle.

TRUDY: (Getting ready to cry again)
                        Aw stop it, will you?

EMMY: (Apologetically)
                        I'm only trying to make you smile, Trudy.
                        Come on, we'll see Mr. Johnson, the lawyer.

TRUDY: (Frightened)
                        What for?

EMMY: To find out if you're really married.

TRUDY: (Indignantly)
                        You're kind of hard to convince, aren't you?

DISSOLVE TO:

D-3   MR. JOHNSON, THE LAWYER, PAST TRUDY AND EMMY

MR. JOHNSON: (Scowling)
                        Certainly she's married.

EMMY: Even with a phony name, Mr. Johnson?

JOHNSON: What's the name got to do with it? Marriage
                        is a matter of fact, not of names. The
                        marriage was celebrated I presume...They
                        usually are.

Emmy looks blankly at Mr. Johnson, then at her sister who
nods in the affirmative.

TRUDY: I, I think so.

                                                        (Continued)

D-3 (Cont'd)

MR. JOHNSON: Well, since you are here on behalf of a
friend who does not wish to appear, all
I can say is that your friend ought to be
ashamed of herself.

EMMY: (Cutting in)
She's a very nice girl...It just happened,
that's all.

JOHNSON: I mean because of her carelessness. The
responsibility of recording a marriage has
always been up to the woman; if it weren't
for them marriage would have disappeared
long since. No man is going to jeopardize
his present or poison his future with a
lot of little brats hollering around the
house unless he is forced to. It is up to
the woman to knock him down and hog-tie him
and drag him in front of two witnesses
immediately if not sooner. Any time after
that is too late. Your friend doesn't
remember the bridegroom's name?

TRUDY: No, sir.

JOHNSON: And she used an assumed name...perfect...
that's really air-tight.

TRUDY: Can't you do anything, Mr. Johnson?

JOHNSON: Well, what for instance?

TRUDY: Maybe divorce him...or annul him?

EMMY: Or sue him for alimony?

JOHNSON: Sue who, annul who? Look: I practice the
law. I am not only willing but anxious to
sue anybody for anything any time, but
they've got to be real people...with names
and corpuses and meat on their bones...I
can't work with spooks. Your friend doesn't
need a lawyer, she needs a medium.

TRUDY: Thank you, Mr. Johnson.

JOHNSON: That will be five dollars...

TRUDY: (Reaching into her bag)
Yes sir.

JOHNSON: ...Which you will kindly hang on to and
buy flowers with on the happy day...for
your friend, of course.

(Continued)

TRUDY: Thank you, Mr. Johnson.

EMMY: You don't have to tell anybody, do you...
                about our friend?

JOHNSON: How could I when I don't even know who she is?

The girls exit.

DISSOLVE TO:

D-4   TRUCKING SHOT - BEGINNING OUTSIDE THE LAWYER'S OFFICE (DAY)

The girls come down the stairs and start walking.

TRUDY: (After a moment)
                I've got to get back to the store. Could
                you get me a sandwich and bring it in ...?
                Swiss on rye.

EMMY: Sure...but the way I look at it: It was a
                man got our friend in the soup...let a man
                get her out of it.

TRUDY: How?

EMMY: (Avoiding her sister's eye)
                Well..she could always get married, couldn't
                she?

TRUDY: How can I get married when I'm already
                married?

EMMY: Don't talk about yourself, we're talking about
                our friend. It's all very well to say she's
                married but when the time comes to prove it.

TRUDY: Are you trying to call our friend a liar?

EMMY: Don't talk so loud.

TRUDY: Well, you'd better not.

EMMY: Look; I'm only fourteen...,my ideas probably
                aren't any good...anyway I was only trying to
                be helpful. Our friend could just marry
                somebody and then one day she could say: "Oh,
                by the way..."

TRUDY: Yes..."there's something I forgot to mention,"
                Only I'm already married, Emmy, Mr. Johnson
                said so.

EMMY: What does he know? Nobody's going to believe
                it, nobody believes good unless they have to;if
                they've got a chance to believe something bad.
                                              (Continued)

TRUDY: But that would be bigamy!

EMMY: Don't talk so loud. How could it be bigamy
                    if you didn't give your right name...you
                    never got married, that was somebody else.

TRUDY: Maybe I could ask some of the other girls
                    who were on the party.

EMMY: If they knew we would have heard about it...
                    You must have slipped away somewhere and done
                    it quietly like a couple of movie stars.

TRUDY: (After a pause)
                    I wonder what Papa's going to say?

EMMY: He probably won't say much, he'll just haul
                    off and shoot Norval so full of holes he'll
                    look like a Swiss cheese...That was Swiss
                    on rye you wanted wasn't it?

TRUDY: Norval! Where does he fit in?

EMMY: He took you out, didn't he? He brought you
                    home didn't he? At eight o'clock in the
                    morning, didn't he? He fits like the skin
                    on a wienie.

TRUDY: Oh, poor Norval...We'd better warn him.

EMMY: We'd better marry him...That would be a lot
                    better.

TRUDY: Marry him! How can you say such things,
                    Emmy?

EMMY: (Coldly)
                    What's the matter with you, he was made for
                    it...like the ox was made to eat...and the
                    grape was made to drink.
                             (She turns back toward a restaurant)
                    I'll get you the Swiss on rye.

FADE OUT:

                    END OF SEQUENCE "D"

FADE IN:

E-1   MR. KOCKENLOCKER, EMMY AND TRUDY - ON THREE SIDES OF THE
       KOCKENLOCKER KITCHEN TABLE - (NIGHT)

       They each take a spoonful of Tapioca pudding, then smile
       under the LENS with jaws moving.

       CUT TO:

E-2   CLOSE SHOT - NORVAL

       He smiles back at them, swallows his Tapioca and sips his
       coffee.

       NORVAL: I'm certainly very glad to see you all
                            again...for awhile I thought you were
                            kinda sore at me, Mr. Kockenlocker.

       CUT TO:

E-3   THE OTHERS - PAST NORVAL

       TRUDY: (Quickly)
                            Papa's bite is worse than his bark.

       EMMY: You said it.

       KOCKENLOCKER: Well, wait 'till you get married and
                            have half a dozen daughters, and see
                            how you feel when some mug brings them
                            home at eight o'clock in the morning.

       TRUDY: You've only got two daughters, Papa.

       KOCKENLOCKER: That's plenty...They're a mess no matter
                            how you look at 'em...a headache 'till
                            they get married...IF they get married
                            and after that they get worse...either
                            they leave their husbands and come back
                            with four children and move into your
                            guest room, or their husband loses his
                            job and the whole caboodle comes back...
                            or else, they're so homely you can't get
                            rid of them at all and they hang around
                            the house like Spanish Moss and shame
                            you into an early grave.

       EMMY: How about sons? They're no bargain
                            either.

       KOCKENLOCKER: That's right, but there's one thing
                            don't happen to them...

                                                        (Continued)

E-3 (Cont'd)

KOCKENLOCKER: (Continued)
                  They never turn into old maids.
                  (He laughs meanly)

His daughters exchange porcelain smiles.

CUT TO:

E-4   NORVAL

NORVAL: You don't make out much of a case for
               marriage.

CUT TO:

E-5   THE OTHERS - PAST NORVAL

KOCKENLOCKER: Wait 'till you try it...You'll settle
                  for half a case.

EMMY: Why don't you and Trudy go out on the front
               porch...We'll do the dishes, won't we Papa?

KOCKENLOCKER: (Vulgarly)
                  In a pig's nose...What?...Oh sure.

DISSOLVE TO:

E-6   TRUDY AND NORVAL - COMING OUT ON THE FRONT PORCH

TRUDY: Comfortable?

NORVAL: Fine, thank you.

TRUDY: It's a good thing I didn't have any designs
               on you or anything...the way Papa talked
               about marriage and all.

NORVAL: I guess if you had designs they wouldn't be
               on me much anyway...I guess.

TRUDY: (With feigned indignation)
               Well I guess they would...if I had any.

NORVAL: Yes, but you haven't, that's what I mean...
               like that night of the party...you could
               of stayed and gone to the show with me, but
               instead you didn't.

TRUDY: (Impulsively)
               I'm sorry I didn't, Norval.

NORVAL: No foolin'?

                                     (Continued)

E-6 (Cont'd)

TRUDY: No foolin'...I wouldn't of got your car
         nicked up or...anything...it was only
         for the boys.

NORVAL: I know...you can't expect a girl to see
         much in a Civilian these days...even an
         unwilling Civilian....if they had uni-
         forms for them it might be a little dif-
         ferent.

TRUDY: I'm not so crazy about uniforms.

NORVAL: (Surprised)
         You're not! Gee I'd give anything to
         wear one.

TRUDY: That's because you're a man.

NORVAL: Lots of women wear them too, like those
         Whackos.

TRUDY: Woman's place is in the home.

NORVAL: That sounds kinda old-fashioned and
         domestic coming from you, Trudy.

TRUDY: Sometimes you just naturally feel old-
         fashioned and domestic, Norval...I guess
         no girl ever gets away from it really...
         She thinks she's away from it and then
         one day something happens and she finds
         out she isn't.

NORVAL: Something like what, Trudy?

TRUDY: (Her chin trembling)
         Something like...falling in love maybe...
         or something.

NORVAL: (After a long pause)
         Why, why...Trudy.
          (He starts to get excited)
         If I didn't know you so well and know
         that nothing could be further from your
         mind a fellow would almost swear you
         were pro, pro...pra, pro...giving him a
         hint.

TRUDY: (Lowering her eyes)
         Would that be...so terrible?

NORVAL: Terrible! It would be marvelous.

                   (Continued)

E-6 (Cont'd)

TRUDY: Well, how much of a hint would you need?

NORVAL: (Getting wildly excited)
Why Trudy, I, I, I...
                (He gets to his feet)
I, I, I, Yi, I, I, I, I...

TRUDY: (Rising and seizing his
                  wrist)
Remember your blood pressure, Norval...I
wouldn't want anything to happen to you
just before you said whatever you were
getting ready to say.

NORVAL: Don't you worry about me, it's just the
surprise of realizing that...ahum...
               (This represents a deep
                  clearing of the throat)
I mean when you've been thinking about...
ahum...something for as...ahum...long as
I have...ahum...don't you know?

TRUDY: Ahum...sure.

NORVAL: And then...ahum...all of a sudden...ahum...
you realize for the first time...ahum.

TRUDY: Take it easy...ahum...Norval.

NORVAL: (Feeling at his head)
That what you've been dreaming ahum...ahum...
about is not only...ahum...not impossible.
               (One of his knees gives
                 away. He straightens it
                 but the other gives away)
But even totally p-pos...ahum...p-p-posp-ppos-
posp-pos -

TRUDY: Norval, stop it!

NORVAL: P-pos p-pos -pppos -pppos -pppos
               (Both knees bend and he starts
               for the floor - desperately)
Trudy, will you marry me?

TRUDY: Norval, this is so sudden!

NORVAL: (Recovering himself)
What do you mean it's so sudden? How can
anything be sudden that's gone on since you
were little kids together...almost since I
can remember I could tell you what you wore

(Continued)

E-6 (Cont'd)

NORVAL: (Continued)
almost at the first fourth of July party
and you weren't hardly any bigger than the
firecrackers...then you remember the Church
lawn party when you sat in the apple-butter
and they blamed me for it and then later at
high school when I took all kinds of subjects I didn't give a hoot about just to be
near you, Trudy...the cooking wasn't so bad,
but the sewing!...and then the older I got
the uglier I got...when I was a kid they
said 'he'll grow out of it'...but I guess
a face like mine you can't grow out of so
easy...it's like it's cast in iron...so I
didn't really blame you when you began looking at the personality kids...with the Greek
profiles and the curly hair cuts.

TRUDY: I did not.

NORVAL: I didn't blame ya...I even bought a thing
once for my nose...but it kept me awake at
night except once when I nearly smothered.

Trudy pats his hand.

NORVAL: It was only for you...it's always been for
you and nobody but you...that's what I went
into the bank for...to get rich and buy you
things some day...any little thing your
heart desired and then it began to look as
if everything I'd always hoped for wasn't
going to be...and you had less and less
time for me...and then not having a uniform
and all...but now, Trudy...now that everything in the world is right here beside me...
everything I've dreamed of all my life...to
have and to hold...to cherish...to protect...
how can you say it's so sudden?

In reply, Trudy bursts into tears.

NORVAL: Why Trudy, what's the matter?

He crosses to her. Trudy renews her sobs and bellows from
now on.

NORVAL: Trudy, stop it...Trudy if I said anything
to hurt your feelings...you know I wouldn't
hurt your feelings for anything in the world
...it's just the other way around.

                                          (Continued)

E-6   (Cont'd)

       NORVAL: (He gets to his knees)
       (Cont'd)   St - st - stttt-st-stop it TTTrudy, you're
                        b-b-b-breaking my heart...the spots, stttop
                        it Trudy.

       TRUDY: (Bawling)
                        I can't do it to you.

       NORVAL: (Excitedly)
                        You can't do what to me, Trudy...the spots...
                        stop it.

       CUT TO:

E-7   MR. KOCKENLOCKER AND EMMY - IN THE KITCHEN

       KOCKENLOCKER: (Looking toward the
                                   front porch)
                        What is he doing now?

       EMMY: I hope nothing went wrong.

       Mr. Kockenlocker starts for the porch followed by Emmy.

       CUT TO:

E-8   TRUDY AND NORVAL

       NORVAL: Trudy, please.

       TRUDY: (Howling)
                        I can't do it to you.

       CUT TO:

E-9   THE NEIGHBORS - ON THEIR FRONT PORCH

       These are the same two we saw in the bedroom. They exchange
       a surprised look.

       CUT TO:

E-10   TRUDY AND NORVAL

       NORVAL: Trudy, please.

       CUT TO:

E-11   DOORWAY OF THE HOUSE

       Mr. Kockenlocker emerges scowling. Emmy, frightened, peeks
       over his shoulder. THE CAMERA PANS them to Trudy and Norval.

       KOCKENLOCKER: (With narrowed eyes)
                        What have you done to my daughter now?
                                                (Continued)

E-11   (Cont'd)

Trudy renews her sobs. Norval opens his mouth and fingers
no, no, no.

KOCKENLOCKER: (Furiously)
          What have you done to her?

NORVAL: (With an effort)
        The spots.

Mr. Kockenlocker looks at Emmy.

CUT TO:

E-12   THE NEIGHBORS - ON THEIR FRONT PORCH

THE WIFE: What did he say?

THE HUSBAND: Something about a pot.

THE WIFE: I just want to ask Mrs. Sneed...
             (Her voice trails off as
             she walks into the house)

CUT TO:

E-13   MR. KOCKENLOCKER, EMMY, TRUDY, AND NORVAL

KOCKENLOCKER: I'm gonna give you just one more chance.

TRUDY: (Blurting it out)
        Leave him alone, Papa...it wasn't his fault.

KOCKENLOCKER: Will you shut up?

TRUDY: Papa, please!

CUT TO:

E-14   THE SIDEWALK IN FRONT OF THE KOCKENLOCKER HOUSE

The Shottish family (or others) are gathered here.

CUT TO:

E-15   MR. KOCKENLOCKER, EMMY, TRUDY AND NORVAL

TRUDY: (Getting to her feet)
        Would you take me for a soda, Norval?

NORVAL: Would I take for a so---oh..well, certainly.

KOCKENLOCKER: Just a minute, just a minute.

EMMY: Papa! Sit down.

                                  (Continued)

E-15   (Cont'd)

She pushes him into a rocking chair, sits on his lap and
throws her arm around him.

KOCKENLOCKER: Will you get off my lap before I...

EMMY: Go on.

TRUDY: Come on, Norval.

They exit.

KOCKENLOCKER: Hey!

Emmy sits back on his lap.

DISSOLVE TO:

E-16   INTERIOR OF NORVAL'S CAR - MOVING - (NIGHT)

NORVAL: You feel better now?

TRUDY: Thank you, Norval.

NORVAL: What made you .... cry?

TRUDY: Oooooh...

She gets ready to cry again.

NORVAL: I'm sorry, Trudy...Was it the thought of
                  marrying me?

TRUDY: Yes, but not the way you think.

NORVAL: (Perplexed)
                  Oh.

TRUDY: I'm in terrible trouble, Norval...and somehow
                  I just naturally turned to you. Like you
                  said that night, you remember, you almost
                  wished I'd be in a lot of trouble sometime so
                  you could help me out of it.

NORVAL: That's right.

TRUDY: Well, you certainly got your wish...I don't
                  spose you'd want to help me out again...I
                  mean you might not like the idea entirely.

Her lips start to tremble.

NORVAL: (Sourly)
             Where's the party tonight?
                          (Continued)

E-16 (Cont'd)

TRUDY: What? Oh no...that party I went to was
        enough of a party for me...for quite a
        while...that was kind of a party to end
        all parties...if you get what I mean.

NORVAL: But, you said you had such a wonderful
        time, Trudy.

TRUDY: Well, I did...in a way but...some kind
        of fun lasts longer than others...if you
        get what I mean?

NORVAL: (Blankly)
        I'm not sure that I do, Trudy.

TRUDY: Maybe I can find some better way to ex-
        plain it.

NORVAL: Maybe you can...

TRUDY: When you asked me to marry you, Norval...
        did you really mean it?

NORVAL: Of course I did.

TRUDY: Could you think of any reason maybe why
        you <u>wouldn't</u> want to marry me?

NORVAL: What would I do with such a reason...I
        <u>do</u> want to marry you.

TRUDY: (Starting to cry)
        I can't do it to you.

NORVAL: Well, now we're back where we started.

TRUDY: Norval, can you keep a secret?

NORVAL: Certainly I can keep a secret.

TRUDY: Cross your heart and hope to die
        And boil in oil
        And stew in lye.

NORVAL: Cross my heart and hope to die.

TRUDY: ...and boil in oil - and stew in lye? -

NORVAL: Sure.

TRUDY: (Slurring the word)
        I'm married.

             (Continued)

E-16 (Cont'd)

NORVAL: You're married. Well, that's no reason
to...YOU'RE WHAT....

He loses control of the car which swerves over to the curb
and crashes into a vehicle which is parked there.

CUT TO:

E-17   LONG SHOT - CAR CRASHING INTO A PARKED CAR

CUT TO:

E-18   NORVAL AND TRUDY - INSIDE HIS CAR - (NOT MOVING)

NORVAL: It didn't do any harm...I misunderstood
you: I thought you said you were married.

TRUDY: I did say I was married.

NORVAL: You did say you were married...you, you,
you...what do you mean you, you, you...
the spots said you were married?

TRUDY: It happened that night.

NORVAL: It happened that night...YOU MEAN THE
NIGHT YOU WERE OUT WITH ME?

TRUDY: (Looking away)
That's right.

NORVAL: (Excitedly)
But that's ttterrible...that's the
terriblest thing I ever, I ever, I ever,
I ever...how could you do such a thing
the spots to me, Trudy?

TRUDY: And that isn't even the worst of it.

NORVAL: (Electrified)
That isn't even the...worst of it? What
could be worse than that?

TRUDY: You're going to make me cry.

NORVAL: Well, go ahead and cry and see if I care
...huh...the spots...who did you marry?

TRUDY: I don't know.

NORVAL: You don't know. WHAT DO YOU MEAN YOU
DON'T KNOW. That's the most ridiculous
statement I ever, I ever, I ever...

(Continued)

TRUDY: It has a "Z" in it...his name had a "Z"
                in it...I think...I don't know any more...
                I've thought so much about it...and the
                more I think about it the less I can
                remember about it...and don't tell me to
                find the name on the marriage license be-
                cause I haven't got any.

Norval opens his mouth.

TRUDY: And don't tell me I can find it under my
(Cont'd)   name in the records because I used a phony
                name I can't remember...and don't ask me
                if I'm sure I'm married because I _am_ sure.

NORVAL: How _can_ you be if there's no rec...record
                ...record...How can you pppossibly have
                the sl-sl-slightest...You don't mean...
                TRUDY!...THE SPOTS!

TRUDY: That's right.

NORVAL: But TTTrudy this is ttterrible...I feel
                ttterrible.

TRUDY: How do you spose I feel?

NORVAL: That's the terriblest thing I ever heard
                of... I, I, I, I...what's your father
                going to think when he finds out and you
                can't give any...I mean you haven't got
                any husband...I mean any proof...I mean
                any, any...who's he gonna

Trudy looks at him silently.

NORVAL: (Suddenly, pointing to himself)
                - THE SPOTS.

TRUDY: I can almost see them myself.

NORVAL: (The dots below represent a long
                            sentence in pure gibberish, not
                            one word of which is clear)
                ·•••

TRUDY: Norval, stop it.

NORVAL: (Holding his head)
                ·•••

TRUDY: Norval, try to concentrate, try to focus.

NORVAL: Ffffocus.
                                    (Continued)

E-18 (Cont'd)

TRUDY: Norval, you'd better take me home.

NORVAL: Ffffocus.

TRUDY: (As to a child)
                    No, home.

NORVAL: H-hhhocus.

DISSOLVE TO:

E-19 INT. KOCKENLOCKER HALLWAY

Trudy comes in and closes the door behind her. As she starts
for the foot of the stairs.

CUT TO:

E-20 MR. KOCKENLOCKER - IN THE SITTING ROOM - READING

He looks up and crosses to the foot of the stairs, which
brings him into the SHOT with Trudy.

KOCKENLOCKER: Now what was all that horsing around on
                    the front porch?

TRUDY: (With a strange dignity)
                    Don't you know there are times when a
                    woman doesn't care to talk.

KOCKENLOCKER: (Indignantly)
                    A woman doesn't care to talk...Only time
                    a woman doesn't care to talk is when
                    she's dead. And where do you get that
                    woman stuff?

TRUDY: (With a far-away look)
                    Or be questioned.

She starts up the steps with tremendous dignity.

KOCKENLOCKER: (Threateningly)
                    Or be what? Why you fresh little...

He starts around the newel post after her.

Trudy sheds her dignity, picks up her skirts and flies up
the stairs and into her room an inch ahead of her father,
who gets the door slammed in his face.

CUT TO:

649

E-21   INT. TRUDY'S ROOM

She leans against the door while locking it. THE CAMERA
PANS FROM HER TO Emmy who is sitting on the edge of the bed.

EMMY: What happened?

CUT TO:

E-22   TRUDY - AT THE DOOR

As she speaks she comes forward and starts to undress.

TRUDY: Oh, just Papa pulling his usual stuff.

EMMY: No, I mean with Norval.

TRUDY: Oh...I couldn't do it to him.

She avoids her sister's eye.

TRUDY: He was so sweet, honey...he said he
                    loved me ever since I wasn't any bigger
                    than a fire hydrant or something, then
                    how he didn't blame me for not loving
                    him because he was so homely in the face
                    and stuff like that, and then...

She starts to gulp.

TRUDY: (Continuing)
                    ...then how he went to cooking class and
                    s-s-sewing class just to be near me...

She starts to yammer.

EMMY: But he's perfect...He could do all the
                    housework.

TRUDY: (Bawling)
                    I couldn't do it to him.

EMMY: Why don't you give yourself up...you
                    ought to have your brains counted.

TRUDY: I just couldn't do it...We'll have to
                    find something else.

EMMY: Where are you going to find another
                    clunk like that one?

TRUDY: Well, there's nothing says you got to
                    have a husband...on the happy day...
                    you take like a widow...

EMMY: Yes, but a widow had one.

                                                 (Continued)

E-22 (Cont'd)

TRUDY: (Belligerently)
                    I had one.

EMMY: You don't have to convince me Trudy....I
                    love you...I know you wouldn't do any-
                    thing wrong...except you take after
                    Papa's side of the family a little. It
                    would hurt me just as much as it would
                    you to have you hurt and...miserable and...
                    and ashamed and everything. That's the
                    only reason I want you to get married.

They both start to sniffle.

EMMY: (Continuing)
                    You can't tell how a town's going to take
                    things...a town that can produce shnooks
                    like Papa...all suspicious and suspecting
                    the worst in everything. There are very
                    few dopes like Norval, honey...... You
                    can't use anybody too snoopy.

TRUDY: (Through her tears)
                    Then maybe...I shouldn't of told him.

EMMY: (Her eyes popping out
                              of her head)
                    You didn't tell him?

TRUDY: (Weeping)
                    Y-y-yes.

EMMY: (Furiously)
                    Oh murder!

Now she bursts into tears of rage, the sisters throw their
arms around each other, flop back on the bed and howl in
unison.

CUT TO:

E-23 HALLWAY - OUTSIDE THEIR DOOR

Mr. Kockenlocker, half in and half out of his nightgown,
comes out of his room, listens and goes over to the door
and pounds on it.

KOCKENLOCKER: (Pounding)
                    What's going on in there? How about a
                    little quiet? Daughters...fooey!

FADE OUT.

                    END OF SEQUENCE "E"

F-1   ELIMINATED
&
F-2

F-3   NORVAL - IN HIS CAGE IN THE FIRST NATIONAL BANK

He looks up as Mr. Tuerck approaches.

MR. TUERCK: Going to lunch?

NORVAL: Yes, sir.

MR. TUERCK: Funny thing happened this morning. Mr.
                Shottish asked me if you had announced
                your engagement yet.

NORVAL: My enga-gagement.

MR. TUERCK: Yes. He had a kinda wild idea that maybe
                you'd eloped or something.

NORVAL: W-w-what would I, would I, would I elope
                for?

MR. TUERCK: What are you so nervous about?

NORVAL: W-why should I b-b-b-e nervous w-wh-who's
                n-n-nervous?

MR. TUERCK: All I mean, Norval, is it isn't any of
                my business what time you get home in the
                morning or how drunk you are when you get
                home...but it is the bank's business.

NORVAL: The b-bank.

MR. TUERCK: That's right. A man in a bank is like a
                fellow crossing Niagara Falls on a tight
                rope...he can not be too careful.

NORVAL: Yes sir, I g-g-get what you mean, Mr. Tuerck.

MR. TUERCK: (Looking back over his shoulder)
                Fathers taking pokes at you and all that
                kind of stuff...very bad for a banker.

NORVAL: You said it...yes sir, Mr. Tuerck...y-y-you
                said it.

MR. TUERCK: Remember it.

NORVAL: Y-y-yes sir.

He knocks a whole tray full of bills and change on the
floor. He stoops to pick them up and peeks to see if
Mr. Tuerck has noticed.
CUT TO:

652

F-4   CLOSE SHOT - MR. TUERCK

He has paused to notice. Now he looks very shrewd, turns
and departs.

DISSOLVE TO:

F-5   OFFICER KOCKENLOCKER - IN THE MIDDLE OF THE STREET

He is having his usual troubles, punctuated by the blasts
of his whistle.

KOCKENLOCKER: Come on, come on - all right, Lady...
                  tell me how to do it.

He changes the direction of the traffic and Mr. Tuerck
crosses the street into the shot with him.

KOCKENLOCKER: Good morning, Mr. Tuerck.

MR. TUERCK: (Jovially)
                  How do you do, Edmund. I am glad to see
                  they haven't run you down yet.

KOCKENLOCKER: I'll probably get it from a horse when I
                  get it.

MR. TUERCK: (After a polite laugh)
                  Heard a rumor one of your daughters was
                  going to get married, any truth in it?

KOCKENLOCKER: One of my daughters! Who told you?

MR. TUERCK: A little bird...we bankers you know...heh,
                  heh, heh...have our own little channels of
                  information. Well, congratulations, Edmund.

KOCKENLOCKER: Well a...come on, Lady will ya...We want
                  you to save gas and all that but a....

He jumps to one side as the car flies past him. While looking after the car indignantly a horse nearly runs him down.

DISSOLVE TO:

F-6   THE TURNTABLE IN RAFFERTY'S MUSIC STORE

Trudy's hand comes into the shot and puts a record on the
turntable. The machine begins to play "Chopin's Funeral
March." THE CAMERA PANS over to Trudy and we see her sitting dejectedly, listening lugubriously to the music. She
reaches for a knob and turns the music up a little higher.

CUT TO:

F-7   MR. RAFFERTY AT HIS DESK NEAR THE CASH REGISTER

He looks indignantly in Trudy's direction, tries to write
in his journal, then slaps it closed and hurries toward
Trudy.

CUT TO:

F-8   TRUDY - LISTENING TO THE MUSIC DEJECTEDLY.

She turns as she hears Mr. Rafferty approaching.

CUT TO:

F-9   MR. RAFFERTY - APPROACHING

As he talks THE CAMERA PANS HIM into the SHOT with Trudy.

MR. RAFFERTY: (Indignantly)
                  For heaven's sake, Trudy, what's the matter
                  with you? "Chopin's Funeral March" again
                  ... "Gloomy Sunday" all day. "A Violet From
                  Mother's Grave" yet...what are you trying
                  to do...drive me into 77B?

TRUDY: (Dejectedly)
                  I'm sorry.

MR. RAFFERTY: What's the matter with you? You'd give the
                  heebie-jeebies to a horse! You got the
                  meloncholic...maybe it's your toots...
                  nothing gives so much trouble like the toots
                  ...now you take me till I had mine hex-rayed
                  did I...WILL YOU TURN THAT THING OFF AND
                  PLAY SOMETHING JOLIER?

TRUDY: Yes sir.

RAFFERTY: You know what it showed in the hex-ray?...
                  I won't cut your appetite. Anyway..now...
                                    (He pushes his uppers firmly
                                    into place)
                  ...a pleasure.

TRUDY: (Turning from putting on
                        another record)
                  I'm all right - I'm just a little bit blue.

The machine starts to play a sentimental Paramount number.

RAFFERTY: Your gallbladder!...now you take me 'till
                  I had my gallbladder hex-rayed was I
                  nauseous!

TRUDY: (Cutting in)
                  There's nothing the matter with me, Mr.
                  Rafferty.
                                          (Continued)

F-9 (Cont'd)

Mr. Rafferty is non-plussed for a second - but only for a
second.

RAFFERTY: (Triumphantly)
                I got it: your feet! 'Till I had my
                feet hex-rayed did I suffer from back
                pains... shooting through here.
                    (Now he demonstrates with
                    his hands)
                My arches was pressing on my nerves
                and shooting pains up my...
                sometimes it would catch me...
                    (He clutches the back of
                    his neck)

                                    (Continued)

TRUDY: It isn't my feet.

RAFFERTY: Then you're in love.

Now he leaps on this theory with joy.

RAFFERTY: (Continued)
                Trudy, you little monkey, you're in love,
                that's wonderful...who is it...don't tell
                me, let me guess: A SOLDIER...one of them
                lieutenants maybe...all right he isn't a
                lieutenant...he'll be a lieutenant.

TRUDY: Mr. Rafferty, please.

She starts to cry.

RAFFERTY: (Desolated - putting his
                         arm on her shoulder)
                Trudy, did I say something...would I try
                to hurt you, Trudy?

The automatic phonograph takes off the record and starts
playing "Chopin's Funeral March" underneath it.

RAFFERTY: Trudy, please WILL YOU TAKE THAT THING OFF...
                and break it...or put it back in the filex.
                Now tell me...what's the matter?

We hear the shop door open and they both turn.

CUT TO:

F-10 NORVAL - COMING IN WITH A LITTLE BUNCH OF FLOWERS IN HIS
     HAND

CUT TO:

F-11 TRUDY AND MR. RAFFERTY

RAFFERTY: Oh ho...aha enough said, two and two is
                four, plus ten percent amusement tax, plus
                five percent federal and three percent un-
                employment.

He laughs at his lousy little joke.

RAFFERTY: Come on now, smile for him when he comes
                in...smile kitsy-kitsy.
                         (He tickles her)
                And no more funeral marches...wedding
                marches...I'll take a powder.

                                              (Continued)

656

F-11 (Cont'd)

He starts toward Norval.

CUT TO:

F-12   NORVAL - COMING IN

RAFFERTY: (Crossing to him)
                        Good evening, Norval.

He takes his hand and shakes it significantly.

RAFFERTY: I know from nothing.

He gives Norval a wise wink, and hurries to his desk.

THE CAMERA PANS Norval into the shot with Trudy.

TRUDY: Hello, Norval.

NORVAL: Hello, Trudy.
                        (Then jerking a thumb
                         toward Rafferty)
          What's he talking about?

TRUDY: I don't know.

NORVAL: The whole town seems to know something.

TRUDY: H-h-how could they?

NORVAL: I don't know...but Mr. Tuerck was saying
          I'd better watch my step and, and...

TRUDY: Why should you watch your step?

NORVAL: I don't know. And then your father came
          in and kind of threatened me.

TRUDY: You didn't tell him anything?

NORVAL: Trudy, how can you say such a thing? I
          mean the way I feel...I couldn't sleep
          all last night, Trudy.

TRUDY: I'm sorry, Norval...I wouldn't want to
          upset you for anything.

NORVAL: You wouldn't want to upset me, Trudy! How
          can you be so brave in the most terrible
          situation I ever, I ever, I ever...

TRUDY: Norval, relax...don't start again...and be
          careful what you say - I'll play something
          to soothe you.
                                 (Continued)

She takes a record at random, puts it on the turntable. It
turns out to be "I Don't Want to Walk Without You."

TRUDY: (Returning to Norval)
                  You better buy some needles.

NORVAL: S-s-sure.

He reaches into his pocket.

NORVAL: I didn't sleep all last night and I don't
                  think I'm ever gonna sleep again until I
                  know you're fixed up.

TRUDY: You can take my word for it, Norval.

NORVAL: I mean you've given me something to live
                  for Trudy, don't be downhearted, don't be
                  blue...don't give up the ship...we'll see
                  it through...it used to be that all I
                  could think of was to get into uniform
                  but now all I can think of is to get you
                  out of trouble. I can't think of anything
                  else...

TRUDY: I don't know how to thank you, Norval.

NORVAL: That's all right. I'll tell you what I
                  figured: We'll take an ad in every camp
                  paper in the country...they make a club
                  rate and we'll say...

TRUDY: But that'll cost you a fortune, Norval.

NORVAL: What does that matter. I've got nine
                  hundred dollars saved up, and to spend
                  it on you would be my dearest wish Trudy.

                  We'll say: 'Party wishing to locate missing
                  Ratzikiwatski. Will pay liberal reward for
                  information leading to his return'...
                  something like that.

TRUDY: You don't suppose they'll think it is a
                  dog, do you?

                              (Continued)

F-13   NORVAL AND TRUDY - <u>IN THE LOCAL NEWSPAPER OFFICE</u>

Norval is going through a handful of mail. The envelopes
are stamped with dog food ads, bargains in orange groves,
electric vitality belts, a million ways to make a million
dollars, the personality that pounces, etc. We hear the
SOUND of the PRESSES.

NORVAL: (Disgustedly)
                We will give you back your vitality with
                dividends...Do you want a body like a greek
                god...Flat-o for flat feet...Do you want to
                retire in thirty-eight years...The naughty
                novelty company...A million ways to make a
                million dollars...
                    (He tosses the envelope on the
                    counter)
                But no Ratzkiwatzki.

TRUDY: Maybe he doesn't read the papers!

NORVAL: Maybe he doesn't read at all.

TRUDY: You mustn't speak that way about the Armed
                Forces, Norval.

NORVAL: Well, what good is he to you? All he's
                doing is stopping people who want to do
                you some good from doing it...the rat.

TRUDY: (Reprovingly)
                Norval!

NORVAL: I'm sorry, but any husband you have to ad-
                vertise for I don't think is worth the
                paper you print him on.

TRUDY: Talking against him isn't going to help
                anything.

THE EDITOR: (Coming in brightly)
                Say Norval, did you ever find that...whatever
                it was you lost?

NORVAL: No.

He turns away.

THE EDITOR: By the way, what <u>is</u> a ... Ratzkiwatzki?

NORVAL: You can search me.

Leaving the editor somewhat surprised, Trudy and Norval
exit.

CUT TO:

F-14 TRUDY AND NORVAL - COMING OUT OF THE NEWSPAPER OFFICE -
      TRUCKING SHOT

      As they come out, we start to move. We stay in playing dis-
      tance ahead of them for the scene.

      NORVAL: You don't remember anything about him
                       except that he had curly hair?

      Trudy shrugs.

      NORVAL: Did he wear glasses?

      TRUDY: Where?

      NORVAL: Well, where do you usually wear glasses?
                       Not on your...

      TRUDY: I don't know.

      NORVAL: Was he tall?

      TRUDY: Probably...I don't know...All I know is that
                       I was dancing with a tall dark boy with
                       curly hair...at least you imagine he must
                       have been tall and dark.

      NORVAL: (Slightly indignant)
                       Oh you do? You think a medium sized man
                       with red hair or even a little short guy
                       as bald as an eagle...

      TRUDY: Don't be vulgar, Norval.

      NORVAL: I'm not vulgar. Why do you just naturally
                       conclude that anybody you dance with would
                       have to be...
                                 (He holds his hand eight
                                 feet in the air)
                       this high with black oily hair?

      TRUDY: You're just jealous.

      NORVAL: (Subsiding)
                       I guess I am...

      TRUDY: Do you think maybe I could divorce him?

      NORVAL: Not unless you could prove you were mar-
                       ried to him first...That's the foundation
                       of divorce...unless there's such a thing
                       as a John Doe divorce...like they have
                       those John Doe indictments...if you can
                       indict a John Doe...you might be able to
                       divorce him.

                                                        (Continued)

                                660

TRUDY: His name wasn't John Doe, it was Ratzki...

NORVAL: I don't know whether it would work or not
                    anyway, Trudy! Maybe you'd just better
                    marry me and...let it go at that.

TRUDY: I couldn't do it to you, Norval...I couldn't
                    let you run the risk of going to jail for
                    twenty years for bigamy...just for me.

NORVAL: Well, you were going to on the front porch
                    ...You didn't mention the twenty years when
                    you let me pro-...pra-prose to you.

TRUDY: I wasn't in love with you then, Norval.

NORVAL: (Galvanized)
                    Trudy! Do you really mean that?

TRUDY: I'm very much ashamed of myself, Norval...
                    for what I almost did to you.

NORVAL: (Excitedly)
                    What are you talking about, Trudy? All
                    you did was give me the chance I've wanted
                    all my life...that I've been waiting for...
                    to show you how much I love you, Trudy...
                    and the kind of love I have for you, Trudy..
                    You've got to marry me, Trudy.

TRUDY: (With sad sweetness)
                    I can't do it, Norval...but I want you to
                    know how much I appreciate your offer...
                    and how much I wish I'd known how sweet
                    you are...a little sooner.
                                   (She squeezes his hand)
                    I want you to know that, and I want you to
                    remember it always...It will be my dying
                    wish...and when they fish me out...I want
                    you to know that my last thought...
                                   (Her lips tremble)
                    was of you.

NORVAL: (Horrified)
                    F-f-f-ish you out! You mean the c-c-c-creek?

TRUDY: It's the only way.

                                   (Continued)

                                   661

F-14 (Cont'd)

NORVAL: (Indignantly)
What are you talking about? That's
the last way...when everything else
has failed! Before I tried that I'd
try bigamy, forgery, burglary...any-
thing.

TRUDY: (Sadly)
The only awful part about it is that
Papa would be <u>sure</u> to shoot you then.

NORVAL: Oh...oh yes...
                  (His voice lets the last
                  sentence trail off into
                  a sort of a mutter. Now
                  he resumes nobly:)
Of course, after <u>you</u> went nothing else
would matter.

TRUDY: (Even sweeter and sadder)
Thank you, dear...We might jump in
together.

NORVAL: There isn't much...water at this time
of the year.

TRUDY: There's a place out about ten miles...

NORVAL: You're not supposed to use your tires
for things like that, Trudy...besides
I'm a very good swimmer...and they say
very good swimmers, no matter how hard
they try...as soon as they lose consciousness, they just s-sw--swim...
right out.

TRUDY: I'm a very good swimmer too, I hadn't
thought of that.

NORVAL: (Emphatically)
Then <u>let's</u> <u>forget</u> the Creek.

TRUDY: (After a pause)
We could tie rocks around our necks.

(Continued)

F-14 (Cont'd)

NORVAL: (Fingering no, no, no)
                  Never.

TRUDY: (After a moment)
                  What's the matter with gas?

NORVAL: (Almost angrily)
                  What's the matter with bigamy?

KOCKENLOCKER'S
VOICE: HEY!

Norval and Trudy turn, startled, toward the porch of her
house.

CUT TO:

F-15 KOCKENLOCKER - ON THE FRONT PORCH - CLEANING HIS SIX-SHOOTER

He has apparatus spread all over the place.

KOCKENLOCKER: Come here.

CUT TO:

F-16 NORVAL AND TRUDY - AT THE GATE

They exchange a frightened look, then the CAMERA PANS them
onto the porch with Mr. Kockenlocker. Make protection
without gun.

KOCKENLOCKER: Want to have a little talk with you.

He blows through the barrel of his gun.

TRUDY: (Nervously)
                  With me, Papa?

KOCKENLOCKER: (Coming down out of the barrel)
                  No, with your gentleman friend there....
                  you go in the house.

TRUDY: Yes, Papa.

Kockenlocker looks through the barrel of the gun again,
blows through it, then barks suddenly:

                        Sit down!

Norval's knees give way under him, he sits on a screwdriver,
raises up, removes the screwdriver, smiles apologetically
and sits down on the trigger mechanism. He removes this
from the seat of his pants with a little jerk, laughs
suddenly and just as suddenly stops.

KOCKENLOCKER: What are you so nervous about?
                                             (Continued)

F-16 (Cont'd)

Norval gestures no, no, no and lays several eggs before
saying:

NORVAL: W-w-who's nervous?

KOCKENLOCKER: There's getting to be quite a little talk
in the town.

NORVAL: Oh.

He fortifies this by gesturing no, no, no.

KOCKENLOCKER: (Working his trigger mechanism
with an iron grip)
Where I come from we don't skulk around in
the bushes, you get me?

He looks around at Norval.

NORVAL: (Inaudibly)
Yes, sir.

KOCKENLOCKER: When we gotta cross the street, we don't
crawl through the sewer to get there!

NORVAL: Y-y-y-yes sir.

KOCKENLOCKER: (Hollering)
When we've got something to say, WE SAY IT!

NORVAL: Yes, sir.

KOCKENLOCKER: When is the happy event?

Norval slips off the edge of the chair.

NORVAL: (Picking himself up off the
floor)
I didn't hear exactly w-wh-wh-at you s-said.

KOCKENLOCKER: When are you and Trudy getting hitched?

NORVAL: (As if delighted to hear this)
Oh!

He bursts into idiotic laughter.

KOCKENLOCKER: (Sternly)
What are you laughing about?

He twirls his revolver on his finger.

10-19-42   (Continued)

F-16 (Cont'd)

NORVAL: Who, m-m-me? I'm not laughing.
                      (He explodes in nervous guffaws:)
                   just something I heard in the b-b-bank today.

KOCKENLOCKER: You haven't answered my question: when are
                   you and Trudy getting spliced?

NORVAL: Oh.

He laughs happily and shakes his fingers no, no, no.

KOCKENLOCKER: There isn't any idiocy in your family, is
                   there?

NORVAL: (Shaking no, no, no after trying
                      three times to form the word
                      'she')
            She won't have me.

KOCKENLOCKER: (Drily)
            Oh, she won't?

NORVAL: No sir, I just...

He points down the street and has some trouble with the
"As" of the next word:

           asked her.

KOCKENLOCKER: (Immediately)
           You didn't ask her right.

He rams a brush through the barrel of his six-shooter.

           You gotta be more forceful in these matters..
           dames like to be bossed...now you take me...

NORVAL: I did my best.

KOCKENLOCKER: You can do better.

NORVAL: (Quickly)
           All I can do is ask.

KOCKENLOCKER: We accept...you're in...

NORVAL: (Sweating)
           Now w-w-wait a minute, w-w-will you?...
           There might be a couple of reasons...a
           couple of details...

KOCKENLOCKER: You can settle the details between you...
           All I'm interested in is results...I'm a
           man who looks at things broadly, see?...
           I'm a man who...
                             (Continued)

F-16 (Cont'd)

NORVAL: Will you just wait a...

KOCKENLOCKER: (Loudly)
                     You gonna go in and ask her or do you want
                     me to do it for you? Where I come from...

By now his gun is reassembled so he fires it twice to see if
it works.

NORVAL: (Shaken)
             I'll go.

He hangs onto the porch rail and exits on rubber legs. THE
CAMERA PANS with him.

CUT TO:

F-17 MR. KOCKENLOCKER - LOOKING AFTER HIM

KOCKENLOCKER: I almost forgot...congratulations.

CUT TO:

F-18 NORVAL IN FRONT OF THE SCREEN DOOR

NORVAL: (Turning politely toward
                                 Kockenlocker)
                     Th-th-thank you.

He smiles and walks through the screen door, into the house.

CUT TO:

F-19 TRUDY - IN THE KITCHEN

She stands nervously in the doorway which leads to the back
shed.

TRUDY: What was that shooting?

CUT TO:

F-20 NORVAL - IN THE DOORWAY FROM THE HALL

NORVAL: (Rubber-legged)
                     N-n-nothing, he was just pr-pr-practicing.

He crosses the kitchen unsteadily and THE CAMERA TAKES HIM
into the SHOT with Trudy.

TRUDY: (Holding her heart)
                     It frightened me.

10-19-42   (Continued)

666

F-20   (Cont'd)

NORVAL: There's nothing to be fr-fr-frightened
about, only he wants us to get ma-m-married
right away, he was very firm ab-ab-ab-about
it.

TRUDY: (Indignantly)
Why?   Oh, you mean because you brought me...

NORVAL: Don't start arguing, will you?   The whole
to-t-town is t-t-talking...You're in a
t-t-terrible s-sp-spot, Tt-t-trudy...
you've either got to m-m-marry me right
away or tell him the t-t-truth...which
would be t-t-terrible.

TRUDY: I can't do it to you, Norval.

NORVAL: What are you talking about?

Now he looks back over his shoulder, then pushes her out
into the lean-to so that they will not be overheard.

CUT TO:

F-21   TRUDY AND NORVAL - COMING INTO THE LEAN-TO

This puts the CAMERA in the BACK YARD and gives us room to
move around.

NORVAL: This is just a lucky break for me, I told
you that...it's just giving me an oppor-
tunity.

TRUDY: But that's bigamy!   I'm married to
Ratzkiwatzki, Norval...I can't keep on marrying people...no matter how sweet they are...

NORVAL: (Dynamically)
WAIT A MINUTE!...Trudy!   I've got it!

TRUDY: Don't get excited, Norval.

NORVAL: Wh-wh-who's excited?   This is air-tight and
w-w-water-tight...It's f-f-fool-proof and
almost legal, Trudy.   And when we get
through you can divorce that b-b-bum and
marry me.

TRUDY: Take it easy, Norval.

NORVAL: It's a cinch!   It's almost an insp-spira-
tion!   Now: will you go to the m-m-movies
with me tomorrow night?...the early show.

F-21 (Cont'd)

TRUDY: Of course I will, Norval, I'll be glad to.

NORVAL: (Triumphantly)
                          All right, that's all there is to it. I'll
                          go get everything ready, I'll go this way.
                                 (He indicates the back gate)
                          I don't want to meet your father just yet.
                                 (He starts for the gate)

TRUDY: (Worried)
                          But wait a minute, Norval.

NORVAL: (Looking back but not
                                  stopping)
                          Don't you worry about anything, this is go-
                          ing to be like f-f-falling off a log!

Saying which, he walks into a branch of a tree and is knocked
flat on his back.

TRUDY: Norval!

She hurries to him and falls on her knees.

CUT TO:

F-22 CLOSE SHOT - NORVAL PAST TRUDY

TRUDY: Did you break anything, dear?

NORVAL: Nothing but my...back.

He clears his throat, whistles, and smiles up at her lovingly,

FADE OUT.

                         END OF SEQUENCE "F"

10-19-42

SEQUENCE "G"

FADE IN:

G-1   CLOSE SHOT - A TRAY OF WEDDING RINGS

THE JEWELER'S
VOICE: Well, well, well, Norval.

CUT TO:

G-2   NORVAL - PAST THE JEWELER - (WE SEE THE TOWN BEYOND)

NORVAL: No, no...my...my aunt in the East dropped
hers down a rat hole - a c-cc-crack in the
floor... so I'm sending her another one as
a surprise...her finger felt kinda naked.

THE JEWELER: (Not believing a word of this)
I see, I see, that's very thoughtful of
you, Norval.

NORVAL: Nothing at all, naturally she wouldn't
want anybody to kn-kn-know it wasn't the
same one she was...my uncle gave her...so
if you just don't say anything about it...
for her sake you know?

THE JEWELER: Not a word, Norval, not a word...

NORVAL: (Handing over a ten dollar bill)
F-f-fine.

THE JEWELER: The secret will die with me.

NORVAL: G-good.

DISSOLVE TO:

G-3   EXT. WINDOW - OF A CLOTHING STORE

Here we see suits, uniforms, hats, etc.

CUT TO:

G-4   INTERIOR - CLOTHING STORE

Here we see Norval and Mr. Swartz.

MR. SWARTZ: I can't do it, Norval. They wrote me a
letter: Wool is very scarce...we gotta
save it for the soldiers.

(Continued)

G-4   (Cont'd)

NORVAL: How about cotton?

MR. SWARTZ: Cotton is very scarce, it says so in the
next paragraph. What for, do you want
for, a uniform for anyway.

NORVAL: I wouldn't want you to tell anybody.

MR. SWARTZ: (Hurt)
Norval!

NORVAL: It's just to wear around the house...you
know, when you've always wanted one.

MR. SWARTZ: (Pointing to it)
How about a Indian suit with feathers?

NORVAL: (Hopelessly)
No it's just...

MR. SWARTZ: (Electrified, grabbing Norval)
Wait! Just to wear around the house?

NORVAL: That's all...in the yard maybe.

MR. SWARTZ: It ain't the latest.

NORVAL: What does that matter?

MR. SWARTZ: (Giving him a feel, muttering
to himself)
7 hat, 36 coat, medium britches, 9 foots.

NORVAL: You got the shoes, too?

MR. SWARTZ: I'll even throw in the gun. Five dollars
for the whole outfit and you're doing me
a favor. You can play soldier till your
feet give out.

NORVAL: Well, that's very kind of you, Mr. Swartz.

MR. SWARTZ: That's very kind of you, Norval.
                         (He starts into the back room)
It just shows you never can tell....

CUT TO:

G-5   MR. SWARTZ - IN THE BACK ROOM

He lifts a 1918 campaign hat off a large bundle, blows a
cloud of dust off it and drops it into a paper bag.

10-19-42   (Continued)

G-5   (Cont'd)

MR. SWARTZ: (Speaking)
                           ...how long you got to hang onto a piece
                           of merchandise...you can have the steel
                           helmet too...I'm glad to get rid of it,...
                           before you get your money out.

As he starts back to the front of the store.

DISSOLVE TO:

G-6   FLORIST'S WINDOW - CLOSE SHOT - A LITTLE BOUQUET

A hand removes it from the shot.

DISSOLVE TO:

G-7   KOCKENLOCKER KITCHEN - (NIGHT)

The girls are wiping the dishes. Mr. Kockenlocker is finishing his coffee. He rises, picks up the paper and starts
out. As he passes his daughter he stops:

KOCKENLOCKER: That Norval talk to you about something
                  again?

TRUDY: I don't know what you're hinting at,
                  Papa...I'm going to the movies with him
                  if that's what you mean.

EMMY: Why don't you leave her alone?

KOCKENLOCKER: Why don't you keep your trap shut?

Emmy deliberately drops the plate in her hand.

KOCKENLOCKER: (Closing his eyes)
                  Daughters.

He stamps out of the room. The girls wait 'till he is gone
before speaking.

TRUDY: And then we get married...and then I get
                  the certificate...and then everything is
                  legal...it just makes the first time more
                  legal!

EMMY: But that's bigamy...just as much as if you
                  married him as Norval Jones.

                                            (Continued)

TRUDY: No, it isn't...they do it all the time...
                                like when a king wants to get married,
                                only he's busy in his kingdom so he can't
                                go to the other kingdom and the other
                                king won't send the princess c.o.d. be-
                                cause he doesn't trust the first king...
                                so they send a kind of a phony bridegroom
                                over and he marries the princess...except
                                he doesn't exactly marry her...it's what
                                you call a marriage by prexy.

EMMY: I didn't know prexies could perform mar-
                                riages.

TRUDY: I didn't either.

EMMY: Well, it's bigamy.

TRUDY: It is not! Because I'm not marrying
                                two different people, don't you see?
                                I'm just marrying Ratzkiwatzki
                                again....it's like you send a check
                                to somebody and it gets lost so you

(Continued)

G-7 (Cont'd)

TRUDY: (Cont'd)	write out another one. That's all we're doing...it's still the same check to the same person, see...for the same amount. It isn't like you wrote two checks to two different people, see? That would be bigamy.
EMMY:	What happens if the first check shows up?
TRUDY:	Why do you have to go and think up things like that?...He's fixed everything up very cleverly! Like how he got the ring and uniform without anybody suspecting anything.
EMMY:	How can a dope do anything clever?
TRUDY:	You mustn't talk about him that way, Emmy. He's one of the most noblest men who ever drew the breath of life.
EMMY:	They're always noble.
TRUDY:	Well, he isn't a dope, and even if he was, it wouldn't be his fault would it?
EMMY:	I didn't say it was his fault, I just said he was a dope.
TRUDY:	(On the verge of tears) But he's got everything figured out !... He says it's going to be like falling off a log.
EMMY:	You know how high you can fall off a log?
TRUDY:	Oh.

She relaxes disgustedly and lets the dish she is wiping fall on the floor.

CUT TO:

G-8   MR. KOCKENLOCKER - OUTSIDE

He half rises out of his chair, then sits down again, a haunted man.

CUT TO:

G-9   TRUDY AND EMMY - <u>IN THE KITCHEN</u>

EMMY: (Picking up the broken dish)
                     Is he coming here in the uniform?

TRUDY: Of course not, stoopid. He only puts that
                   on when we get way out in the country...in
                   a field or something.

EMMY: He'll probably get chased by a bull.

TRUDY: (Dissolving in tears)
                   Don't be so mean and sour about everything,
                   Emmy...here it was almost like going on a
                   picnic and now...

EMMY: (Putting her arms around her
                      sister)
                   It's only because I'm worried about you
                   Honey...if only I could go along and keep
                   you out of trouble.

TRUDY: (Desperately)
                   But, he's got everything figured out.

EMMY: How can a shnook figure anything out?

TRUDY: Oh, Emmy.

She starts to cry.

EMMY: (Taking her in her arms)
             I'm sorry.

A platter crashes to the floor between them.

CUT TO:

G-10   MR. KOCKENLOCKER - <u>ON THE FRONT PORCH</u>

He looks as if his reason were abandoning him. He starts
to rise out of his chair then sinks back again.

KOCKENLOCKER: (To Norval)
                Oh.

CUT TO:

G-11   NORVAL

THE CAMERA PANS HIM into the shot with Kockenlocker.

G-11 (Cont'd)

NORVAL: Good evening.
                    (He smiles most
                    ingratiatingly)
                Taking Trudy to the m-m-movies.
                    (He laughs hilariously)

KOCKENLOCKER: What's so funny about that?

NORVAL: Oh, n-n-n-nothing.
                    (He laughs like a hyena then
                    clears his throat)
                Shall I tell her I'm here...
                    (He clears his throat)
                ...or will you?

KOCKENLOCKER: What do you want me to do...fire a salute?

NORVAL: (After an unhappy laugh)
                Very f-f-funny.

KOCKENLOCKER: You remember what I told you yesterday?

NORVAL: Yes, sir.

KOCKENLOCKER: Keep thinking about it?

NORVAL: Yes, sir.

He clears his throat.

KOCKENLOCKER: Movie is a very good place...you can hold
                hands.

NORVAL: S-s-sure.

He clears his throat.

KOCKENLOCKER: (Bringing the palms of his
                    hands together)
                Snuggle up.

NORVAL: F-f-fine.

KOCKENLOCKER: You get the idea?

NORVAL: P-p-p-erfect.

KOCKENLOCKER: You don't want me to come and sit behind
                you?

NORVAL: (With gestures)
                No, no, no...no, no,no,no...no, no, no...
                no, no, NO.

10-19-42   (Continued)

675

G-11 (Cont'd)

KOCKENLOCKER: I got you. Then I guess that's about all.
        (He turns and bellows)
        TRUDY!

Norval reacts, and we hear a plate crash in the kitchen.

KOCKENLOCKER: They ain't giving away a set of dishes
        tonight are they?

CUT TO:

G-12 TRUDY AND EMMY - IN THE KITCHEN

TRUDY: I guess he's here.

She looks at the broken dish.

EMMY: It doesn't matter...good luck.

TRUDY: Thanks, honey...should I take anything?

EMMY: What for? To go to a movie.

TRUDY: That's right.

She takes a deep breath, crosses her fingers and knocks
on wood. They start out of the kitchen.

CUT TO:

G-13 KOCKENLOCKER FRONT PORCH

The girls join Norval and their father.

NORVAL: (Excitedly)
       Hello, Trudy...guess we're going to see
       some pretty good m-m-m-movies tonight.

TRUDY: (Also very falsely jovial)
       You said it, N-n-norval.

KOCKENLOCKER: (Sourly)
       You gonna start that stuff now?

TRUDY: Well, goodbye, Papa...goodbye, Emmy.

EMMY: (Kissing her)
       Goodbye, honey.

KOCKENLOCKER: What's all this goodbyeing to see a couple
       of bum features?

NORVAL: Th-th-three features.

10-19-42   (Continued)

G-13 (Cont'd)

TRUDY: (Quickly)
"The Bride Wore Purple," "The Road To Reno,"
and "Are Husbands Necessary?"

KOCKENLOCKER: And t hen home.

NORVAL: Y-y-you said it.

KOCKENLOCKER: No boogie woogie.

EMMY: Papa, why can't you be more refined?

KOCKENLOCKER: What?

EMMY: (Pushing the two away)
Goodbye...and watch your step.

She crosses her fingers and holds them high.

KOCKENLOCKER: (Turning to her)
Listen you.

Suddenly Emmy bursts into tears and throws her arms around
her father's neck.

KOCKENLOCKER: (Stupefied)
What's going on around here anyway?

He sits heavily in his chair and takes Emmy on his lap.
The chair collapses into kindling wood.

FADE OUT:

END OF SEQUENCE "G"

10-19-42

SEQUENCE "H"

FADE IN:

H-1   TRUDY AND NORVAL - MOVING CAR - (NIGHT)

TRUDY: Well...here we go kids...How far is it?

NORVAL: About twenty-five miles...There's a Justice
                    of the Peace.

TRUDY: You got the uniform?

NORVAL: It's in the back.

TRUDY: And the ring?

NORVAL: It's in the uniform.

TRUDY: How do you look in it?

NORVAL: I haven't tried it yet; it will be all
                    right...Now: there's one thing we've got
                    to settle on - what was his first name?

TRUDY: Oh, you mean Ratzkiwatzki?

NORVAL: Naturally.

TRUDY: Does he have to have a first name?

NORVAL: Of course he has to have a first name...
                    everybody has a first name...even a dog has
                    a first name...even if he hasn't got a last
                    name.

TRUDY: Well...I don't know...I had an uncle called
                    Roscoe.

NORVAL: (Not liking it from the start)
                    Roscoe! He eats 'em alive!

TRUDY: What?

NORVAL: That's a snake eater's name.

TRUDY: (Resentfully)
                    Well, it was my uncle's name.

NORVAL: How about Hugo?

TRUDY: Phooey.

NORVAL: Well, do you like Otis...

Trudy shapes her lips to say phooey, but Norval continues:

        that was my father's name.

10-19-42   (Continued)

678

H-1   (Cont'd)

TRUDY: (Catching herself in time)
                     No. I'm sorry.

NORVAL: It doesn't matter. You could call him
                     Montmorency for all I care.

TRUDY: Phooey.

NORVAL: Well...what goes good with Ratzkiwatzki?

TRUDY: Nothing.

NORVAL: (After a pause)
                     How about Ignatz?

TRUDY: Ignatz! You'd have to take bicarbonate
                     with that one.

NORVAL: Ignatz Ratzkiwatzki...that fits all right.

TRUDY: Phooey.

NORVAL: It's all very well to sit there and keep
                     saying phooey...but I've got to learn a
                     name before we get there.

TRUDY: All right, Ignatz.

They both laugh.

NORVAL: It's funny, having almost our first fight
                     on the way to the...altar.

TRUDY: I guess it wasn't such a bad fight...more
                     like people have when they're picking out
                     a name for their....

Suddenly she stops in embarrassment.

NORVAL: (Noticing her embarrass-
                         ment)
           Don't think about that...remember what it
           says in the Bible: "Sufficient unto the day
           is the evil thereof!"...and there isn't go-
           ing to be any evil, Trudy...never for you.

TRUDY: (Blinking her eyes)
           Thank you, Norval.

NORVAL: (Reaching into the back)
           I got you these...

He hands her the little bouquet in the box.

TRUDY: (Opening the box)
                    Oh, gee, Norval...they're so pretty.
                        (She starts to snuffle)

NORVAL: Don't do that, please Trudy...

He puts his arm around her and she snuggles up close to him,
her head on his shoulder.

NORVAL: It's just that...I feel almost as if it
                    was me marrying you, Trudy.

TRUDY: I wish it were, Norval....so much.

NORVAL: (Exultantly)
                    You really mean that, Trudy?

TRUDY: Of course I do.

NORVAL: Oh, Trudy!

He starts to kiss her and the car starts right off the road.

TRUDY: (Catching it in time)
                    Look out!

Norval regains control of the car and looks ahead happily
with a big lip print across his mouth.

DISSOLVE TO:

H-2 A SECONDARY HIGHWAY IN THE COUNTRY - (NIGHT)

Norval's car approaches slowly. The CAMERA PANS OFF IT ONTO
A Motel marked: "The Honeymoon Motel - Hot and Cold Running
Water - Justice of the Peace - Marriages Performed," etc.etc.

H-3 NORVAL AND TRUDY - IN A SLOWLY MOVING CAR

NORVAL: There it is.

TRUDY: (Clutching her heart)
                    Gee whiz.

NORVAL: Now, just keep cool, there's nothing to...
                              (He clears his throat)
                    worry about...we'll just go some place and
                    I'll...
                              (He clears his throat)
                    put on the uniform.

TRUDY: Where're you going to go?

                                                   (Continued)

680

H-3 (Cont'd)

NORVAL: Well, I figured some b-bb-ushes somewhere...
                       so nobody will see me come out. I mean,
                       instead of a m-m-mm-otel or anything.

TRUDY: I think the b-b-b-bushes are b-b-better.

NORVAL: Don't get exc-exc-cited.

TRUDY: I w-w-won't.

DISSOLVE TO:

H-4 SOME B-B-BUSHES

The car pulls into the SHOT and Norval gets out.

NORVAL: (Getting the uniform out
                        of the back)
                Just k-k-keep c-c-cool. Don't be n-n-nervous
                about anything...thing.

TRUDY: I'll keep a lookout.

NORVAL: F-f-fine. If you hear anybody c-c-coming
                just wh-wh-whistle like a wh-wha-whipporr-
                will.

TRUDY: H-h-how does it go?

Norval tries to whistle like a whippoorwill but his nervousness makes it come out like the laugh of a hyena.

TRUDY: (After a couple of his efforts)
                Doesn't that sound more like a hyena?

NORVAL: No, a hyena goes more like this.

He continues to make the same sound.

TRUDY: I can make a noise like a dog: ooup, owoop...

NORVAL: All right, anything will do.

He goes behind the bushes. Trudy pins the flowers on herself and starts to repair her make-up. Unable to see very
well, she gets out of the car and stands in front of the
headlights.

CUT TO:

H-5 A MIDDLE-AGED MAN APPROACHING

He looks at Trudy in surprise.

CUT TO:

She hears the man's footsteps, looks at him as he comes into
the SHOT and barks like a dog. The man stops in his tracks
and looks back at her.

THE MAN: Did you say something?

TRUDY: Who me...Oh, no.

THE MAN: I'm sorry, I thought you said something.

He turns to go. Now he looks toward the bush which conceals
Norval.

TRUDY: Owoop.

THE MAN: (Turning)
                  Must be a dog around here.

TRUDY: (Nervously)
                  I didn't see any.

THE MAN: I said there must be a dog around here.
                  I love dogs.

He whistles for a dog. Norval answers with his imitation of
a whippoorwill from behind the bushes.

THE MAN: It's a jackal!

TRUDY: N-n-no it isn't.

THE MAN: I said, it's a jackal.

He starts cautiously for the bushes.

TRUDY: (Desperately)
                  Owoop...owoop...

THE MAN: (Turning to Trudy)
                  There's two dogs.

He whistles for it. Norval answers with his imitation.

THE MAN: (Turning)
                  He's coming closer.

TRUDY BARKS desperately.

THE MAN: I love any kind of a dog: big dogs,
                  little dogs, long dogs, short dogs.

TRUDY: Is that so?

                                              (Continued)

THE MAN: I even like those little naked ones with
                the poppy eyes.

TRUDY: That's very interesting.

THE MAN: If there were more dogs in the world and
                less people it would be a better world --
                much better.

TRUDY: (Desperately)
                That's very interesting.

THE MAN: Did you know there's no insanity amongst
                dogs?

TRUDY: Is that a fact?

THE MAN: Well, bow-wow.

He leaves.

TRUDY: (To the bushes)
                He's gone.

NORVAL'S
VOICE: All right.

TRUDY: Are you dressed?

NORVAL'S   Almost.
VOICE: (Then appearing)
                Maybe you can help me a little.

He appears in the lights of the car and now we see for the
first time his uniform in its full glory. The campaign hat
is a size too big and the chin strap gets in his mouth. The
tunic is a little too small and ducks up behind. The
breeches are too big and droop terribly in the seat. The
shoes are enormous and studded with hobnails. One spiral
puttee hangs around his knee like a concertina and the other
one is dragging behind him. He carries his street clothes
over his arm.

NORVAL: It isn't a...very good fit.

TRUDY: There seems to be something wrong with
                it, Norval.

                                          (Continued)

NORVAL: This must be the Cavalry or something....
                 I haven't seen any like it around here.

TRUDY: (Pointing to the puttees)
                 What are those things?

NORVAL: They must be to go around your legs...
                 You can't go bare-legged.

TRUDY: Maybe it's a tropical uniform....like
                 General MacArthur wears.

NORVAL: He didn't look like this in any pictures
                 I saw.

He clutches the seat of the pants and tries to pull them up
There is a ripping sound.

TRUDY: What happened?

NORVAL: I'm afraid to find out.

Now he reaches behind him and pulls off an extra Cavalry
seat which he looks at dismally.

TRUDY: Norval!

NORVAL: (Feeling)
                 There seems to be another seat left.

Trudy peeks cautiously and sees that he is quite respectabl

TRUDY: (Seizing the seat of
                                   his breeches)
                 Can't you hoist them up a little?

There is an immediate ripping sound.

NORVAL: (Desperately)
                 Don't do that. How many seats do you
                 think these pants have?

TRUDY: I'm sorry.

NORVAL: How do I look?

TRUDY: It's your inside I like to look at...
                 that's where you look the best.

After giving her a look, Norval puts one foot on the bumper
and starts to work on the spiral puttee. As he works with

10-19-42   (Continued)

H-6 (Cont'd)

it, not rolled up, but at its full length, this is a very
difficult job. There are yards and yards of it.

TRUDY: Let me help you.

NORVAL: (Pettishly)
                  Not around both legs...look out what
                  you're doing.

Trudy squats down and passes the puttee back and forth to him.

TRUDY: (After a while)
                  Now put the other foot up.

NORVAL: (Beginning to lose
                  his balance)
                  Hey, you wrapped me to the bumper!

TRUDY: Look out.

She tries to save him and they both fall in a heap.

DISSOLVE TO:

H-7   INT. OF THE JUSTICE OF THE PEACE'S SITTING ROOM - (NIGHT)

This is modern and in keeping with the Motel. The Justice is
reading the newspaper and listening to some Boogie Woogie.

HIS WIFE: (Entering)
                  Another army couple, Henry.

JUSTICE: They want a marriage or a cottage?

HIS WIFE: The ceremony.

JUSTICE: (Rising)
                  All right. They got witnesses?

HIS WIFE: No, I'll call Sally.

JUSTICE: That crackpot.

He exits.

H-8   THE JUSTICE'S OFFICE

Trudy and Norval stand nervously on our side of the counter.

NORVAL: J-j-just...t-t-take it easy...It will
                be over in a m-m-minute.

                                        (Continued)

H-8 (Cont'd)

    TRUDY: I wish it were over now.

    NORVAL: There is nothing to be n-n-nervous about.

    During this the Justice of the Peace has come in behind
    them.

    THE JUSTICE: Good evening.

    Norval leaps forward and his knees start to shake and bend
    under him. He turns towards the Justice of the Peace.

    JUSTICE: Thinkin' of gettin' married...good idea.
                    The names please.

    TRUDY: G-g-gertrude K-k-k-kockenlocker.

    JUSTICE: How was that again?

    During the next speech, Norval's knees start to give.

    TRUDY: G-g-gertrude...G-g-g-ertrude.

    JUSTICE: Now take it easy, there's nothing to be
                    skeered of...people do it every day...
                    the bad part comes later.

    By now Norval's chin is practically down on the counter.

    TRUDY: (With an effort)
                    Gertrude Kockenlocker...k.o.c.k.e.n. -
                    l.o.c.k.e.r.

    JUSTICE: That's better, and yours young man?

    TRUDY: (Surprised at his position)
                    Norv - Ignatz -

    She nearly bites her tongue off and grabs him by the seat
    of the pants and starts to hoist him up.

    CUT TO:

H-9 NORVAL AND TRUDY - PAST THE JUSTICE OF THE PEACE

    NORVAL: (Shooting up like a
                                    jack-in-the-box)
                    Igna-na-natz Radadada-Radadadada-Radarada
                    RATZKIWATZKI.

    CUT TO:

10-19-42

H-10   REVERSE SHOT - JUSTICE OF THE PEACE - PAST THE
        OTHERS

        JUSTICE: (Wiping something out of his eye)
                      How was that again?

        Norval starts straight for the floor and Trudy catches him
        by the seat of the pants. As she starts to boost him up -

        CUT TO:

H-11   TRUDY AND NORVAL - PAST THE JUSTICE OF THE PEACE

        NORVAL: (Straightening up rigidly)
                      Ignatz Ra-ra-ra-ra-ra

        JUSTICE: Take it easy, will you?

        TRUDY: Nor...Ignatz...

        She bites it off in the middle.

        NORVAL: I.g.n.a.t.z.

        TRUDY: R.a.t.z.k.y...w.a.t.z.k.y.

        JUSTICE: K.z....what?

        TRUDY AND   (Together)
        NORVAL: Ratzkiwatzki.

        CUT TO:

H-12   JUSTICE OF THE PEACE - PAST THE OTHERS

        JUSTICE: That's close enough...Bride's residence?

        TRUDY: 17 Genesee Street, Morgan's Creek.

        JUSTICE: Morgan's Creek. Ever been married before?

        Trudy looks at Norval.

        JUSTICE: (Looking up)
                      I said, you ever been married before...
                      that's a simple question.

        TRUDY: No, sir.

        JUSTICE: Groom's residence?

        Norval's knees start to go and Trudy gets a hold of his
        pants.

10-19-42   (Continued)

H-12 (Cont'd)

      JUSTICE: (Seeing both their heads at
                                 counter level)
                    What are you doing down there?...What's
                    the groom's residence? Where do you live,
                    in a tree?

      CUT TO:

H-13   TRUDY AND NORVAL - PAST THE JUSTICE OF THE PEACE

      NORVAL: (He slurs the name of the
                                   camp totally)
                    Camp Smum...

      JUSTICE: Camp what?

      NORVAL: Smum...

      JUSTICE: Where is it located?

      NORVAL: (Pointing far away)
                    In a...ahum...way out in a Smum country.

      JUSTICE: Suppose I just put U.S. Army?

      NORVAL: F-f-fine.

      CUT TO:

H-14   THE ENTRANCE HALL OF THE MOTEL

      The wife is opening the door to Sally who is removing her
      apron.

      THE WIFE: Thank you, Sally.

      SALLY: Oh, I just love it. It's such a privilege
                    to help launch young lovers on the sea of
                    matrimony...oh, dear. Is she pretty, it
                    always helps so?

      THE WIFE: They're always pretty in that pink light.

      They hurry out.

H-15   JUSTICE OF THE PEACE'S OFFICE

      JUSTICE: (As he sees the women enter)
                    Fine. This is Miz Sally Blair and my wife,
                    who'll act as witnesses for you, Miss
                    Gertrude Kockenlocker and Mr. Ignatz Ratast:
                    Watastki...something like that..or should
                    that be _Private_ Ignatz...and the rest of it

10-19-42   (Continued)

NORVAL: Well... M-m-mister is all right.

SALLY: (Impulsively)
                     Oh, I do hope you'll be happy... so many
                     of these marriages go on the rocks.

TRUDY: (Doubtfully)
                     Thank you.

SALLY: Are you certain sure that you love each
                     other?

JUSTICE: What do you think they came here for?

SALLY: Oh, I know but are they <u>sure</u>?

NORVAL: S-s-sure.

JUSTICE: (To Sally)
                     What more do you want?

SALLY: (To the happy couple)
                     Do you want lots and lots of little babies?
                     Do you long for the patter of little footsy-
                     wootsies?

JUSTICE'S   Of course they do, Sally.
WIFE:

JUSTICE: You better lay off or I won't let you be
                     witness any more. Now let's get down to
                     business.

SALLY: I always say a childless home is like a
                     tomb.

JUSTICE: All right. Ignatz Razly Wazly, do you
                     take this woman, Gertrude Sockenbocker,
                     for your lawful wedded wife, to have and
                     to hold, to cherish and to keep forever
                     till death do you part?

NORVAL: (Sinking to the floor)
                     I...ahum...I, I, I...ahum....I, I, I...

They all open their mouths to help him.

NORVAL: (Triumphantly)
                     I d-do!

They all sigh with relief.

JUSTICE: Well, congratulations.

Norval starts shaking hands with all.

                                                        (Continued)

HW   THE MIRACLE OF MORGAN'S CREEK   11-2-42   H-15-14
(91-92)
H-15   (Cont'd)

JUSTICE: Wait a minute. You're not married yet.
Gertrude Krockendocker do you take Ignatz
Razzberry...Razzby Wadsgy for your lawful
wedded husband, to have and to hold in
sickness or in health, to love, honor and
cherish till death do you part...
                (Sally bursts into tears.
                Justice looks at Sally)
so help you God?

TRUDY: (Explosively)
           I do!

JUSTICE: Then give me the ring.

NORVAL: (Triumphantly)
           Th-there!

They smile proudly.

JUSTICE: (Taking the ring)
Put it on her third finger and repeat
after me: With this ring I thee wed.

NORVAL: Wi-wi-wi-wi-with...th-th-th-th...

JUSTICE: You don't have to say it, just think it.

NORVAL: (In a dying gasp)
With this ring I thee w-wed.

JUSTICE: (Surprised)
For heaven's sake! Then with the authority
vested in me by our sovereign state I now
pronounce you man and wife.
                (Norval and Trudy kiss)
That will be two dollars please, and that's
all there is to it.

NORVAL: (Reaching happily for
                his money)
That made me a little n-n-nervous.

JUSTICE: (Cracking his little joke)
If you know what it was like, it would make
you still nervouser.

JUSTICE'S   (Reprovingly)
WIFE: Jake!

By now Norval has found that he has forgotten to change his
money into his uniform.

TRUDY: (Reaching into her bag)
           I've got it.

SALLY: (To the Justice's wife)
She shouldn't start paying her own way so
soon.
                           (Continued)

H-15 (Cont'd)

JUSTICE: (Receiving the money)
     Fine.

He signs the marriage certificate, passes out a receipt
sheet, points out a place and says:

JUSTICE: Sign here.

NORVAL: (Sighing happily)
     I certainly feel better.

He beams at them all and signs. The Justice takes the
receipt and hands out the certificate, after slipping it
into an envelope which contains a cooking folder.

JUSTICE: There you are...and a little cook book
     goes with it...with best wishes from those
     who may have to eat the cooking.

NORVAL AND   (Together - and to all)
TRUDY: Thank you very much...goodbye, goodbye.

JUSTICE: (Jokingly)
     Call again.

SALLY: And don't forget the pitty patter...as I
     always say, a childless home is like a
     homeless child.

TRUDY AND
NORVAL: We won't. Thank you very much.

JUSTICE: (Looking up over the receipt sheet)
     Just a minute.

Norval and Trudy stop.

JUSTICE: Who's Norval Jones?

TRUDY: Norval!

Norval goes into a paroxysm of pure gibberish, punctuated
by silences and no, no, no wavings.

JUSTICE: (Producing a big six-shooter)
     Lock the door, Maria. This man is an
     abductor.

Now Sally starts to attack Norval. She grabs a double fist-
ful of his tunic (which doesn't do it any good) and shakes
him.

10-19-42   (Continued)

H-15 (Cont'd)

SALLY:
                                (Hysterically)
                        You double-dyed deceiver. You wolf in cheap
                        clothing...leading this poor lamb astray for
                        your own vile ends...and a fate worse than
                        death.

She starts to slap him with one hand after the other. While
Norval is defending himself as best he can, Trudy runs forward to protect Norval.

TRUDY:
                        You leave him alone...He didn't mean me
                        any harm.

SALLY:
                        I can read his intentions like a book,
                        and each one is viler than the others...
                        You leper.

She attacks Norval again.

TRUDY:
                                (Defending him)
                        You leave him alone.

JUSTICE'S
WIFE:
                              (Pulling on Sally)
                        Stop it, Sally. It isn't any of your
                        business.

SALLY:
                                (Turning on her)
                        Well I just guess it is. I guess I know my
                        bounden duty when I see it! I just guess...

JUSTICE:
                                (With one hand over the phone)
                        SHUT UP.
                                (Then into the phone:)
                        Get me the military police.
                                  (Then to the others in the room:)
                        Now shut up...That goes for you too, Sally.
                        Don't let them talk to each other, Maria.
                                  (Then into telephone)
                        I said: Get me the military police...the M.P.

TRUDY:
                                (Desperately)
                        But he isn't a soldier.

NORVAL:
                                (Aghast)
                        T-t-trudy.

JUSTICE:
                        Oh he isn't hunh?
                                (Then into the phone)
                        Get the Sheriff over here.
                                (Then to Norval)
                        Then what are you doing in that uniform...
                        wait a minute...

                                          (Continued)

H-15 (Cont'd)

JUSTICE: (Then into the phone)
(Cont'd)   Get me the Secret Service...in the U.S.
                  Marshal's office...and get the Marshall too,
                  while you're at it...and the State Police.
                            (Then to Norval)
                  Trying to pull a fast one, hunh...on a poor
                  old country hick.

     DISSOLVE TO:

H-16 THE COUNTY SHERIFF'S OFFICE - EXTERIOR - (NIGHT)

     It is plainly and appropriately marked on the window. The
     Sheriff and his deputy come out and hop into a car, and it
     zooms away.

     DISSOLVE TO:

H-17 EXTERIOR - U.S. MARSHAL'S OFFICE - (NIGHT)

     The window mentions something about this being the local
     branch of the Secret Service. Two young men hurry out and
     hop into a car.

H-18 THE JUSTICE OF THE PEACE'S OFFICE

     Trudy and Norval sit miserably in the corner. The Justice's
     wife and Sally wait meanly.

TRUDY: (In tears)
                  He didn't want to do me any harm...He
                  wanted to do me some good.

SALLY: The law has another name for it.

JUSTICE: With different degrees...first degree,
                  second degree, third degree...like that.

TRUDY: Well...if we did anything wrong, I did
                  half of it.

Norval gestures no, no, no.

SALLY: You poor misguided little lamb.

TRUDY: Oh, phooey on you...Why don't you give
                  yourself up?

SALLY: (To the Justice's wife)
                  Gratitude.

JUSTICE'S   They never want to be saved...I've seen it
WIFE: time and time again.

                                          (Continued)

693

H-18 (Cont'd)

We hear the ROAR of the Jeep outside and a distant siren.

JUSTICE: Here they are.

He crosses toward the door. Trudy and Norval back into the corner.

H-19 CLOSE SHOT - TRUDY AND NORVAL

She points to the electric light switch which is near them and the window beside it.

TRUDY: (In a whisper)
      Norval.

She reaches for the switch and all the lights go out. Sally and the Justice's wife SCREAM.

JUSTICE'S
VOICE: Stop that...help.

He starts firing his revolver in the air.

CUT TO:

H-20 EXTERIOR - OF THE JUSTICE OF THE PEACE'S - (NIGHT)

Two M.P.'s are getting out, drawing their guns. We hear a SHOT from the inside and two women screaming. The State Police arrive on moaning motorcycles, immediately followed by the Sheriff and Pete, the U.S. Marshal and the Secret Service men. We hear another SHOT and more SCREAMS from inside.

THE SHERIFF: Draw your gun, Pete.

FIRST M.P.: There's a riot inside.

Pete immediately fires his gun twice in the air.

SHERIFF: Not out here.

FIRST M.P.: Follow me, men.

They dive up the stairs. As they do so, THE CAMERA PANS ov onto Trudy and Norval who run around the side of the house, jump into a car and beat it.

CUT TO:

H-21 DARKENED INTERIOR - OF THE JUSTICE OF THE PEACE'S OFFICE

The Justice is trying to follow Trudy and Norval out of the window but his women-folk are restraining him.

JUSTICE: Will you let go of me?

                  (Continued)

H-21 (Cont'd)

JUSTICE'S
WIFE: You'll break your neck, Jake.

JUSTICE: Let me out of here.

FIRST M.P.:   (Tackling the Justice)
                      I got you, Bo.

Sally SCREAMS.

THE SHERIFF: (Rushing in)
                      Hold your fire, Pete.

The chandelier is immediately shot off the ceiling. The
women scream.

THE JUSTICE'S   Will you let go of me? I'm the Justice of
VOICE: the Peace.

He kicks somebody in the face.

SHERIFF'S   Ouch! Oh, you are, well I happen to be the
VOICE: Sheriff of this county.

We hear a sock.

JUSTICE'S
VOICE: Wow!

The women scream and the riot becomes general punctuated
with ouches, wow's and 'oh you will, will you's.' Now a
flashlight flashes over the fighting mass.

US MARSHAL'S   Hold everything in the name of the law.
VOICE: Where is the prisoner?

JUSTICE OF   (Sticking his head out from between
THE PEACE: Pete's legs which are in turn
                      buried in the mass)
            They got away, you dumb clunk...before you
            got here.

DISSOLVE TO:

H-22   TRUDY AND NORVAL - DRIVING ALONG - (NIGHT)

TRUDY: (Very nervously)
            Don't go over thirty-five miles an hour
            whatever you do.

NORVAL: I won't. I'm w-w-watching it like an eagle.

10-19-42   (Continued)

H-22 (Cont'd)

TRUDY: (Looking around)
            This is no time to be arrested for sp-speedi.

NORVAL: You...said it.

TRUDY: You better get out of that uniform quick.

NORVAL: That's right...you drive, I'll ch-ch-change
            in the back.

He starts to climb in the back.

TRUDY: Be careful.

NORVAL: You got it?

TRUDY: (Slipping over into the driver's
                      seat)
            I've got it...and whatever happens, Norval
            even if we have to spend the rest of our
            lives in the penetentiary...I want you to
            know I'll always be grateful to you.

She turns half around to kiss him.

NORVAL: Thank you Trudy.

He tries to kiss her, loses his balance and falls behind
the front seat like a side of beef.

TRUDY: Are you alright?

NORVAL: (Sticking his head up)
            I'm alright, but they're not here.

TRUDY: What?

NORVAL: M-m-m-my clothes.

TRUDY: Well, they must be there.

NORVAL: Well, they're not.

TRUDY: Well, who could have taken them?

NORVAL: (Looking around)
            Holy mackeral!

TRUDY: What's the matter?

NORVAL: We stole somebody else's car.

H-22   (Cont'd)

TRUDY: (Aghast)
         No.

NORVAL: (Pointing at the speedometer)
        And you're going forty-five.

TRUDY: I'm sorry I'll....

We hear the whine of a siren and the headlight of a motorcycle flickers in the back window.

FADE OUT:

END OF SEQUENCE "H"

10-19-42

FADE IN:

J-1   KOCKENLOCKER AND EMMY - ON THE FRONT PORCH

Kockenlocker is cleaning his six-shooter. Emmy seems very
restless. She looks at her watch as she walks up and down.
Now she sits on his lap.

KOCKENLOCKER: Git off of my lap... what's the matter with
                  you?

EMMY: (Tensely)
                  I've got a right to sit on your lap, haven't
                  I? I'm your daughter, aren't I?

KOCKENLOCKER: That's what your mother told me.

EMMY: I'm nervous.

KOCKENLOCKER: What about?

EMMY: You don't hear a police siren, do you?

KOCKENLOCKER: A police siren? That's a tree toad.

EMMY: I keep feeling I hear a police siren.

KOCKENLOCKER: How could you hear a police siren when there
                  ain't one in town?

EMMY: I don't know.

We hear a police SIREN.

EMMY: I thought I heard it again then.

KOCKENLOCKER: How could you hear a police siren when
                  there...

We hear a police SIREN.

KOCKENLOCKER: (Continuing)
                  ...ain't one in town.

He twirls his finger in his ear. Now we hear a police siren
very close.

EMMY: What's that... a hoot owl?

KOCKENLOCKER: That's a...

Now he scowls past THE CAMERA and rises slowly to his feet.

CUT TO:

10-19-42

J-2   THE STREET IN FRONT OF THE KOCKENLOCKER HOUSE - (NIGHT)

Flanked by State Motorcycle Cops and an ever-increasing
number of townspeople, the car Norval stole has just arrived.
Almost simultaneously we see the arrival of the M.P.'s in the
jeep, the Secret Service men in their car, and Pete in the
Sheriff's car. Gun in hand, the Justice of the Peace gets to
the street and ushers Trudy and Norval toward the Kockenlocker house. The U.S. Marshal follows, also gun in hand,
and behind him come the Secret Service men, Pete and the
townspeople.

JUSTICE: (Importantly)
                   Make way, please, make way.

The CAMERA PANS the group up to the porch.

TRUDY: (Arriving at the porch)
                   Hello, Papa.

CUT TO:

J-3   KOCKENLOCKER AND EMMY - PAST THE OTHERS

EMMY: Oh, Trudy.

She runs and throws her arms around her sister's neck.

KOCKENLOCKER: What's all this...what are all you cops
                   doing in my town?

JUSTICE: (Pointing to Norval)
                   Did you ever see this man before?

KOCKENLOCKER: Certainly, I seen him before. What are you
                   doin' in that outfit, Norval? I thought
                   you went to the movies.

JUSTICE: (Triumphantly to all)
                   All please take notice that his name is
                   Norval and that that is not his regular
                   outfit.

KOCKENLOCKER: Well, who said it was...Come in the house
                   here.

DISSOLVE TO:

J-4   MR. JOHNSON, THE LAWYER - AT A WALL TELEPHONE

His wife hovers near.

MR. JOHNSON: He did what?...in a fake uniform!...All
                   right Edmund, I'll be right over.
                        (He hangs up; then to his wife)
                   Norval is in some kind of a mess with the
                   Kockenlocker girl.

MRS. JOHNSON: I don't believe it.

                                              (Continued)

699

MR. JOHNSON: (Reaching for his hat)
                       Nobody asked you to.

DISSOLVE TO:

J-5   THE KOCKENLOCKER FRONT ROOM

Here we see Norval, Trudy, Emmy, Mr. Kockenlocker, the
Justice, the M.P.'s, the Sheriff, Pete, the U.S.Marshal,
the State Police, and the Secret Service men, plus as many
neighbors as can look through the window, the door and
around the front hall.

KOCKENLOCKER: (Coming in from the hall)
                       His lawyer will be here in a minute.
                          (Now he turns to Norval:)
                       Are you nuts or something? What's the
                       idea of the get-up?

FIRST M.P.:   (To Norval)
                       What war do you think you're in, Buddy?

SECOND M.P.:   The ghost of the A.E.F.

FIRST M.P.:   (Reaching down inside Norval's
                           collar:)
                       Let's see your dog tags, General...No more
                       dog tags than feathers on a fish.

SECOND M.P.:   What camp you from, soldier?

FIRST M.P.:   (Examining Norval's insignia)
                       U.S.Navy on one side and cavalry on the
                       other.

SECOND M.P.:   He's a horse marine! I always wanted to
                       see one.

SHERIFF: Do you mind if I examine the evidence,
                       Corporal?

FIRST M.P.:   Sergeant, if it's all the same to you.

TRUDY: Why don't you leave him alone? I can ex-
                       plain to my father what happened.

JUSTICE: Yes, but can you explain it to the judge?

KOCKENLOCKER: What judge? What's the charge?

FIRST SECRET   I fear there may be several.
SERVICE MAN:

KOCKENLOCKER: All right what are they?

                                              (Continued)

J-5   (Cont'd)

SHERIFF: (To Kockenlocker)
                    If it's all the same to you, I'm the Sheriff
                    of this county and will conduct the investi-
                    gation.

KOCKENLOCKER: Yeah? Well, you happen to be in the town-
                    ship of Morgan's Creek and I happen to be
                    the Town Constable, so if anybody's going to
                    conduct an investigation...

U.S. MARSHAL: As a matter of fact, the matter is Federal,
                    as a matter of fact, so if it's all the same
                    to you, gentlemen...

He starts to lay a heavy hand on Norval's shoulder. The
First M.P. catches his hand.

FIRST M.P.:   The way I learned it, any guy in a uniform
                    is a soldier till proved different, so we'll
                    just take him over to the camp.

SHERIFF: Take your hands off my prisoner.

FIRST M.P.:   Listen, Sheriff.

Now they all start talking at once, saying lines which I
will not bore you with in this script. In the middle of
this Mr. Johnson makes his appearance holding a hand high.

JOHNSON: I'm Mr. Johnson, the lawyer, I represent
                    Norval Jones...why Norval what are you doing
                    in your boyscout outfit?

SHERIFF: (Shrewdly)
                    Boyscout outfit?

FIRST M.P.:   He's a mouthpiece! He knows it's a U.S.
                    uniform...don't fall for that stuff.

JOHNSON: (Indignantly)
                    What are you talking about? That's a boy-
                    scout outfit if I ever saw one. I remember
                    very well when you joined the scouts...
                    I was saying to Mrs. Johnson only the other
                    day...

Norval shakes his head sadly in the negative.

JOHNSON: Oh, it isn't.
                    (He glares at Norval, gives the
                    others a quick look, then attacks
                    again)
                    Of course it isn't! I remember now: The
                    Woodsmen of America! I remember when your
                    axe came! I said to Mrs. Johnson: "I hope
                    he isn't going to chop down the whole..."
                    No?

J-5 (Cont'd)

JOHNSON: (This last as Norval has again
(Cont'd)   shaken his head in the negative)
Very well, Norval.
(He turns to the others)
What is the alleged charge...? It being
understood that we admit nothing.

All together start talking, mentioning the various charges.

CUT TO:

J-6   FRIENDS AND NEIGHBORS - ON THE FRONT PORCH

From inside the house we HEAR the ANGRY ABADABA as we go
to SPOT SHOTS of these people.

LADY NEXT   He took Trudy to a Motel...with a false
DOOR: name.

A NEIGHBOR: What was its real name?

AN OLD MAID: They ought to shoot him.

SECOND OLD   Maybe they will....
MAID:

CUT TO:

J-7   THE NEIGHBOR'S HUSBAND

NEIGHBOR'S   I can understand everything but the
HUSBAND: uniform. Why did he put on a uniform?

THE OLD MAID: So she'd run off with him of course.

A MAN: (Happily)
This should be in all the papers...It's
the biggest thing since the mad dog on
Fourth of July.

(Continued)

J-7   (Cont'd)

        A NERVOUS   You say there's a mad dog?
        WOMAN:

        CUT TO:

J-8   MR. JOHNSON - IN THE MIDDLE OF THE MESS

        MR. JOHNSON: Gentlemen, gentlemen, just a minute...one
                           at a time, please.

        CUT TO:

J-9   KOCKENLOCKER - NEXT TO HIS DAUGHTERS

        KOCKENLOCKER: Come here.
                                     (He pushes his daughters
                                     through the crowd)

        CUT TO:

J-10   THE KITCHEN

        Kockenlocker pushes his two daughters in ahead of him and
        closes the doors.

        KOCKENLOCKER: Now give it to me quick. What happened?

        TRUDY: Oh, Papa.

        She starts toward him.

        KOCKENLOCKER: (Backing away)
                           Never mind the 'Oh Papa'...What happened?

        TRUDY: Oh, Papa.

        She throws her arms around his neck, which lands him on a
        kitchen chair and her on his lap.

        KOCKENLOCKER: Now what happened?

        EMMY: Everything.

        KOCKENLOCKER: (To Emmy)
                           You go upstairs to bed...This ain't for
                           fourteen-year-olds. Go on now.

        EMMY: (Sitting on his other knee)
                           Oh phiffle.

        KOCKENLOCKER: Will you get off my lap and get out of
                           here?

        TRUDY: She knows all about it, Papa.

J-10 (Cont'd)

KOCKENLOCKER: Oh she does, does she? Well how about
letting your old man in on some of the
dirt?...Or am I being too snoopy?

EMMY: (To Trudy)
You think it's wise? He'll blab it all
over town.

KOCKENLOCKER: (Threateningly)
Listen, Ladder-legs...

TRUDY: It'll be all over town anyway now,

EMMY: Even the...secret?

KOCKENLOCKER: The secret!
                  (He points to the people
                  in the front room)
This is some secret.

CUT TO:

J-11   MR. JOHNSON - SURROUNDED BY THE OTHERS

MR. JOHNSON: (Consulting a paper)
All right now, just a minute...not that we
admit any of this you understand..we've got:
perjury, abduction...I don't know where you
get this attempted...

THE SHERIFF: He took her to a Motel.

MR. JOHNSON: (Shrugging)
You said it was the office of the Justice
of the Peace!

THE SHERIFF: It was still a Motel...as low a form of...

JUSTICE OF   If it's all the same to you, that happens
THE PEACE: to be my Motel.

SHERIFF: I'm sorry, Jake.

MR. JOHNSON: But he took her there to marry her.

FIRST M.P.:   Under a phony name.

MR. JOHNSON: (Acidly)
Would you mind keeping your nose out of
this...It has already been established
that the matter is not military.

FIRST M.P.:   As long as we're here, it's military.

                                   (Continued)

THE U.S.   The matter is Federal.
MARSHAL

STATE   Partly...but don't forget the State.
POLICEMAN:

SHERIFF: And don't forget the County.

FIRST M.P.:   And remember the Army.

SECRET   The Secret Service will have some-
SERVICE MAN: thing to say later.

MR. JOHNSON: (Consulting his paper)
                   Impairing the morals of a minor.

He shrugs his shoulders.

THE SHERIFF: (Doggedly)
                   He took a minor to a motel, didn't he?

SECOND M.P.:   And what a motel!

MR. JOHNSON: (To the M.P.)
                   Will you keep out of this?
                               (Then to the Sheriff)
                   It was your friend, Jake's Motel wasn't it?
                   ...Practically...a...a...I can't think of any
                   word pure enough.

SHERIFF: You don't have to. I've been there.

JUSTICE: (Threateningly)
                   Now listen, Henry.

SHERIFF: (Exploding with laughter)
                   When we come up tonight they started out
                   the windows.

JUSTICE: (Furiously)
                   They probably thought it was on fire.

SHERIFF: (Controlling his laughter)
                   Sure...their shirt-tails was on fire.

MR. JOHNSON: All of this is very illuminating, but it
                   isn't getting my client anywhere.
                               (He looks at his pad)
                   Impersonating a member of the armed forces.
                               (He shrugs)
                   It isn't what he did, it's why he did it.

FIRST M.P.:   It isn't where he's been, it's where he's
                   going.
                                       (Continued)

J-11   (Cont'd)

    MR. JOHNSON: (After giving him a look)
                             And finally espionage and suspicion of be-
                             ing the agent of a foreign government!
                             Really gentlemen, I ask you.

    SHERIFF: And stealing an automobile.

    MR. JOHNSON: And stealing an automobile.

    He shrugs helplessly.

    CUT TO:

J-12   KOCKENLOCKER AND HIS DAUGHTERS - IN THE KITCHEN

    KOCKENLOCKER: Now, give me that again.

    TRUDY: Norval was trying to save me, Papa.

    KOCKENLOCKER: I'll bat his brains out.

    EMMY: (Sitting on his knee)
                             Norval was trying to save her, Papa. Can't
                             you get anything through your skull?

    KOCKENLOCKER: I'll grab him by the gizzard and I'll bounce
                      him up against the wall and then...

    He coughs with emotion and nearly strangles.

    EMMY: (Pounding his back - to Trudy:)
                             What happened?

    TRUDY: Everything was perfect...He put on the
                      uniform and played Ratzkiwatzki all the
                      way through and then...when it came time
                      to sign for the certificate...he signed
                      it Norval Jones.

    EMMY: I hope he gets life! I told you what you
                      could expect from that picklehead.

    TRUDY: You mustn't talk about him that way, Emmy.
                      He was only trying his best.

    EMMY: Imagine if he hadn't been really trying.

    KOCKENLOCKER: Who signed what? Who was Katzenjammer...
                      and where does he tend bar?

10-19-42   (Continued)

J-12 (Cont'd)

EMMY: It was Norval, Papa...You wouldn't understand anything about it.
(Then to Trudy)
But you got the certificate...you didn't
muff that?

TRUDY: I haven't got it.

KOCKENLOCKER: What certificate?

EMMY: Her marriage certificate...Why didn't you
get it?

TRUDY: He pulled a gun, and then he telephoned...

KOCKENLOCKER: (Understanding something
at last)
Who pulled a gun, that Norval?

EMMY: Don't try to understand, Papa.

KOCKENLOCKER: Listen, you!

TRUDY: And then all those policemen came and...
that's all.

EMMY: Then who's got the certificate?

TRUDY: I don't know, the Justice I guess.

KOCKENLOCKER: What certificate?

EMMY: Her marriage certificate.

TRUDY: To Ratzkiwatzki.

KOCKENLOCKER: To Ratzkiwatzki! I told Jones to marry
you.....

EMMY: She's already married, Papa...perfectly
respectably to a gentleman called Ratzkiwatzki...only she can't prove it...She
hasn't got the certificate...It's just one
of those things.

TRUDY: So tonight I married him again.

EMMY: Just to get the certificate, don't you see?

KOCKENLOCKER: (Firmly)
No.

TRUDY: (As to a child)
You have to have a certificate.

10-19-42   (Continued)

J-12 (Cont'd)

EMMY: So she married Norval.

KOCKENLOCKER: She married Norval!

TRUDY: To prove I was married to Ratzkiwatzki.

Kockenlocker looks unbelievingly at each of his daughters
then straight into the CAMERA.

TRUDY: But then he signed the wrong name and now
they've got him...and we're in the soup.

KOCKENLOCKER: I'll shoot him.

TRUDY: He didn't sign the wrong name on purpose,
Papa.

KOCKENLOCKER: I'll shoot him anyway.

EMMY: The one you'd want to shoot is Ratzkiwatzki,
Papa.

KOCKENLOCKER: (Pointing toward Norval)
Well, isn't he Ratzkiwatzki?

TRUDY: No, I married him a long time ago.

KOCKENLOCKER: When?

TRUDY: The night I was out with Norval.

EMMY: Can't you understand anything?

Kockenlocker grabs his head to keep it from exploding.
Now he looks up as Mr. Johnson comes through the sliding
doors.

CUT TO:

J-13   MR. JOHNSON - COMING THROUGH THE DOORS

JOHNSON: They can't agree on anything, Edmund...
each one wants to put him in his own jail...
and if they do we won't even be able to
find him again, let alone get him out...
Now have you got anything against him.

By now the CAMERA has brought Mr. Johnson into the shot
with Kockenlocker.

KOCKENLOCKER: Nothing except a kick in the pants.

10-19-42   (Continued)

J-13   (Cont'd)

JOHNSON: All right. I'll tell you what you do: You
take him down and lock him up in <u>your</u> jail
and they can draw lots for him tomorrow....
Meanwhile, we can sift the whole thing down...
It's perfectly ridiculous: They've got about
nineteen charges against him.

TRUDY: He didn't do any of those things.

JOHNSON: (Mimicking her)
He didn't do any of those things....He did
<u>all</u> of those things...in the eyes of the Law.
                  (Now he turns to Kockenlocker)
Will you do that for me, Ed?

KOCKENLOCKER: (Rising from under his daughters)
            Yeah.
                  (He starts away, then turns back and
                  looks at his daughters)
And what you two ought to have is a good
shellacking..Daughters!

CUT TO:

J-14   NORVAL AND THE M.P.s - IN THE MIDDLE OF THE GROUP

FIRST M.P.:   Why don't you get wise to yourself,
Soldier...Dames ain't that hard to get.

Now Johnson and Kockenlocker come into the group followed
by Trudy and Emmy.

KOCKENLOCKER: (Dropping a heavy hand on Norval)
            You're under arrest...Follow me.

Everybody starts talking at once.

KOCKENLOCKER: (At the top of his lungs)
Quiet! One more crack out of youse guys
and I'll lock you <u>all</u> up.
                  (He catches the first M.P.'s eye and
                  gives him a wink. Now he starts
                  to move Norval)
Come on, Ox Brains.

TRUDY: (Throwing her arms around Norval's
                  neck)
            Oh Norval.

NORVAL: I'll be all right, Trudy. Don't you worry.

TRUDY: I'll knit you something.

PETE: You'll have lots of time.

10-19-42   (Continued)

J-14 (Cont'd)

KOCKENLOCKER: (To Pete)
Who asked you anything? Put that gun away
before you shoot something.
(Then to Norval)
Come on now.
(Then to Trudy and Emmy)
You get back in the kitchen. I ain't
finished with you.

CUT TO:

J-15   EXTERIOR - KOCKENLOCKER HOUSE - (NIGHT)

The loafers move back as Kockenlocker comes out leading
Norval. The whole gang follows.

SOME VOICES: Shame on you, Norval Jones. That'll
teach you to besmirch the name of our
fair city...lynch him.

KOCKENLOCKER: Quiet.

By now we've heard the motor cops pull away. As the people
pass out of the SHOT, Trudy and Emmy come out and stand silhouetted in the doorway. Now they put their arms around
each other.

DISSOLVE TO:

J-16   INTERIOR - OF THE JAIL

SHOT from the exterior through the barred window. We do not
see this is through the window, however, until we PULL BACK.
Kockenlocker shoves Norval into the cell roughly and slams
the door in his face and shoves the other people out of the
jail.

KOCKENLOCKER: All right, that's all, folks. Leave the guy
some air...Don't breathe it all up on him.

As the people back out, THE CAMERA PULLS BACK and catches
them coming out the door.

SHERIFF: (Handing Kockenlocker a pad)
Just sign here please: "One prisoner
in good order."

KOCKENLOCKER: Okay.

FIRST M.P.:   I'll take one of those.

THE MARSHAL: Me, too.

(Continued)

J-16 (Cont'd)

KOCKENLOCKER: Okay, okay, who's next?   Clear the side-
                walk folks...Go on home...Go on now or
                I'll pinch somebody for loitering.

He glares around at them as they move away.

CUT TO:

J-17 THE JUSTICE OF THE PEACE - WATCHING THE OTHERS GO

Certain that he and Kockenlocker are alone, he sidles over
to him.

JUSTICE: (Mysteriously)
                I wouldn't want this to go no further, see?
                But I figure you and your daughter is in
                enough trouble without having to annul this
                marriage and go through all that rigmarol.
                You get me?

KOCKENLOCKER: Not quite.

JUSTICE: I could of called the cops before the cere-
                mony instead of after, couldn't I? If I
                don't write it on the books, it ain't a
                marriage is it?

KOCKENLOCKER: (Getting the idea)
                Oh....That's certainly mighty white of you
                Brother.

JUSTICE: That's all right...I might ask you a favor
                some day...who knows?...Here's your two
                dollars...There was no marriage...She was
                saved in the nick of time.

KOCKENLOCKER: (Genuinely touched)
                That's mighty white of you Brother....
                mighty white.

JUSTICE: (Producing the certificate)
                And here's the last evidence: the certifi-
                cate...Now you see it...
                            (He tears it up rapidly)
                now you don't... Not a trace.

KOCKENLOCKER: (Crunching his hand in an
                             iron grip)
                Thank you, Brother.

JUSTICE: Forget it....I might call on you some day.
                            (He winks at him
                             heavily, waves and departs)

Kockenlocker looks after him and shakes his head...his
faith in man restored.
DISSOLVE TO:

J-18   TRUDY AND EMMY - SITTING IN THE FRONT ROOM OF THE KOCKENLOCKE
RESIDENCE

They have apparently both been crying and are now holding
hands.

EMMY: (After a sniff)
              I wonder who else you could marry.

TRUDY: Emmy! How can you be so heartless? I'll
              love Norval to my dying day...How could I
              even look at another man...I...I think he's
              the most wonderful man that ever lived.

EMMY: Yes, but he's going to be in jail Trudy,
              for a long time...He can't do you any good
              in stripes, Honey...You can't be so choosey.

TRUDY: (Dissolving in tears)
              Emmy.
                         (Now they look around
                          as the door BANGS)

CUT TO:

J-19   KOCKENLOCKER - COMING IN FROM THE HALL

KOCKENLOCKER: Well...you fixed him! And you certainly
               give us a good name in the town. You
               spend all your life behaving yourself...
               then they find your daughter in a, in a...
               lovely mess.
                         (He sits down and puts his
                          face in his hands)

EMMY: Don't take it that way, Papa.

KOCKENLOCKER: (Looking up and glaring
                          at her)
              Don't take it what way, Papa? Don't take
              it what way, Papa. You're just a kid...
              You can duck down the alleys...Me, I gotta
              stand out in the middle of the street and
              take it...from every louse in town.

TRUDY: I'm terribly sorry, Papa...
                         (She starts to cry)
              You told me not to go out that night.

KOCKENLOCKER: Yeh...well I could be wrong too, you know...
               but why don't you come to me if you're
               worried about something? The trouble with
               kids is they always figure they're smarter
               than their parents...never stop to think if
               their old man could get by for fifty years
               and feed them and clothe them, he maybe

                                        (Continued)

KOCKENLOCKER: had something up here to get by with...
(Cont'd)   Things that seem like brain-twisters to
                 you might be very simple for him...like
                 this for instance...
                              (He waves the two dollar
                              bills at them. Then tosses
                              them in Trudy's lap)
                 There's your two bucks...You never got
                 married tonight...You got nothing to
                 worry about.

TRUDY: (Palely)
                 What?

KOCKENLOCKER: I got the guy to tear up the certificate...
                 Just a little politics...and if you'd
                 come to me in the first place...

EMMY: You got the guy to tear up the certifi-
                 cate...

TRUDY: Oh.
                              (She collapses on her sister's
                              shoulder)

KOCKENLOCKER: (Irritated)
                 What's the matter with you? If nobody
                 knows you're married to this Katzenjammer
                 and it was all by mistake anyway...with
                 false names a corpse couldn't dig up...
                 why do you have to go around proving
                 things? Why can't you be practical?

EMMY: (To her sister)
                 Shall we tell him...or let him linger?

KOCKENLOCKER: (Vulgarly)
                 Tell him what?

TRUDY: (Very simply)
                 I'm going to have a baby.

KOCKENLOCKER: (Repeating quietly)
                 You're going to have a baby...
                              (He holds this for a count of
                              three then leaps to his feet
                              as if shot out of a gun and
                              hollers at the top of his
                              lungs)
                 WHAT DO YOU MEAN YOU'RE GOING TO HAVE A
                 BABY!

                                            (Continued)

J-19 (Cont'd)

EMMY: (Quietly)
                      I told you he'd blab it all over town.

TRUDY: That's why we wanted the certificate.

EMMY: The one you got the guy to tear up,
                      dear Papa.

Kockenlocker looks at his daughters, a stricken man. Now
he walks over and looks out the window. From here he looks
back after a moment.

KOCKENLOCKER: (Quietly)
                      Did Norval know about this...when he asked
                      you to...marry him...?

TRUDY: Yes, Papa.

KOCKENLOCKER: So he gets charged with seduction,
                      abduction, imitating a soldier, repairing
                      the morals of a minor, swiping a car...
                      perjury...he'll be lucky if he gets life...
                      then when your little surprise package
                      happens...he'll probably get some more.

TRUDY: You've got to let him escape, Papa.

KOCKENLOCKER: Oh sure, and take my pension along with
                      him I've been working for for seventeen
                      years...and land in the hoosegow besides.

EMMY: Couldn't you think of some bright way of
                      doing it?...You're always getting bright
                      ideas.

KOCKENLOCKER: Listen, Zipper-puss, some day they're
                      just gonna find your hair ribbon and an
                      axe some place...nothing else...the
                      mystery of Morgan's Creek.

TRUDY: Papa, that really isn't being helpful.

KOCKENLOCKER: (Bitterly)
                      Well, what do you want me to do, learn
                      to knit?
                      (He starts for the door)
                  I'm going out for a walk.

DISSOLVE TO:

J-20 NORVAL - SITTING ON HIS BED - IN THE CELL

He is finishing taking off his puttees. Now he looks up at
the SOUND of the key in the lock.

CUT TO:

J-21 KOCKENLOCKER - THROUGH THE BARS

We see him come into the jail, leave the outer door open,
then come to the inner door and open that. Now the CAMERA
PANS him into the shot with Norval.

KOCKENLOCKER: Trudy told me what you done for her...
at least what you tried to do...I didn't
understand.

NORVAL: That's all right. I'd just as soon she
hadn't told you though...The less people
know about it the better it's going to
be for her.

KOCKENLOCKER: It's too bad it had to turn out like this.

NORVAL: I'll be all right.

KOCKENLOCKER: What do you mean you'll be all right? You
know what they got lined up against you?...
What did you have to take a minor to a motel
for anyway? That's no place to take a minor.

NORVAL: I'm not even thinking about that...I'm so
worried about Trudy.

KOCKENLOCKER: Well...all she's worried about is you.

NORVAL: Poor Trudy! To think I've got to be locked
up in here the very time she needs me most
...if I could just get out for awhile...
I bet you I could find that skunk...I bet
you I could...

KOCKENLOCKER: I couldn't do it Norval... it would cost
me my job...if I conspired in any way.

NORVAL: Oh I didn't mean that, Mr. Kockenlocker...
I wouldn't do anything to get you in trouble
...just when Trudy needs you so much.

KOCKENLOCKER: If you got out it would have to be without
any help from me...in any shape or form
whatsoever...You'd have to do it all by
yourself.

10-20-42   (Continued)

J-21 (Cont'd)

NORVAL: I wasn't thinking of anything like that,
                       Mr. Kockenlocker.

KOCKENLOCKER: (Suiting the action to the words)
                       If I was to turn my back on you...carelessly
                       ...and you happened to grab my blackjack
                       and hit me over the konk with it, that
                       would be something else.
                                 (He closes his eyes and braces
                                 himself for the blow)

NORVAL: As if I'd do anything like that.

KOCKENLOCKER: (Disgustedly)
                       Of course not.
                                 (Then after a pause:)
                       Or if you made a sudden dive for it, pushed
                       me over behind the bunk...and beat it.
                                 (He ends up behind the bunk)

NORVAL: As if I'd do anything like that to you.

KOCKENLOCKER: (Coming up from behind the bunk)
                       How did you do in school?

NORVAL: Who me?...Fine.

KOCKENLOCKER: Is that so?
                                 (He thinks for a moment, then says:)
                       Kinda stuffy in here, ain't it?

NORVAL: I hadn't noticed it...

KOCKENLOCKER: (Rudely)
                       Oh yes you had....I'LL GO AROUND THE BACK
                       AND OPEN THE WINDOW...it works from the
                       outside...way around in back.

NORVAL: (Occupied with his troubles)
                       Thank you very much.

CUT TO:

J-22 NORVAL

He watches Kockenlocker go but no thought dawns upon his
face. THE CAMERA PANS up to the window behind him. Kockenlocker comes into the SHOT and looks down upon Norval speculatively. He even makes a little gesture signifying
"vamoose."

KOCKENLOCKER: Hey.

CUT TO:

10-20-42

J-23 NORVAL

He looks up, then climbs up on the cot - which brings him
into the SHOT with Kockenlocker.

KOCKENLOCKER: I'm up in a tree.

NORVAL: Are you?

KOCKENLOCKER: It's a good thing you didn't run away just
now...I forgot to lock the door and it
would take me five minutes to get down.

NORVAL: Don't you worry.

At this the branch breaks, Kockenlocker falls out of the
SHOT like so much pig iron.

NORVAL: Are you hurt?

He hurries past the CAMERA.

CUT TO:

J-24 KOCKENLOCKER LYING ON THE GROUND - UNDER THE TREE

Norval hurries around the corner of the jail, then crosses
to Kockenlocker and gets down beside him.

NORVAL: Are you hurt, Mr. Kockenlocker?

KOCKENLOCKER: (Prone)
It just knocked the wind out of me...I'm
all right...Only I ain't going to do any
running for the next hour or so...not if
you give me a million...and my gun is way
over there.
(He points vaguely)
It slipped out of my hand.

NORVAL: I'll get it for you.

Norval returns with the gun at which Kockenlocker throws his
arms in the air.

KOCKENLOCKER: All right you got me, Pal...Don't shoot...
I know when I'm licked...Just lock me in the
jail...The keys are in my left pocket...I
know you're going to escape...but I can't
help it...I can't do anything about it...
My car is right down in front of my house
and if you need any gas there's a can with
five gallons in my woodshed... but you
wouldn't take that from me would you, Pal?

10-20-42   (Continued)

J-24 (Cont'd)

NORVAL: Of course I wouldn't, Mr. Kockenlocker.

Mr. Kockenlocker lowers his hands and puts them on his
hips, then looks straight into the camera.

KOCKENLOCKER: (After a moment)
                        Maybe I can make it clearer, Norval...
                        Cheese it, there's a car coming.

They get in the shadow of the tree.

CUT TO:

J-25   KOCKENLOCKER'S CAR - COMING TO A STOP IN FRONT OF THE JAIL

Trudy and Emmy get out and look around cautiously. Now they
reach into the car and lift out a meat saw and axe, a crow-
bar, a shovel, a small stepladder and some rope. They advance cautiously toward the jail. As they get under the
window:

TRUDY: (Whispering)
                Norval.

Suddenly they start in terror. THE CAMERA PANS to Kockenlocker and Norval coming around the jail.

KOCKENLOCKER: What do you think you're doing?...You
                        get back to bed.

TRUDY: Papa, he isn't guilty of anything.

EMMY: Why isn't he in his cell?

KOCKENLOCKER: How about keeping your trap shut...He
                        escaped...Can't you see he's got me
                        covered...Don't shoot, Norval.

TRUDY: (Understanding)
                Oh, Papa.
                        (She hugs him)
                They won't fire you, will they?

NORVAL: Of course they won't. I just picked up
                        his gun for him. I'm not going anywhere.

KOCKENLOCKER: All right, I give up. See if you can do
                        anything with him.

TRUDY: (Putting her arms on Norval's
                        shoulders)
                        I want you to go away, Norval, don't you
                        understand? I couldn't bear to have you
                        in trouble on top of everything else.

10-20-42   (Continued)

J-25 (Cont'd)

NORVAL:	But it would just make things worse, Trudy... Your father would lose his job... They might...
EMMY:	Don't worry about Papa, he's just an old crook anyway.
KOCKENLOCKER:	Listen.
NORVAL:	They might suspect you too, Trudy...and even Emmy...
EMMY:	I'm only fourteen...don't worry about me.
TRUDY:	All right but then I'll come into court, when they try you, and I'll tell them everything that happened...and what a fix I was in...and how you nobly tried to help me.
NORVAL:	(Almost irritated) But I don't want you to do that...Nobody will believe the truth, Trudy...They'll just think you're doing it for me...Let it go the way it is...Don't waste everything we've done so far...They can't send me up for very long... and anyway I won't mind because I'll be doing it for you, Trudy... I'll be happy about it...every day I'll think: Well, this is for Trudy...and as soon as I get out we'll straighten it out somehow and then we'll get married again, but really Trudy...and for always and always,
TRUDY:	You just make me cry but you're not helping anything,
NORVAL:	Don't cry Trudy.
TRUDY:	(Throwing her arms around his neck) Oh Norval.
KOCKENLOCKER:	(After exchanging a disgusted look with his youngest) How about that guy you was gonna find... if you could just get out.
TRUDY:	(Seizing at straws) That's right! Maybe you could find Ratzkiwatzki. Of course you could...anyway it's worth trying.

NORVAL: Do you really think so, Trudy?...If I
                        really thought so I'd track him to the
                        ends of the earth.

TRUDY: Of course you can.

NORVAL: But I haven't got any car.

KOCKENLOCKER: Steal mine.

EMMY: It's insured.

NORVAL: (Vascilating)
                        If I was really sure it was for you, Trudy.
                        I'd need a little money...I've got nine
                        hundred dollars in the bank only it's in
                        bonds...Do you think it would be wrong if
                        I took nine hundred dollars in cash and
                        left my bonds?...I've got a key at the
                        house.

EMMY: It might be wrong but it would be very
                        handy.

KOCKENLOCKER: All we needed was a little bank robbery.

J-26   INTERIOR OF THE BANK

        Through the glass windows we see Kockenlocker's car come
        to a quiet stop. Inside are Norval, Kockenlocker and his
        daughters. Norval appears in his business clothes, looks
        around cautiously and hurries to the door, unlocks it and
        comes into the bank. He goes through his cage door, starts
        for the safe and falls over a large adding machine. As he
        picks himself up, Kockenlocker hurries into the bank.

KOCKENLOCKER: (Whispering)
                        What's the matter?

NORVAL: (Pulling himself to his feet)
                        I tripped on an adding machine.

        Saying which, he pulls over an automatic change maker.
        Trudy and Emmy run into the bank.

TRUDY: What happened?

EMMY: Why don't you look what you're doing?

NORVAL: (In a whisper)
                        It's very hard to open the safe without
                        turning on the alarm.

10-20-42   (Continued)

TRUDY: Can you do it?

NORVAL: Oh yes.

Saying which, he swings the little safe door open and forty
bells go off and blast the stillness of the night.

TRUDY: Norval!

KOCKENLOCKER: Beat it.

Norval counts approximately nine hundred dollars with the
speed of a magician and runs after the others to the car,
falling over only the adding machine and the change maker.
The car whizzes out of the shot.

CUT TO:

J-27   THE TOWN JAIL

Norval's car whizzes into the shot. Kockenlocker and his
daughters leap out.

NORVAL: Goodbye Trudy. I won't f-f-fail you.

TRUDY: Don't let them catch you.

KOCKENLOCKER: Beat it.

The car zips away.

KOCKENLOCKER: Come here you two, quick.

He picks up the rope Emmy had brought and runs into the
jail, followed by his daughters.

CUT TO:

J-28   INTERIOR OF THE JAIL

Kockenlocker hurries in and starts winding the rope around
himself.

KOCKENLOCKER: Tie me up quick.
                   (Both girls go to work
                   on him)
                   Not so hard. What are you trying to do...
                   strangle me? All right, that's tight
                   enough...Now give me a little bump on the
                   head...Take the blackjack out of my pants
                   and lock the door and beat it home and
                   hide the keys.

10-20-42   (Continued)

J-28 (Cont'd)

TRUDY: Yes, Papa.

KOCKENLOCKER: Now a little clunk on the head.

TRUDY: Which side?

KOCKENLOCKER: Any side.

Trudy gives him a little bump on the forehead.

KOCKENLOCKER: (Disgustedly)
                    Harder!...But not too hard,

Trudy gives him another little bump.

KOCKENLOCKER: (Irritably)
                    Harder. How could that put anybody out?

Trudy gives him another gentle pat.

KOCKENLOCKER: (Loudly)
                    Is that all the harder you can hit? For
                    heaven's sake will you try to do one
                    thing right?

EMMY: (Impatiently)
                    Oh here.

She takes the blackjack out of her sister's hand and fells
her father like a poled ox.

FADE OUT:

                    END OF SEQUENCE "J"

10-20-42

FADE IN:

K-1   THE GOVERNOR AND THE BOSS AT THE TELEPHONE

They are listening impatiently.

GOVERNOR: Wait a minute, wait a minute, never mind
                the details: Is the girl married or isn't
                she married? It's a matter of State honor...
                ...a matter of public weal.

THE BOSS: Let me talk to him.

CUT TO:

K-2   THE EDITOR AND MR. RAFFERTY - AT THE TELEPHONE

THE EDITOR: But that's what I've been trying to tell
                you, Mister Governor, nobody knows...She
                said she was married, but then she went
                out and married Norval...so how could she
                have been?

MR. RAFFERTY: (Indignantly)
                What are you talking? Soitanly she was
                married.
                        (He snatches the phone out
                        of the Editor's hand)
                Soitanly she was married, Mister Governor.
                Vould she tell a lie? I known her all
                her life only dat shnook Norval...

CUT TO:

K-3   THE GOVERNOR AND THE BOSS - AT THE TELEPHONE

They look at each other in surprise at the change of accent.

MR. RAFFERTY'S   (Faintly)
VOICE: ...had to take her out and do it under
                a phony name, it shouldn't happen, vich
                started all the trouble.

THE BOSS: (After a look at the Governor)
                Was sagst du?

CUT TO:

K-4   MR. RAFFERTY AND THE EDITOR

MR. RAFFERTY: (Delightedly)
                Mister Governor.........................
                ....
                ....

The dots above denote a nameless foreign language in which
Mr. Rafferty enthusiastically starts telling the story of
the policeman's daughter.
11-23-42

                            723

K-4 (Cont'd)

      THE EDITOR: (Indignantly)
                       Hey.

      CUT TO:

K-5 THE GOVERNOR'S SECRETARY - TAKING THE CONVERSATION IN
     SHORTHAND

     He looks up perplexedly, then around for help.

     CUT TO:

K-6 THE GOVERNOR AND THE BOSS

      THE GOVERNOR: Hey.
                                 (Then into the phone)
                     How about in English?

      THE BOSS: It would be quicker like this.

      CUT TO:

K-7 THE EDITOR AND MR. RAFFERTY

      THE EDITOR: (Snatching the phone away from
                                  Mr. Rafferty)
                     I'm very sorry, Mister Governor. Nobody
                     knows whether she's married or not.

      MR. RAFFERTY: Will you shut up?

      CUT TO:

K-8 THE GOVERNOR AND THE BOSS

      THE GOVERNOR: Well, she's got to be married, that's
                     all there is to it...we can't have a
                     thing like that hanging over our fair
                     state...besmirching our fair name.

      THE BOSS: You said it, Guv.

      THE GOVERNOR: Where is the father now?

      CUT TO:

K-9 THE EDITOR AND MR. RAFFERTY

      THE EDITOR: In jail.

      CUT TO:

K-10 THE GOVERNOR AND THE BOSS

      THE GOVERNOR: I thought you said he escaped.

11-23-42   (Continued)

K-10 (Cont'd)

    THE BOSS: He did say he escaped.

    CUT TO:

K-11 THE EDITOR AND MR. RAFFERTY

    THE EDITOR: Yes, but he came back and got caught
                     again.

    MR. RAFFERTY: It shouldn't happen.

    CUT TO:

K-12 THE GOVERNOR AND THE BOSS

    THE GOVERNOR: When?

    THE BOSS: Yes.

    CUT TO:

K-13 THE EDITOR AND MR. RAFFERTY

    THE EDITOR: Yesterday. It must have been around six
                     o'clock, I guess, because Mr. Tuerck was
                     still in the bank for the Christmas Club
                     and Mr. Rafferty was still in his store.

    MR. RAFFERTY: It was closer to seven.

    DURING THIS LAST WE HAVE SLOWLY DISSOLVED TO:

K-14 THE STREET IN FRONT OF THE KOCKENLOCKER HOUSE - (NIGHT)

    Kockenlocker's old Dodge pulls up and Norval gets out. His
    coat collar is turned up. He looks around furtively, then
    starts for the Kockenlocker house. Suddenly he stops in
    amazement.

    CUT TO:

K-15 THE KOCKENLOCKER HOUSE - (NIGHT)

    Dead leaves have drifted onto the porch. Some boards have
    been nailed over a broken window. A sign is loosely nailed
    to a porch pillar. It says: FOR SALE.

    CUT TO:

K-16 NORVAL

    He seems quite lost. He looks up and down the street in
    perplexity, then goes slowly back to the car.

    DISSOLVE TO:

11-23-42

K-17 THE FRONT OF THE JOHNSON HOUSE - (NIGHT)

The windows are gaily lighted and a Christmas wreath is
nailed to the door.

CUT TO:

K-18 NORVAL COMING THROUGH THE GATE

THE CAMERA PANS him up the steps. He rings the doorbell.
Mrs. Johnson opens the door and blinks into the darkness.

MRS. JOHNSON: What is it, please?...Why Norval! What
                  are you doing here?
                       (Now she remembers his
                        predicament)
                  Come in, dear.

CUT TO:

K-19 THE INTERIOR OF THE JOHNSON HOUSE - (Possible revamp of
Kockenlocker's)

Mr. Johnson is just getting out of his chair.

MR. JOHNSON: Why hello, Norval, I'm glad to see you're
                  all right.
                       (He shakes Norval's hand as
                        the latter and Mrs. Johnson
                        comes into the SHOT)

NORVAL: How do you do, Mr. Johnson.

MR. JOHNSON: What are you doing in Morgan's Creek?
                  Do you think it's wise?

NORVAL: I just came to see Trudy, but there's a
                  FOR SALE sign on the house...I wonder if
                  you could tell me where they moved?

MR. JOHNSON: I don't think anybody knows.

MRS. JOHNSON: They left about six months ago, Norval.

NORVAL: (Aghast)
                  Six months ago! But I've been writing
                  to her for six months...I never got any
                  answers.

MR. JOHNSON: They left kind of hurriedly, Norval, right
                  after he was discharged by the town council.

NORVAL: (Horrified)
                  Discharged! What for?

Mrs. Johnson looks away.

MR. JOHNSON: Something to do with the escape of a
                  prisoner...They didn't quite believe it.

11-23-42   (Continued)

K-19   (Cont'd)

NORVAL: (Pointing to himself)
You mean me?

MR. JOHNSON: I guess so, Norval.

NORVAL: Does that mean he lost his pension, too?

MR. JOHNSON: Oh yes.

NORVAL: But that's terrible...I was only trying
to help Trudy...looking for somebody I
never found...but you wouldn't know about
that...or would you?

MR. JOHNSON: (In a dead legal voice)
I don't know what you're talking about,
Norval.

NORVAL: Good! That's something anyway.

MR. JOHNSON: I mean I don't know as a resident of this
town...and neither does anyone else..what
I might know as a lawyer is entirely between me and the Bar Association.

NORVAL: I see...anyway, now that I'm home and ready
to give myself up. I guess they'll take
Mr. Kockenlocker back on the Force all right,
don't you think?

MR. JOHNSON: I hardly think so, Norval. In the first
place nobody knows where the family went and
then there's a new man in the job, he's held
it for six months now, they probably wouldn't
feel right about discharging him, and besides you know what Mr. Kockenlocker is like
...He didn't exactly take it lying down when
they fired him...He left on very bad terms
...They had to take six stitches in Mr.
Tuerck alone.

NORVAL: Poor Trudy.

MR. JOHNSON: Poor Mr. Tuerck.

MRS. JOHNSON: It was ghastly, Norval.

MR. JOHNSON: You haven't asked for my advice, Norval, and
it certainly isn't up to me to advise you to
evade the law...but since you were kinda
dragged in to this situation...and it's
practically forgotten now anyway...and the
Kockenlockers have gone...and no doubt
taken root somewhere else...they may even
have changed their name, why don't you do
the same?
                            (Continued)

K-19 (Cont'd)

MRS. JOHNSON: I'm sure it would be wiser, Norval.

NORVAL: But I've got to find Trudy, Mrs. Johnson,
      she must be in terrible trouble now...
         (He counts rapidly on his fingers)
      at least if her father had his job...

MR. JOHNSON: Oh, he probably has some kind of a job...
      there's a great shortage of men.

NORVAL: You haven't any idea at all where they went?

MR. JOHNSON: I haven't, Norval. They gave him twenty-
      four hours to get out of town...or Mr. Tuerck
      would have prosecuted.

MRS. JOHNSON: He was very battered.

MR. JOHNSON: I've given you the very best advice, Norval,
      you must do as your conscience dictates, but
      if there were that many charges pending
      against me, you wouldn't see my coat tails
      for the dust...even if they didn't press the
      Kockenlocker charges there is still the
      uniform, and the jail break, and the bank
      robbery and the...

NORVAL: (Horrified)
      Bank robbery! I only took my own money.

MRS. JOHNSON: Oh, I'm so glad, Norval.

MR. JOHNSON: So am I...but that isn't exactly what Mr.
      Tuerck allowed us to understand.

NORVAL: (Backing away)
      Holy m-m-moses...goodbye, Mrs. Johnson,
      goodbye, Mr. Johnson...thank you for...
      not turning me in, anyway.

MR. JOHNSON: (In a legal voice)
      I'm your counsel, how could I turn
      you in?

NORVAL: Goodbye.

MRS. JOHNSON: (Impulsively)
      Goodbye, dear.
       (She puts her arms around him)
      Would you like to take some fruit cake
      with you?

11-23-42   (Continued)

K-19 Cont'd)

NORVAL: No thank you, Mrs. Johnson, I'm afraid
                   I couldn't swallow it.

MRS. JOHNSON: (In tears)
                   Merry Christmas, dear.

NORVAL: Merry Christmas to you.

He looks at them one last time, then departs like a thief
in the night. Mrs. Johnson enters her husband's arms and
cries softly.

DISSOLVE TO:

K-20 EXT. OF RAFFERTY'S MUSIC STORE - (NIGHT)

Through the window we see Mr. Rafferty escort a customer
to the door, then open the door for him.

MR. RAFFERTY: Merry Christmas.
                        (Suddenly he does a double-
                        take at something he sees)

CUT TO:

K-21 ELIMINATED

K-22 NORVAL - <u>COMING ACROSS THE STREET</u>

He comes slowly forward. As he gets near the CAMERA we PULL
BACK past Mr. Rafferty and find that we are inside the Music
Store.

MR. RAFFERTY: (Aghast)
                Norval!

NORVAL: Hello, Mr. Rafferty.

MR. RAFFERTY: (Undecided)
                Well...come in, what are you standing there
                like a convict.

Norval comes in. Mr. Rafferty closes and locks the door behind him.

MR. RAFFERTY: Get away from the window...come here...
                I'll show you a radio.

THE CAMERA PANS them deeper into the store. As they enter a
booth -

CUT TO:

K-23 CLOSE SHOT - RAFFERTY AND NORVAL

MR. RAFFERTY: (Showing a radio)
                This is a very nice model...It plays longer
                and louder and cheezier than anything...

NORVAL: (Interrupting)
                Where's Trudy?

MR. RAFFERTY: I know from nothing...did you find him?

NORVAL: You mean...
                (He makes a vague gesture)

MR. RAFFERTY: Ratinski or however.

NORVAL: No.

MR. RAFFERTY: Iyiiyiyiyiyi.

NORVAL: She must have got the name wrong...I've
                seen a million names...There's nobody by
                that name.

MR. RAFFERTY: Iyiyiyiyiyiyi.

NORVAL: Do you know where she is?

MR. RAFFERTY: I know from nothing.
                (Now he looks all around
                  and adds)
                I got her hid.

11-24-42   (Continued)

K-23 (Cont'd)

NORVAL: (Seizing his hand)
                  Thank heaven! Is she all right?

MR. RAFFERTY: Is she all right! She's all right and
at the same time she's...how would you
feel?

NORVAL: Where is she?

MR. RAFFERTY: (Looking all around)
One time I bought a little farm...buying
farms is a disease. Can you see me with a
plow...I got the whole family, they're all
right...Kockenlocker milks it, Emmy skims
it and Trudy drinks it.

NORVAL: Does anybody suspect anything?

RAFFERTY: Suspect what? Who knows where it's my farm?
I got trouble alone myself finding it. I
got everything fixed. She'll have it on the
farm...It's my sister's grandson and who
knows from what?

NORVAL: Is she happy?

MR. RAFFERTY: Is she happy! She's happy and at the same
time she's...well...they lost their house,
he lost his job, he lost his pension, she
lost her husband...she's happy.

NORVAL: Poor Trudy.

MR. RAFFERTY: Poor Trudy! You ain't exactly in a bed of
roses yourself.

NORVAL: Could I see her?

MR. RAFFERTY: If I can find it...It takes almost a
Columbus...you got a car?

NORVAL: I've got Mr. Kockenlocker's.

MR. RAFFERTY: You got gas...don't tell me how.

NORVAL: Yes.

MR. RAFFERTY: All right, we'll take 'em a toikey. I'll go
next door by the market.

NORVAL: (Reaching in his pocket)
              I'll pay for it.

MR. RAFFERTY: You'll pay for it! Who's farm is it...if you
want to spend your money...buy Bonds!

DISSOLVE TO:
11-24-42

K-24   MR. TUERCK - AT HIS DESK - IN THE BANK - (NIGHT)

He finishes a report, arises, puts on his hat and coat and leaves the bank.

CUT TO:

K-25   MR. RAFFERTY AND NORVAL - IN FRONT OF THE MUSIC STORE (NIGHT)

They are putting the turkey into the car.

CUT TO:

K-26   MR. TUERCK - LOCKING THE DOOR OF THE BANK - (NIGHT)

He looks toward Rafferty's Music Store, looks away, then looks back quickly. He narrows his eyes, takes a long look then hurries back into the bank. A second later he reappears with a big automatic in his hand.

CUT TO:

K-27   NORVAL AND MR. RAFFERTY - GETTING INTO THE CAR - (NIGHT)

MR. RAFFERTY: We'll buy at the bakery a Plum Pudding.
Nothing gives so much indigestion but
at the same time...

Norval turns his head toward the bank and his gaze fixes in horror.

MR. RAFFERTY: (Unaware of this)
...so much pleasure like a Plum Pudding...
except a fruit cake. One time when I
was a boy...

Mr. Tuerck's automatic comes slowly into the picture. THE CAMERA PULLS BACK to hold Mr. Tuerck.

MR. TUERCK: Good evening, Mr. Rafferty...and you, Mr.
Jones...I wondered if you'd come back.
(He puts a police whistle
to his lips and blows
stridently)

DISSOLVE TO:

K-28   ELIMINATED.

K-29   EXT. LITTLE FARMHOUSE IN THE SNOW - (NIGHT)

Against the window shade we see the silhouette of a Christmas
tree and the shadow of Kockenlocker working on it. We hear
the strains of a HARMONIUM.

DISSOLVE TO:

K-30   KOCKENLOCKER DECORATING THE CHRISTMAS TREE IN THE FRONT ROOM
OF THE LITTLE FARMHOUSE

The CAMERA PANS from him onto Emmy who is playing the harmonium. As Emmy looks around the CAMERA PANS onto a chaise
longue in front of a crackling fire. Only Trudy's hand is
visible hanging over the side.

CUT TO:

K-31   KOCKENLOCKER - AT THE CHRISTMAS TREE

KOCKENLOCKER: Anyway, it's going to be a white Christmas
...Why don't you say something?

As there is no answer he crosses to the chaise longue and
sits down. Now he takes Trudy's hand.

KOCKENLOCKER: How about a little smile, huh?

CUT TO:

K-32   BIG HEAD OF TRUDY

She smiles up at her father but not very gaily.

CUT TO:

K-33   KOCKENLOCKER - PAST TRUDY

KOCKENLOCKER: (Huskily)
                      You gotta have more confidence in the,
                      the Almighty...or whatever it is that
                      makes the wheels go round...All right,
                      it's almost Christmas...where was he
                      born?...in a cow shed! You might be
                      waiting for the President of the United
                      States....you gotta have more confidence.

CUT TO:

K-34   BIG HEAD OF TRUDY - AS SHE SMILES

CUT TO:

K-35   EMMY - AT THE HARMONIUM

She looks around at her father, then around a little further,
then back at her father.

                                                           (Continued)

K-35 (Cont'd)

EMMY: Speaking of cowsheds, did you remember
                             to milk Bessie tonight, Papa?

CUT TO:

K-36 KOCKENLOCKER - PAST TRUDY

KOCKENLOCKER: Yes, I remembered "to milk Bessie
                             tonight, Papa."

CUT TO:

K-37 EMMY - AT THE HARMONIUM

EMMY: Then what's she doing in the kitchen?

CUT TO:

K-38 KOCKENLOCKER - PAST TRUDY

KOCKENLOCKER: What?
                                    (He rises and starts
                                     for the kitchen)
                             Will you get out of here?

CUT TO:

K-39 THE DOORWAY OF THE KITCHEN

Bessie is half into the parlor.

BESSIE: (Speaking)
                  Moo.

KOCKENLOCKER: (Coming into the SHOT)
                  Come on, get out of here.
                             (He starts to push her out)

CUT TO:

K-40 BIG HEAD OF TRUDY

TRUDY: (Laughing)
                  Poor Papa.

CUT TO:

K-41 EXT. OF THE FARMHOUSE - (NIGHT)

Kockenlocker's car pulls into the SHOT. Mr. Rafferty gets
out, crunches through the snow to the door and knocks. Under
his arm he holds the turkey.

                                              (Continued)

K-41 (Cont'd)

EMMY: (Opening the door)
               Hello, Mr. Rafferty...it's so good to see
               you.

CUT TO:

K-42   INT. THE FARMHOUSE - REVERSE SHOT

Emmy closes the door behind Mr. Rafferty.

MR. RAFFERTY: I've brought a turkey.

EMMY: Thank you Mr. Rafferty.

She takes the turkey. THE CAMERA PANS Mr. Rafferty to a
position next to the chaise longue. He takes Trudy's hand.

MR. RAFFERTY: Hello.
                    (He sits down on the chaise longue)
               You feel good hunh...it's natural.

TRUDY: Thank you Mr. Rafferty...and for all your
               kindness...I don't know where we would
               have been without you.

MR. RAFFERTY: What are you talking...it's a privilege...
               the doctor will come from the next town...
               then he goes back to his town and forgets
               it...you got nothing to worry about...it
               will be as quiet as a buttered eagle.
                    (He squeezes her hand and
                    smiles nervously)

EMMY: (Coming into the SHOT)
               Would you like a cup of tea Mr. Rafferty?

MR. RAFFERTY: Thank you.

Emmy exits.

MR. RAFFERTY: How's Papa?

TRUDY: Fine, thank you. He's milking Bessie.

MR. RAFFERTY: Dat Bessie, I remember her...never
               satisfied...I brought Papa back his car.

He looks at Trudy uneasily.

CUT TO:

K-43   BIG HEAD - OF TRUDY

TRUDY: But Norval had it...you mean he came back...
               where is he...why didn't he come out with
               you?

CUT TO:

K-44   MR. RAFFERTY - PAST TRUDY

MR. RAFFERTY: (More uneasily yet)
He didn't find anybody while he was away,
Trudy.

CUT TO:

K-45   BIG HEAD OF TRUDY

TRUDY: (Indignantly)
Well, that's no reason not to come out
and see me...he ought to know better than
that...when I've been waiting so long to
see him so, so anxiously.

CUT TO:

K-46   MR. RAFFERTY - PAST TRUDY

MR. RAFFERTY: (Avoiding Trudy's eye)
That ain't why he didn't come, Trudy they
caught him again...he's in the clink.

TRUDY: (Starting to cry)
Oh, Mr. Rafferty...

MR. RAFFERTY: Now, now, now what good is this...you've
got something else to think about...so
he's in jail...so he'll get out...someday.

TRUDY: (Starting to sit up)
I'll go right back to Morgan's Creek and
tell them everything...they'll have to drop
the charges when I tell them what he did...
and why.

MR. RAFFERTY: (Holding her back on the
                       chaise longue)
Trudy, what are you talking...how about your
reputation? We spend six months planning,
fixing everything, building up a secret...
now you got to build it down over night?

TRUDY: I've got to.

MR. RAFFERTY: All right, you don't care about yourself...
how about your father, ain't he in enough
trouble, how about your sister, how about me,
how about...anyway they wouldn't believe you.

TRUDY: They will when they see me.

(Continued)

K-46 (Cont'd)

     MR. RAFFERTY: (Starting to get furious)
                          Trudy, vill you listen to...what's the
                          use...I love you for it.
                               (He takes her in his arms and
                                 pats her on the back)
                          There, there, there.

     EMMY: (Coming into the SHOT)
                          Here's your tea, Mr. Rafferty.

     MR. RAFFERTY: (To heaven)
                          Tea! Wait till your Papa hears.

He and Emmy look toward the kitchen.

CUT TO:

K-47   KOCKENLOCKER - <u>COMING INTO THE KITCHEN WITH A PAIL OF MILK</u>

He stamps the snow off his feet, then comes forward.

     KOCKENLOCKER: That cow'll think twice before she asks
                         <u>me</u> to...
                                 (He slips on a potato peel
                                 or something and does a
                                 108 with milk)

<u>FADE OUT.</u>

<u>END OF SEQUENCE "K"</u>

FADE IN:

L-1   MR. RAFFERTY'S CAR - IN FRONT OF THE MORGAN'S CREEK FIRE-
       HOUSE

       Rafferty and Kockenlocker are standing alongside of it
       looking in.

       KOCKENLOCKER: You've still got time to change your mind.

       RAFFERTY: Why don't you Trudy... Look: I'll get him
                        out on bail and, and
                        (His voice trails off)

       CUT TO:

L-2   TRUDY - IN FRONT SEAT - OF THE CAR

       We see Emmy in the back seat.   Trudy shakes her head "no".

       CUT TO:

L-3   KOCKENLOCKER AND RAFFERTY - ALONGSIDE THE CAR

       RAFFERTY: All right.
                        (He indicates the way in
                        to Kockenlocker and says:)
                        After you.

       They go into the fire house and disappear around the hook
       and ladder wagon. The CAMERA ANGLES UP past the fire
       house sign and onto the second floor windows.

       DISSOLVE TO:

L-4   THE TOWN COUNCIL ASSEMBLED

       At the head of the table we see the Mayor. Next to him
       sits Mr. Tuerck. On one side we see Mr. Ziegler, the jewel-
       er, Justice Meade Woodson, Mr. Shottish, Mr. Swartz, the
       clothier, Mr. McNanny, the proprietor of the movie theatre,
       Dr. Meyer, and Mr. Glumpf. On the near side of the table
       we see a matching number of less important people plus two
       women. In the background we see Mr. Johnson, the Sheriff,
       Pete, the Secret Service men, the U.S. Marshal, and the
       two M.P.s.

       MR. JOHNSON: I just want to be fair about this, Mr. Mayor
                        ...It isn't because I represent Norval...
                        but the Kockenlockers have gone...in disgrace
                        ...where...deponent sayeth not...Norval has
                        lost his job...We'll never hear from him
                        again...It's the day before Christmas...let
                        us show a little of the yuletide spirit...
                        withdraw the charges...wipe the slate clean
                        and forget the whole thing.
                                                    (Continued)

L-4 (Cont'd)

MR. TUERCK:	(Slapping the table) And I say bushwaw! Either we make an example of this man or we're opening the doors and inviting crime in to dinner.
MR. JOHNSON:	Piffle.
MR. TUERCK:	It may be piffle in your book... (He picks up a piece of paper) but I say that breaking and entering, theft, perjury, impersonating a soldier, impairing the morals of a minor, jail-break with or without conspiracy, etc., etc., are not piffle.
MR. JOHNSON:	Piffle.
MR. TUERCK:	(Belligerently) You say that just once more...
MR. JOHNSON:	Piffle.

Mr. Tuerck starts to get up.

THE MAYOR:	Gentlemen, please.

Mr. Tuerck sits down again.

THE MAYOR:	There is a great deal to be said on both sides...
JUSTICE WOODSON:	If I may interrupt Mr. Mayor, it seems to me...
FIRST M.P.:	It's for the Army. The matter is military.
MR. JOHNSON:	Yes, well the matter is not military as I have already pointed out...
THE SHERIFF:	I still happen to be the Sheriff of this county.
THE U.S. MARSHAL:	The matter is and was Federal.
FIRST SECRET SERVICE MAN:	Beyond the shadow of a doubt.
MR. JOHNSON:	(Wearily) Here we go again, boys.
KOCKENLOCKER'S VOICE:	Hoy.

All turn to look.

CUT TO:

L-5   KOCKENLOCKER AND RAFFERTY - AT THE HEAD OF THE
       CIRCULAR STAIRS

Near the stairs we see the brass pole leading to the floor
below.

KOCKENLOCKER: My daughter wants to see you.

MR. RAFFERTY: Right away.

They come forward.

CUT TO:

L-6   THE COUNCIL - AROUND THE TABLE

MR. TUERCK: (Angrily)
                        What are you doing in Morgan's Creek? I
                        warned you that if you ever showed up again..

KOCKENLOCKER: (Coming into the SHOT)
                        Oh yeah?

THE MAYOR: Gentlemen, gentlemen, is this the Christmas
                        spirit? What is it that you want Mr.
                        Kockenlocker?

KOCKENLOCKER: My daughter wants to tell you about Norval..
                       why he done what he done...she says when
                       you hear what she's got to say...you'll
                       never prosecute him.

MR. RAFFERTY: Impossible.

THE MAYOR: (After looking around)
                      Well...bring her up. We must hear both
                      sides...always.

MR. TUERCK: That is strictly the bunk! Women are always
                      trying to take the blame for men...it's
                      what you call the mother instinct.

KOCKENLOCKER: (Furiously)
                      Well you can listen to her can't you, you
                      dumb...

MR. RAFFERTY: (Shaking a finger under Mr. Tuerck's
                       nose)
                      Or I'll take my business out of your bank
                      so quick it will make your hair sizzle.

THE MAYOR: Bring her up.

KOCKENLOCKER: I'm afraid you'll have to come down...she
                      don't feel very good.

MR. TUERCK: Is that so...well, well, well...
                                                      (Continued)

740

L-6 (Cont'd)

KOCKENLOCKER: Yes...what about it?

In the moment of silence which follows we hear Emmy's voice
SCREAM "Papa". All turn. We hear footsteps pounding up the
iron stairs. Emmy bursts into the room, hysterically
frightened.

EMMY: Papa...Trudy has...

MR. RAFFERTY: (Hysterically)
Vot? Well what are you standing there?
(He looks down the table)
Doctor, quick.

The doctor grabs Emmy and runs down the stairs. There is
now a general exodus. Kockenlocker stands in the middle,
stunned for a moment. As Mr. Tuerck starts by him he snaps
out of it.

KOCKENLOCKER: Just a minute you.

MR. TUERCK: (Threateningly)
Now you watch yourself, Edmund.

KOCKENLOCKER: You watch yourself.

Suddenly Mr. Tuerck shoves somebody between himself and
Kockenlocker and makes a dive down the stairs. Kockenlocker
watches him go, then sees the brass pole, grabs it and
slides down.

CUT TO:

L-7 THE BOTTOM OF THE CIRCULAR STAIRS

Mr. Tuerck is hurrying around and around them.

CUT TO:

L-8 HIGH CAMERA SHOT - KOCKENLOCKER WATCHING TUERCK COME DOWN

Now he spits on his hands and lunges out of the SHOT.

CUT TO:

L-9 MR. TUERCK - TAKING OFF BACKWARDS

Kockenlocker dusts his hands and leaves.

DISSOLVE TO:

L-10 LOW CAMERA SHOT - OF THE MORGAN MEMORIAL HOSPITAL

CUT TO:

11-27-42

L-11   DOCTOR MEYER - <u>IN THE CORNER OF THE DELIVERY ROOM</u>

He is adjusting his gloves. Behind him a shadow is going
through the usual scooping motions. THE CAMERA PANS Doctor
Meyer across the room, a nurse puts a mask over his nose and
hands him a stethoscope. Now he comes straight to the
CAMERA. He raises his gloved hand to beat the pulse.

DOCTOR MEYER: Ready.

He places the end of the stethoscope just under the CAMERA
and starts to beat time. Now his eyes blink in surprise.
His finger comes to a stop. He looks around at someone then
starts again. He seems to have trouble catching the beat
like a rookie trying to get in step with a column. He looks
around again, unsanitarily twirls his finger in his ear, replaces the stethoscope, then listens. THE CAMERA PUSHES IN
to: CLOSE UP including his eyes and his nose. As it does
so we hear the deafening beat of the war drums in an African
jungle. The doctor's eyes bug out in surprise.

CUT TO:

L-12   <u>THE UPPER HOSPITAL CORRIDOR</u>

Here we see Rafferty, Kockenlocker and Emmy. Kockenlocker
nurses his right knuckles vaguely then wanders over to a
window and looks down. He reacts unpleasantly to what he
sees.

CUT TO:

L-13   HIGH CAMERA SHOT - <u>DOWN ONTO THE STREET</u>

Here we see a group comprising of the Mayor, Mr. Ziegler,
the jeweler, Justice Meade Woodson, Mr. Shottish, Mr. Swartz,
Mr. McNanny, Mr. Glumpf, the other members of the council
plus two women, Mr. Johnson, the Sheriff, Pete, the Secret
Service men, the U.S. Marshal, the two M.P.s, and the newspaper editor. Now Mr. Tuerck walks out of the drug store
across the street and joins them. He is slightly bandaged
and very indignant. He points up to the hospital and shakes
a warning finger. The newspaper editor takes down his
threats, then starts for the hospital. While this has been
going on quite a few gossips, including Cecelia and her
mother have joined the group.

CUT TO:

L-14   KOCKENLOCKER, EMMY AND MR. RAFFERTY - <u>IN THE UPPER HOSPITAL
CORRIDOR</u>

KOCKENLOCKER: (Turning away from the window)
           Some secret.

RAFFERTY: So they know! So what do they know?

11-27-42   (Continued)

L-14 (Cont'd)

They turn toward the stairs.

CUT TO:

L-15   THE NEWSPAPER EDITOR ARRIVING ON THE SECOND FLOOR

THE EDITOR: Have you any statement to make?

THE CAMERA PANS him into the group:

                 Any little item of general interest?

KOCKENLOCKER: How would you like a punch in the nose?

MR. RAFFERTY: (Confidentially)
                 What would it cost to keep this quiet?

THE EDITOR: (Hurt)
                 Mr. Rafferty...

Before he can say more they turn and look down the corridor.
A nurse hurries out of the delivery room and hurries past
the group. They watch her go rigidly. Now an expression of
horror comes over all their faces. They clutch each other.

CUT TO:

L-16   A NURSE COMING OUT OF A ROOM - WHEELING AN OXYGEN TANK

THE CAMERA PANS her into the shot with the miserable group.
As she hurries by them she tosses them a line.

THE NURSE: It's a boy.

She hurries away.

RAFFERTY: (Exultantly)
                 A boy! Trudy...wonderful!

He seizes Kockenlocker and starts doing a war dance with him.
Emmy turns away and starts to cry.

THE NEWSPAPER
EDITOR: Congratulations, Edmund.

KOCKENLOCKER: (Sourly)
                 For what?

RAFFERTY: (Philosophically)
                 A boy is a boy!

NOTE: THE REST OF L-16 (CONTINUING ONTO PAGE L-8) IS
WRITTEN, CONTAINS NOT ONE CENSORABLE LINE, HAS BEEN SENT TO
MR DeSYLVA, AND WILL BE RELEASED AT THE PROPER TIME.

11-27-42   (Continued)

743

L-16 (Cont'd)

CONTINUATION

OF

L-16

11-27-42   (Continued)

<u>BALANCE</u>

<u>OF</u>

<u>L-16</u>

DISSOLVE TO:

L-17   A WESTERN UNION OPERATOR - PAST THE SHOULDER OF A TRAINED NURSE

THE OPERATOR: WHAT!

He sits down to his spider and the CAMERA WHIPS DOWN with him.

L-18   INSERT - THE SPIDER

The operator's hand rattles it violently.

DISSOLVE TO:

L-19   <u>THE EDITOR'S OFFICE</u> - OF A GREAT METROPOLITAN DAILY

Through the partition in the back we see the city room. A boy runs in and hands a piece of paper to the editor. The editor does an enormous take-em, then files out into the city room holding the paper high and shouting at the top of his lungs.

DISSOLVE TO:

11-27-42

L-20   THE SPIDER RATTLING AWAY

DISSOLVE TO:

L-21   NEWSPAPER HEADLINE:

NOTE: INSERT TO BE RELEASED LATER

DISSOLVE TO:

L-22   THE SPIDER - RATTLING AWAY

DISSOLVE TO:

L-23   MUSSOLINI'S OFFICE - <u>IN ROME</u>

LOW CAMERA SHOT.   Some shiny boots run past us and end up in a tiny figure leaning over a great desk.

CUT TO:

L-24   MUSSOLINI READING A TELEGRAM

He slaps the desk a furious blow, then pops his fingers into his mouth and assumes an expression of pain.

DISSOLVE TO:

L-25   THE SPIDER - RATTLING AWAY

DISSOLVE TO:

L-26   HITLER'S TENT - <u>IN RUSSIA</u>

It is very cold.   Hitler and some generals, with their backs to us, are poring over some maps.

CUT TO:

L-27   TWO GUARDS <u>ON EITHER SIDE OF THE TENT FLAP</u>

An excited officer hurries through here clutching a piece of paper. The guards spring to attention. The officer goes out of the SHOT.

CUT TO:

L-28   HITLER AND HIS GENERALS WITH THEIR BACKS TO US

The officer runs into the shot, kicks his heels and salutes. Hitler turns around and we see that it is Hitler. He reads the piece of paper sourly, re-reads it in horror, then rises, pounds the field table and starts an epileptic oration.

DISSOLVE TO:

L-29   A NEWSPAPER HEADLINE

It reads: "HITLER DEMANDS RECOUNT"

SLOW DISSOLVE TO:

-11-27-42

L-30 NORVAL - IN HIS CELL

He is shivering with cold. He rises and THE CAMERA PULLS
BACK. He comes to the window and looks through the bars.

NORVAL: Hey...could somebody get me a bl-bl-blanket
                 ...I'm fr-freezing to death...Hey.
CUT TO:

L-31 INT. OF THE FIRE STATION - SHOOTING OUT PAST THE FIRE ENGINE

People are hurrying by, but nobody stops.

CUT TO:

L-32 NORVAL - BEHIND THE BARS

NORVAL: (Shivering)
                 What's going on any-anyway?
                      (He blows on his fingers)
DISSOLVE TO:

L-33 THE GOVERNOR AND THE BOSS - AT THE TELEPHONE

THE GOVERNOR: (The instant he is in the clear)
                 Well get him out.

THE BOSS: And step on it.

CUT TO:

L-34 THE EDITOR AT THE TELEPHONE - PAST MR. RAFFERTY

THE EDITOR: How can I Mr. Governor...with all those
                 charges against him?

MR. RAFFERTY: How?

CUT TO:

L-35 THE GOVERNOR AND THE BOSS - AT THE TELEPHONE

THE GOVERNOR: By dropping the charges, you dumb cluck.

THE BOSS: You weal head.

THE GOVERNOR: Get me that banker on the phone.

THE BOSS: His charter is cancelled.

THE GOVERNOR: And that Justice of the Peace.

THE BOSS: His license is revoked and his motel is
                 condemned.

THE GOVERNOR: And that Sheriff.
11-27-42   (Continued)

747

L-35 (Cont'd)

THE BOSS: He's retired...He's too old.

CUT TO:

L-36 THE EDITOR AND MR. RAFFERTY

THE EDITOR: Do you want the M.P.s and the U.S.Men?

CUT TO:

L-37 THE GOVERNOR AND THE BOSS

THE GOVERNOR: What have they got to do with it? That was
a State Militia uniform.

THE BOSS: I can see it from here.

THE GOVERNOR: As a matter of fact he's a Colonel in it.
I'm bringing him his commission tomorrow.

THE BOSS: Retroactive as of last year...

CUT TO:

L-38 THE EDITOR AND MR. RAFFERTY

MR. RAFFERTY: (Excitedly)
                The marriage!

THE EDITOR: There's only one more thing, Mr. Governor:
the marriage.

CUT TO:

L-39 THE GOVERNOR AND THE BOSS

THE GOVERNOR: (Roughly)
                What's the matter with her marriage? She's
married to Norval Jones! She always has been.
The guy married them, didn't he? The boy
signed his right name, didn't he?

CUT TO:

L-40 THE EDITOR AND MR. RAFFERTY

THE EDITOR: But he gave his name as Ratzkiwatzki.

CUT TO:

L-41 THE GOVERNOR AND THE BOSS

THE GOVERNOR: He was trying to say Jones...he stuttered.

THE BOSS: What are you looking for, needles in a
haystack?

CUT TO:

11-27-42

L-42   THE EDITOR AND MR. RAFFERTY

    THE EDITOR: But how about the first Ratzkiwatzki?

    CUT TO:

L-43   THE GOVERNOR AND THE BOSS

    THE GOVERNOR: He's annulled.

    THE BOSS: Scnook.

    CUT TO:

L-44   THE EDITOR AND MR. RAFFERTY

    THE EDITOR: Who annulled him?

    CUT TO:

L-45   THE GOVERNOR AND THE BOSS

    THE GOVERNOR: I did.

    THE BOSS: Retroactive...

    THE GOVERNOR: He's out of the picture.

    THE BOSS: He was never in it.

    THE GOVERNOR: Now get me those guys on the phone.

    THE BOSS: Who do they think they are anyway?

    THE GOVERNOR: Fooling with the honor of our fair state.

    THE BOSS: They'll find out.
                (He pats the Governor on the
                 shoulder)
            Nice work Daniel.

L-45a   NORVAL - IN HIS CELL

He sits despondently on the cot, blowing on his hands, now
he rises and does some embryonic Swedish exercises. We
hear a CLANK, Norval looks up hopefully, then steps back
in surprise.

    NORVAL: Why...h-h-hello Mr. K-K-K-ockenlocker.
                (His teeth play the castanets)
                Gee I'm glad to see you...I didn't know
                you were back on the force...how's Trudy?

    CUT TO:

L-45b   KOCKENLOCKER - ON THE OTHER SIDE OF THE BARS

For the first time we see him in the full magnificence of his Chief's uniform.

KOCKENLOCKER: She's asleep, but you'll be able to see her in a few minutes.

NORVAL: Oh gee! You don't know what it's been like not seeing her all this time.
(Then suddenly)
Say! Are you sure it's all right? I wouldn't want to get you in wrong again.

KOCKENLOCKER: (Astonished)
Get me in wrong?
(He points to his cap)
I'm the Chief! Where have you been?

NORVAL: Right here.

KOCKENLOCKER: (Getting it)
Right here! You mean you haven't heard about; about...you mean you don't know about, about...

NORVAL: About what?

KOCKENLOCKER: About Trudy?

NORVAL: (With growing excitement)
You mean...she's had it? Is that why she's asleep?

KOCKENLOCKER: Has she had it.

CUT TO:

L-45c   THE NEWSPAPER EDITOR, RAFFERTY AND SWARTZ - BURST INTO THE CELL

Swartz carries a package.

THE EDITOR: Here it is Norval...try on the pants.

SWARTZ: Never mind the pants...the coat!

NORVAL: (Backing away from the box)
What is it?

RAFFERTY: The uniform! You think it's a snake or something?

NORVAL: (Repeating mechanically)
The uniform.

THE EDITOR: (Excitedly)
From the Governor!

RAFFERTY: Who else?

KOCKENLOCKER: (Quietly)
You'd better come and see your wife.
(Continued)

750

NORVAL: But I'm not m-m-m...

KOCKENLOCKER: (At the top of his lungs)
                OH YES YOU ARE and boy you'd better not try
                to get out of this one.

DISSOLVE TO:

L-46   A BIG CROWD - IN FRONT OF THE MORGAN MEMORIAL HOSPITAL

There are many news photographers present.

KOCKENLOCKER'S Come on clear off the sidewalk...get
VOICE: going there...leave the hospital a little
                air will you...come on move on there.

CUT TO:

L-47   KOCKENLOCKER PUSHING THE DUMFOUNDED NORVAL THROUGH THE CROWD

NORVAL: You say we're really married?

A TOUGH NEWS-   (Who has been pushed)
PHOTOGRAPHER: Who are you?

KOCKENLOCKER: The Chief of Police among other things,
                you want to make something of it?

A VOICE IN   That's the father with him.
THE CROWD:

There is a wild hurray and people start shaking Norval's hand
to the accompaniment of the flashes of flashbulbs. Norval
looks around in astonishment.

CUT TO:

L-48   THE UPPER HOSPITAL CORRIDOR

Doctor Meyer is guarding the door which is faced with another
crowd of news photographers.

DR. MEYER: No, no, no.....she's just waking up and
                nobody goes in except the father.

KOCKENLOCKER'S
VOICE: Gangway...come on clear away there.

A VOICE: Here he comes.

CUT TO:

751

L-49   KOCKENLOCKER, RAFFERTY, SWARTZ AND THE NEWSPAPER EDITOR
PILOTING NORVAL THROUGH THE CROWD

Norval is resplendent in a State Militia Colonel's uniform.
Again Norval has his picture taken and his hand shaken.

DR. MEYER: (Seeing him)
              Aha.....congratulations.
                      (He shakes Norval's hand)
              ...go in please...shh.
                      (He opens the door just a lit-
                      tle and Norval starts through)

CUT TO:

L-50   TRUDY AND EMMY - IN THE SOFTLY LIGHTED ROOM

Emmy sits beside the bed, she turns and puts her fingers to
her lips.

CUT TO:

L-51   NORVAL - COMING INTO THE ROOM

His eyes are full of tears, he comes forward on tiptoe and
THE CAMERA PANS him into the shot with Emmy. She kisses him
gently on the cheek, then admires his uniform with a gesture, and they look down at the bed.

CUT TO:

L-52   TRUDY ASLEEP

Norval's head comes into the SHOT. She smiles in her sleep,
then opens her eyes.

TRUDY: (Very gently)
              Norval.

NORVAL: (Taking her hand)
              Trudy.

TRUDY: (Very softly - pointing to
                          his uniform)
              You look so beautiful.

NORVAL: You look so beautiful.

TRUDY: I love you.

NORVAL: Your father said...I don't understand how
              exactly....
                      (He points to his uniform)
              I don't understand anything...but we're all
              married now...for ever and ever.

(Continued)

L-52 (Cont'd)

TRUDY: (In a whisper)
                  I'm very happy.

NORVAL: I love you.

TRUDY: You're a papa now.

NORVAL: I feel like one...and I will be always...
                  as good as I can.

TRUDY: (After a smile)
                  Was it a boy or a girl?...We've got to
                  pick a name for it.

NORVAL: I'll find out.

TRUDY: I'm so happy.

THE CAMERA PANS him up into the shot with Emmy.

NORVAL: (In a whisper)
                  Was it a boy or a girl?

Emmy gives him a long fishy stare then motions with her
finger for him to follow her. They go out a side door, such
as those that lead through a bathroom to an adjoining room.

CUT TO:

L-53   TRUDY

She closes her eyes and sighs happily.

CUT TO:

L-54   A SMALL CORRIDOR

Emmy and Norval are down at the end of this coming toward
us. As they approach, the CAMERA PULLS BACK and we see that
some plate glass separates them from us. THE CAMERA PULLS
BACK a little further and we find that we are shooting up at
Norval over some foreground pieces. The SOUND in this room
would indicate that it is the baby room. Norval looks all
the way over from the left to the right and then back again.

Now he points an inquiring finger at the different foreground pieces. Emmy looks at him in amusement then whispers
something in his ear. Norval becomes galvanized. He hangs
onto the glass and his mouth shakes. He turns and runs away.

CUT TO:

753

L-55   TRUDY SLEEPING

We HEAR some pounding footsteps. She wakes up and sits up,
a little alarmed.

CUT TO:

L-56   NORVAL - COMING INTO THE ROOM ON TWO WHEELS

He skids, falls down, picks himself up, then comes rubber-
legged, yammering, to the side of the bed.

TRUDY: (Frightened)
                    What's the matter darling? What was it?

NORVAL: Th-th-the th-th-the th-th-the THE SPOTS.

He sinks into Trudy's arms as the doors burst open behind
and the Doctor, Kockenlocker, the Editor, Mr. Rafferty and
Emmy come into the SHOT.

                            THE END

Unfaithfully Yours

On October 30, 1946, Howard Hughes informed Sturges by telephone that their partnership of twenty-six months was dissolved. "In spite of their estrangement," says James Curtis, "Sturges continued to work away on *The Sin of Harold Diddlebock*."[1] A preview of the film had been set for a theater in Westwood, California, in early November and took place on schedule with Hughes in attendance. "He laughed not once during the entire experience," notes Curtis. "When the lights came up, both Francie [Ramsden] and Preston turned at once to Hughes. His seat was empty."[2] Sturges decided that the two-and-a-half-hour film could be tightened and "spent the next thirty-three hours in a cutting room with Francie and editor Stuart Gilmore. He reduced the running time to ninety-one minutes and at that he was satisfied."[3] On November 29 there was a preview of the recut *Diddlebock* at the Warners Theater in Huntington Park, California. Audience response at the event was measured by Sturges's "Laugh Meter," the registrations of which were divided into four levels:

> Force 1 – Chuckle: 79
> Force 2 – Laugh: 32
> Force 3 – Hearty: 19
> Force 4 – Yell: 10

Sturges used his laugh meter results to convince producers, when necessary, that his "cut" of a film worked well with audiences, hence that it should not be tampered with; but he also used them for his own guidance in fine-tuning a film before release. On December 2, for instance, Sturges wrote a single page of "Notes after Huntington Beach Preview," which contained nine suggestions for further improving the film's pace, mainly through small editing changes.[4] His brief preface to the numbered suggestions is, oddly, one of his few statements on pace—that quality for which, perhaps more than any other, his films are celebrated:

I will endeavor to recall those parts of the film during which I, as the author and director, felt a certain embarrassment and wished to Christ we would get to the next step sooner. By step, I mean of course, those scenes or series of events I am reasonably sure of from the first preview and reactions in the projection rooms.

Sturges's acute sense of pace, and what impeded it, is also important for understanding the fate of *Unfaithfully Yours*: Darryl F. Zanuck and Sturges were to square off on precisely this issue, particularly as it bore on the question of the film's length.

When the dissolution of the Sturges-Hughes partnership became known, Sturges received a number of offers, from Paramount, MGM, Samuel Goldwyn productions, and—the one he accepted—from 20th Century-Fox. Studio chief Zanuck had wanted Sturges for Fox since *The Great McGinty*. With a contract dated December 13, 1946, Sturges sold Fox, for $50,000, a story he had written in December 1933. The title of the story was *Matrix* and it concerned a beautiful woman who rejected the love of a rich, dynamic man in favor of an often-drunk, weak one, who blamed others for his failures—a hopeless case who somehow aroused the main character's maternal instincts. Apparently no one but Sturges had ever liked the story or seen a movie in it. Fox may have acquired it as a way to acquire Sturges, but the studio did send out publicity stating that Sturges would direct *Matrix* at Fox with Gene Tierney.

On February 13, 1947, Sturges signed a contract formalizing his arrangement with Fox. He was to receive $7,825 per week for thirty weeks beginning March 10. His plan until that time was to see *Diddlebock* on its way to a successful release. A final preview in Inglewood, California, was held on February 5. On February 18 the film had its world premiere in Miami. According to Curtis, "The audience was responsive, the reviews enthusiastic, and the ensuing business brisk. In subsequent engagements—in Portland, San Francisco, and Fort Wayne, Indiana—the film performed admirably."[5]

In his film projects, Hughes was a mogul but not really a producer; he was guided by his aesthetic sense, such as it was, not the need for profit. Above all, he was not swayed by audience response. *He* thought *Diddlebock* was slow and overlong, so in May 1947, before the film had had a Los Angeles or a New York booking, he pulled it from release. With the help of Stuart Gilmore, Sturges's longtime editor, Hughes cut nineteen minutes from the film, which he renamed *Mad Wednesday*. Further, he entirely eliminated the banker character played by Rudy Vallee, an actor whom Hughes detested![6] After several announced release dates, Hughes actually released the film in January 1950 through his newly acquired company, RKO.

Meanwhile, back at Fox, the *Matrix* project was running into trouble. One wonders whether Zanuck had decided in advance of the contract not to film *Matrix* or if he did so—as he later claimed—only after careful thought. He makes that claim in a three-page letter to Sturges on February 20, 1947, just eighteen days before Sturges's contract with Fox was to begin. *Matrix* is mentioned only late in the letter; its main body concerns what Zanuck wishes Sturges to do instead.

> I am really embarrassed in writing you and primarily at what may appear to be my negligence in getting to you at this late date. I have never been so busy in my life as I have been in the last three months with *Forever Amber, Captain from Castile, The Late George Apley, The Ghost and Mrs. Muir* and *The Foxes of Harrow*—all in the mill at the same time. I really have been in a whirl . . .
>
> I will get right to the point.

The clutch of films Zanuck mentions is more impressive as a group perhaps than as individual titles. Is there really a good film in the bunch? In any case, Zanuck's recitation makes them all sound like pure gold and that sound, far from prefatory to his point, *is* his point. He continues:

> We have just completed a remarkable film with Betty Grable. It is called *Mother Wore Tights,* and it has turned out to be one of the most delightful and unusual films which has come out of the studio. It is a distinguished film in every respect and Grable rises to both comedy and dramatic heights which she has never previously been anywhere near. . . . This means I can never again put Betty back in the obvious musical comedies where she originally rose to popularity. It means I must find for her story material which is off the beaten track and not in the standard musical formula.
>
> Betty is going to have another baby and she will be ready to work again in September. More than anything else, I would like you to write and direct a picture with her. After *Mother Wore Tights* she cannot go backwards. She is one of the three biggest solo stars in our Industry and she must go forward. I know it is unreasonable for me to place an order with you for a project like this, yet I have the feeling that you will come up with something that is fresh and original and will give her an opportunity to go on.
>
> She has become quite an actress. She has always been a damned good comedienne, but now she seems to have her feet or her legs more solidly upon the ground. I feel she is capable of, as an example, Kitty Foyle or a delightful comedy like your own *The Miracle of Morgan's Creek.* Betty's amazing popularity . . . comes from the fact she is so completely an American girl. There is a sort of down-to-earth tarty sparkle to her and nothing at all pretentious. You feel she is a nice girl in a nice way, and yet you feel if you tried hard enough, you might be able to make the grade. Anything which Carole Lombard could have done, I am convinced she can do, and the remarkable part is she is only twenty-six years old.
>
> Perhaps if you come in and had a talk with Julian Johnson and went through some of our material or some of our past subjects, you might come up with a springboard for an idea.
>
> On the subject of *Matrix,* I was frankly not very enthusiastic—and neither was Julian. We discussed it at length before I got into all of my other studio complications a couple of months ago and I sincerely do not believe it has the freshness or originality

associated with your previous accomplishments, and frankly I don't think you are too crazy about it although I have never discussed it with you.

I just sense this. I am not saying it cannot be licked but somehow I have the feeling even though the relationship were developed and motivated in your usual style it would still be less than great.

To get back to Grable, this is an acute Studio problem, and if you can help me in solving it, it will indeed be more than a service. After you have seen Julian, I look forward to seeing you. In the next week or so, I should be over the hurdle of most of my problems.

Sturges replied on February 24:

As I have no 20th Century Fox stationery as yet, I am answering your very nice letter of February 20th on the paper of the moribund California Pictures Corporation.

Orsatti [Sturges's agent] is arranging a meeting with Julian and in the meantime I have started thinking myself . . . going back through the pieces I have written to see which would most closely have fitted Miss Grable. I am glad to report that I have written a few which would have suited her perfectly. Having done it before, it should not be too difficult to do it again.

As far as *Matrix* is concerned, I will be delighted to take it back and give you something else instead. It is one of the two stories I have carried around in my head since landing in Hollywood, one of the two stories I tried for many years to persuade someone to let me direct. No one has ever seen eye to eye with me on it. The other story was called *The Biography of a Bum* but was released as *The Great McGinty*. I am quite aware of the fact that the modest success of the one does not assure the reception of the other but I am enormously fond of the story and will surely make it some day if my strength holds out.

I will communicate with you as soon as I have seen Julian.

These documents, which seal the fate of *Matrix,* are themselves the matrix of Sturges's fate at Fox and, indeed, in Hollywood generally. A producer tells Sullivan in *Sullivan's Travels,* "At the salary you're getting, I can't afford to argue with you." This was roughly Sturges's own position at Paramount, as his ability to make *The Great Moment* testifies. Sturges drew the largest salary of his career at Fox but by that time the formula had somehow reversed itself: "At the salary I'm getting, I can't afford to argue with you (producer)." It is also true that with the war over and veterans returned, times had changed in Hollywood as elsewhere. The cost of making films had sharply increased and audience tastes were different. Some highly regarded filmmakers seemed to have lost touch with the postwar audience: Capra, Lubitsch, and Sternberg, among others. Betty Grable was not the only one in need of a Hollywood future; every reputation was up for grabs and had to renew itself, fast, or die.

The Grable vehicle Sturges undertook to write and direct, a comedy like

Morgan's Creek for a different Betty, turned out to be a comic Western with music called *The Beautiful Blonde from Bashful Bend.* Just how and when this lowering of ambition took place is not clear from the available correspondence. "Once Sturges had consented to do a picture with Grable," says James Curtis, "Zanuck went to work selling him on a treatment called *The Lady from Laredo.*"[7] This was a story by Earl Felton that Fox had purchased, although when it had done so and how long the story itself was are not clear. (A three-page synopsis of the story was prepared by a Fox staff writer on February 18, 1947, two days before Zanuck's long letter to Sturges!) In any case, at some time, in some place, and in some manner, Sturges bought the whole Zanuck package and on June 11 he began taking notes on the project, which he called at that time *Teacher's Pet.* What Sturges had done between March 10, his starting date at Fox, and June 11 is not entirely clear—being convinced by his employer perhaps. He also screened twenty-three Grable films to prepare for the project—a few week's work at least—and he may have sketched some film ideas of his own before succumbing to Zanuck's Western idea.

Having begun June 11, Sturges received a Zanuck memo on July 21, setting forth

our exact production situation with Betty Grable and Technicolor. Grable reports to us on September 1st and we have a Technicolor commitment which starts September 15th. This means that if we were ready to go into production on September 15th or no later than September 22nd it would solve all of our problems.

As you know, you have been on this assignment for 18 weeks. This entitles us to 16 more weeks time which expires November 8th. By starting production on the dates I have specified we should be able to come within your guaranteed time as well as Miss Grable's guaranteed time.

As you know, the construction of sets, no matter how small or ordinary, has become a big-time business in our industry. It is vital for the Production Department that they have your first-draft script no later than the first week in August if they are going to be able to make the starting date.

In addition to this it is even more vital that I have the script, even though you still have polish work to do on it. I have twice avoided talking to Miss Grable about the assignment as I did not want . . . to be in a position of going out on a limb until I have actually read the screenplay.

"At the present writing," Sturges replied the same day,

what with throwing away stuff I haven't liked, I have about forty pages of shooting script. This need not alarm you as I spritz dialogue like Seltzer water once I know where I'm going. The French playwright, Jean Racine, when asked how his new play was coming, replied happily: "It is all finished . . . I have nothing more to do but write it down." That is the present condition of *The Blonde from Bashful Bend.*

I have at last discovered its theme and its wherefore, its characters and their view-points, its settings and its climaxes. I have looked at every foot of film in which Miss Grable has appeared and have come to like her immensely. I think I know how to write for her now. . . . I will close now as the first week in August is nearly upon me and there are some hard nights ahead including this one.

Sturges was, or at least made himself sound, still quite cheerful at this point. He may even have been pleased, after a spell of Hughesian ambiguity, at the hard deadline. He submitted an unfinished, eighty-three-page draft on August 19, along with a list of sets. Zanuck sent a four-page memo on August 22 saying, in addition to some suggestions for improvement, how pleased he was with the script to that point. Sturges wrote back the same day to say how pleased he was that Zanuck liked the script. It was only an afterthought that Zanuck passed along in a memo on August 25 that shattered the good feeling:

In my letter to you I forgot to tell you that we are going to make the picture in black-and-white and not Technicolor. Confidentially, Technicolor is a luxury we cannot afford at this moment with our foreign market gone.

The last is a reference to the British Labor Government's recent imposition of severe restrictions on the number of foreign (i.e., American) films that could be exhibited on British screens. These measures, designed to protect and expand the English film industry, all but wiped out Hollywood's crucial foreign market. 40 percent of its world gross came from foreign markets and 85 percent of that 40 percent came from England. Producers and many others in Hollywood railed against what became known as the English quota system—Sturges himself (indirectly) denounced it in several of the drafts of *Unfaithfully Yours*. Without the quota crisis, however, there might never have been an *Unfaithfully Yours*. Sturges would have proceeded directly to *Bashful Bend* and, as thanks for his "service" to Zanuck, been bounced from Fox and, possibly, from Hollywood itself.

Sturges was stung at the loss of color. He wrote seven drafts of a reply to Zanuck, noting in one of them, "It is now a little past five a.m. Tuesday morning and I have been sitting here since 10:00 o'clock last night." Another draft observes, "Miss Grable is the natural child of color. Without it and your wonderful idea of presenting her as you have she would long since have disappeared from the screen." At some point in his dark night of the soul, however, Sturges glimpsed an opportunity, as his letter to Zanuck the next day makes clear.

I cannot tell you how depressed I am at the prospect of making the B. FROM B.B. or any picture of this type in black and white. They simply do not hold together and I would be completely remiss in my job as producer if I failed to tell you that it would be very much wiser and better for all concerned to let me get to work immediately on a script of my own type which does not depend quite so much on jokes and luscious color for its acceptance.

One such is my Symphony Story that Ernst Lubitsch can tell you about. Boyer has always liked it and could probably be persuaded to play in it, possibly opposite Miss Grable. I have always refused to sell this story as I wanted to save it for my own company, but since you have already paid me a great deal of money and I feel a grave emergency exists, I would be willing to part with it.

Zanuck wrote back on August 28, presumably after speaking or corresponding further with Sturges: "The new arrangement seems to be very satisfactory—providing you are able to do the new job as rapidly as you anticipate. Otherwise it becomes quite obvious that we will be confronted with a serious problem . . . Unless it is possible to do your screenplay on SYMPHONY STORY in eight weeks after you finish the writing job on BASHFUL BEND, then I will really be over a barrel." Writing back the same day, Sturges undertook to work "with the speed of an antelope to finish THE BLONDE and then write, produce, and direct and edit THE SYMPHONY STORY." He also noted that "James Mason has expressed a desire to do a picture with me and . . . I am quite certain THE SYMPHONY STORY would appeal to him . . . especially the part, which is quite funny incidentally, in which he slaughters a courtroom full of people with an ax." Zanuck wrote back on August 29 saying that Mason was involved in a lawsuit with David Rose that would take more than a year to clear up, hence "you would be making a mistake to write the story expressly for him."

On October 8, 1947, Sturges finished the first complete draft of what he had come to call *The Beautiful Blonde from Bashful Bend*. To Zanuck, at least, this must have seemed well less than antelopine velocity. The writing of a complete *BBBB* script had taken Sturges from June 11 to October 8, nearly four months. This does not include March 10–June 10, Sturges's first salaried months at Fox, which Zanuck regarded as time and money spent on the Grable project.

But a complete script for Sturges's next project—described in his August 26 letter to Zanuck as "my Symphony Story"—was finished on December 2, well within the eight weeks promised.[8] Actually called *Unfinished Symphony,* this story, which Sturges had presumably enclosed with his letter or sent the next day, is nineteen pages long and undated.[9] It was "first written," Sturges later said, in 1932, referring perhaps to a story sketch or first draft. He did not send the story to producers until August and September 1933, however, which was probably when he had finished a showable version. Sturges rarely sat on projects; he sent them out as soon as they were done. The idea for *Unfinished Symphony* had occurred to Sturges in December 1932, while he was writing *The Power and the Glory* in an office at Universal. He later said: "I had a scene all written and had only to put it down on paper. To my surprise, it came out quite unlike what I had planned. I sat back wondering what the hell had happened, then noticed that someone had left the radio on in the next room and realized that I had been listening to a symphony broadcast from New York and that this, added to my thoughts, had changed the total."[10] Self-authored as it is, the anecdote does not quite connect with the 1933 story or the 1948 film. Sir Alfred is not the unaware, passive listener to music that Sturges was; he has chosen, or approved, the selections he plays, which he knows intimately, and his conducting both summons and shapes the music that in turn shapes his fantasies. Music maker and listener, producer and consumer, the auditory signals he conveys with his hands return to him as sensations for his ear and thus complete a circuit: he is, in both senses, a conductor. Considered as narrative, his situation is partly Wilde's life (or thought) imitating art, partly the modern artist ensnared by his own creation—and altogether more complex than the story of the radio in the next room. Nevertheless, many Sturges critics and biographers recount the story as the project's true genesis. Even the host of cable television's American Movie Classics invokes it before a showing of *Unfaithfully Yours*: it's the anecdote to tell if you're telling only one.

Two early responses to *Unfinished Symphony* are still of interest. In a letter dated October 17, 1933, Sol M. Wurtzel of Fox found the subject "interesting and colorful, but I do not believe it will click with the average movie audience." In a letter of September 16, Jeff Lazarus of Paramount also found the story interesting, particularly because "different from the run-of-the-mill stuff." "However," he noted,

in spite of that, we can't quite see a successful feature picture in it. One of the most dangerous kinds of subjects to handle are those in which we discover at the finish of the seventh reel that it all really didn't happen. Once in a while they come through but, on the whole, they are too much of a gamble.

In October 1947, Sturges was gambling—at high stakes—that there was a successful feature picture in his 1933 story. It begins with two charwomen in the balcony of a great auditorium reacting comically to blasts from the rehearsing orchestra below:

The balcony of the great auditorium is dark except for a work-light. Two charwomen are at work, one with a carpet sweeper, the other with a pail of soapy water and a rag. At a blast of music from the stage Mrs. Smythe drops her Bissell, glares at Mrs. Mulligan: "That gave me a turn, that did. I never seem to get used to it." "Fierce," says Mrs. Mulligan. "You'd think they'd know their bloody pieces by now. They been playin' them long enough."

"We come now to the orchestra," the story continues:

First, with a PANNING shot from the conductor's stand which pivots slowly through 180 degrees, we see it in its entirety. There is a sharp rapping and the musicians stop. The voice of the maestro criticizes the rendition of the last passage and we are introduced to the various musicians in turn. Some are roundly abused, some are coaxed, and some are praised faintly. We see now the maestro himself: a handsome man of forty-five. Obviously not an American, his nationality is not easily guessed. He is, like all great musicians, a cosmopolitan rather than a foreigner. He denounces them roundly again then, without much hope, says: "Once more, now . . . from bar sixteen, and try to do it right this time." He starts to lead. After a few seconds he pulls out his watch and looks at it.

[INSERT of Watch] [He] raps on his music stand . . . the musicians stop and he speaks: "That's a little better, but it's still terrible. You must do better tonight. That's all." He throws down the stick and hurries off the stand.

A dissolve to a shot of a diamond-studded woman's wristwatch is followed by the shot of a very pretty young woman. The maestro arrives, full of apologies. He kisses his wife's hand and tells her how much he has missed her. "He is obviously madly in love with her and she seems very fond of him." To prove her love she even dances with him. He is a fearful dancer and she laughs at him. The dance ends, they return to their table and "a beautiful gigolo appears." He kisses the wife's hand, is introduced as a friend of her sister Lily's, and asks her to dance—a tango as it turns out. "She looks at her husband who says: 'Certainly.' He watches them, frowning slightly, then shrugs his shoulders and laughs." Lily arrives with her husband and when she in turn dances with the gigolo, whose name is Tito, her husband's extreme jealousy is revealed. The contrasting reactions of the two unnamed husbands seems the principal point of the scene: "The maestro is full of love and confidence. His brother-in-law believes that only the most careful watchfulness will keep the horns off his head."

"We come now to the maestro and his wife dressing for the concert," Sturges continues. They have just finished dinner and carry on a gay conversation, he from his room, she from the bathroom-dressing room where she is making up. As he tightens his white waistcoat, the strap tears off the back. He looks for a safety pin on his dressing table then, at her suggestion, on hers.

He looks for it, finds one, and while adjusting it, notices a letter protruding from her handbag. He looks at it for a moment, then we flash back to his conversation with his brother-in-law. We return to the maestro. He picks up the letter, and looks at it speculatively. He puts it down again and adjusts the pin in his waistcoat. He picks it up once more and throws it down angrily and starts out of the room. He stops, hesitates, and returns to the letter.

His wife asks if he found the pin. He says: "Yes." She offers to adjust it for him. He says it's already done. Slowly he lifts the letter and reads it. We INSERT the letter. It begins: "My darling" and ends with "Your adoring Tito." It mentions last night and wonders when "once more we shall enjoy paradise together." Slowly the maestro lowers the letter. Like an automaton he returns it to the handbag.

The maestro walks out of the room, sinks onto his bed and puts his hand over his eyes—"He is a stricken man." At the concert hall, his manager asks him if he is ill. The maestro tells him he is not and walks slowly out onto the stage. From the podium he looks up at the box occupied by his wife, who, with her sister and the rest of the assembly, applauds wildly. The maestro bows, "turns his back upon us and raps on his music stand."

He raises the baton and waits for complete silence. He lowers the baton slowly and quietly come the strains of a great, noble piece. We move around in front of him and look up into his face as he leads his musicians. It is full of suffering. We move closer to him until his face fills the whole screen. Closer yet until one eye fills the screen. Still closer 'til the pupil of his eye, infinitely magnified, turns the screen black. The music rises to a crescendo now.

We FADE IN slowly on the living room of the maestro's apartment. The music continues strong. A door opens and the maestro, preceded by his wife, enters the room. The music fades enough for us to hear their conversation.

The maestro's wife tells him how great he was tonight; he sinks into a chair. Then, pulling her onto its arm, he tells her about the letter. She starts to draw away but he holds her gently and asks her not to be frightened, that he could not understand music so well if he did not also understand human emotions.

He realizes, he says, that he is old and ugly, no fit mate for her beauty. He does not blame her for what she has done, rather he blames himself for having forced her to look for youth and beauty surreptitiously. . . . He thanks her for the two years of joy she has given him—two such years should be enough for any man. He will give her all the money she needs . . .

She tells him how kind and generous he is. He thanks her, rises and kisses her gently. He tells her to pack her things.

The music gets louder. He goes slowly into the next room, sits at his desk, and draws toward him a large cheque book. He begins to write a cheque then sobs, and buries his face in his arms. The music is very loud as we DISSOLVE TO the maestro.

His face fills the screen. The tears are rolling down his cheeks. We TRUCK BACK slowly as he concludes the first piece on the program.

The applause, including that of his wife and sister-in-law, is loud and long. His brother-in-law claps until he notices and scowls at a handsome young man in the next box. The maestro takes another bow, "waves his musicians to their feet, then waves them down again." He raises his baton, then lowers it,

bringing forth a very different piece of music. Less noble, less detached, more of the earth and its people and emotions that are human. Again we pass into the interior of his mind and his thoughts return us to his apartment.

As before, the living room is empty, the door opens and the maestro, preceded by his wife, enters the room. She tells him how proud of him she is and how much she adores him. He says he has to go to Cleveland that night. She says she'll be lonely and he suggests "you get that fellow Tito, or whatever his name is, to take you dancing." She resists then agrees, calling Tito when she thinks she's alone. The maestro listens at the door then tiptoes to his room and packs frantically. He then takes from a top shelf a case containing an old-fashioned straight razor.

He opens this, takes out the razor and smiles at it insanely. The music gets louder. Holding the razor open in his hand he tiptoes across the room and peeks in at his wife through the partly open door. The music gets louder still. He holds the razor behind his back and slowly opens the door. We CUT to his wife.

She is making herself pretty in front of a long mirror. In the mirror she sees somebody moving. She frowns slightly, then turns slowly, lipstick in hand. The music grows louder. She begins to look scared. We see the maestro advancing. He is smiling crazily. His right hand is held in back of him. She begins to back away, then cowers against the mirror. He steps close to her and clutches her throat as she starts to scream. He forces her back on the bed. We see a CLOSE SHOT of her hand clutching the bed clothes. The music reaches its climax, then grows distant as the hand relaxes.

We then see the maestro as he walks out of the bathroom, drying his hands. He throws the towel in the suitcase, closes it, puts on his hat and coat, "then takes an envelope into which he puts a pearl necklace, several bracelets, some rings, and, last of all, the razor [and] puts the envelope in his pocket." Tito arrives, the maestro takes his overcoat, then leads him into the living room. He calls to his wife to hurry up, then shakes Tito's hand and leaves for his train, pausing to empty the contents of the envelope into the pocket of Tito's fashionable overcoat.

We DISSOLVE TO: A judge, sentencing Tito to hang by the neck until he is dead. At this there is a wild burst of hysterical laughter. Everyone in the courtroom turns and looks at the maestro who is laughing crazily. The laughter continues as we DISSOLVE back to the maestro concluding his second piece.

He is laughing hysterically. There is great applause. The concert master nudges the violinist next to him and points to the maestro. The violinist shrugs his shoulders and tunes his fiddle.

Lily remarks to her sister that the maestro seems to be laughing about something. The wife responds, "Probably something funny in the score. Music means so much more to him than to people like us." "I suppose so," says Lily, who turns slightly to steal a glance at the beautiful young man in the next box. At this, her husband clears his throat ominously.

The maestro raps on his music stand. The applause ceases and he begins his final offering of the evening. The music this time is noble, without being sentimental. It has a true passion, not the exaggerated passion of a rhapsody. The maestro conducts with infinite sadness. He turns and looks at his wife for a second, then looks at his musicians suspiciously. They look back at him in surprise, the stolid double-bass players, the comic flutists, the romantic cellists, and the anxious tympanist. His thoughts wander again. We are in the living room.

Again the maestro enters preceded by his wife, again she compliments him on the concert and adds that he should be very happy. It was the most unhappy day of his life, he says, and walks into his room. She follows and he tells her he has read the letter. She asks him what he is going to do. He says he was going to let her go but now he can't do it and that he also thought of killing her and hanging the guilt on her lover, but that was melodramatic and stupid. Instead, he says, he is going to kill her and then himself. "I'm ready," she says, bidding him good-bye and forgiving him.

He pulls the trigger, then raises the gun to himself. The two shots come almost simultaneously. He clutches the desk, then falls forward and tries to take her in his arms.

We return to the concert. The maestro is clutching his music stand. He looks very ill. The music comes to an end, he throws down his baton, and goes quickly into the wings. The musicians look after him in astonishment.

Lily wonders if he is ill and the maestro's wife jumps up, telling her sister that she'd better not come, and then hurries out of the box. Backstage the maestro tells his wife he does not want to see anyone, then puts on his coat and "asks her roughly if she is ready to go home." Surprised, she says of course she is. Once home, he stalks into his room and slams the door. He walks up and down nervously, clenching and unclenching his hands.

Slowly he goes to his desk. He pulls his cheque book toward him, opens it and unscrews a fountain pen. He writes the date on the cheque, starts to write his wife's name, then hurls the fountain pen in the corner and jumps to his feet. For a moment he looks in the direction of his wife's bedroom, then turns slowly and goes into the bathroom. He opens the medicine cabinet and from the top shelf, takes down a razor case. From this he takes out the straight razor and looks at it horribly. He opens the razor and feels its sharpness against his thumbnail. Then he puts the blade against the back of his hand, draws it quickly and makes a little cut. As the blood runs down his hand he shakes his head and throws the razor in the wash basin. It clatters as it falls. He turns back into his room, goes to his desk, pulls open a drawer and looks at the revolver in it. He picks it up, and breaks it to make sure it is loaded. As he hears a step he looks behind him, puts the revolver in the drawer, and almost closes the drawer.

His wife enters the maestro's room and says: "Darling, I wish you weren't this way just tonight . . . I'm so worried I'm almost sick and I'd like to . . . to talk to you." From this point to its end, the story is written in dialogue, as follows:

    HE: What do you want with me?

    SHE: I'm afraid there's going to be an awful scandal.

HE: You're right, there is going to be.

SHE: How did you know?

HE: Never mind how I know.

SHE: (With sudden intuition)
        Good heavens, did you read the letter?

HE: Suppose I did?

SHE: Well then you can imagine how worried I am. She stuck it in my
        bag this afternoon after that nasty little gigolo passed it to her . . .
        she was afraid Otto would look in her bag . . . he's such an old
        snooper you know.

HE: (Haltingly)
        She stuck a letter in your bag?

SHE: Yes. I know I shouldn't have looked at it, but she's always been
        such an idiot . . . and I am older than she is . . . so I read it and
        I'm worried to death. I'm afraid it really has happened now and
        it's only a question of time till Otto finds out she's been untrue to
        him, she's such an idiot, and then there'll be hell to pay and we'll
        all be dragged through the mud.

The Maestro points his finger and looks at her as if he'd never seen her
before in his life. He speaks in a whisper: "Your . . . your sister?"

SHE: (Furiously)
        Yes, the little fool.

HE: The letter was to her?

SHE: Naturally.

HE: (Still pointing)
        She's been untrue to Otto?

SHE: (Looking away)
        I'm afraid so.

HE: (Rapturously)
        But she should be, my angel. Imagine that oaf, that lout, that
        boor, that ridiculous individual supposing for one instant that he
        could have that beautiful woman all to himself.

SHE: What's the matter with you, are you crazy?

HE: (Joyously)
        Certainly I am. Don't you know that your sister is one of the
        most beautiful women in the world . . . the conceit of that
        idiot! . . . don't you know there's only one woman in the whole
        universe more beautiful, more lovely, and more perfect than your
        adorable sister?

SHE: Who?

HE: (Taking her shoulder)
<u>You</u>, my beautiful darling, <u>you</u>.

He kisses her passionately and holds her at arm's length.

HE: A thousand poets dreamed for a thousand years and then you
were born. Go put your things on. I want to go dancing.

SHE: But, but . . .

HE: But nothing. I tell you I want to go dancing. I want to hold you
in my arms and jump around the room to this ridiculous jazz
music. I want everybody to see you . . . to know that I adore you
and that you adore me . . . you do adore me, don't you?

SHE: (Innocently)
Of course I do, silly.

HE: Then run quick and get ready, I am impatient to go.

SHE: (Laughing)
All right, darling.

She pauses in the doorway:

But what was the matter with you before?

HE: (Adjusting his tie)
Something too stupid, my dear, too idiotic, and too completely
unimportant to mention. Hurry up, I will buy lots of champagne
tonight.

SHE: I like champagne.

She exits.

[THE END]

Compared to the 1948 film, at least, there is perhaps something unsavory about Sturges's early story. The conductor is by turns abusive to his players and subservient to his wife, who is evoked before we see her with a shot of her diamond-studded wristwatch, which she may be holding up to show the conductor he is a few minutes late, as does the young man on the beach to his woman friend in *Un chien andalou* (1928). The conductor, full of apologies for his offense, is madly in love with her, whereas she seems to be only fond of him. When she dances with the "beautiful gigolo" after her turn with her clumsy husband, one feels again the disenchanted ambience. The story perhaps belongs to the spirit, as well as to the era, of *Child of Manhattan,* Sturges's 1932 play about a New York taxi dancer who ends up the mistress of a multimillionaire, which critics found "offensive," "coarse," and "tawdry."

Sturges's 1933 story was the point of departure for all of his 1947–1948 work on the project, but he does not once in his notes refer to it directly.

Rushed as he was by Zanuck, he was not able to start again from scratch, as he had done so often in the past. However, he might, to keep his mind free, have pretended to do so.

His first note was taken on October 15, 1947, and consisted of a single sentence on a page: "The conductor changes place with musician during disagreement." Is this moral imagination—the conductor and a musician seeing through the other's eyes to resolve a dispute? Or is it arrogance—the conductor showing a seasoned player how to play his instrument? The notes that follow, and the 1933 story that precedes it, suggest the latter interpretation.

Beneath this one-sentence note is a line and beneath the line the following speech, presumably by the conductor:

Personally I think that music is a secondary art . . . that should be served with some other art . . . like gravy is served with meat . . . personally I don't like gravy all by itself . . . and that's the way music all by itself affects me . . . it is a secondary art that should be served with sex or drama . . . you ought to take it lying down on a soft couch . . . with a turkey leg in one hand and a beautiful girl in the other . . . not sitting in a straight dusty chair . . . like a lecture on market trends.

The conductor may be arrogant but he is not pompous: he takes neither classical music nor (perhaps) himself too seriously. Sturges considered the point important enough to frame it in a number of ways and try it out in a variety of contexts until, after tireless revising, it fell "effortlessly" into its rightful place.

The next page in the notes is undated and is headed "MUSICIAN TYPES IN ORCHESTRA." Under the heading is a column of names: Lionel Stander, Torbin Meyer, Mikael Rasumny, Tall thin Russian, Mischa Auer, Franklin Pangborn. On the next page is a single name, Alberto Garcia-Ferrari, which was most likely a name he considered for the conductor, and on the page after that:

What actors actually look like the orchestra leaders they would represent:

Toscanini . . . . Paul Lukas
Bruno Walter . . . .
Sir Thomas Beecham . . . . Monte Wooley
Alfred Coates . . . . Charles Coburn?
Jose Iturbi . . . . Akim Tamiroff
Leopold Stokowski . . . . Paul Henried

Another column, presumably the names of candidates to play the conductor, appears on the next page:

CORNEL WILDE
REX HARRISON
TYRONE POWER

JOHN SUTTON
HENRY FONDA
MARK STEVENS
RONALD COLMAN
Richard GREENE
J. Carroll Naish
VICTOR MATURE
FREDERICK MARCH
CHARLES BOYER
GEORGE RAFT (?)
PAUL HENREID.

To list players for an undefined character may seem odd, but for Sturges it was surely part of the character-defining process itself. This exercise presupposes, however, that the star personae mentioned have firmer outlines and more fixed, harder-edged qualities than the still-nebulous fictional character— a revealing comment on the star-as-commodity in Hollywood.

On October 17, Sturges wrote his first page of dialogue. The conductor, called Sir Alfred for the first time, is in rehearsal with his orchestra.

SIR ALFRED
Gentlemen, gentlemen, I see here two small "F's" with their arms around each other which I have always been led to believe means Fortissimo . . .
(he leans toward the Concert Master)
. . . or does it mean something else in America, doctor?

DR. SCHULTZ
(uncomfortably)
You know as well as I do . . . I mean better than I do . . . what it means, maestro . . . of course it means Fortissimo.

SIR ALFRED
I rejoice in your reassurance . . . I had always thought that music was a universal language and did not change from continent to continent or even peninsula . . . we are faced then with the small interlaced "F's" with which Mr. Beethoven indicated to us . . . his musical heirs and assigns forever . . .
(his voice begins to swell)
. . . that he wanted this part to be played Fortissimo . . . is there anyone here who thinks Mr. Beethoven was temporarily uninspired? . . . Oh I know it is not customary to follow slavishly the indications of the masters . . . we "interpret" them and to the extent that we change their simple and clearly stated wishes we feel that we have grown (otherwise how could we push them around?) and they have diminished . . . the rarest quality among men is the ability to execute an order exactly as they are asked to

do it . . . without improvement . . . without embellishment . . .
without change. . . . I have made some small success by playing
exactly what I saw before me in black and white . . . without fear
or the general underplaying dictated by the so-called canons of
good taste . . . Mr. Beethoven has asked that we play this part
loud . . . and so long as I am on the podium that is exactly what
Mr. Beethoven is going to get . . . once again from three bars
before "C."

He raises the baton and brings it down with a house shaking crash.

As we have seen, Sir Alfred's lack of pomposity was stressed by Sturges
early on; endowing him with a humane attitude toward his orchestra took
much longer. The Sir Alfred of these passages, like the conductor of the 1933
story, is steeply condescending and a bully of the podium. To distinguish this
behavior from pomposity may be hair-splitting. As for Sir Alfred's ribald
paean to turkey leg, girl, and thou, music, his first torrent of abuse might erase
it from viewer memory.

On October 18, Sturges wrote another page with a single sentence: "Nearly
every musician in a symphony orchestra is a disappointed virtuoso." The
word, "disappointed," suggests failure, envy, and perhaps sullenness. This
portrait of orchestra musicians steeped in resentment is the reverse angle of
the portrait of the conductor as condescending autocrat—a perfect, repellent
match.

Later on the 18th, Sturges turned his attention to the topic of the conductor's fantasies during the concert. He wrote a page headed "The Concert,"
which describes—and, in relation to the 1933 story, reverses—two of the
conductor's fantasies, placing first the episode in which Sir Alfred shoots his
wife and then himself, and second the one in which he forgives her and writes
her a check for fifty thousand dollars. (The episode in which Sir Alfred murders Daphne and frames her lover is omitted.) At the bottom of the page
Sturges adds, appropriately, a *P.S.* to himself:

The important thing is to make clear to the audience, through the camera movement,
that we are going into the maestro's mind and seeing with him the scenes after the
concert that he is seeing beforehand.

The film succeeds so well in "making clear" the relations between reality and
fantasy and, far more difficult, the respective tenses involved, that we may
not appreciate what a feat it was to do so. Sturges's word for the scenes that
take place inside Sir Alfred's head is *prospects,* which is a far better word
than theorists of narrative have come up with for what might be called future possible. ("Flash-forward," which has been applied to *Easy Rider* and
some Alain Resnais films, clearly is not useful here.) The precisely prospective tense of these scenes did not prevent Zanuck from referring to them as
"retrospects."

According to another item Sturges wrote on the 18th,

The note which starts the fireworks could be from the maestro's wife to her sister . . . the following words scribbled in pencil: "Be very careful . . . he suspects . . ." She is referring of course to her sister's husband.

It is as though Sturges's reconsideration of the concert fantasies has led him to reconsider how the conductor comes to suspect his wife in the first place. On October 21, in any case, Sturges recast the origin of Sir Alfred's wife-doubting for the first time in fourteen years. It is interesting in this respect that he also regarded it as a way to lengthen the project, that is, to fill out his 1933 story to feature film dimensions:

I may be able to gain length in the following way: by not making it quite so easy to find out what his wife has done to him. For instance: his concert manager who is also his brother-in-law might ask him if he is broad-minded and then when the maestro has replied, "not vulgarly so, why?", his brother-in-law might remind him of the fact that his wife is younger than he, that she spends considerable time in the company of his secretary who is about her own age . . .

Maestro: I am the one who arranged that.

Brother-in-law: You will not be the first to be hoist by your own petard.

Maestro: How about your own wife? She's two years younger than mine and you aren't exactly my junior.

Brother-in-law: I have her watched every so often.

Maestro: What do you mean watched?

Brother-in-law: By detectives, what do you think?

Maestro: You mean to say people actually use detectives . . . I mean outside of detective stories?

Brother-in-law: What are you talking about? Did you ever look in the classified 'phone book? It's full of detectives . . .

Maestro: Pew.

Brother-in-law: What?

Maestro: I think it stinks, if you will forgive the vulgarity, although why I should ask anyone who employs detectives to forgive anything vulgar I shall never know, as I would consider that the nadir of crass vulgarity.

Brother-in-law: Nevertheless, my musicians aren't laughing at me.

Maestro: Your musicians? Since when have you had any musicians? What do you mean my musicians are laughing at me?

Brother-in-law: Oh nothing. If you haven't noticed it I'm sorry I mentioned it.

Maestro: I wish I'd kept up my boxing . . . I would certainly enjoy giving you a good thrashing . . . although I'd probably hurt my hands on your thick skull and come out the loser.

A shorter note written the same day reduces this dialogue to one sentence: "The concert manager who is a thorough boor wastes no time in sowing the seed of uneasiness in the mind of his brother-in-law." That seed was not likely to grow into murderous fantasy, however, unless reinforced by some piece of physical evidence, some Shakespearean handkerchief or a letter protruding from a handbag. Unsure what device to use, Sturges refers here to "some action" by the concert manager's young wife that casts "by implication, an innuendo upon her sister who is married to the great Sir Adam," as Sir Alfred is called in this and one other passage only. What first prompts Sir Alfred's doubt is no longer the story's letter but the infectious suspicions of a brother-in-law who perhaps has something to prove: they (women) are all the same (unfaithful). It is also true, of course, that the brother-in-law's poisonous seeds do not fall upon barren ground.

On a page written on October 22, Sturges jumped ahead to sketch a number of possible plot turns. First he considers different versions of a note that Sir Alfred might find and misunderstand: "A note in Sir Adam's wife's handwriting . . . would be interpreted by the brother-in-law and Sir Adam as being a note from Sir Adam's wife to the young male secretary, whereas actually it is from Sir Adam's wife to her sister."

A second entry on the same page has the maestro's wife indignantly denying interest in her husband's secretary: "That jelly bean! I like men . . . with beards . . . who work and sweat . . . and amount to something in the world . . . men with ugly faces like you, darling . . . Tony is prettier than I am . . . you won't have to worry about the Tonys . . . just keep an eye on your double bass player." The wife responds vigorously and forthrightly to her husband's suspicions, which presumes that, instead of nursing his supposed betrayals, Sir Alfred has actually told his wife what was bothering him. The only difficulty with such an enlightened scene is that it would have ended the film, as John Ford said of the Indians' odd failure to shoot the horses drawing the title conveyance in *Stagecoach* (1939).

A third entry, an unfinished dialogue between Sir Alfred and a detective, actually has the former consult the latter to have his wife watched.

The detective: "How much are you prepared to spend?"

Sir Alfred: "What has that got to do with it?"

*"You stuffed moron!"—Sir Alfred roughs up August:
Rudy Vallee and Rex Harrison in* UNFAITHFULLY YOURS.

The detective: "How much do you want to find out?"

Sir Alfred: "Oh," then after a pause, "Could you do this for me
                   without my telling you who I am?"

The detective: "What do I care who you are . . . so long as you pay the
                   bills."

Sir Alfred: "I see . . . I suppose you'd have to know who my wife
                   was though."

The detective: "Well, what do you think?"

Sir Alfred: "Couldn't I point her out to you from behind a news-
                   paper kiosk or something . . . and then you . . . sleuth
                   her from then on."

The detective: (after a pause) "I got you. Who have you been reading
                   lately, Sherlock Holmes?"

Sir Alfred: "How was that?"

The detective: "You would like to *shadow* her" [no period in original]

Such flying stabs as this rarely survive in the work of Sturges or other writers; they probably disappear more often into wastebaskets or are screened out

before pen touches paper or fingers touch keys. Such an attempt may limber up the imagination or, on the contrary, catch its overheated spill; but also, by reversing the premise of a project, it may test its validity, its struts and stresses. That a premise can be turned around says something about it and—who knows?—may reveal the outline of a superior project, in which case the work done so far is dropped and the task of working out the implications of the new premise is begun.

Two last pages written on October 22 sketch more of the dialogue between Sir Alfred and his brother-in-law. Then, from the 23rd to the 25th, Sturges wrote a twelve-page draft sequence of the film's opening that centered on the brother-in-law, named here for the first time August Henschler III, who has come to call on Sir Alfred.

After the main titles during which we have seen various shots of a symphony orchestra, its conductor always from the back, we FADE IN ON A DOWN SHOT of a magnificent limousine pulling up to a Park Avenue curb. From this gleaming apparition, shining in the morning sun, the huge doorman ushers forth a slender gentleman in his early forties. He is conservatively dressed, hatted and pince-nezed; he walks in a conservative manner and his voice is conservative. Conservatively speaking, he has millions.

August bids good morning to the doorman, asks his chauffeur to wait, and asks the hotel clerk to announce him to Sir Alfred de Carter (whose full name also appears here for the first time). A cut to Sir Alfred's apartment shows Tony, Sir Alfred's secretary, picking up the phone and telling his employer that his brother-in-law wishes to see him.

> SIR ALFRED
> What the devil does he want? Tell him I'll call him back and then remind me to forget it.

Here for the first time is Sir Alfred's detestation of his brother-in-law. Gone, never to be revived, is the suggestion that August is Sir Alfred's concert manager—a relationship that requires, at a minimum, trust and respect and, if possible, friendship. Tony explains that August is in fact downstairs and Sir Alfred reluctantly agrees to see him. While August is on his way up, Sir Alfred resumes a dictation he has been making—"now where were we?" Tony replies, ". . . Although I doubt that I shall be in Porthole this season . . ."

> SIR ALFRED
> Porthaul . . . P-o-r-t-h-a-u-l . . . although I doubt that I shall be in Porthaul this season, I shall most certainly avail myself of your charming offer at the earliest opportunity . . . yours most affectionately, Alfred de Carter . . . what a charming little village in the heart of that most beautiful of all states . . .

TONY

Mitchigan

SIR ALFRED

You can't fool me . . . I know it's pronounced Michigan. And you know why it is the most beautiful of all states and Porthaul is the most beautiful of all hamlets and Genesee street is the most beautiful of all streets?

TONY

(sardonically as he opens some more mail)

No . . . tell me again.

SIR ALFRED

(stropping his razor for the finish)

Because the most beautiful half of the most beautiful pair of sisters in the most beautiful of all worlds . . . came from there . . . directly to me . . . I suppose I've told you how we met . . . [Tony looks up, says nothing, looks back at the mail.] how the train broke down because the tracks were washed out . . . we were playing in Canada and the local Baldwin man asked me if I would listen to his daughter play at the high school concert . . . and I said "Cripes, Sir Alfred, we're in for it that's what we are" . . . and we had to take a punt to get there . . . and I said "Murder, there'll be no getting away from here at all unless I swim" . . . and then . . . I looked into her eyes . . . and the world began anew for me.

We hear a buzzer and Sir Alfred's face falls.

This is the first appearance of the Porthaul story, which will appear in different forms and in different contexts in all subsequent drafts, including the final script, reprinted below (pages 13–15 and 104–112). Its function in each case is to stress Sir Alfred's love for his wife, which it does by recalling their romantic, love-at-first-sight encounter. To be sure, its placement here is unlikely—a reminiscence trumped up by a fortuitous letter—and awkward—squeezed as it is between August's call from the lobby and his arrival upstairs; but it serves to show us, before August plants suspicion, Alfred in love. The great conductor bores his secretary by telling him, yet once more, how he met his wife and how rapturously he loves her. This construction is also questionable in that Tony is presented as an intimate friend of Alfred's as well as his secretary, and hence is introduced too sympathetically if we are later to believe that he cuckolds his good friend. A larger defect is that we have not yet seen Sir Alfred's wife, the object of his raptures, and that he declares his love for her to Tony rather than to her. This is remedied in later versions when we see the couple rapturously together before Sir Alfred's suspicions are aroused.

In any case, in the middle of the Porthaul story, August arrives and Tony is sent down to the hotel barber to have Sir Alfred's razor honed, with instruc-

*Sir Alfred attends the comic soprano in the Porthaul
episode cut from UNFAITHFULLY YOURS.*

tions to return in a few minutes—"we have many letters to get off before
rehearsal." Several pages of light skirmish between Sir Alfred and August
follow, centering chiefly on two huge boxes of flowers that arrive for Sir Alfred's wife—the first, according to Sir Alfred, "very probably the ones I ordered for her earlier this morning." When August suggests he find out who
sent the second box, Sir Alfred says,

> That is a matter entirely between Lady de Carter and her
> florist . . .
>   (then after a pause, quite seriously)
> Bantering to one side, August . . . when two magnificent girls
> like your beautiful wife and <u>my</u> beautiful wife . . . condescend to
> marry a couple of old door posts like yourself and myself . . . even
> though we <u>do</u> have millions, and one of us at least is fairly well
> preserved although I will not say which one . . . it does not be-
> hoove us to behave like jealous boys . . . The only emotion we
> have any right to evince is: gratitude.

Odd perhaps, given his dislike of August, that Sir Alfred rhapsodizes
to him about his own wife—and her sister, August's wife. In any case, he

777

continues in this vein for two more speeches, including the line, "the fact that this beautiful creature loves me . . . is the catalyst that transforms each dull day into an exciting adventure." At this point in the conversation, August, in his characteristically negative way, seizes the initiative:

> You are positive she loves you?
>
> SIR ALFRED
> I am certain of it.
>
> AUGUST
> I am not certain that <u>mine</u> loves <u>me</u>.
>
> SIR ALFRED
> I wouldn't be either if I were in your place.
>
> AUGUST
> Oh you wouldn't.
>
> SIR ALFRED
> No because by instinct a woman will always try to be what her man thinks she is . . . if he doubts her she will give him cause to doubt her . . . just as the man who is frightened of dogs . . . gets bit.
>
> AUGUST
> Not having your high-faluting theories at my command . . . I put some detectives on her.

As before, Sir Alfred is appalled by the vulgarity of this act and hopes the news was bad—"a man who employs detectives should never be disappointed." August says he found out that the sisters went out dancing with Tony, Sir Alfred's secretary. "In view of the fact I sent them I know it very well indeed," answers Sir Alfred. After more discussion, August prepares to leave, noting that he has tried to do Sir Alfred a service but that if he wants his musicians, his friends, the critics, and all of New York laughing at him, that is his business. Sir Alfred says "(savagely at the very last moment) What did you come here to tell me?" at which point the draft ends.

How to proceed from this point was a problem that Sturges addressed in the days that followed. On October 27 and 28, he wrote a nineteen-page draft of the film's opening that, for the first time in his work on the project, was typed in the format of a studio script, probably by a secretary that Sturges hired. The October 27–28 draft follows the twelve-page October 23–25 draft exactly for seven and a half pages and with mainly minor changes for two and a half pages after that. There is then a major divergence in the form of a digression that Sturges allowed himself in the later draft as Sir Alfred and August discuss their wives' lavish spending habits. As before, August complains about his wife's extravagance and Sir Alfred extols the pleasures of a free-spending spouse, particularly a young and beautiful one. Now, however, Sir Alfred reinforces his point by proposing to sing a little ditty of his own composition—"The Miser's Love Song." August, who generously provides dialogue hooks at all stages of the project, repeats the title with exclamation: "The Miser's Love Song!"

> SIR ALFRED
> (moving to the piano at which he plays
> standing up)
> That's right . . . a very rich friend of mine always complaining
> about his girl . . . my uncle as a matter of fact . . . I had him say:
> (he accompanies himself as he <u>speaks</u>
> the lines)
> I really had to get rid of you . . .
> Your extravagance was driving me wild.
> The value of money was beans to you honey . . .
> Financially you were a child . . .
> Although a delicious one.
>
> So last night I built a fire
> A sentimental pyre
> To sear the wounds . . . of my desire
> An overdraft or two
> Some statements overdue . . .
> My only memories of you.
>
> But as the flames destroyed
> Your last expensive trace,
> I heard your silver laugh again . . .
> I saw your elfin face.
> And as the embers died
> A voice within me sighed:
> Those are the ashes of your heart you fool . . .
> Those are the ashes of your love.
>
> As he plays the final chord, he repeats: "The Miser's Love Song."

It is difficult to imagine anyone but Rex Harrison playing this scene. (Imagine James Mason, for example.) Harrison had not been cast at this point but he was under consideration and interested. Here Sturges appears to have anticipated, by seven years, the actor's speak-singing in *My Fair Lady*. However, the scene never appeared in another draft and neither Harrison nor anyone else, except the typist, probably ever saw it.

The draft continues as before with August admitting to having hired detectives to follow his wife and Sir Alfred berating August for his bad manners. Also as before, August mentions that both wives were seen dancing with Tony and Sir Alfred replies that he sent him to do so. In this draft, however,

779

Sir Alfred does not demand to know why August has come; instead August takes his hat, gloves, and stick and leaves, while both men pretend cordiality. The scene continues as Sir Alfred

> closes the door after his brother-in-law, then crosses to the window and looks down into the street. After this he goes toward his wife's bedroom, starts to put his hand on the knob, then takes his hand away, looks at the door a moment longer, then turns on his heel and walks to the living room door. He opens it.
>
> CUT TO: THE LIVING ROOM
>
> Twenty characters spring to their feet and address Sir Alfred at once.
>
> CUT TO: SIR ALFRED – IN THE DOORWAY
>
> He looks at the people stonily, as if they were speaking in a language he did not understand, then closes the door firmly in their faces.
>
> CUT TO: SIR ALFRED – IN HIS STUDY
>
> He turns from the door, crosses to his wife's bedroom door again, puts his hand on the doorknob and leaves it there a long moment before slowly and soundlessly opening the door.
>
> CUT TO: LONG SHOT – A DARKENED BEDROOM
>
> The crack of light widens on the sleeping Daphne, then narrows again and the shadowy figure of Sir Alfred goes past the CAMERA and stops as he looks down at his young wife.
>
> CUT TO: CLOSE SHOT – DAPHNE SLEEPING
>
> CUT TO: CLOSE LOW CAMERA SHOT – UP AT SIR ALFRED
>
> He looks at his wife in sadness and perplexity.
>
> CUT TO: A LITTLE DOG – IN THE CHAIR NEAR THE BED
>
> It is eyeing Sir Alfred. It growls.
>
> CUT TO: He turns and gives the animal a hostile look.
>
> CUT TO: DAPHNE – CLOSE SHOT
>
> In her sleep she turns toward her little dog, opens one eye and says:
>
> DAPHNE
>
> Sh!
>
> Now she looks up at her husband, blinks, smiles lovingly and speaks.
>
> DAPHNE
>
> Good morning, Alfie . . . did you sleep well?
>
> CUT TO: LOW CAMERA SHOT – OF SIR ALFRED

SIR ALFRED
(with great precision)
Wonderfully, thank you . . . like an ox! Now go back to sleep, I'll see you later.

He smiles mechanically, turns and strides out of the room.

CUT TO: CLOSE SHOT – DAPHNE

Looking after him, frowning. Now she pushes herself up on one elbow and looks over at the little dog.

DAPHNE
What's the matter with him?

The draft characterizes Sir Alfred as sad and perplexed; as described, however, his actions seem menacing, if not actually murderous. The scene—which belongs more in a *film noir* than in a sophisticated comedy—continues, appropriately, with Tony's return of Sir Alfred's newly sharpened razor, whereupon the secretary is confronted by his employer: "How long have you been taking Daphne dancing . . . while I was away?" Tony says that it only happened once when he ran into Daphne. Sir Alfred appears or pretends to be mollified until Tony, "trying for a conversational lightness," asks if it was Mr. Henschler who told him about the incident. Sir Alfred "looks back at Tony without replying then opens the door and disappears into a room full of people."

Sir Alfred's accusing Tony, like his silent menacing behavior toward Daphne, leaves too little for the concert fantasies. If Sir Alfred is shown as acting on his suspicions now, then his fantasies at the concert will seem a pale extension of those actions rather than a vivid substitute for them. Compared even to incomplete action, the fantasies will seem insipid, perhaps even like cowardly avoidance. The concert fantasies work only if they are a substitute for action altogether—because the man who entertains them lives in his mind and his music. That, in any case, is the plan of the final script and the film. There he is shown to be irritated with Daphne and Tony before and during the concert, but his restraint keeps his behavior within bounds—it is taken by them as "temperament." Then when Alfred tries to put his fantasies into practice—after the concert—he makes a farce of it.

The generous and confident Sir Alfred who urged his wife to dance with his secretary gives way in the October 27–28 draft to a more conventional husband. He construes Tony's guilty behavior as evidence that he is having an affair with Daphne, never imagining that the affair is with August's wife. Later that evening, after his concert, Sir Alfred will learn the truth; in the meantime, Sturges implies, there are sufficient "proofs" of his wife's infidelity to fuel his fantasies at the concert itself. Since he has tipped his hand to Tony, however, he can hardly imagine framing him with murder. Indeed, if he is certain enough of the couple's guilt to fantasize their murders at the concert, why not fire Tony now or, on the contrary, pretend to know nothing of the affair? A one-page scene fragment written later on October 28 has Sir Alfred, "after calming down a little," call August a "poor stupid gook."

AUGUST
(recoiling)
I forgive your language on the ground that you are excited.

SIR ALFRED
I didn't ask your forgiveness and I may still punch you in the nose at any instant . . . don't you understand that when two beautiful creatures like Barbara and Daphne marry a couple of old doorposts like you and me . . . no matter how many millions we have . . . or how well preserved at least one of us is, the only emotion that we have any moral, spiritual or honorable right to display . . . is gratitude . . . deep, rich, round and fulsome gratitude.

All draft scenes are, by definition, transitional; a few, like this one, actually show transition taking place. The hostility between Sir Alfred and August reaches a new intensity here: the stage of name-calling, if not yet of shouting, has been reached, and for the first time there is a threat of physical violence. But what occasions Sir Alfred's fury, from which he calms down sufficiently to hurl insults and threaten punches? Can it merely be August's admission that he set detectives on his own wife? A more likely response to that admission is what we have seen in the earlier drafts: a shocked, barbed criticism or two, followed by Sir Alfred's reassertion of confidence in his wife—she went dancing with Tony because Sir Alfred sent him to do so. Sturges now has Sir Alfred angered in the extreme—enraged—and then, as in the earlier drafts, wax sentimental, and adjectival, in his appeal for the gratitude of old doorposts to young wives. In a three-page draft written later the same day, Sturges decided why Sir Alfred was so angry and dropped, for the time being at least, references to gratitude and old doorposts:

AUGUST
When you left for Philadelphia last week, Alfred, and asked me to keep an eye on your wife for you, I naturally accepted as I would expect you to do the same for me if I were going to . . . let us say: Pittsburgh . . .

SIR ALFRED
(puzzled)
Yes?

AUGUST
What I didn't know was that I would have to fly down to Palm Beach for a slight illness of my mother . . .

782

SIR ALFRED
(dryly)
I'm sorry to hear it.

AUGUST
. . . to return to your wife you asked me to keep an eye on her
which you may believe I would, as your brother-in-law, gladly
have done . . .

SIR ALFRED
(totally nonplussed)
But my dear fellow you are attaching much too much importance
to all this . . . I said "keep an eye on Daphne" as I might have said
take good care of her for me or "take her to the pictures with you
some night if she's lonely" that's all . . .

AUGUST
I thought you said "keep an eye on her for me."

SIR ALFRED
I presume I must have, but how could you from Palm Beach so . . .

AUGUST
(lamely)
With detectives.

SIR ALFRED
(horrified)
With detectives!

This new tack solved a number of story problems for Sturges and at the
same time opened the way to later scenes, as a brief note written later the same
day indicates: "Immediately after burning the report on his wife's activities
Sir Alfred realizes that there is probably a carbon copy of it down at the
agency. This takes him there to have that destroyed also." This note is followed in turn by a scene fragment:

DAPHNE
I got so worried I got up in the middle of the night and went to his
room to ask him . . . I didn't dare telephone because August is the
kind of man who would have his wire tapped.

SIR ALFRED
(deliriously happy)
He most certainly would . . . how you've penetrated his vulgarity.
Now tell me more . . . I'm enjoying every syllable of it.

Still another passage has Sir Alfred ask Daphne after August's visit: "(ap-
ropos of nothing) Do you love me?"

DAPHNE
(pointing to the bed)
Well what would I be doing here if I didn't?

SIR ALFRED
(getting to his knees)
You lovely thing.

He takes his wife in his arms.

SIR ALFRED
Would you like to meet me at Lalott's after rehearsal.

DAPHNE
What for?

SIR ALFRED
I'd like to buy you a dress.

DAPHNE
I don't really think I need . . .

SIR ALFRED
Oh yes you do . . . you haven't a thing to wear . . . And then will
you have an expensive lunch with me?

DAPHNE
Yes darling . . .

Reordered, these fragments suggest, if they do not quite constitute, a new
story outline. August's new revelation—that he set detectives on Daphne—
leads plausibly to, and retrospectively justifies, the barely controlled anger of
Sir Alfred that fit so oddly into the earlier passage. August somehow manages, in the hailstorm of Alfred's outrage, to hand him a copy of the detective's report on Daphne, which Alfred burns without reading. However, the
incident leaves him with enough doubt to ask Daphne if she loves him. Her
answer reassures him and he invites her to meet him, following his orchestra
rehearsal, for a dress-buying and lunch. He then visits the detective agency to
obtain and destroy the original of the report in their files. The placement of
this visit is uncertain: whether it is to occur before, after, or instead of the
dress shop visit and/or lunch. But its function in the plot as a whole is certain:
to convince Sir Alfred, shortly before the concert, of his wife's infidelity.

Catching up with his new plot outline—the most important story development since the 1933 original—took Sturges some time. On November 1 and
2, after two days away from the project, he wrote a twenty-three-page draft
that went only slightly beyond August's new revelation and Sir Alfred's outraged "With detectives!" The draft did have a new opening, however.

After the credits during which we have seen various SHOTS of
a symphony orchestra, its conductor always from the back we

FADE IN

1 THE TICKET WINDOW – IN THE LOBBY OF A
CONCERT HALL

Next to the window there is a large eight-sheet of SIR ALFRED
de CARTER, Bart., superb in mustache, imperial and slightly-
puffed-at-the-temples hair. The lithographer has caught him in
the act of conducting an orchestra, his baton held high, his eyes
sparkling with enthusiasm. The head of a long queue of ticket
buyers is purchasing his tickets at the window. Now the CAM-
ERA STARTS TRUCKING along the queue. To do this it goes
out on the sidewalk, then makes a turn, follows the queue up to
the corner, then goes around the corner and comes finally to rest
on the last person in the queue, my friend Jose Iturbi. He puffs
out his cheeks and blows through his lips signifying that he
thinks the queue ahead of him is very long. We hear a limousine
door slam too, and the CAMERA PANS over to a magnificent
town car. The chauffeur opens the door and out pops August
Henschler III. From his drooping pince-nez to the last button on
his spats, he spells conservatism. He would appear to be about
the age of Rudy Vallee. He exchanges an owlish look with Jose
Iturbi, then starts for the head of the queue. As he moves forward, Mr. Iturbi hollers after him indignantly:

MR. ITURBI
Hey!

August, now in full motion, "acknowledges this only with a slight backward look." The camera takes him around the corner, then "down past the
long line of music lovers of all nationalities, races and hair cuts," then finally
into the lobby and up to the window. August asks for and receives promptly
"my box for tonight." The first and second in line complain—"How about waiting your turn like the rest of us, buddy?" and "Is this a Democracy or isn't it a
Democracy?" To the latter August replies: "(putting his tickets away) This is
a republic . . . although founded on Democratic principles . . . if you don't believe it, look it up . . . Good morning." Sturges adds: "He marches conservatively out of the SHOT." (Why did conservatives in the forties, fifties, and
sixties so often tell one to look things up, as though the [conservative] truth
were written down somewhere, fixed and unchanging?)
    Sturges dissolves from this new scene to another, a seven-and-a-half-page
scene with Sir Alfred, a jeweler, and (later in the scene) Tony in Sir Alfred's
apartment. The jeweler has made a house call, as it were, and brought a generous supply of his merchandise with him; Sir Alfred is browsing, in his dressing gown, for a bracelet to give Daphne. He has picked out the one he likes—
"By Jove . . . that's a real blinder, isn't it?" he says. A telephone rings and the
camera pans "across the table to a French 'phone just as a new hand picks

it up. The CAMERA follows the hand up onto a very handsome young man [Tony]." The caller is August, who wishes to see Sir Alfred; the latter seeks to postpone the meeting, indefinitely if possible, until Tony informs him that August is downstairs and wishes to come up. Alfred's disappointed and re-signed remarks at having to see August are now counterpointed with his interest in jewelry. "I suppose I'll have to have this . . . it will look so pretty on her little wrist," he says to the jeweler, after which, Sturges notes, he "sighs happily." While waiting for August's arrival from downstairs, Sir Alfred now tells the "Porthole, Michigan" story—his and Daphne's ecstatic first meet-ing—to the jeweler! This is, to say the least, awkward, even if preferable, for reasons discussed above, to his telling it to Tony. The Jeweler says, after the story:

> Gee, that's like a poem, Sir Alfred.

> SIR ALFRED
> My life has been like a poem since that night.

> THE JEWELER
> Porthole, Michigan . . . you'd never think it . . . you want that gift wrapped, Sir Alfred?

> SIR ALFRED
> No, no . . . just a piece of tissue paper . . . maybe I can slip it on her wrist while she's sleeping.

> THE JEWELER
> Beautiful . . . but don't forget to have it insured . . . these dames!

> CUT TO: TONY – AT THE TELEPHONE

> TONY
> I'm doing that now.

What Sturges thought of the November 1 and 2 opening is nowhere recorded. It seems to me less a serious draft than a kind of lark, if a delightful one. In any case, on November 3 and 4, Sturges returned to, and comprehensively recast, the opening of the film, which now focuses on Sir Alfred's arrival from London by airplane. This became, with one major change, the opening of his first screenplay draft, which was begun on November 7 and finished on December 2. Thus it is not too much to say that Sturges's decision to have August hire detectives to follow Daphne set off a chain reaction that led to a new story outline, a new opening for the film, and that pivotal moment in the development of any Sturges script—the transition from the writing of notes and draft scenes to the writing of a complete screenplay version.

The December 2 script was followed by two versions written in 1948: a January 15 screenplay and a February 10 screenplay, the final script, which is reprinted below. The two later scripts were written under the pressures of censorship and Zanuck, respectively—constraints that are discussed in detail below. If our immediate focus is the December 2 script, it is because that is the only version that Sturges wrote free of external restrictions. Also, as the first screenplay version, it occupies a pivotal place between the story and the notes and drafts that precede it and the screenplay versions and film that succeed it.

As the December 2 script begins, we see, at the beginning of the main titles, "a huge trans-Atlantic plane flying through the sunlit clouds high over the ocean." As the sun sets, the sky gets dark and the lights go on in the plane. Following the main titles, there is a dissolve to the navigator inside the plane, who is calling LaGuardia field but getting no response. The camera pans up and around to the door behind the navigator—"Here we see a very pleasant looking man in his late thirties, his face adorned with a mustache and imperial." As the man looks down at the navigator anxiously but sleepily, a little girl's voice says "Sir Alfred."

The man with the imperial looks around in surprise, then down below the SHOT. The CAMERA PANS down to include a little girl of seven whose grimy little mitts hold an autograph book and a pencil with which she has been poking the gentleman.

The child says something indistinguishable, the gentleman beams, takes the pencil, and signs his name in the book. Just as he finishes he looks up at the navigator and we hear "the voice of LaGuardia Field." The scene pivots at this point to the control tower "of LaGuardia or some other great airport," then cuts to the loudspeaker in a corner of the airport waiting room through which the arrival of a flight from London is announced. The camera then pans up to a glass window through which we see the cocktail bar of the terminal and, seated "just near us . . . two very pretty and very fashionably dressed young women, a very handsome well-dressed young man, also in his twenties, and a very conservative looking gentleman in his early forties in a drooping pince-nez." Amidst loud music and room chatter, the quartet debates, with much hostile byplay between August and Barbara, whether or not the arrival of the London plane has just been announced. Finally, after four and a half pages of this, Daphne asks a waiter to "let us know the minute the London plane is announced" and he replies, putting down another round of drinks, "Oh, it's here." Daphne grabs Tony and rushes out of the shot, "neatly avoiding everything except the tray full of drinks which she knocks to the floor."

There is a dissolve to Sir Alfred coming through the gate from the field. "He looks around anxiously past the other passengers, then sees someone and speaks with medium happiness." The man he greets, whom we see in the next shot, is Sir Alfred's concert manager, described in the script as "A LARGE DARK IMPRESSARIO – IN A COAT WITH A FUR COLLAR." "His name is Hugo Hammock," Sturges notes, "and he speaks with a slight accent."

Hugo embraces Sir Alfred and tells him that a concert scheduled for later has
been pushed up to tomorrow. "Oh that's all right," says Sir Alfred,

> we'll have plenty of time . . . I'll rehearse in the morning . . . after all it's
> the men that count . . . all I have to do is wave a stick.

> HUGO
> Says you!

> SIR ALFRED
> Don't worry about it Hugo. I've been through much tighter spots than
> that . . . what I'm worried about is . . .

> Suddenly his face lights up, he throws wide his arms, and shoves Hugo
> to one side.

> CUT TO: DAPHNE – RUNNING THROUGH THE CROWDED
> WAITING ROOM

> DAPHNE
> (in wild excitement)
> Darling!

> She throws her arms around her husband's neck and three news photog-
> raphers appear from nowhere and flash their cameras.

There is a dissolve from the embrace to "A MAGNIFICENT LIMOU-
SINE – OF THE MOST EXPENSIVE MAKE IMAGINABLE. We photograph it from a CAMERA CAR just ahead as it moves through Astoria."
Oblivious to everyone else, Sir Alfred and Daphne engage in love talk, which
seems to unnerve Barbara in particular.

> DAPHNE
> Then I'm going to take you right home and put you to bed . . . first you'll
> take a nice hot bath, and then you'll put on some nice silk pajamas . . .
> and then I'll serve you a nice cold bottle of champagne . . . I was able to
> get some Bollinger Brut '28 . . . and then . . .

> SIR ALFRED
> (huskily)
> And then what?

> CUT TO: BARBARA AND AUGUST

> BARBARA
> Open the window and get me some air, will you? . . . look, Jake . . . why
> don't we get out of here and take a taxi?

There is a dissolve to the next day, specifically to a two-column newspaper
photograph of Sir Alfred and Daphne with Hugo "beaming in the background."

In the draft of November 3 and 4, it is Tony's voice that begins to read the caption, which includes Sir Alfred's remark to a reporter, "Britain is hungry for music." There is then a cut to Sir Alfred shaving with "an old-fashioned straight razor":

SIR ALFRED
(continuing Tony's sentence)
. . . and for a great many other things, unfortunately . . . principally food. Our dear leaders . . . and I don't mean just in England, I mean everywhere, have finally enacted so many rules and regulations that NOTHING moves any more, and the whole secret of prosperity is: rapidity of circulation (or movement). Food, money, everything has to move . . . and the faster the better . . . from shore to shore, from hand to hand . . . and there is no reason why it shouldn't, we have plenty to move everything in, but they would hardly listen to a musician . . . so . . . I hope only they find it out . . . before it is too late, however all that is magnificently depressing and hardly the way to start a morning.[11]

In the December 2 script, we see, as before, the photograph of Sir Alfred and Daphne in the newspaper and hear a voice reading its caption. That voice is no longer Tony's, however, but Hugo's:

HUGO'S VOICE
(not forgetting the accent)
"Sir Alfred deCarter, Baronet, arrives in time. Noted conductor shown with his bride of a year who greets him at LaGuardia Field."

HUGO AND TONY – IN SIR ALFRED'S STUDY

Tony is typing a letter on a noiseless typewriter while Hugo reads the paper aloud.

HUGO
(shaking his head from side to side)
Alfie, Alfie . . . If I had your secret . . . would I be a dog!

Tony, typing on a noiseless typewriter, is now seen but not heard. How much better that the later-imagined sexual threat comes not from a confidant but from the silent, barely noticed one who is always there but, at the same time, not there. The leap that turns such a person into the wrecker of one's home has an air of creative paranoia about it, whereas suspecting one's best friend, as Tony seems to have been in earlier drafts, seems hackneyed. Even better, Alfred now has in Hugo a bantering partner closer to his own weight, whose observations about life and love are worth hearing and whose manner of expression is original.

Hugo asks Sir Alfred at some point "how a brilliant man like you, with a beautiful young girl like you got can get away from here and leave her alone . . . surrounded by woollufs." Sir Alfred replies:

> If she married me it must be because she liked me better than the other wolves . . . if she likes me better . . . what is there to worry about?

HUGO
(waving him away)
Theories . . .

SIR ALFRED
That's right . . . and not the kind you lift out of books either . . . the kind you come by the hard way. You see, Hugo, I have no faintest wish or desire to think of myself as the lord and master of that dream of loveliness reclining in the next room . . . when I was very young and first married I tried out that role . . .
(he waves a finger in the negative)
. . . I think all young men adopt it more or less naturally . . . and what a stupid ugly role it is . . .
(he shakes his head in reminiscence and then speaks very dryly)
. . . my second marriage was to another musician and naturally went flat . . . we found it impossible to harmonize . . . my third attempt nearly succeeded . . . it came within a fraction of an inch . . . which is all you need to miss a bus by . . . my fourth was just a shipboard romance picked up on the rebound . . . I'm sorry to have to mention it . . . BUT NOW: I don't want to be the only man that angel sees or is fond of . . . I just want to be the favorite man . . . the one she is fondest of . . . the lover, not the proprietor . . . O-o-o-h . . . the lover in law, in all probability, since this is the Twentieth Century and it's always nicer for the children . . . but still: the lover.

This speech, which might be called the Five Marriages of Man, may be credited not only to Sturges and Sir Alfred but also to the character of Hugo. Alfred could never have spoken of these things, or in this way, to Tony. This peroration by Sir Alfred, informed perhaps by the many marriages of Sturges, can only be forthcoming to the right listener. "Fine theories," Hugo repeats, "but I tell you: you give them an inch . . . they'll take the tape measure . . . I know what I'm talking about." "How many times have you been married?" Sir Alfred asks. "Once," says Hugo, whereupon Sir Alfred demands: "Then what do you know about marriage? . . . you're like a fighter who has had only one fight." Hugo replies, after a slight pause, "But *what* a fight."

A huge box of flowers is delivered for Daphne and the ensuing exchange is now between Alfred and Hugo. Alfred refuses to peek at the card, as Hugo suggests, to see who sent them. Instead he builds a fantasy about "some poor devil who nearly committed suicide the day she married me":

> Once each year, on the day that he and my dear wife graduated from Sunday School together in Porthole, Mitchigan . . . he sends her this little bunch of violets . . . or could it be Lillies [sic] of the Valley?

> HUGO
> (looking at the box)
> In this box it could be a skeleton! He could send himself.

Admonishing Hugo not to be gruesome, Alfred returns to his discourse.

> Now: Am I to pry into this pitiful little rite . . . uncover this pathetic little secret . . . assert my largely debatable prerogatives as a husband and drag into the cold blue daylight this humble offering from a tear-stained past?

> HUGO
> You shoulda been an obituary writer.

> SIR ALFRED
> I might easily have been. Music was only a sideline which happened to succeed.

Hugo notices the flowers were sent from a florist in the lobby and Alfred recalls "in mock relief" that *he* ordered the flowers early that morning.

The phone rings, and Tony announces that August is downstairs and wishes to see Alfred, who reluctantly agrees. While August ascends—on the world's slowest elevator—Alfred departs the room and is next seen opening the door to Daphne's bedroom. The menacing quality of the earlier draft is gone; having no reason to suspect Daphne, Alfred now stands in the doorway, holding the box of flowers, "looking down at all this prettiness." Daphne "sits bolt upright, starts to scream, then sees her husband."

> DAPHNE
> (startled)
> Alfred! What's that, a coffin? Aw, you sweet . . .

> She puts her arms around his neck. Without removing her arms Sir Alfred reaches into the box and starts pulling out flowers.

> DAPHNE
> They're beautiful . . . who are they from?

> SIR ALFRED
> "From whom are they?"

> DAPHNE
> I don't know and I don't want to guess . . . those are the kind of guesses that shorten marriages.

One who corrects one's spouse's grammar at such a moment deserves the answer Sir Alfred receives. He erred even earlier perhaps by contortedly taking flowers out of the box with Daphne's arms already around him. For what are flowers, one may ask, if not to secure the embrace of the beloved? The flowers, answers Sir Alfred, "are from the most devoted, the most humble . . . and the most fortunate of your many admirers." Then:

> Without saying a word Daphne kisses him very warmly.

> SIR ALFRED
> (putting his arms around her)
> Do you know why Porthole, Mitchigan, is the most beautiful hamlet in the United States and Genessee Street is the most beautiful of all its avenues?

Alfred rather unbelievably chooses this intimate moment to tell his story about—Daphne corrects his pronunciation—Porthaul, Michigan. Daphne knows the story well—she was there—but is perhaps for that very reason a more plausible listener than Tony or August or a jeweler who makes house calls. The story goes on for three and a half pages, after which, following some banter about eyes and other body parts, Alfred asks Daphne to meet him at Lalotte's to buy a dress and then to come with him to the Colony to partake of a very expensive lunch. There's no one she'd rather partake with, says Daphne, whereupon "Sir Alfred hugs her very close and is about to kiss her when we hear Tony's voice" announcing August's arrival. Standing in the doorway Sir Alfred has left open, Tony's appearance is nevertheless so unexpected that his voice causes the lovers to "spring apart as they look around." Tony apologizes and closes the door behind him as Daphne suggests to Alfred that he send August away as soon as possible "then come back and talk to me some more." That thought is "full of health . . . I'll see what I can do," says Alfred as he leaves her bedroom. Alfred greets August, Hugo and Tony leave at August's request, and then begins the dialogue between Alfred and August, which lasts for slightly more than ten pages.

In the December 2 script that dialogue begins on page 29, which is much later than in all earlier drafts. If August's revelations are sufficient to launch the plot by themselves, then Alfred's encounter with August can be delayed— this is what Sturges seems to have discovered in writing his first screenplay version. Postponing that encounter allows him to add, among other things, the scenes showing Alfred and Daphne in love. This is much superior to having Alfred rhapsodize about Daphne in her absence and eliminates his role as an Ancient Mariner who stoppeth one of three—Tony, Hugo, or the jeweler— to tell his Porthaul story.

Near the end of the exchange between Alfred and August, Alfred takes the detective's report from August, tears it up, drops it in a wastebasket and, once August has gone, "picks up the wastebasket, then drop kicks it out into the hall." Following this, he "takes two deep breaths and forces an artificial smile, then goes through the door which leads to his wife's apartment." She is on the phone making an appointment at Lalotte's. When she finishes, Alfred complains about August: "there are times I am glad I haven't an ax in my hands."

DAPHNE
That Hershey Bar . . . I'm getting a little worried about Barbara because I know what I'd do if I were married to him myself . . . also for other reasons which I'll talk to you about later.

SIR ALFRED
You didn't do anything you shouldn't while I was away, did you? I mean like falling in love with anybody . . . or anything like that?

Alfred is so preoccupied with his own imagined betrayal that he does not take Daphne up on why she is worried about her sister. Daphne's explanation for that, and other things, must wait until the end of the script. Meanwhile she answers Alfred's question with one of her own: "How could I fall in love with anybody when you took my heart with you?" "Do you really love me?" Sir Alfred persists, to which Daphne replies, "What would I be doing here if I didn't?" To this he says, evidently calmed, "I'll buy you two dresses at Lalotte's . . . and if there's time we'll go by Cartier's." "Were you like this to all your wives?" "I don't think so . . . no." "I don't think so either or you never could have got away from them . . . they never would have let you go . . ." To this Alfred replies, "The only trouble with you is . . . I never want to go away from you to do anything . . . however music calls." Daphne "blows him a kiss from the end of her forefinger," which is followed by a cut to Sir Alfred, who "looks at his wife for a second, then comes straight to us. THE CAMERA PULLS BACK a little as he bends over and kisses Daphne full on the lips." When the kiss has run the legal limit, Sturges notes, it is interrupted by Pepper Pot, Daphne's dog, who "looking on sourly . . . gives a short bark." "If I'm going to rehearse at all . . . I think I'd better leave now," says Alfred, to which Daphne replies, "I think your words are full of wisdom," whereupon he departs.

Even a husband and wife could not be implied to have had or to be about to have sex—this was so fundamental an axiom of Hollywood censorship that Sturges observed it before the censors, indeed before anyone, had seen his script. Thus the absurdity of Alfred's flower throwing when Daphne just wants to make love, of his telling stories like Scheherazade to prevent a consummation he strongly wishes, and of his dragging himself off to rehearse his orchestra just as he is about to attain his desires. In short, the prohibitions of censorship have contaminated the character of Sir Alfred himself. Avoiding this was a Hollywood screenwriter's conundrum: how to create highly dynamic, sexualized characters who never have sex, or even come near it. Each of their days had to be like Don Giovanni's final day—a series of tantalizing encounters that go awry through circumstance. Where the Don curses, however, they had to remain cheerful, and hopeful, throughout.

The December 2 script seems schizophrenic: it represses Alfred and Daphne on the day of the concert but appears to indulge them on the night before. Alfred's plane arrives after sundown and Hugo tells him the concert has been postponed until the following day. The enticing schedule that Daphne outlines is thus an evening program: hot bath, silk pajamas, dinner in bed, cold champagne. Alfred's "And then what?" may seem, under the circumstances, underly sex suggestive; why, unless he prefers talking-about to doing, does he have to ask? The next morning, in any case, Alfred is up and at 'em with Hugo, Tony, and the soon-to-arrive August. When he ducks in to see Daphne before and after his meeting with August, there is no reference between them to the night before—not the least reminiscence or secret smile. Working retroactively, censorship here puts in question the lovemaking we were sure had taken place. Indeed the couple's passion on concert day seems long unfulfilled—it flares repeatedly, even if, like a mechanical log, it does not combust.

The root problem of the December 2 script is that Alfred has too much time on his hands. Both the January 15 script and the February 10 script, reprinted below, eliminate most of Alfred's free time and thereby restore his theoretical vigor—God knows he'd dally with Daphne if he could. Alfred, who has flown overnight, arrives in the morning and is told by Hugo that the concert scheduled for the next day will take place that evening. Alfred has not slept on the plane, so Daphne says she will take him home, put him in a hot tub, "and then rub you with alcohol . . . and then put you in some nice, clean, cool, silk, freshly laundered pajamas . . . ["How heavenly," Alfred says.] And then we'll have our little nap . . . and then I'll wake you up with a nice frosted bottle of Brut Champagne . . . I found some Pol Roger '34 . . . and then . . . [exchange between Barbara and August] . . . and by then it should be easily about 11:30 . . . ["And then some," says Barbara.] Thank you, darling . . . so then you'll go down and rehearse your men . . . oughtn't that be enough time, Hugo?" Hugo agrees, pointing out that the musicians are experienced and have played the concert selections a few thousand times. "Of course it'll be time enough . . . ," says Alfred, "putting his arm around his adored one" and kissing her on the cheek.

Time enough for what, we might ask, for we have now landed on the old Hollywood runway: constant teasers about sex, and undeniable drifts toward sex, punctuated in each case by a circumstantial obstacle or a retrospective denial. Here the irreducible circumstance is that Alfred is fatigued by his flight and needs a nap if he is to rehearse at midday and conduct in the evening. Champagne, the cinema's universal solvent for sexual reluctance, is now applied for waking up rather than going to bed. We see Alfred and Daphne later, he still in bed smiling sleepily, Daphne sitting on the floor next to him, each holding a glass of champagne. This, we suppose, will be their sole opportunity until after the concert. A touch of the old difficulty remains, however: Alfred seizes the opportunity to tell his Porthaul story. Daphne resists— "The way you've built this thing up," she says—but then succumbs to the story's romanticism and they kiss. Tony, whose knock on the closed door Alfred and Daphne do not hear, brings with him the day's business, which later includes August. Between his discussion with the latter and his departure for rehearsal, Alfred—as before—brings flowers to Daphne and asks if she really loves him. He is reassured by her answer and happily asks her to meet him at the dress shop and then have lunch. Then, as before, he departs for his rehearsal.

The rehearsal scene, for the viewer, is another kind of consummation—seeing Alfred do his stuff as the great conductor he's been said to be by his intimate friends. Eight pages long, the rehearsal scene begins with a shot of the tympani player of a great orchestra. "We are playing Schubert's Marche Militaire," Sturges notes, "and the gentleman is quite busy." Additional shots and notes follow:

EIGHT DOUBLE-BASS PLAYERS

They bow wonderfully in unison (the word bow rhymes with dough, not cow).

HORNS

Thrillingly they sound the attack.

CELLI

They are as busy as the rest.

SECOND FIDDLES

in wonderful unison their bows rise and fall.

FIRST FIDDLES

Why are these the elite of the orchestra? Because the Concert Master is a first fiddle? Anyway they are playing beautifully.

SIR ALFRED

in his short sleeves. Singing at the top of his voice he leads the men with much gaiety, turns the pages of the score with a slap. Suddenly he looks out and across at the triangle player.

TRIANGLE PLAYER

with the rest of the drum section visible behind him. He is doing his best with the triangle but it is nothing spectacular.

Sir Alfred raps for quiet and conveys to "Mr. Triangle" his thought that Schubert meant the triangles here "to convey the jingle jangle of the chains and metal harness rather than a strict beat . . . I have occasionally jingled two triangles together and it was quite effective." The triangle player tries this and Sir Alfred, apparently satisfied, makes no answer. He addresses himself instead to the entire orchestra:

If you don't mind . . . and since we've stopped anyway . . . May I ask you to play the Fortissimo as if they were marked Fortissimo and the Pianissimo as if they were marked Pianissimo? I know it's old-fashioned in these days of loose interpretation but I believe Schubert would feel better about it. Now: Two bars before "C" . . . one, two, three, four.

The two halves of the orchestra start off off-beat and Sir Alfred immediately raps for quiet.

SIR ALFRED

Gentlemen, I am in love . . . nothing you can do is going to spoil my day . . . again from two measures before 'C', if possible together, but in any case with deep feeling.

He starts them off skillfully. He consults his wrist watch then mops himself as he conducts happily. The piece now comes to a strong end.

SIR ALFRED

Splendid, splendid . . . good enough for them.

Sir Alfred looks at his watch and says to the Concert Master, "Shall we take five for the union, doctor?" Sir Alfred lights a cigarette and "courteously extends the light to one of his musicians." After the light, the musician's thank you, and Sir Alfred's welcome, we hear

an oboe player trying out a new reed by playing a theme in Boogie Woogie. Sir Alfred places his hand on the musician near him to stop him from talking.

OBOE PLAYER

He plays a little more of the Boogie Woogie, then stops, adjusts his reed, then plays it again. As he plays a shadow falls on him. After an instant he feels the presence of someone, stops suddenly and looks up sheepishly.

The oboist apologizes to Sir Alfred—he was just breaking in a new reed. Alfred replies, "But it's perfectly magnificent. Do you suppose anyone has ever done the . . . . in Boogie Woogie before? (To the orchestra) I wonder if you would do me a little favor . . . just for my private pleasure . . . and, I suppose, ... 's intense displeasure." "Would you like to hear it in Boogie Woogle?" asks Dr. Schultz, the Concert Master. "Enormously . . . have we all the Boogles and Woogles we need?" "If we can't do it, who is?" says Schultz, walking back to his desk beside Sir Alfred. The latter says to the orchestra, "I'll start you off and I suppose the corruption will come in about the beginning of Bar Four." At Schultz's suggestion, the first double bass starts it off—"He does a wonderful Boogie Woogie bass which is taken up by the seven other double-bass players." Rapping on his stand, Sir Alfred says, "All right . . . here we go . . . and then I am leaving you until tonight."

Sturges again describes various sections of the orchestra, this time for their participation in the boogie-woogie. Sir Alfred "starts the orchestra . . . with wonderful movements of the baton," but when he comes to Bar Four he stops beating time, folds his arms, and looks first at the double bass players then at each of a number of other instrument groups, in effect conducting the orchestra with eyes and head movements. When the improvisation is well under way, Sir Alfred "collapses into a chair with laughter."

Sturges cuts from the convulsed Sir Alfred to a queue of ticket buyers in the concert hall lobby, where "an intruder," who is the detective from Sir Alfred's hotel, has, to the consternation of those behind him, appeared at the head of the line and "pushed his head into the window." We do not hear what he says but soon Hugo appears and takes the detective backstage to see Sir Alfred. The orchestra is nearing the end of "the Marche Militaire in Boogie Woogie"; Alfred "picks up his baton and brings them in safely," then bids his players good-bye until the concert that evening.

As Alfred walks off the rehearsal stage, according to the December 2 script, "he comes face to face with Hugo and the [hotel] detective." The latter asks to see him alone and, reluctantly, Alfred takes him to his dressing room to hear what he has to say. In the ensuing scene, which reads very much as it appears in the film, the detective presents Alfred with a pasted-together version of the report that Alfred had torn up and sent flying into the hall that morning. Extremely angered, Sir Alfred showers the detective with invective, then asks him to light a match, which he uses—while it is still in the hand of the startled detective—to ignite the report. Thrown again into a wastebasket, the burning report sets fire to the room's curtains.

After some hapless fire fighting before the professionals arrive—an interval of farce—Alfred calls Daphne at the dress shop. Distractions at both ends of the line—a fire chief's questions; an acerbic couturier—make communication difficult, but they agree to meet at the restaurant for lunch. Sturges dissolves from the phone call to a shot of Sir Alfred

> entering a fashionable restaurant. He has changed his clothes and carries gloves and stick. We see the street or Rockefeller Plaza or something like that behind him. He hands his hat and stick to an attendant. (page 49)

The film's presentation of the brief restaurant scene is unexpectedly delightful. Negotiating briskly an elegant maze Sir Alfred knows well, Harrison conveys the conductor's pleasure and excitement. The day has been turbulent—plane, August, hotel detective, fire—and Sir Alfred seems to wish for no more than a pleasant lunch with his wife. His sense of honor will not let him, however. Enjoy Daphne's company as he might, he will set off instead, knightlike, to stamp out the last innuendo upon her reputation, even if it is only a document, like hundreds of others, rotting in a detective's files.

In the restaurant Alfred sees Daphne and Tony and, crossing to them, "suddenly he stops as he finds himself passing August and Barbara." Alfred demands to know what they are doing there and why they are not lunching with Daphne and Tony. "We didn't wish to intrude . . . ," August says coldly, still smarting from Alfred's word-lashing that morning. "They looked so cute together," Barbara adds "witchily." "They do look cute together," Alfred agrees, "I'm the one who feels like an intruder . . ." (In the film he says simply: "Why shouldn't they look cute together?") Alfred pats Barbara's cheek—"I'll see you later, pretty one . . ." (The film includes the line but not the pat)—and crosses to Daphne. He kisses her hand, she apologizes for having gone ahead with lunch, and they then discuss why August and Barbara have been so cool. Daphne hasn't the faintest notion why Barbara should behave as she has and asks Tony if he does. Why should Tony have a faint notion, asks Sir Alfred, and Tony, "with the trace of nervousness," agrees he does not. (Tony's telltale nervousness was carried over in the January 15 script but then dropped; it does not appear in the final script or film.)

Daphne asks Alfred about the fire in his dressing room—"What was it, darling . . . a bad review, or something like that?"

SIR ALFRED
Something like that . . . it was very unimportant . . .
(he glares across the room at his brother-in-law)
. . . after all it takes all sorts, I suppose, to make a world . . . you have to take the sour with the sweet.

CLOSE SHOT – AUGUST AND BARBARA

With a forkful of food almost in his mouth August recoils from Sir Alfred's glare, then looks nearsightedly at the forkful of food and recoils from it.

BARBARA
(coolly)
Are you going to eat it or just hold it there.

AUGUST
(coming back to life)
Oh . . .

He pops the forkful of food into his mouth.

SIR ALFRED – DAPHNE AND TONY

SIR ALFRED
(suddenly and furiously)
By Jove!

He slaps the table and rises to his feet.

DAPHNE
(startled as she grabs his sleeve)
What's the matter, darling?

798

SIR ALFRED
Excuse me just one second . . . I'll be right back.

August rises to his feet "as if hoisted by a rope" as he sees the approaching Sir Alfred. Alfred asks August if "those people" (i.e., the detectives) would be apt to have "additional copies of that which I did you know what with this morning . . . because I will not have them around!" August advises him to "forget the whole thing and concentrate on your music"; he will tell them to dispose of those things at the earliest opportunity. Sir Alfred says "viciously" that he will tell them himself and asks for their card—which he is sure August carries around in case of emergency. Alfred takes the card, glances at it, rips it in four, and puts it carefully in his pocket. He returns to Daphne, sits down and tells her that he's just remembered something that he wishes to attend to at once and asks to be excused. Daphne reminds him that he has had nothing to eat and he asks her if she'll be kind enough to have a sandwich for him at the hotel later. Of course she will, she says, ascribing his nerves to the plane flight. In addition to the sandwich she'll have "some beautiful very old scotch," then he can take a hot shower and "then we'll take a nice long nap until it's time to dress for the concert." He tells her he feels better already, rises, kisses her hand and leaves.

The scene at the detective agency begins with Sir Alfred stepping out of a taxicab. "This shot," Sturges notes, "is through a first floor plate-glass window in the type of New York building which was formerly a brownstone front but now has plate-glass store windows on two levels: the basement and the first floor. Backwards on the glass we read (that is those of us who can read backwards, like printers) Sweeney's Detective Agency . . ." (page 55).

The camera, following Sir Alfred's sight line, sees in the window "a sinister face looking down at us while eating a sinister-looking sandwich in a rather sinister way" (page 55). Sir Alfred mistakes the man for Sweeney and, once inside, unloads his invective upon him, saying, "after a long accusing look,"

I suppose you call this . . . a business?
SANDWICH EATER
(truculently)
Well what would you call it?

SIR ALFRED
(furiously and oratorically)
I would call it a criminal invasion of the rights of decent people
. . . an assault upon the very privacy which is the cornerstone of
self-respect . . . an infamous pursuit without shame or ethics, dedi-
cated to the destruction of honor and the substitute for it of all that
is low, bestial and despicable in the human heart . . . a vile calling,
masquerading in the cloak of respectability, but actually sprung
from the cesspools of humanity . . . the seepage of civilization . . .
(page 56)

After more of the same, a furiad without bounds, the man with the sandwich rises and says that he is the tailor from next door who was just there to
eat his lunch—"I mean I was trying to eat my lunch" (page 57)—and answer
the telephone. Sir Alfred has fired his big guns at the wrong target. When the
true Sweeney arrives—"Here he is now climbing," says the tailor—Alfred is
deflated. Another surprise is that Sweeney turns out to be a music-lover and
an ardent fan of Sir Alfred's. His unexpected adulation seizes the initiative of
the exchange and sets Sir Alfred back on his heels. Sweeney concludes a long
litany of praise for Sir Alfred by saying,

> There's you up here
>   (his hand nearly touches the ceiling)
> ... and then ... there's nobody ... no second ... no third ...
> maybe way down here Arturo: a poor fourth. (page 58)

Sir Alfred counterthrusts with an assertion of music's "moral and antisep-
tic powers" which should elevate and purify "its disciples, lifting them out of
and above professions like this ... so spare me your compliments ... the flat-
tery of a footpad is an insult in itself" (page 59). Sweeney perceives soon
enough that "you're just hurt ... I can see it ... you read that report and naturally it upset you ..." and "drops a consoling hand on Sir Alfred's shoulder"
(page 60). Alfred orders his hand off and Sweeney counters:

> Don't get sore at me! What have I got to do with it? I suppose it
> was me that went down to thirty-four-o-six in the middle of the
> night wearing only a negligee and stayed for thirty-eight minutes
> ... I suppose that's the part that bothered you ... it usually is ...
> (page 60)

It is evident from Sir Alfred's reaction that he has not read the report, so
Sweeney hands him the only copy, which Alfred slowly tears to bits. When
he returns home—after, we learn later, having seen a double feature at a
moviehouse—he is very short with Daphne. He takes the sandwich she has
prepared and the Scotch, goes into his study and closes the door. After a moment he steps into the hallway, looking at the numbers on the doors. When he
comes to 3406 and knocks, Tony's voice bids him enter. Sir Alfred goes in,
walks around the apartment, looks out the window, looks at the bathroom,
looks at the bed, and leaves without saying a thing. The two pages that
conclude this sequence chronicle the increasingly strained relations between
Daphne and Sir Alfred. Daphne's exit from his study—she slams the door
after her—is followed by a shot of Sir Alfred

> looking after her. He snorts and continues unbuttoning his shirt.
> Suddenly he stops, crosses the room violently to the desk contain-
> ing the revolver, snatches the sandwich off the plate and bites into

*Sir Alfred tears up the last report as the admiring
detective looks on: Edgar Kennedy (his last role)
and Rex Harrison.*

it viciously. He washes it down with a big gulp of whiskey and
soda.

FADE OUT

The next scene, following a FADE IN, begins with a "HIGH CAMERA
SHOT" down on the concert hall where Sir Alfred is about to conduct his
orchestra.

All versions of what became *Unfaithfully Yours* divide into two parts at
this point—the preconcert events on the one hand and the concert and postconcert events on the other. The belief in his wife's betrayal that Alfred arrives at in the preconcert day leads to his fantasies at the concert that night.
The 1933 story had what we might call a single-stage process of arousing Sir
Alfred's jealousy (i.e., he pulls an incriminating letter out of his wife's handbag). In his October–November 1947 notes and drafts, Sturges had worked
toward a two-stage process through which the jealousy results: Sir Alfred's
contamination by the innately suspicious August and then his discovery of
some physical evidence to corroborate his doubts. Considered in retrospect,
the plan was dubious to begin with, requiring as it did an overly rapid, overly

convenient confirmation of Alfred's suspicions. Indeed, Sturges never quite got to the second stage in his draft scenes. The first stage too was gradually undermined as Alfred's dislike of August grew with each succeeding draft— until he seems determined to resist *any* August influence, let alone assume his predisposition to jealousy.

More fundamentally, the problem with the two-stage model was the developing character of Sir Alfred himself. In the 1933 story and the early 1947 notes, his character was still unspecified, hence the emphasis in those texts on sheer plot device, particularly on the means by which Sir Alfred comes to suspect his wife. However, as the character of Alfred evolved, his ethical standards rose and his devotion to his wife increased. Thus Sir Alfred is appalled at the investigation of Daphne by detectives and refuses to read their report. Indeed he goes to great lengths to destroy any extant copy. It is only through the loquacity of an unexpectedly admiring detective that he learns its essential content. Thus the mechanism through which Sir Alfred's jealousy is finally aroused is now rooted in his character. As for Sturges's earlier goal of "gain[ing] length . . . by making it not quite so easy to find out what his wife has done to him," that too is no longer accomplished by external circumstances but by Sir Alfred's refusal to doubt his wife's loyalty.

Sturges's 1933 story was schematic and somewhat gimmicky. The idea of a conductor having three fantasies about his wife while playing three pieces of music is a plot concept that takes little more than a sentence or two to outline. In his 1947 work Sturges recognizes immediately that the story needed fleshing out and that characterizations had to be provided for the ciphers who propelled its plot. What Sturges did between October 15, 1947—when he took his first note on the project—and February 23, 1948—when he made the final changes to his final script—went well beyond such minimal requirements. He developed the characters of Alfred and Daphne and their relationship; he revealed Daphne's "infidelity" not all at once but in oscillations of Alfred's belief and disbelief; he postponed Alfred's suspicions for half the film by relaying the information he refuses through brother-in-law, house detective, and private detective; and he filled in—lovingly—the details of Alfred's work as a conductor and of orchestral music-making more generally. These were incremental changes, gradually achieved, that eventually became a transformation. In the process, a rather disembodied project on music's power to shape fantasy became a project on a troubled day in the life of a celebrated conductor. The concert fantasies remain the focus of the final script but the lines that converge there are far longer and more complex than those of the story. The fantasies themselves are richer and more resonant because they now concern multifaceted characters. Each episode becomes, in effect, a different page on which the relationship between Alfred and Daphne might be written.

*   *   *

The 1933 story devotes 4 1/2 pages to the preconcert events and 14 1/2 pages to the concert and postconcert events. The December 2 script devotes 82 pages to the preconcert events and 79 pages to the concert and postconcert events. Coming between the story and the screenplay were the October–November 1947 notes and drafts, which were devoted almost exclusively to reinventing the preconcert events—a process in which the 1933 story played little part.

By contrast, the concert and postconcert events changed rather little from the 1933 story to the final film. Retained by all subsequent versions were the story's three concert fantasies, Alfred's farcical attempts to put them into practice after the concert, and the concluding reconciliation between Alfred and Daphne. In expanding the story's 14 1/2 pages to 79 pages, the December 2 script fleshed out the story's treatment and added many details—the newly complex characters of Alfred and Daphne required this. (With a few exceptions, including the reconciliation scene and the third fantasy episode, those 79 pages were carried over virtually unchanged in the January 15 and February 10 scripts.)

There were other changes as well. A note Sturges took on October 18 reverses the order of the first two fantasies, putting the murder first and the forgiveness and check-writing second. This order, which was followed by all script versions and the film, proved to be definitive. Also, in place of the story's murder-suicide, the December 2 script substitutes Alfred's proposing a game of Russian roulette to Tony—the survivor to win Daphne. Alfred takes the first spin, which turns out to be fatal, and the episode ends.

The film's most spectacular effect—the camera's apparent passage through Sir Alfred's eye as each concert fantasy begins—is described quite explicitly in the 1933 story (see page 766 above). The December 2 screenplay added a number of further subtleties to this effect and to the concert fantasies more generally. Consider its description of the first episode.

> Now after a pause the CAMERA PUSHES IN until his eyes, eyebrows and nose fill the screen. After this we PUSH IN still closer until one eye fills the screen and finally so close that the pupil of one eye, which is to say blackness, fills the screen. Now that we are in Sir Alfred's mind a very, very slow FADE IN begins and we find ourselves in Sir Alfred's study on a CLOSE-UP of the antique village orchestra clock. It comes to 11:30. There is a whirring sound and the leader beats out the first eleven notes of Jingle Bells. The sound of the orchestra is not abated much but the bells probably cut through all right.

Sturges describes Alfred and Daphne—just returned from the concert—walking through the door, down the hall, and into Sir Alfred's study.

> Daphne comes to a stop a foot ahead of her husband and looks ahead nervously . . . probably a little guiltily. Sir Alfred, behind her, rolls his

eyes toward her without turning his head, like an actor playing an Oriental. Daphne does not look quite the same as the last time we saw her. Her make-up is a little more obvious . . . Her eyes more heavily beaded. She seems to have very much less character than before. She speaks only when spoken to. She does not seem to move of her own vo- lition. She looks cheaper. She looks like an unfaithful wife. Sir Alfred, on the other hand, looks, if anything, handsomer than before. Any little defects he may have had are gone. Slowly he removes his coat and muf- fler then takes Daphne's fur coat from her shoulders. This seems to bring her to life.

DAPHNE
(with a big smile)
Thank you, darling.

Sturges's descriptions reveal how far his sense of the concert fantasies had developed since the 1933 story. That sense is further elucidated by a cover letter that accompanied the transmittal of the December 2 script to a Mrs. Jungmeyer, who apparently worked in Fox's story department, perhaps as its head.

The "prospect scenes" (we looked it up in the dictionary and this seems to be the op- posite of "retrospect") are of course written by Sir Alfred himself which is why he does not bother to give anyone else a line or even a movement. I presume that will come through to the audience.

In that he controls the demeanor of his fantasy figures—their performances, as it were—Sir Alfred is not only the writer but the writer-director of his fantasies.

Alfred's farcical attempts to put his three fantasies into practice grew from three pages in the 1933 story to what is in all three screenplay versions a twenty-three-page comic set piece (see pages 123–145). Because of space lim- itations, a comparison of the script and film versions of this passage must be omitted here.

The final postconcert event is the reconciliation of Daphne and Alfred. A scene devoted to this event provides the ending for the 1933 story, for all three script versions, and for the film. The December 2 script is the only version whose ending adheres to the story's ending. In both cases it is not Daphne but her sister who is having an affair with the rival the conductor sus- pects. In the story Daphne's sister has hidden Tito's note to her in her sister's handbag, where Alfred finds it. In the December 2 script, the matter is more complicated.

Despite Alfred's bizarre behavior after the concert, Daphne confides to him that she is terribly worried. While Alfred was in England, August called her at 1:30 one night to ask if Barbara was with her. Daphne had suspicions about Barbara and told August, incorrectly, that Barbara had been with her until moments ago. Daphne then hurried down to Tony's room—"3406," says Alfred "in a strange voice." At first Tony did not want to let her in, but could not leave her in the hall, so he let her in—where she found Barbara. Daphne told her younger sister "to get the heck out of there," that August had called and that she'd told him Barbara had just left. "And so," Daphne continues, "she put on her . . . things and . . . just before she went out I had a hunch . . . I got on a chair and looked out the transom with a mirror, and there was a big jerk peeking around the corner near the back elevator . . ." "Sweeney!" says Sir Alfred "in a strangely contented voice." Daphne then relates that they waited and waited—"thirty-eight minutes," says Alfred. When some people came down the hall, the detective "went back near the elevator and I shoved Barbara out the door . . . and then I told Tony what I thought of him and left . . ."

Alfred is so delighted to find that Daphne was loyal to him that he suggests they go to "the vulgarest, most ostentatious, loudest and hardest to get into establishment that this city affords" and, once there, that they consume "magnums of champagne." He also asks her to do him a great favor.

> Would you put on your lowest cut and most vulgarly ostentatious
> gown . . . and the largest and vulgarest jewels that you possess.
> (page 151)

On December 9, Zanuck wrote a three-page memo to Sturges praising the December 2 script but noting, among other things, that "we have a censorship problem":

(a) We cannot indicate that Barbara has actually had an affair with Tony.
(b) We cannot indicate that she has actually gone to his bedroom at the hotel unless we prove to the audience and the censors that she went there for a nightcap or a little indiscreet flirtation.

Specifically to be eliminated is the dialogue in which Daphne tells Alfred she is worried about Barbara—"the audience may wonder why she hasn't told him more." Also, "Sir Alfred condones the illicit romance by permitting Tony, his secretary, to remain in his employ even though Tony has been involved with his wife's sister."

Also, Zanuck continues,

the Catholic Church Legion of Decency is concentrating on a campaign against divorce and immorality. As a matter of fact they will object strenuously to this story on one point alone and this is the fact that Sir Alfred has been married five times. They will also pick on any number of little lines or pieces of business that may tend to indicate that we treat marriage or marriage laws lightly. In order to get our theme accepted we must be practical and shrewd enough to avoid all of the little things that offend them. Thus by doing so we could manage to squeeze through our basic theme. If, however, on one hand we show that Daphne is virtuous and innocent but her sister, Barbara, is promiscuous, then we haven't got a chance.

"So that we do not invite trouble," Zanuck continues, he asked Colonel (Jason S.) Joy (Fox's liaison with the censors) not to submit this present script to the Breen Office. "I would rather make our own corrections first and get out the new version and then have our battle on it." Zanuck's advisories, which were probably based upon a preliminary evaluation by Joy, accurately reflected Breen Office standards of that time. References to, even strong hints of a Barbara-Tony affair had to go, as did Alfred's "Five Marriages" speech and other references to his earlier marriages. Sturges accomplished these tasks, apparently easily and apparently without serious damage to the project, in his second script draft of January 15, 1948, which was duly submitted to the Breen Office. The latter's official report, dated January 23, was one and a half pages long, short by Sturges standards, and on the whole rather mild: deletion of two references to Alfred's multiple marriages that Sturges had not caught; elimination of Alfred's response to Daphne's list of what they will do when they get home—"And then what?"—as "overly sex suggestive"; the usual reminders on "intimate parts of the body—specifically the breasts of women" being "fully covered at all times"; a warning against "unduly prolonged" kisses "that might prove offensive in the finished picture," et cetera.

Zanuck had obliquely raised the issue of length in his December 9 memo:

I believe you will get most of your footage out of the earlier sections. All of it is very amusing and delightful and I had the impression that we were slow getting started. I am sure this tightening up will be easily and adroitly accomplished.

Zanuck may have hoped that Sturges would shorten the script on his own but the second draft, finished January 15, cut only two pages from the December 2 draft: from 161 to 159 pages. From the script's opening, zoned by Zanuck for reduction, Sturges had cut only three pages—the rehearsal scene starts at page 39 rather than 42. Zanuck wrote Sturges on January 20 that he was as enthusiastic as ever about the project and believed it improved, but "there is no question but what we are considerably over-length . . . I am sure that you will agree with me that some definite cuts will have to be made." The next day Zanuck wrote Sturges again, referring to a footage estimate of the script that was being prepared:

I am certain . . . it will reveal that *The Symphony Story* in its present form is about three or four thousand feet overlength. In the good old days this would not have bothered me but under the economic conditions of today it presents an impossible barrier. . . . Today even a great picture that costs too much money does not break even. . . . I think we should aim toward getting twenty or twenty-five pages out of the script. I can see an elimination of fifteen pages that I believe will drop out readily and improve the mood and tempo of the film. Perhaps a shrinkage of dialogue will account for the balance.

On January 23 Zanuck sent Sturges a copy of the script with passages crossed out and comments typed in. These include, Zanuck says in a cover note, a number of my suggested eliminations and also my impressions of certain episodes in the story. . . . My eliminations were made as a result, not only of the budget and the footage chart but also as a result of my feelings about the tempo of the picture as a whole. I believe that many of the cuts that I have suggested should be made even if we had no cost problem. I hope you agree with me.

The entire second part of the rehearsal scene, in which Alfred has the orchestra play a classical piece in boogie-woogie, was one of Zanuck's longest cross-outs (five and one half pages); he accompanied it with these typed-in remarks: "If we cannot reduce the budget we must drop this entire episode," which is very good "but it has no story content and it is an extravagance we cannot afford." Sturges acceded, in this instance, to Zanuck's wishes; in the final script and film, the end of the orchestra's run-through of an overture to be played that evening is the end of the rehearsal sequence itself.

Sturges wrote and submitted his final script, as the dates on its pages indicate, in two parts: 54 pages on February 10, 1948; the rest, 100 pages, on February 13. Zanuck wrote Sturges on the 10th:

I read the new version up to page 54. I think the cuts are wonderful. I do not think they hurt the story at all, as a matter of fact I think they improve not only the tempo but the mood.

Zanuck's note was virtually an OK to go ahead with production—which was to begin February 18—on the script as it stood.

On February 13, Sturges wrote Gaston Glass of Fox:

Herewith the balance of the script. Please tell Molly Mandaville that it is now in 10,800 feet and that I think it is wise not to hold up the mimeographing any longer. I will get the last 300 feet out as quickly as I can, if possible before I start shooting, but in any case in plenty of time to prevent my shooting something which will afterwards not be used.

On February 18, having read the balance of the final script, Zanuck wrote Sturges a two-page letter praising the "eliminations" that had been made but recommending further cuts and revisions. Most of these reiterate earlier suggestions that Sturges had ignored. Zanuck recommends trimming pages 16–19—Tony's list of the people who want to see Sir Alfred and the latter's witty responses. What Zanuck really seems to object to is the children's orchestra gag (pages 18–19), "the least amusing of the five various comedy items you use in this sequence." Zanuck also feels, though he did not cite page numbers "that we have entirely too much at Madame Lalotte's":

Here again it is not a question of footage but I feel that something is retarding us. It is a question perhaps of only a few speeches. But I am anxious to get to the next story point.

Zanuck's major objections, however, have to do with (1) the Porthaul, Michigan story that Alfred tells Daphne on pages 13–15, which he feels needs trimming; and (2) "the third retrospect episode," as he calls it, in which Alfred fantasizes Russian roulette between himself and Tony as Daphne looks on. Zanuck's typed-in note to the January 15 draft had called for the episode's total elimination:

It is my opinion that we are compelled to lose one "dream" episode — it is the only way we can come within the budget and the footage requirements. Also, I have the feeling that three episodes wear thin. The first episode, of course, is the best, by far. I like the second episode next best, but it is the most expensive [because of the interpolated Porthaul scene]. However, if we can drop the third episode I suppose we can afford the second. But one must go, and personally I believe the story will be improved thereby.

By the time he had read the (February 10) final script, as his February 18 letter shows, Zanuck had softened: "I liked the idea immensely but I believe this sequence will be benefitted if it is further trimmed." Despite Sturges's improvements, Zanuck still felt:

you will benefit if you boil down further . . . particularly the dialogue that comes just ahead of the challenge to fight Tony. . . . I am not thinking of footage in making this urgent recommendation. I feel that an elimination will be highly beneficial if we can come to the point of the scene very quickly because by now the audience will accept an abbreviation because we have already set the pattern with the previous retrospects. Any further dilly-dallying, no matter how amusingly written, will prove to be a delay. Of this I am convinced.

On February 23—his last work on the final script—Sturges rewrote episode three. His four replacement pages (117–120/121), called "blue" pages, greatly sharpened the entire episode, shortening the earlier version by one page and "pointing" its dialogue. Zanuck responded the same day: "I read the new blue pages that came through based on the shortened scenes and I think the cuts are excellent." Sturges saved the third episode, chiefly, by improving it. Zanuck's desire to cut one episode, apparently not a bluff, strains musical credibility. Sturges's program—two overtures and a medium-length tone poem (Tchaikovsky's *Francesca da Rimini*)—hardly makes an evening as it is. A concert consisting of two overtures is unconvincing—little more than a joke.

Unfaithfully Yours became the official name of the project on February 10, eight days before shooting started. Zanuck wrote Sturges on that day: "It looks like we have got the title cleared on *Unfaithfully Yours*. Therefore the revised version of the *Symphony Story* should be mimeographed under the title *Unfaithfully Yours*." Zanuck's communiqués to Sturges during shooting were, relative to his usual outpouring, rather few. He wrote Sturges on February 20 that the first day's shooting was well acted—"both Rex and Linda played it well" and "the tempo was brisk and lively," but

frankly I was slightly disappointed in the quality of the photography. It did not seem to be rich enough. I felt their faces were on the brown side. There didn't seem to be

Daphne as mask in the first prospect of UNFAITHFULLY YOURS: Linda Darnell and Rex Harrison.

quite enough sparkle and life to the scene. It all appeared rather gray and a sort of dark gray. It is my belief that this picture must reek with brilliance. By this I do not mean that everything should be lit up but it should have a plush and rich feeling. What was your impression?

Zanuck's question was perhaps less "What is your view?" than "What are you up to that you shouldn't be?" Sturges wrote back the same day:

I agree with you entirely about the necessity for sparkle in the photography in the comedy parts of *Unfaithfully Yours,* and I am reasonably certain that we have that in the negative. I felt also that the print was a touch on the dark side. This matter has already been corrected.

Nevertheless, Zanuck wrote Sturges again on February 27:

I am not at all happy about the photography. I think it is very spotty and uneven. At times Rex looks muddy and dirty, and while it is not totally bad I certainly do not believe it measures up to the standard of the photography of our other pictures in this category on the lot.

Sturges distinguishes the comedy parts of the picture from, implicitly, its noncomedy parts, which surely include, at a minimum, the concert fantasies.

809

Zanuck, on the contrary, sees the picture as undividedly belonging to a certain filmic category—traditional sophisticated comedy perhaps—that must receive a standard and undifferentiated visual treatment (i.e., "reek with brilliance" and "have a plush and rich feeling"). It does seem to occur to Zanuck that sophisticates like Alfred and Daphne may not wish to reek with anything and may pointedly eschew as well "a plush and rich feeling." It is questionable whether Zanuck entirely understood the project, which might be considered a romantic comedy gone sour or a *film noir* with comedy and farce.

Zanuck's February 27 letter did not limit itself to cinematography but also included the Sturges-owned domain of pace:

> I still believe that you are playing the long scene too fast. I refer to the master scene between Rudy Vallee and Rex Harrison. I noticed that when you took the closeups you deliberately slowed the action down by at least 20% and in my opinion the close shots are much more effective than the rapid long shots for the simple reason that you have a chance to digest what the actors are saying. The tempo in the long shot is so rapid that you get the feeling that it is nothing but talk, talk, talk, and it comes so rapidly you have no chance to completely appreciate the fine quality of the dialogue. . . . This does not mean that I do not like the scene. I only wish it was all taken at the same tempo as the close shots. When dialogue comes so rapidly it sounds more like a rapid recital than actually a scene between two people.

Zanuck's calling for more footage was a novelty but not one that Sturges savored. Five days later, on March 3—1948 was a leap year—Sturges wrote to Zanuck:

> I have just sent over to your projection room the early scenes of UNFAITHFULLY YOURS exactly as I would have cut them had we not had a meeting the day before yesterday and had you not voiced any fears concerning part of the casting. In other words, I have left out those jokes and setups which did not come off, left in those that did and kept the camera on that part of the set which seemed most interesting at the moment.
>
> I sincerely hope the film will speak more convincingly for itself than any arguments I could advance, that your confidence in me will be to some extent restored and that for the sake both of this film, and for my very necessary authority with the people I work with, if I am to be of any value to this company, that you will reconsider what sounded very much like a pre-judgment and let me continue with an easy heart in the making of a film that should do us all a little good.

Sturges's note kept Zanuck off his back for what must have seemed an eternity of uninterrupted work—seventeen days. In the meantime Sturges had shot, among other things, footage of the orchestra's playing music—for the rehearsal scene and for the three concert pieces. This process allowed Sturges to thank Alfred Newman, Fox's brilliant and multitalented music director, for "the beautiful job that you so kindly did for me in conducting the *Semiramide* and *Tannhauser* Overtures. . . . I cannot tell you how thrilled and grateful I am." Writing to Sturges on March 20, however, Zanuck was not pleased:

Zanuck didn't get it: film noir style in UNFAITHFULLY YOURS, figure 1. The conductor as villain: Rex Harrison as Sir Alfred de Carter.

I am, of course, delighted by the humor you have managed to get into the musical numbers. I also note, however, that from being more than one day ahead of schedule you are now approximately a day and a half behind schedule having unfortunately lost this time in the musical numbers. I assume you have worked out ways and means of picking up the lost time from here on. I am now certainly glad that we eliminated the boogie-woogie number if for no reason than the element of time and cost.

Are you possibly going to be able to use twenty per cent of the material you have shot in the musical numbers? I am certain that you have some editorial scheme in mind.

Harrison's conducting is magnificent and I think it is the best photography we have had so far in the picture.

Sturges replied on March 22, thanking him for the nice things said in his note and assuring him the day and a half would be made up without difficulty.

As to the footage shot in the various setups of Mr. Harrison and the musicians, it is re-grettably necessary in each setup to include the whole section we are using so that the cutters may have the freedom to go to any angle they need at any measure of the piece.

I am reasonably certain that I have made no unnecessary setups, but it is typical of this type of sequence that each cut has to be longer than usual.

Film noir style in UNFAITHFULLY YOURS, *figure 2.
Daphne (Linda Darnell) before the murder,
already fragmented.*

Again, my congratulations on your well-merited triumphs of Saturday night. [Academy Awards for *Gentleman's Agreement*: Best Picture, Best Director (Kazan), Best Supporting Actress (Celeste Holm).]

Sturges probably finished shooting on April 20, as a number of sources suggest, but assembling a rough cut, including the trick shots into Harrison's face and a preliminary sound dub, seems to have taken another two weeks. In any case, the film was screened for Zanuck for the first time on May 5. In a letter the next day, Zanuck congratulated Sturges "for last night."

Film noir style in UNFAITHFULLY YOURS, *figure 3. Sir Alfred (Rex Harrison) about to break a phonograph record after the murder of Daphne.*

It is an excellent picture in every respect. Whether or not it is completely a commercial picture in these peculiar box office days . . . Perhaps our story is too brilliant or our aim is too high but in any event your job is excellent in each and every category.

We spent too much money on the picture. We shot a week longer than we should have. We should have paid more attention to the footage chart as the final picture was even longer than the footage estimating department said it would be . . .

I had a chance to reflect on the picture and I am sure that all of the cutting suggestions that I made last night should be followed. I have also had a chance to discuss it informally with some of the boys who saw it last night and I am passing the following things along to you.

(a) Everyone thought the first rehearsal music should be used in a shorter version. It was excellent but overdrawn.

(b) No one had any real liking for the Porthaul, Michigan episode. They all admitted that it has laughs but they believe the comedy song is so out of key with the rest of the picture that it actually might have the effect of spoiling the overall flavor of perfection. One by one the boys brought up this particular point. I know you are going to try to boil it down and I will be anxious to see it when you have got it down to length as

813

this seems to me to be the one place we went completely out of character and got from gentle satire to broad burlesque.

(c) Everyone feels that we are absolutely marking time until Rudy Vallee has his first scene with Rex and that it is essential that we lose every second we can up to this point.

A Sturges letter on May 7 thanked Zanuck "for your most courteous, charming and encouraging letter" but noted, "I presume that part of the job of being the head of a great studio consists of telling the directors that they could have done it in half the time if they had really put their can to the grindstone, or however the metaphor goes, so I do not hold it against you. I normally work seventeen hours a day but will try to do more in the future." "Seriously speaking," Sturges continued in a new paragraph,

your letter made me very happy, and I hope Unfaithfully Yours will be merely the first of a series of successes, both commercial and pride-satisfying, for your excellent company.

The cutting is proceeding well, and I have come upon some methods for shortening the scenes we felt needed shortening without losing those parts of them which I believe do good to the picture.

Zanuck wrote back on May 10 explaining his remark about shooting a week too long on the picture.

I am sure you will be the first to agree that it is a very good thing we eliminated certain sequences, such as the Boogie-Woogie rehearsal sequence and other costly items. The present length of our picture clearly indicates that we could also have dispensed with certain sequences that we wanted to cut but which for one reason or another we left in the script. These items probably consumed the better part of a week's work. . . . It is not part of my job as the head of a studio to tell every producer or director that he did a good job but could have done it quicker. As our association lengthens you will learn that I make a habit of not kidding myself or my associates. UY is an excellent picture in every respect. It is also entirely out of line from the standpoint of cost. In these very precarious box office days I do not think that we are entitled to make a comedy drama that assembles in more than 13,000 feet, and therein lies the so-called "added week" I was referring to in my previous note. . . . If you are unable to make all of the cuts that we discussed when I ran the picture please let me know because then I will want to run the picture again before we do another dubbing job before we get it ready for a sneak preview. If, however, you have been able to make all of the cuts then I do not need to see it again before we are ready for the sneak preview.

Sturges replied the next day:

Thank you very much indeed for your note of May 10th. The cutting is proceeding well and the cuts will all be completed in time for the preview.

I am delighted to report that the Sersen Department [Fred Sersen, Fox's special effects man] has come through with four of the most magnificent shots I have ever seen, and I have been looking at pictures for some time, commencing with The Great Train Robbery at a children's birthday party in 1903 at Green Lake, Wisconsin. I believe you will be as thrilled with these shots as I am. They are probably the most important shots in the picture, being those in which we go into Sir Alfred's mind and on one occasion return from it.

Considering the length of the picture in the first assembly: I sincerely do not believe the script was much too long. Considerable attention was paid to the Production Department estimate. What happened was that I, like most directors, was tempted on the set to enlarge and embellish some of the scenes, as opportunities presented themselves, gaining thereby some laughs and some beauty but also, unfortunately, some footage. I think it is all going to come out pretty nicely, however, financially and otherwise.

I have two terrific new titles, one for Miss Grable and one for somebody else, but I don't dare tell them to you for fear you will register them in the name of Twentieth Century-Fox, whereas they are actually my own personal property having occurred to me in the gents' room at the Players.

The preview was set for June 3 in Riverside, California. On May 27, Sturges asked Zanuck's permission to bring to the preview, among others, Edwin Gillette to take a laugh meter reading. Zanuck replied the same day that he never used "a laugh meter or other mechanical contraption in editing a film," but he had no objection to Sturges's doing so and "fully approve[d]" the rest of Sturges's guest list also.

Zanuck wrote Sturges that day, "Here's wishing you very good luck for tonight. I will see you at the theatre after the preview is over. In discussing the reaction of the audience I would like to talk exclusively with you and the film cutter. We will use the manager's office. I told Lew Schreiber to tell you that in my opinion it would be a great error to dedicate the film to anyone." As no other reference to a proposed dedication of *Unfaithfully Yours* is found in the Sturges papers, it remains a mystery, as does the identity of the dedicatee.

The morning after the preview, Zanuck wrote Sturges a letter marked CONFIDENTIAL:

There were 94 walk-outs last night. This does not include the ones that walked out and returned. The walk-outs occurred as follows: A small number left at the start of the first concert number, a larger group left at the start of the second concert number, but the largest group of all left at the conclusion of the second concert number and before the third concert number started.

In talking with the manager today, who called me, he feels after talking with his customers that everyone loved the comedy values in the picture and thought that it was as funny as *Sitting Pretty* which was also previewed at this theatre. The only complaints were on the over-all length of the picture and, of course, the musical numbers. These really seemed to stop the picture completely like an extraneous song in a musical. The only other criticisms concerned the serious part of the love story. They loved the comedy love scenes, but when Harrison got romantic in a serious vein and became rather poetic, they felt that this was out of key with the wonderful humorous spirit of the whole picture.

We must realize, just in confidence, that audiences to date have accepted Rex as a wonderful actor, but as a character man, and I believe this is the reason that last night they razzed him every time he put on the heavy love look. Of course by eliminating entirely the Michigan episode we cut out the worst part of this.

I will look forward to seeing it on Wednesday with all the cuts made.

On June 7, Zanuck forwarded to Sturges additional preview cards that had arrived in the mail. Zanuck noted that people either enthused about the film or detested it. "It is my opinion," he concluded, "that the length of the picture, the repetition and the long dull spot in the middle were primarily responsible for the majority of the critical cards. I am certain that editing will remedy this problem."

Zanuck wrote Sturges on June 11:

At my request, the Cutting Department was to give me this morning information on the length of the picture that I would see tonight. I was advised to date that only 1100 ft. had been eliminated from the film. If this figure is incorrect, I am sorry.

The picture was previewed in 2 hours and 6 minutes. To bring it in the neighborhood of 1 hour and 45 minutes, which was the time we agreed upon, meant of course the elimination of approximately 21 minutes of footage.

We now face a release problem. A picture of this size must inevitably be in the hands of the advertising and sales department eight weeks prior to the pre-release date.

I am certain we can finish up the picture in its entirety tonight and be able to turn it over for final score and re-recording no later than Monday.

Later on the 11th, Zanuck wrote Sturges another letter marked CONFI-DENTIAL:

I am extremely disappointed to learn that we have eliminated only 1200 ft. since the preview. After the reaction in Riverside it is, in my opinion and also the opinion of the public that we previewed, at least twenty minutes overlength.

Because this has been primarily your undertaking I have allowed you to take more time on the editing of this film than on any other film in the history of 20th Century-Fox—I would say more time by 300%. We are now facing a deadline on the release problem. Under these circumstances it is therefore necessary that I assume the responsibility for the further editing of the picture.

I intend to complete the cutting job on the film tonight and turn it over tomorrow to the music and re-recording department for the final job.

There is no dialogue continuity for *Unfaithfully Yours* in the Sturges papers, so it is difficult to know exactly (1) what Sturges shot; (2) what he included in his two-hour, six-minute preview version; and (3) what he removed in the 1,300 feet that he took out before Zanuck took control of the editing. Without this information, it is difficult to gauge exactly the effects of Zanuck's cuts. What we do have for comparison are Sturges's final script and the release version of the film, and Zanuck's statements of what he wished cut. The latter are especially useful since Zanuck made each point on at least two occasions and, in Sturges's case at any rate, never seems to have changed his mind on any of them. (Useful as it is, however, a dialogue continuity has no information about nondialogue scenes, especially important in the music passages of *Unfaithfully Yours,* or about the length, images, and editing patterns of the scenes whose dialogue it records.)

As Zanuck said in his May 6 letter, he wished to "lose every second" until Rudy Vallee has his first scene with Rex—"everyone feels that we are absolutely marking time . . . up to this point." Zanuck had expressed a similar judgment in his typed-in comments in the January 15 script: "It is my opinion we must cut everything we can until the plot starts—and the plot does not start to work for us until August arrives in the next episode." The consistency of Zanuck's remarks over nearly four months shows his clarity of mind but also makes one wonder about the "everyones" who agree with him. One recalls in this respect the title of Mel Gussow's biography of Zanuck: *Don't Say Yes until I Finish Talking.*

Zanuck stresses narrative not only as *a* value but as the supreme value in Hollywood filmmaking. I discussed above the transformation of the project from the 1933 story's plot-centeredness to the script's emphasis on character—what might be called "Alfred's Day." Sturges had never done a project like this before, just as he had never before made a film lasting two hours and six minutes. *Unfaithfully Yours* was the experiment he made at this juncture of his career just as *The Great McGinty* and *Sullivan's Travels* and *The Miracle of Morgan's Creek* were at others. More than most directors, Sturges was constantly changing—his only surprise is not to surprise us. Despite its length, *Unfaithfully Yours* did not require a leisurely pace; Zanuck rankled at the breakneck speed of the Alfred-August exchange. At that point and elsewhere in the film, Harrison was obliged to spit out his lines at a speed not required of him by Shaw or Coward. At stake in the film was not only pace but an expanded scale of relevant detail: the variety and range of Alfred's experience, including his roller coaster emotional states, the many and diverse characters he encounters, and his distinctive reactions to each, including Harrison's amazing variations in mood and in vocal pitch and rhythm. Each of Zanuck's cuts reduced the variety and range of Alfred's experience and of our sense of him, Daphne, and the other characters.

The reader can see what was cut from the script before August's arrival by comparing it to the finished film. The brief scene with reporters at the airport was eliminated—Alfred is a celebrity and it is plausible that he be interviewed. He has just returned from England, so—in all script versions—he is questioned and responds on the subject of England. In the final film, however, he is just said to have returned from England and it is left at that. When Daphne and he fight about her many dresses and the poverty of English women, it seems to come out of the blue. Even the children's orchestra gag (pages 18–19), admittedly unfunny in itself, shows us a sour Sir Alfred and thereby gives us a fuller picture of him.

Zanuck almost surely reduced the length of the rehearsal scene. May 6: "everyone thought the first rehearsal music should be used in a shorter version. It was excellent but overdrawn." March 20: "Are you possibly going to use twenty per cent of the material you have shot in the musical numbers?" The last, Zanuck said following the June 3 preview, "really seemed to stop the picture completely." How much music-making Sturges included in his two-hour, six-minute version we will probably never know. Sturges makes high and exhilarating drama of the rehearsal footage we see: that he let the tension lapse in the rest seems unlikely. Even if the rehearsal went on and on, burned a hole in the screen, it might be esteemed by modern viewers as fascinating "excess."

Zanuck's intention to cut the Porthaul, Michigan episode was clear and multisignaled. Sturges, it must be admitted, refused to listen. Why had he, by the way, included both Alfred's telling the Porthaul story to Daphne early in the film and a full-scale filming of it for the second fantasy episode? In addition to its importance to Sir Alfred himself, perhaps Sturges meant it to be a kind of control upon the second fantasy episode. If the Porthaul passage appeared in the episode without prior reference, the viewer might doubt its actuality—perhaps Alfred is fantasizing this "past" of the couple as well as its immediate future. This seems to confirm Zanuck's position—either both Porthauls or neither—but the briefest early reference would have sufficed to establish the incident's objective status. The finished film retains only a fleeting Porthaul reference, which now just hangs there with no place to go.

As written, the Porthaul sequence has no clear tonality; all would depend upon how it was directed, which, unfortunately, we will probably never know. After his and Hugo's initial consternation at the flood-stalled train, Alfred might have found himself on a wonderful, even dreamlike adventure, heading out in a duckboat with the suddenly appearing Baldwin man into the unknown. Even the amateur musicale they come to might be presented as magically strange rather than farcical. This would make the discovery of Daphne the extension and capstone of the dream, with Alfred a kind of sleepwalker through it all. Sturges's more usual method, it is true, would be to play it as a combination of high verbal comedy and farce.

Zanuck's remarks suggest that it was shot this way. He wrote Sturges on May 6 that "no one had any real liking for the Porthaul, Michigan episode" but then concentrated his criticisms on a small detail—what he calls the episode's "comedy song," which is presumably the following:

A fat seventeen-year-old coloratura. She is accompanied by her mother, also very fat, who is giving the Baldwin quite a thumping. Before each high note her face takes on a desperate expression.

Zanuck's reference is somewhat ambiguous—probably just the song, but possibly the Porthaul episode as a whole is "out of character"; the film here goes "from gentle satire to broad burlesque," "spoiling the overall flavor of perfection." Three brief notes Sturges took on February 21, a day after shooting had begun, suggest an even more farcical treatment of the passage than appears in the script:

While Jimmy Conlin [the Baldwin man] tries to row the boat he falls into the water and Stander reaches in after him.

Stander [Hugo] has to push boat because Conlin drops oar, suddenly Stander steps into a hole and disappears below water level.

While boat goes along we see a crate with a cat on it floating by as well as tops of mail boxes and picket fences.

Whether these jottings were incorporated into the passage during shooting is not clear.

When he wrote Sturges on June 4—the morning after the preview—Zanuck raised a different point. The audience—which not only thought like Zanuck but wrote like him—"loved the comedy love scenes, but when Harrison got romantic in a serious vein and became rather poetic, they felt that this was out of key with the wonderful humorous spirit of the whole picture." Zanuck's next remark—"they razzed him every time he put on the heavy love look"— at last sounds something like a forties audience and it touches on a real problem: how does any actor convey what Sturges asks here—instantaneous, life-transforming love at first glance?

Farce the Porthaul episode almost certainly had, and this has structural implications for the film as a whole. The dressing room fire and subsequent hosing of everyone in sight is the film's only farcical episode until Alfred's postconcert attempt to act out his fantasies. Some farce between these points—in the second episode's Porthaul sequence—might have made the other farce passages seem less isolated and abrupt. It might also have fit well and complemented nicely the elegiac quality of the second episode itself, which emphasizes, by way of the *Tannhäuser* Overture, forgiveness for past misdeeds. To have Alfred fondly recall the start of a relationship now crumbling might have enlarged and deepened the episode—all the more so for including in his reverie farce as well as romance. What is more melancholy upon such an occasion than recalling the happy disasters of the past?

Zanuck's cut was technically deft in that what remained afterward was still a superbly crafted and complete film. Unlike Hughes, Zanuck was rational.

He wanted a film that audiences would flock to and that he could live with as studio head. That did not include films—like *Unfaithfully Yours*—that would not find their audience until years later.

Unfaithfully Yours, like many films, tends to disprove mechanistic descriptions of "the Hollywood system" or "classical Hollywood" as turning out a standardized product. The reality was far more dialectical than that. Sturges declined to write and film the streamlined narrative that Zanuck early on urged him to do. Zanuck tried to impose his views on the project after the fact, but could only do so in a limited way. It is also true, however, that aside from his filming of *The Beautiful Blonde from Bashful Bend* (1949), *Unfaithfully Yours* was Sturges's last work as writer-director in Hollywood.

NOTES

1. James Curtis, *Between Flops: A Biography of Preston Sturges* (New York: Harcourt Brace Jovanovich, 1982), 219.

2. Ibid.

3. Ibid. Donald Spoto, whose version is slightly different, says that Hughes objected to the film's prolonged slapstick, the endless sequences with the tethered lion, and the forty-minute excerpt from *The Freshman*. Sturges cut an hour of footage and recommended this trimmed, ninety-two-minute version to Hughes. See Spoto, *Madcap: The Life of Preston Sturges* (Boston: Little, Brown, 1990), 209.

4. One item called for adding an inset of Miss Otis in a scene, to show where Harold is going as he rises from his desk and leaves the frame; another called for a different take of a scene to replace one in which the principals' heads moved too much. These too are arguably matters of pace, or bear upon it: determining how long it takes, or seems to take, to pass through a particular scene; and how smoothly one does so.

5. Curtis, *Between Flops,* 220.

6. Ibid.

7. Ibid., 225.

8. Censorship problems anticipated by Zanuck led to a January 15, 1948, script and Zanuck's insistence on shortening the January 15 script led to the February 10 script, reprinted below. Sturges took advantage of these required occasions to make his own changes and improvements.

9. Exactly what version of his story Sturges sent to Zanuck is unclear. The text of the story in the Sturges papers at UCLA has many cross-outs in the first three pages, in effect comprising a revision of it. In the story summary that appears on pages 764–770, I restored the crossed-out passages regarding the conductor (pages 764–765), but not those regarding the charwomen (page 764). The original opening passage is as follows:

> The balcony of the great auditorium. It is dark except for a single work-light, shedding a dismal radiance from within its grille. Two elderly charwomen are at work, the one with a carpet sweeper, the other with a pail of soapy water and a

rag, washing the painted plaster back of the family circle. Comes now a blast of music from the stage far below. Mrs. Smythe drops the handle of her Bissell, clutches her heart and looks at Mrs. Mulligan indignantly. The latter looks over the plaster work with disgust. The music stops as suddenly as it began.

Mrs. Smythe speaks whiningly: "That give me a turn, that did. I never do seem to get used to it."

"Fierce," says Mrs. Mulligan.

MRS. SMYTHE: (Touching her back)
God knows, the work is hard enough without 'avin' to listen to them and their blasted re'earsin' all the time. Why do they 'ave to re'earse?

MRS. MULLIGAN: Search me.

MRS. SMYTHE: You'd think they know their bloody pieces by now. They been playin' them long enough.

MRS. MULLIGAN: The wonder to me is that people will pay good money to hear that stuff.

MRS. SMYTHE: There's no accountin' for tastes.

A terrific blast of music comes from below. Mrs. Smythe clutches her heart again, then wearily pushes her Bissell up and down. Mrs. Mulligan rings out her cloth and returns to the painted plaster.

We come now to the orchestra, etc.

Handwritten at the bottom of the story's second page is an alternative to the conductor's brief speech to his musicians after he raps on his music stand: "'You are the finest musicians in the world and the proof is you get the biggest salaries. Consequently I cannot criticize your playing and all I can say is: 'Beethoven stinks!' That's all.' He throws down his stick and hurries off the stand."

10. Curtis, *Between Flops*, 227–228.

11. A discarded page of the November 3–4 draft has a longer version of this speech:

England, I mean everywhere have finally enacted so many rules and regulations that NOTHING moves any more. Imagine England hungry . . . when Belgium . . . forty miles away . . . is choked with food . . . all natural laws like the law of supply and demand and the survival of the fittest and the law of diminishing returns have been replaced by artificial rules and regimentation. Whatever you feel like doing is probably against the law. Part of it is an effort to drive out the old aristocracy and maybe that's a good thing . . . these silly sirs and milords and my lieges and your grace and your excellency . . . but in driving them out they have replaced them with a new aristocracy of crooks and shysters and regulation wormer-arounders and shrewd money changers in illegal currency and black marketeers in various shades of blackness. They are the ones who get what honest men cannot . . . when I was a little boy, England was a free port, which means there was no duty on anything . . . practically anything . . . one could bring practically anything except dogs into England without fuss or feathers and how one did! What beef! What lamb! What oysters from Brittany and butter from Denmark and cheese from Normandy and goose livers from Alsace and oranges from Spain and olive oil from Italy and dates from Egypt and figs from Malta and cigarettes from Turkey and caviar from the Volga and Pilsener beer! And good herring out of the North Sea . . . it was really the Island of Plenty and it's nice to have known it at least once. Then I went to Dresden to study harmony and I got my first taste of the muddling and meddling that exists everywhere today. Everything was verboten . . . it was verboten to walk on the grass, to pick flowers, to roller skate on the sidewalk, to fly kites on the street . . . I thought the Germans were very funny people . . . so unEnglish . . . but now that we've defeated them we seem to have absorbed a lot of their habits.

Both of Sir Alfred's speeches denouncing "rules and regulations" that impede the free circulation of money and goods may also be read as Sturges's denunciation of the English system of quotas for foreign films. In the final script and film, Sir Alfred's peroration on economics is cut to a very brief remark which completes a newspaper interview with Sir Alfred himself: "[Britain is hungry for music] and for a great many other things, unfortunately a little harder to produce."

"UNFAITHFULLY YOURS"

Screenplay

by

Preston Sturges

❉ ❉ ❉

<u>Revised F i n a l</u>
February 10, 1948

823

2/10/48

"UNFAITHFULLY YOURS"

After the trademark we:

DISSOLVE TO:

1   LONG SHOT - A SYMPHONY ORCHESTRA PLAYING

The main titles DISSOLVE in over this and during them
we PUSH IN straight toward the conductor's back so that,
by the time we have given the last credit (and modesty
forbids my mentioning whose that is) we are on the conductor's rear. In other words the screen is black.

DISSOLVE TO:

2   A BIG TRANS-ATLANTIC PLANE - ROARING TOWARD US THROUGH
THE FOG - DAY

After a nice piece of this:

DISSOLVE TO:

3   A BLACKBOARD IN AN AIR TERMINAL

It is ruled in the customary way. It appears that
Flight three forty-nine from London due at 9:00 A.M. is
late because of poor visibility. Over and above the
distant Abadabba of voices in the terminal we hear the
Information Man's voice,

                    INFORMATION MAN'S VOICE
          I tell you you have nothing to
          worry about...the plane is per-
          fectly safe...

By now the CAMERA has pulled far enough back for us to
see the Information Man who holds a telephone to his
ear as he faces his interrogators,

                    INFORMATION MAN
          ...they just ran a little short on
          gas...on account of all that fog,
          that's all...so they put down in ...
                    (he speaks into
                    the telephone)
          ...give me that one again, Max...
          Aroostock?
                    (he looks past the CAMERA)
          ...Aroostock.

2/10/48   2.

4   CLOSE SHOT - HUGO STANDOFF

He is a large gentleman in a long grey coat with an
Australian Opossum collar. Above this there is a jaunty
grey Homburg hat with a feather on the side of it.
Between the hat and the collar there is his face. While
he is talking to the Information Man we continue to
PULL BACK revealing first the two beautiful girls who
flank him and then, following the laws of perspective,
the equally beautiful young Tony and the somewhac
pickled-looking multi-millionaire, August Henschler.

                        HUGO
                (indignantly and with
                a slight Russian accent)
            Aroostock! And where is Aroostock
            supposing to be it shouldn't happen?

5   THE INFORMATION MAN - PAST THE OTHERS

                        INFORMATION MAN
                (vaguely)
            Well it's in the uh...the uh...
            that is to say I presume...
                (now he listens into
                the telephone, then
                speaks with much
                assurance)
            ...Oh...it's in the general neigh-
            borhood of Nova Scotia.

6   HUGO, DAPHNE, BARBARA, TONY AND AUGUST

                        HUGO
                (with a fine
                Russian sneer)
            Is dot so? And from dis general
            neighborhood you can tell me maybe
            how he is tonight at Philharmonic
            a concert conducting? By telewision
            I am presuming...

                        DAPHNE
                (sincerely frightened)
            Is it a very bad fog? Make him
            tell me the truth, Hugo.

                        HUGO
                (reassuringly)
            Of course it ain't.

7   THE INFORMATION MAN - PAST THE OTHERS

                        INFORMATION MAN
              It's hardly a fog at all. Madam...
              it's more of a mist really...more of
              a...
                        (now he puts the
                        phone back to his
                        ear)
              ...yes, Max?

8   HUGO, DAPHNE, BARBARA, TONY AND AUGUST

                        HUGO
                        (reassuringly)
              ...Just something to make the
              engines run better.

                        DAPHNE
                        (frightened)
              You're sure.

                        INFORMATION MAN'S VOICE
              Correction please...

                        DAPHNE
                        (putting her hand
                        to her throat)
              What is it?

.9   INFORMATION MAN - PAST THE OTHERS

                        INFORMATION MAN
              ...It was not Aroostock...it was
              Antigonish.

10   HUGO, DAPHNE, BARBARA, TONY AND AUGUST

                        HUGO
                        (with a fine snarl)
              Well ain't dot someting!
                        (he turns to the others)
              It ain't Aroostock...it's
              Antigmonish...
                        (now he looks sideways
                        at the Information Man)
              ...And where is dis mud hole... if
              I ain't too optimistic?

11   INFORMATION MAN - PAST THE OTHERS

                        INFORMATION MAN
              In the general neighborhood of...
              Nova Scotia...I believe...

2/10/48

12   HUGO, BARBARA, DAPHNE, TONY AND AUGUST

                  HUGO
      What a neighborhood!

               INFORMATION MAN'S VOICE
      Yes Max?

                DAPHNE
      Hugo, please try to find out...

               INFORMATION MAN'S VOICE
      Correction please...

Hugo puts a hand on Daphne's arm.

13   INFORMATION MAN - PAST THE OTHERS

               INFORMATION MAN
      Thank you, Max.
        (he puts the telephone
        back on its stand)
      It turns out it wasn't Antigonish,
      after all. It was Apohaqui...and
      it didn't get there...it left
      there...nearly two hours ago.

14   HUGO, DAPHNE, BARBARA, AUGUST AND TONY

                  HUGO
      Apohaqui!

                DAPHNE
        (urgently)
      Then where is it now?

                  HUGO
        (with bitter sarcasm)
      In the general neighborhood of
      Nova Scotia...where else?

15   INFORMATION MAN - PAST THE OTHERS

               INFORMATION MAN
        (with fine sarcasm)
      Far, far from it, my friend...
        (he points)
      As a matter of fact it's coming
      in there directly behind you.....
      what an airline!

16   HUGO, DAPHNE, BARBARA, AUGUST AND TONY

                              DAPHNE
                           (weakly)
                  I feel as if I were going to
                  faint.

                              TONY
                           (taking her arm)
                  Don't do that.

                              BARBARA
                           (taking her
                           other arm)
                  Come on, stoopid.

        They go out of the shot.

                              AUGUST
                           (to the Information
                           Man)
                  There is one very reassuring
                  thing about airplanes....they
                  always come down.

        He hurries after the others and the Information Man
        gives him a slight double-take.

                                              LONG DISSOLVE TO:

17   TWO BIG HEADS - DAPHNE PAST SIR ALFRED

        They are kissing affectionately.

18   HUGO, BARBARA, AUGUST AND TONY

                              BARBARA
                  They can't do it much longer...
                  it's against the law.

                              HUGO
                  Am I glad to see you, Alfie! Are
                  you a sight for eyesores! Again
                  Wolfgang can't conduct! Again he
                  has intestinal flue!..Confidentially
                  I think his trouble is bratvurst...
                  intestinal bratvurst!...so your con-
                  cert got to be shoved up...tonight
                  we are giving it yet...one more hour
                  and I had to...

217

/10/48

19   TWO BIG HEADS - DAPHNE PAST SIR ALFRED

They come up out of the kiss.

SIR ALFRED
(gently)
And did you think of me every night?

20   HUGO, BARBARA, AUGUST AND TONY

HUGO
I guess I been talking to myself...
(now he notices
nobody is paying
attention to him)
...I guess I'm sure of it.

21   TWO BIG HEADS - DAPHNE PAST SIR ALFRED

DAPHNE
(tenderly)
Of course I did, my love.

SIR ALFRED
And did you take my picture to bed
with you?

DAPHNE
Of course I did, my darling...every
single night.

22   BARBARA, AUGUST, HUGO AND TONY

BARBARA
(after taking a long
look at her sister)
Are they kidding? If she wasn't my
own sister I'd have a name for her
that'd make her hair curl.

August removes his pince-nez, starts polishing it, and
opens his mouth to speak.

AUGUST
I uh...

BARBARA
Sh-h-h, why couldn't I have married
a member of the nobility instead of
you?

(CONTINUED)

9

217

22 (Cont.)

                    AUGUST
          There are some American families
          quite as aristocratic as anything
          to be found even in the most
          dilapidated parts of Europe.

                    BARBARA
          Yes, sweetie, but not yours...
          don't forget I have seen them.

She makes a face like a Mongolian Idiot, then returns
her attention to the lovers and August continues polishing his pince-nez.

23   TWO BIG HEADS - DAPHNE AND SIR ALFRED

                    SIR ALFRED
          And did you dream of me after you
          went to sleep?

                    DAPHNE
          Every single night, my love...only...
          I didn't sleep very well.

                    SIR ALFRED
               (in a very low tone)
          Neither did I, my darling...naturally.

24   BARBARA AND AUGUST WITH PARTS OF TONY AND HUGO TIPPED IN

                    BARBARA
          Will somebody get me an ice pack?
               (then noticing August
               polishing his pince-nez)
          Put them back on your nose and learn
          something...

She looks back at her sister.

25   TWO BIG HEADS - DAPHNE AND SIR ALFRED

                    DAPHNE
               (tenderly)
          At least did you get some rest on
          the plane last night?

                    SIR ALFRED
          Frankly, not a particle.

                                        (CONTINUED)

25 (Cont.)

                              DAPHNE
               Then I'm going to take you right
               straight home and put you in a
               nice hot tub, and then...

26   BARBARA AND AUGUST WITH PARTS OF TONY AND HUGO TIPPED IN

                              BARBARA
                           (to August)
               You see what I mean? The only
               place I feel like putting you is
               on ice.

                              HUGO
                        (almost shocked)
               Now, Barbara...

                              BARBARA
               I can't help it...I'm just terribly,
               terribly honest...I told him when I
               was his secretary I could never learn
               to love him...but he wouldn't believe
               me.

                              HUGO
                    (consolingly to August)
               Deep down under everything I'm sure
               she loves you...deeply.

                              BARBARA
                        (shocked to Hugo)
               How can you be such a liar!

27   TWO BIG HEADS - DAPHNE AND SIR ALFRED

                              DAPHNE
               ...and then rub you with alcohol...
               and then put you in some nice,
               clean, cool, silk, freshly laundered
               pajamas...

                              SIR ALFRED
                        (shaking his head)
               How heavenly.

28   BARBARA, AUGUST, TONY AND HUGO

                              BARBARA
                        (narrowing her eyes)
               Will somebody kindly take me out
               of here and throw some air on me...

                                           (CONTINUED)

2/10/48

28 (Cont.)

She pretends to fan herself.

> AUGUST
> (disapprovingly)
> I don't really think they ought
> to do this in public.

> BARBARA
> (giggling)
> Of course it's better to do it in
> public than not to do it at all...

29   TWO BIG HEADS - DAPHNE AND SIR ALFRED

> DAPHNE
> And then we'll have our little
> nap... and then I'll wake you up
> with a nice frosted bottle of Brut
> Champagne...I found some Pol Roger
> '34...and then...

30   BARBARA, AUGUST, HUGO AND TONY

> BARBARA
> (pointing this
> out to August)
> You see? Some men just naturally
> make you think of Brut Champagne...
> with others you think of prune
> juice.

August starts laughing merrily and then looks suspiciously at his wife.

> BARBARA
> You have nothing to laugh at.

31   TWO BIG HEADS - DAPHNE AND SIR ALFRED

> DAPHNE
> ...and by then...it should be easily
> about 11:30...

32   BARBARA, AUGUST, HUGO AND TONY

> BARBARA
> And then some.

33   TWO BIG HEADS - DAPHNE AND SIR ALFRED

> DAPHNE
> Thank you, darling...so then you'll
> go down and rehearse your men...
> (she looks out
> of the shot)
> ...oughtn't that be time enough,
> Hugo?

34   HUGO AND THE OTHERS

> HUGO
> Look: so they pushed the concert up
> to today...so the boys didn't start
> taking fiddle lessons yesterday...
> the pieces they have played before...
> a few tousand times.

35   TWO BIG HEADS - SIR ALFRED AND DAPHNE

> SIR ALFRED
> (putting his arm
> around his adored
> one)
> Of course it'll be time enough...

He kisses her on the cheek.

36   HUGO AND THE OTHERS

> HUGO
> It ain't as if you was a rehearser
> anyway...
> (he turns to
> August)
> ...he's a hypnotizer...out of what
> dogs have I seen him coax it out.

37   TWO BIG HEADS - SIR ALFRED AND DAPHNE

> SIR ALFRED
> Oh no you haven't...it's the men
> who really count...all I have to
> do is wave a little wand a little...
> and out comes the music...

> DAPHNE
> (very sweetly)
> A little magic wand, darling...
> dipped in a little stardust.

As Sir Alfred turns to look into her eyes:

38   TWO NEWSPAPER REPORTERS AND THREE NEWSPAPER CAMERAMEN

                            FIRST REPORTER
                  Will you hold it please, Sir Alfred?

39   TWO BIG HEADS - SIR ALFRED AND DAPHNE

                            SIR ALFRED
                            (amiably)
                  I shall be honored.

Daphne smiles prettily as the flashes go off. They
close their eyes.

40   THE TWO REPORTERS AND THE·THREE CAMERAMEN

                            SECOND REPORTER
                  Could you tell us something about
                  England, Sir Alfred? Could you
                  give us some kind of a lead, like:
                  would you say that England is
                  hungry for music?

41   SIR ALFRED AND DAPHNE - PAST THE REPORTERS

He holds his wife tightly to him.

                            SIR ALFRED
                  I'm a little too happy at the
                  moment to be truly deepdish...but
                  I would say that England is hungry
                  for everything...and I would add
                  that it is a great pity in this
                  world of plenty...a very great pity.

                                                DISSOLVE TO:

42   CLOSE SHOT - AN ANTIQUE PORCELAIN CLOCK

on top of which are animated figurines representing a
four-piece village band led by a bandmaster with his
back to us.

On the face of the clock we see that it was made by de
Carter &'Sons, Purveyors to His Majesty, or whatever
they put on the face of old English clocks. The minute
hand moves a fraction to show a quarter to eleven, there
is a whirring sound and we hear the first seventeen
notes of Jingle Bells stiffly punctuated by the leader's
baton.

                                                (CONTINUED)

2/10/48   12.

43   HUGO AND JULES - IN SIR ALFRED'S STUDY

Hugo is glaring at the clock, Jules is arranging some
clothes in the background.

                        HUGO
                (going to the piano
                and finishing the
                tune with irritation)
        Dah, dah, dah, dah, do! Don't that
        drive you nuts...always hanging up
        on the meat hook like that?

                        JULES
        Except once an hour when it terminates,
        I confess it is quite irritating, sir,

44   TONY - COMING IN FROM THE FOYER

He closes the door behind him, but while the door was
open we heard a little Abadabba.

                        TONY
        I suppose I ought to wake him up...
        if he's going to see anyone before
        the concert.

                        HUGO
                (tolerantly)
        Give him a coupla minutes...ain't
        you ever been in love?

He pounds out the Tristan and Isolde theme with crashing chords.

                                    DISSOLVE TO:

45   DAPHNE AND SIR ALFRED - IN HER DARKENED BEDROOM

One shaft of sunlight comes through the curtains. Sir
Alfred still in bed smiles sleepily, a glass of champagne
in his hand. Daphne sits on the floor next to him also
holding a glass of champagne. Next to her we see the
bottle in its cooler.

> SIR ALFRED
> (after a swallow)
> You do everything so well.

> DAPHNE
> (sweetly)
> You taught me, darling.

She takes another sip of champagne.

> SIR ALFRED
> (dreamily)
> Do you know why Porthole, Mitchigan
> is the most beautiful hamlet in all
> of the United States?...and Mitchigan
> itself the most beautiful of these
> States...although very rainy...

> DAPHNE
> I suppose it doesn't rain in England.

> SIR ALFRED
> ...and Genesee Street is the most
> beautiful of all fashionable
> thoroughfares?

> DAPHNE
> In the first place it's Porthaul...
> h-a-u-l, Michigan, which rhymes
> with Squishigan, and you know it
> perfectly well...and in the second
> place...

> SIR ALFRED
> (putting his
> arm around her)
> ...because the most beautiful half
> of the most beautiful pair of the
> most beautiful sisters in all this
> beautiful world came from there...
> directly into my arms.

(CONTINUED)

45 (Cont.)

                    DAPHNE
               (dryly)
     It's too bad bigamy is illegal in
     this country or you could have had
     the pair of us.

                    SIR ALFRED
     Don't be immoral...how fondly I
     remember it...we were on our way
     to Canada for the annual Music and
     Fur Trapping Festival...we didn't
     win that part of it...when sud-
     denly the train stopped with a
     jerk...and a jolly good thing it
     did as the tracks had just floated
     away,

                    DAPHNE
     The way you've built this thing
     up.

                    SIR ALFRED
     The local Baldwin man nailed me
     at once of course, there's one in
     every town and he always nabs me,
     and asked me if I would kindly
     listen to his small daughter play
     the sliphorn at the local high
     school concert...just to get my
     opinion of her talent, you know
     the "now that you're 'ere Sir
     Alfred" approach, "it would make
     me extremely 'appy..."

                    DAPHNE
               (taking him by
               the throat to
               strangle him)
     It was not a high school concert,
     it was a charity concert....and
     it wasn't a sliphorn, and you know
     it perfectly well...and whatever
     else my poor father does, he most
     certainly doesn't drop his aitches...
     like some people's fathers I've
     heard a few rumors about.

                              (CONTINUED)

45 (Cont.1)

                              SIR ALFRED
                         (ignoring all this)
                    ...so we got into a punt to row over
                    there and I said: "Jeepers, Sir
                    Alfred, we're in for it now all right,
                    all right...there's no way out but to
                    swim for it..." so we got there and
                    pretty soon the Baldwin man sidled up
                    dragging his ugly brat behind him...and
                    suddenly I looked up and straight into
                    her eyes...and a hundred harps glissed
                    into E Flat Major...and my heart
                    flopped over in me in a complete somer-
                    sault...and the world began anew.

     There is a knock on the door which neither of them hear.
     Daphne puts her lips against his and melts into his arms.

46   THE DOORWAY OF THE ROOM

     Tony enters, looks toward the bed in some discomfiture,
     then turns to tiptoe out and knocks over the champagne
     cooler. As he stoops to pick it up:

47   SIR ALFRED AND DAPHNE

     They turn and look at Tony.

                              SIR ALFRED
                         (good-naturedly)
                    Isn't it customary to knock before
                    entering a bedroom...or am I just
                    old-fashioned?

48   TONY - BY THE CHAMPAGNE COOLER

                              TONY
                    I did knock, Sir Alfred.

49   SIR ALFRED AND DAPHNE

                              SIR ALFRED
                    I'm extremely sorry, I didn't hear
                    you.

                              DAPHNE
                         (laughing)
                    It must have been those harps.

                              SIR ALFRED
                    Now that you're here would you care
                    for a glass of champagne?

50   TONY - NEAR THE DOOR

                         TONY
              No, thank you...I just wanted to
              make sure you were awake and ask
              you what to do about the morning
              delegation of crackpots...among
              them a lady reporter who wants to
              know why you conduct with a stick.

51   SIR ALFRED AND DAPHNE

Daphne gets up, goes around the bed and opens the curtains.

                       SIR ALFRED
              What does she expect me to use,
              an umbrella?

52   TONY - IN THE DOORWAY

                         TONY
              She says Stokie uses just his
              hands.

53   SIR ALFRED AND DAPHNE

Daphne is getting a dressing gown for him out of the
closet.

                       SIR ALFRED
                  (lighting a cigarette)
              Yes, but they're so beautiful...
              so large and white...
                  (he looks at his own)
              ...mine look more like nutcrackers.

                        DAPHNE
                  (holding out the
                   dressing gown)
              Here, darling.....

Sir Alfred starts putting it on.

54   TONY - IN THE DOORWAY

                         TONY
              She also wants to know why you con-
              duct from a score.

55   SIR ALFRED AND DAPHNE

                           SIR ALFRED
                  Because I'm one of the few living
                  conductors who can actually read
                  music...I took lessons in it and
                  paid good money for them...I also
                  play an instrument: the flageolet
                  ....don't forget to tell her that.

                           DAPHNE
                  You fool.

56   TONY - LOOKING AT A PAD IN HIS HAND

                           TONY
                  Mr. Pedasta, your concert master,
                  would like to discuss the finger-
                  ing in the fourth, fifth and sixth
                  bars before letter H in the
                  Tannhauser Overture.

57   SIR ALFRED AND DAPHNE

        With a perplexed look on his face he rapidly goes
        through the fingering on an imaginary violin.

                           SIR ALFRED
                  The fingering is standard...what's
                  the matter with him?

58   TONY - NEAR THE DOOR

                           TONY
                       (looking at his pad)
                  He says because it is the Paris
                  version...with the Venusberg music...
                  do you want the French fingering?

59   SIR ALFRED AND DAPHNE

                           SIR ALFRED
                       (laughing)
                  Of course...that old story...tell
                  Mr. Pedasta I'll walk to rehearsal
                  with him and we'll discuss it on
                  the way.

        He gets up and crosses to the dressing table to brush
        his hair.

2/10/48

60   TONY - BY THE DOOR

                    TONY
          Certainly, Sir Alfred...then
          there's a citizen who wants you
          to endow the de Carter Foundation
          for the Diffusion of Serious Music.

61   SIR ALFRED - BRUSHING HIS HAIR

                    SIR ALFRED
          Throw him out...there's nothing
          serious about music...it should be
          enjoyed flat on the back...with a
          sandwich in one hand, a bucket of
          beer in the other....and as many
          pretty girls about as possible...
          it is a secondary art that adds to
          the joy of living...sandwich eating
          is a primary art.

                    DAPHNE
                  (to Tony)
          If you repeat a word of this stuff...

62   TONY - IN THE DOORWAY

                    TONY
          And then there's a gentleman who
          wants you to conduct an all chil-
          dren's orchestra of a hundred and
          fifty with no child over eleven.

63   SIR ALFRED AND DAPHNE

      Sir Alfred clutches his head and Daphne howls.

                    SIR ALFRED
          What is the matter with these
          monsters? When I was a child of
          eleven I played Hop Scotch! They
          play Shostakovich!

64   TONY - BY THE DOOR

                    TONY
          This takes place in the open
          air among the giant redwoods.

841

65   SIR ALFRED AND DAPHNE

                              SIR ALFRED
                  You will tell the gentleman that I
                  am broken hearted to have to de-
                  cline, but I am allergic to them...
                  they make me sneeze.

          Daphne puts her hand over her mouth.

66   TONY - BY THE DOOR

                              TONY
                  The redwoods...

67   SIR ALFRED AND DAPHNE

                              SIR ALFRED
                       (delighted with his joke)
                  No...musicians under eleven!

          He and Daphne fall into each other's arms and roar with
          laughter.

68   TONY - IN THE DOORWAY

          He opens his mouth to speak, then exits and closes the
          door after him.

69   SIR ALFRED AND DAPHNE

                              SIR ALFRED
                       (to Daphne)
                  The only trouble with you is: I never
                  feel like getting up...I never feel
                  like getting dressed...I never feel
                  like going out into the world to
                  wrestle it and bring it to its knees
                  ...I think the successful, energetic
                  men must all have been married to
                  women who looked like gargoyles...
                       (he tilts her sur-
                       prised chin up and
                       kisses her on the cheek)
                  ...I will now leap into a cold shower.

          He exits rapidly. Daphne stares after him in open
          mouthed amusement.

                                                 DISSOLVE TO:

70   CLOSE SHOT - THE ANTIQUE CLOCK

        The minute hand arrives straight up on eleven o'clock,
        and the little village orchestra plays the entire
        Jingle Bells ending in a whirring sound. Before it
        gets to the end we:

                                                CUT TO:

71   HUGO - BEATING TIME WITH HIS CIGAR

                                HUGO
                            (happily)
                    At last.

        We hear a buzzer. Hugo goes to the door to the hall
        and opens it revealing a little page boy with an
        enormous box of flowers.

                                THE BOY
                    Some flowers for Lady de Carter.

72   SIR ALFRED'S BATHROOM

        His face covered with soap - a straight razor in his
        hand - he sticks his head out and speaks gaily:

                                SIR ALFRED
                    What is it, Hugo?

        He comes further out and we see that he is dressed ex-
        cept for buttoning his shirt and putting on a tie.

73   HUGO AND THE BOY - AT THE DOOR

                                THE BOY
                    Some flowers for Lady de Carter,
                    Sir Alfred.

                                HUGO
                            (taking them)
                    I'll take 'em.

74   SIR ALFRED

        Feeling for money he comes forward and the CAMERA PANS
        him into the group at the door.

                                SIR ALFRED
                    How nice.

                                            (CONTINUED)

74 (Cont.)
                            SIR ALFRED (Cont.)
                         (he feels in his pocket
                         and finds nothing)
                    Give him a dollar, Hugo.

                                HUGO
                    A dollar!

He pulls out his money reluctantly.

                                SIR ALFRED
                    It's only sixty-two and one-half
                    cents you know...
                              (he takes a dollar
                              from Hugo and
                              presses it into
                              the boy's hand)
                    ...there's sixty-two and one-half
                    cents for you.

                                THE PAGE BOY
                              (happily)
                    Thank you, Sir Alfred, I'll pretend
                    it's a dollar.

Hugo closes the door and Sir Alfred takes the large box
from him and looks at it.

                                SIR ALFRED
                              (amiably)
                    Now I wonder who sent her these?

                                HUGO
                    Why don't you grab a look and treat
                    yourself to a surprise?

                                SIR ALFRED
                    It isn't any of my business...they're
                    probably from some poor devil who
                    was madly in love with her and nearly
                    perished when she married me who once
                    each year on the anniversary of their
                    last farewell sends her this little
                    bunch of snapdragons...or could it
                    be hollyhocks?

                                HUGO
                    In that box it could be a skeleton...
                    he could'a sent himself.

                                SIR ALFRED
                    Don't be gruesome, Hugo.

2/10/48

75   TONY - COMING INTO THE FOYER

                    TONY
         I see they came, Sir Alfred...I
         tried to get all long stemmed
         roses but they must have filled
         out with chrysanthemums.

    By now the CAMERA has PANNED him into the shot with
    the other two.

                    SIR ALFRED
              (pointing first to
              the flowers then to
              himself)
         Oh these are the uh...flowers
         that I uh...

                    TONY
         ...that you asked me to send on
         the way in this morning...I
         scratched out the name on one
         of your cards and wrote instead
         "For my love."

    For one fleeting instant Sir Alfred's expression hardens,
    then he answers amiably.

                    SIR ALFRED
         Well that was remarkably efficient...
              (now he hands Tony
              the razor)
         ...thank you very much...and have
         this honed for me, will you? It's
         duller than one of my brother-in-
         law's jokes.

                    TONY
              (taking the razor)
         Mr. Henschler is on his way up
         by the way...

                    SIR ALFRED
              (indignantly)
         What does he want?

                    TONY
         He did not inform me.

                              (CONTINUED)

75 (Cont.)

                        SIR ALFRED
But I've already <u>seen</u> him once
today...I mean to say just because he's married to my wife's
sister doesn't entitle him to,
to. .what a BORE he is!

                          HUGO
Look: he's got a hundred million
dollars...don't be expecting also
Jolly Miller! (or Happy Hooligan
or Abbott and Costello or Jack
Benny and Mary Livingston or Fred
Allen and Rochester).

                        SIR ALFRED
I have a few million <u>myself</u>, you
know...but that doesn't entitle me...

                          HUGO
You ain't got a <u>hundred</u> million...
it's that last zither that cooks
the goose. (or: that chokes the
jokes).

                        SIR ALFRED
That <u>miser</u>...every fur coat he
gives his wife he inherited from
his grandmother...every diamond
is from his aunt...every pearl is
from his...

                          HUGO
Stop...you're breaking my heart.

                        SIR ALFRED
I know it's stupid of me to allow
him to annoy me so, but do I haunt
<u>his</u> hotel constantly sending messages
that I'm on my way up to see <u>him</u>...?
Do I use that vaguest of all relationships: two strangers who marry sisters
...as a wedge for the purpose of...

                          JULES
                (opening the door
                 from the foyer)
Mr. August Henschler.

                                        (CONTINUED)

75 (Cont. 1)

>   SIR ALFRED
> Good morning again, August...
> what happy updraft wafts you
> hither?

>   AUGUST
> Well I uh...

>   SIR ALFRED
> Do you wish to see me alone or in
> committee?

>   AUGUST
>   (smiling coldly from
>   Tony to Hugo)
> Well...if it wouldn't be too much
> trouble?

>   HUGO
>   (starting for the
>   foyer)
> Remember you got a lot of jerks
> waiting for you in the next room
> ...when you get through in here.

>   TONY
>   (starting for the
>   foyer)
> I'll take the razor down to the
> Barber Shop...

>   SIR ALFRED
> If you don't mind I'll continue
> dressing.

>   AUGUST
> I don't mind at all...now let me
> see the best way to begin.

>   SIR ALFRED
> At the beginning.

>   AUGUST
>   (after a cool smile)
> Quite so...you are no doubt aware,
> Alfred, that I have a deep sense
> of family obligation?

>   (CONTINUED)

75 (Cont.2)

> SIR ALFRED
> (vaguely surprised)
> I was not aware of it but I am
> willing to accept your word for
> it.

> AUGUST
> ...and we are brothers-in-law,
> aren't we?

> SIR ALFRED
> I'm afraid we are and there isn't
> a blasted thing we can do about it.

> AUGUST
> (after laughing
> coolly at this
> little joke)
> Oh...it may come as quite a shock
> to you, Alfred, to realize that I
> don't actually relish being your
> brother-in-law any more than you
> relish being mine.

> SIR ALFRED
> (stupefied)
> No!

> AUGUST
> But yes!
> (he removes his pince-
> nez and starts to
> polish them)
> In the first place, I hate music...
> which does not relieve me from
> having to snore through every
> blasted soiree you promulgate...

> SIR ALFRED
> Soiree!

> AUGUST
> (coldly)
> Precisely...in the second place
> I am embarrassed about the pro-
> duct your family made its money
> out of...and in the third place...

(CONTINUED)

75 (Cont.3)
                          SIR ALFRED
                     (returning to a more
                      normal dislike)
          I think it's quite as good as sucking
          mortgages if you should happen to
          ask me.

                            AUGUST
                       (pleasantly)
          It may be but I prefer mortgages...
          lastly: as a humble American the only
          titles I have any use for are in the
          Title Guaranty & Trust Company.

                          SIR ALFRED
                       (chillily)
          I see...you have my deepest sympathy,
          August, but I am a baronet, I am a
          band leader, and my family's product
          has kept England on time since
          Waterloo...I regret it but there it
          is....now if I may inquire again as to
          the reason for this happy visitation...

                            AUGUST
          I will come to the point at once:
          when you left for England and asked
          me to keep an eye on your wife, dur-
          ing your absence...

                          SIR ALFRED
                       (blankly)
          I asked you to keep an eye on my
          wife...

                            AUGUST
          I naturally accepted in the same
          spirit I would expect you to display
          if I asked you to keep an eye on my
          wife while taking off,let us say,
          for Zanzibar.

                          SIR ALFRED
          When are you leaving?

                            AUGUST
          I said "if."

                          SIR ALFRED
                       (disappointed)
          Oh.
                                            (CONTINUED)

75 (Cont.4)

> AUGUST
> What I didn't know...and I don't
> see very well how I could have...
> was that my dear mother who is
> probably Public Hypochondriac No.
> 1, would wire for me the same day
> asking me to join her in Palm Beach...
> because of a slight indisposition.

> SIR ALFRED
> (coldly)
> I am distressed to hear it,...I
> suppose she's related to me also -
> in some way...

> AUGUST
> So faintly that it is hardly worth
> mentioning.

> SIR ALFRED
> (slightly mollified)
> Good...I'm sorry anyway.

> AUGUST
> Oh we're quite used to it...if it
> isn't one part of her that's ailing,
> it's another and she seems to have
> so many parts...for a woman of her
> age, that is...however, to return to
> our muttons: you asked me to keep
> an eye on your wife and I want you
> to know that had it been possible
> for me to do so I would gladly have
> done so.

> SIR ALFRED
> I don't doubt it for a second but -
> if it was too much trouble or in-
> convenient in any way...

> AUGUST
> Nothing is too much trouble for the
> busy man...if you ever want anything
> done always ask the busy man...the
> others never have time...you asked
> me to keep an eye on your wife and...

(CONTINUED)

75 (Cont.5)

> SIR ALFRED
> You keep repeating: "Keep an eye
> on your wife" as if it had some
> special meaning...I don't know
> exactly what you're leading up to
> but I feel my back hair rising.

> AUGUST
> Well, you see, Alfred, being a
> little nearsighted I couldn't very
> well keep an eye on her from Palm
> Beach...
> (he laughs coolly)
> ....nevertheless I did not fail you...

> SIR ALFRED
> (interrupting him)
> Again something is happening to my
> back hair...I have no recollection
> of saying anything at all to you at
> the airport except possibly "Goodbye"...
> if I did say: "Keep an eye on my
> wife for me" I meant find out if she's
> lonely some evening and if she is,
> take her to the movies...you and
> Barbara.

> AUGUST
> But you didn't <u>say</u> that...you said:
> "Keep an eye on <u>my</u> <u>wife</u> for me."

> SIR ALFRED
> (exasperated)
> Suppose I did...how could you
> possibly do it from Palm Beach?

> AUGUST
> (as if it were
> the simplest of
> all problems)
> With detectives.

> SIR ALFRED
> (parrot-like at
> first as he does
> not understand)
> With detectives...

(CONTINUED)

75 (Cont. 6)

<pre>
                    SIR ALFRED (Cont.)
                   (then suddenly under-
                    standing, at the top
                    of his lungs)
        ...WITH DETECTIVES! You stuffed
        moron...
                   (he seizes August
                    by the necktie and
                    with the iron grip
                    of a conductor nearly
                    carries him into the
                    corner of the room)

                    AUGUST
                   (trying to free
                    Sir Alfred's
                    hold on his tie)
        Control yourself, Alfred control
        yourself...this is entirely un-
        called for...kindly release my
        scarf.

                    SIR ALFRED
                   (growling like a lion)
        You dare to inform me you have had
        vulgar footpads in snap brim fedoras
        sluicing after my beautiful wife?

                    AUGUST
                   (desperately as he
                    is half strangled)
        I believe it's called sleuthing,
        Alfred...Alfred please! Kindly
        let go of my shirt, you're tearing
        it...there's nothing to be so up-
        set about, good Heavens...I merely
        had her tailed and...

                    SIR ALFRED
                   (nearly bursting
                    with rage)
        You merely had her what! I give
        you my solemn word, August...if
        I don't regain control of myself
        in the next few seconds...concert
        or no concert...I'll pick up that
        lamp and beat this walnut you use
        for a head into a NUTBERGER...I
        believe they are called!
</pre>

                                        (CONTINUED)

2/10/48

75 (Cont.7)

                          AUGUST
                     (strangling)
          Please try to k-keep co-cool,
          Alfred.

                          SIR ALFRED
                     (furiouser and
                     furiouser)
          K-keep c-cool, Alfred, my sainted
          aunt...I AM OUTRAGED!

He gives August such a shaking that the collar comes
off his suit.

                          AUGUST
          P-please Alfred.

                          SIR ALFRED
          Low as my opinion of you has always
          been August...little as I have ever
          expected from you in the way of
          chivalry or even common dignity...
                     (August's coat starts
                     parting over one of
                     his shoulders)
          ...today you have sunk below even
          yourself...this is the sewer!...
          the nadir of good manners!

                          AUGUST
          I really think you're exaggerating
          a little, Alfred...I've always used
          detectives to some extent and so
          has my whole family...one of my
          aunts even married one of them...
          although I must admit she was quite
          elderly at the time.

                          SIR ALFRED
          Then your whole family is contam-
          inated...no man who employs detec-
          tives should ever be disappointed...
          I hope every time you've engaged
          these vermin you've discovered you
          had antlers out to here...

                                        (CONTINUED)

75 (Cont. 8)   SIR ALFRED (Cont.)
                                  (he indicates a
                                  pair of horns
                                  six feet wide)
                    ...that you were the laughing stock
                    of the city...and that you came
                    crawling out of the agency your
                    face aflame...your briefcase stuffed
                    with undeniable evidence of your
                    multiple betrayal...dishonor drip-
                    ping from your ears like garlands
                    of seaweed...

                              AUGUST
                    I forgive your insults on the grounds
                    that you are excited, Alfred.

                             SIR ALFRED
                    I forbid you to forgive me anything
                    on any grounds whatsoever and I may
                    still punch you in the nose at any
                    instant...now go away and never
                    speak to me again unless it is in
                    some public place where your silence
                    might cause comment...and embarrass-
                    ment to our wives.

        August moves away then starts to pull a paper out of his
        ruined coat.

                              AUGUST
                    I don't suppose you'd be much in-
                    terested in the operative's report
                    then...

                             SIR ALFRED
                                  (snatching it away
                                  from him savagely)
                    Oh yes I would! Give that to me!
                                  (he glares at it)

                              AUGUST
                    ...Although it contained a couple
                    of passages that I for one...

                             SIR ALFRED
                    That you for one what?

        He tears the back of the document in two, then putting
        the halves together, tears it again and again into long
        strips which he drops into the wastebasket.

                                                  (CONTINUED)

75 (Cont.9)

                    SIR ALFRED
          Now go away before I do the same
          to you.

August looks at him uneasily for a moment, puts on his
hat, crosses to the door, opens it and hesitates there.

                    AUGUST
                  (miserably)
          I suppose I'll be seeing you at
          the concert tonight...I've already
          bought the tickets...

                    SIR ALFRED
          I suppose you will...I'm usually
          there on the nights I conduct.

                    AUGUST
          I see,.. I uh...

He makes a hopeless gesture then exits and closes the
door after him. Sir Alfred watches him go, then
suddenly strides to the wastebasket, picks it up, throws
open the door and drop-kicks the basket out into the
hall. After this he bangs the door violently, breathes
deeply, forces a smile which is far from genuine and
goes toward his wife's apartment. On the way he
snatches up the large flower box.

76   DAPHNE - NEARLY DRESSED FOR LUNCH

                    DAPHNE
                  (startled)
          What's that supposed to be?...
                  (then guessing)
          ...Oh, you angel...

76-A   SIR ALFRED - COMING THROUGH THE DOOR

The CAMERA PANS him over into the SHOT WITH Daphne.

                    SIR ALFRED
          I think it's supposed to contain
          flowers although it might easily
          turn out to be a rowing machine.

                    DAPHNE
                  (leaning over the box)
          You sweet love...I don't know where
          we'll find enough pots to put them
          in but...

                              (CONTINUED)

855

                    SIR ALFRED
                (looking at her
                closely)
        You really do love me, don't you?

                    DAPHNE
                (gently)
        I don't know what I'd be doing
        here if I didn't.

                    SIR ALFRED
                (gently)
        I don't either...I'm going to
        rehearsal now but I wish you'd
        meet me at LaLotte's about one
        o'clock on the way to lunch.

                    DAPHNE
        What for?

                    SIR ALFRED
        Because you haven't a thing to
        wear...and I would like to buy
        you a little something...would
        you do that for me?

                    DAPHNE
                (pointing)
        But I have closets full of...

                    SIR ALFRED
        And then lunch with me?

                    DAPHNE
        Of course I will...but I really
        don't need anything...

                    SIR ALFRED
        It says here in very small type...
        by the way you didn't do anything
        you shouldn't while I was away,
        did you?...I mean like falling
        in love with anyone else... or
        anything like that?

                                        (CONTINUED)

76-A (Cont.1)

                              DAPHNE
How could I fall in love with
anyone else when you took my
heart with you?

                            SIR ALFRED
No man ever got a better answer
than that...I'll see you at
LaLotte's.

                            DAPHNE
Yes, my darling.

                                          FADE OUT

FADE IN

77   TYMPANI PLAYER OF A GREAT ORCHESTRA

He has four kettle drums around him. The orchestra is
playing Rossini's Semiramide Overture. He bounces up
and down on the balls of his feet in time with the beat,
then does that exciting stuff that leaps from one drum
to the other.

78   THE BRASS

There is a wonderful part for them in the beginning of
the Overture...the only way I can think of getting that
in the picture is by starting the rehearsal further up
and skipping some subsequent parts.

79   THE WOODWINDS

Rossini also provided a part for them.

80   THE PICCOLO

It might have a girl player. She plays a wonderful and
wonderfully difficult solo.

81   TEN DOUBLE BASS PLAYERS

They saw away thrillingly in perfect unison, the growl
of their huge instruments in the foreground, the rest of
the orchestra in the background. (This will be done by
sweetening the sound track before dubbing. The same
method will be used with the other closeups of instruments if it seems advisable.)

82   THE CELLI

They bow or pluck according to the music.

83   THE VIOLAS

They sing sonorously.

84   SECOND FIDDLES

Facing left their bows rise and fall in wonderful unison

85   FIRST FIDDLES

Their bows in just as perfect unison, they play beautifully.

REVISED - "UNFAITHFULLY YOURS" - 2/16/48   36.

86   SIR ALFRED

In a turtle-neck sweater. He is singing at the top of
his lungs. He leads the men with much gaiety, a cigarette hanging from his smiling lips. Just after a mild
cymbal crash Sir Alfred looks up and scowls past the
CAMERA.

87   CLOSE SHOT - DR. SCHULTZ - THE CYMBALS PLAYER

Bouncing up and down on the balls of his feet he crashes
the discs together.

88   SIR ALFRED - CONDUCTING

During the dialogue he continues conducting and turning
the pages.

                         SIR ALFRED
                    (as the music drops to
                    a lower level for a
                    few bars)
          Keep on, gentlemen, please, I don't
          want to waste your time...
                    (then looking across
                    the orchestra)
          Dr. Schultz...
                         DR. SCHULTZ
          Yes, Sir Alfred?
                         SIR ALFRED
          Yours is one of the most ancient and,
          insofar as I'm concerned...most re-
          vered instrument in the orchestra...
          when Egypt was young, your instrument
          was old...I have been looking at you
          but I can't hear you.

89   DR. SCHULTZ

                         DR. SCHULTZ
          I was afraid of being a little loud,
          Sir Alfred...you know: wulgar.

90   SIR ALFRED

                         SIR ALFRED
          Be wulgar by all means...but let me
          hear that brazen laugh...and let us
          remember always that there is nothing
          refined about music...

The music engulfs him at this point and he conducts
vigorously. He looks at his watch.

91   INSERT OF WATCH

It is quarter to one.

217
(Sturges)

92   DR. SCHULTZ IN HIS POSITION ABOUT FIVE FEET FROM
       THE BASS DRUM

       He looks at his music, turns the page, then hurries
       around the back platform and down and around in back-
       stage (a crane will help us here) until he comes to
       the percussion trunks. With lightning speed he opens
       a low well-used trunk about one yard square and re-
       moves from it a pair of enormous cymbals.

93   HUGO AND THE HOTEL DETECTIVE - BACKSTAGE

       They look at the cymbals player in surprise.

94.   DR. SCHULTZ - HOLDING THE HUGE CYMBALS WELL SEPARATED

       He takes to his heels and hurries back on stage.
       (The boom helps again here.) Just as he is passing
       the surprised Sir Alfred his cue comes and he crashes
       the huge cymbals right where he is, surprising and
       delighting Sir Alfred and nearly knocking the Concert
       Master off his chair. Now he hurries up out of the
       shot.

95   SIR ALFRED - CONDUCTING WONDERFULLY

       He flips over the pages of the score and beams at the
       retreating cymbals player.

96   DR. SCHULTZ - WENDING HIS WAY THROUGH THE OTHER
       MUSICIANS

       Again a cue catches him. He turns and lets go a mighty
       crash which is reacted to by the musicians nearest him.

97   SIR ALFRED - FROM DR. SCHULTZ'S VIEWPOINT

       He brings the wonderful overture to its thrilling end,
       pausing merely to remove his coat before doing so.

                         SIR ALFRED
                     (as it finishes)
           Splendid, gentlemen, splendid....it
           is already much too good for them...
           to make it any better would be a
           total waste of effort...besides which
           I have an appointment with a beauti-
           ful young woman.
                     (he consults
                     his watch)
           ...I will see you tonight.

       He picks up his coat and starts off stage.

98   HUGO, AND THE HOTEL DETECTIVE - BACKSTAGE NEAR THE OPEN
        DOOR TO THE GREEN ROOM

        Through this we see Jules laying out some clothes. From
        the stage proper we hear the conversation of the musi-
        cians putting away their instruments.

                              HUGO
                Look: he is a busy man...I'm his
                manager...he ain't got time to hang
                around and talking with...

                         THE DETECTIVE
                        (indignantly)
                You think I'd skip my lunch and ankle
                all the way over here if what I had
                to show him wasn't red hot?

                              HUGO
                Yas...

                         THE DETECTIVE
                Well that's where you're wrong, see?

99   SIR ALFRED - APPROACHING THEM RAPIDLY

                            SIR ALFRED
                What is it, Hugo?

        The CAMERA PANS him into the shot with the other two.

                              HUGO
                This gink says he's got something
                for you...he's from the hotel.

                         THE DETECTIVE
                And I ain't a gink, I'm the detective
                there...you remember me, don't you,
                Sir Alfred?

                            SIR ALFRED
                Oh yes, I think I've seen you skulk-
                ing about...you are what is known as
                the house "dick" aren't you?

                         THE DETECTIVE
                That's me...could I see you alone a
                minute?

                                                   (CONTINUED)

217

2/10/48   39.

99 (Cont.)

                        SIR ALFRED
                    (not too warmly)
        I suppose so...but I won't enjoy it
        ...Come along...

They start toward the dressing room.

100   THE GREEN ROOM

        Sir Alfred comes in with the detective and the CAMERA
        PANS him over to Jules who hands him a towel.

                        JULES
        Beautiful music, sir, just beautiful.

                        SIR ALFRED
        Thank you very much.
                    (then to the
                    detective)
        Now what do you want? Wait outside
        a moment, will you, Jules?
                    (then to the
                    detective)
        I'm sorry if I sound sharp but I feel
        extremely unsympathetic toward all
        detectives this morning.

                        THE DETECTIVE
        It's all in the line of duty with
        me, boss...it just shows you the
        kind of service we're givin' you at
        The Towers, that's all....we don't
        know just how it got into the hall...
        we're investigating that...but we
        found it and saved it for you...I
        glued it together myself.

He pulls out the very much patched-together operative's
report and tenders it to Sir Alfred.

                        SIR ALFRED
                    (taking the report
                    without enthusiasm)
        I see...you read it, I presume?

                        THE DETECTIVE
        Just enough to glue it together.

                                        (CONTINUED)

862

100 (Cont.)

>   SIR ALFRED
> I see...you concluded that when I
> tear papers up into small bits...
> throw the bits into the waste-
> basket...and kick the wastebasket
> out the door...it is because I am
> trying to save the papers which
> make up the documents. Is that
> correct.

>   THE DETECTIVE
>   (uneasily)
> Well, we didn't know, Sir Alfred...
> the head maid seen this basket
> come flying out and she called me
> and I just used my own judgment,
> that's all.

>   SIR ALFRED
> Very astute! Do you customarily
> shove your nose this deep into
> other people's business?

>   DETECTIVE
> Look boss, as far as I'm concerned..

>   SIR ALFRED
> Have you a match at least?

>   DETECTIVE
> Hunh?

>   SIR ALFRED
>   (irritably)
> A match! One of those little wooden
> things you scratch on the side of
> a match box.

>   DETECTIVE
> Yes sir.

He pulls a large kitchen match out of his pocket.

>   SIR ALFRED
> Will you light it, please?

>   DETECTIVE
> Yes sir.

He lights it with his thumbnail.

>   (CONTINUED)

100 (Cont.1)

SIR ALFRED

Now, get it going well...that's fine
...now hold it steady...

He holds the operative's report to the match until it is
burning brightly.

SIR ALFRED

You see?...it was very important to
me...I hope you don't know any way
of bringing it back to life this
time.

DETECTIVE

No, sir.

SIR ALFRED
(after throwing the
torch into a metal
wastebasket over by
the window)

In that case, why don't you get back
to your work at the hotel...there may
be some very important things you
have to do...such as spying on decent
people by looking through keyholes or
standing on ladders....or picking
through the garbage!

DETECTIVE
(miserably)

Look, boss...I'm sorry...all I meant
to do was....LOOK OUT!

He spins Sir Alfred around and points to the curtain
over the wastepaper basket which is going up in flames.

DETECTIVE

Cheezit!

Now he shoves Sir Alfred out of the room.

DETECTIVE

Help!

101   BACKSTAGE - OUTSIDE OF SIR ALFRED'S ROOM

102   STAGE DOORMAN

Leaping to his feet.

(CONTINUED)

102 (Cont.)

STAGE DOORMAN

Hunh?

DETECTIVE'S VOICE
Where's the hose?

The stage doorman hurries to the wall, seizes a little
hammer on a chain and breaks the glass to a firebox. He
pulls the plunger, then hurries to a box containing folded white firehose and a nozzle. He yanks this out and
starts unscrewing the water valve.

103 DETECTIVE

standing in doorway of Sir Alfred's dressing room. The
glow of the fire and the smoke are visible behind him.
His arms are spread to prevent anyone's entrance into
the room.

DETECTIVE
Keep cool, folks...everything's going
to be all right...the most we can lose
is this side of the building...if the
company gets here in time which they
probably...

104 DOORMAN

rushing toward us, dragging limp hose. Suddenly he
seizes the nozzle more firmly and the hose stiffens like
an angry snake and a powerful jet of water shoots past
the CAMERA, while a leak where the hose joins the nozzle,
sends a cloud of spray up in the doorman's face. Hugo
hurries to help him.

105 DETECTIVE

in the doorway. He stands like Horatio at the bridge.

DETECTIVE
Keep coo...

At this he gets the water right in the face. It knocks
him backwards into the smoking room.

106 DOORMAN

holding hose nozzle. Blinded by the spray, he starts
to lose his balance from the power of the water. Sir
Alfred hurries to his assistance, and also gets a face
full of spray.

107   DOORWAY OF SIR ALFRED'S ROOM

        The detective appears and tries to come out.

108   SIR ALFRED AND DOORMAN

        Squinting through the spray, Sir Alfred aims the nozzle
        a little differently as a couple of violinists come to
        help hold the hose.

109   DOORWAY OF SIR ALFRED'S DRESSING ROOM

        The detective who has almost managed to get out, now
        gets the stream again and goes down like so much pig
        iron. We hear the fire sirens arriving outside. The
        detective reappears on hands and knees and starts out
        under the stream.

110   SIR ALFRED, STAGE DOORMAN AND TWO VIOLINISTS

        holding hose. Ducking the spray, Sir Alfred starts
        bending the hose downwards, both eyes closed. The door-
        man helps him do it.

111   DETECTIVE - IN DOORWAY

        Slowly he is slid back into the smoking room.

                                                    DISSOLVE TO:

REVISED - "UNFAITHFULLY YOURS" - 3/4/48   44.

112   A CORNER OF LALOTTE'S SHOWROOM

In the foreground we see some full-length mirrors re-
flecting doors to dressing rooms. Beyond the mirrors
we see more of the very elegant shop. Daphne's reflection advances toward the mirror wearing a dazzling
evening gown. Madame LaLotte and a saleslady and a
young assistant come with her. Some models come toward
us from beyond the mirrors.

                    DAPHNE
               (pointing to one
               of the models)
          I wonder if that one would look
          better? How much is it?

                    SALESLADY
          Six hundred.

                    MADAME LALOTTE
          What a bargain... why don't you take
          'em both? Turn around again, dollink.

                    DAPHNE
          At six hundred dollars!

                    MADAME LALOTTE
          You're only rich once... take it from
          me.

                    DAPHNE
          I'm not going to choose any of them
          until Alfred gets here... it was all
          his idea anyway... I didn't really
          need anything.

                    MADAME LALOTTE
          I didn't hear you.

                    DAPHNE
          I told him I really didn't need any-
          thing.

                    MADAME LALOTTE
          Vot is becoming to dese girls...
          nudists?

                    A YOUNG GIRL
               (joining the group)
          Will you take the telephone, Lady
          de Carter? It's Sir Alfred.

The saleslady immediately picks up the telephone and
hands it to Daphne.

                                        (CONTINUED)

217
(Sturges)

112 (Cont.)
                    MADAME LALOTTE
          What a lollypop.

                    DAPHNE
          Hello...hello, sweetie love...
          where are you, you're late?

                    MADAME LALOTTE
          Late!

113   SIR ALFRED - IN A PHONE BOOTH BACKSTAGE OF CONCERT HALL

      We are SHOOTING from the wall's side so that through the
      glass behind him we see firemen with axes and policemen
      and excited musicians. Sir Alfred is quite wet and
      looks like hell, but his good humor is unchanged.

                    SIR ALFRED
              (into the telephone)
          I'm dreadfully sorry, darling,
          there's been a little excitement
          down here...I'll join you as soon
          as I get into some dry trousers.
          Some silly ass set fire to my
          dressing room...did you find some
          pretty dresses?

114   DAPHNE - IN THE MIDDLE OF ROOM AT LALOTTE'S

                    DAPHNE
              (excitedly)
          Never mind the dresses...what do
          you mean some silly ass set fire
          to your dressing room?

                    MADAME LALOTTE
              (hastily)
          What do you mean "never mind the
          dresses?"...never mind the fire.

                    DAPHNE
          Sh! Who did you say set fire to
          it?...No!...
              (then putting her
              hand over the phone)
          ...he set fire to it himself.

                    MADAME LALOTTE
              (as if to herself)
          Oh ho...insurance.

                    DAPHNE
          Sh...
              (then into the telephone)
          ...I can't hear you, darling, with
          all those bells going off.

868

REVISED - "UNFAITHFULLY YOURS" - 3/4/48   46.

115   SIR ALFRED - IN PHONE BOOTH

Just outside the phone booth is the fire chief in a white
hat knocking at the door.

                    SIR ALFRED
            I said if you see anything pretty
            be sure to buy it.

                    DAPHNE
            But I don't want to buy anything.

                    MADAME LALOTTE
            Look: Live and let live.

                    SIR ALFRED
            Buy several...it's always nice to
            have a change...I've told Tony to
            pick you up for lunch.

He flaps the door open.

                    THE CHIEF
            Are you the party that started
            this confloration?

                    SIR ALFRED
            Yes, and I'll be with you in just
            a second, Colonel.

He flaps the door closed.

                    SIR ALFRED
            I have to answer some questions
            now, darling, there's a nobleman
            in a white hat waiting outside the
            booth for me.

116   DAPHNE - IN GROUP AT LALOTTE'S

                    DAPHNE
            You didn't get in any trouble,
            darling, I mean...I'll come right
            over...you didn't get burned?

                    MADAME LALOTTE
                (worried)
            What are you talking!...

117   SIR ALFRED - IN PHONE BOOTH

The chief in the white hat waits patiently outside.

                                    (CONTINUED)

217

117 (Cont.)

                              SIR ALFRED
                         (laughing)
          Quite the contrary...I'm sloshing
          wet but I don't think I'm in the
          slightest trouble...
                         (he flaps the door
                         open)
          ...I'll be with you in just one
          second, General.
                         (he flaps the door
                         closed)
          ...GOODBYE, my darling...I'll join
          you at the earliest possible moment.

118   DAPHNE - AT TELEPHONE

                              DAPHNE
          Goodbye, my love.

                              TONY
                         (coming in from in
                         front of the shop)
          Hello, Daphne, I've come to take you
          to lunch.

                              DAPHNE
                         (hanging up the phone)
          Oh, hello, Tony...I'll be ready in
          a minute. It wasn't too serious,
          was it?

                              TONY
                         (reassuringly)
          I don't think so.

                              MADADE LALOTTE
                         (looking suspiciously at
                         Tony then back at Daphne)
          Who's the Hershey bar?

                                        DISSOLVE TO:

119   SIR ALFRED

entering a fashionable restaurant. He has changed his
clothes and carries gloves and stick. We see the street
or Rockefeller Plaza or something like that behind him.
He hands his hat and stick to an attendant.

                    A MAITRE D'HOTEL
                      (bowing)
              Sir Alfred.

                         SIR ALFRED
              Hello, Louie, is my bride here?

120   DAPHNE AND TONY - AT A TABLE

Daphne, wearing a very smart tailored suit, is waving
violently. Apparently she and Tony have almost finished
lunch.

121   SIR ALFRED AND HEAD WAITER

                         SIR ALFRED
              There she is.

                         LOUIE
                      (snapping his fingers
                       to someone ahead of
                       Sir Alfred)
              Conduisez Monsieur au 44.

The CAMERA PANS with Sir Alfred as he crosses toward
Daphne. Suddenly he stops as he finds himself passing
August and Barbara.

                         SIR ALFRED
                      (surprised)
              What are you doing here?
                      (he indicates
                       Daphne and Tony)
              Why aren't you all lunching together?

                         AUGUST
                      (coldly)
              We didn't wish to intrude...

                         BARBARA
                      (witchily)
              ...they looked so cute together.

                                        (CONTINUED)

121 (Cont.)

> SIR ALFRED
> (looking at his
> wife and Tony)
> They <u>do</u> look cute together...
> However...
> (then to Barbara)
> I'll see you later, pretty one...

He pats her cheek, then moves toward Daphne and Tony
and the CAMERA ROLLS with him, passing by people who
stare at and whisper to each other about this celebrated
and handsome man.

> SIR ALFRED
> (as he reaches his wife
> and kisses her hand)
> My darling, I'm terribly sorry...
> thank you so much, Tony, for bring-
> ing her.

> DAPHNE
> I was just famished, sweetie love,
> I <u>had</u> to eat...and you're <u>awful</u> to
> buy me three dresses...and <u>I adore</u>
> you for it...now tell me all <u>about</u>
> the fire...did you burn down the
> whole place or only the back half?

> SIR ALFRED
> I'm sorry to disappoint you but it
> was only a curtain...and part of a
> venetian blind...and of course the
> window...glass breaks so easily,
> you know...probably most of the
> damage was from the water...and I
> think they broke a leg off the piano.

> DAPHNE
> (laughing)
> How did you start it...the fire?

> SIR ALFRED
> I would like to say that I began
> to think about you...and then stood
> too near the curtains...
> (he laughs and so does
> Daphne)
> ...actually I was burning a piece
> of paper I didn't care to have in
> the world...and <u>it</u> set fire to the
> curtains.

(CONTINUED)

121 (Cont. 1)

                    DAPHNE
You mean something like a bad review,
or something? But you never have
any!

                    SIR ALFRED
Something of that nature...anyway
it was very unimportant...
        (now he looks across
        the room at his brother-
        in-law)
...why aren't Barbara and August
sitting with you?

                    DAPHNE
I haven't the slightest idea...they
seemed quite cool.

                    SIR ALFRED
They seemed or he seemed?

                    DAPHNE
They both seemed.

                    SIR ALFRED
What has she to be cool about?

                    DAPHNE
What has he to be cool about?

                    SIR ALFRED
That's another matter...he might
have misunderstood something I
said...or taken it the wrong way...
        (then suddenly)
...By Jove!

He slaps the table and rises to his feet.

                    DAPHNE
        (startled)
What's the matter, darling?

                    SIR ALFRED
Excuse me just one second...I'll
be right back.

He strides out of the SHOT. Daphne and Tony exchange
a worried look.

122   AUGUST AND BARBARA

August rises to his feet as if hoisted up by a rope as
he sees the approaching Sir Alfred.

                    SIR ALFRED
                (first to Barbara)
        Excuse me, Barbara...I have just had
        a revolting thought, August: would
        those people who shall be nameless
        be apt to have additional copies of
        that which I did you know what with
        this morning...because I will not
        have them around

                    BARBARA
                (to August)
        And if you can figure that out
        you're smarter than I think you
        are.

                    AUGUST
                (after sneaking a
                look at his wife)
        Why don't you forget the whole thing
        and concentrate on your music, Alfred.
        I will tell them to dispose of those...
        things at the earliest opportunity.

                    SIR ALFRED
                (viciously)
        Thank you...I will tell them myself...
        give me one of their cards...I
        suppose you carry them around with
        you in case of emergency...

                    AUGUST
                (opening his zipper
                within a zipper wallet)
        I...may have one.

                    BARBARA
        What's all the mystery?

                    SIR ALFRED
                (pretending to make
                a joke)
        The mystery is that you are married
        to a square from Delaware...if you
        are familiar with the appellation...

                                        (CONTINUED)

874

122 (Cont.)

> BARBARA
> That's no mystery...the whole world
> knows it.

> AUGUST
> (producing a card and
> laughing at the joke
> at the same time)
> There you are, Alfred...but I still
> think...

> SIR ALFRED
> (glaring at the card)
> Thank you very much indeed.

He nearly spits on it, then tears it in four, puts it
carefully in his pocket.

> SIR ALFRED
> Thank you.

He stamps out of the SHOT.

> BARBARA
> What's the matter with him...he's
> getting nuttier than you are.

> AUGUST
> Probably something he didn't eat...
> since he merely entered and exited.

123   DAPHNE AND TONY

Sir Alfred enters the SHOT and sits down.

> DAPHNE
> (grabbing his sleeve)
> You weren't challenging August to a
> duel? I saw you passing cards around.

> SIR ALFRED
> (scornfully)
> A duel! I would take him by the back
> of the neck and drop him in a dust
> bin! I've just remembered something,
> darling, that I wish to attend to at
> once so if you'll be kind enough to
> excuse me...you take care of the
> lunch, Tony.
>   (CONTINUED)

123 (Cont.)

                    DAPHNE
        But you haven't had anything to eat,
        darling.

                    SIR ALFRED
        I don't feel like anything to eat
        just at the moment...maybe you'll
        be kind enough to have a sandwich
        for me at the hotel later.

                    DAPHNE
                (soothingly)
        Of course I will...you're all ner-
        vous, darling...it's that plane
        flight... you come back to the hotel
        and I'll have a lovely sandwich all
        ready for you and some beautiful
        very old scotch...and you'll feel a
        lot better...

                    SIR ALFRED
                (kissing her hand
                and arising)
        I feel a lot better already...I'll
        see you in a little while, my love.

He hurries out.

                    TONY
                (after quite a
                long pause)
        For one terrible moment I wondered
        what he and August were talking
        about.

                    DAPHNE
                (after a pause and
                without changing
                her expression)
        Ask for the bill.

Now she gives Tony a long look.

                                        DISSOLVE TO:

217

124   DOWN SHOT ON SIR ALFRED - STEPPING OUT OF TAXICAB

This shot is through a first floor plate-glass window in
the type of New York building which was formerly a brownstone front but now has plate-glass store windows on two
levels: the basement and the first floor. Backwards on
the glass we read (that is those of us who can read backwards, like printers) Sweeney's Detective Agency...
Investigations...Secret Service...Special Information.
The CAMERA PANS Sir Alfred half way across the sidewalk.
Now he stops, reads and turns his head further to one
side.

125   LOW CAMERA SHOT - UP AT SWEENEY'S WINDOW

The CAMERA holds the lettering for a moment, then PANS
to one side onto a sinister face looking down at us while
eating a sinister-looking sandwich in a rather sinister
way.

126   DOWN SHOT - ON SIR ALFRED

He reacts to this face, then sets his jaw and comes up
the stairs. The CAMERA FOLLOWS him through the glass
front, takes him past the tailor shop on the same landing
and brings him into the agency, through the buzzer-
ringing door.

                         SIR ALFRED
                     (after a long
                      accusing look)
                 You are Mr. Sweeney?

He spits out the word Sweeney as if it meant snake.

127   SANDWICH EATER

He looks Sir Alfred up and down in a sinister way before
replying with a slight accent.

                         SANDWICH EATER
                 Who me? Why not O'Brien? What do
                 you want to see him about?

                         SIR ALFRED
                     (coming into the shot)
                 About...business I suppose...I sup-
                 pose you call this...a business?

                         SANDWICH EATER
                     (truculently)
                 Well, what would you call it?

                                        (CONTINUED)

877

127 (Cont.)

He takes a large bite of his sandwich which nearly
strangles him as he reacts to the violence of Sir
Alfred's answer.

> SIR ALFRED
> (furiously and
> oratorically)
> I would call it a criminal invasion
> of the rights of decent people...an
> assualt upon the very privacy which
> is the cornerstone of self-respect...
> an infamous pursuit without shame or
> ethics,   dedicated.to the destruction
> of honor and the substitution for it
> of all that is low, bestial and des-
> picable in the human heart...

> SANDWICH EATER
> (waving his sandwich in
> a token of surrender)
> Look, mister...

> SIR ALFRED
> I'm not finished...a vile calling,
> masquerading in the cloak of re-
> spectability, but actually sprung
> from the cesspools of humanity...
> the seepage of civilization...

The sandwich eater puts down his sandwich.

> SIR ALFRED
> Does that answer your question?

> SANDWICH EATER
> Completely.

He starts to put his sandwich back in his mouth.

> SIR ALFRED
> (during this final
> diatribe, the Sandwich
> Eater, unable to get a
> word in, waves No, No,
> with his finger)
> A so-called profession that introduces
> into the world of decent folk, and for
> their entrapment, the methods of rogues,
> knaves and blacklegs, the standards of
> traitors and spies...the scruples of
> jackals, vultures and other scavangers...

(CONTINUED)

127 (Cont.1)

> SANDWICH EATER
> (rising)
> Look, mister, I'm the tailor from
> next door...I'm just here to eat
> my lunch... I mean I was <u>trying</u> to
> eat my lunch... and answer the tele-
> phone... a favor that's all.
> (he starts for
> the door)
> ...with much of what you got to say...
> and believe me whatever you are do-
> ing you are wasting your time, you
> should be in Congress...confiden-
> tially I agree....but what good is
> that going to do you... about a blue
> serge suit my opinion is worth some-
> thing...but about ethics?
> (he gets one hand
> on the doorknob)

> SIR ALFRED
> (defeated)
> Then where is the director of this
> enterprise?

> SANDWICH EATER
> (pointing)
> Here he is now climbing...good day.

> SIR ALFRED
> (stonily)
> Good day.

He watches the tailor go out and Mr. Sweeney come up:
a large man in his fifties.

> SIR ALFRED
> (watching him come
> through the door)
> You at last are Mr. Sweeney, I trust?

> MR. SWEENEY
> (expansively)
> And <u>you</u> are Sir Alfred de Carter.

He seizes Sir Alfred's reluctant hand and crushes it in
both of his.

> (CONTINUED)

127 (Cont. 2)

                              MR. SWEENEY
                        (dreamily)
                  How I've looked forward to this mo-
                  ment, Sir Alfred! I was to your
                  maiden concert in this country...
                  your dee-but...down there at
                  Aeolian Hall...people said 'What
                  do you want to hear that limey for?
                  What does he know about music? It
                  takes an Eyetalian or a Rooshian
                  or a Dutchman to bring it out good,'
                  but something inside of me said give
                  the limey a chancet...and I did!

                              SIR ALFRED
                        (coldly)
                  Did you...

                              MR. SWEENEY
                  And am I glad I did! That hunch has
                  paid off in golden dividends! I
                  haven't missed one of your concerts
                  ...within the metropolitan area, of
                  course...I don't follow you to you
                  know...South Dakota...the WAY you
                  handle Handel, Sir Alfred! For me
                  nobody handles Handel like you do...
                  there's you up here...
                        (his hand nearly
                        touches the ceiling)
                  ...and then...there's nobody...no
                  second...no third...maybe way down
                  here Arturo: a poor fourth.

                              SIR ALFRED
                  That is largely debatable, in any
                  case what I came to see you abou....

                              MR. SWEENEY
                        (carried away)
                  And your Delius...
                        (he closes his eyes
                        and shakes his head
                        from side to side)
                  ...delirious. Usually I have my
                  tickets as soon as they're printed
                  ...that change in schedule loused
                  me up a little...but I'll get in
                  somehow...

                                              (CONTINUED)

217

127 (Cont.3)

                         SIR ALFRED
          I am bitterly sorry to hear that
          you are a music lover...

                         MR. SWEENEY
                    (shocked)
          Hunh?...I live for music...why
          without music I wouldn't have...

                         SIR ALFRED
                    (interrupting icily)
          ...as I had always believed that
          music had certain moral and anti-
          septic powers quite apart from its
          obvious engorgement of the senses
          which elevated and purified its
          disciples, lifting them out of and
          above professions like this...
          infamy.

                         MR. SWEENEY
                    (terribly hurt)
          Sir Alfred!

                         SIR ALFRED
          So spare me your compliments...the
          flattery of a footpad is an insult
          in itself!

                         MR. SWEENEY
                    (pleadingly)
          You mean a flatfoot, don't you, Sir
          Alfred? You don't mean a footpad...

                         SIR ALFRED
                    (emphatically)
          I mean a footpad! And now that I
          know you like them...I will probably
          cut Handel and Delius out of my pro-
          grams forever.

                         MR. SWEENEY
                    (as if Sir Alfred
                    had threatened to
                    cut out his liver)
          Now don't talk like that, Sir Alfred.

                         SIR ALFRED
          So kindly refrain from telling me any
          other of your musical favorites...and
          poisoning those for me also!

                                        (CONTINUED)

127 (Cont. 4)

                    MR. SWEENEY
                 (very sympathetically)
        You're just hurt...I can see it...
        you read that report and naturally
        it upset you...ah, we fall for these
        little dames and try to believe
        they're in love with us...when every
        morning our shaving mirror yells
        they can't be...'til one day we find
        out youth belongs to youth...like
        you just done...and then...

He drops a consoling hand on Sir Alfred's shoulder.

                    SIR ALFRED
                 (bristling)
        Take your hand off me!

                    MR. SWEENEY
                 (holding wide his arms)
        Don't get sore at me! What have I
        got to do with it? I suppose it was
        me that went down to thirty-four-o-
        six in the middle of the night wearing
        only a negligee and stayed for
        thirty-eight minutes...I suppose
        that's the part that bothered you...
        it usually is...

                    SIR ALFRED
                 (startled)
        Thirty-four-o-six!

                    MR. SWEENEY
        I think that was the number of the
        room...I got it here someplace...
        if you want it...

He unlocks the file and starts looking for the report
without stopping his conversation.

                    MR. SWEENEY
        ...but that's only circumstantial
        evidence...why don't we give her the
        benefit of the doubt...maybe she
        couldn't open her toothpaste...you
        was in England...so she goes down
        and gets this guy to do it for her...
        maybe she seen a mouse in her room...
        and it upset her and she wanted com-
        pany...o'course that one's kind of thin...

                                        (CONTINUED)

127 (Cont. 5)

> MR. SWEENEY (Cont.)
> BUT LET'S GIVE HER THE BENEFIT OF
> THE DOUBT ANYWAY...maybe she woke
> up out of a bad dream...and without
> thinkin' where she was goin'...she
> slipped into a neglijay and...

He makes a helpless gesture and puts on a pince-nez,
and pulls out the correct report.

> SIR ALFRED
> Are you presuming to discuss the
> Lady de Carter, my wife?

> MR. SWEENEY
> (innocently)
> Well, you read it, didn't you? I
> thought that's why Henschler said
> he was taking the copy...Holy Moses!
> (he hands him
> the report)
> ...here...sit down some place.

> SIR ALFRED
> (in a dead voice as
> he takes the copy)
> This is the only copy?

> MR. SWEENEY
> Yeah...that's the original.

Slowly Sir Alfred tears it to bits.

> MR. SWEENEY
> You're a wise man...I been through
> it...only I wasn't as smart as you
> are...so I lost my piano...and my
> savings...and a little shack I had
> down to the beach...and her...so
> what have I got now...maybe I
> shouldn't be saying this, but if
> it was me I'd never have 'em tailed...
> I'd never try to find out nothin'...
> I'd just be grateful for whatever
> they was willing to gimme...a year...
> a week...an hour...

During this Sir Alfred has stood quietly tearing the
remains of the report into ever and ever smaller bits.

(CONTINUED)

127 (Cont. 6)

> Now he turns and crosses to the door; he pauses here for
> a second and Mr. Sweeney looks at him compassionately.
> Now Sir Alfred reaches into the inside of his coat pock-
> et, takes out a dozen tickets, separates two from the
> rest, and returns to a position near Mr. Sweeney, then
> throws the two tickets on the desk.

SIR ALFRED

> For tonight.

> He turns, goes through the door and lightly down the
> steps. Mr. Sweeney picks up the two tickets and quite
> sadly waves them after the retreating Sir Alfred.

FADE OUT

FADE IN

128   DAPHNE - AT TELEPHONE

She is partly and attractively dressed. Her dressing
table is visible behind her, and beyond that the open
door to her bathroom.

> DAPHNE
> I just thought he _might_ be, that's
> all.

129   BARBARA - IN HER BEDROOM

She is also half dressed and her maid (white) is busy
in the background.

> BARBARA
> (into the telephone)
> I'm sure he isn't...but wait a
> minute...I'll go and ask Casanova.

She gets up, crosses to a door and opens it.

130   AUGUST - AT HIS DRESSING TABLE

He is in evening clothes but still in shirt sleeves. At
the moment he is busy counting his roll. We see the
door opening and Barbara appears in the mirror beyond
him.

> BARBARA
> Daphne wants to know if you've seen
> anything of Alfred...he seems to
> have disappeared.

> AUGUST
> (after jumping slightly
> to the unexpected voice)
> No, I haven't...but we're not on the
> best of terms anyway, so...

131   BARBARA - IN HER ROOM

> BARBARA
> O.K.
> (she closes the
> door and returns
> to the telephone)
> No, he isn't, sweetie...there's
> nobody here but Sitting Bull...
> counting his money in the other
> room...what time do you want me
> to pick you up?

217

132   DAPHNE - AT TELEPHONE

                         DAPHNE
          Well, if he doesn't show up pretty
          soon, there may not be any concert...
                    (while she said
                    this a wedge of
                    light fell upon her
                    and she turned and
                    looked out of the
                    picture)
          ...wait a minute...the great man is
          just coming in...make it about seven-
          thirty, darling...unless we just want
          to pick up some hamburgers on the way
          ...you do whatever you like.
                    (then, as a quick
                    afterthought)
          What fur are you wearing so I won't
          wear the same...all right, baby.

     She hangs up.

133   SIR ALFRED - SILHOUETTED IN DOORWAY TO HIS STUDY

     Daphne's last words come over him.

134   DAPHNE

     Getting up from the telephone.

                         DAPHNE
          What happened to you, darling?
          Tony and I were terribly worried...
          I finally sent him to get dressed
          anyway.

     She walks toward him and the CAMERA PANS her over to
     him.

                         DAPHNE
          I've had your sandwich all ready...
          I've had the ice all ready for your
          drink...I've had the bed all ready
          for your nap...where have you been?
          ...I bet you've been out with some
          girls!

                         SIR ALFRED
          Girls! Hah!

                                        (CONTINUED)

134 (Cont.)

                          DAPHNE
                    (putting her arms
                    around his neck)
          Where have you been, sweetie?   I've
          been awfully worried about you.

                          SIR ALFRED
          I have been to the movies.

                          DAPHNE
                    (stupefied)
          The movies!

                          SIR ALFRED
          I saw a very long picture about a
          dog, the moral of which was that
          the dog is man's best friend, and a
          companion feature which questioned
          the necessity of marriage for eight
          reels and then concluded that it
          was essential in the ninth.

                          DAPHNE
                    (soothingly)
          Alfred.

                          SIR ALFRED
          There was also something about
          Time Marching On and a newsreel
          of the British Royal Family
          christening something or other
          and a lot of people saved from a
          sinking freighter and a picture of
          a cat that had its kittens in a
          harmonium...which made ghostly
          music and frightened a harlem con-
          gregation nearly out of its wits.

                          DAPHNE
                    (putting her hand
                    on his forehead)
          You feel quite hot.

                          SIR ALFRED
          I am anything but quite hot.

                          DAPHNE
          Why didn't you take me to the movies
          ...I love the movies.

                                        (CONTINUED)

134 (Cont. 1)

> SIR ALFRED
> There are times when a man wishes
> to be alone...this was one of those
> times...any further questions?

> DAPHNE
> Well, of course not, darling...
> would you like...would you like
> me to run a nice hot bath for you?

> SIR ALFRED
> Do I appear to need one?

> DAPHNE
> (nearly in tears)
> Well of course you don't, darling,
> I, I just...

> SIR ALFRED
> If I decide that I need, "A nice
> hot bath," I will draw one...if I
> don't, I won't.

> DAPHNE
> You're going to make me cry...Won't
> you take your sandwich anyway,
> darling?
> (she picks it up
> and puts it in
> his hands)
> You can't go all day and all night
> without eating.

> SIR ALFRED
> (gruffly)
> Thank you for your solicitude.

He steps into the study and closes the door. Daphne
looks at the door for a second, puts the back of her
hand to her mouth, bursts into tears, staggers blindly
toward her bed and throws herself upon it.

135   SIR ALFRED - IN HIS STUDY

He stands quietly in the middle of it for a moment, then
goes to the door and opens it. He steps into the hall,
pulls the door within six inches of closing.

217

136   SIR ALFRED - IN HALL

        He walks down this and the CAMERA PRECEDES him. As he
        passes the doors he takes note of the numbers: 3425,
        3423, 3421, 3419...presently he stops and looks grimly
        at the number.

137   INSERT - NUMBER ON THE DOOR

        It is 3406.

138   SIR ALFRED - LOOKING AT DOOR

        He looks at it for a long moment, then knocks firmly
        three times.

                              TONY'S VOICE
                    Come in...

        Slowly Sir Alfred opens the door.

139   INSIDE OF DOOR

        It opens slowly and Sir Alfred comes in. Now he closes
        the door behind him.

140   TONY - AT HIS CHIFFONIER

        He is already dressed in a very well-fitting tail coat,
        and has paused in the act of brushing his hair. He is
        so surprised at Sir Alfred's visit that he says nothing.

141   SIR ALFRED - IN FRONT OF DOOR

        He advances into the room and the CAMERA PANS him PAST
        Tony as he crosses to the window, looks out of it, looks
        into the bathroom, looks at the bed, then goes to the
        door, opens it and leaves without a word.

142   TONY - IN FRONT OF CHIFFONIER

        He watches Sir Alfred go without betraying the slightest
        emotion. Now he resumes brushing his hair but changes
        implements after a moment as he finds he is trying to
        do it with a shoehorn.

                                        DISSOLVE TO:

143   TRUCKING SHOT - AHEAD OF SIR ALFRED - IN HALL

        After a moment he reenters his apartment.

144   SIR ALFRED - IN HIS STUDY

He closes the door and goes to the window and looks out.
After a moment he looks at his wrist watch and removes
his coat, tiepin and necktie. While unbuttoning his
shirt, he stops suddenly, crosses to his desk and opens
the right-hand upper drawer.

145   INSERT - CLOSE SHOT OF A REVOLVER

146   SIR ALFRED

Looking down at the revolver. Suddenly he looks up and
closes the drawer hastily.

147   DOOR TO DAPHNE'S ROOM

It is opening. She comes in, in a lovely evening gown,
carrying a big whiskey and soda.

                    DAPHNE
                 (hesitantly)
         I don't know what's the matter with
         you...and I don't know what's the
         matter with my zipper either...will
         you see if you can close it?

148   SIR ALFRED

He looks at his wife sourly for a moment, then speaks.

                    SIR ALFRED
         Come to the light.

149   DAPHNE

She comes forward. As she passes the desk she puts the
whiskey and soda down on it next to the sandwich, and
the CAMERA PANS her into the shot with her husband.
Sir Alfred puts on his glasses, examines the problem,
gives three yanks on the zipper, then zips it up so
hard that the zipper and the top back of the dress remain in his hand.

                    DAPHNE
             (turning and clutching
              her dress together)
         Well that's a fine thing...what's
         the matter with you...now I'll have
         to put on something else.

                                        (CONTINUED)

149 (Cont.)

> SIR ALFRED
> Then put on something else...you
> certainly are not suffering from
> any shortage...the women of England
> are· lucky to have <u>one</u> dress.

> DAPHNE
> (dismayed)
> What's that got to do with <u>me</u>?

> SIR ALFRED
> You are after all married to an
> Englishman.

> DAPHNE
> Well, I didn't ask you to buy me all
> these dresses...I can't stop you
> from buying me dresses...you're
> <u>always</u> saying I'll meet you at so
> and so's and buy you a dress...you
> <u>know</u> you do...if you're so worried
> <u>about</u> how English women are dressed
> there's nothing to stop you from
> sending them all to them instead...
> it wouldn't bother me any... I don't
> <u>like</u> clothes!

> SIR ALFRED
> I have sent the women of England
> plenty.

> DAPHNE
> Then shut up about it...

> SIR ALFRED
> I forbid you to speak to your hus-
> band in that tone!

> DAPHNE
> That's right, strike me, you brute!
> (she waits a
> moment but
> nothing happens)
> So you don't dare.

> SIR ALFRED
> Go away and get dressed for the con-
> cert...this really should be a mag-
> nificent concert.

(CONTINUED)

149 (Cont. 1)

> DAPHNE
> (starting out)
> Maybe I will go to the movies in-
> stead.

> SIR ALFRED
> Culturally they might suit you bet-
> ter.

> DAPHNE
> And I thought my <u>sister</u> had married
> the jerk! Give me <u>that</u> zipper!

She snatches it from him, exits and slams the door
after her.

150   SIR ALFRED

Looking after her. He snorts and continues unbuttoning
his shirt. Suddenly he stops, crosses the room violently to the desk containing the revolver, snatches
the sandwich off the plate and bites into it viciously.
He washes it down with a big gulp of whiskey and soda.

> FADE OUT

FADE IN

151   HIGH CAMERA SHOT - FROM MIDDLE OF STREET - DOWN ON EXT.
      OF CONCERT HALL - NIGHT

      We look over the cars into the lobby. We see the queue
      at the box office, the doorman and the policeman control-
      ling the traffic. As the cars discharge their fashion-
      able cargoes and are hurriedly shooed away:

152   NEWSPAPER PHOTOGRAPHERS

      At corner of lobby one of them steps forward and raises
      his camera.

153   MME. POMPODOUR AND DEAF GENTLEMAN

      Expert at this sort of stuff the old lady beams toothily
      as the flashlight goes off.

154   HUGO - IN THE LOBBY

      He bows happily as the dowager goes by from a position
      near the ticket takers.

155   MR. SWEENEY AND THE TAILOR

      marching quietly into the lobby, proud of their tickets
      and showing it. They are wearing tuxedos. As they hand
      in their tickets:

156   BACKSTAGE - CONCERT HALL

      Sir Alfred comes in, his hat turned low over his eyes,
      and his overcoat collar turned up.

                         STAGE DOORMAN
                Good evening, Sir Alfred.

                         SIR ALFRED
                    (almost inaudibly)
                Evening.

                         A CELLIST
                    (with cello - hurry-
                    ing in after Sir Alfred)
                Evaning, maestro...I'ma terribly
                sorry I'ma little late.

                         SIR ALFRED
                    (gloomily)
                No importance.
                                          (CONTINUED)

2/13/48

156 (Cont.)

                    CELLIST
          Thank you, maestro, thank you.

He hurries by. From force of habit Sir Alfred starts
into his blackened dressing room. At the last moment
he notices a piece of molding that has been tacked across
the door with a hand-lettered sign: "Please Keep Out."
He looks around in perplexity then roars at the top of
his voice:

                    SIR ALFRED
          Jules! Where are we?

157   A DOOR

It flies open and reveals a little old English valet.

                    JULES
          Right in 'ere, Sir Alfred...it's a
          bit of a squeeze but our regular
          room 'ad a bit of a blitz.

                    SIR ALFRED
          Quite all right.

He enters the room and Jules closes the door behind him.

158   MR. SWEENEY AND THE TAILOR

coming around the outside aisle in auditorium. An usher-
ette (check this) is leading them. With each step toward
the front seat they look prouder but there is a spatter
of applause (check this) as the musicians come on the
stage.

159   STAGE OF CONCERT HALL

The orchestra comes on from the wings. Most of the instruments have already been tuned off stage (I believe)
but there is still some tuning to be done.

160   MR. SWEENEY AND TAILOR

They are now in their seats. They open the programs and
look at them with great anticipation. It is possible
that the cover of the programs bears the same shot of
Sir Alfred that we saw as an eight-sheet in the lobby.

161   HIGH CAMERA SHOT - DOWN ON EXT. OF CONCERT HALL

       August Henschler's magnificent automobile (possibly a
       1948 Rolls Royce) pulls into the curb. As the doorman
       throws open the door:

162   CLOSE SHOT - INTO CAR - PAST DOORMAN

       First Tony, then August, then Barbara, then Daphne are
       helped out. The jewels and furs on the two girls are
       the best. Also they are not similar.

163   NEWSPAPER PHOTOGRAPHERS

       They all hurry forward.

164   TRUCKING SHOT - AHEAD OF DAPHNE, TONY, BARBARA AND
       AUGUST

       The two girls smile prettily as the bulbs flash. Tony
       does nothing. August smiles a little phonily.

165   TRUCKING SHOT - TOWARD HUGO

                          HUGO
                       (happily)
              Good evening, good evening.
                       (then in a slightly
                       lower tone)
              What a house....did you deliver the
              maestro in the back?

                          DAPHNE
              Yes and he's as cross as a bear
              with a sore paw.

                          BARBARA
                       (to her sister)
              I'd rather have yours sore than
              mine all smiling.

                          DAPHNE
              From the way he was tonight you
              can have him.

                          BARBARA
              It's a deal.

                          HUGO
              It's nothing but talent...he'll sweat
              it all out before he gets to the end
              of intermission.
                                        (CONTINUED)

165 (Cont.)

DAPHNE
(fervently)
Well I hope so.

BARBARA
Mine doesn't even sweat...he doesn't
do anything.

The girls go past us as Tony and August get close to us.

AUGUST
(speaking confi-
dentially)
Music!...let's hope it isn't a long
one anyway.

166   SIR ALFRED

sitting glumly in his dressing room. His coat is off
and Jules is massaging the back of his neck.

SIR ALFRED
Are you in love Jules?

JULES
Oh devotedly, sir.

SIR ALFRED
What would you do if you found out
your wife was untrue to you?

JULES
(bursting out
laughing)
Untrue to me? I think it's most unlikely Sir!...first of all where
would she find anybody...and in the
second place if she'd wanted someone
better than me she could've 'ad him
easy enough...I was awful ugly when
I was young, sir...begging your
pardon but what would you do, sir,
since we're asking questions...

SIR ALFRED
You mean if...my wife...

JULES
Yes sir...purely supposititious and
'ypothetical naturally...

(CONTINUED)

166 (Cont.)

                         SIR ALFRED
                    (after a pause)
          I don't know...
                    (he narrows
                    his eyes)
          I really don't.

                         JULES
                    (laughing)
          As if anybody could be untrue to
          you, Sir!

     There is a knock on the door and in the mirror behind
     Sir Alfred we see the door open and a head appear.

                         THE HEAD
          Three minutes, Sir Alfred.

                         SIR ALFRED
          Thank you...and thank you, Jules.

                         JULES
                    (taking a towel
                    off Sir Alfred's
                    shoulders)
          You're most welcome, Sir Alfred.

     As Sir Alfred looks at his watch, we:

                                             DISSOLVE TO:

167   A BOX

The CAMERA PULLS BACK as Daphne, Barbara, Tony and
August are ushered in. As they arrange themselves and
the two beautiful girls throw off their furs, the peopl
in the neighboring boxes watch them with fascination.

168   DOWAGER

we saw before. She raises her opera glasses.

169   AN OLD DIPLOMATIC TYPE OF GENTLEMAN

He curls his mustaches.

170   LOW CAMERA SHOT - UP AT BOX

The sisters look very lovely.

171   HIGH CAMERA SHOT - MR. SWEENEY AND TAILOR

Mr. Sweeney looks up at the box and shakes his head a
little sadly. The tailor notices him and follows his
glance. He twists his head so far that his collar flie
open and nearly hits Mr. Sweeney in the nose. Mr.
Sweeney points out to the tailor what has happened and
the latter repairs the contretemps with some embarrassment.

172   DAPHNE AND BARBARA

The beautiful sisters, almost in unison, take out their
vanity cases and start repairing their lip rouge.

173   A MIDDLE-AGED GENTLEMAN - IN NEXT BOX

He is watching them practically with his tongue hanging
out.

174   DAPHNE AND BARBARA

Without having looked at him Barbara has nevertheless
seen the guy. With a faintly amused look and an imper-
ceptible jerk of the head she tells her sister to take
a gander at the mug. Daphne turns frankly and the
CAMERA PANS with her as she looks right in to the fat-
head's tonsils. The latter yanks his head back, snaps
his mouth closed and looks out over the audience.
Daphne explodes with laughter and the CAMERA PANS back
to include Barbara who laughs also but not so whole-
heartedly. Now there is a thunder of applause and the

(CONTINUED)

217

174 (Cont.)

      Lights dim (check this). The girls look toward the
      stage. Barbara, Tony and August start clapping perfunc-
      torily. Daphne looks at the stage and she looks as if
      she is about to cry, then as if it were wrung from her
      she applauds wholehearted.

175   BOOM SHOT - STAGE RIGHT AND PART OF MUSICIANS

      Sir Alfred is striding toward the podium, superb in his
      London made Hammerclaw. The CAMERA BOOMS in to him as
      he crosses the stage so that we are in a tight full
      length shot by the time he has reached the podium and
      taken his third bow. Before turning around to his music
      he looks grimly at his box.

176   DAPHNE, BARBARA, TONY AND AUGUST

      All are applauding. Daphne stops applauding and surrep-
      titiously blows her husband a little kiss.

177   HIGH CAMERA SHOT - SIR ALFRED

      He turns his back upon us, picks up his baton and raps
      on the metal shade. The applause dies out except for
      that from two pairs of hands which comes out very
      sharply. Sir Alfred looks back over his shoulder for
      a quick glance and gives a slight double take.

178   MR. SWEENEY AND TAILOR

      They are beating their palms enthusiastically. Now
      they nudge each other and stop a little lamely. The
      tailor's collar flies open again and he grabs it desper-
      ately.

179   SIR ALFRED

      He looks sourly down at this, lifts his eyes for one
      second to his wife, then turns, raps quickly on the
      light shade, raises his arms high and brings them down
      to the thunder of the opening measure of a bloody,
      militaristic piece. The CAMERA BOOMS back slowly to
      include the entire orchestra.

180   THE BOX - CONTAINING BEAUTIFUL SISTERS, TONY AND AUGUST

      They watch spellbound.

899

181   CLOSE SHOT - SIR ALFRED FROM BACK

        We stay on him for a moment then PAN on to the Concert
        Master, and the first two stands of first fiddles. Now
        the CAMERA TRUCKS along the first fiddles until it en-
        filades the double basses.

182   CELLI

        At the proper moment we:

183   SECOND FIDDLES

        After watching their beautiful work we:

184   WOODWINDS

        After a little of these we:

185   BRASS

        Just as they raise their instruments. After this we:

186   TRICK SHOT ON SIR ALFRED

        about twenty feet away and on level with his eyes. We
        start PUSHING IN as he conducts the martial music. We
        come closer and closer until we are on a big head of
        him. The suffering in his face is very obvious from
        this distance. Now after a pause the CAMERA PUSHES IN
        until his eyes, eyebrows and nose fill the screen.
        After this we PUSH IN still closer until one eye fills
        the screen and finally so close that the pupil of one
        eye, which is to say blackness, fills the screen. Now
        that we are in Sir Alfred's mind a very, very slow FADE
        IN begins and we find ourselves in Sir Alfred's study
        on a CLOSEUP of the antique village orchestra clock.
        It comes to 11:30. There is a whirring sound and the
        leader beats out the first eleven notes of Jingle Bells.
        The sound of the orchestra is not abated much but the
        bells probably cut through all right. Now the CAMERA
        PANS over to the door leading to the foyer. This door
        is open and at the end of the foyer we see the door to
        the hall open and Sir Alfred comes in preceded by his
        wife. They walk slowly toward us and into the study.
        Daphne comes to a stop a foot ahead of her husband and
        looks ahead nervously...probably a little guiltily.
        Sir Alfred, behind her, rolls his eyes toward her with-
        out turning his head, like an actor playing an Oriental.
        Slowly he removes his coat and muffler then takes
        Daphne's fur coat from her shoulders. This seems to
        bring her to life.

                                                      (CONTINUED)

186 (Cont.)

SIR ALFRED
(looking at her
strangely as he
removes her cape)
I trust you enjoyed the concert?

DAPHNE
I thought you were wonderful, darling.

SIR ALFRED
Thank you...I felt quite inspired
tonight...did you have a peculiar
feeling you were hearing me conduct
for the last time?

DAPHNE
(frightened)
For the last time!

SIR ALFRED
Women get premonitions about things
sometimes...such as that their husbands are going to die...or even
that they are going to...pass on
I believe it is called in America...
or things of that nature.

DAPHNE
(frightened)
Why should I have any such thoughts
as that?

SIR ALFRED
It could have been the music...
which does strange things sometimes...
very strange things...I think that
after all that sombre music of mine...
you should hear something lighter...
something gayer...something nearer
your age....as a sort of antidote...
how would you like to go dancing?

DAPHNE
Wouldn't that be wonderful.

SIR ALFRED
(watching her carefully)
Yes, wouldn't it?... I have to talk to
Hugo about the South American tour for
awhile...but I might be able to join
you later...certainly I will try very
hard.
(CONTINUED)

186 (Cont.1)

> DAPHNE
> Join who later?

> SIR ALFRED
> (blandly)
> You and...whoever was fortunate
> enough to take you dancing....at
> my expense of course...I should
> insist upon paying.

> DAPHNE
> (puzzled)
> But I don't think I want to go
> dancing without you....I can't
> think of anyone I'd care to go
> out with.

> SIR ALFRED
> Think hard.

> DAPHNE
> I am thinking hard...but I can't
> think of anybody.

> SIR ALFRED
> (very off-handedly)
> How about Tony?

> DAPHNE
> (watching him out
> of the corner of
> her eyes)
> Tony! Oh you mean Tony...why should
> I want to go out with Tony?

> SIR ALFRED
> I merely suggested Tony because he
> is my secretary and therefore con-
> venient...because he is a very fine
> looking young man and you must look
> well together...especially dancing...
> because being seen with him, since
> it is well known that he is my
> secretary, will cause no raised eye-
> brows or remarks behind the napkins..
> and finally because he has my com-
> plete confidence.

> DAPHNE
> But he's such a bore.

(CONTINUED)

186 (Cont.2)

                         SIR ALFRED
          Obviously he is not as amusing as
          I am.
                    (he laughs uproar-
                    iously and so does
                    his wife)
          ...but I'm not asking you to fall
          in love with the young man...I'm
          only asking you to let him take
          you dancing.

                         DAPHNE
          Well if you really want me to...

                         SIR ALFRED
          I really want you to.

                         DAPHNE
          ...I don't suppose there could be
          much harm to it.

                         SIR ALFRED
                    (archly amused)
          How could there be?

                         DAPHNE
          I'll go and call him then.

                         SIR ALFRED
                    (quickly)
          Do you know his room number?

                         DAPHNE
                    (rigidly)
          I can get it...from the operator...
          I guess.

                         SIR ALFRED
          Of course...and what will you wear?

                         DAPHNE
                    (pointing to her.
                    dress)
          You think I should change...just
          for Tony?

                         SIR ALFRED
          Tony is a very handsome young man...
          you mustn't talk about him that way.

                                        (CONTINUED)

186 (Cont.3)

> DAPHNE
> I've never noticed it.

> SIR ALFRED
> I'm sure you haven't...nevertheless
> I'd wear something a little younger...
> a little less...conservative...not
> as if you were going out with...me.

> DAPHNE
> You mean like that purple one...
> with the plumes at the hips?

> SIR ALFRED
> Yes. Why not the one with the plumes
> at the hips? You go and call Tony
> and tell him to pick you up in...
> (he looks at his
> watch)
> FIFTEEN MINUTES EXACTLY...then put
> on the purple dress...with the plumes
> at the hips.

He licks his lips a little nervously after saying that.

> DAPHNE
> (happily)
> All right, darling.

She kisses him on the cheek, picks up her fur coat and
practically skips out of the room. Sir Alfred smiles
after her and the music grows louder as his smile
hardens. The instant her door closes he becomes the
man of action. Swiftly, surely, without a superfluous
movement, he removes from a cupboard, sets up, complete
with microphone, plugs into the wall and loads with
record ready for receiving a message, a portable, automatic record changing, thirty-three and one-third to
seventy-eight R.P.M. recording unit. Now after looking
over his shoulder to see that he is unobserved, he slides
the unit into the bathroom, enters the bathroom, and
closes the door after him.

187   SIR ALFRED - IN BATHROOM

Partly in the mirror, partly directly, we see him reach
for a switch on the machine.

188   INSERT - CLOSE SHOT - RECORDING UNIT

Sir Alfred's hand comes into the SHOT and turns a switch
to "Loud." Now his hand goes to a knurled knob which
has attached to it a little pointer. The little pointer
is at seventy-eight R.P.M. Sir Alfred's hand turns it
to thirty-three and one-third R.P.M. Now his hand goes
to the "On" and "Off" switch, twists it to "On" and the
record begins to rotate.

189   CLOSE SHOT - SIR ALFRED - PICKING UP MICROPHONE

                         SIR ALFRED
                    (into the microphone
                     stretching the words)
                 He-e-l-p! H-e-e-l-l-p!

Worried about the loudness of his own voice he stops,
unhooks a large terry cloth robe and puts it over his
head, practically obscuring himself and the microphone
from our view. Now he continues to record.

                         SIR ALFRED
                     (stretching the
                          words)
             H-e-e-l-p! H-e-e-l-p! H-e-e-l-p!
             H-e-e-l-p!.. St-o-o-p, T-o-o-ny...
             St-o-o-p...O-o-o-h...O-o-o-h...
             A-h-h-h...A-h-h-h...H-e-e-l-p...
             H-e-e-l-p...Please have pity.
             What did I ever do to you except
             love you...take my jewels if you
             want them, but spare me for the
             love of Heaven...Help, help...

Now he pulls back the terry cloth robe, lifts the recording arm off the record and puts down the playback
arm. Now he turns a little knob and immediately we
hear in Sir Alfred's own voice: Help, help...(a long
pause) help, help, help, help, stop, Tony, stop. Now
Sir Alfred reaches for the knurled knob.

190   INSERT - KNURLED KNOB

Sir Alfred's hand comes into the SHOT and twists it so
that the little pointer moves from thirty-three and
one-third to seventy-eight.

191   SIR ALFRED

Instantly the voice rises in a howling portamento and
lands shrilly in the upper register. We hear the

                                            (CONTINUED)

191 (Cont.)

    desperate callings of anguished woman.

                    THE RECORDER
        O-o-o-h, O-o-o-h, Ah-h-h, Ah-h-h,
        Help, Help. Please have pity...
        what did I ever do to you except
        love you...take my jewels if you
        want them...but spare me for the
        love of Heaven...help...help...

    Sir Alfred smiles insanely at the recorder as it comes
    to the end of the message, then stops it, turns the
    knurled knob back to thirty-three and one-third, removes
    the playing arm, and puts the cutting arm back, placing
    the needle carefully in the right groove, and then after
    putting the terry cloth robe over his head again, picks
    up the microphone, turns on the machine and continues
    his recording in long stretched words:

                    SIR ALFRED
        Help, help, stop, Tony...murder..
        police...murder...A-a-a-a-a-a-a-h.

    This last as a gurgling sound reminiscent of that made
    by Chaliapin at the death of Boris Godounoff. It is a
    cheerful sound like someone drowning just under the
    surface of his own blood.

192   DAPHNE - IN HER BEDROOM

    She is at the telephone. Her cheerful confidential tone
    is made a little more confidential still by the fact
    that she has already removed her dress and is in a very
    pretty slip. While talking, she squirts a little perfume
    on herself with a one-hand atomizer. Her smile at this
    point is slightly lewd.

                    DAPHNE
            (into the telephone)
        You're sure you don't mind, Tony...
        you're sure it won't be too, too
        much trouble? All right, honey...
        he says in fifteen minutes exactly...
        but that was about two minutes ago...
        so if you're in a hurry....all right.

    She hangs up, does a little dance step, then reaches
    into her closet for the purple dress with the plumes
    at the hips. As she starts to get into it:

193   CLOSE SHOT - SIR ALFRED'S BATHROOM - DOOR

It opens and he looks around it cautiously. Reassured,
he opens the door rapidly and comes out with a record.
The CAMERA PULLS AHEAD of him as he carefully places
the record in the drawer of his desk. Now he hurries
back into the bathroom and we notice that the recording
unit has been taken apart and put back into its travel-
ing arrangement. Sir Alfred picks it up and glides
lithely with it to the cupboard from which he first got
it. He puts it all away without a superfluous movement,
then hurries back to his bathroom, opens the medicine
cabinet, removes his straight razor from the lower
shelf, glares maniacally toward his wife's bedroom, then
starts sharpening the razor on a strop hooked under the
medicine cabinet. After a moment he closes the door a
little and we see only his hands, the strop and the
razor.

                                        SLOW DISSOLVE TO:

194   DAPHNE

in the purple dress with the plumes on the hips. We see
her full length before her mirror as she preens herself.
Now she picks up a lipstick and moves closer to the mirror as she starts doing her lips. At this the CAMERA
PANS slowly toward the door. The music grows frighten-
ingly in volume and excitement during the PAN. Arrived
at the door, we see that it is opening very slowly. At
first there is just a crack of light and we see one of
Sir Alfred's eyes, then both eyes and his face as he
looks into the room with a suggestion of a superior smile
After watching Daphne for a few seconds he starts opening
the door further.

195   FAIRLY CLOSE SHOT - DAPHNE AND HER REFLECTION IN MIRROR

This is shooting down over her left shoulder. As she
moves a little we see Sir Alfred's reflection in the mirror about two seconds before she does. Now she sees him
too, and her pleased smile fades first into a look of
puzzlement and then into one of vague alarm. Lipstick in
hand, she turns slowly and stands with her back to us
looking at her husband. The CAMERA has naturally PULLED
BACK with her.

196   SIR ALFRED - AT DOOR

The latter continues to open slowly until Sir Alfred is
fully revealed to us, his left hand on the doorknob, his
right hand hidden behind his back. Now he drops his left
hand limply to his side.

197   DAPHNE - AT DRESSING TABLE

She puts her left hand to her throat and her fingers play
nervously. Now she looks at the lipstick in her right
hand as if she had never seen it before, then puts it on
the dressing table behind her. She points questioningly
with her left hand toward Sir Alfred's hidden right arm
then puts her left hand to her mouth and bites her fin-
gernails.

198   SIR ALFRED - IN DOORWAY

Still wearing his mysterious smile, he puts his left hand
behind him, then closes the door with his right. After
this, with both hands behind him, he comes forward in the
small purposeless steps of a man walking up and down in a
waiting room. He seems in no hurry.

199   DAPHNE - BY HER DRESSING TABLE

She backs away a little as Sir Alfred comes into the shot
his hands behind his back. As the light comes from the
dressing table, we do not see too well what he has in his
hand. Suddenly his left hand shoots out and tears her
beautiful dress from her shoulders, her pearls from her
neck. Now his right hand flies up through the shot and
out of it. Daphne has seen what he has in his hand. She
starts to yammer and points weakly to his hand. Now she
opens her mouth to scream. His left hand seizes her by
the hair, and the CAMERA PANS with her as she is bent
back on the bed. Still her fascinated eyes fix upon the
one object. Suddenly she closes her eyes and winces to
avoid seeing what she is about to see.

200   CLOSE SHOT - UP AT SIR ALFRED'S FACE

His expression is maniacal as, almost rhythmically, he
does some jerky violent movement with his arms.

201   DAPHNE'S HAND - CLOSE SHOT

It jerks spasmodically on the bed, the fingers crisped
in pain. Now the little hand relaxes, shudders once
more, then slowly dies.

                                        SLOW DISSOLVE TO:

202   SIR ALFRED'S HANDS

drying each other with a towel. The CAMERA PULLS BACK
and we see that we are in Daphne's bathroom. Sir Alfred
finishes drying, then in a most businesslike way picks
up his straight razor and dries it. Now, after examining
it closely, he picks it up carefully with the handkerchief and goes through the door into Daphne's room, the
CAMERA PRECEDING him. He looks down out of the shot for
a moment, sneeringly.

203   CLOSE SHOT - DAPHNE'S FOOT - ON BED

The little high-heeled slipper is partly off.

204   SIR ALFRED - LOOKING DOWN AT DAPHNE'S FOOT

He looks at his wrist watch, then turns quickly and
switches on a late model radio-phonograph combination
with record changer. As the dial dims a little after its
first brightness, Sir Alfred leaves the room, carefully
holding the razor on the handkerchief.

205   SIR ALFRED'S STUDY

He enters quickly, puts the razor carefully on his desk,
gets the razor case from the bathroom and puts it next
to the razor, then opens the drawer and takes out the
phonograph record. With this he hurries back into
Daphne's room.

206   DAPHNE'S ROOM

Sir Alfred comes in with the phonograph record and goes
directly to the radio-phonograph combination.

207   INSERT - RADIO-PHONOGRAPH COMBINATION AND SIR ALFRED'S
        HANDS

The hands arrange a stack of nine phonograph records.
Now the top six records are lifted up and the home recording, which looks quite different, is placed so that
it will be the fourth record to play. After this the six
records are replaced and the switch turned from "radio"
to "phono."

208   SIR ALFRED - AT RADIO-PHONOGRAPH

Certain that this is all ready he crosses to the telephone which has a long cord, avoids looking at the bed,
then puts the telephone on a little table and practices
going out the door and placing the little table with the
telephone on it against the inside of the door so that it
will be knocked over when the door is opened. Having assured himself that this can be easily done and that two
of his three props are now ready, Sir Alfred looks at his
watch, then goes out to his study.

209   SIR ALFRED'S STUDY

Sir Alfred enters, goes to his desk, arranges some papers
looks at his watch again, then picks up a magnifying
glass and the razor with the handkerchief and examines it
once more for fingerprints when the buzzer sounds. He
puts the razor back on his desk, his handkerchief back in
his pocket, puts on his glasses and picks up some papers
from his desk before going to the door and admitting Tony

                        SIR ALFRED
                    (jovially)
            There you are my boy...
                    (he slaps him
                    on the back)

                                        (CONTINUED)

910

217

209 (Cont.)

> SIR ALFRED (Cont.)
> ...it's extremely kind and devoted
> of you to take my place for tonight
> with Daphne...which I hardly presume
> amuses you as no doubt you like older
> women...
> (he laughs merrily)
> ...but you know what I told you when
> I first engaged you...twenty-four
> hours a day and not a minute less
> would be the least I would need you.

> TONY
> (with a faintly
> amused look)
> I'm very glad to be of service, Sir
> Alfred...any service...any time...

> SIR ALFRED
> I don't doubt it for an instant, my
> boy...maybe I can do something for
> you some day...who knows?

He laughs a trifle insanely, then calls toward his wife's
bedroom.

> SIR ALFRED
> Darling, Tony is here.

He cocks his head, listens for a moment, then speaks
smilingly.

> SIR ALFRED
> Ah, she didn't hear me...but you know
> what girls are like...when they're
> dressing...and putting on something
> extra special...to go dancing with
> such handsome young men as you.

He winks at him gayly and pats him on the shoulder. Tony
smirks a little conceitedly.

> SIR ALFRED
> I do wish I didn't have to talk
> business with Hugo...how lucky you
> are...however...

He takes off his glasses and starts putting his papers in
his pockets. Then quite offhandedly:

(CONTINUED)

217

209 (Cont. 1)

> SIR ALFRED
> (pointing to
> the razor)
> By the way, I don't think that bar-
> ber did an awfully good job on that
> razor...you did ask him to hone it,
> didn't you?

> TONY
> (looking down at
> the razor without
> touching it)
> Of course I did...have you tried it?

> SIR ALFRED
> Well not actually, but...

He stops talking as Tony reaches slowly for the razor and
picks it up.

> TONY
> Of course I don't know much about
> these old-fashioned razors...

> SIR ALFRED
> (beaming contentedly)
> Naturally not...at your age.

> TONY
> Isn't there something about taking
> a hair from your head.

> SIR ALFRED
> That's right...now you are doing much
> better.

> TONY
> (yanking a hair
> from his head)
> Thank you.

> SIR ALFRED
> (as Tony begins
> the experiment)
> No, no...hold the blade in your hand
> ...that's right...hold it firmly...
> that's right...now draw the hair along
> the razor's edge.

(CONTINUED)

209 (Cont. 2)

> TONY
> (surprised)
> It cut it.

> SIR ALFRED
> (pleased)
> Well, by Jove, I am surprised...
> (he laughs
> ruefully)
> ...that ought to be sharp enough for
> almost anything...just put it back
> in the case and not a word to the
> barber...I don't want him to cut my
> throat the next time I go down there...

He laughs happily and Tony does likewise while returning
the razor to its case.

> SIR ALFRED
> (taking the
> case from him)
> Thank you very much. I'll be off
> now. I don't want to keep Hugo wait-
> ing...maybe I'd better just tell
> Daphne you're here...otherwise these
> girls keep you waiting all night.
> (he calls toward
> the bedroom)
> Darling...

And walks out of the study.

210   DAPHNE'S BEDROOM

Sir Alfred enters smilingly. The instant he is out of
Tony's view his expression becomes maniacal. He glares
back once toward Tony, then opens the razor case, pours
the razor out onto his handkerchief, opens the blade by
holding it with a handkerchief, then with a cat-like
tread crosses to the bed. The CAMERA PANS no further
than Daphne's feet. Holding the razor gingerly Sir Alfre
reaches outside the shot and seems to manipulate it for
an instant. Now he comes back into the shot and examines
his hands very carefully including under the nails. Reassured he hurries to the radio-phonograph combination and
reaches inside.

211   INSERT - WORKS OF THE RADIO-PHONOGRAPH

Sir Alfred's hand comes into the shot and pushes a button.
The turntable begins to spin, the tone arm raises of

> (CONTINUED)

211 (Cont.)

itself, the first record falls onto the turntable and the
tone arm settles upon it. Gay music begins.

212   SIR ALFRED - AT RADIO-PHONOGRAPH

He looks at his watch, then picks up and closes the razor
case, then hastens to the door. He takes the doorknob
in his left hand, looks at the bed one last time and
waves at it.

                    SIR ALFRED
          Good night, darling.

Now he picks up the little table with the telephone on it
and as he closes the door reaches around and places the
table in front of it. He now removes his arm, leaving
the door about six inches open.

213   SIR ALFRED'S STUDY

                    SIR ALFRED
               (entering with
               the razor case)
          Now she's playing music...but she
          won't be long...and she's put on a
          wonderful gown for you, Tony...purple
          with plumes at the hips.

                    TONY
          I am lucky.

                    SIR ALFRED
               (putting the razor
               case in his medicine
               cabinet)
          Yes...I think you'll be quite bowled
          over...when first you see her in it...
          don't be impatient...it's really
          quite worth waiting for...good night.

                    TONY
          Good night.

Sir Alfred puts on his hat, looks once more at his watch
and exits cheerfully. As he closes the door:

                                        DISSOLVE TO:

214   BRONZE FLOOR INDICATOR

above an express elevator. It moves slowly, as an elevator coming down from the thirty-fourth floor takes quite
a little while. As the indicator points to the elevator's imminent arrival the CAMERA PANS down and the
doors open. Glancing surreptitiously at his watch Sir
Alfred comes out and walks toward the hotel desk.

215   HOTEL DETECTIVE

lolling near the desk.

                    THE DETECTIVE
          Good evening, Sir Alfred.

                    SIR ALFRED
               (coldly)
          Good evening...have you seen any-
          thing of my manager, Mr. Hugo
          Hammock?

                    THE DETECTIVE
          No, I ain't, boss.

                    SIR ALFRED
               (looking at his watch)
          I will ask the operator...maybe he
          has called.

He walks out of the shot.

216   HOTEL SWITCHBOARD

Two operators sit here side by side. The near one looks
up as Sir Alfred enters.

                    FIRST OPERATOR
          Good evening, Sir Alfred.

                    SIR ALFRED
          Have there been any calls for me?
          I've been expecting my manager,
          Mr. Hugo Hammock...

                    THE OPERATOR
          I haven't had any, Sir Alfred.
               (she turns to
               the other girl)
          Maizie, did you have any calls for...

Suddenly Sir Alfred's muscles tighten, his eyes narrow,
and he pulls his wrist watch up close to his face.

217   TONY - IN SIR ALFRED'S STUDY

He is smoking a cigarette and idly looking at a magazine. As he turns a page we hear a terrible scream.
The high voice from the next room: "Help, help!" Tony
staggers to his feet and drops the magazine. The high
voice from the next room: "Help, help!" Tony runs
toward Daphne's bedroom.

218   DAPHNE'S BEDROOM

The door flies open, the table falls, the telephone
crashes to the floor with.its bells jingling and Tony
trips over the wire and falls headlong toward the bed.
The high voice: (piercingly) "Help, help, Stop, Tony,
Stop, O-o-h, O-o-h, A-h-h, Ah-h-h."

                         TONY'S VOICE
             Daphne, where are you...Ah - Oh-h-h!

This last is to indicate the scream of a man.

219   SIR ALFRED AND TELEPHONE OPERATORS

and presently the house detective.

                         FIRST OPERATOR
                    (wildly excited)
             It's your apartment, Sir Alfred...
             it's Lady Daphne...she's calling
             for help...she said: "Tony, Stop,
             Tony."

Suddenly she screams out of sympathy with the screams
from upstairs.

                         SIR ALFRED
                    (nearly in tears)
             Do something! Do something!

                         TELEPHONE OPERATOR
                    (weeping)
             Stop, Tony, Stop!

220   HOUSE DETECTIVE

running toward us. He is followed by some guests.
CAMERA PANS them into the shot with Sir Alfred and the
telephone operator.

                         DETECTIVE
             What's the matter!

                                           (CONTINUED)

220 (Cont.)

>   SIR ALFRED
>   (to telephone operator)
>   Call the police!
>   (then to detective)
>   Upstairs, quick, follow me!

>   FIRST OPERATOR
>   Send the police quick...I want a
>   policeman...this is the Hermitage
>   Towers...there's been a murder!

>   MAIZIE, THE SECOND OPERATOR
>   (also weeping)
>   Now there's just music playing...
>   she must be dead.

>   DISSOLVE TO:

221   DAPHNE'S BEDROOM

It is dimly lit. The phonograph is still playing gayly.
Tony, disheveled, torn, and bloody from his fall, faces
us past Sir Alfred, the house detective and the guests.

>   TONY
>   (hysterically)
>   I tell you I had nothing to do with
>   it! You know that, Sir Alfred...
>   I was just where you left me waiting
>   for her, then I heard her scream and
>   ran in here.

>   HOUSE DETECTIVE
>   Will somebody turn off that blasted
>   music?

>   SIR ALFRED
>   Oh, Tony, Tony, what have you done?

He crosses to the radio-phonograph, then reaches into
it.

222   INSERT - RADIO-PHONOGRAPH COMBINATION

Sir Alfred's hands into the shot pick up the six top
records and lift them up.

223   SIR ALFRED - AT PHONOGRAPH

He smashes the records to the floor, then reaches into
the phonograph again.

224   INSERT

Sir Alfred's hands pick up the home recording, and breaks
it in pieces.

225   SIR ALFRED - BY RADIO-PHONOGRAPH COMBINATION

                          SIR ALFRED
              There's something on the floor
              there...Oh, Tony!   It's the razor.

While everybody is looking at the razor, he slips the
remains of the home recording into his pocket. As one
of the guests goes near the razor, the house detective
speaks sharply:

                        HOUSE DETECTIVE
              Don't touch that...it might have
              fingerprints on it.

                                          DISSOLVE TO:

226   NEWSPAPER - WITH PHOTOGRAPHS OF DAPHNE, SIR ALFRED AND
        TONY

We read "Sentenced Today in Love Triangle Murder Case."

                                          DISSOLVE TO:

227   A JUDGE

sitting on a bench.

                              THE JUDGE
                    ...and to be taken to the place of
                    execution and there electrocuted
                    until dead.

(Look up an English sentence for here as that is probably the kind Sir Alfred would be more familiar with).

228   TONY

standing before the judge. Over him we hear the end of
the sentence. As it is finished there is a wild peal of
laughter. Tony turns apathetically.

229   JUDGE

He turns and looks with a mildly shocked expression.

230   SIR ALFRED

He is doubled up with laughter, as he holds his sides.
Under this the background music begins to get very loud.

231   CLOSEUP - SIR ALFRED

laughing. The lighting is a little different but not
very much so. The music is still louder. The CAMERA
PULLS away from him, and we see him laughing and conducting violently as he approaches the end of the first piece
in the concert hall. He flips the pages insanely and
redoubles his laughter.

232   CONCERT MASTER AND FIRST VIOLIN

They are laughing without knowing just why they are
laughing.

233   DOUBLE BASS PLAYERS

They grin ferociously as they saw their terrible beat.

234   TYMPANIST AND CYMBAL PLAYER

They laugh as they help bring the piece to its crashing
climax.

235   MR. SWEENEY AND TAILOR

Showing all their teeth, they are helping Sir Alfred
bring the piece in in tempo.

236   DAPHNE - BARBARA - TONY AND AUGUST

The beautiful girls watch and listen ecstatically, their
lips parted, their bosoms heaving. Tony sits excitedly
forward in his chair. Even August is beating time in a
conservative manner and showing his teeth a little.

237   SIR ALFRED

With tremendous gestures he brings the piece in under
the wire. The last sixteen bumps shake the building.
As he finishes, he bows his shoulders as if to receive
the shock of the tremendous applause.

238   TAILOR AND MR. SWEENEY

They are on their feet applauding and yelling.

239   DAPHNE - BARBARA - TONY AND AUGUST

The girls and Tony are on their feet jumping up and down
and yelling "Bravo!" The boxes near them are similarly
caught up in the wave of enthusiasm.

240   SIR ALFRED - FROM BACK

Still bowed he turns and looks unhappily at the audience.
Now with an infinitesimal nod of the head he acknowledges the audience's acclaim. Slowly as the applause
redoubles he looks up at his beautiful wife.

241   CLOSE SHOT - DAPHNE IN BOX

Her eyes are filmed with tears and her little hands
don't make noise any more as they applaud.

242   HIGH CAMERA SHOT - ON SIR ALFRED

Slowly he lowers his eyes. Now he breaks the baton in
his hands, throws it on the stage, then turns and
motions his musicians to their feet. As the applause
continues, he hurries off stage. The violinists applaud
him with their bows on the backs of their fiddles as he
passes.

243   MR. SWEENEY AND TAILOR

They applaud excitedly. The tailor starts standing on
the seat better to look, but Mr. Sweeney shakes his head
in the negative and helps him down.

244   DAPHNE - BARBARA - TONY AND AUGUST

Daphne blows her cheeks out, indicating that she is
exhausted, then sits down and fans herself with her
program.

245   SIR ALFRED'S DRESSING ROOM

Jules is waiting with a bath towel over his shoulder.
Sir Alfred hurries in, removing his tie. Jules helps
him strip to the waist, throws some alcohol on him, then
dries his back while Sir Alfred takes care of the front.
Now Sir Alfred starts into a dry shirt. The door flies
open and Hugo appears.

                         HUGO
                    (emphatically)
              Never!

                         SIR ALFRED
                    (quietly)
              What?

                         HUGO
              Never in the history of music...
              never since the invention of that
              most beautiful of all instruments:
              the symphony orchestra...has it been
              played like you just done...Toscanini
              would die of jealousy...Koussevitsky
              would shoot himself...Stokowsky would
              enter a convent...and all the others
              would dry up and blow away.

                         SIR ALFRED
              Don't flatter me.

                         HUGO
                    (indignantly)
              Flatter you! Compared to the truth
              I am insulting you...what did you
              have in your head? What visions
              of eternity...Armageddon...the final
              battle of the planets and the end of
              creation...was you looking at...to
              bring music like that out of that
              bunch of cat scratchers?

                         SIR ALFRED
                    (dryly)
              You'd be enormously surprised if
              you knew Hugo...thank you, Jules.
              Well, here we go.

He exits, putting on his tail coat.

246   AN ELECTRICIAN AT A DIMMER BOARD - BACKSTAGE

As Sir Alfred approaches, he dims his house lights.

247   SIR ALFRED

walking out onto apron and starting across stage. He
turns and smiles a little sadly at the explosive applause that greets his appearance.

248   MR. SWEENEY AND TAILOR

They rise, beat their palms and holler "Bravo!"

249   TRUCKING SHOT - BESIDE SIR ALFRED

He does a slight double-take upon recognizing them, then
despite the mood he is in, he evinces some lugubrious
amusement. Now, dropping the smile from his face, he
looks up at Daphne.

250   DAPHNE - BARBARA - TONY AND AUGUST

Daphne and Barbara are doing their lips, unconscious or
disdainful of the crowd below. Suddenly Barbara sees
Sir Alfred. She nudges Daphne who leaps to her feet to
applaud, dropping, naturally, her lipstick and vanity
case over the edge of the box.

251   DEAF GENTLEMAN AND MADAME POMPADOUR

He reacts slightly to the vanity case nicking him on the
dome. Then places his hand on the top of his head and
looks straight up. The old lady next to him, sitting
under an enormous pompadour scooped out on top like a
nest, removes Daphne's lipstick from it, looks at it
with displeasure, and also looks straight up.

252   DAPHNE - BARBARA - TONY AND AUGUST

                         DAPHNE
                   (mouthing the word
                    very distinctly)
               I'm terribly sorry.

                         TONY
                     (rising)
               I'll go down.

                                              (CONTINUED)

922

217

2/13/58   101.

252 (Cont.)

                        AUGUST
                 (leaning way forward
                  and looking down)
               What happened?

        His pince-nez falls off.

253   BALD-HEADED GENTLEMAN AND OLD LADY

        From the nest on top of her head the old lady removes
        the pince-nez, looks at them with displeasure, tries
        them to see if they suit her eyes, then looks straight
        up.

254   SIR ALFRED

        reaching the podium. The applause becomes deafening and
        he turns and bows perfunctorily. The applause gets
        stronger and Sir Alfred invites the musicians to rise.
        As they do so:

255   TONY

        hurrying down main stairs. The CAMERA PANS him down and
        around, then follows him a little way on the lower level.

256   SIR ALFRED

        waving the musicians down. The house lights dim a little
        further and Sir Alfred looks at the audience patiently
        as they quiet down. Now he turns, opens the music, picks
        up a fresh baton, and is about to raise it when we hear
        laughter. Sir Alfred throws down the baton, turns slowly
        and looks into the audience. At what he sees his eyes
        narrow.

257   DEAF GENTLEMAN - MADAME POMPADOUR AND TONY

        Tony is talking so softly that he cannot be heard at all.
        Mostly he points to the box above them in explanation of
        his presence. He moves his lips but we hear nothing.

                        DEAF GENTLEMAN
                      (to the old lady)
                 What did he say...I can't hear a
                 word he says.

                        MADAME POMPADOUR
                 He says he's sent down from up there
                 for the...loot...

                                              (CONTINUED)

923

257 (Cont.)

BALD-HEADED MAN
Yes, but he might be a crook who...

There is a roar of laughter from the audience followed
by shushing.

258   SIR ALFRED

He watches the goings on with some displeasure. Now he
looks up above at Daphne.

259   CLOSE SHOT - DAPHNE

Almost in tears of embarrassment. She explains in
pantomime that she dropped something and is terribly
sorry,

260   SIR ALFRED

He folds his arms and waits stonily.

261   TONY

bowing as he receives jewelry and glasses. He hurries
out the side door.

262   SIR ALFRED

looking after him coldly. Now he turns, raps on the
shade, then lifts his baton high and starts the
Tannhaüser Overture. We stay on this SHOT almost long
enough for Tony to get back to the box,

263   DAPHNE - BARBARA AND AUGUST

Tony enters with the recovered jewelry and gives it back
to Daphne and August. Now Barbara starts to whisper
something in Tony's ear and Daphne shushes her ferociously.

264   TRICK SHOT - ON SIR ALFRED

As he leads and follows the score we again push into his
mind.

                                          LONG DISSOLVE TO:

265   CLOSE UP - ANTIQUE VILLAGE ORCHESTRA CLOCK

It comes to eleven-thirty and there is a whirring sound

                                          (CONTINUED)

924

265 (Cont.)

and the leader beats out the first eleven notes of
Jingle Bells. Now the CAMERA PANS over to the door
leading to the foyer. This door is open and at the end
of the foyer we see the door to the hall open and Sir
Alfred comes in preceded by his wife. Now they come
into the study. Daphne stops and looks dismally into
the distance. Sir Alfred removes her fur coat, puts his
hands on her shoulders and talks past her ear.

                    SIR ALFRED
          Poor baby.

Slightly startled, Daphne starts looking back over her
shoulder.

                    DAPHNE
          Wh-why?

                    SIR ALFRED
                (quietly)
          Because you know...that I know...
          you can feel it...and it's made you
          all small and ashamed...and unhappy
          ...as if we could control our love
          ...lead it by the hand like an
          obedient child...and order it to do
          our bidding...

                    DAPHNE
                (very nervously)
          I don't know what you're talking
          about.

                    SIR ALFRED
                (quietly)
          Yes you know what I'm talking about
          ...because Love took you by the hand
          and led you, albeit shyly and reluc-
          tantly, into the presence of this
          beautiful young man and said: See,
          little Daphne, what I had intended
          for you?...gaze upon your destiny...
          see how gently the tendrils of his
          lustrous hair curl behind his ears...
          see how respectfully he lowers his
          silken lashes when addressing you...
          but notice the spark that leaps from
          his skin to yours when accidentally
          your hands meet...notice the way

                                        (CONTINUED)

265 (Cont.1)

                          SIR ALFRED (Cont.)
your poor heart skips its beat when
his eyes at last are raised and come
to rest in yours...feel the warm
blood tingling and spreading inside
you as it rushes upward when your
nostrils reach the warm perfume of
his breath and deeply draw it in to
mix with yours...

                              DAPHNE
                        (anguished)
No, no...

                             SIR ALFRED
                        (gently)
I don't blame you, darling...you
didn't want to...I am the one to
blame....entirely and alone...and
I'm deeply ashamed, Daphne...for
what I have done to you...

                              DAPHNE
You...ashamed...
                        (she starts to weep)
I'm the one.

                             SIR ALFRED
No, darling...
                        (he seats her in
                        a sofa beside him
                        and pats her hand)
...the one who knows the most
carries the responsibility. He and
he alone must judge the chances of
success...or failure...a union between a man of the world...a seasoned
traveler and a child from Porthole,
Michigan.

                              DAPHNE
                        (weeping)
P-Porthaul...

                             SIR ALFRED
I'll never remember it...a baby
with bows in her hair...
                        (Daphne puts her
                        nose under his ear)
...that wonderful night...

                                        DISSOLVE TO:

266   BELL-CLANGING AMERICAN LOCOMOTIVE - NIGHT

It is moving about one mile an hour in a torrential
rain. The engineer is holding a lantern outside, trying
to see the tracks which are invisible. Now he shakes
his head in the negative and brings the engine to a
stop.

                         ENGINEER
                  (to the fireman who is
                  peering over his shoulder)
            It's no soap...as far as I'm con-
            cerned I've been as far as I'm
            going...what they need here is a
            sea captain...

                         FIREMAN
                  (laughing oafishly)
            Ha, ha, ha, that's a good one, Jake.

                         ENGINEER
            I'm going to take her back to the
            station.

He blows a long blast on the whistle, reverses his
link mechanism and opens the throttle a little. The
engine starts to move backwards. The CAMERA STAYS with
him.

                                          DISSOLVE TO:

267   SIR ALFRED - HUGO - A FEW MUSICIANS AND A PORTER -
        IN VESTIBULE OF A PULLMAN CAR

The door is open, but the trap that fits over the
steps has not been raised. The porter holds his arm
across the opening.

                         SIR ALFRED
            I say...now we seem to be going
            backwards.

                         HUGO
            We got to go forwards...Canada is
            that way...we are giving a concert!

                         PORTER
                  (politely)
            Yes suh, you sure are...but not to-
            night you ain't...unless you is givin'
            it right here.

                                          (CONTINUED)

267 (Cont.)

                         HUGO
                  (indicating the rain)
            What is the name of this swamp?

                         PORTER
            This heah is Porthaul, Michigan...
            it enjoyed the highest precipitation
            of rainfall last year of any town of
            its size in the North Central States.

                         SIR ALFRED
                      (politely)
            I can well see how it might have.

                         PORTER
                      (proudly)
            Yes suh, I seen one whole street...
            the houses and all...slowly float
            away...

                         SIR ALFRED
            You better send some telegrams,
            Hugo.

                         HUGO
            Do you suppose the telegraph office
            floated away, too?

                         PORTER
            No suh, it's made of brick.

                         SIR ALFRED
            Then it probably sank.

            Now a small, cheerful party is PANNED into the SHOT.
            He immediately starts to move to keep opposite Sir
            Alfred.

                         THE BALDWIN MAN
            Sir Alfred de Carter...are you Sir
            Alfred de Carter?

                         SIR ALFRED
                      (mildly)
                  Yes...

268   THE BALDWIN MAN

        past Sir Alfred.

                                              (CONTINUED)

268 (Cont.)

                    BALDWIN MAN
                (moving along
                in the wet)
        Well doggone if I ain't glad to see
        yuh...I am the Baldwin man...the
        local representative of your exclu-
        sive piano.

He seizes the hand rails, swings himself up to the
platform and nearly falls out backwards.

                    SIR ALFRED
                (grabbing him)
        Look out!

                    THE BALDWIN MAN
                (shaking Sir Alfred's
                hand)
        This is an unexpected surprise, a
        pleasure and an honor, Sir Alfred.
        While you're here my house is yours
        and you got to be here tonight any-
        way...everything's washed out ahead
        and behind you...you know, Sir Alfred,
        they say great opportunities make
        great men and normally I wouldn't
        get to ask you a favor, I wouldn't
        even get to meet you probably even
        though I am the Baldwin man and you
        do use our piano exclusively...but
        I got a daughter playing at the
        charity concert tonight...and I
        said to myself if I can just swan-
        dangle that Sir Alfred de Carter...
        Baronet...himself in person...
        just like he looks in the magazines...
        to my daughter's concert...well she's
        made that's all...she can give les-
        sons the rest of her life as the
        prodigy of Sir Alfred de Carter,
        Baronet...she might even give a
        real concert sometime...

                    HUGO
                (clutching his head)
        Gevalt...are you crazy or something?

                                    (CONTINUED)

929

268 (Cont. 1)

>   BALDWIN MAN
>   (crushed)
> I suppose I am asking a lot...
> well, you can't say I didn't try...

>   SIR ALFRED
>   (quietly)
> I shall be delighted to attend...
> your daughter's concert...I had a
> first concert too, you know.

>   BALDWIN MAN
>   (seizing his hand
>   deliriously)
> You mean that, Sir Alfred?

>   SIR ALFRED
>   (very graciously)
> I have never meant anything more.

>   BALDWIN MAN
> WHOOPEE!

                                    DISSOLVE TO:

269   SIR ALFRED - HUGO AND BALDWIN MAN -

in a collapsible duck hunter's boat.

The Baldwin man is rowing. Sir Alfred holds an umbrella
over himself.

>   BALDWIN MAN
>   (enthusiastically and
>   at the same time
>   apologetically)
> It's just this last part is a little
> wet...I didn't think we ought to
> risk it in the car.

>   HUGO
>   (indignantly)
> In a car! A submarine! What did
> you say this joint was called?

>   BALDWIN MAN
>   (happily)
> Porthaul, Michigan.

                                    (CONTINUED)

269 (Cont.)

> HUGO
> (looking around)
> You mean <u>Lake</u> Michigan.

He makes a move and the boat rocks violently.

> BALDWIN MAN
> (warningly)
> <u>Look</u>...out! Or we might get a
> little wet.

> HUGO
> A little wet! You should feel
> where I'm sitting.

> BALDWIN MAN
> (as the boat
> reaches some steps)
> And here we are...all safe and
> sound...

> HUGO
> That's what you think.
> (saying which he
> slips and sits a
> little in the
> water)

DISSOLVE TO:

270   CLOSE SHOT

A fat, seventeen-year-old coloratura. She is accompanied by her mother, also very fat, who is giving the
Baldwin quite a thumping. Before each high note her
face takes on a desperate expression.

271   SIR ALFRED, HUGO AND BALDWIN MAN - STOCK PEOPLE

in a mass of steaming humanity. The three of them
assume the same desperate expression as the coloratura,
as they try to help her over the hard passages. In the
middle of this Hugo looks at Sir Alfred with an expression of such horror that the latter explodes into his
handkerchief. Even the Baldwin man looks a little ill-
at-ease and applauds gratefully when the piece ends.
Now he gets to his feet and goes over by the piano.

(CONTINUED)

271 (Cont.)

                              BALDWIN MAN
                    And now, ladies and gentlemen, and
                    distinguished guests...Sir Alfred
                    de Carter, Baronet, and Sir Hugo
                    de...I mean <u>Mr</u>. Hugo de...ahem....

          He clears his throat.

272   SIR ALFRED AND HUGO

          Sir Alfred is still having a little trouble with his
          handkerchief.

                                    HUGO
                    Standoff!

273   BALDWIN MAN - BY PIANO

                              BALDWIN MAN
                    How was that?

274   SIR ALFRED AND HUGO

                                    HUGO
                    Standoff...like in Mexico.

275   BALDWIN MAN - BY PIANO

                              BALDWIN MAN
                    Oh...and Mr. Standoff his friend
                    from Mexico.
                              (he gives Hugo
                              a little hand)
                    ...it is my great pleasure to intro-
                    duce for your approval and edifica-
                    tion...my own daughter: Miss Daphne
                    Delehanty...that's my name too.

276   SIR ALFRED AND HUGO

          Sir Alfred is still bent over into his handkerchief.
          He is shaking with laughter. Now he wipes his eyes,
          looks up vaguely and suddenly does a double-take and
          becomes rigid.

277   A TALL YOUNG GIRL

          in a white, lace dress with a little train. Her long,
          dark hair falls to her shoulders where it curls under

                                                    (CONTINUED)

277 (Cont.)

slightly. With the echo of a smile and perfect poise
she bows her head, kicks her train back and curtsies
as if she were being presented at court.

> DAPHNE
> Sir Alfred.

278   SIR ALFRED AND HUGO

Gravely, almost grimly, and to Hugo's astonishment
Sir Alfred rises to his feet as if lifted by all the
laws of chivalry. Now he bows slightly, comes forward,
takes the young girl's hand and lifts her to her feet.

> SIR ALFRED
> I can only say that...
> (the words fail
> him and he fin-
> ishes lamely)
> ...please play for me.

He leads her to the piano, then, instead of resuming
his seat, he arranges himself in the curve of the piano.

279   DAPHNE

From Sir Alfred's position. She smiles faintly, then
with perfect poise plays, and very well too, a Chopin
Nocturne.

280   CLOSE SHOT - SIR ALFRED

As he listens to her. This is the love of his life and
he knows it.

281   DAPHNE - PLAYING PIANO

From Sir Alfred's point of view. Slowly, she raises
her eyes and looks at him with quiet assurance. This
is the love of her life...and she knows it.

> DISSOLVE TO:

282   SIR ALFRED AND DAPHNE - ON PORCH OF HER FATHER'S HOUSE

Behind them are the rain and the mist and some shrubbery.
A little light comes from inside the house.

> (CONTINUED)

282 (Cont.)

> SIR ALFRED
> (choked with emotion)
> It is ridiculous...it is absurd...
> you don't know me at all...I
> might be the ogre of ogres seducing
> you away for my own foul purposes...
> but I want you to marry me tonight
> or tomorrow or whenever the preacher
> next performs...and then come away
> with me, my love.

> DAPHNE
> (quietly)
> Of course.

Sir Alfred takes her hand and covers it with kisses.
Softly she smoothes his hair.

DISSOLVE TO:

283   SIR ALFRED AND DAPHNE

Her nose is still under his ear.

> SIR ALFRED
> And so you see...we tried our best..
> I couldn't understand music as well
> as I do if I didn't understand the
> human heart a little...don't cry,
> little lady...neither of you has
> done anything wrong...youth belongs
> to youth...and beauty to beauty...

He pats her and rises gently and crosses to his desk,
takes out a large checkbook, takes a large quill pen
from an alabaster stand and starts to write.

284   INSERT - CHECK

Already written we see: Daphne de Carter. The pen now
fills out the rest of the check for fifty thousand
dollars.

> SIR ALFRED'S VOICE
> I want you to be rich and comfortable
> and free...I don't want you to worry
> about rent and clothing...

285   SIR ALFRED - SIGNING THE CHECK

He picks it up and looks toward Daphne.

> SIR ALFRED
> ...and food and other unromantic
> things that should always be pro-
> vided for you...
>> (he crosses to her,
>> pats her head, then
>> takes one of her hands)
> ...that little head was never
> made to worry nor those little
> hands to work...
>> (he picks up the hand
>> and kisses it tenderly)
> ...only to love...to love so
> dearly...

He blinks away a tear.

86   DOWN SHOT - DAPHNE CRYING

287   CLOSE SHOT - SIR ALFRED LOOKING DOWN

The lighting is a little different. He is also crying.
The CAMERA PULLS back and we see him finishing the
second piece of the evening.

288   CONCERT MASTER

The tears are rolling down his nose and his partner at
the first stand is having a little duct trouble also.

289   OBOIST

The tears are rolling down his cheeks as he plays the
last sad notes.

290   MR. SWEENEY AND TAILOR

Mr. Sweeney is crying into his handkerchief. The tailor
wipes his nose with his finger.

291   DAPHNE - BARBARA - TONY AND AUGUST

Daphne's eyes are glazed with tears. She holds a small
handkerchief close to her mouth. Even August removes
his pince-nez and examines the steam on them with some
surprise.

292   SIR ALFRED - FROM BACK

He brings the piece quietly to a close. There is a
little silence before the applause comes rolling down
the aisles, like thunder in the Catskills. Quietly he
turns and bows, looks quickly at his wife, then walks
off the stage.

293   DAPHNE - BARBARA - TONY AND AUGUST

                         DAPHNE
                    (to Tony)
          Come on.

Followed by Tony she hurries out of the box.

294   AUDIENCE APPLAUDING

295   SWEENEY AND TAILOR APPLAUDING

296   STAGE RIGHT

From audience's point of view. Sir Alfred comes out reluctantly and bows. Before leaving, his eyes automatically find Daphne's box. He stops and stares rigidly.

297   BARBARA AND AUGUST - IN BOX

Daphne and Tony conspicuous by their absence.

298   SIR ALFRED - LOOKING UP

He turns and goes backstage.

299   BACKSTAGE

Sir Alfred walking away from us toward his dressing
room.

                    DAPHNE'S VOICE
          Darling...

Sir Alfred turns.

300   IRON STEPS

Coming up from auditorium level. Daphne is hurrying
toward us followed by Tony.

                    DAPHNE
               (enthusiastically)
          I just couldn't wait until the end...
          I had to tell you now how wonderful
          it is...it's just wonderful.

                    TONY
          Wonderful!

                    SIR ALFRED
               (as they reach him)
          I am relieved to hear it...I thought
          it was slightly overdone...every
          emotion exaggerated...every forte a
          fortissimo...every piano a pianissi-
          mo...every tutti a boiler factory.

                    DAPHNE
               (putting a hand
               on his shoulder)
          It was just wonderful.

                    SIR ALFRED
          Yes, you've already said that...
          both of you. Now if you'll forgive
          me a moment...there's a towel
          waiting...

                                        (CONTINUED)

937

300 (Cont.)

> DAPHNE
> Can I help you, darling?

> SIR ALFRED
> I have Jules waiting for that...
> excuse me.

He turns and walks toward the open door of his dressing
room where Jules is visible with a towel.

301 DAPHNE AND TONY

They exchange a look and Daphne shrugs and, considerably
hurt, they start back toward the auditorium.

> DISSOLVE TO:

302 BARBARA AND AUGUST

> BARBARA
> What d'you say?

> AUGUST
> I said you look exceptionally pretty
> tonight.

> BARBARA
> I can't imagine why I should.

> AUGUST
> Maybe it's the music.

> BARBARA
> With me music goes in one ear and
> out the other.

Daphne and Tony come in.

> BARBARA
> Did you go back...how is he?

> DAPHNE
> I don't know what's the matter with
> him.

> AUGUST
> Too much temperament...give me the
> simple viewpoint.

> (CONTINUED)

302 (Cont.)

                    BARBARA
              (coldly)
          You got it, boy...you don't have to
          ask for it.

 Now they look out of the shot as there is a burst of
 applause.

303   SIR ALFRED - COMING OUT ONTO THE APRON

      He crosses to the podium, bows twice in response to the
      applause, then starts the third piece of the evening.
      This time he plays at least thirty seconds before we go
      to the trick shot.

304   TRICK SHOT ON SIR ALFRED

      We go into his mind again....(it might be interesting at
      some point to see the whole orchestra from the conductor's
      viewpoint reflected on something black and shiny, then
      PULL BACK and see it is the pupil of the conductor's eye).

                                        DISSOLVE TO:

305   VILLAGE ORCHESTRA CLOCK

      It strikes eleven-thirty, the CAMERA PANS OVER and again
      we see Sir Alfred and Daphne coming into their apartment,
      only this time Tony comes with them. As they come into
      the study, Daphne exchanges a frightened look with Tony.

                    DAPHNE
              (looking at her
               husband)
          What is it, Alfred?

                    SIR ALFRED
          First of all I want to apologize to
          you both for being so abrupt with you
          backstage at the concert...but somehow
          when you happen to be perfectly aware
          of the fact that your wife is your
          secretary's mistress....

                    DAPHNE
              (clutching her throat)
          Alfred!

                    TONY
              (moving into a position
               behind Daphne)
          Sir-r-r-r-...Alfred.
                                        (CONTINUED)

939

305 (Cont.)

                         SIR ALFRED
          Oh, didn't you know I knew? Don't
          try to hide behind Daphne, Tony...
          you will never hide from me.

                         TONY
                    (livid)
          I don't know...what you're...talking
          about.

                         SIR ALFRED
          You know precisely what I'm talking
          about, both of you...you have been
          dreading this moment...hoping against
          hope it would never come...but knowing
          inside your secret hearts that it
          would, and now that the moment has
          arrived...
                    (they both start
                    guiltily)
          ...you are wondering what I'm going
          to do, aren't you?...knowing that I
          hold all the cards...and that the
          unwritten law will protect me to the
          end. I thought of killing you, my dear...
          I cut your throat with my razor...your
          head nearly came off...
                    (he turns to Tony)
          ...but it was your fingerprints they
          found on the razor, Tony, and you
          they burned...screaming your innocence...
          it's a relief to hear that in the past
          tense, isn't it?
                    (he sneers - then
                    turns to Daphne)
          ...then...such is human idiocy...I
          forgave you...
                    (Daphne clutches her
                    hands hopefully. He
                    roars with bitter
                    laughter)
          ...wrote you an enormous check...and
          grew maudlin over the necessity of
          youth for youth...where and why is
          this necessity?...by what logic does
          it flourish?...what is so precious
          about a young female?...no, no, Daphne
          ...you shall have no money and Fate
          will decide which man you are to have...
          and how much of a man he is...

                                        (CONTINUED)

305 (Cont. 1)

                              SIR ALFRED (Cont.)
                         (he reaches into his desk,
                         pulls out a revolver, breaks
                         it and empties the six bullets
                         into his hand)
          Here we have all the necessary appar-
          atus for a genuinely amusing game,
          Tony, invented by some Czarist offi-
          cers who cared little for their lives,
          but much for bravery and the conquest
          of emotion...the idea is to play it
          with a perfectly steady hand...
                         (he smiles at the
                         sweating Tony with
                         diabolic pleasure)
          ...of the six bullets...I remove
          five...one only goes back into the
          cylinder...which I spin like this
          ...for the lucky winner...the odds,
          then, are one to five for... five to
          one against...better than I have had
          in many a casino...so you see it is
          not really very dangerous at all,
          Tony, and will vouchsafe you a mag-
          nificent opportunity to show Daphne
          how brave you are...how icy cool in
          the face of this...small adventure
          ...I'll spin it once more now...
                         (he does so)
          ...just in case you have peeked,
          and then...
                         (he forces the revolver
                         into Tony's hand)
          ...as the seducer of my wife and
          the destroyer of my home...you shall
          have the honor of playing the first
          hand of this enthralling little game
          called: Russian Roulette... exciting,
          isn't it?

                              TONY
                         (inarticulately - his
                         eyes starting from his
                         head - his mouth yam-
                         mering)
          No-o...

                              DAPHNE
                         (seizing Tony's
                         coat sleeve)
          Stop, Alfred, stop!

                                             (CONTINUED)

                              941

305 (Cont. 2)

SIR ALFRED

But what a fuss we are making...
     (then suddenly seizing
     the barrel of the re-
     volver)
...No, no, Tony...not at me...at
your temple...
     (he forces the gun
     up to Tony's temple)
...like this: NOW...cool and collected...with nerves of steel...
with steady hand and cheerful eye,
Mr. Anthony Windborn, the celebrated
wife stealer...will demonstrate the
...

TONY
     (yammering cravenly)

No-o, no-o..., Sir Alfred, please.

DAPHNE
     (sinking to her knees)

Alfred...I beseech you...

SIR ALFRED
     (with heavy sarcasm)

Can it be that I detect a thread
of saffron in this otherwise perfect
fabric?...come, come, Tony...you
the fearless cavalier...you hesitate?
...then watch me closely while I
show you how it's done...I spin the
wheel of fortune once more, you see,
and then...with a rigidly steady
hand...and without quaverings or
sniveling yammerings...I will ask
you to notice, Daphne...I place the
muzzle here...
     (he puts it to
     his temple)
...and with a simple godspeed in
case I should be...
     (he smiles sweetly)
...unfortunate...I pull the trig...

There is a deafening explosion. The side of his forehead becomes black and shiny and he slumps into the
arms of the screaming Daphne and the yammering Tony.
The music swells as we:

DISSOLVE TO:

306   SIR ALFRED

finishing last piece of his concert. He seems weak and
nerveless. He clutches the lecturn to hold himself erect.

307   CONCERT MASTER

He nudges his partner to look at Sir Alfred, then looks
behind him at the next desk to see if they have observed
Sir Alfred's condition.

308   MR. SWEENEY AND TAILOR

looking greatly alarmed. Mr. Sweeney raises half out of
his seat, as if to go to the assistance of a friend.

309   DAPHNE - BARBARA - TONY AND AUGUST - IN BOX

Daphne also has felt the alarm. Her hand is on her
sister's shoulder as she stands looking at her husband.

310   MED. CLOSE - SIR ALFRED

as he leads the last bars he regains control of himself.

311   DAPHNE - BARBARA - TONY AND AUGUST - IN BOX

Reassured by his appearance, Daphne slowly sits down
and fans herself.

312   SIR ALFRED - FROM BACK

He brings the piece to a glorious finale and turns to
the applause and waves his men to their feet. The deafening applause continues.

313   CLOSE SHOT - SIR ALFRED

He looks at the audience, up once at the box, and strides
off stage. The CAMERA PANS with him. The audience which
thinks he is taking bows continues to applaud.

314   JULES - IN WINGS NEAR DOUBLE BASS PLAYER

He is applauding from a stepladder or something. Below
and behind him we see Sir Alfred hurry into his dressing
room and emerge a second later putting on his hat and
coat. He starts for the stage door.

315   MR. SWEENEY AND TAILOR

They applaud violently but they are beginning to wonder
why it takes Sir Alfred so long to come out and take his
bow.

316   DAPHNE - BARBARA - TONY AND AUGUST

They also look worried.

>   DAPHNE
>   (to the rest of them
>   although this prob-
>   ably cannot be heard)
>   Let's go backstage.

They start out.

317   MR. SWEENEY AND TAILOR

Their applauding is beginning to run down. The tailor
examines the palms of his hands and blows on them, then
he and Sweeney exchange a glance and loyally redouble
their applause. We leave them beating their mitts violently.

>   DISSOLVE TO:

318   SIR ALFRED

coming into the dark foyer of his apartment. His hat is
turned down, the collar of his coat turned up, as he
looks over his shoulder like a conspirator, comes forward
a few steps, then says:

>   SIR ALFRED
>   Is anybody here?

He looks into the empty living room as he passes it and
comes into his study, and turns on the desk lamp. Now
the first notes of Jingle Bells come to startle him. He
turns guiltily and looks at the clock.

319   VILLAGE ORCHESTRA CLOCK

It shows eleven o'clock and so, for the first time, we
see the leader play out the entire piece.

320   SIR ALFRED

He looks at the clock in a somewhat sinister manner, then
crosses to his bathroom with a catlike tread and looks
behind the door to make sure there is no one there.
After this he looks longly toward Daphne's room, then
starts toward it.

321   DAPHNE'S ROOM

It is dark. Sir Alfred appears and stands silhouetted
in the doorway. He looks toward the bed with some

>   (CONTINUED)

321 (Cont.)

distaste, then crosses to the radio-phonograph combination and turns it on. Instantly he snaps his fingers in
irritation at his stupidity. In the light of the dial
he looks at the knob he has touched, then examines his
fingers. Now he looks for a handkerchief. In doing so
he reveals his wet and rumpled shirt. He feels it for
dampness and pulls his coat tightly together again.
After this he picks up the tail of his coat and starts
wiping the knob with this, but as it does not seem very
practical, he crosses to the door of Daphne's bathroom.
As he is about to grab the knob of the door, he suddenly
remembers and snatches his hand back as though the knob
were red hot. He picks up the tail of his coat again,
seizes the knob through it, and in a very sure and
efficient manner silently yanks the door open. He is
instantly rewarded by a beam of brilliant light and a
piercing woman's scream. He is blown back into a sitting
position on the bed.

322   HOTEL MAID

sitting on a laundry receptacle. Startled by Sir
Alfred's appearance, she has fallen back on this, clutching her heart and a large stack of face towels. She is
a stout, elderly party in uniform, a ring of keys chained
to her waist. At the moment she is flushed, breathing
heavily and looking past the CAMERA very indignantly.

323   SIR ALFRED

Rising from the bed where he landed.

                    SIR ALFRED
                  (accusingly)
            What are you doing in there?

324   MAID - IN BATHROOM

                    MAID
                  (with a strong
                   Irish brogue)
            I'll give you three guesses, Sir
            Alfred.

She rises panting, but still clutching her heart.

                    MAID
            Sure and it's the likes of me that
            could be layin' here dead at this
            moment with the likes of you creepin'
            up on them in long black overcoats.

325   SIR ALFRED

                           SIR ALFRED
              Yes, will you tell me what color
              overcoat you like, and I'll wear
              it... What are you doing in there,
              anyway, at this time of night?

326   MAID - IN BATHROOM

                           MAID
              Sure and I remembered I'd forgotten
              to remember the face towels when I
              come in at seven so thinkin' every-
              body was out...

327   SIR ALFRED

                           SIR ALFRED
              I see...well I'll have one of them,
              please.

As he reaches for it, the radio, now warmed up, comes
crashing in.

                           RADIO
                    (in four part harmony)
              Are you rosy? Are you pink?
              Are you frisky like a mink?
              If you're not,
              Try a pot
              Of Woolfan's LAX-A-TEA.

Sir Alfred takes the towel, crosses to the radio-phonograph and switches it off with the towel.

                           OLD MAID
                    (going past him)
              Goodnight, sir.

                           SIR ALFRED
                    (shortly)
              Goodnight.

He watches her until he hears the outside door click,
then gets back into his mood. He wipes the knob, then,
not quite sure how well this method works, does it again
with a little spit. While cleaning off the knob, he has
rested his left hand on the edge of the console. Realizing this just in time, he cleans the whole top of it off
with spit, while doing so he places one hand against the
side of the instrument. Now, with one backward glance
into the room, he goes out.

328   SIR ALFRED'S STUDY

He comes in, looks at his hands, and crosses to a chiffonier, opens one of the top drawers with his towel and
removes a pair of thick fur-lined gloves. After putting
these on, he takes one look around to make sure that he
is alone and crosses to the cupboard we have seen before,
opens the door, and reaches for the recording unit which
happens not to be there. Now he gets on a chair to look
higher, but there is no more recording unit than feathers
on a fish. Absentmindedly he picks up one of a pair of
Christmas present book ends in the form of a nude mother,
shaped like an alligator but with a face like a gargoyle,
suckling her egg-shaped child. He reacts unpleasantly
to this, puts it back in the cupboard, then looks at a
cupboard on the other side of the room. He gets down
from the chair, crosses to the other cupboard, puts the
chair below it, climbs up and opens the cupboard. No
more recording unit than feathers on a flute (just to
give you a little variety). Idly he frowns at an opened
gross of conductor's batons, lying there like a package
of noodles, seizes one and tries it out, then sticks it
back with the others, gets down from the chair and looks
very pensive. Suddenly his face shows that an idea has
come to him. He coughs slightly, looks at his wet shirt,
pulls his coat tighter, then strides rapidly out of the
study toward the living room.

329   DARKENED LIVING ROOM

Sir Alfred appears silhouetted against the foyer, feels
for the switch which does not seem to work with the big
gloves, then comes blindly toward a lamp on a little
table next to a chair. His knee finds the table just
before his hands find the lamp, and the lamp falls to
the floor with a heavy crunch. The light goes on.

330   SIR ALFRED

with his hand still in a standing lamp next to piano.
He examines the slight wreckage, then with one efficient
double movement, sets the table on its feet and the lamp
on it at the same time. He starts to move away but as
the table has now only three legs, the lamp crashes to
the floor again, landing this time on the marble hearth
and really fixing itself up. Sir Alfred looks at it
crossly, then continues toward a high cupboard next to
the mantelpiece. He opens this and steps back to look.
There at last is a heavy black case with a handle and
about a hundred feet of assorted cables and plug-ins on
top of it. Without a second's hesitation, he places a
small antique cane-bottomed chair under the cupboard,
steps nimbly upon it, reaches the handle of the black
suitcase. It is apparently very heavy. He starts yanking
it.

331   SIR ALFRED'S FEET ON CANE-BOTTOMED CHAIR

        With one more yank, the feet go ripping through the seat.

332   SIR ALFRED'S UPPER HALF

        He is clinging to the handle of the suitcase and the
        edge of the shelf, looking anything but pleased. Now
        his movement upset the hundred feet of cable which drape
        themselves around his neck.

333   SIR ALFRED'S FEET

        They have some difficulty locating the edge of the chair
        around the missing seat. However, they finally do so.

334   CLOSE SHOT - SIR ALFRED AND BLACK SUITCASE

        As we are a little higher than he is, we can see into
        the cupboard much better than he can. For instance, we
        see another black suitcase behind the one he has a hold
        of. We see, also, a rather ornate flower vase, which is
        moved along with the suitcase and also some light bulbs
        along the front of the suitcase, concealed from Sir
        Alfred by the fact that his eyes are below the shelf. He
        looks down to make sure that his feet are safe, then
        inches the suitcase toward the front of the shelf with
        little jerks. The vase and bulbs move right along, of
        course.

335   CLOSER SHOT - SIR ALFRED

        Noticing that his nose has come in contact with the edge
        of the shelf below (or some object sitting upon it), he
        stops and wipes off the nose print with a little spit
        applied to a finger of a glove. Now he seizes the handle
        above him, grunts as he gives an extra hard yank and
        ducks as the vase flies past him.

336   THAT PART OF FLOOR

        where vase is about to land. Far from disappointing us,
        it lands explosively.

337   LOW CAMERA SHOT UP AT SIR ALFRED

        as he looks down at the flower vase cursing silently.
        Now he gives another yank on the suitcase and receives
        a shower of light bulbs which explode like French
        Seventy-Fives as they reach their various destinations.

338   SIR ALFRED'S FEET

        on edges of little chair. To the music of the exploding
        bulbs, one foot slips through the seat. The other one
        starts to wobble.

339 SIR ALFRED'S UPPER HALF

Clutching desperately to the heavy suitcase, he starts
to go. The suitcase shoots out horizontally, parting
from the handle and Sir Alfred goes down vertically to
the crackling of the disintegrating chair.

340 A FRENCH WINDOW

This is just beyond the piano and leads to a little
balcony. The black suitcase minus its handle flies
through the glass and lands on the balcony.

341 COLLAPSING CHAIR WITH A LARGE BULB UNDER IT

Sir Alfred comes through the remains of the chair, explodes the bulb and sits for a second still holding the
handle of the suitcase. The cable is still around his
neck and his hat now sits sideways. During this fall
the glass has been tinkling musically on the balcony.
Now Sir Alfred rises crunchingly, removes part of the
bulb from the seat of his overcoat and goes to the French
window. As he opens this he steps back hurriedly as one
of the upper panes, no longer held by its cross-bar,
falls to the stone. Now Sir Alfred opens the window,
brushes the broken glass off the top of the suitcase,
then picks it up minus its handle with both hands, puts
it on a low table in the room. After this he removes
the cable from around his neck, plugs one end into a wall
outlet, then looks for a receptacle on the side of the
suitcase into which to plug the other end. He does not
see any, so feels with his gloved finger for one. As
there is none on the side, he puts the wire between his
teeth and feels underneath. There does not seem to be
any here either. Now he tries pushing the button catch
release. He tries in four different directions but
nothing happens. After this he remembers to flip up the
U-shaped safety hasp, then again tries opening the suitcase by pushing the button catch in four different directions, but nothing happens. Beginning to show his teeth,
Sir Alfred grabs a corner of the suitcase and worries it
a little. He now finds that the top was damaged in the
fall, and by breaking off the edge of the top he is able
to get his gloved hand under the top. He yanks on this
a few times, then puts his foot on the table and exerts
all of his strength. There is a loud splintering and
the top comes off revealing, to his horror, a roulette
wheel, hundreds of chips, a cribbage board, checkers,
chessmen, plain and poker dice, casting cups and a Mah-
Jong set. He is unable to move for a moment, then picks
up the heavy box and starts back toward the cupboard
with it. Unfortunately, the fall has damaged the case a

(CONTINUED)

341 (Cont.)

little more than he has realized, and half way to the
cupboard the bottom falls out depositing everything
already mentioned on the floor, plus a few loose packs
of cards, scoring pads, pencils, chess and backgammon
boards. (At this point we are four minutes and fifty
seconds from Sir Alfred's entrance into the apartment.
His trip in a taxicab from the hall to the hotel could
have been accomplished in about four minutes. The trip
from downstairs to the thirty-fourth floor, or 340 feet,
in about 20 seconds, at a half a second per floor. Pre-
suming it took Daphne and her party five minutes to reach
Sir Alfred's dressing room through the crowd and that she
allowed another five minutes to elapse before being persuaded he was not in the building, she should be calling
up about now.) Sir Alfred glares wolfishly at this mess,
then, determination strong upon his face, he places another small cane-bottomed chair under the cupboard, but
this time, having learned his lesson, tries his weight on
it before getting up. He is not disappointed because his
foot goes through it at first trial. Now he puts the
chess board over the cane and steps up on it. THE CAMERA
GOES UP with him as he steps to the ledge of the cupboard
in order to see still higher. Up here at last he sees
the second black suitcase and grabs its handle.

                    SIR ALFRED
          So there you are.

He starts pulling it out to the edge. The 'phone rings.
As Sir Alfred stares evilly toward the study, his wet
shirt at last begins to do its work and he is seized by
a desire to sneeze. He fights this for a few seconds,
then gingerly climbs down and hurries to the study.

342   STUDY

Sir Alfred comes in and picks up the telephone and again
is seized by this desire. His lip twitches, his nose
wiggles and the only sound that he can make is an idiotic
yammering.

                    DAPHNE'S VOICE
               (tinnily through
               the 'phone)
          Hello, hello...

343   DAPHNE - IN SIR ALFRED'S DRESSING ROOM IN CONCERT HALL

Beyond her we see Barbara, Tony, August and Hugo. Beyond
them are crowds of well-wishing spectators and hurrying
musicians.

                                        (CONTINUED)

343 (Cont.)

> DAPHNE
> (worried)
> Hello...who is this...it sounds
> like a talking dog. .

>   JULES
>   (hurrying in)
> The stage doorman said he left
> while they were still applauding.

>   HUGO
>   (tapping his
>   forehead)
> He's nuts...

>   DAPHNE
> Hello!

344   SIR ALFRED - AT TELEPHONE

His lip twitching violently he makes a ghastly gasping
sound, a sort of a cross between a snore and the sounds
of whooping cough and the croup.

>   DAPHNE'S VOICE
>   (tinnily)
> Hello, hello...

Now Sir Alfred's lungs are full. He opens his mouth
cavernously.

345   DAPHNE AT TELEPHONE

She has just time to say one more hello before the explosion comes through and startles her so she drops the
instrument on the floor.

>   BARBARA, TONY, AUGUST,
>   HUGO AND JULES
>   (together)
> What's the matter?

>   DAPHNE
>   (wiggling her finger
>   in her ear)
> It was like an explosion.

>   HUGO
>   (picking up the
>   telephone)
> Hallo...hallo, Alfie...where are you?

346   SIR ALFRED

                              SIR ALFRED
                          (crossly into
                           the telephone)
                  Well where do you think I am since
                  I'm here answering the 'phone?

347   HUGO - AT TELEPHONE

                                 HUGO
                          (into the 'phone)
                  What happened to you?

                                DAPHNE
                          (terribly worried)
                  Is he all right?
                          (she takes the
                           'phone away
                           from Hugo)
                  Darling, are you all right...what
                  happened to you?

348   SIR ALFRED AT TELEPHONE

                              SIR ALFRED
                  Yes, I merely felt a slight...
                  yak...yak...yak...

349   BARBARA - AT TELEPHONE

                               BARBARA
                  I can't understand him....

                                AUGUST
                          (taking the telephone)
                  Let me try.

                  He gets the sneeze full in the ear and it shoots the
                  glasses off his nose and onto the floor.

                                 HUGO
                          (taking the 'phone
                           away from him)
                  Hello...Alfie?...we'll be right up....

350   SIR ALFRED - AT TELEPHONE

                              SIR ALFRED
                  I don't <u>want</u> you up here...you might
                  just...send my wife home...if she has
                  nothing better to do...goodbye.

                                            (CONTINUED)

350 (Cont.)

>He hangs up and hurries out of the study toward the
>living room.

351   HUGO AND OTHERS IN DRESSING ROOM

                              HUGO
                        (into the dead
                        telephone)
                  Hallo, hallo...
                        (then, hanging up)
                  He don't want nobody but Daphne.

                              DAPHNE
                        (taking Tony's arm)
                  Then take me home quickly, Tony...
                  we'll grab a cab...

                              HUGO
                        (after they leave)
                  Is there any insanity in his family?

                              BARBARA
                  I don't know...there's plenty in
                  mine...

>She looks mildly at her husband. Suddenly August gets
>it and, minus his pince-nez, gives her a near-sighted
>double take.

352   CLOSE SHOT - HUGO

                              HUGO
                  We'd better go over...you never
                  can tell widda musician...it's
                  de vibration!

                                        DISSOLVE TO:

353   SIR ALFRED AND RECORDING UNIT

He's working against time now and he constantly looks at
his wrist watch. The recorder is open, and from a receptacle in the cover he takes a disk and puts it on the
turntable. Now he lifts out the small microphone and
picks up a booklet of instructions, takes it over to a
better light and with some difficulty gets his glasses
out of his pocket and puts them on his nose.

354   INSERT - BOOKLET

We read: Directions for thirty-three and one-third -
seventy-eight R.P.M. simplicitas home recording unit.
"First thing to remember about the simplicitas home recording unit is that it is so simple a child can operate
it successfully. Merely follow the instructions to the
letter and you cannot go wrong. Remember what goes in
must come out. At seventy-eight RPM the record will
play brilliantly for two minutes and fifty-six seconds
At thirty-three and one-third RPM it will play nearly
seven minutes but the quality will not be quite so
brilliant. You must be the judge. To change from
seventy-eight RPM to thirty-three and one-third RPM
merely lift the cam dog A-1-a-3 (see simplified diagram
Page 6)

355   SIR ALFRED - LOOKING AT BOOKLET

With difficulty he turns to page six.

356   INSERT - SIMPLIFIED DIAGRAM ON PAGE SIX

If this is the simplified one we are glad they didn't
print the other one. The drawing represents a smear of
partly drawn gear wheels, dotted lines, symbols for
electrical wiring with little tags attached to different
places variously labeled A-1, A-2, A-3, A-4, etc.
A-1-a, A-2-a, A-3-a, A-4-a; A-1-b, A-2-b, A-3-b, A-4-b;
A-1-a-1, A-1-a-2, A-1-a-3, A-1-a-4, etc. Sir Alfred's
thumb comes into the shot near the A-1-a-3 label.

357   CLOSE SHOT - SIR ALFRED PAST BOOKLET

Now with difficulty he goes back to the first page
where we read the continuation of the instructions:

358   INSERT - INSTRUCTIONS

...and holding it between the thumb and index finger of
the left hand....

359   SIR ALFRED PAST BOOKLET

He reaches into the recorder and seizes something between the gloved fingers of his left hand. Now he
returns to the booklet.

360   INSERT - BOOKLET

        ...push the sliding spindle shaft bell crank rotator
        (B-1-a) in and over.

361   SIR ALFRED - PAST BOOKLET

        He wets his gloved finger and goes again to page six.
        He now goes back to the first page, then back to page
        six, now placing the booklet on the table, he seizes a
        knob near him in the recorder between the index and
        thumb of his left hand, then carefully watching the in-
        structions of the book he reaches his right hand over
        his left, grabs something in the machine and looks back
        at the instructions. Needing to see the diagram, he
        releases his left hand and passes it under his right
        armpits, wets the index finger and turns the page. Now
        he moves his left hand back into the machine and puts
        his right on the instruction book. With some dismay he
        finds the sliding spindle shank bell crank rotator be-
        tween the thumb and index finger of his right hand.
        Suddenly he reacts to a click and light starts flashing
        intermittently in the machine. Seizing the microphone,
        Sir Alfred starts hollering into it: Help, help...
        Oh-h-h....Ah-h-h-h...Sto-o-p....what did I ever do to
        you... (now he realizes what he has done...) ... take it
        again from the beginning...realizing the absurdity of
        this, removes the record, turns it over and gingerly
        puts the cutting arm down again. The machine still
        flashes so it is apparently still working.

                              SIR ALFRED
                         (after looking over
                         his shoulder and con-
                         sulting his watch)
                   H-e-e-l-p, h-e-e-l-p, murder, police,
                   he-e-l-p...he-e-l-p...spare me, spare
                   me...what did I ever do to you, Tony,
                   that you should do this to me...
                   he-e-l-p. he-e-l-p, Oh-h-h, A-h-h-h.

        He lifts the cutting arm off, looks at his watch again,
        looks nervously toward the door, then wets his finger,
        turns the book of instructions back to Page One.

362   INSERT - BOOKLET OF INSTRUCTIONS

        Directions: To change from thirty-three and one-third
        RPM to seventy-eight RPM is merely the reverse of the
        previous operation. Seizing cam dog A-1-a-3 between
        the index finger and the thumb and holding it out of
        gear, grasp the sliding spindle shaft bell crank
        rotator (B-1-a) and pull it out and under.

363   SIR ALFRED - READING BOOKLET

He looks over to the table, picks up the sliding spindle
shank bell crank rotator (B-1-a) and looks at it. Now
he reaches back into the machine and somehow gets rid of
it. After this he goes back to Page One, turns to Page
Two, then, consulting the booklet carefully, twists a
knob which causes the flashing light to go off and a loud
hum to go on. He turns another knob which reduces the
hum somewhat, then still consulting the booklet, places
the playing arm on the record, then braces himself for
the piercing screams which are to issue forth. There is
a long surface sound during which he clenches his fists
and watches the machine diabolically. Suddenly, like a
clap of thunder, a voice, obviously that of the mountain
god, Jehovah, two and a half times deeper, growlier and
more resonant than any basso ever heard comes out in room
shaking volume. The windows rattle and a last loose
piece of glass falls to the stone balcony. As Sir Alfred
glares at the machine in open mouthed disgust:

364   FOYER

We hear the sound of the turning lock and Daphne hurries
in with Tony behind her. They stop in dismay at the
voice of Doom which at the moment is saying:

                    VOICE OF THE MOUNTAIN GOD
                         (very loud)
           H-e-e-e-1-1-1p, h-e-e-1-1-p...

Daphne lets out a wild scream and rushes past the CAMERA
followed by the stupefied Tony.

365   SIR ALFRED - AT RECORDING UNIT

Gloved, overcoated, his hat on sideways, sitting in a
mass of broken glass, broken bulbs, broken chairs, with
chips, playing cards, Mah-Jong symbols and general flot-
sam and jetsam, not to mention the curtain flapping in
the broken window behind him, his appearance would be
frightening enough even without the voice of Doom which
at the moment is croaking out:

                    VOICE OF THE MOUNTAIN GOD
                Spare me, spare me, what did I ever
                do to you...

Sir Alfred turns and looks in startlement at the doorway.

366   DOORWAY OF LIVING ROOM

Daphne appears and lets out a piercing scream. Tony
appears behind her.

367   SIR ALFRED - IN MIDDLE OF HIS MESS

He grabs the tone arm in a powerful grip, rips it off
the machine entirely and throws it into the fireplace.
Now he seizes the record, breaks it in pieces, throws
the pieces in the fireplace and sneezes.

368   DAPHNE AND TONY - IN DOORWAY

Quite frightened, Daphne comes forward, Tony follows
after. The CAMERA PANS them into the shot with Sir
Alfred.

                         DAPHNE
               Are you all right, dear?

                         SIR ALFRED
                    (majestically)
               Why shouldn't I be all right?

He removes his hat, starts pulling off his gloves.

                         DAPHNE
                    (pointing to the dis-
                    aster on the floor)
               What were you...

                         SIR ALFRED
                    (icily)
               I was making an experiment...people
               do you know...without them there
               would be very little progress in this
               world...I believe I am well within my
               rights...in doing what I like...in my
               own house...am I not? We say in
               England that an Englishman's home is
               his castle...

                         DAPHNE
               Well of course you have your rights,
               darling.
                    (she begins to be
                    seized by a desire
                    to laugh)
               ...but you've made a kind of a mess
               out of your castle.

Tony sniggers.
                         SIR ALFRED
                    (instantly)
               And what are you laughing at?...did
               I invite you here...do you have to
               be in my house morning, noon and
               night...kindly wait in thirty-four...
               oh...six until I send for you.

                                        (CONTINUED)

368 (Cont.)

>   TONY
>   (nonplussed)
>   Well, certainly, Sir Alfred...
>   I was only...

>   SIR ALFRED
>   (violently)
>   And spare me your explanations
>   until I ask for them!

>   DAPHNE
>   (coming to Tony's
>   defense)
>   What has he done? You're acting
>   like a bear with a sore...

>   SIR ALFRED
>   (narrowing his eyes)
>   That's right, defend him!

>   DAPHNE
>   (bravely)
>   Well, why shouldn't I defend him?

>   TONY
>   I'll be in thirty-four oh six.

He does a quick fade.

>   SIR ALFRED
>   (after him)
>   Craven...

>   DAPHNE
>   Let me feel your head.

>   SIR ALFRED
>   (starting out of
>   the room to get
>   away from her)
>   I don't wish my head felt, thank
>   you...except for marrying you my
>   head has functioned quite well for
>   quite some time.

He exits toward his study, tripping slightly over a
cable. Daphne looks after him in stupefaction, then
follows him slowly, kicking little things out of her way.

369   SIR ALFRED - COMING INTO THE STUDY

He looks around malevolently, starts to sneeze but
manages to strangle it. He watches Daphne cunningly
as she comes in behind him and makes an effort to
speak nonchalantly.

                    SIR ALFRED
          By the way I uh...won't be able
          to take you dancing tonight.

                    DAPHNE
          Why...who are you taking?

                    SIR ALFRED
          I mean you'll have to be taken by
          somebody else...I have other plans.

                    DAPHNE
          Taken where?

                    SIR ALFRED
               (crossly)
          Dancing!

                    DAPHNE
          Who told you I wanted to go dancing?
          I feel about as much like dancing as...

                    SIR ALFRED
          Wouldn't you like to go dancing with
          Tony?

                    DAPHNE
          With Tony! Have you ever seen Tony
          dance? I saw him once with Barbara.
          He gets up on his toes and bends you
          over sideways 'til you think he's
          going to take off...compared with
          him you dance like Arthur Murray.

                    SIR ALFRED
          I don't need any compliments, thank
          you.

                    DAPHNE
          You're not getting any...besides,
          the way you've been behaving I feel
          about as much like dancing as I do
          like cutting my throat...all I feel
          like doing is crying.

                                   (CONTINUED)

369 (Cont.)

                          SIR ALFRED
                     (rigidly)
          How did you happen to use that
          simile?

                          DAPHNE
          What's a simile?

                          SIR ALFRED
          A simile is a...
                     (he opens his mouth
                     and shapes it for
                     a sneeze)
          ...a simile is a...yak, yak, yak...
          a simile is a...

He sneezes violently.

                          DAPHNE
          What you need is a good hot bath.

                          SIR ALFRED
          Why are you always trying to put
          me into a hot bath...I begin to
          find it sinister.

                          DAPHNE
          Would you like a hot toddy then?

                          SIR ALFRED
                     (exasperated)
          I don't want anything hot at all...
          I am sweating now.

                          DAPHNE
          You mean perspiring, darling.

                          SIR ALFRED
                     (raising his voice)
          I don't mean perspiring...if I say
          I'm sweating, I'm sweating...

He peals off his overcoat and reveals himself in his,
by now, terribly wrinkled evening clothes, lamentable
shirt, and concertina pleated collar.

                          SIR ALFRED
          Now if you would be kind enough
          to go to your room...I would like
          to disrobe.

                                        (CONTINUED)

369 (Cont.1)
                          DAPHNE
            You talking to me?

                          SIR ALFRED
            Unless you have someone concealed
            under the rug, I imagine that I am.

                          DAPHNE
            Well, go ahead and disrobe...oh...
            aren't we getting fussy...go into
            your strip-tease...I will retire
            to my own compartment...

With her nose in the air she marches out of the room.

                          SIR ALFRED
                    (looking after her)
            Hah!

Now he peals off his coat, collar and tie and after
looking toward her bedroom he stamps into the bathroom,
throws open his medicine cabinet and starts looking for
his razor. There is a reprise of the razor-killing
music while he lifts out half the contents of the lower
shelf. He raises his eyes thoughtfully to the top
shelf, reaches into the shelf over and behind the
bottles and knocks into the washbasin only two small
glass vials as he brings down the razor case. Now he
opens it, looks at it fiercely, then strops it. After
this, he examines the blade again and puts the edge
against his thumb to see how sharp it is. At this the
music stops abruptly.

370   DOORWAY TO DAPHNE'S ROOM

It opens and she speaks gently.

                          DAPHNE
            Darling..

Sir Alfred reacts as if jabbed by a trident, nicks his
thumb and lets the razor fly high in the air and clatter
into the bathtub as he pops his thumb into his mouth.

371   DAPHNE

hurrying in. The CAMERA PANS her into the bathroom.

                          DAPHNE
            Did you hurt yourself, darling?

                                            (CONTINUED)

371 (Cont.)

                    SIR ALFRED
                (taking his thumb
                out of his mouth)
Nothing of the slightest importance,
thank you.
                (he pops his thumb
                back into his mouth)

                    DAPHNE
                (dismayed)
You cut yourself...I'll bandage it
for you.

                    SIR ALFRED
                (reaching for a box
                of band-aids but not
                taking his thumb out
                of his mouth)
I'll bandage it myself, thank you.

Of course not a syllable of this is clear.

                    DAPHNE
                (all concerned)
What did you say, dear?

                    SIR ALFRED
                (taking his thumb
                out of his mouth)
I said I'll manage quite nicely,
thank you.

He takes the top off the box, puts his thumb back in
his mouth and shakes the band-aids out. They all fall
into the washbasin.

                    DAPHNE
                (taking charge)
Oh, here...

Very expertly she puts some alcohol on a piece of
cotton, wipes the little wound and says:

                    DAPHNE
Hold that.

Now she peels the gauze from a band-aid, removes the
cotton from Sir Alfred's thumb and quickly applies the
band-aid all around his thumb.

                        (CONTINUED)

371 (Cont.1)

                         DAPHNE
                       (gently)
          There...does it hurt very much?

                         SIR ALFRED
          No.

                         DAPHNE
          I'm glad.

Now she holds the dressing gown out for him, pushes him
into it, then arranges a hand towel around his neck in
the shape of an ascot.

                         DAPHNE
          If you won't take a bath, at least
          don't catch your death of cold.

The middle or check-writing music now comes softly over
us.

                         SIR ALFRED
                       (hesitantly)
          You do like to do little things for
          me, don't you?

                         DAPHNE
          Not when you're like this I don't.

The soft music stops as suddenly as it had begun.

                         SIR ALFRED
                       (after looking at
                        her for a moment)
          I will forgive you, anyway.

The music starts again.

                         DAPHNE
                       (indignantly)
          Forgive me for what?

The music stops.

                         SIR ALFRED
                       (beginning to
                        get angry again)
          You know what I'm forgiving you for,
          so just hold your tongue...

He pulls open his desk drawer and slaps his great checkbook on the desk.

                         SIR ALFRED
          ...lest I change my mind.

                                        (CONTINUED)

371 (Cont.2)

                         DAPHNE
        Well, go ahead and change your mind.

                         SIR ALFRED
                    (reaching for the
                    long fountain pen in
                    the ornate stand)
        I'll change my mind if I <u>wish</u> to
        change my mind...
                    (he struggles with
                    the pen which is stuck
                    in the swivel holder)
        ...and if I don't wish to change my
        mind...
                    (he succeeds in get-
                    ting the pen out,
                    slaps the checkbook
                    open and starts
                    writing a check)
        ...I won't change my mind...
                    (he shakes the pen
                    to try to coax some
                    ink out of it)
        ...is that clear?

        Now he writes again but with no results.

                         SIR ALFRED
                    (with thinly dis-
                    guised fury)
        If it were possible just for once to
        have a little ink in the fountain
        pens in this house...as they do in
        well <u>run</u> houses!...

                         DAPHNE
        I know...like in England.

                         SIR ALFRED
        Precisely...like in England.

                         DAPHNE
                    (pointing)
        Try the other one...we drive on the
        right-hand side over here.

                         SIR ALFRED
        That's a bright remark.

                                        (CONTINUED)

371 (Cont.3)

He seizes the right-hand pen which is also stuck. With
much twisting, he works it loose and starts to write.
Now he looks down at his checkbook which is covered
with ink, then at his hand which is covered with ink,
then at the pen, the end of which is missing...only a
rubber stump being evident.

                    SIR ALFRED
               (rising and throwing
                down the second pen)
          Very well...I will not forgive you.

He pulls open the right-hand drawer. Now the third
music reprises as he lifts out his revolver, looks at
Daphne and sneers.

                    DAPHNE
               (a little frightened
                for the first time)
          What's the matter with you?

She points nervously at the revolver.

                    SIR ALFRED
          You're not laughing quite so hard
          now.

                    DAPHNE.
               (pointing to the
                revolver)
          What are you going to do with that?

                    SIR ALFRED
               (breaking the
                revolver)
          Have you ever heard of Russian
          Roulette?

                    DAPHNE
          Certainly...I used to play it all
          the time with my father.

                    SIR ALFRED
               (irritated)
          I doubt that you played Russian
          Roulette all the time with your
          father.

                                   (CONTINUED)

371 (Cont.4)

He discovers the cylinder of his revolver is empty.

                    SIR ALFRED
          Where are the...

                    DAPHNE
          Well, I certainly did...you play it
          with two packs of cards...and we
          used to play it for a cent a game
          and whoever gets the card on the
          other card first...

                    SIR ALFRED
          That is Russian Bank. Russian
          Roulette is a very different amuse-
          ment which I can only wish your
          father had played continuously...
          before he had you.

                    DAPHNE
          What are you talking about?

                    SIR ALFRED
          Where are the bullets for this
          revolver?

                    DAPHNE
          You told me to get rid of them.

                    SIR ALFRED
          I told you to get rid of them?

                    DAPHNE
          Don't you remember? You said it
          was dangerous to have them around
          the house...that somebody might
          shoot himself?

Sir Alfred throws the revolver into the wastepaper
basket. He looks so pathetic that Daphne puts a
sympathetic hand on his shoulder.

                    DAPHNE
          I don't know what's the matter with
          you, darling...I suppose something
          went wrong in England, but I wish
          you weren't like this just now...
          because I'm really terribly worried.

                                        (CONTINUED)

                        SIR ALFRED
You should be.

                        DAPHNE
                (surprised)
Well, I am...
                (then suddenly)
What do you know about it?

                        SIR ALFRED
                (ominously)
Much, much more than you think,
probably.

                        DAPHNE
Then you can imagine how I feel.

                        SIR ALFRED
I can imagine nothing of the kind...
and I don't wish to.

                        DAPHNE
That's just because you don't like
him.

                        SIR ALFRED
                (indignantly)
Yes, well, if you can tell me any
reason why I should like him...
the drinks are on me...

                        DAPHNE
Oh, I know he's a jerk, but still...
you feel a little sorry for him...he
called me one night while you were
in England...about one-thirty in the
morning.

                        SIR ALFRED
Oh, he did.

                        DAPHNE
He wanted to know if Barbara was
with me.

                        SIR ALFRED
How was that his business?

                                        (CONTINUED)

967

371 (Cont.6)

                          DAPHNE
                       (simply)
                Well, he's married to her.

                          SIR ALFRED
                Who is married to her?

                          DAPHNE
                August.

                          SIR ALFRED
                What does he have to do with it?

                          DAPHNE
                       (as if talking
                        to a child)
                He's her husband.

                          SIR ALFRED
                Who's her husband?

                          DAPHNE
                August...you ought to know him...
                he's your brother-in-law.

                          SIR ALFRED
                Wait a second...you mean August
                called you up...

                          DAPHNE
                At one-thirty in the morning.

                          SIR ALFRED
                ...to ask if Barbara was here?

                          DAPHNE
                That's right...but she wasn't.

                          SIR ALFRED
                Then why did he call you?

                          DAPHNE
                Because she told him...she was
                here...he was checking on her.

                          SIR ALFRED
                Well, where was she?

                                              (CONTINUED)

371 (Cont. 7)

> DAPHNE
> (looking away)
> I had a suspicion...that I didn't
> want to have...you know she's always
> so frank about not liking August and
> everything...that you begin to think
> she really <u>does</u> like him and is just
> saying these things because that's
> her way of being funny...but I really
> think she <u>doesn't</u> like him,..and when
> she says these things, she means
> them...only we're expected to copper
> them twice...that's one of my father's
> expressions...

> SIR ALFRED
> I'm afraid he has the advantage of me.

> DAPHNE
> Anyway, I didn't dare tell August she
> wasn't here...and I didn't dare call
> her where I thought she was...because
> the kind of a man who checks up on
> his wife is the kind of a man who
> hires detectives...and has telephones
> tapped.

> SIR ALFRED
> You are entirely correct.

> DAPHNE
> So, I told him that she'd been with
> me and just left...and then I hurried
> down there...just in case...

> SIR ALFRED
> (rigidly)
> You hurried down where?

> DAPHNE
> You won't tell anybody?

> SIR ALFRED
> Why would I advertise these things?

> DAPHNE
> To Tony's room.

(CONTINUED)

371 (Cont.8)

SIR ALFRED
(in a strange voice)
Thirty-four-o-six!

DAPHNE
That's right...when I got there I
was about to knock and then I
noticed the door was open about an
inch...almost as if I had been
·expected...I knocked anyway...but
there wasn't any answer so I went
in...there wasn't anybody there...
but I had the feeling somebody had
been there...a very short time
before...I don't know whether it was
cigarette smoke...or perfume...or
just the warmth of human bodies...
anyway there wasn't anybody there
now so I started for the door to go
back to our apartment...and then
suddenly I realized how terrible it
would look...if anybody saw me
coming out of Tony's room...you
know, because he's about my age and
to anyone who didn't understand how
I feel about you it would look...you
know how dumb some people are...so
just before I ·went out I took a
little mirror...I forgot to tell you
there was a handbag in the room...
Tony told me afterwards Barbara had
forgotten it at lunch and he hadn't
had a chance to return it yet....
(she looks at her
husband a moment
before continuing)
...so I took this little mirror and
held it over my head like this...so
I could look out the transom and
make sure there wasn't anybody in
the hall...and right there...just
near the freight elevator...I saw
this big jerk peeking around the
corner.

SIR ALFRED
What big jerk?

(CONTINUED)

217

371 (Cont. 9)

                        DAPHNE
          I don't know...a great big old
          gorilla...with a face like an
          orangutang...looking right straight
          at my door.

                        SIR ALFRED
                   (loudly and
                   rapturously)
          Sweeney the detective!

                        DAPHNE
                   (surprised)
          What?

                        SIR ALFRED
          Nothing darling...not worth remem-
          bering...just an English joke.

                        DAPHNE
                   (not understanding
                   but too interested
                   in her own story
                   to care)
          I thought he might be a detective...
          except you'd never expect anybody
          who looked that much like a detective
          to actually be one...anyway I waited
          ...and he waited...and I waited...and
          we waited...

                        SIR ALFRED
                   (triumphantly)
          Thirty-eight minutes!

                        DAPHNE
                   (unaware of the
                   meaning in his mind)
          I don't know how long it was...it
          seemed more like thirty-eight years
          ...I began actually to feel guilty
          ...I don't know why...I've never
          been in a man's room before...
          except yours...and that old baboon
          just stood there as if he was nailed
          there...finally I heard some people
          coming down the hall and he must
          have heard them too because he went
          slinking back toward the elevator...

                             (CONTINUED)

371 (Cont. 10)

> DAPHNE (Cont.)
> his rubber shoes creaking...what a
> jerk...so I slipped out without a
> sound and I was starting to run when
> I heard a tearing sound...and there
> was the train of my negligee caught
> in the door...and the baboon heard
> it too because suddenly he stuck his
> kisser around the corner...so I just
> gave him a haughty stare...tore the
> train off and went home.

> SIR ALFRED
> (stifling his
> laughter)
> So it is really dear August who is
> to be congratulated on all this...
> and how richly he deserves it -- you
> wonderful child...to tell me all this.

> DAPHNE
> Tell you what, darling? I have no
> secrets from you.

> SIR ALFRED
> (quietly)
> Would you do me a great big favor?

> DAPHNE
> What?

> SIR ALFRED
> Would you put on your lowest cut and
> most vulgarly ostentatious gown...
> and the largest and vulgarest jewels
> that you possess.

> DAPHNE
> Hunh? But I thought that you didn't
> feel...

> SIR ALFRED
> (gaining in voice)
> And then would you accompany me to
> the vulgarest, most ostentatious,
> loudest and hardest to get into
> establishment this city affords?

(CONTINUED)

371 (Cont. 11)

> DAPHNE
> But your cold, darling?

> SIR ALFRED
> There is nothing the matter with me
> that a couple of magnums of champagne
> won't cure...I happen to feel like
> celebrating...I want to be seen in
> your exquisite company...I want the
> whole world to know that I am the
> most fortunate of men...in the
> possession of the most magnificent of
> wives...I want to swing in champagne
> and paint the town not only red but
> red, white and blue...I want every-
> body to see how much I adore you...
> > (he takes her
> > in his arms)
> ...always have adored you...revere
> you and trust you...also how much,
> I hope, you have of warmth for me.

> DAPHNE
> (very simply)
> But, my darling, I worship you.

> SIR ALFRED
> (pushing her away)
> Then let's not waste time in words...
> go put on your most outrageous dress...

> DAPHNE
> Shall I wear the purple with the
> plumes at. the hips?

> SIR ALFRED
> (as if he had been
> struck with a crowbar)
> The purple with the plumes at the
> hips?

> DAPHNE
> (illustrating it)
> You know...it's cut down on one
> shoulder...and the coq feathers
> shoot up off the left hip...like
> the tail of a comet?

(CONTINUED)

371 (Cont. 12)

> SIR ALFRED
> (gravely)
> Wear the purple with the plumes at
> the hips...like the tail of a
> comet...and let it be a <u>purple</u>
> <u>lesson</u> to me...

> DAPHNE
> (happily)
> All right, my darling.

She starts to hurry out then pauses in the doorway.

> DAPHNE
> What was the matter with you tonight?

> SIR ALFRED
> Something so vulgar...so utterly
> contemptible and unworthy of a love
> like yours...that I beg of you never
> to make me tell you.

Daphne comes close to him and the CAMERA STARTS PUSHING
IN.

> DAPHNE
> (softly)
> But of course I won't, my darling...
> I know what it's like to be a great
> man...that is I don't really...but...
> having so many responsibilities and
> so much tenseness...and watching out
> for and...protecting so many people...

Sir Alfred pulls her tightly to him and kisses her
devotedly. As her hands tighten behind his neck:

372   BARBARA, AUGUST, HUGO AND TONY - COMING TOWARD US IN THE
      FOYER

We see the door to the hall open behind them... They slow
down at what they see.

373   TWO BIG HEADS - SIR ALFRED AND DAPHNE

They come out of the kiss. Daphne's eyes are still
closed.

(CONTINUED)

273 (Cont.)

                                  SIR ALFRED
                             (huskily)
A thousand poets dreamed a thousand
years...and then you were born...my
love.

As they start to kiss again:

374   BARBARA, AUGUST, HUGO AND TONY - IN AS TIGHT A FOUR AS
       POSSIBLE

They are watching fascinated. August removes his pince-
nez and polishes it.

                                   BARBARA
                           (passing the back of
                           her hand lightly over
                           her forehead)
Would somebody kindly take me out
of here and get me a glass of ice
cold beer?...this is getting <u>very</u>
<u>monotonous</u>.

                                           FADE OUT

                            T H E   E N D

Designer:	UC Press Staff
Compositor:	Prestige Typography
Text:	10/12 Times Roman
Display:	American Typewriter
Printer:	Malloy Lithographing, Inc.
Binder:	John H. Dekker & Sons